An Introduction to Political Theory

9th Revised Edition

Other Important Books by Dr. O.P Gauba:

- Western Political Thought
- Indian Political Thought
- Contemporary Political Ideologies
- Social and Political Philosophy
- Political Ideas and Ideologies
  (Understanding Political Theory—Major Concepts and Debates)
- Reading Gandhi

NATIONAL
PAPERBACKS
4230/1, Ansari Road, Darya Ganj, New Delhi 110002

AN INTRODUCTION TO POLITICAL THEORY

O. P. GAUBA
Formerly Associate Professor
Department of Political Science
School of Open Learning
University of Delhi

National Paperbacks
4230/1, Ansari Road, Darya Ganj
NEW DELHI 110002

•

Branch :
Hyderabad Publishers and Distributors
Plot No. 28, 2nd Floor, Ganesh Nagar Colony
West Marredpally, Secunderabad-500026
Mob : 9395314841, e-mail : hpdhyd@gmail.com

•

•

Price: ₹ 550

•

First Edition	:	1981
Seventh Edition	:	2014 (Thoroughly Revised)
Eighth Reprint	:	2017
Fifteenth Reprint	:	October, 2018
Eighth Edition	:	2019 (Thoroughly Revised)
Seventh Reprint	:	2021
Ninth Edition (Thoroughly Revised)	**:**	**2021**
Third Reprint	:	2022
Fourth Reprint	:	2023
Fifth Reprint	:	2024
Sixth Reprint	**:**	**2024**

•

Printed in India at
Avon Printers, Loni Road, Delhi

•

ISBN: 978-93-88658-33-1

e-mail: nationalpaperpacks2018@gmail.com / Ph. 011-41040710, 47014602 [922-0220]

Preface

The present book *An Introduction to Political Theory* has been in circulation since 1981. In the meantime, its contents were revised, enlarged and upgraded, and its style of presentation was improved to make it reader-friendly and richer in content. The author is grateful to the academic community whose more than one generations have accepted and encouraged this modest attempt.

The purpose of this introductory work is to examine the major issues of the ever-expanding field of political theory from various reference points including liberal, libertarian, Marxist, neo-Marxist, communitarian, elitist, pluralist, socialist, social-democratic, moralist, ecological, Gandhian, feminist and subaltern perspectives. The issues examined here include the nature and significance of political theory, concept of ideology with a short description of major ideologies (liberalism, Marxism, socialism, fascism, anarchism, Gandhism and feminism), nature of politics and various approaches to its study such as empirical, normative, behavioural, post-behavioural as well as interdisciplinary approach, concepts of state and sovereignty, imperialism, colonialism, neo-colonialism, impact of globalization, grounds and limits of political obligation, various dimensions of law, power, citizenship, human rights, liberty, equality, justice, common good, democracy, development, under-development, sustainable development and political development, etc.

An attempt has been made to combine analytical and critical approaches to the various problems while avoiding a doctrinaire mode of thought. Any stand taken on an issue is sought to be substantiated by suitable arguments, illustrations and data. I make no claim to suggest a final solution to any problem of the present-day world. In my opinion, an author's job is adequately done if he is able to bring out the complexities of the problems and indicate the possible ways to find their answer, so that he inspires his readers to think for themselves rather than look for ready-made solutions!

For the seventh edition of this book, the entire text of the previous edition was given a facelift. In particular, the following topics were substantially revised and augmented: Ideology as a set of ideas; Ideology as a science of ideas; Neo-liberalism; Socialism; Post-behavioural Revolution; Marxian Analysis;

Interdisciplinary Approach; State and Nation; Gandhian Perspective on the State—the Concept of *Swaraj;* Pluralist Perspective on the State; Gandhian Perspective on Political Obligation; Sources of Law; Power, Authority and Legitimacy; Gender Perspective on Power; Group Perspective on Power; Nature of Liberty; Freedom as Emancipation and Development; Idea of Equality; Liberty and Equality; Feminist Perspective on Justice; Significance of Multiculturalism; Pluralist Theory of Democracy; Development and Environmentalism; and Concept of Political Development.

Besides, the following new topics were inserted in appropriate contexts: Interface with Geography; Interface with Anthropology; Interface with Law; Postmodern Perspective on Power; Nature of Democratic Citizenship; Debate on the Status of Human Rights; and Amartya Sen's Concept of Development-Oriented Freedom.

This new eighth edition represents a thoroughly revised, improved and updated version of all previous editions. Its reader-friendly features have been further refined and enhanced. It is hoped that the academic community will continue to receive this book with the same fervour as heretofore.

Constructive suggestions will be most welcome. Please e-mail your suggestions to *ompgauba@gmail.com*

New Delhi

O. P. GAUBA

वादे वादे जायते तत्त्वबोध:

(Ancient Indian Saying)

It is through articulation of diverse opinions that the truth would be finally revealed.

Contents

Flowcharts, Comparative Charts and Diagrams

1

Nature and Significance of Political Theory

AS HUMAN BEINGS we live in society. Society includes many institutions like family, school, religious organization, polity, etc. Every institution serves some specific purpose. It involves some organization and use of authority. Authority implies a relationship of command and obedience where the command is generally regarded to be reasonable. Mild protests, if any, would not upset the authority.

[I] NATURE OF POLITICAL THEORY

WHAT IS POLITICAL?

When an organization is designed to regulate the whole community, it takes the character of polity. Polity, therefore, denotes an organization where rules are made and decisions are taken for the whole community, and authority is exercised over each member of the community. The term 'political' refers to something related to a polity, that is 'public', as distinguished from private or something applicable to a limited number of persons. Sheldon S. Wolin, in his *Politics and Vision* (1960), has beautifully summed up the characteristics of the 'political' as follows:

> Of all the authoritative institutions in society, the political arrangement has been singled out as uniquely concerned with what is 'common' to the whole community. Certain functions, such as national defence, internal order, the dispensing of justice, and economic regulation, have been declared the primary responsibility of political institutions, largely on the grounds that the interests and ends served by these functions were beneficial to all of the members of the community.

The state is an essential component of polity which enjoys a unique position among social institutions. It is so important that Aristotle, ancient Greek philosopher, described man by nature a 'political animal'. Living in a state was so natural for a person that he who lived outside the state or who did not need a state was either a beast or an angel!

The terms 'polity', 'politics' and 'political' are derived from the Greek word 'polis' which stood for ancient Greek city-state. The Greek city-states were relatively small communities which were separated from each other by geographical barriers like forests, mountains and seas. Each city-state had evolved a compact social life and culture where all institutions and activities were knit together. These institutions and activities which were aimed at securing 'good life' for the community were regarded to be the part of 'politics'. However, in the present-day society the scope of politics is not regarded to be so comprehensive. Today we draw a distinction between public and private spheres of human life, and confine the usage of the term 'politics' to the institutions and activities falling in the public domain. Thus the decisions of cabinet and parliament, election campaigns and other activities of political parties, people's movements seeking change in law and public policy, etc. belong to politics but the object of our faith and worship, the content of our education, art and culture, etc. do not properly belong to the sphere of politics until some regulation thereof is required to maintain public order and safety!

SCOPE OF POLITICAL THEORY

After identifying the nature and scope of the 'political', we are now ready to understand the nature of political theory. The term 'theory' stands for a systematic knowledge. Thus 'political theory' refers to a systematic knowledge of political phenomena. What type of knowledge do we require about the political phenomena in the realm of political theory?

Broadly speaking, political theory is concerned with three types of statements—(1) *Empirical statement,* which is based on observation, through sense-experience alone, that is the experience gained through sight, sound, smell, taste and touch of the concrete phenomena; (2) *Logical statement,* which is based on reasoning (*e.g.* 'two plus two is four'); and (3) *Evaluative statement,* which is based on value-judgement (*e.g.* 'men are born free and equal'). Political science, as distinguished from political philosophy, relies only on empirical and logical statements. It is argued that correct observation and correct reasoning by different persons would lead to the similar conclusion; hence empirical and logical statements are capable of verification. On the other hand, it is alleged that evaluative statements are based on individual or group preferences which differ from individual to individual or group to group; there is no reliable method of determining what is right or wrong, good or bad; one cannot scientifically discover the purpose of the universe or human life. Champions of *Positivism* sought to build political science and other social sciences (*e.g.* sociology, economics, history, etc.) on the foundations of the methodology of natural sciences (*e.g.* physics, chemistry, biology, etc.). Then the exponents of *'Logical Positivism'* argue that evaluative statements have no empirical content or logical structure; they are the expressions of subjective reflection or emotional preference. Likewise, champions of scientific method for the study of politics insist on a 'value-free' or 'value-neutral' approach.

Political Philosophy

Political philosophy refers to a branch of learning which is primarily concerned with moral and substantive dimensions of politics. Its central problems include the pursuit of good life, questions pertaining to norms and values, good and evil, virtue and vice, means and ends, right and wrong, and visions of an ideal state and society. Political philosophy inquires into the foundations of political life, grounds of political obligation, and moral worthiness of different political systems. It makes use of philosophical and historical method in determining the goals of public life. A major part of political philosophy coincides with moral and social philosophy.

Positivism

Positivism refers to the view that relies on scientific method as the only source of true knowledge. It rejects superstition, religion and metaphysics as pre-scientific forms of thought. It holds that all knowledge is ultimately based on sense-experience (*i.e.* the experience gained through sight, sound, smell, taste and touch). Hence, the method used in the natural sciences (e.g. physics, chemistry, biology, etc.) must be adopted for any genuine inquiry in the field of social sciences.

Logical Positivism

Logical positivism refers to a school of thought founded by German sociologist Max Weber (1864-1920) and the members of Vienna Circle (Moritz Schlick, Ludwig Wittgenstein, A.J. Ayer, etc.) in the early decades of the twentieth century. It holds that reliable and valid knowledge in any field of inquiry can be obtained only by empirical method (*i.e.* the observation based on sense-experience). The questions concerning values are beyond the scope of scientific knowledge; hence it is not possible to obtain reliable knowledge about them.

In any case, political theory cannot be confined to the so-called scientific knowledge. It is equally concerned with determining values which come within the purview of political philosophy. We cannot accept the view that values are based on individual or group preferences. On the contrary, values do have a sound logical structure unless we mistake them for biased statements. Upholders of different values can be invited to have a dialogue, to have an opportunity to understand each other's point of view, to convince each other and probably to agree on certain universal principles to judge the validity of values. Determination of values is the basis of a sound public policy or decision. If we abdicate this responsibility, it may fall in irresponsible hands, with disastrous consequences. Hence, political theory must comprehend both political science and political philosophy.

Dwelling on the nature of political theory, George Catlin (*Political Quarterly;* March, 1957) significantly observed: "The theory (of politics) itself is divided into *political science* and *political philosophy.*" Pleading for combining the study of political science with sociology, Catlin asserted: "It is the supreme virtue of the fusion of sociology and political science that it could enable us to be sharp-eyed for *the phenomena of control* in its many forms, over all the processes of the whole social field" (*ibid.*).

Then defining the scope of political philosophy, Catlin explained: "Our concern here... is with the kingdom of ends or final values...So soon as a man begins to ask, 'What is for the national good?' or 'What is the good society?', he is asking questions in philosophy" (*ibid.*). In short, Catlin proceeds to identify the nature of political theory by pointing to its two important components— political science and political philosophy. As he has suggested, political science deals with the facts of political life (*i.e.* what is the real situation and which laws govern our actual behaviour) while political philosophy is concerned with values (*i.e.* what is right or good for us).

Andrew Hacker (*Political Theory: Philosophy, Ideology, Science;* 1961) also dwells on these two major components of political theory but he introduces some new factors to elaborate the issue. Hacker writes: "Every political scientist plays a double role. He is part scientist and part philosopher... no theorist can make a lasting contribution to human knowledge unless he works in the realms of both science and philosophy. The scientific part of a theory can only achieve coherence and significance if the writer has a preconceived idea or the goals of political life." Commenting on the role of political science, Hacker observes: "The theorist whose pursuit is political science is interested in describing and explaining the realities of political behaviour. He attempts to draw up generalized propositions about the actual relations between states and citizens and about the role of power in society" (*ibid.*). About the role of political philosophy, he comments: "The theorist whose interest is in writing political philosophy, on the other hand, is concerned with prescribing the goals which citizens, states and societies ought to pursue. His aim is to generalize about right conduct in the political life and about the legitimate uses of power" (*ibid.*). Adequate knowledge of political science is essential for a sound political philosophy. As Hacker points out, "The philosophical parts of a theory must be informed by a profound understanding of the fact of political life. The best political philosophers have always been well aware of the existing realities; they have given intense and systematic study to the needs and capabilities of man and society" (*ibid.*).

Fuller scope of political theory may be understood with reference to its focus and its method of study. One point of its focus is the study of political concepts and ideas. For this purpose, normative-philosophical method is regarded to be suitable. Another point of its focus is the study of political institutions and behaviour. For this purpose, descriptive-scientific method is regarded quite suitable. It is necessary that each problem of political theory should be studied by the proper method.

> In practice political decisions usually entail a mixture of empirical and moral judgements... in politics 'refusing to decide' is simply deciding to allow others to decide for you.
>
> Robert Dahl (*Modern Political Analysis;* 1977)

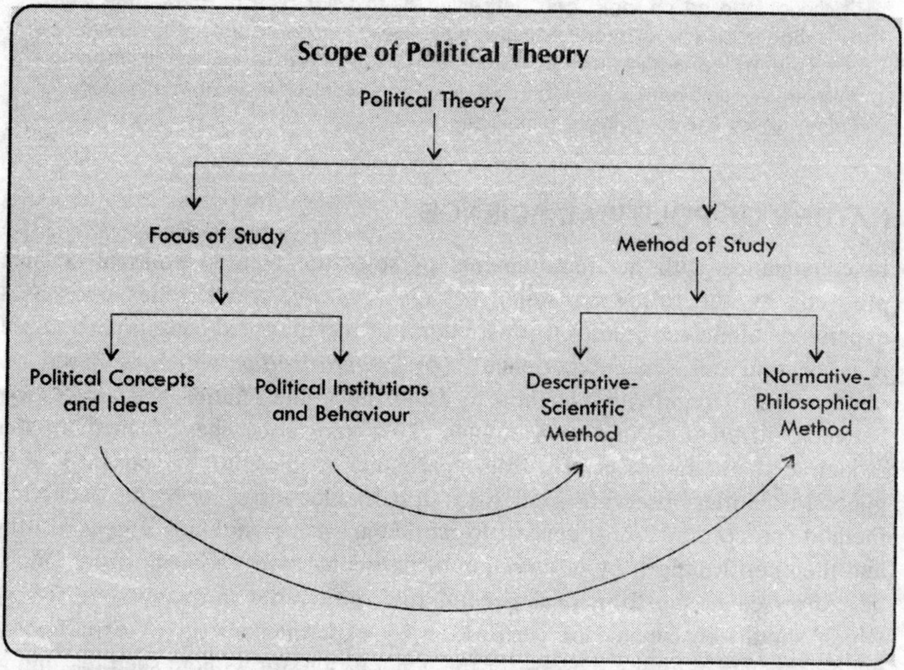

Scientific Method

Scientific method refers to the method of study which focuses on the observation of facts through sense-experience (that is the experience obtained through sight, sound, smell, taste and touch), inquires into their relationship and the laws governing this relationship. Its purpose is to obtain reliable knowledge about facts and give explanation of events. The use of scientific method in the study of politics is an essential feature of political science.

Normative Method

Normative method refers to the method of study which seeks to determine as to what we *ought to* do. It is the arena of reflection on our values and ideals. It is concerned with the judgement of good and evil, right and wrong. While agreement on certain principles on these issues is possible, nobody can claim to have a final word in this behalf. Each party is expected to advance sound arguments to substantiate its stand.

Philosophical Method

Philosophical method refers to the method of study which seeks to construct basic concepts in order to solve the riddles of the universe and human society. It raises certain basic questions and inquires as to which of the phenomena are capable of observation, and which of them are beyond our observation by sense-experience. In order to understand the things beyond our observation, we try to build a system of thought based on logic, and determine as to what type of knowledge would be reliable, and what type of knowledge would not be reliable. The knowledge obtained by normative method is also duly recognized under the philosophical method. A combination of normative and philosophical method in the study of politics gives rise to political philosophy.

NATURE OF POLITICAL SCIENCE

In consonance with the requirements of scientific method political science proceeds by the following steps: (*a*) *Observation,* which relies on sense-experience alone and rules out supernatural or metaphysical causation (because it is beyond our sense-experience); (*b*) *Generalization* which is based on observation of regularities leading to establishing the relation and correlation between different factors or variables. This may either be obtained by the inductive method (proceeding from 'particular to general', *i.e.* arriving at a general rule after observing similarities in particular cases), or by the deductive method (proceeding from 'general to particular', *i.e.* postulating a general rule and then confirming it by observation of particular cases). Generalization must be expressed in the form of a general rule, preferably in quantitative terms, which should be capable of verification by experimentation; (*c*) *Explanation* which consists in giving reasons for the general rule, for without such reasoning any observation of correlation might be a mere coincidence; explanation alone will make particular events, situations or tendencies meaningful; and finally, (*d*) *Prediction and Prescription* so that in the light of known facts and general rules, their possible outcome could be known and measures for achieving such objectives as higher efficiency, stability, satisfaction, etc., could be suggested.

Behavioural approach exemplifies the scientific approach to the study of politics. It insists on studying the actual behaviour of human beings in a political situation rather than describing salient features of political institutions and their legal position. In the behavioural approach formal political institutions are dissolved into 'systems' and 'processes' so as to focus attention on the actual behaviour of political actors, which alone is capable of scientific study. However, *post-behavioural approach* insists on making the achievements of political science subservient to human values and ends. Hence, it heralds revival of concern with 'values' without compromising scientific method for the study of 'facts'. In short, post-behaviouralism calls for application of political science for overcoming the prevailing crises in various spheres of human life.

NATURE OF POLITICAL PHILOSOPHY

It is sometimes alleged that political science deals with the 'real' while political philosophy deals with the 'ideal'. According to this viewpoint, political science inquires into what men and women actually *do* in a political situation while political philosophy tries to determine what they *ought to do* in keeping with the ultimate good or purpose of human life. But this view does not define the scope of political philosophy adequately. Political philosophy may properly be recognized by its *'critical' function.* As D.D. Raphael *(Problems of Political Philosophy;* 1976) significantly observed: "It is true that some of the classical political philosophers have set out ideal forms of society, but ... this has not been their central concern. Even in Plato, the purpose of depicting an ideal society is to criticize existing society and to promote understanding of general social concepts such as justice." According to Raphael, the fundamental purpose of traditional philosophy has been the critical evaluation of beliefs: "Philosophy differs from science in that science seeks explanation while philosophy seeks justification" *(ibid.).* The term 'justification' implies the attempt to give rational grounds either for accepting or rejecting the beliefs which are usually taken for granted.

Another closely related function of political philosophy is the *clarification of concepts.* As Raphael has pointed out, many of these concepts—such as the concept of society, authority, social class, justice, liberty and democracy—are not only highly general but also vague. Clarification of such concepts involves three related purposes: analysis, synthesis and improvement of concepts. Analysis of a concept involves specifying its elements, often by way of definition, such as defining sovereignty as supreme legal authority. Synthesis of concepts implies showing the logical relationships between two concepts, such as showing that the concept of a right involves that of an obligation. Improvement of a concept implies recommending a definition or use that will assist clarity or coherence, such as recommending that the concept of sovereignty should be applied only to the legal authority of a state, and not to its coercive power.

CONCLUSION

It may be conceded that political philosophy deals with the needs, objectives and goals of human life which cannot be scientifically ascertained. But these can always be discussed by the right-thinking people, argued on the basis of available data and reasoning, and some acceptable point may be reached at the current level of our social consciousness. Most of the arguments can be picked up for further scrutiny from the long tradition of political thought, new arguments can be introduced thereto and conclusions drawn from the expanding horizons of our knowledge. Hence, the search for values and a critical review of our position is an ongoing process which justify the continuing pursuit of political philosophy. In fact political philosophy itself arose from a critical reflection of political activity which existed long before the advent of political philosophy. It exemplified the Socratic function of 'speaking truth to power'.

Hacker particularly cautions us to distinguish political theory from 'ideology'. A theory–whether it takes the character of science or philosophy–must be dispassionate and disinterested. When a theorist has no personal interest in any political arrangement, "his vision of reality and his image of the good life will not be clouded, nor will his theory be special pleading... The intention of ideology is to justify a particular system of power in society. The ideologue is an interested party; his interest may be to defend things as they are or to criticize the status quo in the hope that a new distribution of power will come into being" (*Political Theory: Philosophy, Ideology, Science;* 1961). When theory is clouded by ideology, it is bound to be distorted. Political philosophy aims at a disinterested search for the principles of the good state and the good society. When clouded by ideology, it is reduced to a rationalization for current or future political and social arrangements. For instance, upholders of capitalism regard private property as most conducive to justice and social progress while upholders of socialism regard social ownership of means of production as the most suitable method of achieving these ends. Similarly, upholders of nationalism place national pride and national interest above any other goal while supporters of internationalism tend to disregard national boundaries to determine the index of human progress. In a nutshell, all ideologies are biased towards partisan ends. Any such bias obstructs our search for truth. Political science demands a disinterested search for knowledge. Ideology focuses on selected parts of social and political reality, and gives its distorted description as well as explanation. On the contrary, scholarly detachment is the keynote of political theory in real sense of the term.

Ideology

Ideology refers to a set of ideas and arguments used to defend an existing or a proposed distribution of power in society. These ideas are accepted to be true by their upholders without inquiring into their validity. The ruling class may propagate its ideology to strengthen its own position while its opponents may use their ideology to mobilize people to replace the existing order by a new one to achieve some great objectives.

[II] SIGNIFICANCE OF POLITICAL THEORY

Political science and political philosophy play complementary roles in the realm of political theory. Significance of political theory may, therefore, be sought in both of these areas.

CONTROL OF SOCIAL LIFE

Scientific analysis of political life enables us to understand and solve the problems of our social life. Just as the knowledge of geology helps us in understanding the causes of earthquake and gives us insights for preventing the havoc caused by it, so political science enables us to understand the causes of conflict and violence in society and gives us insights for preventing their outburst. Just as the knowledge of physics enables us to generate electricity from our thermal and water resources, so the knowledge of political science enables us to secure development of society from our human resources. Just as the knowledge of medical science enables us to control and cure various diseases of human body, so political science guides us to find remedies of political instability and various types of social crises.

SOCIAL CRITICISM AND RECONSTRUCTION

Political philosophy is primarily concerned with right and wrong, good and evil in social life. When we find something wrong in our society and polity, we look for logical grounds for criticizing it and speculate about the creation of a good society. A galaxy of political philosophers like Plato, Aristotle, St. Augustine, Machiavelli, Hobbes, Locke, Rousseau, Hegel, Marx, Mill and Macpherson have analysed the prevailing ills in society and they have given their own schemes of social reconstruction. We cannot accept any of these proposals as the final truth. But they give us ample insights into the possible ills of social life and their remedies. We can draw our own scheme of social reconstruction on the basis of these insights. For example, Plato brilliantly exposed the *modus operandi* of selfish and cunning politicians in a democracy. Machiavelli vividly described the character of selfish and greedy people. Marx identified the sources of conflict between the owners and non-owners of property, and Macpherson exposed the intricacies of power structure in contemporary society which obstructs the way to creative freedom of individual. We can draw valuable insights from their thought for finding remedies to the existing ills in the present-day society.

CLARIFICATION OF CONCEPTS

Political philosophy helps us a lot in the clarification of concepts used in the analysis of social and political life. In fact the clarification of concepts in each area of study—whether science or philosophy—is essential for the development of knowledge. This task is particularly difficult in the field of political theory. As Sheldon S. Wolin has pointed out: "There is the widespread tendency to utilize the same words and notions in describing non-political phenomena that we do in talking about political matters. In contrast to the restricted technical usages of mathematics and the natural sciences, phrases like 'the authority of the father', 'the authority of the church', or 'the authority of Parliament' are evidence of the parallel usages prevailing in social and political discussions" *(Politics and Vision;* 1960).

So when we use the terms of common parlance in political discourse, it is very important to determine their technical meaning. Moreover, the terms like authority, social class, liberty, equality, justice, democracy, etc. may be applied by different schools of thought to indicate different ideas. Political philosophy tries to determine their precise meaning which should be acceptable to the upholders of different ideologies. Agreement on the meaning of the terms of political discourse does not necessarily mean that they come to accept each other's viewpoint. But it certainly paves the way for their dialogue. For example, if a liberal and a socialist accept the same meaning of 'freedom' or 'equality', they are likely to appreciate each other's viewpoint more readily.

As long as precise meanings of the terms of political discourse are not determined, some people may apply them so cleverly as to conceal a weak point of their argument. Some selfish leaders and demagogues may use these terms to mislead people by creating an emotional appeal and evading reason, and autocrats may apply them to legitimize their oppressive regimes. as Mussolini (1883-1945) did in Italy.

Again, a precise and widely accepted definition of a term enables each thinker to build his argument on a sound footing. *As every innovative mechanic need not invent a wheel to assemble a new machine, so every new thinker need not devise new terminology to present his point of view.*

ENCOURAGEMENT TO MUTUAL RESPECT AND TOLERATION

The tradition of political theory encourages a dignified debate between upholders of different points of view. Most political philosophers from ancient times till the present-day have been dwelling on some common problems and giving us new insights. As Andrew Hacker has significantly observed: "Political theory is a never-ending conversation among theorists. And while the greatest of the debates are never resolved, the criticisms which the writers make of each other are always most vivid and illuminating... Politics is, after all, the most democratic of sciences. The final judgements concerning political reality and the good life are the responsibility of all who undertake the study of theory" *(Political Theory: Philosophy, Ideology, Science;* 1961).

When we follow the tradition of political philosophers, it inspires us to understand each other's viewpoint. It gives us an opportunity to identify the strengths and weaknesses of our thought, to convince others and be convinced by others when truth is discovered. In short, political theory generates mutual respect and toleration among us and prompts us to resolve our differences peacefully.

CONCLUSION

Broadly speaking, political theory consists of political science and political philosophy. These two branches of political theory taken together perform three functions which are recognized as the functions of political theory: (*a*) Description; (*b*) Criticism; and (*c*) Reconstruction. Political science mainly relies on empirical method, that is the knowledge based on our practical experience which is supposed to be most reliable. Hence it specializes in 'description'. Political philosophy being concerned with value-judgement specializes in 'criticism' and 'reconstruction'.

Advocates of positivism, neo-positivism (logical positivism) and behaviouralism wish to confine political theory to the sphere of political science. They argue that evaluative statements are based on individual or group preferences which differ from individual to individual, and from group to group. There is no reliable method of determining what is right or wrong, good or evil; one cannot scientifically discover the purpose of the universe or human life. Hence the questions of value-judgement should be dropped from the purview of political theory altogether.

However, since the advent of post-behaviouralism (1969) and consequent upon the revival of political philosophy in the 1970s and 1980s, there has been a renewed emphasis on values in the realm of political theory. It is now argued that value-judgement serves as an essential guide to social policy. Indifference to value-judgement will leave society in the dark. The emerging concerns with environmentalism, feminism, human rights and social justice for the subaltern groups, etc. call for exploring the new horizons of value-judgement. If political theory tends to relinquish this important function, it may be grabbed by some less competent agency. As David Held *(Political Theory Today;* 1991; Editor's Introduction) has pointed out: "Taken as a whole, the tasks of political theory are unquestionably demanding. In the absence of their systematic pursuit, there is always the danger that politics will be left to the ignorant and self-interested, or to those simply with a 'will to power'."

Thus, all the functions of political theory have now become very important and urgent in the present-day world where most of our problems are assuming global dimensions and they are being recognized as the problems of humanity as such.

[III]
DEBATE ON THE DECLINE OF POLITICAL THEORY

Political theory implies an intellectual effort to attain a systematic knowledge about the goals and methods of politics. In this sense, it has a long tradition spreading over two-and-a-half millenniums. However, in mid-twentieth century the exponents of new political science began to question the continued relevance of the traditional political theory.

David Easton, an American political scientist, in his *Political System: An Inquiry into the State of Political Science* (1953) asserted that the traditional political theory was based on mere speculation. It was devoid of acute observation of the political reality. In order to lay scientific foundations of the study of politics, it was necessary to rescue it from the study of classics and the history of political ideas. Easton argued that the traditional political theory was the product of the turmoil that characterized the past ages. It particularly flourished in Greece in pre-Plato days, Italy in the fifteenth century, England in the sixteenth and seventeenth centuries, and France in the eighteenth century which were the days of widespread social and political upheaval. It had no relevance in contemporary society.

Easton also pointed out that there has been no outstanding political philosopher after Marx (1818-83) and J.S. Mill (1806-73). Why live parasitically on a century-old ideas? Easton argued that while economists and sociologists had produced a systematic study of human behaviour in their respective spheres of investigation, political scientists had lagged behind. They failed to acquire suitable research tools to account for the rise of fascism or communism and their continuance! Again, during the Second World War (1939-45) economists, sociologists and psychologists had played an active role in the decision-making process, but political scientists were ignored.

Easton, therefore, appealed for building up a behavioural political science, closer to other social sciences, to take its due place in the decision-making process. He suggested that while traditional political theory was primarily concerned with evolving suitable values for society, modern political science need not make efforts in this direction. He believed that values represent individual or group preferences relative to the social conditions in which these are developed. Contemporary society would evolve its own value system from its own experience and insight. Political scientists should only focus on building causal theory to explain political behaviour.

Causal Theory

Causal theory refers to the theory that explains the relation between cause and effect. In other words, it inquires into the cause of what happens; and anticipates what will happen if certain cause is present.

However, Easton changed his view after one-and-a-half decades. In his presidential address to the American Political Science Association in 1969, he launched his 'post-behavioural' revolution. In fact, Easton was trying to convert political science from a 'pure science' to 'applied science'. He insisted that scientific investigation should enable the contemporary society to tide over the prevailing crisis. This also involved a renewed concern with values which were sought to be excluded in the earlier behavioural approach.

The debate on the decline of political theory which appeared in 1950s was also joined by some other prominent writers. Thus, Alfred Cobban in his paper on 'The Decline of Political Theory' published in *Political Science Quarterly* (1953) argued that political theory had lost its significance in capitalist as well as communist systems. Capitalist systems were inspired by the idea of 'libertarian democracy' whereas there was no political theorist of democracy. Capitalist system was characterized by an overwhelming role of bureaucracy and the creation of a huge military machine. Political theory had practically to play no role in sustaining this system. On the other hand, communist systems were characterized by a new form of party organization and the rule of a small oligarchy. Political theory had taken a back seat under these systems.

Cobban pointed out that Hegel and Marx were interested in a small part of the universe. Hegel was primarily concerned with 'territorial state' and Marx with 'proletariat class'. They wanted to discover what was predestined within their respective frames of reference. Contemporary politics was operating on such a large scale that it could not be analysed in the light of any partial or narrow theory. Besides, logical positivists who sought to concentrate on facts to the exclusion of values were also responsible for the decline of political theory. However, Cobban came to the conclusion that all was not yet lost. Political science has to answer questions which the methodology of social sciences (*i.e.* the methodology akin to that of the natural sciences) may not be able to answer. It must evolve criteria of judgement which will revive the relevance of political philosophy.

Then Seymour Martin Lipset in his *Political Man: The Social Bases of Politics* (1960) argued that the values of the contemporary society had already been decided. In the United States, the age-old search for 'good society' had come to an end because they had already achieved it. The prevailing form of democracy in that country was "the closest approximation to the good society itself in operation". Thus, Lipset too questioned the continued relevance of political theory in those days.

Indeed, the exponents of behavioural approach sought to strengthen scientific basis of the study of politics and to delink it from political philosophy. But the champions of political philosophy never approved of their stand. Leo Strauss in his famous paper 'What is Political Philosophy?' published in *Journal of Politics* (1957) and in 'An Epilogue' to *Essays on the Scientific Study of Politics* (edited by Herbert J. Storing; 1962) argued that the new science of politics was, in fact, a symptom of the alleged decline of political theory. By adopting positivist approach, it had ignored the challenge of normative issues. Empirical theory of politics asserts equal importance of all social values. It denies that certain things are intrinsically high while others are intrinsically low. Thus, it obliterates the distinction between men and brutes as if it destroys the identity of clean water by mixing it with dirty water.

Commenting on this debate, Dante Germino in his *Beyond Ideology: The Revival of Political Theory* (1967) argued that in most of the nineteenth century and early twentieth century there were two major causes of the decline of political theory: (*a*) the rise of positivism which led to the craze for science; and (*b*) the prevalence of political ideologies culminating in Marxism. But now it was again in ascendancy, particularly in the political thought of Michael Oakeshott, Hannah Arendt, Bertrand de Jouvenal, Leo Strauss and Eric Voegelin. This list was expanded by Germino in a subsequent paper 'The Contemporary Relevance of the Classics of Political Philosophy' (*Handbook of Political Science*, ed. by Fred I. Greenstein, Nelson W. Polsby, Vol. I; 1975). The new political thinkers added to this list included: John Rawls, C.B. Macpherson, Christian Bay, Robert Nozick, Herbert Marcuse, Jürgen Habermas, Alasdair MacIntyre and Michael Walzer. The works of these writers had revived the grand tradition of political philosophy.

Germino suggested that in order to understand the new role of political theory it was imperative to identify it with political philosophy. Political philosophy is a critical study of the principles of right order in human social existence, involving inquiry into right and wrong. It is neither reductionist behavioural science where everything is reduced to sense-experience, nor opinionated ideology which accepts some principles to be true without inquiring into their validity. It comprehends both the knowledge of facts and the insight with which that knowledge is comprehended.

According to Germino, political philosophy deals with perennial problems confronting man in his social existence. Detachment is not ethical neutrality. A political philosopher cannot remain indifferent to the political struggle of his times as a behaviouralist would claim. In short, behavioural political science concentrates on facts and remains neutral to values. Political philosophy cannot grow along with positivism which abstains from a critical examination of any social situation. The gulf between traditionalist and behaviouralist components of political theory is so wide that they cannot be 'reunited'. Any theory separated from the perennial concerns of political philosophy will prove to be irrelevant.

Germino laments that the behavioural political theory has often implicitly or uncritically endorsed the policies and practices of the established order instead of performing the Socratic function of 'speaking truth to power'. He warns that full recovery of critical political theory cannot be achieved within the positivist universe of discourse.

Herbert Marcuse (1898-1979) has significantly pointed to the risk involved in the demand for scientific study of society and politics. He has argued that when the language of social science attempts to conform to the language of natural science, it tends to lend support to the *status quo*. In this context, scientific terminology is sought to be defined in terms of such operations and behaviour that are capable of observation and measurement. This leaves no scope for a critical vision in the scientific language. For instance, when people's participation is sought to be estimated on the basis of the numbers of voters who turn up at elections, we do not question whether the prevailing electoral system is conducive to the spirit of democracy! When we adopt this method of study, social science no longer remains an instrument of social inquiry; it becomes an instrument of social control.

In any case, since 1970s the dispute between political science and political philosophy has largely subsided. While David Easton had shown a renewed concern with values in his post-behavioural approach, the exponents of political philosophy did not hesitate in testing their assumptions by empirical method. Earlier, Karl Popper (1902-94), an eminent exponent of scientific method, had sought to recommend certain social values. Now John Rawls (1921-2002) adopted empirical method for arriving at his principles of justice. Then C.B. Macpherson (1911-87) attacked the empirical theory of democracy propounded by Joseph Schumpeter (1883-1950) and Robert Dahl (1915-2014), and advanced his own radical theory of democracy. Herbert Marcuse and Jürgen Habermas (1929-) have shown a strong empirical insight in their critical analysis of the contemporary capitalism. It is now widely held that political science, like other social and natural sciences, enables us to strengthen our means but we will have to resort to political philosophy to determine our ends. Means and ends are interdependent. Hence, political science and political philosophy play complementary roles in our social life.

2

Concept of Ideology

IN THE REALM of political theory, the term 'ideology' is applied in two contexts: (*a*) a set of ideas which are accepted to be true by a particular group, party or nation without further examination; and (*b*) the science of ideas which examines as to how different ideas are formed, how truth is distorted, and how we can overcome distortions to discover true knowledge.

[I]
IDEOLOGY AS A SET OF IDEAS

In this context, ideology means a set of those ideas which are accepted to be true by a particular group without further examination. These ideas are invoked in order to justify or denounce a particular way of social, economic or political organization. In this sense, ideology is a matter of faith; it has no scientific basis. Adherents of an ideology think that its validity need not be subjected to verification. Different groups may adhere to different ideologies; hence differences among them are inevitable. Ideology, therefore, gives rise to love-hate relationship, which is not conducive to scientific temper. Examples of some ideologies are: liberalism, capitalism, socialism, Marxism, communism, anarchism, fascism, imperialism, nationalism, internationalism, etc.

Scientific Temper

Scientific temper refers to an inclination to rely on scientific method for discovering truth and acting on the truth so discovered. It does not subscribe to miracles, magic or sorcery. It draws conclusions only from scientific evidence and reason, and rules out any role of abstract forces or supernatural causes, movements of heavenly bodies, acts of ghosts or evil spirits, etc. in regulating human life, as science and superstition do not go together.

IDEOLOGY, POLITICS AND POLITICAL THEORY

A group will invoke its ideology to determine the best system of government, the basis of right to rule and the procedure for the selection of rulers. Broadly speaking, it answers the following questions: Who should rule? How rulers should be selected? According to what principles should a government operate? And, what institutions should be maintained or replaced for the realization of those principles? When an ideology is used to defend an existing system or to advocate a limited or a radical change in that system, it becomes a part of politics. A political ideology may lend legitimacy to the ruling class or it may involve an urge for revolution. It, therefore, signifies the manipulative power of a dominant class or of a social movement.

An ideology is action-oriented. It presents a cause before its adherents and induces them to fight for that cause, and to make sacrifices for its realization. For example, nationalism may inspire people to sacrifice their wealth or life for defending the freedom of their nation. But communalism may induce hatred among people towards members of another community and prompt them to destroy life and property of innocent persons. One stream of fundamentalism, based on obscurantism, has given rise to worldwide terrorism.

Fundamentalism

Fundamentalism refers to an extremely orthodox view of religion which regards the contents of its scripture to be literally true, and firmly adheres to its teachings. So it accepts the description of supernatural events and divine miracles included in the scripture with full faith. It does not recognize any scientific knowledge that contradicts the contents of the scripture.

Obscurantism

Obscurantism refers to an approach, policy or viewpoint which tends to project the world in such a form that ordinary people are unable to attain true knowledge thereof. It believes in concealing the truth and preventing its knowledge to reach the ordinary people who continue to be guided by superstitions.

In the sphere of politics, conflicting ideologies may be invoked to defend conflicting norms or ideals. Of these, some ideals may be designed to serve some vested interests, and some ideals may seek to challenge irrational beliefs and conventions, and thus pave the way for progress. For example, ideology of imperialism may be invoked to encourage the exploitation of colonial territories and their people, while environmentalism may be invoked to save humanity from the curse of atmospheric pollution and depletion of valuable natural resources.

Coming to political theory, it may be observed that in many cases political theories and political ideologies are described by the same terminology. For instance, the terms 'liberalism', 'socialism', 'communism', etc. are applied to describe certain political ideologies as well as political theories. Do they indicate identical things? Some writers think it is so. At times a political theory seems to justify and prescribe a course of action as if it were a political ideology. The genesis of a political theory may be sought to be explained in the light of stresses and strains emanating from actual politics. Sometimes, clash of some political theories may be explained in the light of a clash in a political situation. That is why G.H. Sabine in his Preface to the first edition of his *A History of Political Theory* (1937) wrote:

> This history of political theory is written in the light of the hypothesis that theories of politics are themselves a part of politics... Reflection upon the ends of political action, upon the means of achieving them, upon the possibilities and necessities of political situations, and upon the obligations that political purposes impose is an intrinsic element of the whole political process.

However, Sabine's view on this issue cannot be accepted as the final word. We must draw a distinction between the origin and the validity of a theory. While it may be conceded that political theories arise from different political situations, yet the study of political theory also includes a critical evaluation of these theories. This critical evaluation involves segregation of truth embodied in these theories from those elements which are the product of political considerations. For example, we denounce Aristotle's defence of slavery and subjugation of women because these were designed to promote the interests of 'freemen' in ancient Greek society. But his explanation of the instability of constitutions stating that the 'power and virtue cannot coexist' must be accepted as valid as it embodies an eternal truth. Similarly, Machiavelli's advice to the Prince to set aside all moral considerations cannot be accepted, but his insights regarding human behaviour can be profitably used in the sphere of diplomacy and statecraft.

It is the critical function of political theory that distinguishes it from the set of ideas which are the product of politics. Politics involves the pursuit of partisan ends. Political ideology is closely related to politics because it involves a passionate search for a better society according to the prescribed model. But political theory involves a disinterested search for a better society. Its goals are under constant investigation and critical examination. Andrew Hacker, in his *Political Theory: Philosophy, Ideology, Science* (1961), has observed that whether we look at the philosophical side of political theory or its scientific side, it is always dispassionate and disinterested. In other words, the theorist has no fascination for a particular political arrangement. His image of a good life is not affected by any prejudice. He does not favour or oppose any particular arrangement without examining its rightness. On the contrary, an ideology is designed either to defend the existing system, or to condemn it in order to prove the superiority of a different system.

If theory is loaded by an ideology, it is bound to be distorted. Political philosophy or political theory calls for a disinterested search for the best system of state and society. Ideology seeks to justify an existing or a future political and social arrangement. Political science calls for impartial observation of political and social reality. Ideology focuses on selected parts of political and social reality, and gives its distorted description as well as explanation. On the contrary, absolute impartiality is the keynote of genuine political theory.

In the realm of political theory, each political theory should be critically examined. Its strong and weak points must be discerned. It should be compared with other relevant theories and evaluated in that light. It is, therefore, imperative to understand ideology as the science of ideas also.

[II]
IDEOLOGY AS THE SCIENCE OF IDEAS

The term 'ideology' was originally devised to describe the science of ideas. In this sense, it seeks to determine how ideas are formed, how they are distorted, and how true ideas could be segregated from false ideas. It was Destutt de Tracy (1754-1836), a French scholar, who first used the word 'ideology' during 1801-15 in his writings on the Enlightenment. He defined it as a study of the process of forming ideas—a science of ideas. Tracy observed that ideas are stimulated by the physical environment; hence empirical learning (*i.e.* the knowledge obtained through sense-experience—sight, sound, smell, taste and touch) is the only source of knowledge. Supernatural or spiritual phenomena have no role to play in the formation of real ideas. Science is founded on these ideas. People could use science for the improvement of social and political conditions.

Although Tracy was the first to use the term 'ideology' in this sense, he was not the first to study the process of formation of ideas. Francis Bacon (1561-1626), an English philosopher, before him, had insisted that knowledge should come from a careful and accurate observation and experience. He held that the knowledge deduced from less scientific methods of inquiry was distorted by false impressions or 'idols'. In short, Bacon and Tracy focused on the validity of knowledge obtained by scientific method, and cautioned us against distorted forms of knowledge.

> All colours will agree in the dark.
>
> Francis Bacon (1625)

In contemporary literature, *the term 'ideology' is applied to the set of ideas which are adopted by a group in order to motivate it for the achievement of predetermined goals.* Science of ideas is now described by different terms, like 'sociology of knowledge' (the term introduced by Karl Mannheim), or 'critical theory' (the term popularized by the Frankfurt School). Science of ideas is used to identify the causes of distortion in the prevailing ideologies. A systematic attempt in this direction began with Marx. Later Lukacs and Mannheim also made significant contributions to this effort.

Sociology of Knowledge

Sociology of knowledge refers to a systematic attempt to inquire as to how our knowledge is determined, conditioned or distorted by our social background. The term was introduced by Karl Mannheim in *Ideology and Utopia* (1929) although earlier sociologists had also made a significant beginning in this direction.

Critical Theory

Critical theory refers to a stream of philosophical thought which maintains that human society has not yet evolved a rational form of existence, which is still to be achieved. Hence it cannot be analysed by the paradigm of natural sciences. All social institutions and behaviour should, therefore, be analysed from the perspective of their deviation from a rational form. This theory was popularized by the Frankfurt School (which was originally set up in 1923). Critical theory is 'interested' in human emancipation, and not in the achievement of a narrow ideological goal. Hence, it cannot be equated with an ideology.

Dimensions of Ideology

Ideology

Set of Ideas (on best system of society and government)	Science of ideas (on how ideas are formed and distorted)
A matter of faith	A matter of critical examination
Characterized by Closed Mind	Characterized by Open Mind
Interested Search for Better Society	Disinterested Search for Better Society
Instrument of Politics	Instrument of Political Theory
Demands Subordination to Authority	Allows Individual to Question Authority

Illustration

Consider the following statements:

(a) God created man in his own image.

(b) Man created God in his own image.

Now the first statement (which occurs in the *Bible, Old Testament*) conveys an issue of faith. It is required to be accepted without questioning, *i.e.* without asking for any evidence to prove it. On the other hand, the second statement (which seems to be the reversal of the first statement) conveys our own experience. It is akin to an empirical statement. Its occurence can be empirically demonstrated. Each community (particularly each religious community) tends to seek the attributes of man in its image of God and other characters of its mythology. So the first statement corresponds to the concept of ideology as 'a set of ideas' while the second statement is concerned with 'the science of ideas'.

VIEWS OF MARX

Karl Marx (1818-83) in *German Ideology* (1845-46) and *A Contribution to the Critique of Political Economy* (1859) dwelled on the nature of ideology. According to him, ideology is a manifestation of 'false consciousness'. In his *A Contribution to the Critique of Political Economy* (Preface), Marx observed:

> In the social production which men carry on, they enter into definite relations that are indispensable and independent of their will; these relations of production correspond to a definite stage of development of their material powers of production. The sum total of these relations of production constitutes the economic structure of society—the real foundation on which rise legal and political superstructures and to which correspond definite forms of social consciousness. The mode of production in material life determines the general character of the social, political and spiritual process of life. It is not the consciousness of men that determines their existence, but, on the contrary, their social existence determines their consciousness.

According to Marx, in the process of social development material needs of people advance, but their social consciousness lags behind. This distorted consciousness or false consciousness is reflected in their ideology. Dominant class at any stage of social development makes use of ideology to maintain its authority. For example, makers of the French Revolution (1789) raised the slogan of 'Liberty, Equality, Fraternity' to enlist support of the masses. But they settled for liberty which served their interest, *i.e.* the interest of the new entrepreneurial class of those days. They did not proceed to win freedom for common man, but stopped after winning freedom for a new dominant class to ensure inviolability of property.

Marx and Engels (1820-95) held that ideology is an instrument for protecting the interests of the dominant class. Thus, bourgeoisie (the capitalist class) needs ideology to maintain itself in power. On the contrary, when proletariat (the working class) comes to power after the socialist revolution, it has no vested interest in maintaining itself in power. It strives to pave the way for 'withering away' of the state itself. It does not want to continue as the dominant class but prepares for transition to the classless society. However, V.I. Lenin (1870-1924) in his *What is to be Done?* (1902) maintained that ideology is not necessarily a distortion of truth to conceal the prevailing contradictions, but it has become a neutral concept which refers to the political consciousness of different classes, including the proletarian class. He argued that the class struggle will continue for a very long time during the socialist phase. So proletariat also needs an ideology—the ideology of scientific socialism for their guidance, lest they are overpowered by the bourgeois ideology.

Scientific Socialism

Scientific socialism refers to a theory of socialism based on the scientific laws derived from the historical analysis. Marx (1818-83) and Engels (1820-95) are the chief exponents of this theory. They held that various stages of historical development are the manifestations of the contradictions in material conditions which necessarily lead human society to the goal of socialism. Whereas Utopian socialism regards socialism as a moral choice, scientific socialism considers it a historical necessity.

VIEWS OF LUKACS

Georg Lukacs (1885-1971), a Hungarian Marxist, in *History and Class Consciousness* (1923) postulated a theory of the dependence of thought on social life, which primarily consisted of class relations of material production. He held that consciousness was always class consciousness. The proletariat, by virtue of its increasing estrangement within the socio-economic sphere, occupied a unique historical position from which it could achieve universal consciousness.

On the nature of ideology, Lukacs maintained that it refers both to bourgeois and proletarian consciousness, without implying a necessary negative connotation. Marxism itself is the ideological expression of the proletariat. Lukacs held that bourgeois ideology is false, not because ideology itself is 'false consciousness', but because bourgeois class situation is structurally limited. In other words, bourgeoisie (the capitalist class) cannot stand on its own. It must exploit proletariat (the working class) to maintain itself. Bourgeois ideology is deplorable because it dominates and contaminates the psychological consciousness of proletariat. However, Lukacs has warned that ideological struggle should not become a substitute for class struggle.

VIEWS OF MANNHEIM

Karl Mannheim (1893-1947), a German sociologist, in his famous essay *Ideology and Utopia* (1929) rejects Marx's theory of ideology on three grounds:

(*a*) 'style of thought' of any group is only indirectly related to its interests; there is no direct correlation between its consciousness and its economic interests; (*b*) all thought is shaped by its social background; hence Marxism itself is the ideology of a class; and (*c*) apart from classes, other social groups, like different generations, also have a significant influence upon consciousness.

Mannheim introduced the term 'sociology of knowledge' to focus on social determination of knowledge. He sought to generalize Marxist framework as a tool of analysis. He held that the false consciousness may be manifested in two forms— ideology and utopia. Ideology represents the tendency of conservation. It relies on the false consciousness to muster support for the maintenance of *status quo*. On the other hand, utopia represents the impetus to change. It relies on the false consciousness by projecting unrealizable principles to muster support for the forces of change. A ruling class makes use of ideology; the opposition may project a utopia. Mannheim declared that Marxist vision of a classless society was nothing short of utopia. Hence, it also makes false consciousness its tool.

Utopia

Utopia refers to the vision of a perfect social and political system where everyone is happy. Originally it signified an imaginary island depicted by Sir Thomas More in his Latin work *Utopia* (1516). In social sciences, this term is applied to designate a set of fascinating but unrealizable principles.

The relative character of all knowledge as postulated by Mannheim makes the knowledge of objective truth extremely difficult. Is there no hope, then, to discover truth? Well, there is a silver lining. Mannheim hinges on the possibility of a 'free-floating stratum' of intellectuals between the contending classes to achieve disinterested knowledge. He hopes that some enlightened individuals within the conflicting groups will realize that their perception of truth is partial; it could be complemented by understanding their opponent's view. Such individuals from both sides will come together with an open mind; they will enter into a dialogue and incessantly strive to arrive at the objective truth. Thus, they will open the way to achieve synthetic common knowledge of the prevailing historical situation and a realistic assessment of actual possibilities. In other words, they will be able to grasp a realistic vision between ideology and utopia.

Mannheim identifies these intellectuals as social scientists. He recommends that these social scientists, who have proved their ability to grasp the objective truth, should be given authority to rule.

Critics argue that Mannheim has created confusion between the origin and validity of knowledge. His extreme relativism contemplates the existence of ideas without upholders. Moreover, giving absolute power to social scientists is fraught with danger of absolutism. They would behave like self-righteous rulers who would refuse to accept any new ideas that may challenge their authority. This tendency must be prevented to pave the way for social progress.

Let these social scientists function as critics of power-holders instead of wielding power themselves. They would better serve as organizers of agitations and demonstrations, journalist and writers, and as 'conscience-keepers' of society.

> Power corrupts; absolute power corrupts absolutely.
>
> *Lord Acton*

[III]
IDEOLOGY AND TOTALITARIANISM

When ideology is conceived as an instrument of motivating people for the achievement of predetermined goals, it comes close to totalitarianism. Some writers, therefore, assert that ideology in this sense is found only in totalitarian systems; it has no place in an open society.

> **Totalitarianism**
>
> Totalitarianism refers to a system of governance in which the state seeks to regulate and control all aspects of life of its citizens—whether public or private. In other words, it seeks to direct all political, economic, social-cultural and intellectual activities of people towards fulfilling certain aims which are determined by the state itself. No citizen has the right or opportunity to oppose or criticize the state, or to propose any new aim.

> **Open Society**
>
> Open society refers to a social and political system where there is a free flow of information regarding public affairs and matters of public importance. Public policy in such a system represents a reconciliation of diverse interests of the people. Power-holders under this system do not claim that they have found the truth. Hence, it encourages freedom of expression among citizens; it shows readiness to adopt new ideas; and permits the citizens to criticize the government.

Famous Austrian philosopher Karl Popper (1902-94), in *The Open Society and Its Enemies* (1945), argued that ideology is the characteristic of totalitarianism; it has nothing to do in an open society. He maintained that science and freedom flourish together in a society which is open in the sense that it is willing to accept new ideas. In contrast, a totalitarian society claims that it has already found the truth, and strives to implement it ruthlessly. Ideology is the tool which enables the state to mobilize its manpower and other resources for a goal which is declared to embody the absolute truth. It does not allow anyone to oppose or criticize the public policy which is exclusively determined by the ruling group. In Popper's view, Western liberal-democratic societies are open societies; hence they do not need an ideology for working smoothly. Citizens of these societies are absolutely free to criticize the existing institutions and structures of power.

> **Minds are like parachutes: they function only when open.**
>
> **Thomas R. Dewar**

Then Hannah Arendt (1906-75), a German Jew philosopher in *The Origins of Tatalitarianism* (1951), defined totalitarianism as a system of total domination, characterized by ideology and terror. It was made possible in recent Europe by three factors: (*a*) the specific political and social position of the Jews which had given anti-semitism (the tendency of hatred toward Jews) a new force; (*b*) imperialism which generated racist movements and worldwide expansion of power; and (*c*) dissolution of European society into uprooted masses, so lonely and disoriented that they could be mobilized behind ideologies.

Thus Popper and Arendt focused on the role of ideology as a tool of totalitarianism. It is interesting to recall that Marx had evolved the concept of ideology in late nineteenth century in order to expose the contradictions of capitalism. Concept of totalitarianism was evolved in early twentieth century to describe the dictatorial way of working of communist regime of the Soviet Union till the end of Stalin-era (1953) and fascist regime of Italy (under Mussolini) and Germany (under Hitler) till the end of Second World War (1945). Both communist and fascist regimes made ample use of their respective ideologies for the mobilization of their citizens toward the achievement of their respective goals. Popper largely focused on the communist regime, and Arendt on the fascist regime to bring out the close correlation between ideology and totalitarianism.

CONCLUSION

Ideology has been variously condemned as the reflection of false consciousness or as an instrument of totalitarianism. But it is not fair to look at all ideologies in this light. In actual practice, different ideologies as sets of ideas will continue to exist as the vehicles of value-systems evolved by different groups. They will be used for motivating people to achieve the goals cherished by their upholders. They may also be used by some groups to convince others regarding their rightful claims. Ideologies do not belong exclusively to dominant classes; oppressed classes also have their own ideologies. They cannot be set aside as 'false consciousness'.

Ideologies could serve as a meeting ground for like-minded people, instead of confining themselves to their tribe, caste, religion, region, etc. They may reflect changing social consciousness on crucial issues. Some ideologies have given rise to strong social movements for the emancipation of various oppressed sections. Some ideologies manifest a deep concern with the future of humanity.

An ideology is identified by commitment to a cause. It rules out personal interest, bias or submission to a particular person, group or dynasty. It signifies a set of coherent ideas—perception of real and ideal from one's own position. It may also be used to make others realize that position. That is how, in the sphere of world politics, developing nations strive to impress upon the advanced nations to adopt humanist attitudes and policies.

[IV]
END OF IDEOLOGY DEBATE

The current status of ideology in the world was reviewed in mid-1950s and in 1960s. In Western liberal-democratic countries, it was declared that the age of ideology had come to an end. These countries looked at ideology as a tool of totalitarianism which had no place in open societies. 'End of ideology' also implied that at the advanced stage of industrial development, a country's social-economic organization is determined by the level of its development, and not by its political ideology. In other words, capitalist and communist countries were bound to evolve similar characteristics at the advanced stage of their industrial development, irrespective of their ideological differences.

Early indications of this view may be found in the proceedings of a conference on 'The Future of Freedom' held in Milan, Italy, in 1955. Edward Shils' report on this conference was published in *Encounter* (1955) under the title 'The End of Ideology'. The conference urged its participants to forget their minor differences and discover common grounds to face the danger of Communism. Daniel Bell observed in the course of his speech:

> Today ideologies are exhausted...In the Western World...there is today a rough consensus among intellectuals on political issues: the acceptance of a Welfare State; the desirability of decentralized power; a system of mixed economy and of political pluralism. In that sense too the ideological age has ended.

This view was confirmed and further elaborated by several Western writers. Ralph Dahrendorf in *Class and Class Conflict in Industrial Society* (1957) argued that the Western societies had entered a new phase of development. They were no longer capitalist societies; they had become 'post-capitalist societies'. The coincidence of economic conflict and political conflict, which was the foundation of Marx's theory, had ceased to exist in the post-capitalist societies. In a capitalist society, the lines of industrial and political conflict were superimposed. The opponents within the industrial sphere—capitalists and workers—met again as bourgeoisie and proletariat in the political arena. In contrast, industry and society have been dissociated in the post-capitalist society. The social relations of the industrial sphere, including industrial conflict, no longer dominate the whole society but remain confined in their patterns and problems to the sphere of industry. In post-capitalist society, industry and industrial conflicts are institutionally isolated. In other words, they remain confined within the borders of their proper realm, and do not influence politics and other spheres of social life. Thus in Dahrendorf's view, the framework of Marxian ideology was no longer suitable for the analysis of the Western societies.

Daniel Bell, in his noted work *The End of Ideology* (1960), asserted that post-industrial societies are prone to similar development irrespective of their ideological differences. They have lesser proportion of workers in industry than in services. In other words, at the advanced stage of industrial development in any country the services sector expands at a faster rate than the manufacturing sector. Besides, it is also characterized by the increasing dominance of technical *elites*. The change in this direction is not affected by its political ideology.

Then Seymour M. Lipset, in *Political Man: The Social Bases of Politics* (1960), significantly observed:

> Democracy is not only or even primarily a means through which different groups can attain their ends or seek the good society; it is the good society itself in operation.

Lipset observed that in the Western democracies the differences between the left and the right are no longer profound; the only issues before politics are concerned with marginal increase in wages, marginal rise in prices, and extension of old-age pensions, etc. He maintained that the fundamental political problems of the industrial revolution have been solved: the workers have achieved industrial and political citizenship; the conservatives have accepted the welfare state; and the democratic left has recognized that an increase in overall state power carries with it more dangers to freedom than solutions for economic problems. The triumph of democracy in the West has made the intellectuals realize that they no longer need ideologies or utopias to motivate them to political action.

W.W. Rostow, in *The Stages of Economic Growth: A Non-communist Manifesto* (1960), built a unidimensional model of economic growth which was applicable to all countries irrespective of their political ideologies. He suggested that all societies pass through five stages of growth: traditional society, preconditions for take-off, take-off, road to maturity and the age of high mass consumption. He believed that the process of development going on at that time in Asia, Latin America, Africa and the Middle East was analogous to the stages of preconditions for take-off and take-off which prevailed in the Western societies in late eighteenth and nineteenth centuries. Rostow asserted that the adoption of different political ideologies played no role in determining the course of economic development in different countries.

J.K. Galbraith, in *The New Industrial State* (1967), identified certain characteristics of advanced industrial societies which correspond to the end of ideology thesis. Galbraith observed that all industrialized societies are destined to similar development. This involves greater centralization, bureaucratization, professionalization and technocratization. These characteristics were visible in Russian as well as American systems although they had adopted as divergent ideologies as communism and capitalism respectively. It means that a country's techno-economic structure is shaped by the level of its industrialization, and not by its distinctive political ideology.

Galbraith claimed that a new ruling class consisting of the bureaucratic and technocratic *elite* had emerged in all advanced industrial societies. This class belonged neither to the working class nor to the capitalists. In liberal societies, the members of this class occupied high positions in an open meritocratic system. Because of high rate of social mobility, they are not attached to particular capitalists. Power in society is vested in bureaucracy and technocracy, and not in capitalists. Galbraith comes to the conclusion that in the contemporary world, emancipation of humanity should be sought in anti-bureaucratism rather than in anti-capitalism.

The end of ideology thesis had a message for the new nations of Asia, Africa and Latin America. It implied that they should focus on their industrial development, and should not run after the mirage of communism as a remedy of their ills. With the collapse of communist systems in East European countries in 1989 (which was followed by a similar collapse in the then Soviet Union in 1991), this view got a new impetus in the form of the *'End of History'* thesis. Francis Fukuyama, in his paper entitled 'The End of History', published in *The National Interest* (1989), argued that the failure of socialism (*i.e.* communism in the present context) meant an unabashed victory of economic and political liberalism. It marked the end point of mankind's ideological evolution and the universalization of Western liberal democracy as the final form of human government. Fukuyama maintained that the liberal democracy contains no basic contradictions and that it is capable of fulfilling the deepest aspirations of mankind. Its victory has heralded an end to the long historical struggle which had obstructed its expansion in the past. This thesis was given wide publicity in the Western press and academic circles as it was suited to their mode of thought.

However, Richard Titmuss, C. Wright Mills, C.B. Macpherson and Alasdair MacIntyre severly criticized the end of ideology thesis. Titmuss observed that the champions of the end of ideology thesis overlook the problems of monopolistic concentration of economic power, social disorganization and cultural deprivation within the capitalist system. C. Wright Mills dubbed the upholders of end of ideology thesis the advocates of *status quo*. In his view, it is an ideology of political complacency which appears to be the only way now available for many social scientists to acquiesce in or to justify the established social structure. So far as human and political ideas are concerned, the end of ideology thesis stands for the denial of their relevance. C.B. Macpherson asserted that the champions of the end of ideology thesis make a futile attempt to solve the problem of equitable distribution within the market society. Alasdair MacIntyre

(*Against the Self-images of the Age;* 1971) significantly observed that the 'end of ideology' theorists "failed to entertain one crucial alternative possibility: namely that the end of ideology, far from marking the end-of-ideology, was itself a key expression of the ideology of the time and place where it arose."

In short, the end of ideology debate, and its latest version are designed to project the supremacy of liberal-democratic system in theory as well as practice. In the contemporary climate of increasing urge for liberalization, privatization and globalization, this idea seems to be riding high. However, it needs a close scrutiny. Collapse of socialism in a large part of the world could be the outcome of human faults in its implementation. Moreover, Western democratic world is by no means an epitome of justice and morality. Human emancipation is a complex venture. There are no readymade answers to all human problems. In devising their solution, relevant ideas from different ideologies may be drawn and examined. Of these, liberalism, Marxism, socialism, fascism, anarchism, Gandhism and feminism are particularly important.

[V]
LIBERALISM

BASIC TENETS OF LIBERALISM

Liberalism is a principle of politics which insists on 'liberty' of individual as the first and foremost goal of public policy. Liberty, in this sense, implies 'liberation' from restraints—particularly from the restraints imposed by an authoritarian state. This principle was evolved in the West in late seventeenth century in order to liquidate feudal privileges of the land-owning class and to create favourable conditions for the new entrepreneurial class to enable them to contribute to social progress.

> **Authoritarian State**
>
> Authoritarian state refers to a state where an individual, a group, an institution, or a set of rules enshrined in a sacred book are regarded as the source of authority, *i.e.* legitimate power; its orders or directions are required to be obeyed by all without questioning.

In fact, *liberalism is not a fixed mode of thought, but an intellectual movement which seeks to accommodate new ideas in order to face new situations and new challenges.* However, its basic tenets may be identified as follows:

(*a*) Man is a rational creature. He has immense potential to contribute to social progress as well as to his own good;

(*b*) There is no basic contradiction between an individual's self-interest and the common interest of society. In fact, the common interest denotes a point of reconciliation between the diverse interests of different individuals;

(*c*) Man is endowed with certain natural rights which cannot be transgressed by any authority;

(*d*) Civil society and the state are artificial institutions created by individuals to serve the common interest. They are entitled to demand obedience from individuals on the condition of fulfilling this function;

(*e*) Liberalism believes in the primacy of procedure over the end-product. It means, if the procedure for arriving at a decision is right, the decision may be accepted to be right. Liberal view of freedom, equality, justice and democracy is a search for right procedure in different spheres of social life;

(*f*) Liberalism promotes civil liberties of the individual, including freedom of thought and expression, freedom of association and movement, personal freedom (which rules out search or arrest without a warrant) and strict compliance with legal and judicial procedure. Any restriction on individual freedom should be meant to ensure equal freedom for others;

(*g*) Liberalism upholds freedom of contract. No individual can accept any obligation without his own consent, and without consideration of mutual benefit. The state would function as an umpire in the enforcement of contracts. However, a contract concluded under pressure, or the one which compromises dignity of the individual, shall be void; and finally,

(*h*) Liberalism holds that public policy should be the product of free bargaining between groups of individuals formed to pursue their specific interests.

In short, *liberalism treats market society as the model of social organization* where role of the state should be confined to the protection of individuals' life and property, enforcement of contracts, and maintenance of minimum common services which would not be undertaken by private entrepreneurs. In liberal view, *the state is a necessary evil.* Liberalism treats the state as the means and individual as the end. It rules out absolute authority of the state.

Early exponents of liberalism include John Locke (1632-1704), Adam Smith (1723-90) and Jeremy Bentham (1748-1832). All of them were English philosophers. Locke is known as the father of liberalism. Smith is known as the father of economics; and Bentham, the founder of utilitarianism. All of them defended the principle of *laissez-faire* which implies least interference of the state in the economic activities of individuals. They are the founders of *classical liberalism* which is called *negative liberalism* because it contemplates negative role of the state in the sphere of mutual interaction of individuals. In late nineteenth century, Herbert Spencer (1820-1903), an English philosopher, sought to reaffirm negative liberalism through the application of the principles of natural sciences to social organization. This version of liberalism paved the way for establishing capitalism in the economic sphere.

Laissez Faire

Laissez faire is a French term which means 'leave alone'. It implied the policy of non-intervention by the state in economic activities of individuals. This phrase was in common usage in mercantile and industrial circles in nineteenth century England and other parts of the world, to express a belief in the freedom of industry and economic activity from state interference.

Capitalism

Capitalism refers to an economic system of the modern age, largely based on industrial production, where means of social production (land, buildings, mines, forests, machinery and capital), distribution and exchange are owned by private entrepreneurs, a large number of workers are employed on wages at the market rate, and economic activity is primarily devoted to private profit. Here workers are free to work anywhere according to their skills and capacities as well as market demand.

BROAD STREAMS OF LIBERALISM

Early liberal theory developed in two main directions: (*a*) individualism; and (*b*) utilitarianism. *Individualism* conceded primacy of the individual as a rational being. It required that individual's dignity, independent existence and judgement should be given full recognition while making public policy and decisions. It means, no individual shall be made to suffer in order to benefit any larger unit of society. According to this view, only an individual can have any rights; family, trade union, corporation or the state cannot have any rights which could be distinguished from the rights of their individual members. Similarly, no social unit can have any interests which could be distinguished from the interests of its individual members. Individualism supports a social and legal system which is based on voluntary transactions between individuals. This view strongly upholds market society model and holds that even taxation should be confined to the provision and maintenance of common services. John Locke and Adam Smith are the early exponents of individualism.

On the other hand, *utilitarianism* stands for 'greatest happiness of the greatest number' where interest of the few may be sacrificed in the interest of the collectivity. Happiness is defined as the balance of pleasure over pain derived from various goods and services, acts and policies. Founder of this school of thought, Jeremy Bentham, observed that nature has placed mankind under two sovereign masters—pleasure and pain. Human behaviour is guided by an urge to obtain pleasure and avoid pain. Moral principles and state policy should aim at promoting 'greatest happiness of the greatest number'. Bentham made no distinction between qualities of different pleasures. He insisted on maximizing the quantity of pleasure. But John Stuart Mill (1806-73) pointed to qualitative differences between different types of pleasure, and thus recognized the variety of tastes of different individuals. Further, he projected the liberty of individual as the highest value. These modifications in utilitarianism tilted it toward individualism and transformed its basic character. Mill also pleaded for taxation of the rich for the benefit of the poor, and thus paved the way for the welfare state.

In the nineteenth century, T.H. Green (1836-82), another English philosopher, sought to add a moral dimension to liberalism and thereby advanced a full-fledged theory of the welfare state. This tradition was further developed by L.T. Hobhouse (1864-1929), Harold J. Laski (1893-1950) and R.H. Tawney (1880-1962)—all of them were English philosophers. Thus, the theory and practice of the welfare state flourished in the first half of the twentieth-century England. This theory contemplates positive role of the state in securing a dignified life to individuals. It is, therefore, called *positive liberalism.*

On the political side, liberalism promotes democracy; on the economic side, it promotes capitalism. Democracy is concerned with fulfilling needs and aspirations of ordinary people, but capitalism results in the concentration of economic power in the hands of the few who may use it against the interests of ordinary people. This situation is sought to be rectified by the mechanism of the welfare state.

Welfare State

Welfare state refers to a state that safeguards liberty of its citizens and provides for various types of social services for their benefit, e.g. social security (financial assistance in case of loss of job or any other source of income, death of the bread-winner, prolonged illness or physical disability or any other calamity), free education, public health, poor relief, supply of essential goods and services like foodgrains, milk, fuel and transport to the needy at subsidized rates. It undertakes the protection of cultural heritage including monuments, museums, libraries, art galleries, botanical gardens and zoological parks, etc. It also promotes higher education and scientific research, etc. to step up intellectual and cultural development of society. A welfare state largely resorts to taxation of the rich to provide for the common services as well as for giving reLief to the poor and the distressed.

NEO-LIBERALISM

Neo-liberalism, neo-classical liberalism or *libertarianism* stands for contemporary version of classical liberalism which seeks to restore *laissez faire* individualism. It denounces the welfare state, opposes state intervention and control of economic activities. Champions of neo-liberalism stand for 'rolling back' the state which has immensely expanded its sphere of activities. The chief exponents of neo-liberalism include F.A. Hayek (1899-1992), an Austrian thinker, Milton Friedman (1912-2006), an American economist, and Robert Nozick (1938-2002), an American philosopher.

> One cannot help a country to maintian its standard of life by assisting people to consume more than they produce.
>
> F.A. Hayek (1976)

In the second half of the twentieth century, these thinkers realized that the theory of the welfare state was inimical to individual liberty, as it involved the forced transfer of resources from the more competent to the less competent. In order to restore individual liberty, they sought to revive the principle of *laissez-faire* not only in economic sphere, but also in social and political spheres. In a nutshell, neo-liberalism upholds full autonomy and freedom of the individual. It seeks his liberation from all institutions which tend to restrict his vision of the world, including the institutions of religion, family and customs of social conformity apart from political institutions. Philosophically it repudiates the deterministic outlook of human life, and maintains that human personality, character, thought and actions cannot be construed as the outcome of his circumstances. In other words, it treats man as the maker of his destiny. It is, therefore, hostile to all social and legal restrictions on individual's freedom of action. In the political sphere, neo-liberalism particularly insists that man's economic activity must be actively liberated from all restrictions to enable him to achieve true progress and prosperity.

All neo-liberals believe in the primacy of the 'spontaneous order' of human relationships as exemplified by free markets. They deplore any politics (notably socialism) which pretends to have definitive knowledge of human needs. No government can have such knowledge. Human needs manifest themselves through the myriad unpredictable transactions between individuals living in a free or open society. If government tries to regulate these activities, it would amount to curtailing their freedom without fulfilling their genuine needs. It would, therefore, be advisable to transfer such decisions to the market which will maximize their choice. In the economic sphere, market exemplifies the arena of individual freedom. In the political sphere, market represents a model of genuine democracy, where votes are traded against welfare benefits, and the cost is borne by the most productive members of society.

Socialism

Socialism refers to an economic system of the modern age, largely based on industrial production where means of social production (land, buildings, mines, forests, machinery and capital), distribution and exchange are placed under social ownership and control, and economic activity is primarily devoted to the fulfilment of social needs.

In the contemporary world, neo-liberalism found practical manifestation through three interrelated principles: liberalization, privatization, and globalization.

> **Liberalization**
>
> Liberalization refers to the policy of removal or relaxation of government control or restriction on economic activity of the people with a view to maximizing its efficiency. It seeks to reduce the state's liability toward welfare of the individuals and promote incentive-based rewards rather than dependence on various subsidies.

> **Privatization**
>
> Privatization refers to the policy of transferring government ownership and control of any sector of economy to private ownership and control in order to improve the standard of its management and to prevent loss to the public exchequer.

> **Globalization**
>
> Policy of globalization holds that economic efficiency can be increased to the maximum if economic activity is allowed to benefit from the resources available at the global scale. It encourages the utilization of capital and machinery available in one part of the world, raw materials in another part, labour in still another part for the process of production and search of markets for the final product all over the world. Its objectives include the minimization of cost of a product, enhancement of its quality and the maximization of profit from its marketing.

Broad Streams of Liberalism

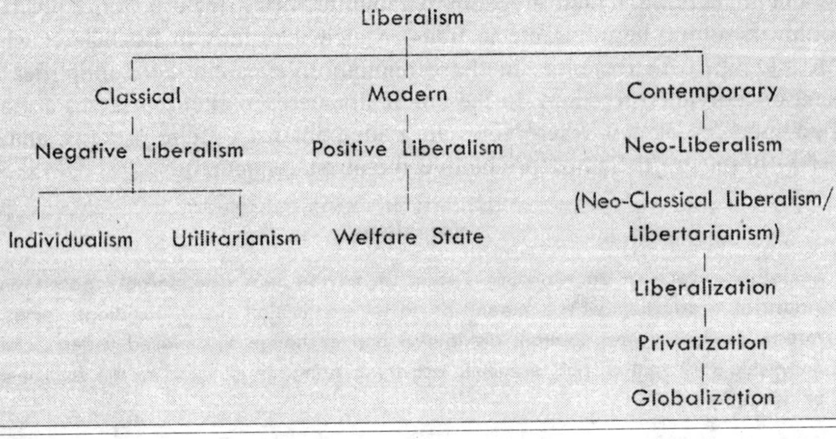

> **The system of property is the most important guarantee of freedom, not only for those who own property, but scarcely less for those who do not.**
>
> **F.A. Hayek (1944)**

A CRITICAL APPRAISAL

Liberalism is, no doubt, a dynamic political philosophy which has responded to the changing needs of time. However, like any other ideology, it has failed to redeem mankind from its predicament. In fact, liberalism has clung to capitalism so firmly that all its new ventures appear to be new devices for sustaining the capitalist system or justifying its existence.

Liberalism Retains Its Bourgeois Character

Liberalism arose in late seventeenth century for the protection of the interests of the *bourgeoisie* (the capitalist class) when political power was wielded by feudal interests. In its early phase, liberalism stood for limiting the power of the state in favour of *laissez-faire* individualism, minimum government and minimum regulation. In pleading for this policy, liberalism insisted so much on freedom of the property-owing class that it set aside all human considerations. As R.H. Tawney, in his *The Acquisitive Society* (1920), observed:

> The story of the struggle between humanitarian sentiment and the theory of property transmitted from the eighteenth century is familiar. No one has forgotten the opposition offered in the name of the right of property to factory legislation, to housing reform, to interference with the adulteration of goods, even to compulsory sanitation of private houses.

Such arguments are no longer advanced. But, at times, the right to property is held sacrosanct even when it is responsible for wide socio-economic disparities, inflicting indignities and injustice on the bulk of mankind.

In a later phase, particularly from early twentieth century when the bourgeoisie themselves came to power, liberalism tended to widen the functions of the state and to support an ever larger degree of regulation. It cannot be denied that the concept of the 'welfare state' was evolved not out of sympathy for the vulnerable sections of society—the peasants, workers and ordinary people—but with a view to enlisting the support of these classes in order to maintain the *status quo.* Thus, in practice, liberalism upholds the capitalist system or *mixed economy* which also creates favourable conditions for the bourgeoisie to maintain their hold on economic as well as political power. The policy of *incremental change,* which implies small and continual concessions to the lower classes, is cleverly devised to contain unrest and to hold the forces of revolution in check. Thus, the welfare state seems to create an illusion of welfare, rather than securing real welfare.

Mixed Economy

Mixed economy refers to a type of national economy which combines some features of capitalism with those of socialism in order to maintain the scope of individual incentives along with adequate provision of social welfare. Under a mixed economy, means of social production may be selectively placed in private sector, public sector and cooperative sector. All sectors are required to function under government guidelines, and all economic activities are sought to be regulated and coordinated through state planning.

Actual Imbalance of Group Interests

Contemporary liberalism upholds representative democracy on the assumption that the state represents the interests of all groups within society and that it ensures reconciliation of conflicting interests. This could be true in the case of some societies but it cannot be demonstrated as a universal phenomenon. In developing nations, it is particularly evident that various groups are not equally conscious of their interests, nor are they equally well-organized, nor equally vocal. Usually, these countries are dominated by 'vested interests'. For instance, in India, a handful of business interests are very well-organized, active and vocal while the tremendously large body of consumers is not adequately organized. Thus, in spite of decisions being taken by representative institutions, in practice, there is an obvious imbalance in the sphere of protection of the interests of various social groups.

CONTRIBUTION OF LIBERALISM

The greatest merit of liberalism lies in initiating the process of replacing traditionalism by modem rationalism. In other words, it asserted that socio-economic relations of men in society, which were hitherto based on 'tradition', should now be based on 'reason'. Since this process was started by the new middle class—the merchants and the industrialists—they were the first to benefit from this change; feudalism was replaced by capitalism not only in the economic sphere, but corresponding changes were brought about in the political sphere as well. This had some evil effects also. The condition of the working classes deteriorated with the success of capitalism. But *once the process of redefining social relations from the point of view of 'reason' had started, it could not be stopped from reaching its logical conclusion*—the rise of socialism. Socialism sought a better deal for the working class on the same principle of 'reason' which was initially invoked by liberalism. Faith in 'reason' is a dynamic force. Liberalism, therefore, did not hesitate to transform itself as and when it was faced with new challenges. This has led to new insights as regards the principles of freedom, equality, justice, democracy, progress, and other human values.

In fact, liberalism is invoked today in two important contexts: (*a*) as a theory of capitalism, and (*b*) as a theory of constitutionalism. So long as liberalism is commended with a view to vindicating the economic relations of the capitalist society, it is bound to suffer from its inner contradictions which must be resolved by invoking human values. On the other hand, when liberalism is invoked as the foundation of constitutionalism requiring suitable curbs on political power, it embodies lasting political values. It is, therefore, bound to survive on this front.

> **Constitutionalism**
>
> Constitutionalism refers to the principle that insists on organization and working of the state according to a constitution so that no organ or office-holder of the state is allowed to use arbitrary power. A constitution not only provides for a framework of government but also prescribes powers of various organs of government and the limits of those powers.

[VI]
MARXISM

WHAT IS MARXISM?

Marxism derives its name from that of Karl Marx (1818-83), a famous German economist and social philosopher of the nineteenth century who is the chief exponent of this theory. It is interesting to recall that this term was unknown in Marx's own lifetime. Friedrich Engels (1820-95), a close friend and collaborator of Marx, once reported the following comment made by Marx himself: "All I know is that I am not a Marxist." Marx probably said so as he did not claim to offer a comprehensive worldview. It is also possible that he did not advance such a claim out of modesty. However, towards the end of the nineteenth century, G.V. Plekhanov (1856-1918), a Russian Marxist, announced that 'Marxism is a whole worldview'. But despite this name, Marxism should not be regarded as a system of thought exclusively belonging to Marx. Marxism, in fact, comprises a rich tradition of social thought—a living tradition, with immense possibilities.

Marxism, in its proper sense, first appeared in the middle of the nineteenth century in response to the oppressive conditions created by the capitalist system. It will be recalled that liberalism arose in late seventeenth century as a philosophy of human freedom, but by the middle of the nineteenth century it had become clear that the classical form of liberalism, with it doctrine of *laissez-faire* and free market economy, had failed to create conditions of human freedom. Liberalism had achieved the goal of establishing capitalism under which a tiny class of capitalists enjoyed special power and privileges at the expense of the large majority of the working class. The legal and political equality sought by the exponents of liberalism had been achieved with tremendous economic inequalities and consequent injustice. Early champions of liberalism had hoped that the elimination of governmental restrictions on business and industry would usher in an era of universal improvement in the material conditions of life. But actual experience showed that unbridled capitalism had produced socially disastrous consequences. The tremendous increase of wealth was cornered by a small section which happened to own the means of social production while the large majority of the industrial population was consigned to a sub-human living. Successful bankers and market speculators increased their wealth by leaps and bounds while the slum-dwelling working classes were living under the constant threat of insecurity, malnutrition, discomfort, disease and death. These developments belied all the humanitarian hopes of universal economic progress.

The first response to these horrible conditions came in the form of an early socialist movement, which opposed the policy of free market competition and drew attention to the deteriorating conditions of the working classes. Early socialists like Saint-Simon (1760-1825) and Louis Blanc (1811-82) in France advocated a more or less centralized economy under state control. Some others sought to project images of model communities governed by the principle of 'free cooperation' instead of 'free competition' as advocated by the capitalist system. Robert Owen (1771-1858) in England and Charles Fourier (1772-1837) in France produced elaborate plans of setting up such model communities. P. J. Proudhon (1809-65) in France hoped to set up a nationwide system of decentralized workers' cooperatives which would bargain with one another for the mutual exchange of goods and services. All these thinkers knew clearly what was wrong with the world, but they were not clear as to what to do about it for they suggested only visionary solutions—far removed from the hard realities of life. In other words, they had arrived at a correct diagnosis of the ills of the capitalist system, but had no clear conception of the remedy. They are, therefore, rightly described as *'utopian socialists'*.

During the decades beginning with the 1830s and the 1840s, the ideas of the utopian socialists were subjected to severe criticism by a group of brilliant writers committed to fundamental social change, notably by Karl Marx, a German scholar, and Friedrich Engels, a young German businessman residing in England. *Marx and Engels sought to replace utopian socialism by scientific socialism for the analysis of social problems and finding their solution.* The solution came in the form of an elaborate philosophy which is now recognized as Marxism. Marx and Engels' *Communist Manifesto* (1848) came out with an interpretation of the role of the working class in the making of past and future history. It also gave a clarion call to workers of all countries to unite for the purpose of securing their own emancipation and, through that emancipation, the freedom of all mankind. Other leading works on this theme include Marx's *A Contribution to the Critique of Political Economy* (1859), *Capital,* Vol. I (1861-79), Vol. II (1885) and Vol. III (1894) (Vol. II and III were edited by

Engels), and Engles' *Anti-Dühring* (1877-78).

In short, Marxism may be defined as a set of political and economic principles founded by Karl Marx and Friedrich Engels in order to lay scientific foundations of socialism. It seeks to understand the problems of human society through historical analysis and treats history as a process of conflict between antagonistic forces and classes. This conflict arises from the faults in the mode of production in which one class comes to gain ownership and control of the means of social production and compels the other class to work on terms and conditions dictated by itself. This conflict reaches its peak in the age of capitalism when it can be resolved only through a revolutionary overthrow of capitalism, placing all means of social production (land, buildings, mines, forests, machinery and capital, etc.) under social ownership and control, enforcing universal labour and ensuring full development of the forces of production.

The original tenets of Marxism—as a scientific system of thought—are identified as *Classical Marxism*. Its chief exponents include, apart from Marx and Engels themselves, V.I. Lenin (1870-1924), a Russian revolutionary and thinker, Rosa Luxemberg (1871-1919), a Polish activist and thinker, and Mao Zedong (1893-1976), a Chinese revolutionary and thinker. The wider implications of Marxism, largely inspired by the humanist thought of the Young Marx, are broadly identified as *Neo-Marxism*. In a nutshell, Classical Marxism holds that private property divides society into dominant and dependent classes with irreconcilable class interests. It is held together only by the ideological power of the dominant class. Human history moves towards its goal of human freedom through the revolutionary destruction of inherent contradictions in society culminating in the emergence of a classless society. Neo-Marxism, on the other hand, seeks to analyse the subtle aspects of the phenomenon of dominance and dependence, distortions in the contemporary civilization and the possible ways to human emancipation.

Young Marx

Karl Marx (1818-83) as the author of his early work is known as Young Marx. This work remained unpublished during his lifetime. It was discovered from the archives of German Social Democrats as late as 1927, and later published as *Economic and Philosophic Manuscripts* of 1844. It is distinguished from Marx's later work which is characterized by scientific rigour. Marx's early work contains his humanist thought on communism, and focuses on the concepts of alienation and freedom. It exposes the dehumanizing effect of capitalism.

MAIN TENETS OF MARXISM

Main tenets of Classical Marxism include— (*a*) Dialectical Materialism; (*b*) Historical Materialism; (*c*) Doctrine of Class Conflict; and (*d*) Theory of Surplus Value.

Dialectical Materialism

Marx borrowed his dialectical method from German philosopher, G.W.F. Hegel (1770-1831) and sought to combine it with his materialism. Hegel had postulated that 'idea' or 'consciousness' was the essence of the universe, and that all social institutions were the manifestations of the changing forms of idea. Idea evolved into new forms because of its inherent tension, exemplified by the clash between *thesis* (partial truth) and *antithesis* (opposite of thesis—again a partial truth) resulting in *synthesis* (which is nearer to the truth). As long as synthesis itself contains partial truth, it takes on the role of thesis and undergoes the same process until this process reaches absolute truth, as manifested in the 'absolute idea' or 'absolute consciousness'.

On the contrary, Marx believed that 'matter' (and not the idea) was the essence of the universe, and that social institutions were the manifestation of changing material conditions. Matter underwent the dialectical process because of its inherent tension, until perfect material conditions, exemplified by a 'rational mode of production', come into existence. Engels, in his *Anti-Diihring* (1878) postulated three laws of material dialectics (or dialectical materialism): (*a*) the transformation of quantity into quality, and *vice versa;* (*b*) the interpenetration of opposites; and (*c*) the negation of negation. These principles signify the process of resolving contradictions of material conditions of human life which paves the way for social progress. Class conflict is also a manifestation of this process.

Historical Materialism

While dialectical materialism *represents the philosophical basis of Marxism, historical materialism represents its scientific basis.* It implies that in any given epoch the economic relations of society—the means whereby men and women undertake production, distribution and exchange of material goods for the satisfaction of their needs—play important role in shaping their social, political,intellectual and ethical relationships. A perfect society will secure all the necessities of life to the satisfaction of all its members. But it would be achieved through a long-drawn process. Initially, internal stresses and strains in material conditions usher in many imperfect forms of society. These conditions tend to attain perfection in the course of historical development.

> **Just as Darwin discovered the law of development of organic nature, so Marx discovered the law of development of human history.**
>
> **Engels' Epitaph at Marx's Graveside (1883)**

According to the Marxist perspective, the structure of society may be understood in terms of its *base* (the foundation or the *substructure)* and *superstructure* (the external build-up). In this building-like metaphor, base consists of the mode of production while superstructure is represented by its legal and political structure, religion, morals, social practices, literature, art and culture, etc. Mode of production has two components—forces of production and relations of production. Forces of production cannot remain static; they have an inherent tendency of development in the direction of achieving the perfect society.

> It is not the consciousness of men that determines their being, but, on the contrary, their social being that determines their consciousness.
>
> Karl Marx (1859)

Forces of production have two components—means of production (tools and equipment), and labour power (human knowledge and skills), Men and women constantly endeavour to devise better ways of production. Improvement in the means of production is manifested in the development of technology. This is matched by the development of human knowledge and skills as required to operate the new technology. Hence, there is the corresponding development of labour power.

On the other hand, relations of production in any given epoch are determined by the pattern of ownership of the means of social production. This gives rise to two contending classes—*haves* and *have-nots*. In earlier stages of historical development, development of the forces of production fails to make any dent in this pattern. In other words, changes in the mode of production bring about changes in the nature of contending classes, but they do not bring about an end of the class conflict. Change in the nature of contending classes is itself brought about by a social revolution. When material productive forces of society come in conflict with the existing relations of production, these relations turn into their fetters. The new social class, which comes to own new means of production, feels constrained by these fetters and overthrows the old dominant class in a revolution. As a result of social revolution, an old social formation is replaced by a new social formation. In this process old contending classes are replaced by new contending classes, but class conflict continues on a new plane. This has been the case till the rise of capitalism, which will be overthrown by a socialist revolution, leading to the eventual emergence of a classless society.

Social Formation

In Marxist thought, social formation refers to a form of organization of society which comes into existence around a specific mode of production. Changes in the mode of production give rise to different social formations which are associated with different historical epochs. Thus, household-based small-scale production gives rise to slave-owning society; large-scale agriculture-based production gives rise to feudal society; and large-scale machine-based production under private ownership and control gives rise to capitalist society.

Marxian View of the Stages of Historical Development

Historical Epoch	*Prevailing Mode of Production*	*Caused by*	*Social Formation*	*Contending Classes*
Ancient times	Household-based small-scale production	Emergence of private property	Slave-Owning Society	Master and Slave
Medieval times	Large-scale agriculture-based production	Rise of Feudalism	Feudal Society	Lord and Serf
Modern times	Large-scale machine-based production	Rise of Capitalism	Capitalist Society	Capitalist and Worker
Future-I	-do-	Socialist Revolution	Socialist Society	Workers in power and the former capitalists under subjugation
Future-II	-do-	Liquidation of remnants of Capitalism	Communist Society	No contending classes as it will be a classless society

Doctrine of Class Conflict

Class conflict or class struggle is an integral part of historical materialism. The opening sentence of *Communist Manifesto* (1848) reads:

> The history of all hitherto society is the history of class struggles.

Here, history means all *written* history. When *Communist Manifesto* was originally written, the pre-history giving account of primitive tribal communities with common ownership of means of production, was not known. When it became known, it was described as 'primitive communism'. *Communist Manifesto* deals with the period beginning with the division of society into antagonistic classes since the emergence of private property. So *Communist Manifesto* proceeds: "Freeman and slave, patrician and plebeian, lord and serf, guild-master and journeyman, in a word, oppressor and oppressed, stood in constant opposition to one another, carried on an uninterrupted, now hidden, now open fight, a fight that each time ended either in a revolutionary re-constitution of society at large, or in the common ruin of the contending classes."

Primitive Communism

Primitive communism refers to a form of communism (classless society with common ownership of means of production) found in primitive societies. At this stage, the instruments of labour were of most primitive kind—the club, the stone axe, the flint knife, the stone-tipped spear, followed later by the bow and arrow. Man's muscular strength was the only motive force employed to operate these elementary tools. These tools were held in common ownership by the members of the primitive community which engaged itself in common labour, e.g. common hunting, common fishing, and the fruits of this common labour were also shared in common. There was no concept of private property, hence no exploitation of man by man.

With the development of forces of production, one mode of production is replaced by another, but class conflict (between the new social classes) reappears under the new social formation. Thus, ancient slave-owning society was characterized by class conflict between master and slave; medieval feudal society by class conflict between lord and serf; and the modern capitalist society by class conflict between bourgeoisie (capitalists) and proletariat (workers).

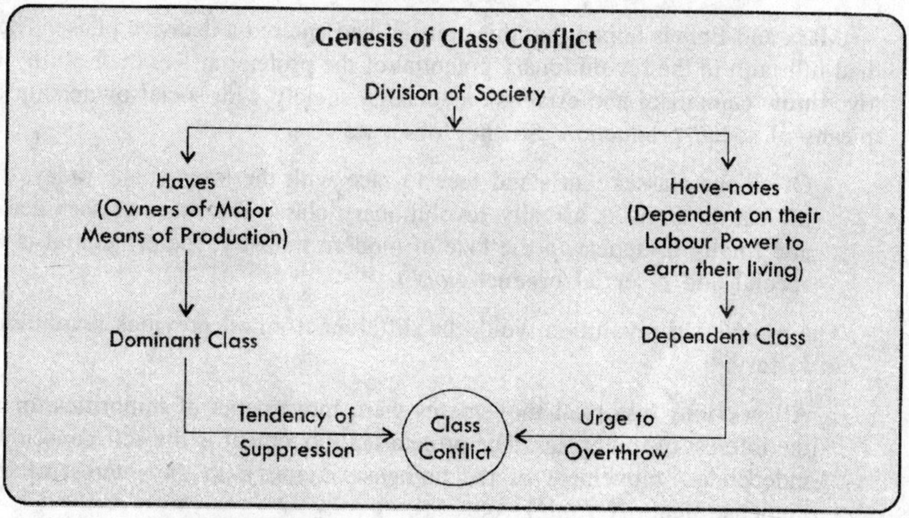

Status of the class conflict in modern capitalist society is described in *Communist Manifesto* as under:

> The modern bourgeois society that has sprouted from the ruins of feudal society has not done away with class antagonisms. It has but established new classes, new conditions of oppression, new forms of struggle in place of the old ones.

Lord and Serf

These were the two contending classes in medieval feudal society. Lord meant the landlord who was the owner of land. Serf meant the peasant who did not own land but cultivated it, and received a small, fixed share of the produce as a return for his toil. Serf was not a full-fledged slave. He could have his family and its belongings, but he could not leave his duty without permission of his lord. Exploitation of serfs was the distinctive feature of feudal society.

Bourgeoisie and Proletariat

These are the two contending classes in modern capitalist society. Engels' note to the English edition of *Communist Manifesto* (1888) reads: "By bourgeoisie is meant the class of modern Capitalists, owners of the means of social production and employers of wage labour. By proletariat, the class of modern wage-labourers who, having no means of production of their own, are reduced to selling their labour power in order to live."

Class conflict in modern capitalist society has appeared in more crystallized form. So *Communist Manifesto* declares:

> Our epoch, the epoch of the bourgeoisie, possesses, however, this distinctive feature: it has simplified the class antagonisms. Society as a whole is more and more splitting up into two great hostile camps, into two great classes directly facing each other: Bourgeoisie and Proletariat.

Marx and Engels hoped that this conflict had entered a decisive phase. They had full faith in the revolutionary potential of the proletariat, *i.e.* their ability to overthrow capitalism and establish a socialist society with social ownership of means of social production. So they observed:

> Of all the classes that stand face to face with the bourgeoisie today, the proletariat alone is a really revolutionary class. The other classes decay and finally disappear in the face of modern industry; the proletariat is its special and essential product *(ibid.)*.

The proletarian revolution would be different from all previous revolutions of history:

> All previous historical movements were movements of minorities, or in the interest of minorities. The proletarian movement is the self-conscious, independent movement of the immense majority, in the interest of the immense majority *(ibid.)*.

According to Marx and Engels, this revolution would bring about the final emancipation of mankind because there is no class below the proletariat which could be subjected to exploitation when the proletariat comes to power. It would place all means of social production under social ownership, make work compulsory for everyone, and develop the forces of production to their full potential. This will pave the way for the emergence of classless society which will mark the end of class conflict.

Theory of Surplus Value

While doctrine of class conflict represents sociological basis of Marxism, theory of surplus value represents its economic basis. It embodies the Marxist critique of capitalism. It is meant to demonstrate how the capitalist mode of production involves the exploitation of working class. *According to Marx, labour is the sole creator of value.* Of the four factors of production, *viz.* land, labour, capital and organization, three factors—land, capital and organization are sterile because they are capable of reproducing only what is put in them. Labour is the only element which produces value in society. In other words, the value of a commodity is the product of labour. The quantity of labour employed in its making should be calculated right from the production of the raw material, processing the raw material, acquiring the sources of energy for its processing, and constructing the required machinery and building for its production. The quantity of labour required in its production is also determined by the average conditions of social production and the average skill of the labour employed.

The actual amount of labour employed in the production of a commodity is called its *natural price.* It differs from its price in the market, or *market price* which fluctuates with the changing conditions of demand and supply. In a free market society, fostered by capitalism, the worker is forced to sell his labour at the market price. When more and more job-seekers come to the market place, the market price of their labour, *i.e.* their wage-rate declines. Their employer—the capitalist exploits their full potential to work but pays them only subsistence wages for their own and their families' sustenance.

Thus, the value produced by the worker may be split into two parts—one part is paid to the worker towards his wages; the other part is pocketed by the capitalist as his profit. This second part is described by Marx as 'surplus value'. Rent and interest are paid from the surplus value. In other words, surplus value denotes the value of the labour done by the worker for which he is not paid at all; it forms part of the capitalist's profit, rent and interest on the sterile elements of production (organization, land and capital). It is, therefore, a glaring example of the worker's exploitation under capitalism.

NEO-MARXISM

Contemporary debates on Marxism focus on the relative importance of its basic tenets and identification of some new forms of domination and conflict emerging in the present-day society. It is no longer believed that the superstructure is wholly dependent on the base. Recognition of a sort of autonomy of the superstructure and interdependence between base and superstructure has led to extensive analysis of various aspects of superstructure.

The ongoing controversies in the arena of Marxist thought largely owe their origin to the work of the Frankfurt School. It was originally set up in 1923 as the Institute of Social Research in the University of Frankfurt, exiled from Germany in 1933 consequent upon the rise of Hitler, and relocated in the United States shortly thereafter. Then after the downfall of Hitler it was reestablished at Frankfurt in the early 1950s. Scholars of this Institute were hostile to capitalism; they were also disillusioned with Soviet socialism. They sought to evolve an alternative path for social development in accordance with the essence of Marxism as understood by them. The ideas evolved by the Frankfurt School are compendiously described as *'critical theory'*, although they do not fit into a single framework. The general outlook of the exponents of critical theory has been described by David Held as follows: "They tried to develop a critical perspective in the discussion of all social practices, that is a perspective which is preoccupied by the critique of ideology—of systematically distorted accounts of reality which attempt to conceal and legitimate asymmetrical power relations. They were concerned with the way in which social interests, conflicts and contradictions are expressed in thought, and how they are produced and reproduced in systems of domination. Through an examination of these systems they hoped to enhance awarenes of the roots of domination, undermine ideologies and help to compel changes in consciousness and action" *(A Dictionary of Marxist Thought,* edited by Tom Bottomore; 1983).

The exponents of critical theory advanced new interpretations of Marxism in several directions and various spheres of learning, including those of philosophy, economics, political science, sociology, anthropology, social psychology, psycho-analysis. music and fine arts, etc. The leading figures of the Frankfurt School—Theodor Adorno (1903-69), Max Horkheimer (1895-1973), Herbert Marcuse (1898-1979) and Jürgen Habermas (1929-), among others, advanced a cultural critique of bourgeois society—particularly in terms of 'technological domination' rather than capitalist domination.

Broadly speaking, contemporary Marxist thought—better known as neo-Marxism—has developed in two directions— humanist and scientific. The humanist strain of neo-Marxism draws particularly on the work of the Young Marx and constitutes the mainstream of critical theory. Its dominant themes are the problems of alienation and ways to human emancipation. Thus, Herbert Marcuse brilliantly portrayed the conditions of alienation in bourgeois society which have reduced the human being to 'one-dimensional man'. He pointed out that capitalism had cunningly anaesthetized the discontent of the oppressed by manipulating the means of communication so as to stimulate trivial, material desires which are easily satisfied. Marcuse argued that human beings should first be made aware of their condition of unfreedom whereafter they will easily find their way to freedom. On the other hand, the scientific strain of neo-Marxism is primarily concerned with its scientific and explanatory character. It is particularly interested in structures as well as relative importance of cultural, ideological and social factors. Thus, Louis Althusser (1918-90), a French communist and philosopher, challenged the humanist themes of Marxist thinking in the early 1960s, and asserted the importance of analysing the deep structures of human societies—especially their modes of production.

CONCLUSION

It is significant that the collapse of socialism in Eastern Europe by the end of 1980s, and its collapse in the former Soviet Union by 1991, followed by the introduction of market economies and multiparty political systems, necessitated new thinking on the adequacy of classical Marxism on which these regimes were based. Moreover, in the People's Republic of China and other countries which still claim to retain their communist systems, necessary changes are being made towards liberalization in keeping with their national needs and aspirations. Now there is no scope of rigidity in maintaining communist systems as it was done during the regimes of Stalin (1879-1953) in Russia and Mao Zedong (1893-1976) in China. Experience has shown that instead of 'withering away of the state' in socialist countries, there has been a collapse of socialist state and consequent return towards liberalism. Champions of classical Marxism try to explain away this situation by alleging that these countries were not really socialist at all!

This is, however, an oversimplification of the issue. It is now becoming increasingly clear that the problem of fighting out the forces of domination and exploitation is no longer confined to the struggle of working class against capitalist class, as originally envisaged in late nineteenth century. The upholders of 'dependency theory' have been arguing that in late twentieth century the focus of struggle has shifted to the fight of the developing nations against the forces of colonialism and neo-colonialism. Other neo-Marxists have amply demonstrated that domination and exploitation in human society assume many complex forms. The framework of Marxism must be modified suitably to tackle all these problems in the contemporary context.

Dependency Theory

Dependency theory refers to the theory that the continued impoverishment of the underdeveloped countries is not generated by their internal conditions like the lack of drive, entrepreneurial spirit, creativity or problem-solving ability. In fact, it is the consequence of their colonial exploitation in the past, and their linkage with the global capitalism in the present, which prevent them from independent development. To overcome this problem they must adopt Western technology but exert their independence in the field of international relations and international trade.

André Gunder Frank (1929-2005), German-American economic historian, and Samir Amin (1931-2018), Egyptian-French Marxian economist, are the chief exponents of dependency theory.

Colonialism

Colonialism refers to the practice under which a nation-state, after consolidating its national power, extends its domination over territories of other countries for exploiting their natural and human resources. The colonial power establishes its own administration in the subject country and takes all resources thereof under its own control.

Neo-Colonialism

Neo-colonialism refers to the practice under which an advanced nation does not maintain its political domination in a foreign territory, but taking advantage of its superior position in the organization of trade and industry, uses the resources of a developing nation as a source of cheap labour and raw materials as well as a big market of its own products. It is a subtle method of economic exploitation of developing nations by the developed nations.

[VII]
SOCIALISM

The term 'socialism' is variously understood and defined by various thinkers and schools of thought. C.E.M. Joad, in his *Introduction to Modern Political Theory* (1924), significantly observed:

> Socialism proves to be a different creed in the hands of its exponents, varying with the temperaments of its advocates and the nature of abuses which have prompted their advocacy ... *Socialism,* in short, *is like a hat that has lost its shape because everybody wears it.*

A large number of works on socialism have evaded the problem of defining it. However, a working definition of socialism is necessary in order to understand its various applications. *The Oxford English Dictionary* defines socialism as 'a theory or policy that aims at or advocates the ownership or control of the means of production—capital, land, property, etc.—by the community as a whole and their administration in the interests of all'. This definition, though not very comprehensive, indicates the chief method and goal of socialism. A more elaborate definition of socialism is found in Joseph A. Schumpeter's *Capitalism, Socialism and Democracy* (1942) where it is defined as:

> that organization of society in which the means of production are controlled, and the decisions on how and what to produce and on who is to get what, are made by public authority instead of by privately-owned and privately-managed firms.

Many other definitions and descriptions of socialism more or less embrace these and similar ideas.

In short, socialism stands for an economic system under which the major instruments of social production (that is the instruments by which production is carried out for consumption by the larger society) are placed under the ownership and control of public authority in order to ensure that they are properly utilized to secure the public interest. It is based on the view that liberty and equality granted to citizens in the political sphere will remain an empty form unless they are accompanied by a reorganization of the economic life of society so as to convert them into substantive rights for citizens. How can socialism be established in society?

It is interesting to note that the varieties of socialism differ from each other because of their different answers to this important question. The distinction between them will help us understand the true character of socialism.

EVOLUTIONARY AND REVOLUTIONARY SOCIALISM

In popular parlance, the term 'socialism' is usually applied to indicate 'evolutionary socialism', that is the kind of socialism achieved by evolutionary process or by degrees, not by wholesale transformation of society in a single stroke. *Evolutionary socialism* may be distinguished from *revolutionary socialism,* which seeks to establish socialism in its totality by overthrowing the capitalist system in a single stroke. In other words, revolutionary socialism seeks to transform the social system thoroughly instead of accepting small concessions for the underprivileged sections. In fact, evolutionary socialism admits an attitude of 'compromise'—compromise between capitalism and socialism, so that the capitalist system is allowed to continue with some changes here and there in the socialist direction. It, therefore, belongs to the liberal tradition. On the other hand, revolutionary socialism makes a direct attack on the prevailing contradictions of the social order. It, therefore, belongs to the Marxist tradition. While evolutionary socialism may also be described as 'liberal socialism', revolutionary socialism may be called 'Marxian socialism'. Evolutionary socialism relies on the democratic method, parliamentary reform and even economic planning on the plea that the interests of the underprivileged sections, especially the working classes, might be represented and taken care of by their representatives and leadership. It is, therefore, coterminous with *'democratic socialism'*. Revolutionary socialism, on the other hand, insists on organizing the working classes for fighting against capitalism so as to overthrow the capitalist order and establish complete socialization of the instruments of production and distribution by revolution.

It is important to note that evolutionary socialism aims at securing the rights of the working classes, especially their economic rights, as a part of the supposed *common interest* of the community. In other words, it seeks to *accommodate* or *reconcile* the interests of the working classes with those of other classes. Thus, it subscribes to the theory of *harmony* or *equilibrium* as the governing principle of social relationships, corresponding to the position taken by modern liberalism. On the other hand, revolutionary socialism repudiates the theory of equilibrium or reconciliation between different interests in society. It seeks to reverse the position of the *dominant* and *dependent* classes of capitalist society, and ultimately to destroy the conditions of domination itself so as to secure a *classless* society. Most of the exponents of evolutionary socialism were associated with Fabian socialism.

DEMOCRATIC SOCIALISM

While Marxism seeks to bring about socialism through revolutionary method, democratic socialism prefers evolutionary or democratic method. Adherents of democratic socialism pay equal importance to democracy and socialism in order to secure social justice. They believe that the goals of democracy and socialism are not separable from each other, both stand for amelioration of the condition of ordinary man. In effect, democratic socialism signifies the use of the democratic method for achieving the socialist goal. It seeks to modify orthodox socialism in some important details.

Partial Socialization of Production and Distribution

Democratic socialists hold that socialism does not require wholesale socialization of the means of social production and distribution. Instead, if some essential means of social production and distribution are placed under state ownership through the democratic process so as to ensure the supply of essential goods and services for the bulk of the population, this would be a substantial achievement in the direction of socialism.

Satisfaction of Moral as well as Material Needs

Democratic socialists seek to expand the goal of socialism. They insist that socialist programme should not be confined to satisfying the material needs of human beings. It should also take care of their moral, intellectual and emotional needs so as to ensure a fuller development of the personality of each individual. Hence, the state should take care not only of food, clothing and shelter for the masses, but also for their education, entertainment, art and culture, etc.

Freedom of Thought and Expression

According to democratic socialists, an atmosphere of freedom is essential for the development of personality. Even if a society has abolished private property, put an end to economic exploitation and managed to satisfy the material needs of all individuals, such conditions will not be conducive to the fuller development of personality without ensuring the freedom of thought and expression, freedom of religion and worship, freedom of movement, and other similar democratic freedoms.

No Form of Dictatorship

Democratic socialism is opposed to all forms of dictatorship, even if it is a 'dictatorship of the proletariat' as expounded by the Marxian theory of socialism. Dictatorship of any kind leads to the suppression of personality; hence it is not conducive to human happiness.

Free Competition for Power

Democratic socialism treats democratic structures—free competition for power among political parties, freedom of pressure groups, parliamentary institutions with an effective role for the opposition, etc.—as essential instruments for achieving the ends of socialism.

Among modern thinkers, Harold J. Laski (1893-1950) has made important contribution to the theory and practice of democratic socialism. Laski has, in fact, sought to combine the ends of socialism with the democratic method of liberalism. In many of his famous works, particularly in his *Liberty in the Modern State (1930), State in Theory and Practice* (1935) *and A Grammar of Politics (1938),* Laski has made a brilliant attempt to combine the concept of liberal freedom with the goal of socialist justice. Then, E.F.M. Durbin, in his *The Politics of Democratic Socialism* (1940), has competently elaborated the tenets of democratic socialism. Many countries of the world today are following the path of democratic socialism. Among these the Scandinavian countries—Sweden, Norway and Denmark—are the most notable. India also claims to follow the path of democratic socialism.

COMMENT

Democratic socialism seeks to provide for democratic rights and civil liberties along with social-economic rights of citizens—a difficult combination indeed! If this could be achieved, it would serve as an ideal scheme for social justice. But democracy is a matter of procedure; it does not prescribe the goals of state policy. Adoption of the goals of social justice in a democratic state largely depends on two factors:

(*a*) Prevalence of a strong and discerning public opinion in favour of the goals of socialism so that those committed to these goals win majority in elections and they have a strong political will to implement their programme; and

(*b*) A strong resource-base for the state which enables it to provide for elaborate public services and social security without resorting to coercion and undue taxation.

If the leadership of a nation is able to motivate the people to work hard to raise production and mobilize resources, democratic socialism will have a good chance. This needs cultivation of a sense of duty, work culture and patriotism among citizens in general—a difficult task indeed! On the other hand, if the leadership resorts to heavy taxation of the relatively well-placed sections, who have improved their standards of living by dint of their talents, efforts, enterprise and frugality, it might mar the incentives and thereby impoverish the resource-base of the nation. This will erode the prospects of maintaining democratic socialism itself.

FABIAN SOCIALISM

Some thirty-five years after the *Communist Manifesto* (1848) was issued, Fabian socialism made its appearance in England. This was the first systematic doctrine of 'democratic socialism' or 'evolutionary socialism' in contrast to Marxian doctrine of 'revolutionary socialism'. Fabian socialists sought to modify Marxian concepts in several ways:

(*a*) They based their economics on the Ricardian law of rent rather than on the labour theory of value;

(*b*) They did not rely exclusively on the working class for bringing about social change but set before themselves the task of 'permeating' the middle class with the socialist message; and finally,

(*c*) They sought to introduce socialism not in a single stroke, but by degrees through state and cooperative ownership of industry, increasing power of labour in legislative and executive offices, growth of trade unions and educational movements and development of social consciousness—through gradual democratization of society in the political, economic and intellectual fields.

Ricardian Law of Rent

Ricardian law of rent refers to a law of economics enunciated by David Ricardo (1772-1823), a British economist. It held that with the growth of industrialization demand for foodgrains rises, and rent on land goes up. So landlords immensely benefit from the growth of capitalism.

Fabian socialism or Fabianism was first developed in England by the Fabian Society (founded in 1884) from which it derived its name. The term 'Fabian' was adopted after the name of a great Roman General, Quintus Fabius (275-203 B.C.), whose tactics in the fight against Hannibal served as a guide for the Society. Thus its motto read: "For the right moment you must wait, as Fabius did, most patiently, when warring against Hannibal, though many censured his delays; but when the time comes, you must strike hard, as Fabius did, or your waiting will be in vain and fruitless."

It will be recalled that Marxian socialism, developed in the late forties of the nineteenth century, had envisaged revolution as an essential medium of change from capitalism to socialism. However, Fabian socialism regarded the transition from capitalism to socialism as a gradual process; it looked forward to the socialization of industry by the peaceful use of economic and political agencies already in hand.

Marxian socialism had relied on the strength of the working class to bring about the transition from capitalism to socialism; Fabian socialism sought to make use of the services of the middle class for developing the technique of bringing about a new social order; it considered arousing the social conscience of the community in favour of the socialist ideal as a significant achievement.

Fabianism, in fact, arose in the wake of the establishment of democracy in Great Britain, especially during the years 1865 to 1885. During this period, the working classes had not only obtained the franchise (right-to-vote) and the legalization of trade unions, but their influence on legislation and the wage-contract was visibly on the increase. In such a state there was no need of a revolution to create a new political mechanism, for it was already in existence and needed only to be used for the social transformation.

The Fabian socialists addressed themselves to the task of making the democratic state an instrument of systematic social reform. Sydney Webb (1859-1947), the leading Fabian socialist, maintained that the mission of the socialists was to acquire knowledge by means of specialized research into the various manifestations of economic and social life, to acquaint themselves with the machinery of legislation and administration, and to place their knowledge and experience at the disposal of all political agencies.

With the new approach, Fabianism was able to attract some very brilliant men of England who became its exponents. Among them George Bernard Shaw (1856-1950), Sydney Webb (1859-1947), Beatrice Webb (1858-1943), Sidney Olivier (1859-1943), Graham Wallas (1858-1932), and G.D.H. Cole (1889-1959) are the most illustrious figures.

AIMS AND OBJECTS OF FABIANISM

The exponents of Fabian socialism, which included many eminent writers, produced a sizeable literature wherein they spelled out their aims and objects. Among these, some are quite outstanding.

Emancipation of Land and Industrial Capital

In pursuance of its socialist mission, the Fabian Society sought reorganization of society by the emancipation of land and industrial capital from individual and class ownership, and vesting them in the community for the general benefit, so that the natural and acquired assets of the community could be equitably shared by all.

This, in effect, meant working for the extinction of private property in land so that individual appropriation in the form of rent and other benefits accruing from private ownership of land could be stopped. In the past, the monopoly of the means of industrial production, industrial inventions and transformation of surplus income had mainly enriched the proprietary class while the worker had remained dependent upon that class for the means to earn a living. Fabianism sought to emancipate the worker through the transfer of the management of industrial capital to the community as a whole.

Equality of Opportunity

The Fabian Society was convinced that the emancipation of land and industrial capital from individual and class ownership would create conditions under which rent and interest would be added to the reward of labour. The idle class, living on the labour of others, would necessarily disappear and political equality of opportunity would be maintained by the spontaneous action of economic forces with much less interference in personal liberty than the existing system entailed.

Dissemination of Socialist Ideas

The Fabian Society aimed at spreading socialist ideas, especially regarding the relation between individual and society in its economic, ethical and political aspects, including the establishment of equal citizenship for men and women. For this purpose, the Fabian socialists sought to use the democratic method of a slow and gradual turning of the popular mind to the new principles of social reorganization. Sydney Webb, writing on the historical basis of socialism in the *Fabian Essays* (1889), edited by George Bernard Shaw, observed that important organic changes can only be: (1) *democratic,* and thus acceptable to a majority of the people; (2) *gradual,* and thus causing no dislocation, however rapid might be the rate of progress; (3) *not* regarded as *immoral* by the mass of the people, and thus not subjectively demoralizing them; and (4) in England, at any rate, constitutional and peaceful.

Webb came out with a new interpretation of democracy in conformity with the socialist point of view. He asserted that democracy consisted in the *control by the people themselves,* not only of their own political organization, but, through that also, *of the main instruments of wealth production; the gradual substitution of organized cooperation for the anarchy of competitive struggle and the consequent recovery of the enormous share which the possessors of the instruments of industry are able to take from the produce.*

Thus, the Fabian socialists were convinced that the spread of socialist ideas would automatically *transform democracy into socialism.*

Universal Education

Sydney Olivier, writing on the moral basis of socialism in the *Fabian Essays,* insisted on the provision of universal education as an essential means of emancipation of the working class. He pointed out that the educational system was an essential instrument of fostering social morality. The idea of the school implied leisure to learn. This meant 'the release of children from all non-educational labour until mind and physique have had a fair start and training'. Education of adults needed a still wider arrangement:

> The schools of the adult are the journal and the library, social intercourse, fresh air, clean and beautiful cities, the joy of the fields, the museum, the art gallery, the lecture-hall, the drama and the opera; and only when these schools are free and accessible to all, will the reproach of proletarian coarseness be done away with.

GERMAN SOCIAL DEMOCRACY

German social democracy, as developed by Ferdinand Lassalle (1825-64), was another important version of evolutionary socialism. Lassalle accepted the Marxian doctrine of economic interpretation of history so far as it implied that the rise of the working class and the consequent decline of capitalism was inevitable in the future society. However, Lassalle evolved a different view regarding the nature and role of the state.

Instead of a violent overthrow of the capitalist state, Lassale suggested that the working class should organize itself into a political party with a view to securing universal, equal and direct suffrage so us to make its power legally effective. Thus, Lassalle envisaged a constitutional and peaceful transition from the capitalist state to a workers' state. In this way, Lassalle sought to redefine the immediate goal of the workers' movement as securing a majority in the democratic legislative organs of the state.

REVISIONISM

Another important school of evolutionary socialism that emerged in Germany itself was the revisionist school led by Eduard Bernstein (1850-1932). It also sought to revise some of the basic tenets of Marxian theory, particularly on the following lines:

(*a*) The class struggle had become less intense because the conditions of the working class had improved rather than deteriorated;

(*b*) The middle class had, in fact, expanded rather than shrunk; and

(*c*) Large areas of industry had remained in small-scale production rather than concentrated in large-scale industries.

Bernstein observed that contemporary social developments did not vindicate Marx's position. He argued: "Peasants do not sink; middle class does not disappear; crises do not grow even larger; misery and serfdom do not increase" (*Evolutionary Socialism;* 1898). Marx had predicted a sharp division between the classes and the greater and greater impoverishment of the working class. These two factors would create a mounting tension in capitalism to such a degree that the system would eventually collapse. Since these predictions were the cornerstones of Marx's revolutionary theory and these did not prove to be true, Bernstein proceeded to reject the case for revolution as well as the scientific basis of the 'scientific socialism'.

Bernstein, therefore, insisted that *socialism should be treated more as a movement than an ultimate goal.* Karl Kautsky (1854-1939) continued to defend Marxian theories which remained the official doctrine of communist parties of Europe, but revisionist tactics became part of the socialist struggle.

Bernstein rejected Marx's materialist interpretation of history which implies the inevitability of class conflict as the road to socialism. Instead of class struggle and class rule, Bernstein preferred democracy, a genuine partnership of all adult citizens in a limited government as their joint enterprise. Liberal democracy was, to his mind, the very substance of socialism.

Liberal Democracy

Liberal democracy refers to the system of governance based on the principles of liberalism and democracy. Liberalism seeks to evolve such rules and procedures that would secure liberty of individual while democracy implies the formation of government with the consent of the ordinary people. Accordingly, liberal democracy is largely identified by the following characteristics: (a) Representative government based on majority rule with due recognition of minority rights; (b) More than one political parties freely competing for political power; (c) Periodic elections based on universal adult franchise; (d) Political offices not confined to any privileged class; (e) Accountability of government to the electorate; (f) Protection of civil liberties of citizens (such as freedom of thought and expression, movement, association and assembly, etc. including freedom to criticize the government); and (g) Independence of judiciary from executive and legislative control.

SYNDICALISM

The socialist movement developed in France and Latin countries in the form of Syndicalism. In fact, Syndicalism originated as a trend in the French labour movement which considers labour unions and their federations as cells of the future sooialist order. It insists on the complete independence of labour unions from political parties. In short: (*a*) Syndicalism accepted the class-struggle theory of Marx; (*b*) it preached abolition of the political state; (*c*) it urged industrial action as the only effective means of bringing about a revolutionary change in society and treated the 'general strike' as a means of securing workers' control over industry; and (*d*) it visualized a social order in which all power would be given to the producer; trade and industrial unions would serve as the economic framework of society.

Syndicalism achieved great ideological success in France in the period between 1899 and 1937. Initially, the movement insisted on the exclusive right of workers to control industry. But after the First World War (1914-18), it expanded its scope and conceded the equal right of consumers in this sphere of control. Syndicalism stood for 'socialization without state'. Its opposition to the state took two major forms: (*a*) the state should have no right in the control of industry; and (*b*) independent economic organizations should be used to restrict and counterbalance the power of the state.

GUILD SOCIALISM

In the first quarter of the twentieth century, there was another socialist movement in England, known as Guild Socialism. In fact, Guild Socialism originated as a trend in the British labour movement which enjoyed great ideological success in the period from 1916 to 1926. It tried to combine the good points of socialism with those of the ancient guild system. In short: (*a*) it upheld the Marxian emphasis on class struggle; (*b*) it stood for the abolition of the wage system and demanded representation of the workers in industrial control; (*c*) it sought to modify Syndicalism by introducing the importance of the consumer side by side with the worker; and (*d*) it sought to abolish the old state which was an instrument of exploitation. However, it insisted that a new organization must be evolved to take charge of the many civic activities necessary to the life of the community. Guild Socialism was strongly opposed not only to communism but also to all forms of collectivistic socialism. It was inspired by that branch of French Syndicalism which sought to restrict and counterbalance the power of the political state by independent economic organizations of workers and consumers. However, British Guild Socialism drifted away from French Syndicalism because of its affinity with the British liberal tradition as manifested in the pluralistic view of society.

Guild System

Guild system refers to a system of organization of work which prevailed in preindustrial communities. A guild, in this sense, refers to an association of craftsmen and artisans that was formed to provide for mutual support, to pass on knowledge to new entrants in the trade, to control craft standards, and to govern new entries into the trade. The guilds enjoyed special prestige and power; membership of a guild was regarded to be a source of privilege.

A CRITICAL APPRAISAL

Evolutionary socialism, in some form or the other, is practised in a large number of countries today. In some countries, especially in the Scandinavian countries, it has brought widespread security and prosperity. In others, such as India, it has secured a marginal improvement in the general standards of living without making an effective dent in the vast socio-economic disparities. It has, therefore, been criticized on various grounds.

No Coherent Doctrine

Evolutionary socialism is criticized because it has no coherent doctrine. There are so many varieties of evolutionary socialism—Fabian socialism, revisionism, syndicalism, guild socialism, parliamentary or democratic socialism, etc.—that it is difficult to identify its essential contents. Different forms of evolutionary socialism accept and reject some or the other tenets of Marxian socialism without evolving suitable alternative strategies. It is, therefore, devoid of any general, unified view, consistent philosophy or programme. Different schools of evolutionary socialism seek to substitute 'class cooperation' for 'class conflict', 'democracy' for the 'dictatorship of the proletariat', and an 'evolutionary method' for the 'revolutionary method'. But they fail to demonstrate how these substitutes can function effectively to attain the socialist goals.

Not Based in the Working Class

Some forms of evolutionary socialism, such as syndicalism and guild socialism, are, of course, based in the working class. But other forms are not so based. For instance, Fabian socialism was exclusively based in the intellectuals of the middle class, with hardly any links with the working class. In effect, it was reduced to an intellectual luxury. It aimed at permeating all classes, but failed to arouse the working class which is the main sufferer under the capitalist system, and which is bound to be the chief beneficiary of the socialist transformation. In fact, Fabian socialism insisted on redistribution of national wealth for the social good, that is for the benefit of all sections of society rather than for a particular section like the workers. In essence, this was nearer the principle of liberalism rather than that of socialism which seeks to tilt the balance in favour of the weaker, exploited, underprivileged and oppressed sections.

Legitimization of the Bourgeois State

Evolutionary socialism seeks to accommodate socialist goals in the operation of the capitalist system. Since capitalism has accepted 'liberal democracy' as its political framework, characterized by universal franchise, periodic elections and free competition for power, it is felt that the people's urge for economic equality cannot be evaded for long by granting them formal equality in the political sphere. It is alleged that the adoption of socialist goals reassures the people, and serves as a 'safety valve' for the capitalist system. In other words, evolutionary socialism is the device to maintain market society system with certain modifications.

However, it may be conceded that no society can function efficiently without adequate incentives. Even 'pure' socialist systems felt the need of introducing a modicum of market principles to maintain efficiency. This mixture of market principles with socialism was called 'market socialism'. This policy was adopted in Yugoslavia after the early 1950s, in Hungary after 1968, in China, Poland, Bulgaria and the former Soviet Union in 1980s. But that too, could not solve the problem of scarcity. This led to bureaucratic corruption and eventual collapse of socialist systems.

Market Socialism

Market socialism refers to an economic system where means of social production are held in public ownership, but allocation of resources is made according to market principles. Thus, product market, labour market and capital market come into existence side by side with the socialist system.

In the present age of disillusionment with 'revolutionary socialism', evolutionary socialism or democratic socialism is the only hope to promote social justice.

Social Justice

Social justice refers to a social policy which seeks to prevent concentration of valuable resources of the community or mankind (wealth, prestige and power) in the hands of the chosen few, and to create a social order which will enable the deprived and underprivileged sections to gain a respectable share thereof by virtue of their ability, effort and need.

CONCLUSION

In spite of some shortcomings, evolutionary socialism is an effective instrument for mitigating the rigours of capitalism. It is definitely better than the crude form of capitalism—a free market economy with unrestrained competition. Evolutionary socialism provides an opportunity to the common people to resist and reduce the harshness of the capitalist class within capitalist society itself. It fails to transform capitalism precisely for want of adequate, organized and consistent public pressure. The capitalist class manages to create an illusion of 'common welfare' by granting small concessions and reliefs to the exploited and hard-pressed sections. Social contradictions continue to thrive in such a situation. Once the exploited sections become conscious of these contradictions and make up their mind to fight them out, the ground is prepared for transformation of the capitalist system.

Even Marxian socialism postulates the emergence of class consciousness and a strong organization of the exploited class for bringing about revolution. If necessary consciousness and organization are present among the exploited sections, it should not be difficult for them to transform the capitalist system even through the ballot box. A combination of democracy and socialism is now regarded as not only possible, but logical and even inevitable. In the ultimate analysis, if democracy is real enough, its success will be reflected in the fulfilment of the aspirations of ordinary people, which are not very different from the socialist goals. It is now being increasingly realized that in highly industrialized modern states, armed revolutions have very little scope of being victorious. The constitutional method of securing the goals of socialism is, therefore, not entirely redundant, provided the exploited classes are on the alert, well-organized, vocal and seriously engaged in building up strong public pressure against the capitalist class.

I hope that socialism does not kill or suppress individuality; indeed I am attracted to it because it will release innumerable individuals from economic and cultural bondage.

Jawaharlal Nehru (1939)

[VIII]
FASCISM

WHAT IS FASCISM?

Fascism stands for a doctrine, ideology or a set of principles underlying the movement founded in Italy by Benito Mussolini (1883-1945) and his followers in 1919. For this purpose, he combined his *fasci* of workers, that is the small groups organized to bring about revolutionary changes in the political structure of Italy, into the *Fascisti.* The word *fasci,* from which the term *fascism* is derived, denotes the bundle of rods bound with a red cord round an axe helve which was borne before the Roman consuls by the Lictors (*i.e.* the magisterial attendants) as the symbol of public power. The word *Fascisti* stood for the movement as well as the party founded to achieve the goals of fascism. In fact, Italian fascism came to have some well-defined goals, as conceived and declared by its leader—Mussolini himself. It also evolved or embraced certain principles—a variety of unrelated principles woven into an incoherent whole, designed to meet political exigencies. That is why fascism never developed into a coherent political philosophy. It only developed into a movement which achieved temporary success in Italy. It was partly adopted by Adolf Hitler (1889-1945) and the Nazis in Germany, Franco (1892-1975) and the Falangists in Spain, and had a marginal following in Britain, France and other European countries. Some writers try to find its parallels in Asia, particularly in Japan, and in some Latin American countries, particularly in Argentina.

Of the three major streams of political thought—Liberalism. Marxism and Idealism—fascism is openly opposed to liberalism and Marxism. It is wedded to the idealist theory, but only to its distorted form. Fascism embraced some theoretical principles only to win the political support of some groups, especially to mobilize a large number of frustrated elements in society. Since these heterogeneous groups had no common interest, no common ideal and no common values, fascism could never evolve a consistent political theory. It never became a part of the mainstream of political theory. The students of political theory look to fascism not for guidance in sorting out theoretical issues, but for understanding 'political pathology'; that is to understand how an adventurous leader like Mussolini or a fanatic leader like Hitler can play upon and exploit the sentiments of different categories of people under abnormal circumstances, and mobilize them for achieving certain goals which they would not approve of under normal mental and social conditions. Sociologists and social psychologists have found rich material for study in the abnormal conditions of society which gave rise to the emergence of fascism.

In politics, fascism is identified with a sick mental attitude which sets aside reason as well as sound moral and social principles for the fulfilment of ambitions of narrow groups. Fascist tendencies pose a danger to peace and freedom in the world. The word 'fascist' is a term of abuse in the present-day vocabulary.

> **Idealism**
>
> Idealism refers to a philosophical outlook which regards 'idea' or consciousness as the essence of the universe and the motive force behind all change. It is the opposite of materialism which comprises the basic principle of Marxism. G.W. F. Hegel (1770-1831), famous German philosopher, has given a vivid account of the idealist interpretation of human history. He regarded all social institutions as the expression of development of idea or consciousness which culminates in the emergence of nation-state. Hegel called for complete subordination of man to the authority of the state for the realization of his freedom. Fascism made use of a distorted version of this theory to muster support for its programme.

DEVELOPMENT OF FASCISM

The development of Fascism chiefly took place during the period between the two world wars (1919-39) in Italy and Germany. It also had some parallel in Japan so that the three countries—Germany, Italy and Japan—eventually formed the 'Berlin-Rome- Tokyo Axis' who were the chief enemies of the Allied Powers in the Second World War (1939-45). In fact, the Second World War was fought to defeat fascism. Fascism was strongly opposed to democracy (if not to capitalism) as well as to communism. That is why the capitalists and the communists joined together to defeat it. William Ebenstein, in his *Today's Isms* (1980), observed:

> Stripped to its essentials, fascism is the totalitarian organization of government and society by a single-party dictatorship, intensely nationalist, racist, militarist, and imperialist. In Europe, Italy was the first to go fascist in 1922, and Germany followed in 1933. In Asia, Japan became fascist in the 1930s, gradually evolving totalitarian institutions out of its own native heritage.

Its chief variants—Italian Fascism and German National Socialism. (Nazism)—arose under somewhat different circumstances but they had many parallels in theory and practice. As R.M. MacIver (*The Web of Government*; 1965) has elucidated:

> Both succeeded in enlisting diverse groups and classes to a programme of expansionist aggression, finding common ground in the respective treatment meted out to them in the Treaty of Versailles—though one was chafing in defeat and the other discontented with the rewards of victory...In both instances a disoriented small-bourgeois group, in a time of social upheaval and economic trouble, found a leader who was master of the

mass appeal. The preceding war had inculcated habits of blind obedience to the command of the superior but the authority behind the command had been discredited. Men were groping for a new myth of authority. They were susceptible to the gospel of new demagogues.

> **Demagogue**
>
> Demagogue refers to a type of political leader who tries to win support of the people by appealing to their emotions rather than by giving rational arguments.

It is significant that both Italy and Germany had lagged behind other countries of Europe, *e.g.* France and Great Britain, in their way to national unification. Their geographical position had prevented them from attaining the status of world powers. Their societies were still in transition; the power was passing from a reactionary aristocracy to the emerging bourgeoisie (the capitalist class), but a strong working class was simultaneously rising and raising its claim to power. Both countries cherished a deep pride in their past cultural distinctions and felt bitterness over less great countries rising to the status of world powers, ignoring their claims. After the First World War (1914-18), many Italians strongly felt that they had been cheated in the matter of distribution of the spoils of victory while the Germans were indignant over the back-breaking war reparations imposed on them by their victors. In short, both Italy and Germany were in the grip of crisis and abnormal circumstances which were responsible for their similar development. As MacIver has argued:

> It is an old story that under conditions of grave stress, with the breaking of tradition, the people, and especially the young, lose the finer cohesion that gives play to the personality of each, and are more easily reduced to the mass, the populace, the mob. Then comes the leader, whether he be a fanatic or an ambitious adventurer, and by his devices and his eloquence advances the process, at length making the mass the instrument of his purposes *(ibid.)*.

Theory of Reaction

The doctrine of fascism arose as a theory of reaction to democracy, socialism and communism. While democracy and communism represented progressive forces of the modern age, fascism sought to promote a movement or a tendency in the reverse direction, in support of the former outmoded, repressive, social and political conditions and policy. According to *Dictionary of Political Science* (ed. Joseph Dunner; 1965):

> Fascism rejects equality and substitutes the principle of hierarchy culminating in a supreme leader or dictator whose will is law. Fascism repudiates individualism and asserts that all values derive from the state, against which the individual possesses no rights; true liberty, consequently, is found only in subjection to state authority. The fascist state requires complete conformity,

> rigid discipline, and unquestioning obedience; force is legitimate which conduces to these ends.

As against the liberal-democratic cult of reason, fascism relies on faith and emotion as the motive force of human actions. Instead of regarding individual as an end and the state as a means, fascism exalts the state as an end and reduces individual to the means. It establishes monopoly of the nation-state in all internal and external matters. It does not tolerate any human association or organization within the state to compete with the state for the loyalty of the individual. Thus, it rejects the pluralistic cult of liberal-democracy. In the international sphere, it does not support international organization for settlement of disputes, and relies upon military solutions.

Fascism repudiates the progressive doctrine of human equality as the basis of their rational organization into nations or other associations. On the contrary, it seeks unity through homogeneity. In Germany, this attitude was embodied in racist doctrines and the programme of liquidation of 'non-Aryan' elements.

The fascist disdain for democracy is reflected in its policy of concentration of political power in the hands of the dictator and a single political party. This is amply revealed in Mussolini's pattern of leadership. As R.M. MacIver, in his *The Web of Government* (1965), has aptly illustrated:

> In one thing he showed consistency throughout his career—his contempt for democracy. Exulting over the 'decaying corpse of the Goddess of Liberty', he proceeded to tear down, piece by piece, the parliamentary structure. He nullified and then abolished all political parties except 'the' party ... He changed his office of premier into that of 'head of the government' ... He made the party the organ of the state, with a hierarchical system of controls from the local party boss to the Grand Council of Fascism. His regime became a personal government of the most extreme type. The members of the party were sworn to boundless obedience to his orders.

Fascism created a peculiar authoritarian system which strived to engender mass enthusiasm for its regime and policies. In the event, Mussolini emerged as an extremely popular leader enjoying immense authority in the state. As MacIver has elaborated:

> He had his personal army, the blackshirt Militia, bound exclusively to his service. The new political structure of fascist dictatorship was built inside the pre-existing system, until all that remained of the old order was a hollow façade. The king still 'reigned', the senate still met, but one man, backed by his disciplined cohorts, commanded Italy *(ibid.)*.

In short, fascism set aside constitutional democracy in order to enhance the prestige and power of the dictator and to establish the hegemony of a single party, commanding unconditional obedience from the people.

Theory of Counter-revolution

Fascism began as a movement demanding revolutionary changes in the social and political structure of Italy. But it soon developed into a force against revolution itself, especially against the revolutionary force of communism. Fascism may also be regarded as counter-revolutionary because it sought to promote concentration of economic control in fewer hands as also to stop diffusion of political power. In other words, it stripped capitalism of its democratic character which could have had some sobering effect on it. While the masses in a capitalist society could use their political power, thanks to the development of democracy, to secure increasing material well-being, fascism ruled out such possibility. Under fascism, the masses are left with no rights or safeguards against their oppression by the ruling clique. In the liberal phase of capitalism, the capitalists are somewhat prepared to pay the price of people's support in the form of some concessions, but when it enters the fascist phase, the capitalists are no longer required to pay that price. Profit-making motive of the capitalists is no longer restrained by people's demands or expectations. The result is lower wages for the workers, inferior general conditions of industry, lowering of taxation upon capital and contraction of social services.

Harold J. Laski, in his *State in Theory and Practice* (1935), observes that so long as the marriage of capitalism and democracy continued, capitalism continued to extend concessions to the masses, giving them a sense of satisfaction. But when it sought to withdraw those concession, it had recourse to fascism:

> Fascism came to rescue capitalism from this dilemma. By the abrogation of democracy, in one form or another, it has entrusted unlimited political power to those who own and control the means of production ... All political parties which deny its purposes have been suppressed. The free trade unions have gone, and, with them, the right to strike. Wages have been reduced either unilaterally by the employers, or with the approval of the state. The right to free criticism has been suppressed; and the power of the electorate to change its government has been withdrawn.

Fascist states also sought to curb individual liberty by obstructing the supply of true news. They brought the press, the wireless, the publishing trade, the cinema and the theatre directly under government control. The neutrality of the civil service was openly abandoned, and even the judiciary was subordinated to the service of fascist ideals. The fascist states built their authority by relying on the loyalty of the armed forces as also by arming the forces of their own partisans. The whole state apparatus was used to advance the interests of capitalism at the expense of the worker. As Laski has illustrated:

> Mussolini has explained that the individual fulfils himself in the fulfilment of the state-end ... Once we examine the actual character of that end in fascist communities, it becomes clear that it implies the sacrifice of the ordinary worker to the capitalist need to make profit *(ibid.).*

In a nutshell, fascism seeks to avert the transformation of the capitalist system into a democratic welfare state or service-state. It tends to maintain the exploitative character of the capitalist pattern of production in the name of national interest, national unity, discipline, industrial peace and higher production, and to save a decadent capitalist system from the revolutionary threat of the oppressed classes.

Fascism also seeks to dilute the revolutionary content of communism by an improvised anti-Marxist theory. It tries to replace materialism by a mystical political idealism. It rejects the theory of class-conflict in favour of the organic unity of the nation-state that claims to represent a unified national interest. It even repudiates the economic motive behind human actions which could give rise to class struggle. As Mussolini himself observed in his famous article in *Encyclopaedia Italiana* (1932):

> Fascism, now and always, believes in holiness and in heroism; that is to say, in actions influenced by no economic motive, direct or indirect. And if the economic conception of history be denied, according to which theory men are no more than puppets, carried to and fro by the waves of chance while the real directing forces are quite out of their control, it follows that the existence of an unchangeable and unchanging class-war is also denied—the natural progeny of the economic conception of history. And above all fascism denies that class-war can be the preponderant force in the transformation of society.

Fascism thus tends to project an image of a unified nation with an indivisible interest to repudiate the theory of class-conflict. It even refuses to rely on reason for arriving at truth. Instead, it eulogizes the creative power of the *myth* to muster the support of all classes in society. As Mussolini said in a speech at Naples in 1922:

> We have created our myth. The myth is a faith, it is passion. It is not necessary that it shall be a reality. It is a reality by the fact that it is a goad, a hope, a faith, that it is courage. Our myth is the nation, our myth is the greatness of the nation.

Hitler similarly created the myth of race and developed his racist doctrine as a counterpart of the fascist image of the nation. He dwelled on the miraculous power of propaganda, especially of false propaganda, in his notorious work *Mein-Kampf* ('My Struggle') (1925-26). Thus, fascism openly sets aside truth and reason for the advancement of its sinister designs and containment of revolutionary forces.

SOCIO-ECONOMIC BASIS

Some writers, such as W.M. McGovern *(From Luther to Hitler;* 1941) and R.M. MacIver *(The Web of Government;* 1965) regard fascism as a movement of the lower middle class. However, when examined closely, this interpretation does not seem to be correct. It may be admitted that fascism particularly appealed to small businessmen, such as individual shopkeepers, who felt their livelihood threatened on the one hand by the rising working class with its revolutionary socialism, and on the other by the monster of monopoly capitalism. But fascism itself did not emanate from any movement launched by the lower middle class. The fascist militia were recruited from a subclass of the tradeless dregs of the working class without class loyalty or self-respect. In fact, fascism sought to muster support from diverse sections of society through false promises, appeals and tactics. To discover the real socio-economic basis of fascism, it is essential to determine which class it sought to serve. As Laski, in his *State in Theory and Practice* (1935) has amply demonstrated, fascism sought to serve the interests of the capitalist class at the expense of the masses, especially the working class. It created the myth of the nation to secure concentration of economic and political control in the hands of the chosen few, and to demand unquestioning obedience and devotion from the masses to the authority so created. As Laski concludes: "Stripped of all its rhetorical trappings Italian fascism appears quite simply as an insistence upon compulsory obedience to a state whose purpose is to protect existing class-relations" (*ibid.*).

Instead of serving the interest of the whole nation, fascism only sought to exploit the prevailing social tensions and crises to bring home the need of absolute authority and unquestioning obedience. William Ebenstein has tried to show that the conditions of capitalism do not by themselves give rise to fascism, but it arises only where democracy is particularly weak:

> Industrialists are not, as a class, any more fascist-minded than other social groups; in countries with strong liberal and democratic traditions, for example, industrialists have neither more nor less faith than other people in the democratic process. But where democracy has been weak, as it was in Germany, Italy, and Japan, it took only a few wealthy industrialists and landowners to supply fascist movements with ample funds *(Today's Isms;* 1980).

Ebenstein observes that even the conditions of economic depression need not necessarily lead to the rise of fascism, but the fear and frustration arising out of economic depression can lead to it:

> In times of depression, fear and frustration undermine faith in the democratic process, and where the faith in rational methods weakens, fascism is the potential gainer. The small businessman blames big business for his troubles; big business puts the blame on the unreasonableness of the labour unions; labour feels that the only way out is to soak the rich; the farmers feel that they are not getting enough for farm products and that the prices they pay for manufactured goods are too high; and—worst of all—there is the large mass of unemployed people *(ibid.)*.

Ebenstein further argues that even the economic suffering caused by unemployment can be mitigated by adequate relief, but the feeling of being useless, unwanted, and outside the productive ranks of society paves the way for the rise of fascism:

> It is among these spiritually homeless that fascism makes serious inroads during a depression: by putting an unemployed person into a uniform, a fascist movement makes him feel that he 'belongs', and by telling him that he is a member of a superior race or nation, such a movement restores some of his self-respect *(ibid.)*.

The basic point made by Ebenstein to vindicate capitalism is, however, not fundamentally different from Laski's view. Th point is that *so long as capitalism can accommodate the democratic aspirations of the people, it is not likely to degenerate into fascism.* Ebenstein is highly optimistic of this potential in capitalism. But Laski further holds that if the marriage between capitalism and democracy is brought to its logical conclusion, it will lead to the transformation of capitalism itself. On the contrary, an unrestrained capitalism would degenerate into fascism by crushing the democratic aspirations of the people.

LIBERAL AND MARXIST CRITIQUES OF FASCISM

Fascism is by no means a systematic doctrine. It is a queer mixture of incongruous elements. In Laski's words:

> Fascism, when closely examined, proves to be nothing more than an ill-assorted rag-bag in which all kinds of remnants from the most diverse philosophies seek, as best they may, to find a place (*The State in Theory and Practice;* 1935).

Fascism sought to mix up different theoretical elements only to evolve an instrument of mass appeal and mass mobilization for the attainment of some political goals projected by an *elite* who happened to control political as well as economic power. Mussolini himself in an article written in 1924 admitted:

> We Fascists have had the courage to discard all traditional political theories, and we are aristocrats and democrats, revolutionaries and reactionaries, proletarians and anti-proletarians, pacifists and antipacifists. It is sufficient to have a single fixed point: the nation. The rest is obvious.

In its attempt to attain practical goals, fascism sought to repudiate both liberalism and Marxism in their essentials. It rejected constitutional government and other vital attributes of liberal-democracy; it equally rejected Marxism. It has, therefore, been criticized by liberals as well as Marxists.

Liberal Critique

Several liberal writers have criticized fascism, particularly because of its totalitarian character and its rejection of democratic methods, human rights, etc. It is important to note that while liberalism is primarily a philosophy of capitalism, fascism also sought to promote capitalism rather out of the way. Liberal writers have taken different positions on this issue. Some of them do not refer to any significant relation between fascism and capitalism. As William Ebenstein has argued:

> The Marxist interpretation of fascism in terms of class (identifying fascism with capitalism in decay) is not borne out by the facts. *Fascism cuts across all social groups*—wealthy industrialists and landowners support it for one reason, the lower middle classes for another, and some blue-collar workers for another still *(Today's Isms: 1980).*

Still others feel that fascism sought to distort the liberal and benevolent character of capitalism by dissociating it from democratic traditions and diverting it from the path of the welfare state.

The main liberal objection against fascism is that it sought to destroy individual liberty by subordinating individual to the absolute authority of the state, and by reducing individual to a means to serve the end of the state. In the second place, fascism sought to accentuate the irrational element in human nature while liberalism pleads for man's freedom treating him primarily as a rational being. Thirdly, fascism repudiates the liberal faith in the natural and social equality of men, through its cult of hero-worship, superiority of the *elite* and racist doctrines. In the fourth place, fascism hits at the pluralistic nature of society by establishing the monopoly of a single political party and eliminating free and open competition for political power. And finally, fascism demolishes constitutional government which is the sole guarantee of human freedom and progress as well as the cardinal principle of liberal-democracy.

Marxist Critique

Marxists deprecate fascism as an attempt to protect capitalism in its decadent phase. By creating the myth of a nation, fascism sought to suppress class-conflict on the one hand, and to thwart any international movement towards communism on the other. Antonio Gramsci (1891-1937), an Italian Marxist who was victimized and tortured by the fascist regime of Mussolini, maintained that the ideological propaganda of the fascists sought to preserve capitalist 'hegemony' and 'structures of domination' which made it acceptable to the ignorant masses. Leon Trotsky (1879-1940) and others argued that the mass basis of fascism was provided by a desperate, rootless, middle class. Some critics argue that the widespread fear of uncertainty in a time of crisis served as the breeding ground of authoritarianism in the fascist countries.

> **Authoritarianism**
>
> Authoritarianism refers to a political outlook that requires everybody and everything to conform to an established order. It sees no need to obtain explicit or tacit consent of those affected by a decision. It does not permit ordinary people to express their independent opinions, demands or preferences and rules out accountability of power-holders to public opinion or popular vote.

CONCLUSION

Some liberal writers, prompted by their equal disdain for fascism and communism, have sought to club the two as 'totalitarian dictatorships'. For instance, R.M. MacIver (*The Web of Government;* 1965) and Alan Ball *(Modern Politics and Government;* 1988) have adopted this classification. This is not only unfair but misleading. Fascism tends to suppress the masses to secure the interests of a tiny class in all spheres—social, economic, political. On the contrary, communism—even when it uses coercion—seeks to distribute benefits to secure the maximum satisfaction of the masses. G.A. Almond and G.B. Powell, in their noted work *Comparative Politics: A Developmental Approach* (1966), have aptly made this distinction:

> Totalitarian systems suppress demands coming from their societies and are unresponsive to demands coming from the international environment. At the same time, they regulate and coerce behaviour in their societies, and seek to draw maximum resources from their populations. Communist totalitarianism differs from fascist totalitarianism in having a strong *distributive* capability as well.

Fascism, besides its retrograde class character, symbolizes a sick mental and political attitude. It fosters anti-human and anti-progressive forces. It seeks to curb liberty and equality and to distort justice. In short, it is a philosophy of the lunatic fringe, champions of terror and violence who advocate superiority of one race, sect, region, religion, language or culture, relegating the rest of mankind to slavery. Unfortunately, fascist tendencies are not dead the world over. Enemies of mankind still thrive in some parts of the world and pose a potential threat to the security of those who do not belong to them, not to speak of those who do not follow them!

> **Fascism...supplied a moral justification for violence; it exploited patriotism to the limit; it subtly rationalized minority rule;... it offered the masses a new religion with a new god to worship.**
>
> C.C. Maxey, *Political Philosophies* (1961)

[IX]
ANARCHISM

WHAT IS ANARCHISM?

Anarchism stands for a mode of thought which holds that society can and should be organized without the coercive authority of the state. Although some indications of this mode of thought could be traced to ancient times, William Godwin (1756-1836), a British political theorist, was the first thinker who argued unequivocally for a stateless society. His *Enquiry Concerning Political Justice* (1793) is regarded to be the first systematic defence of anarchism. However, it was P.J. Proudhon (1809-65), a French philosopher, who was the first to call himself an anarchist. As an ideology anarchism had its greatest influence in late nineteenth and early twentieth centuries, when several revolutionary movements in Western countries favoured this mode of thought.

Anarchist thinkers have one common aim—abolition of the state. But they widely differ as to how the state should be abolished, and what type of organization should be evolved to replace it. So they by no means form a homogeneous group. They include a wide variety of thinkers ranging from the defenders of extreme form of socialism to the champions of extreme form of individualism. All anarchists agree on the need to dispense with compulsory forms of authority, culminating in authority of the state. However, most anarchists recognize the rational form of authority, particularly the authority of experts. *e.g.* scientists and doctors in their respective fields, as also the moral authority of collective decisions taken in a genuinely democratic manner. They are mostly averse to hierarchical forms of authority, *e.g.* churches, armies, bosses of capitalist enterprises, and impersonal bureaucracies.

Of the several schools of anarchist thought, the following are particularly important: philosophical anarchism, socialist anarchism, revolutionary anarchism, anarcho-syndicalism, pacific anarchism, and libertarian anarchism.

PHILOSOPHICAL ANARCHISM

Philosophical anarchism rejects the idea of legitimate authority in the sense that no individual, whether state official or not, has the right to command the obedience of another. Individual autonomy, as conceived morally, requires individuals to act according to their own judgements. Because of its focus on individual, this school of thought is also called *'individualist anarchism'*. It was originally founded by Godwin himself in his essay *Enquiry Concerning Political Justice* (1793). Then Max Stirner (1806-56), a German philosopher, in *The Ego and his Own* (1845) argued that every individual is the unique one who truly 'owns himself'; he recognizes no duties to others, and does what is right for himself, within the limit of his might. In contemporary thought, Godwin's line of argument was endorsed by R.P. Wolff (*In Defense of Anarchism;* 1970).

Accordingly, philosophical anarchism has little scope to encourage cooperation among individuals or to evolve their formal organization. Its upholders are generally suspicious of authority, yet they recognize the rational authority of experts within their fields of competence and the moral authority of basic social norms, such as 'contracts should be kept'. If politics is defined as the art of persuading others when they do not agree, then philosophical anarchists may also recognize even political authority, but not the coercive authority of the state. So, if members of a commune or workers' cooperative actually participate in decision-making, their decisions may be deemed morally binding.

SOCIALIST ANARCHISM

Socialist anarchism insists on freedom of individual, defined as the capacity to satisfy his needs. It regards social and economic equality as a necessary condition to secure maximum freedom of all. In its view, social and economic equality is incompatible with capitalist private property and the state. It, therefore, rejects both. P.J. Proudhon (1809-65), a French philosopher, is regarded the chief exponent of socialist anarchism. He postulated 'mutual aid' as the appropriate method of achieving its goal. It is, therefore, also called *'mutualism'*.

Proudhon argued that liberty or freedom is the mother, not the daughter, of order. All political parties are a variety of despotism. Power of the state and power of capital are coterminous. So the proletariat cannot emancipate itself by acquiring and using state power. On this ground, Proudhon criticized Marx's idea of establishing 'dictatorship of the proletariat' as a way to human emancipation. Instead of violent method of overthrowing capitalism, Proudhon recommended the peaceful method of direct action and the practice of mutualism for evolving all new social order. He proposed that society should be organized as a network of autonomous local communities and producers' associations, linked by 'the federal principle'. Each person might possess his means of production (tools and equipment, land, etc.) either singly or collectively, but should only be rewarded for his labour. This system will eliminate the elements of profit and rent, and ensure a high degree of equality.

Dictatorship of the Proletariat

According to Marxism, dictatorship of the proletariat refers to a form of organization of the State that comes into existence when organized working class overthrows capitalism and assumes full control of political power. It is characterized by the socialization of the major means of production, *de novo* planning of material production so as to serve social needs, provide for an effective right to work, education, health and housing for the masses, and further development of science and technology so as to multiply material production to achieve greater social satisfaction.

Exchange of goods and services between different voluntary associations will be based on the principle that each party will seek only an equivalent for what it offered to the other. This will be supplemented by the establishment of a mutual credit bank which would lend to producers at a minimal rate of interest, covering only its cost of administration. Proudhon firmly believed that this system of mutual aid would promote social solidarity.

Proudhon's experiments on these lines proved to be a failure in actual practice. But his French disciples played an influential role in the early years of the First International (founded by the London Working Men's Association in 1864).

Philosophy of socialist anarchism was further developed by Peter Kropotkin (1842-1921), a Russian thinker. In *Mutual Aid—a Factor of Evolution (1890-96)*, Kropotkin argued that the principle of 'the struggle for existence and survival of the fittest' as enunciated by Charles Darwin (1809-82) in the field of biological evolution, does not apply to the sphere of social relations. On the contrary, sociability is, under all circumstances, the greatest advantage in the struggle for life, and therefore the natural condition of all evolutionary beings. If human beings are not corrupted by the state and law, they would develop bonds of instinctive solidarity which would make government unnecessary. Kropotkin favoured a system of 'communism' where everything belongs to everyone, and distribution is made according to needs. Kropotkin's version of socialist anarchism is called *'communist anarchism'*.

REVOLUTIONARY ANARCHISM

Revolutionary anarchism is still another version of socialist anarchism. Mikhail Bakunin (1814-76), a Russian revolutionary, is regarded the chief exponent of revolutionary anarchism. It is called revolutionary because of its reliance on the revolutionary method of achieving the goal of anarchism. Since it believes in collectivization of the means of social production, it is also called *'collectivism'*. Bakunin stood for the strategy of encouraging popular insurrections. It was envisaged that during the course of these insurrections, capitalist and landed property would be expropriated and collectivized, and the state would be abolished. It would be replaced by autonomous, but federally linked, communes.

Commune

Commune refers to an organized group of people or families who work together, live together, and share the fruits of their common labour for common use.

Bakunin projected the vision of a socialist society which would be organized from below upwards, not from above downwards. To foster the spirit of revolt among the oppressed, revolutionary anarchists adopted the tactic of 'propaganda by the deed'. This would start with local insurrections, and then include acts of assassination and terrorism. They sought to establish a collectivist system in which each group of organized workers would be managing their own means of production. The distribution of the proceeds would be made according to collective decision. It was generally assumed that rewards would be proportional to labour, at least for the foreseeable future. Revolutionary anarchists opposed the authoritarian element in Marx's communism.

ANARCHO-SYNDICALISM

Anarcho-syndicalism or *syndicalist anarchism* is another version of revolutionary anarchism. Georges-Eugene Sorel (1847-1922), a French philosopher, was its chief exponent. It was based on the idea to turn trade unions into revolutionary instruments of class struggle. Instead of 'communes' (as envisaged by communist anarchism), anarcho-syndicalism sought to make trade unions the basic units of a new society. In his important work *Reflections on Violence* (1908), Sorel argued that law and institutions of every enduring society contain a form of structural violence. Capitalist system is itself an epitome of violence. Unjust violence should be fought with just type of violence.

Sorel commended the method of 'general strike' as the fit instrument for the workers to fight against capitalism. He recommended the use of 'myth' to mobilize masses into action. The power of 'general strike' could be exaggerated to elevate it to the level of a 'myth' which should be used to mobilize workers for mass action. Since Sorel relied on organized groups to overthrow capitalist state, and provide for its alternative, he is not regarded a full-fledged anarchist.

Myth

Myth stands for an idea or a story that refers to some wonderful or miraculous qualities of something. It is believed to be true by its upholders although there is no evidence to prove it. The concept of myth as a political tool was developed by Georges-Eugene Sorel (1847-1922), French philosopher. Sorel suggested the use of myth to stimulate mass action, particularly the resort to 'General Strike' by workers to make them realize their unique collective strength. Sorel argued that validity of the myth was unimportant as long as it resulted in the desired action.

PACIFIC ANARCHISM

In contrast to revolutionary anarchism, pacific anarchism stands for abolition of the state in a peaceful manner. It advocates anarchism on moral grounds. Its chief exponent, Leo Tolstoy (1828-1910), the Russian novelist, was inspired by 'the law of love', expressed in the Sermon on the Mount (delivered by Christ himself). This made him denounce the state as 'organized violence' and to call on people to disobey its immoral commands. Tolstoy argued that the state tried to fight one evil with another evil, *i.e.* with the help of police and military force. Private property enables the few to lead a luxurious life by exploiting others' labour. Both of them should be abolished for the regeneration of humanity. Mahatma Gandhi (1869-1948), the Indian philosopher, was inspired by these ideas in developing his philosophy of non-violence.

In any case, Tolstoy did not advance any concrete programme for the abolition of the state.

LIBERTARIAN ANARCHISM

Libertarian anarchism represents the contemporary version of 'individualist anarchism'. Its beginnings may be traced to Herbert Spencer (1820-1903), a

British philosopher. Spencer's concept of 'blessedness of anarchy' envisages the development of 'market society' to a stage where the state is dissolved and society becomes self-regulated. Its contemporary exponents include F.A. Hayek (1899-1992), an Austrian economist and Robert Nozick (1938-2002), an American philosopher. Libertarianism stands for the revival of *laissez faire* individualism which believes in minimum interference of the state in economic activities of people.

F.A. Hayek, in *Law, Legislation. and Liberty,* Vol. 1: *Rules and Order* (1973), observed that social order exists independently of the state—an order spontaneously generated, a product of human sociability. This natural order does not need supplementing by an order imposed from above. Then Nozick in his *Anarchy, State and Utopia* (1974), argued that the state has no legitimate powers beyond the functions of protection, justice and defence; it is not authorized to engage in redistributive transfers among its citizens who were originally its clients. In Nozick's view, legal rights are the product of voluntary exchanges. An ideal state would be one which completely stays away from regulating voluntary exchanges between individuals. It would approximate to anarchy. For Nozick, anarchy refers to the status of a self-regulated society where government is not required to exercise its regulatory function.

In short, libertarians stand for restricting the role of the state to minimum possible level. They do not recommend to abolish the state altogether. The contemporary exponents of 'rational choice' theory also advance similar arguments. M. Taylor, in his essay *Community, Anarchy and Liberty* (1982), argued that social order is a 'public good'. It cannot be divided and nobody can be excluded from its benefits, yet people under the conditions of 'anarchy' will cooperate voluntarily to create it. For libertarian anarchists, the state is not merely a necessary evil; it is a positive evil. They advocate the idea of 'natural society', a self-regulated, pluralistic society in which power and authority are radically decentralized.

Broad Streams of Anarchism

The Stream	*Chief Exponents*
Philosophical Anarchism	William Godwin (1756-1836), British political philosopher, Max Stirner (1806-56), German philosopher
Socialist Anarchism	P.J. Proudhon (1809-65), French philosopher, Peter Kropotkin (1842-1921), Russian philosopher
Communist Anarchism/ Revolutionary Anarchism	Mikhail Bakunin (1814-76), Russian revolutionary and philosopher
Pacific Anarchism	Leo Tolstoy (1828-1910), Russian writer and philosopher
Anarcho-Syndicalism	Georges-Eugene Sorel (1847-1922), French philosopher
Libertarian Anarchism	Herbert Spencer (1820-1903), British philosopher, F.A. Hayek (1899-1992), Austrian economist

A CRITICAL APPRAISAL

Anarchism is based on a fascinating idea. However, it takes a too optimistic view of human nature. If human nature were so benign as envisaged by anarchists, and society could become self-regulated without interference of the state, the ills afflicting human society under the state would not have arisen at all which the anarchists want to remedy.

Moreover, in the contemporary world which is severely afflicted by the problems of worldwide terrorism, crime and environmental pollution. the need of regulation has become all the more evident and pressing. It is now felt that authority of the state is inadequate to deal with these gigantic problems. There is an urgent need to strengthen the machinery of global governance in order to regulate the present-day world which would supplement authority of the state. Anarchist vision is terribly inadequate to deal with this situation.

However, various schools of anarchism draw our attention to the tyranny of economic and political power which makes the life of people so miserable! Its significance lies in devising suitable means to curb that power. That will restore justice in society and pave the way for human emancipation.

[X] GANDHISM

Gandhism derives its name from that of Mahatma Gandhi (M.K. Gandhi) (1869-1948), Indian social and moral philosopher. His social and political thought is compendiously described as Gandhism. He did not write any treatise on his philosophy. His thought is scattered in a large number of notes and pamphlets as well as his *Autobiography (My Experiments With Truth;* 1929). He even denied the existence of 'Gandhism'. But as the time rolled on, it revealed the immense possibilities of application of Gandhian principles to various social, economic and political situations, and their relevance is steadily increasing. It proved that Gandhian way of thinking has not only its distinct identity, it is a full-fledged worldview. That is precisely the basis of Gandhism.

POLITICS AND ETHICS

As a moral philosopher, Gandhi treated ethics as the guiding star of all human behaviour, including politics. Gandhi's ethics was based in moral teachings of all religions, although he paid special attention to time-honoured Hindu religion *(sanatana dharma).* He expressed his firm faith in the *spiritualization of politics.* This meant that if politics was to be a blessing and not a curse to mankind, it should be informed by the highest ethical and spiritual principles. In other words, politics should be guided by high moral standards, and not by expediency.

Gandhi believed in purity of means as well as ends. Only right means should be adopted for the pursuit of right ends. He strongly refuted the idea that 'end justifies the means' or that 'if a noble end is achieved by adopting ignoble means, their use would be excused'. As Gandhi himself observed:

> They say 'means are after all means'. I would say 'means are after all everything'. As the means so the end ... Realization of the goal is in exact proportion to that of the means. This is a proposition that admits of no exception
>
> (*Selections from Gandhi*, by Nirmal Kumar Bose; 1948).

Gandhi was convinced that if we take care of our means, end will take care of itself. Means and ends may be compared to the seed and the tree respectively. The nature of tree is determined by the nature of seed. Only the right type of seed will grow into the right type of tree. As you sow, so shall you reap. *He that soweth vice shalt not reap virtue.* Again, means and end may be compared to the action *(karma)* and its consequence *(phala).* Man has full control over his action, not over its consequences. That is the famous teaching of *Bhagwad-Gita*—Hindu sacred book.

Means and ends are the two sides of a coin. They cannot be separated. Immoral means cannot be used to achieve moral ends. If used, they will vitiate the end itself. Wrong way can never lead to a right destination. The authority founded on fear and coercion cannot inspire love and respect among people. Gandhi adopted the path of *satyagraha* (reliance on the force of truth) for achieving the goal of *swaraj* (independence from the foreign rule) because this path was as sacred as its destination. *Satyagraha* involved the practice of *ahimsa* (non-violence) which embodied the right course of action. So Gandhi declared: "For me, *ahimsa* comes before *swaraj.*"

For Gandhi, the terms 'spiritual', 'religious' and 'moral or ethical' conveyed the same idea. They taught man to abstain from vice and follow the path of virtue. In Gandhi's view, the essence of all religions was identical. God of Hindus was not different from God of Muslims or God of Christians. All religions taught piety and charity towards fellow-beings. No religion was superior or inferior to any other religion. Religious tolerance was the keynote of social harmony. Gandhi's notion of religion was aptly expressed in his own words:

> By religion, I do not mean formal religion, or customary religion, but that religion which underlies all religions, which brings us face to face with our Maker
>
> (*The Mind of Mahatma Gandhi,*
> compiled by R.K. Prabhu and U.R. Rao; 1945).

For Gandhi, adherence to religion was the part of his pursuit of truth. This very pursuit induced him to participate in politics. He believed that politics bereft of religion was nothing short of a death trap, which kills the soul. So

Gandhi wrote in his *Autobiography:*

> My devotion to Truth has drawn me into the field of politics; and I can say without the slightest hesitation and yet in all humility, that those who say that religion has nothing to do with politics do not know what religion means.

In short, politics and ethics were inseparable in Gandhian system of thought.

TRUTH AND NON-VIOLENCE

Devotion to truth is the essence of Gandhism. But how to discover truth? It is as difficult as finding God Himself. In Gandhi's view, God and truth are inseparable. Devotion to God can be carried out through devotion to His creation, particularly through the service to the down-trodden. As Gandhi wrote in *Harijan* (1939):

> I recognize no God except the God that is to be found in the hearts of the dumb millions. They do not recognize His presence; I do. And I worship the God that is Truth or Truth which is God, through service of these millions.

Non-violence is also the part of pursuit of truth. Non-violence or non-injury *(ahimsa)* literally means abstention from violence in one's behaviour towards other living beings. This represents only the negative side of non-violence. On positive side, it implies love of all. We should extend our love not only to those who love us, but also to those who hate us. In Gandhi's own words:

> It is non-violence only when we love those that hate us. I know how difficult it is to follow this grand law of love. But are not all great and good things difficult to do? Love of the hater is the most difficult of all. But by the grace of God even this most difficult thing becomes easy to accomplish if we want to do it
>
> (*Selections from Gandhi,* by Nirmal Kumar Bose; 1948).

In Gandhi's view, even the intention to harm somebody or wishing him ill is a form of violence which should be eschewed. Hatred or malice to anyone is also violence. Acquiring material things beyond one's immediate need is also a form of violencc bccause thereby we deprive others of their share. Even the acts of spreading atmospheric pollution and damaging public health amount to violence. Thus, *the principle of non-violence embraces all rules of good citizenship and human decency.*

When it comes to confrontation with injustice, non-violence does not imply showing weakness. Non-violence is not the resort of the weak; it is the power of the strong—of course, his moral power. This power comes from the firm adherence to truth. When one fights for a just cause, and shows firm faith in truth, it results in the 'change of heart' of the mighty opponent and makes him bend. In short, *non-violence is the art of gaining victory over physical force by spiritual force.* Non-violence is the method of self-purification. Practitioner of non-violence gains ample power to defeat the forces of untruth.

Gandhi's technique of struggle against the mighty British Empire was throughout based on the principle of non-violence *(ahimsa).* His method of civil disobedience and *satyagraha* (reliance on the force of truth) were strongly based on non-violence. His doctrines of trusteeship and the vision of a classless society are also the manifestation of his adherence to truth and non-violence.

DOCTRINE OF TRUSTEESHIP

Broadly speaking, Gandhi believed in simple living, at the level of production as well as consumption. He gave primacy to simple technology over heavy industries. Simple technology had the capacity of mass employment, whereas advanced technology would create vast unemployment, particularly in a country like India, and would promote consumerism with all its ill effects. Gandhi preferred 'production by the masses' over 'mass production' by heavy machinery. However, he realized that it was not feasible to switch over to the new system abruptly.

Consumerism

Consumerism refers to a social outlook that tends to regard the consumption of goods and services as a great virtue and a source of social prestige. Under its influence, sublime values of life like self-control, public spiritedness and artistic tastes are relegated to the back-seat.

Wider use of simple technology could be kept in mind in the course of future expansion. The existing system of large-scale production may be allowed to continue with necessary changes in the attitude of the owners of means of production. As Gandhi wrote in *Amrita Bazar Patrika* (1934):

> What is needed is not the extinction of landlords and capitalists, but a transformation of the existing relationship between them and the masses into something healthier and purer.

For the transformation of this relationship, Gandhi enunciated his doctrine of trusteeship. It urges landlords and capitalists not to consider themselves as the sole proprietors of their possessions, but only as 'trustees' of a gift bestowed upon them by God for the service of humanity. Gandhi realized that the existing system had become oppressive because of the moral decline. If the organizers of agriculture and industry could be persuaded to act as public servants, they would win wide public respect instead of the existing hatred. The tendency of class conflict would be replaced by the spirit of class cooperation. Gandhi relied on the power of truth and non-violence *(ahimsa)* to accomplish 'change of heart' of the rich and resourceful members of society.

Critics point out that the vision of 'change of heart' of the rich is a fascinating idea, but it is hardly realizable in actual practice!

VISION OF A CLASSLESS SOCIETY

Gandhi's faith in human equality made him a strong votary of a classless society. He realized that the division of labour among different individuals was inevitable. However, class division of society was not directly related to division of labour. It was the product of a mindset in which one type of labour, *i.e.* physical labour was regarded as inferior to another type of labour, *i.e.* mental labour or mere leisure. Gandhi sought to create a sense of equality among people by making 'bread labour' compulsory for all.

The gospel of *'bread labour'* expected everybody to do physical labour towards production, at least to compensate for the bread that he consumes. Bread is symbolic of various items of one's physical consumption. When everybody does physical labour, apart from the performance of other functions suited to his aptitude and qualifications, nobody will look down upon physical labour. This will create a sense of 'dignity of labour' throughout society, which will promote a sense of equality among people transcending the prevailing division of labour. This attitude would even create a sense of equality between the rich and the poor.

Gandhi stood against discrimination among human beings on the grounds of gender and faith. In other words, he championed equality between men and women as also between the adherents of different religions. In short, he wished to create a classless society by transforming the attitude of people towards the sources of discrimination in society. He insisted on moral regeneration of society for which adherence to truth and non-violence was indispensable.

GANDHISM AND MARXISM

Both Gandhi and Marx were deeply concerned with the plight of the down-trodden. Both stood for a classless and stateless society. It is sometimes felt that their philosophies were akin to each other. But on deeper analysis, it is revealed that their differences were more pronounced than their similarities.

Gandhi was a spiritualist; Marx was a materialist. Gandhi treated religion as a moralizing force; Marx dubbed religion 'the opium of the people'. Gandhi favoured simple technology; Marx relied on advanced technology as a liberating force. Gandhi attributed the division of society into classes to a mental outlook based on the contempt for physical labour; Marx held the existence of private property responsible for this division. Gandhi believed in class cooperation; Marx regarded class conflict as the instrument of social transformation. Gandhi enunciated the doctrine of trusteeship for resolving the conflict between the rich and the poor; Marx exhorted the proletariat to overthrow capitalism.

Comparative Study of Marxian and Gandhian Views

The Issue	*Marxian View*	*Gandhian View*
Philosophical Basis	Materialism; Scientific Socialism	Spiritualism; Moral Individualism
Attitude toward Religion	Negative; an ideological instrument for the protection of private property	Positive; a moralizing force; equal respect for all religions
Attitude toward Technology	Positive; necessary for full development of the forces of production	Negative; use of heavy machines stunts moral growth and creates vast unemployment
Basis of Classes	Division of society into owners and non-owners of means of social production	Mental outlook based on contempt for physical labour
Recommended Relation between Classes	Class Conflict	Class Cooperation
Way to Achieve Classless Society	Overthrow of capitalism; Social ownership of means of social production; Universal labour; Fullest development of technology	Doctrine of trusteeship: moral persuasion of capitalists to regard themselves as 'trustees' of public property; restore 'dignity of labour': universal 'bread' labour requiring everybody to do physical labour
Nature of the State	An instrument of class domination involving oppression and exploitation of the dependent class	An instrument of coercion of individuals; a soulless machine for enforcing rules and regulations without human sensitivity or a sense of moral responsibility
Way to Achieve Stateless Society	After full development of the forces of production in a classless society, the state will 'wither away'	When everybody follows the principle of non-violence *(ahimsa)* and becomes self-disciplined and self-regulated, the state will become redundant
Image of Future Society	A self-regulated society ruled by the principle: 'from each according to his ability, to each according to his need'	A self-regulated society comprised of self-disciplined individuals having minimum needs, with a sense of moral responsibility towards social needs

Moral Individualism

Moral individualism refers to a philosophical principle which regards individual as an end-in-itself, endowed with 'dignity'. Accordingly, no human being can be treated as a means to serve an end which lies beyond his conscious existence; no worldly thing can be treated as more valuable than a human being; and no human being can accept an obligation except at his own free will.

Gandhi saw the state as a soulless machine for the coercion of individuals; Marx the saw it as the instrument of class domination. Gandhi hoped that when non-violence is adopted as a universal principle, society will become self-regulated and state would become redundant; Marx anticipated that after socialist revolution and the fullest development of the forces of production, 'the state will wither away'. Gandhi's vision of the future society consists of self-disciplined individuals having minimum needs with a sense of moral responsibility towards social needs; Marx's vision of the future consists of a self-regulated society ruled by the principle—'from each according to his ability, to each according to his need'.

[XI] FEMINISM

Feminism stands for the concern with the status and role of women in society in relation to men. It holds that women have suffered and are still suffering injustice because of their sex; hence it seeks effective measures for the redressal of that injustice. In short, it implies a voice of protest against the inferior status accorded to women in society, which is the product of the institution of *patriarchy,* and not based on reason.

Patriarchy

It literally means 'rule of the father'. Originally this term was used to describe a social system based on the authority of male head of the household. Now it is applied to denote male domination in general, including its occurrence in labour market as well as domestic division of labour.

Early feminism emerged in the wake of Enlightenment, which sought to enlarge the scope of 'rights of man' so as to include equal rights of women therein. In Britain, free-thinking women like Mary Wollstonecraft (1759-97) and Harriet Taylor (1807-59) made a fervent appeal for equal rights of women. Later, John Stuart Mill (1806-73), in his essay on *The Subjection of Women* (1869), argued that women were by no means less talented than men and hence deserved equal rights with men. In the contemporary world, the issue concerning the status of women may be understood by drawing a distinction between sex and gender.

> **Enlightenment**
>
> Enlightenment refers to an intellectual movement of eighteenth century France, Germany and Great Britain. It was a period when people's religious and political life was set free from obscure and orthodox beliefs and new light was shed on the conduct of human affairs. This led to the growth of a new outlook, informed by reason and committed to the authority of scientific research and discovery. Old superstitions were discarded, old fears were dispelled, and a new faith in the knowledge obtained by scientific method was developed.

SEX AND GENDER

At the outset, it is necessary to understand the distinction between sex and gender in the sociological context. When we use the term 'sex', its scope is limited to biological differences such as reproductive function and secondary characteristics such as body hair and breast development. But the term 'gender' refers to cultural ideas that construct images and expectations of both females and males. Nature has divided human race between men and women, but their status and role in society are determined by our culture. When we speak of women as 'fair sex' or 'weaker sex' or when we invoke the etiquette of 'ladies first', our attention is not confined to the biological fact, but we have already entered the realm of culture.

> **Culture**
>
> Culture refers to the set of values, beliefs, symbols, modes of thought and behaviour, styles of art and various skills evolved by the members of a community in order to streamline its social life. These factors contribute to the establishment of a distinctive identity of the community in question.

In social sciences and literary criticism, the term 'gender' is used to indicate the differences in social status of man and woman, particularly to refer to the fact that women are placed in a lower status in relation to their intrinsic worth. Feminist thought focuses on gender perspective that calls for cultural transformation of society. It implies the right ordering of status of women in relation to men in social and political life.

Culture usually refers to certain distinctive features of different communities. However, some typical attitudes towards gender can be found throughout the civilized world. These attitudes tend to divide male and female personality traits and behavioural tendencies into two opposite patterns. These patterns may be described as *masculinity* and *femininity* respectively. Masculinity, for example, typically includes aggressiveness, logical outlook, control of emotional expression, and attitude of dominance, while femininity is associated with peacefulness, intuitiveness, emotional expressiveness, and submissiveness. Some variations in these characteristics are possible in different social contexts. For example, a wife may be relatively submissive to her husband, but as a mother she may not be so towards her children. Moreover, the degree of submissiveness of a woman may vary from one case to another.

In any case, relative dominance of man and relative submissiveness of woman represent almost universal cultural traits, which are not directly based on their biological differences. Broadly speaking, these are the products of the social organization based on patriarchy and its institutions, the division of labour in the family and the competitive and exploitative character of the economic system. From this perspective, the concepts of masculinity and femininity serve as instruments of social control that reinforce male dominance. So if a woman tends to behave in an authoritarian manner, particularly towards men, her behaviour is termed to be indecent. In short, the expectations attached to differential roles of men and women serve as the foundation of gender inequality in society.

Jean-Jaques Rousseau (1712-78), a French philosopher, in his essay *A Discourse on the Origin of Inequality* (1755), had distinguished between natural inequality and conventional inequality. Natural inequality describes the inequality of age, health, beauty, physical and intellectual capacities of different people, which were created by nature. These inequalities are largely unalterable. On the other hand, conventional inequalities represent disparities of wealth, prestige and power among different individuals. These inequalities are the product of our social arrangements. We can undertake a critical examination of these inequalities from the point of view of justice, and can reduce them by altering our social arrangements. In other words, conventional inequalities are alterable. In the present context, the division of society into two sexes—male and female—represents natural inequality, while gender inequalities are the product of convention and culture. These inequalities can be questioned and removed wherever they are found objectionable. So the issues relating to sex and gender may briefly be shown by the following chart:

Issues Relating to Sex and Gender

The Issue	**Division of Society into Men and Women**	
Point of Division	Sex	Gender
Basis of Division	Product of Nature	Product of Culture
Symptom of Division	Natural Inequality	Conventional Inequality
Character of Division	Unalterable	Alterable

Recent thinking on the subject has led to a voice of protest against gender-based discrimination, accompanied by the commitment to improve the position of women in society. It seeks restoration of justice for women who remained deprived of equal status and opportunities vis-à-vis men since earliest times. Their condition in the present-day society is reflected in the following report:

> Women constitute half the world's population, perform nearly two-thirds of its work hours, receive one-tenth of the world's income, and own less than one-hundredth of the world's property *(United Nations Report,* 1980).

The condition remains more or less unchanged today.

It has now been proved beyond doubt that biological differences between man and woman do not justify inferior status of women. On the contrary, cultural factors have contributed to accentuate even the biological differences between men and women. The rapid improvement in women's athletic records in recent decades is an indication that social norms had shaped biology and restricted women's physical development. Feminist anthropologists have pointed out that in some ethnic groups physical differentiation between men and women is not as prominent as in others. The present status of women is chiefly the product of social arrangements. Women often spend most of their time in domestic work and in rearing children. Most women do not get an opportunity to develop their own personality. They are made to believe that the proper sphere of their activity is within their household and that they need not take interest in public life. From the beginning, girls are taught to pay more attention to personal relations, not to personal success. Boys are taught to be firm, assertive and aggressive; girls are taught to be obedient, shy and submissive. Boys are encouraged to become doctors, engineers and lawyers; girls are encouraged to become school teachers, nurses or secretaries. The experience gained by women in their own professional life does not help them to take up a political career.

In the light of the growing social consciousness against various forms of injustice in sooicty, the position with regard to the status of women needs to be reviewed, challenged and changed. Indeed, feminist theory and movement urge that women's situation and the inequalities between men and women should be treated as central political issues. All streams of feminist thought focus on the causes and remedies of women's inequality, subordination or oppression.

If injustice against women has existed since earliest times, why has it come to the forefront only in recent times? It may be recalled that at the early stages of social organization, biological differences between men and women necessitated certain division of labour between them. Men who were physically strong and stable chose to go out for hunting and other hazardous jobs. Women who were constrained to undertake child-bearing and rearing chose to remain at home and perform household jobs. The system was based on mutual care and adjustment, and did not involve any significant level of resentment.

With the development of technology, sweeping changes took place in other parts of social organization, but the prevailing division of labour between men and women remained more or less unchanged. With the evolution of various forms of power, man as head of the family, of the clan, and of the tribe acquired more and more power but woman largely continued to hold the subordinate position. Woman was given some concessions and exemptions from strenuous and hazardous tasks as she was regarded the 'weaker sex'. As she was sexually (and also perhaps emotionally) vulnerable, she was not allowed to mix with strangers. Shyness was eulogized as a woman's ornament. She was encouraged to decorate herself and her beauty was admired in poetry, music, paintings and other works of art. In civilized society, she was recognized as the 'fair sex', endowed with special dignity. Manners like 'ladies first' were evolved to confirm that dignity. Helping 'a damsel in distress' was admired as an act of chivalry among men. However, in spite of so much importance accorded to woman in social life, she was systematically deprived of her share in power. She was given security but not an opportunity to learn certain things that would make her as competent as man, and thereby vindicate her claim to equality. In particular, she was deprived of the right to ownership of property, right to vote and opportunities of education and higher learning even though these deprivations had no logical connection with her biological status as a woman. Early voices demanding rights of women particularly focused on these issues.

When Mary Wollstonecraft (1759-97) published her essay *Vindication of the Rights of Woman* (1792), woman was not only restrained from voting, but was deemed unfit for education, was debarred from many occupations, and had no legal right to own property. She had no real right to divorce even if her husband abused her. Wollstonecraft forcefully challenged the prevailing belief in female inferiority and demanded equal rights for women. She argued that women, like men, are rational individuals and should have equal rights. She established the principles on which campaigns for women's right to education, employment, property and the vote were later built up. John Stuart Mill (1806-73), in *The Subjection of Women* (1869), sought to demonstrate that women were in no way inferior to men in their talents, and pleaded to give them full legal and political rights.

In the nineteenth century, feminist theory largely focused on removing educational and professional barriers from woman's life. The reforming spirit behind these campaigns was often quite militant which culminated in early twentieth century struggles for women's suffrage. More recent demands of this movement in the Western world focused on women's employment rights, equal pay for equal work, and equality in social benefits, taxation and so on.

In the contemporary world, further advancement in technology, diversification of business, industry, administration, arts and professions, etc. and the increasing demand of new skills, talents, and professional competence, have given women the opportunity of proving their abilities. They have also been encouraged to acquire higher qualifications and training and to seek respectable careers. It is now realized that women are fit to perform most of the jobs that men do, and for which they were not considered fit earlier. Equal rights for women are no longer questioned in enlightened circles.

BROAD STREAMS OF FEMINISM

Feminist theory has evolved into various schools of thought. Of these three are particularly important: (*a*) Liberal feminism, (*b*) Radical feminism, and (*c*) Socialist feminism.

Liberal Feminism

Liberal feminism represents the earliest trend in feminist thought. It seeks amelioration in the condition of women in pursuance of the policy of liberalism. It advocates suitable reforms in the liberal institutions already existing in Western countries. It opposes any revolutionary change. Mary Wollstonecraft, the early exponent of liberal feminism, sought to establish fundamental equality between men and women within the existing framework of liberal democracy. She argued that both man and woman are essentially rational creatures. But women were deprived of education as well as opportunity to participate in public life. Under the circumstances, woman was cast in the image of an emotional and playful creature rather than a rational creature.

Then John Stuart Mill, another exponent of liberal feminism, sought to demonstrate that women were in no way inferior to men in their talents, and pleaded to give them full legal and political rights. Mill argued that society as a whole was losing out if it did not make good use of the rational qualities of women as well as men. He maintained that a more equal relationship between man and woman as marriage partners would ameliorate the qualities of life for both men and women. He advocated reform of the property laws so that women retained rights to their property after marriage.

Among the contemporary exponents of liberal feminism, Betty Friedan (1921-2006), American writer and activist, is most notable. In her most famous work *The Feminine Mystique* (1963), she argued for measures to ensure substantive equality for women in the sphere of work as well as in politics and private life. In *The Second Stage* (1983), she underlined the continued significance of home, family and children for women. Friedan resembles Mary Wollstonecraft and Mill insofar as she does not want to overturn contemporary liberal society. She asserts that the liberal creed of autonomy and self-determination of the individual should be applied to women as well as men. She advocates widespread access to créche and similar facilities to enable women to combine effectively their professional careers and family responsibilities. Friedan is regarded as an inspirational figure for second wave liberal feminists.

Another important contemporary exponent of liberal feminism is Carole Pateman (1940-). She is widely known for her synthesis of conceptual problems in liberal democratic theory with the theory of the patriarchal basis of sexual politics. In her famous essay *The Sexual Contract* (1988), she particularly attacked the misconception that the liberal theory of the 'Social Contract' had overthrown the concept of patriarchal rule.

In a nutshell, liberal feminism accepts the liberal assumptions about the value to be accorded to individuality and freedom, but campaigns to achieve their equal realization for women as well as men. This is the most popular stream of feminist movement, but it is not considered to be very influential.

Radical Feminism

Radical feminism focuses on the all-pervading male domination in society and calls for overturning of gender oppression. Although it arose in mid-twentieth century, its early hints are found in early twentieth century, particularly in the writings of Virginia Woolf (1882-1941), English novelist and essayist. In her famous essay A *Room of One's Own* (1929), Woolf dwelled on how men socially and psychically dominate women. She argued that women are simultaneously victims of themselves as well as of men by acting as mirrors to men. Then Simone de Beauvoir (1908-86), French novelist and author of *The Second Sex* (1949), sought to challenge Sigmund Freud's (1856-1939) famous dictum 'Anatomy is destiny' (of woman) when she asserted: 'A woman is not born but made.' She argued that the dependent, derivative status of woman as 'the other of man' was the product of her upbringing in society. She exhorted women to strive to transform their status and life-style across all social and cultural reference points.

Another prominent exponent of radical feminism, Shulamith Firestone (1945-2012), in her celebrated work *The Dialectic of Sex* (1970), argued that women's subordination could not be understood as a symptom or an aspect of some deeper or more comprehensive system of domination, such as racism or class-based division of society. Historically, women constituted the first oppressed group; their subordination could not be eliminated by the changes such as the elimination of prejudice or even the abolition of class society.

Firestone claimed that the basis of women's subordination was ultimately biological. In other words, human reproductive biology was responsible for considering women the weaker sex. Moreover, the survival of women and children required that infants should depend on lactating women, and women, in turn, should depend on men. Happily the material conditions for ending this hitherto inevitable dependence had finally been achieved in the twentieth century with the advent of reliable contraception, baby foods and 'test-tube babies'. These technological developments provided women the means of freeing themselves from the tyranny of their reproductive biology and diffusing the child-bearing and child-rearing role to society as a whole, men as well as women.

Then Kate Millett (1934-2017), in *Sexual Politics* (1971), argued that the relationship between the sexes was based on power and further sustained by an ideology. It was similar to the relationship between classes and races. Hence, it should be treated as a political relationship. Basing her analysis of women's subordination on Max Weber's (1864-1920) theory of domination, Millett argued that men have exercised domination over women in two forms: through *social authority* and *economic force*. Time had now come to smash these implements of man's domination. Shulamith Firestone and Kate Millett are regarded to be the two pillars of radical feminism, who exercised enormous influence on developing the Women's Liberation Movement in 1970s.

Socialist Feminism

Socialist feminism recognizes twofold division of capitalist society into (*a*) men and women in which men dominate; and (*b*) capitalists and workers in which capitalists dominate. It holds that here capitalists as well as men are the beneficiaries of women's subordination. Establishment of socialism is, therefore, the necessary condition of women's emancipation.

Initially, Charles Fourier (1772-1837), French social critic and socialist philosopher, argued a case for socialist feminism at the beginning of the nineteenth century. He stood for a version of socialism that would be based on equality between men and women. He envisaged a form of social organization in which men and women would enter into group marriages and live in small communities where all men and women would be treated as equal partners. The children born out of these marriages would be brought up together by their common parents without discrimination: boys and girls would get identical treatment.

Later, Friedrich Engels (1820-95), co-founder of Marxism as a close associate of Karl Marx (1818-83), provided a classic account of the origin of gender inequality. In his *The Origin of the Family, Private Property and the State* (1884), Engels argued that the origins of sexual inequality may be traced to the establishment of patrilineal descent, that is the practice of tracing kinship through the line of father to son and then to grandson, etc. It arose with the advent of private property as a mechanism to ensure that property remains with male descendants only. Engels hoped that the arrival of socialism would abolish both private property and the domestic servitude of women.

Evolution of Feminism

First-wave feminism refers to women's suffrage movements of late nineteenth and early twentieth centuries. Its exponents argued that men and women were equal as regards their intellectual and emotional capacities and needs; so the rights enjoyed by men should be equally extended to women. In their view, women's interests were not reducible to those of their husbands.

Second-wave feminism refers to the resurgence of activist feminism in late twentieth century, particularly in 1960s and 1970s. Its exponents attacked on male violence towards women, particularly sexual violence. They rejected feminine norms such as sexual submissiveness and participation in beauty practices. They advocated the liberation of women from the enforced domesticity and insisted on establishing female solidarity and sisterhood.

Post-feminism insists that women should see themselves as agents, and not as victims within the existing social system. Focus on the incidence of violence against women would undermine their real role. The exponents of post-feminism argue that sexuality should be considered a liberating force; all consensual sex should be celebrated. In their view, there is no clash between sexual equality and participation in beauty practices and gendered dress. Women should only focus on their material equality with men.

Sheila Rowbatham (1943-), the contemporary representative of this school, advocated a participatory, decentralized approach to social change that contemplates linking of the struggles of all oppressed groups. In her best-known historical writings—*Women, Resistance and Revolution* (1972) and *Hidden from History* (1973)—Rowbatham tried to reclaim the past for women as a source of knowledge and strength that could contribute to their present struggle. She continued this approach in *The Past is before Us* (1989). As a Marxist, she maintained that the struggle for women's liberation is essentially bound with the struggle against capitalism. She has shown from historical evidence that class exploitation and women's oppression are closely linked phenomena. She argued that the success in these spheres can be achieved only through combining these struggles.

EMPOWERMENT OF WOMEN

A general awareness of the exploitation of women on various fronts like social, cultural, political and eonomic fronts has led to strong protests manifested in Women's Liberation Movement, which emerged in the United States since the early 1970s. Soon this movement also spread to Europe and other parts of the world. The movement focused on equal rights and status for women in a male-dominated society. Some prominent organizations associated with this movement were: National Organization for Women (NOW), Boston's Bread and Roses, Berkeley Women's Liberation Group, Women's Radical Action Project, Women's Equity Action League (WEAL), National Women's Political Caucus (NWPC), etc.

Broadly speaking, Women's Liberation Movement demanded a truly equal treatment of men and women. It required that many of society's myths, values and beliefs concerning status and role of women in society should be fundamentally reassessed and changed. These changes must embrace the patterns of work and family life, social behaviour, decision-making, politics, religion and education. Even the more personal and private domain of sexuality needed to be redefined. These demands led to a widespread debate on diverse issues concerning women. These include day-care facilities for children, development of a non-sexist vocabulary (*e.g.* the term 'chairman' should be replaced by 'chairperson'), and setting suitable norms for the representation of women in the mass media, including advertising. These debates have not only led to the enactment of new laws in some countries, but also to the worldwide acceptance of new norms protecting the dignity of women.

In India, some important legislation concerning the protection of women includes: the Immoral Traffic (Prevention) Act, 1956; Dowry Prohibition Act, 1961; Indecent Representation of Women (Prohibition) Act, 1986; and the Commission of *Sati* (Prevention) Act, 1987. Female foeticide was sought to be prevented by the enactment of the Prenatal Diognostic Techniques (Regulation and Prevention of Misuse) Act, 1994. The recent legislation concerning empowerment of women includes Hindu Succession (Amendment) Act, 2005 (which gives equal right to daughters in joint family property) and Protection of Women from Domestic Violence Act, 2005.

Feminists also assert that until the condition of equal participation of women in public life is fulfilled, the concept of citizenship cannot be brought to its logical conclusion. In India, a beginning in this direction has been made by making reservation of one-third of the seats in *panchayats* for women. This will encourage women to join politics at grass-root level. By and by their representation at this level can be increased to one-half, and provision can also be made for their adequate representation in legislative assemblies and parliament. The opening up of vast opportunities of higher education for women would also prove to be instrumental to their larger representation in administration and high-profile professions. In this way, the idea of equal citizenship can be fully realized from the feminist point of view.

Feminists argue that even after getting full citizenship in law, women continue to suffer from subjection in their social life. From 1960s and 1970s the status of women in society and polities has become the centre of attention. Earlier it was usually thought that after establishing legal equality of men and women, women were not left with any issue of complaint. After the extension of right-to-vote to women, there were some studies on voting behaviour. It was found that women's participation in voting was lower in comparison to men. To explain this situation it was argued that women were largely interested in private and domestic affairs; they were less interested in politics and public affairs and probably they had no time to attend to these matters.

However, when the size of the family began to shrink and more and more women took up jobs, the above explanation regarding women's sphere of interest was no longer held to be valid. Again, it was noticed that more and more women were taking part in voting, but their share at various levels of political authority had remained insignificant. While the electorates of various countries of the world had nearly fifty per cent women, their share at the level of political representation was far below that of men. Membership of women in the legislatures of Western Europe was less than ten per cent. Women's share in British House of Commons was less than five per cent. The situation in the United States House of Representatives was not very different. But the situation in the Scandinavian countries was not that bad. In Sweden and Denmark, women's membership of legislatures amounted to twenty-six per cent; in Norway, this figure was thirty-four per cent. In recent years, these figures have slightly gone up.

In the sphere of international politics, the representation of women is still meagre. In November 1990, thirty-four Heads of Government of European countries gathered to sign the historic Charter of Paris for the New Europe. The gathering marked the end of the Cold War. In newspaper headlines it was described as the 'end of an era'. But feminists ask: "Which era had come to an end?" In any case, it was not an end of the patriarchal era. In the group-photo of these thirty-four heads of government, only two women could be spotted after a thorough search.

These were: Gro Brundtland, Prime Minister of Norway, and Margaret Thatcher, Prime Minister of Britain. Two days after this Conference, Mrs. Thatcher also resigned, and a man replaced her as Prime Minister. In this situation, what is the consequence of granting full political rights to women if their representation in public life remains so negligible? Happily, however, by the end of 2005, Germany had elected its first woman Chancellor. By the beginning of 2006, Chile and Liberia had elected their women Presidents. Then in 2007, India and Argentina had the distinction of having women Presidents.

In the countries outside Europe and America, women' representation is very insignificant at the level of political authority although some women have been successful in attaining top positions. Sri Lanka, Israel, India, Pakistan and Bangladesh have the record of having women Prime Ministers or Heads of Government. But on the whole, the number of women holding high offices is very small. Some women have excellent record of performance in various important positions, like those in legislatures, cabinets, bureaucracy, diplomacy, journalism, legal profession, fine arts, academics and scientific research, etc. This record is enough proof of the potential of women's power. But it is no proof of the opportunities open to women as their share in these positions continues to be very meagre.

CONCLUSION

Currently, there are two broad views concerning equal rights for women: (*a*) one view is that there is no difference between men and women as regards their capabilities; hence they should be governed by the same laws; and (*b*) another view is that women are essentially different from men—biologically, culturally and socially; they should be given equal opportunities to develop and apply their distinctive capabilities along with equal rights. Thus, women could be exempted from hazardous tasks, like underground mining and working in night shifts. Similarly, women should be entitled to maternity leave and related benefits, arrangements for maintenance and custody of children after divorce, etc. Besides, in order to compensate women for their under-representation in important positions, reservations for women should be made in the seats for higher learning, appointments, seats in legislatures, etc. They should also be given tax concessions in order to encourage them to work for additional income. This view seems to be more reasonable and is widely endorsed.

Worldwide concern for gender justice was expressed in *Human Development Report,* 1995, issued by the United Nations Development Programme (UNDP). It sought to include the 'gender-related development index' (GDI) for a group of 130 countries (out of a total of 174 countries included in the report). Further, it also included the estimation of the 'gender empowerment measure' (GEM) or the extent to which women participate in a country's economic and political life. According to this report, Sweden, Finland, Norway and Denmark came out on top with the highest GDI and GEM scores, indicating the virtual absence of any gender bias in their development process. The most gender-biased societies, with scores under 0.3 (compared to a maximum possible value of 1.00) are mostly African or Islamic nations. India ranks 99 in terms of GDI of the 130 countries included in the report.

The present report defines gender equality as follows:

> Moving towards gender equality is not a technocratic goal—it is a political process... It requires a new way of thinking—in which the stereotyping of women and men gives way to a new philosophy that regards all people, irrespective of gender, as essential agents of change.

Significantly, the report does not find any correlation between gender bias and a country's economic development. A poor economy like Cuba, which ranks 72 on Human Development Index (of the 174 countries), ranks 47 on the GDI and 16 on the GEM (of the 130 countries). Commending China and Cuba for their support of women, the present report observes:

> Countries applying socialist models used social and political mobilization to achieve rapid and equal progress in education and health for women and men and to engineer social transformations to expand opportunities for women.

It is interesting to note that there is no essential correlation between GDI and GEM in many cases. This means that they have given adequate attention to health care and education of women, but no adequate share in the exercise of power. This is illustrated by the case of 'economic tigers' of East Asia where in spite of substantial improvement in the level of development of women, they have been denied a tangible share in economic and political power, in an essentially male-dominated society.

In a nutshell, feminist perspective on justice calls for securing the overall development of women, including improvement of their health and education as well as giving them adequate share in economic and political power.

> Among the rude people, the women are generally degraded; among civilized people, they are exalted.
>
> James Mill (1773–1836)

3

Nature of Politics

THE TERM 'POLITICS' is applied to a particular social phenomenon as well as to a systematic study of that phenomenon. When Aristotle, ancient Greek philosopher, adopted *Politics* as the title of his famous work, he used the term to indicate a distinct branch of study. Some modern writers have frequently used the term 'politics' in this sense. For example, Henry Sidgwick (*The Elements of Politics;* 1891), Harold J. Laski *(A Grammar of Politics;* 1925, and *An Introduction to Politics;* 1931), G.E.G. Catlin *(Systematic Politics;* 1965), J.R. Lucas *(The Principles of Politics;* 1967), and Seymour Lipset *(Politics and the Social Sciences;* 1969), have treated 'politics' as a particular subject of study. Similarly, when we speak of 'Comparative Politics' or 'International Politics' as branches of study, we refer to 'politics' in the sense of a discipline. In some universities, 'Politics' and 'Political Science' are used as interchangeable nomenclatures for their academic departments. For instance, the University of Mumbai has a Department of Civics and Politics while the University of Delhi maintains a Department of Political Science. A similar variation can be seen in the 'Gokhale Institute of Politics and Economics' and the 'London School of Economics and Political Science'. In short, the term 'politics' is often used synonymously with 'political science'.

[I]
POLITICS AS A PROCESS

Whether we use the term 'politics' or 'political science', our subject of study is always concerned with a particular type of human activity, also described as 'politics'. What is the nature of that activity?

At the outset, a reference may be made to the layman's image of politics. Alan Ball, in his *Modern Politics and Government* (1988), has indicated two problems arising from the general impressions about political activity. In the first place, 'it is often assumed that politics is only concerned with the public sector, with parliaments, elections, cabinets, and has little relevance to other spheres of human activity'. Secondly, 'there is the danger of confusing politics solely with party politics, that it is somehow concerned with having a political opinion, or that it at least implies a distaste with the intrigues and tricks of party politicians seeking power'. In other words, a layman thinks of politics in terms of public meetings, processions, slogans, demonstrations, demands, strikes, tear-gas, lathi-charge as well as elections accompanied by false promises and false reports on their fulfilment. Such vague assumptions are the reason why politics often gets dubbed the 'last resort of scoundrels'. Ernest Benn has sarcastically described politics as 'the art of looking for trouble, finding it where it exists or not, diagnosing it wrongly, and applying the wrong remedy'. That is why politics is sometimes condemned as a 'dirty game'; why students are advised to keep away from politics; and why judges and other intellectuals are expected to keep themselves above politics.

For a systematic study of politics, it is essential to dispel such confusion and to lift politics from the arena of vague impressions to the level of scientific precision. The word 'politics' itself is derived from the Greek word 'polis' which denoted ancient Greek city-state. The activities of citizens in their role as members and operators of the state were termed by ancient Greek thinkers as 'politics'. Thus, from the very beginning, 'politics' came to be associated with the 'state'. In fact, traditional writers have considered 'political science' as the 'science of the state', and have devoted themselves: (*a*) to a study of the institutions of the state; and (*b*) to developing ideas concerning the nature of a perfect state. However, modern writers have increasingly recognized that 'politics' does not operate strictly within the framework of an institutional set-up but permeates the entire social fabric. Accordingly, 'politics' is now treated as a *social process* rather than an aggregate of the formal institutions of the state. How does this *process* operate?

State

State refers to the set of institutions within a society which are responsible for taking public decisions, making and enforcing law, maintaining justice, public safety as well as public order. In order to perform these functions effectively, the state is always armed with supreme legal authority. In actual practice, functions of the state are performed by government.

THE POLITICAL SITUATION

Politics as a process operates in a particular situation which may be termed as a 'political situation'. According to Alan Ball (*Modern Politics and Government;* 1988), 'political activity ... involves disagreements and the reconciliation of those disagreements'. In other words, 'the essence of the political situation' is 'conflict and resolution of that conflict'. Some earlier authors had also made this point. Stephen L. Wasby *(Political Science—The Discipline and its Dimensions: An Introduction;* 1972) similarly observed: "Where there is politics, it is said, there is controversy; where there are issues, there is politics. Where no controversy exists, where no issues are being debated, politics does not exist." J.D.B. Miller *(The Nature of Politics;* 1962) had pointed to the 'use of government' in the process of conflict-resolution in a political situation:

> Political activity ... arises out of disagreement, and it is concerned with the use of government to resolve conflict in the direction of change or in the prevention of change ... Politics, to be distinguished as a recognizable activity, demands some initial disagreement between parties or persons, and the presence of government as a means of resolving the disagreement in some direction.

In a nutshell, the political process postulates the existence of disagreement or conflict, and efforts for the resolution of that conflict through the authority of government. Thus, every situation involving a conflict and efforts for its resolution cannot be called a 'political situation'. An example of a political situation given by Alan Ball does not appear to be a fit case. He says: 'Two children in a nursery with one toy which they both want at the same time present a political situation ... The two children could resort to violence, with the stronger claiming the toy, or the mother could appear and use her stronger position to arbitrate between the quarrelling children.' This example suffers from two defects. In the first place, it refers to a 'private' conflict between two children which does not qualify for being a political situation. Similarly, a dispute between husband and wife on the family budget does not present a political situation. Only that conflict can be considered the proper subject of politics which arises at a 'public' level, *i.e.* in which two or more major groups are involved in any social setting, whether local, regional, national or international, or at the economic, cultural, linguistic, religious or ethnic plane. In other words, a political conflict is always concerned with 'public' issues, not with private issues; it demands a 'universal' solution, not a solitary one. In common parlance, we talk of the politics of church, university or a factory. But as long as this so-called politics is confined to a single organization with little effect on public life, it cannot be considered the proper subject of study in political science.

In the second place, Alan Ball's example contemplates 'resort to violence' as one of the possible methods of conflict-resolution. But, properly speaking, resort to violence or war does not qualify for a political solution. No doubt, some political disputes do culminate in war, but war is a symptom of the failure of a political solution. On the contrary, a political solution emanates from negotiation, persuasion, arbitration, compromise, pressure, counting of votes or any similar tactic short of war. In any case, the solution is supposed to be acceptable to the parties involved in the dispute. How is this made possible?

POLITICS AS 'AUTHORITATIVE ALLOCATION OF VALUES'

The political solution of a conflict is made acceptable to the parties concerned because of its 'authoritative' character. According to David Easton *(The Political System: An Inquiry into the State of Political Science;* 1953), politics is concerned with the 'authoritative allocation of values' for a society. This short but compact definition involves three terms which must be understood clearly. These are: 'values', 'allocation', and 'authoritative'. By 'values' he means the 'things considered valuable, whether they be spiritual or material'. By 'allocation' he means distribution of these things to various individuals or groups; this is accomplished through policy which consists of a 'web of decisions'. Decision refers to the 'selection among alternatives'; policy implies arriving at a decision as well as its implementation: 'a policy is authoritative when the people to whom it is intended to apply or who are affected by it consider that they must or ought to obey it'. In other words, 'authority does not signify the use of brute force; it denotes the capacity to secure more-or-less willing compliance from its subjects for a particular decision or course of action'.

> **The need for social policy stems from the very character of a society.**
> **David Easton (*The Political System;* 1953)**

In this way, politics as the 'authoritative allocation of values' represents a universal social phenomenon. In the words of David Easton himself, "Every society provides some mechanisms, however rudimentary they may be, for authoritatively resolving differences about the ends that are to be pursued, that is for deciding who is to get what there is of desirable things. An authoritative allocation of some values is unavoidable."

Thus, Easton's observations add a new dimension to our earlier formulation regarding the nature of politics. It brings in the element of authoritativeness to the process of conflict-resolution. Geoffrey K. Roberts *(A Dictionary of Political Analysis;* 1971) has given an elaborate definition of politics which brings out its important characteristics. At the outset, he has made it clear that the term 'politics' refers to 'both an activity and to the study of that activity'. Then he proceeds: "As an activity, politics is the process in a social system ... by which the goals of that system are selected, ordered in terms of priority both temporally and concerning resource allocation, and implemented." Taking a liberal view of politics, Roberts holds that the political process 'involves both cooperation and the resolution of conflict by means of the exercise of political authority, and if necessary, coercion'. Elucidating the scope of politics, Roberts observes that it 'usually involves the activities of groups of various kinds, including sometimes groups of a specifically political type, such as political parties'. As regards its peculiar character, the political process 'is distinguished from other social processes by its concern with the 'public' goals of the society'. Whereas 'economics' may be concerned with public or private allocation of resources, 'politics' is exclusively concerned with the 'public' allocation of resources in pursuance of 'public goals'.

Easton's View of Politics as 'Authoritative Allocation of Values'

- Values = things considered valuable, whether spiritual or material
- Allocation = distribution of these things to various individuals or groups
- Authoritative = a situation when the people affected by an order think that it is worth obeying

GENERAL CHARACTERISTICS OF POLITICS

It is significant that the extent of involvement of individuals and various groups in politics depends upon the level of their *'politicization'*. The term 'politicization' may be applied either to issues (*e.g.* politicization of caste) or to human beings. In the latter case it implies the drawing of individuals or groups into political activity, particularly giving them a role in the making of public decisions. Thus, an absolute monarchy—where all public decisions are taken by the monarch and his close associates—exemplifies the low level of politicization. In contrast, ancient Greek city-states represented the high level of politicization by drawing all 'freemen' into political activity; yet it was by no means universal since it excluded the very large majority of slaves and aliens. Again, under a military dictatorship politicization is confined to the military junta. It is only under a democracy that politicization is intended to be universal. However, when an emergency is declared, politicization is restricted to the ruling groups as long as the declaration of emergency is in operation.

Democracy

Democracy refers to a form of government where ultimate authority to take public decisions is vested in the ordinary people or their representatives so that public policy is designed to conform to the will of the people and to serve the interests of the people.

Accordingly, the salient features of 'politics' as a *social process* may be identified as follows:

Politics Involves Conflict or Dispute Regarding Allocation of Values

A political situation necessarily involves a conflict or dispute regarding allocation of rare and valuable resources in society. If something is valuable but available in abundance, there will be no dispute for its allocation. If something is both valuable and rare but the people are just complacent or ascetic, there is hardly any possibility of conflict over its allocation. Conflict occurs when something is valuable, rare and desired by many, thus giving rise to a political situation. It is the clash of interests or conflicting claims or expectations of rewards that give rise to politics. Some of the examples of prevalent 'values' of society involved in the political process are: power, enlightenment, wealth, well-being, health, skill, affection, rectitude and deference. In concrete terms, conflicting claims may be advanced by various groups for the allocation of bus service, schools, hospitals, public parks, markets, offices, business and employment opportunities, etc. in their favour.

Politics is Concerned with Public Goals and Decisions

All conflicts for resource-allocation do not give rise to a political situation. Politics is exclusively concerned with the conflicts involving public goals and public issues requiring public decisions for their resolution. For instance, a conflict between worker and employer, between customer and trader, between tenant and landlord, between the passengers on the same bus or between the users of the same road or of different roads meeting at a crossroad becomes a public issue when it is concerned with broad categories of people and calls for a solution at the public level. A conflict between husband and wife on some petty domestic affair does not present a political situation. But if it takes the form of a question of respective claims of men and women in the context of their mutual relationships demanding solution at the public level, it becomes a political question and a fit subject of politics. As Michael Curtis *(Comparative Government and Politics;* 1978) has rightly observed: "The student of politics is normally concerned with inquiry into matters of public concern, with the behaviour and acts that may concern a society as a totality or which may ultimately be resolved by the exercise of legitimate coercion."

Politics Requires Authoritative Decisions

The resolution of a political conflict is meaningful only when it is treated as binding by those who are affected by the decision embodying the resolution. According to David Easton, a policy may be accepted as authoritative on several grounds: 'moral, traditional or customary, or purely from fear of consequences' *(The Political System;* 1953). In other words, authority involves 'legitimacy' or 'power' or both. For instance, when some seats in a public bus are reserved for 'ladies only' or when certain posts in bureaucracy or seats in legislatures are reserved for the scheduled castes and scheduled tribes, this allocation is treated as 'legitimate' due to the prevailing belief that the weaker sections are entitled to special protection. The rich pay higher taxes, particularly income tax and wealth tax, for maintaining government hospitals, schools and public transport at cheaper rates, which are largely meant for the benefit of the poor. The rich cannot refuse to pay this tax on the plea that it is not utilized for their benefit, since it involves authoritative allocation. On the other hand, the poor are made to pay large sums in the form of say, sales tax or excise, on each commodity of their use, sharing the burden for the maintenance of police, defence, etc. which are chiefly meant for the protection of the property of the rich. The poor, too, cannot refuse to pay this tax since it involves authoritative allocation. Then there is a machinery to implement the authoritative decisions which symbolizes application of force or threat of physical force or coercion for the enforcement of a particular 'value-allocation'. An authority is always backed by law, executive orders, custom and a strong public opinion in its favour on the one hand, and by police, magistrates and prisons on the other. However, no authoritative allocation can be treated as eternal or unalterable. It holds the field until a new arrangement is established as authoritative.

Authority	=	Power + Legitimacy
Power	=	Ability to use force to make others obey one's commands
Legitimacy	=	The quality of being considered lawful, *i.e.* right or correct according to the prevalent standards of morality, common good or social justice.

Politics Involves Interest Groups

A political situation arises from a clash of interests of several large groups of society. These groups must be conscious of their particular interests, and be more or less organized for pursuing those interests. The conflicting claims and demands for the 'authoritative allocation of values' emanate from these 'interest groups',which require policy decisions. Political parties appear on the scene with a view to formulating large policy proposals incorporating the interests of their support-groups according to their respective ideologies.

Interest Groups

In a liberal democracy, interest groups refer to the groups of people who organize themselves for pursuing their specific, collective interest. They try to serve their interest through obtaining the support of public opinion by publicizing their viewpoint widely, and pleading to government to mould its policy to suit their interest. Examples of interest groups are: trade unions, lawyers associations and chambers of commerce and industry.

While each interest group is concerned with pursuing the specific interest of its members, political parties normally seek to serve larger interest of the community by projecting a point of reconciliation between diverse interests of the various sections of society.

Politics is an Instrument of Conflict-Resolution

The end-product of the political process is supposed to be the resolution of the conflict from which the process had started. On this point, there is a divergence between liberal and Marxist viewpoints. The liberal view of politics holds that politics is an instrument of reconciliation of the various conflicting interests in society. On the other hand, Marxist view of politics asserts that the interests of the two major social classes—the 'haves' and 'have-nots' (the property-holders and the propertyless)—are irreconcilable, and that so long as society remains divided into classes, there is no possibility of conflict-resolution. A classless society, according to the Marxists, symbolizes not only the end of the conflict but the end of politics itself.

[II]
DIFFERENT VIEWS OF POLITICS

Politics has been defined as a process through which an 'authoritative allocation of values' is made in society. Now this is not an independent or a closed process, but takes place within the larger arena of the social process. By 'process' we mean the sets of interactions among the components of a system. So where there is a process, there is a system. The political process constitutes a political system. But the political system itself is a sub-system of the larger social system. That is why the political process has been described as a dimension of social process.

Since process implies interaction among the components of a system, and the political process itself is a component of the social system, there are interactions between politics and other components of the social system, such as economy and culture. The products of these interactions are 'political economy' and 'political culture' respectively.

If politics is a dimension of the social process which arises from conflicting demands and interests of various sections of society, what is the nature of that conflict and what is the outcome of this process? In order to answer this question, different positions can be taken. Of these, liberal, Marxist and communitarian views are particularly important.

Liberal view of politics is based on liberalism which coincides with the tradition of thought beginning with John Locke (1632-1704), English philosopher. This view concedes the existence of conflict between various interests within the society, but holds that this conflict is not very deep. Different groups are willing to and capable of evolving such arrangements wherein their conflicts would be resolved. Marxist view, on the other hand, is based on Marxism which owes its origin to the ideas developed by Karl Marx (1818-83), Friedrich Engels (1820-95), both German philosophers, and their followers. This view attributes all social conflict to the existence of two antagonistic classes—haves and have-nots (*i.e.* those who own the means of social production, and those who live by their labour), and holds that their interests are irreconcilable. This conflict can be resolved only by switching over to a 'classless society', that is by socializing all major means of production and introducing universal labour. Apart from these two divergent views of politics, a third view of politics has also become popular in the recent decades although its origins may be traced to an earlier stream of political thought. This is called 'communitarian' view of politics. It holds that there is no real conflict in the society. The impression of conflict arises from misunderstanding of our real interest—the common good which comprehends everybody's real interest. This view redefines politics as the pursuit of the common good rather than as an attempt at resolution of some pre-existing conflict.

Communitarianism arose from the criticism of liberalism as a means to human happiness. It holds that the modern man enjoys better conditions of living, but his economic security has failed to make him happy for want of emotional security. He feels lonely in a huge crowd around him. He lives in society without the sense of belonging to it. Communitarianism seeks to restore the broken bond between individual and society. It makes the individual realize that he owes his existence and personality to society. Different individuals are not isolated units but they constitute the threads of the social fabric. They can serve their interest by serving the common interest, not by seeking their self-interest individually. While liberalism insists on the rights of the individual, communitarianism focuses on his duties and obligations. Early indications of this view may be traced to Aristotle (ancient Greek philosopher), Jean-Jaques Rousseau (1712-78), G.W.F. Hegel (1770-1831) and T.H. Green (1836-82). Its contemporary exponents include Alasdair MacIntyre (1929-), Charles Taylor (1931-), and Michael Sandel (1953-), etc.

THE LIBERAL VIEW

Politics as State or Group Activity

The liberal view of politics upholds the pluralistic view of society. According to this view, different individuals pursue their interests as members of different groups. There are a large number of groups in society, more or less organized, which seek to serve the interest of their members against the conflicting interests of competing groups. In other words, each of these groups is not only conscious of its particular interests but actively pursues them with a view to securing the authoritative allocation of values in its favour. For instance, a workers' union seeks to serve the interests of the workers which may clash with the interests of the employers. But employers have their own organizations seeking their interest. Similarly, producers and consumers, landlords and tenants, suppliers and customers, etc. seek to serve their respective interests through their organized groups. In this sense, politics has been described as a 'group activity'.

Since the authoritative allocation against the demands and claims of various groups is made by the state, the liberal theory also regards politics as a state activity. In other words, demands and supports (such as obedience to laws and regulations, payment of taxes, etc.) emanate from various interest-groups while policies and decisions are delivered by the state. Thus, politics according to this view, is a group activity as well as a state activity.

As a Process of Conciliating Interests

According to the liberal standpoint, different groups have conflicting interests, yet we can identify the 'common interest' which will reconcile the diverse interests of the competing groups. Politics is essentially an instrument of conflict-resolution. In other words, whenever there is an apparent clash of interests between several groups, some way can always be found to ensure the reconciliation of their conflicting interests. For instance, you can always form a rule or evolve a policy which will satisfy the parties to a dispute, such as the employer and the worker, the producer and the consumer, the supplier and the customer, the landlord and the tenant, or those travelling by different vehicles meeting at a cross-road. In short, politics enables the organized power of society to evolve a legitimate and just solution of their problems and controversies. Any conflict, disagreement or dispute arising in society is capable of resolution by conciliation and legitimate coercion. Thus, politics is an instrument of securing order and justice in society.

As a Means of Promoting the Common Good

Since there is a 'common interest' behind the conflicting interests of various groups, and politics is an effort to discover and pursue that 'common interest', it is naturally a means of promoting the 'common good'. The 'common good', according to liberal theory, accommodates the interests of all parties involved in the conflict. Thus, the entire process of politics is regarded as an instrument of progress. Awareness of the conflicting interests amongst various groups and their interaction leads to an awareness of the 'common interest'. Thus, at one point, the contending groups are prepared to accept the solution which is conducive to the 'common good'. This means that not only a compromise between contending parties is possible, but that you can also evolve a policy that will ensure better conditions for workers and higher profits for employers; 'a reasonable price' which will satisfy both the producer and the consumer, the supplier and the customer; a 'queue system' which will facilitate the distribution of rationed commodities; or the 'red and green signal system' which will provide order and safety to the users of cross-roads. This concern for the 'common good' has led us to the concept of the modern 'welfare state'.

THE MARXIST VIEW

Primacy of Economic Interests

According to the Marxist point of view, political institutions and activities are shaped by the prevailing economic system, especially the mode of production. All social relations, including political relations, are determined by the prevailing economic relations in society. Conflicting economic interests are, therefore, the motive force behind all politics. While the liberal theory envisages innumerable political situations and clash of interests on multifarious issues—*e.g.* economic, linguistic, cultural, religious, ethnic, etc.—the Marxist theory regards the clash of economic interests as the fundamental issue of social conflict. In its view, other issues are superficial and their resolution, if any, cannot end the conflict. In other words, if the economic issue is solved, all other issues will automatically disappear. Conversely, if the economic issue is evaded, settlement of all other issues will be a futile exercise.

Politics as an Instrument of Class Domination

According to the Marxist theory, conflict and politics arise in society because its system of production is not organized on a 'rational basis'. A rational system of production implies: (*a*) highest advancement of technology so as to get maximum production; (*b*) social ownership of the means of production and distribution; and (*c*) implementation of universal labour so as to maximize material production for the fulfilment of social needs. Only a rational system of production is conducive to genuine cooperative effort.

But under capitalism and in earlier stages, production is not organized on a rational basis. A small minority manages to corner ownership of the major means of production and forces the rest of the population to live on hard labour. The emergence of private property has divided society into two classes—the 'haves' and the 'have-nots' , the masters and the servants, the exploiters and the exploited— whose interests are irreconcilable. Politics and the state are the product of this division of society—they continue to serve the interests of the dominant class. As Friedrich Engels (*The Origin of the Family, Private Property and the State;* 1884) has elaborated:

> Because the state arose from the need to hold class antagonisms in check ... it is, as a rule, the state of the most powerful, economically dominant class, which through the medium of the state, becomes also the politically dominant class, and thus acquires new means of holding down and exploiting the oppressed class. Thus, the state of antiquity was above all the state of the slave-owners for the purpose of holding down the slaves, as the feudal state was the organ of the nobility for holding down the peasant serfs and bondsmen, and the modern representative state is an instrument of exploitation of the wage labour by capital.

Class Interests are Irreconcilable

The division of society into antagonistic classes gives rise to class-conflict or class struggle. All politics ensues from this class struggle. As Marx and Engels, in their *Communist Manifesto* (1848), have observed:

> The history of all hitherto existing society is the history of class struggles ... Freeman and slave, patrician and plebeian, lord and serf, guild-master and journeyman, in a word, oppressor and oppressed stood in constant opposition to one another, carried on an uninterrupted, now hidden, now

open fight, a fight that each time ended either in a revolutionary reconstitution of society at large, or in the common ruin of the contending classes.

This class-conflict is irreconcilable by its very nature. Politics cannot resolve this conflict. On the contrary, politics is used by the dominant class to suppress the conflict. This gives the impression of a voluntary compromise, but in reality it is a compromise imposed by the dominant class on the dependent class. It even creates an 'illusion of consent' by propagating the ideology of the ruling class.

Ideology

In Marxist theory, ideology refers to the set of ideas, beliefs and arguments which are used to lend legitimacy to the rule of the dominant class. It projects and promotes a value system under which even the exploitation of the dependent class seems justified.

So long as society remains divided into classes, state and politics will continue to be used as the tools of the dominant class for the suppression of the dependent class. This process will continue even after the 'socialist revolution', but in the 'reverse gear'. In other words, while capitalism is characterized by the exploitation of the workers by the capitalists, socialism (popularly dubbed communism) is characterized by the suppression of the dispossessed capitalists by the workers (proletariat) in order to forestall a counter-revolution and to pave the way for the blossoming of communism—a classless society. With the elimination of the classes, class-conflict will disappear and state and politics would no longer be required; the state will 'wither away'. Thus, according to Marxism, the antagonistic interests of the classes cannot be reconciled by the process of politics. The end of class-conflict marks an end of politics itself.

THE COMMUNITARIAN VIEW

Politics is the Arena of Mutual Cooperation, Not of Conflict

According to the communitarian view, the essence of human nature lies in the spirit of cooperation, not of conflict. Hence mutual aid or cooperation is the foundation of political organization. Aristotle had argued that the relation between individual and the state was similar to that between an organ and the organism. The state was an indispensable instrument of good life for all human beings. Hence, different individuals must cooperate with each other in order to secure good life for everyone. Modern communitarians postulate a similar role of the individual in a larger social and political organization.

Communitarians tend to argue that an individual develops his identity, talents and pursuits in life only from his place in the community. Community represents a set of social relationships based on sharing common characteristics, common values and common interests. In order to flourish in life, an individual requires a place in a well-functioning community. Whereas liberals encourage each person to define and seek his own 'good' within the political structure, communitarians direct him to discover and pursue his 'good' as an integral part of the 'good of the community'. This can be accomplished only through cooperation, not through competition.

Politics is Instrumental to the Pursuit of the Common Good

The idea of the common good is the keynote of communitarianism. Its notion of the common good is different from that of liberalism. Liberalism holds that if each individual is allowed to pursue his self-interest, common interest would be served automatically as a consequence. On the contrary, communitarianism does not believe that different individuals could have genuinely different interests. It does not recognize even their right to pursue self-interest apart from the interest of the community itself.

Liberalism holds that an individual is not indebted to society for his existence and his potentialities; hence he is absolutely free to pursue his self-appointed goals. In contrast, communitarianism believes that the individual owes his existence and his potentialities to society; hence he has no right to apply these potentialities in the so-called self-interest, disregarding the interest of society. His commitment to society is an essential feature of his personality. Alasdair MacIntyre *(After Virtue;* 1981) argues that the individuals can develop and promote virtue only through cooperative human activity. It is designed to achieve such standards of excellence which human beings are capable to achieve. If the state allows 'socially disconnected' individuals to pursue their so-called 'self-appointed goals', the result would be social disintegration and moral disaster. In fact, the process of such disintegration has already started in some modern liberal states as evident in the prevalence of crime and violence, the breakdown of the family, and the widespread drug-abuse.

Charles Taylor *(Philosophical Papers;* 1985) attacks the liberals' 'atomistic' conception of human beings which ignores the fact that a human being must be 'situated' in a society in order to develop his personality. Similarly, Michael Sandel *(Liberalism and the Limits of justice;* 1982) criticizes the liberals' conception of disjointed nature of the people. Sandel views human nature as 'embedded' in a particular time, place and culture. He insists on creating a 'deeper commonality' informed by 'shared self-understanding' as well as affection. In a nutshell, the communitarian view treats politics as a human activity concerned with the identification and pursuit of their common interest.

CONCLUSION

The chief difference between the liberal and the Marxist points of view regarding the nature of politics lies in their different notions about the nature and source of the conflict from which politics emanates, the prospects of conflict-resolution, and the utility of politics itself. Ralph Miliband, in his *Marxism and Politics* (1977), has significantly observed:

> In the liberal view of politics, conflict exists in terms of 'problems' which need to be 'solved'. The hidden assumption is that conflict does not, or need not, run very deep; that it can be 'managed' by the exercise of reason and good will and a readiness to compromise and agree ... The Marxist approach to conflict is very different. It is not a matter of 'problems' to be 'solved' but of a state of domination and subjection to be ended by a total transformation of the conditions which give rise to it.

Apparently, the liberal approach seems to be based on 'reason' and devoted to 'justice'. But the difficulty with this approach is that it fails to distinguish between 'compromise' and 'cooperation'. 'Compromise' can be effected without creating the conditions of 'freedom'. Real 'cooperation' among members of different groups or classes can be generated only after elimination of the conditions of 'dominance' and 'dependence' in their social, cultural as well as economic life. Liberal writers use 'compromise' and 'cooperation' synonymously which obscures the whole issue.

According to liberal theory, conflict is not only capable of resolution, but plays a positive role in the progress of society. As Ralph Miliband has further elaborated, in liberal view the conflict 'is not only civilized, but also civilizing'. It is not only a means of resolving problems in a peaceful way, but also of providing new ideas, ensuring progress, achieving ever-greater harmony, and so on. Conflict is 'functional', a stabilizing rather than a 'disrupting force'. On the other hand, Marxist theory regards conflict as 'dysfunctional'. It is symptomatic of a rift within society which tends to perpetuate the practice of exploitation until its character is transformed by a 'socialist' revolution. The so-called resolution of conflict by liberal methods is in reality a poor consolation: 'The antagonisms are irreconcilable, and the notion of genuine harmony is a deception or a delusion, at least in relation to class societies' *(ibid.)*. According to this viewpoint, genuine harmony in society can be achieved only when the real source of the conflict—the division of society into antagonistic classes—is eliminated, *i.e.* when a classless society comes into existence. The experience of the socialist revolutions in the twentieth century, especially those of the former USSR (1917) and the People's Republic of China (1949) and working of their systems, has, however, demonstrated that the dream of a 'classless' society is extremely difficult to realize. Moreover, the conditions of 'dominance' and 'dependence' exist in society at many subtle levels and they operate in many subtle ways at the national and international levels. Justice can only be achieved when these conditions are closely scrutinized and straightened, and not by arriving at vague 'compromises'.

Finally, the communitarian view sees no basic conflict between the interests of different members of society. Accordingly, a uniform, common interest is the natural characteristic of each community. It need not be established artificially in any society. It is only to be discovered and identified. When the people are able to see their common interest, they naturally tend to cooperate in its pursuit.

None of these views of politics may be treated as universally acceptable. *Liberal view is suited to a society which is not afflicted by wide disparities of wealth, prestige and power. Marxist view may be applied to a society sharply divided into dominant and dependent classes, where dependent class is not left with any alternative for peaceful solution of their problems. And communitarian view would be suitable for a society whose members are largely satisfied with their status and are prepared to cooperate to improve their lot.* If a society is characterized by wide disparities of power and differences of opinion, it would be futile to look into its problems from the communitarian point of view.

Different Views of Politics

The Issue	*Liberal View*	*Marxist View*	*Communitarian View*
Nature of Politics	Means of Reconciliation of Conflicting Interests	Means of Suppression of Class-conflict	Means of Pursuit of the Common Good
Status of the Individuals	Disconnected, Independent Units	Members of Conflicting Classes	Mutually connected Units
Structure of Society	Set of Independent Individuals	Set of Antagonistic Classes	Set of Intellectually and Emotionally United Human Beings
Notion of the Common Good	Stage of Equilibrium between Conflicting Interests	Not Discernible in a Class-Divided Society where Class Interests Dominate	Uniform Good that Comprehends the Good of Each Member of Society
Nature of Conflict	Not Very Deep which can be Resolved Easily	Very Deep Conflict between Classes which cannot be Resolved	No Real Conflict within a Community
Way to Progress	Conflict-Resolution	Revolution	Social Solidarity
Basic Principle	Liberty	Equality	Fraternity
Suited to	A Society not afflicted by wide disparities of wealth and power	A Society sharply divided into dominant and dependent classes	A Society whose members are largely satisfied, and prepared to cooperate
Exponents	Locke, Bentham, J.S. Mill, Laski, Robert Dahl	Marx, Engels, Lenin, Gramsci, Mao	Rousseau, Green, MacIntyre, Sandel, Charles Taylor

Social Solidarity

Social solidarity refers to a condition in which members of a society identify themselves with that society, and feel bound to support it. All sections of society display a strong faith in the basic values of society and devotion to its basic interests. They are inclined to combine their resources and energies for the fulfilment of its goals and objectives even if they are required to sacrifice their self-interest. Social solidarity lends strength and stability to a society.

Liberty

Liberty refers to a condition in which an individual does not face unreasonable restraints while making full use of his abilities in fulfilling his self-appointed goals.

Equality

In liberal theory, equality refers to 'absence of discrimination'. In Marxist context, equality implies a condition in which individuals are not divided into dominant and dependent classes due to private ownership of the major means of production: all members of society enjoy similar status as workers.

Fraternity

Fraternity refers to a sentiment that informs the members of a community who share a common culture, common values, an awareness of the common good, and engage in the common effort to achieve a social goal.

What is morally wrong cannot be politically right.

Donald Soper (1966)

It is our character that supports the promise of our future—far more than particular government programs or policies.

William J. Bennett (1989)

4

Approaches to the Study of Politics

[I] INTRODUCTION

> **Science is nothing but trained and organized common sense.**
>
> **T. N. Huxley**

DISTINCTION BETWEEN METHOD AND APPROACH

In the sphere of social sciences, the terms 'method' and 'approach' are applied rather loosely, and sometimes even interchangeably. To be precise, as far as possible, in their usage, distinction may be drawn between the two. Method is a more general term which refers to a particular way of doing something. In a systematic study, method may be defined as the procedure of inquiry by which reliable knowledge could be obtained and reliable conclusions could be drawn. Examples of methods are: scientific method, inductive method, deductive method, comparative method, etc. On the other hand, approach is a wider term which comprehends not only the method (*i.e. how* to inquire) but also the focus of our study *(i.e. what* to inquire) in order to understand the given phenomenon.

Vernon Van Dyke *(Political Science: A Philosophical Analysis;* 1960) has aptly defined the scope of approach: "An approach consists of criteria of selection—criteria employed in selecting the problems or questions to consider and in selecting the data to bring to bear; it consists of standards governing the inclusion and exclusion of questions and data." Commenting on the distinction between approach and method, Dyke has further pointed out: "In brief, approaches consist of criteria for selecting problems and relevant data, whereas methods are procedures for getting and utilizing data."

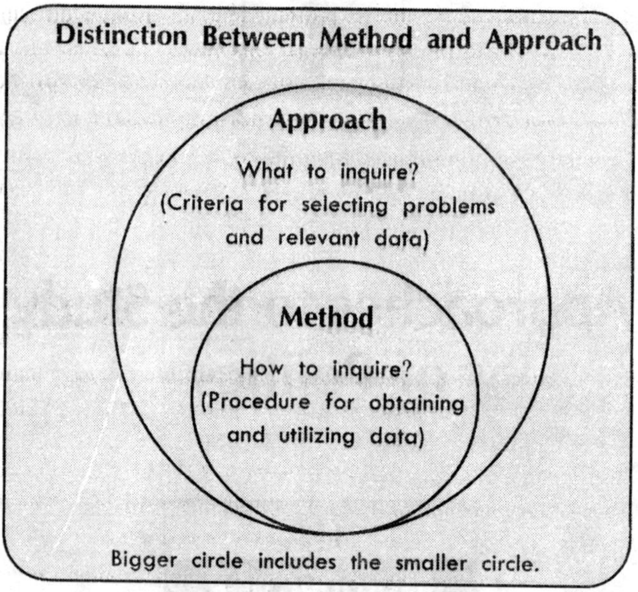

It may, however, be observed that an approach is usually wedded to a particular method while a method is not always wedded to a particular approach. That is why an approach suggests the relevant method also. Thus, behavioural approach is wedded to scientific method (because behaviour of several actors in a political situation is capable of scientific study) while the normative approach is wedded to philosophical method (because norms and values can only be determined philosophically, not through scientific method). Then, philosophical approach and historical approach suggest the use of philosophical method and historical method respectively although they also point to their respective focus of study. Again, empirical approach to the study of politics leads us to 'political analysis', and several models of political analysis (*e.g.* systems analysis, structural-functional analysis and decision-making analysis) in fact point to several methods adopted under this approach (although these are loosely referred to as 'political system approach', 'structural-functional approach' and 'decision-making approach' respectively).

TRADITIONAL *VERSUS* CONTEMPORARY APPROACHES

The study of politics has a very long tradition. Several approaches have been adopted for this purpose. Broadly speaking, the approaches which remained largely in vogue till the end of the Second World War (1939-45) are described as traditional approaches while those which were developed thereafter are known to be contemporary approaches. As Alan Ball (*Modern Politics and Government;* 1988) has rightly suggested, the use of the label 'traditional' is neither a criticism nor a refutation of the obvious fact that they still play an important role in modern political studies. In other words, the traditional approaches to the study of politics have not become all outdated, but they are no longer favoured by the champions of the contemporary approaches. It is not possible to furnish any comprehensive lists of the traditional or contemporary approaches. Truly speaking, they do not represent watertight compartments, although some of their distinctive features might be identified. A few decades ago it was argued that the contemporary approaches focus on facts while traditional approaches focus on values. This view is no longer upheld. Hence, the distinction between empirical and normative approaches cannot be treated as coterminous with the distinction between traditional and contemporary approaches.

However, it is true that the traditional study of politics was dominated by the study of philosophy, history, law and institutions. Hence, *philosophical, historical, legal and institutional approaches are usually identified as traditional approaches.* On the other hand, contemporary approaches are faced with the problem of the identity of the discipline. They particularly focus on phenomenon of politics as a process as manifested in the behaviour of different actors in a political situation which is sought to be studied by scientific method. Hence, *'behavioural approach' is a typically contemporary approach.* Then politics as a process is sought to be analysed by using *different models of political analysis.* All these models fall *within the purview of the contemporary approach.* Moreover, contemporary political science seeks to enrich itself by utilizing the relevant findings of other social sciences which leads us to the *interdisciplinary approach.* Hence, *interdisciplinary approach is also a contemporary approach.*

EMPIRICAL AND NORMATIVE APPROACHES

Although contemporary political science gives prominence to empirical approach and traditional study of politics was dominated by normative approach, it cannot be assumed that the distinction between empirical and normative approaches coincides with the distinction between contemporary and traditional approaches. In fact, some features of empirical as well as normative approaches are found both in the traditional and contemporary approaches. For instance, when we turn to traditional political theory, we find that Aristotle's analysis of the causes of revolution (or rebellion), Montesquieu's theory of separation of powers and Marx's analysis of the exploitation of the working classes are rich in empirical content. Then, in contemporary political theory Karl Popper's advocacy of incremental change, F.A. Hayek's defence of libertarianism, C.B. Macpherson's concept of creative freedom and Rawls's theory of justice are very rich in their normative content. What is the distinction between empirical and normative approaches?

Broadly speaking, the empirical approach seeks to discover and describe *facts* whereas the normative approach seeks to determine and prescribe *values.* The empirical approach primarily relies on the observation through sense-experience (*i.e.* sight, sound, smell, taste and touch); it aims at making an empirical statement which is concerned with *'is'* whereas the normative approach aims at making a normative statement which is concerned with what *'ought to be'* or *'should be'*. However, these forms of expression cannot be followed literally as the criterion of distinction between the two approaches. The crucial point is that an empirical statement is concerned with a situation which can be observed by our sense-experience, which can be verified by repeated observation and whose accuracy can be tested. On the other hand, a normative statement tends to express preference for a particular type of order as dictated by a sense of duty or universal need or by commitment to a moral principle or ideal. While strong arguments may be advanced in support of a normative statement, it is not capable of being discovered, described or verified by our sense-experience. For example, 'what is justice'—this question may be answered in several ways, such as 'justice is treating equals equally, and unequals unequally', or 'justice is giving equal freedom and equal opportunity to all provided that any departure from equal distribution will prove beneficial to the least advantaged', etc. Now all such answers purporting to define what is justice express a variety of value preferences; none of them is based on empirical observation or is capable of empirical verification. So in spite of using the 'is' form, they are by no means empirical statements.

Then there could be a statement requiring something to be done for the fulfilment of a definite purpose or condition. For instance, we may say, 'everybody *ought to* vote in election in order to make democracy work' (fulfilment of a purpose) or 'if democracy is to work, everybody *ought to* (or should, or must) vote in election'. Now these types of statements are certainly empirical statements in spite of using the 'ought to' form, because their contents can be empirically verified or falsified. To be sure, a normative statement requires something to be done in order to serve an *intrinsic value*—which is an end-in-itself (*e.g.* the truth, the good, the beautiful). On the other hand, an empirical statement requiring something to be done is intended to serve an *instrumental* value—which is a means to some higher end (*e.g.* 'do regular exercise to improve your health' or 'grow more trees to reduce environmental pollution'). In short, *it is the content of a statement, not its form, which makes it empirical or normative.*

Intrinsic and Instrumental Values

When something is desired, aimed at or commended purely for its own sake, rather than as a means to anything else, *i.e.* as an end-in-itself (e.g. the truth, the good, the beautiful), it represents an intrinsic value. On the other hand, when something is commended because it serves as a means to another end (e.g. natural resources, energy and planning), it represents an instrumental value.

Critics of the normative approach argue that the empirical approach is objective whereas the normative approach is subjective. T.D. Weldon, in his *Vocabulary of Politics* (1953), maintained that a political philosophy is like a matter of taste; one can only state one's taste and go away—there is no point in arguing. This is a biased view. While there may exist several schools of thought upholding different interpretations of, say, freedom, equality and justice, a dialogue between these schools can always be opened. Those holding different viewpoints can always come together to evolve or arrive at certain basic principles of reasoning by which they can prove or disprove different points. It is not like a matter of individual taste which can be stated but which cannot be defended.

The terminology adopted by empirical and normative approaches for approval or disapproval of any proposition creates confusion at times. The categories 'true or false', 'right or wrong' may have different meanings in the contexts of, say, mathematical and moral questions. It is sometimes assumed that empirical approach refers to 'true or false', 'right or wrong' as absolute categories while normative approach treats them as conditional. However, it is now widely accepted that even scientific principles are largely tentative. Nobody can claim to have found the final truth in the realm of matter, not to speak of the realm of mind. Scientific principles in the sphere of nature as well as society can be treated as valid until they are falsified by some new discovery. In politics, particularly, we cannot afford to abstain from acting until a very high level of scientific validity is achieved. As Robert Dahl has rightly pointed out: "In politics, 'refusing to decide' is simply deciding to allow others to decide for you" *(Modern Political Analysis;* 1991*)*.

Finally, the empirical approach remains largely *descriptive* while the normative approach is mainly *prescriptive*. Empirical approach seeks to discover laws that are unalterable (*e.g.* law of gravitational force). Hence, they are beyond man's control; one can discover and describe them. Normative approach is concerned with laws and conditions largely created or adopted by human society, which are alterable (*e.g.* laws governing property and public order). One can examine how far they are morally right or wrong and then prescribe the right course. Incidentally, in the normative approach prescription may be preceded by description. For instance, Plato and Aristotle had given description of their experience before prescribing their respective solutions. On the other hand, in the empirical approach description may be followed by prescription or suitable recommendations for the achievement of some obvious goals, such as economy and efficiency, or some specified goals, such as health and stability. Moreover, empirical approach can render immense help in examining the grounds of a normative argument. For example, Aristotle prescribed harsher punishment to a slave than to a freeman for the same crime, on the ground that a slave is less sensitive to punishment. Empirical approach has now established beyond doubt that men are not more or less sensitive to punishment because of their status as freemen or slaves. This is a sufficient reason to reject Aristotle's prescription in this behalf.

Champions of empirical approach have been very vocal in criticizing the normative approach on the ground that there is no 'scientifically valid' or reliable method of determining what is morally right or wrong. The supporters of normative approach do not condemn the empirical approach as such, but they criticize its indifference towards values, particularly its ignorance of discrimination between higher and lower values. As Leo Strauss has emphatically stated: "By teaching the equality of values, by denying that there are things which are intrinsically high and others which are intrinsically low as well as by denying that there is an essential difference between men and brutes, it unwittingly contributes to the victory of the gutter" *(Essays on the Scientific Study of Politics,* edited by Herbert Storing; 1962).

The state of estrangement between empirical and normative approaches, wherever it exists, will prove disastrous. There is an urgent need to build a bridge between the two approaches which will be beneficial not only for their respective upholders, but also for the human civilization itself.

Distinction between Empirical and Normative Approaches

The Issue	*Empirical Approach*	*Normative Approach*
Chief Concern	Facts (it *is* so.)	Values (It *ought to be* so.)
Focus of Inquiry	Real	Ideal
Designed to	Discover	Determine
Nature of Inquiry	Scientific and Descriptive	Critical and Prescriptive
Based on	Sense-experience and logic	Speculation and logic
Result of Inquiry	Verifiable	Debatable
Criteria of Validity	True and False	Right and Wrong

[II]
TRADITIONAL APPROACHES

Philosophical, historical, legal and institutional approaches to the study of politics may be taken to represent the mainstream traditional approaches.

PHILOSOPHICAL APPROACH

In the first place, the philosophical approach is concerned with the clarification of concepts used in a particular discipline. As Vernon Van Dyke *(Political Science: A Philosophical Analysis;* 1960) has significantly observed:

> A philosophical analysis is an effort to clarify thought about the nature of the subject and about ends and means in studying it. Put more generally, a person who takes a philosophical approach to a subject aims to enhance linguistic clarity and to reduce linguistic confusion; he assumes that the

> language used in descriptions reflects conceptions of reality, and he wants to make conceptions of reality as clear, consistent, coherent, and helpful as possible.

Secondly, the philosophical approach aims at evolving "standards of right and wrong" for the purpose of a critical evaluation of the existing institutions, laws and policies. As Dyke has elaborated:

> It may denote efforts to arrive at truth through the use of reason. The truth sought may be normative, descriptive, or prescriptive. The object of philosophic inquiry in this sense is to establish standards of the good, the right, and the just, and to appraise or prescribe political institutions and practices in the light of these standards *(ibid.)*.

Most of the classical political theory represents philosophical approach. Its themes are generally concerned with moral reasoning which cannot be subjected to scientific test although the empirical aspect of such reasoning can always be questioned. Moreover, the moral aspect of such reasoning can also be questioned from the viewpoint of our 'modern consciousness'. For instance, Kant's concept of 'human dignity' which rules out any type of slavery, is closer to modern consciousness than Aristotle's defence of slavery. Then so many political thinkers upheld certain notions of 'human nature' which can now be examined in the light of the findings of the contemporary psychology and social sciences. Hence, the philosophical approach does not simply rely on the political thought of the past; it is a subject of current and continuous debate.

Most of the classical thinkers, proceeding from a hypothesis about human nature, dwelled on two main themes: 'art of government' and 'grounds of political obligation'. Aristotle postulated: 'man is by nature a political animal', and then elaborated his views on these two subjects. Machiavelli mainly dwelled on the 'art of government' on the assumption of the very selfish and ungrateful nature of man. Thereafter, 'art of government' ceased to be a part of mainstream political theory. Hobbes mainly focused on the grounds of political obligation; his absolutist view of political obligation was carried on by Rousseau and Hegel on different grounds. Locke was probably the first thinker to repudiate this absolutist view and to postulate 'rights' of the individual against the state. That is why Locke is regarded as the pioneer of individualism which later developed into liberalism. Kant proceeding from different premises evolved the concept of 'human dignity'. J.S. Mill sought to explore the limits of political obligation by defining the conditions of state intervention. T.H. Green developed his theory of rights on moral grounds and sought to limit the authority of the state. Laski similarly tried to build an elaborate system of individual rights. John Rawls revived Kant's notion of 'rational negotiators' to build his theory of justice. On the other hand, Marx sought to demolish political obligation by identifying man's position in a social class, and projected the working class as an agent of revolution. Neo-Marxists have been looking for alternative instruments as well as alternative strategies of revolution.

Political Obligation

Political obligation refers to the set of conditions which determine as to how far, when and why individual is obliged to obey law and the commands of political authority. This may be accompanied by such duties as the payment of taxes, participation in voting, jury service and military duty, etc. which are considered to be necessary for the maintenance of political institutions.

In a nutshell, political philosophy mainly dwelled on the logic behind grounds and limits of political obligation. Concepts of individual rights and revolution are the by-products of this debate. Conceptions of freedom, equality and justice are extensions of the theories of rights. The concept of democracy denotes an effort to translate the concept of individual rights into concrete political institutions. Again, concepts of authoritarianism, totalitarianism and fascism, etc. largely represent the negative side of this effort.

Fascism

Fascism refers to an anti-democratic theory advanced by Benito Mussolini (1883-1945), the Italian dictator, which eulogized nation-state as the supreme moral authority. It exhorted people to set aside all rules, conventions and legal limitations, and religiously follow the dictates of their leader in pursuit of national glorification.

Of the contemporary champions of the philosophical approach to the study of politics, Leo Strauss (1899-1973), American philosopher, is the most outstanding. According to Strauss, political science and political philosophy are coterminous. They denote an attempt to obtain true knowledge of political things as well as the standards of the right and the good. Political philosophy is a product of our quest for good life and good society. Values as well as facts are indispensable part of political philosophy which enable us to undertake a critical and coherent analysis of political institutions and activities. Without such analysis, assumptions regarding the political things take the character of opinions. Political philosophy seeks to replace opinion by knowledge, as originally postulated by Socrates. Strauss has severely criticized the contemporary behavioural approach which insists on 'value-free analysis' and thus destroys the essence of true knowledge of politics.

HISTORICAL APPROACH

The term 'historical approach' to politics may be used in two senses. Firstly, it may denote the process of arriving at the laws governing politics through an analysis of historical events, that is events of the past, as exemplified by the theories propounded by Hegel and Marx. Karl Popper (1902-94), Austrian philosopher has described this approach as 'historicism'. It implies that historical processes are determined by their inherent necessity which are beyond the control of human ingenuity. Popper has criticized historicism because it insists on discovering what is inevitable, and then advocates totalitarian methods for its realization, as Hegel and Marx have done for the realization of their respective visions of future society. In the second place, historical approach stands for an attempt at understanding politics through a historical account of political thought of the past, as exemplified by George H. Sabine's *A History of Political Theory* (1937).

According to Sabine, the subject matter of political science coincides with the major themes of discussion in the writings of the well-known political philosophers—Plato, Aristotle, Hobbes, Locke, Rousseau, Bentham, Mill, Green, Marx and others. Leading examples of the questions raised by these philosophers are: what ideals are sought to be realized through the state; what is the meaning of freedom and equality; what are the grounds and limits of political obligation, etc.? Sabine points out that each political theory is advanced in response to some specific situation. It is necessary to recapitulate the circumstances under which a particular theory was produced for understanding its relevance to the present situation. Moreover, any political theory is not only a product of history, it also served as an instrument of moulding history by its ideological force. However, all great political theories are valid for all times.

Critics of the historical approach point out that it is not possible to understand the ideas of the past ages in terms of the contemporary ideas and concepts. Moreover, ideas of the past are hardly any guide for resolving the crises of the present-day world which were beyond comprehension of the past thinkers. David Easton (*The Political System;* 1953) warned against living 'parasitically on ideas a century old' and failing to develop a 'new political synthesis'. This challenge to historical approach of course encouraged the development of the 'behavioural approach'. However, the recent revival of interest in values has led to a renewed interest in the rich heritage of political thought for evolving guiding principles for our own age. For instance, John Rawls (1921-2002) has built his celebrated theory of justice by drawing on the methodology of Locke and Kant and by rejecting the utilitarian philosophy of Bentham and Mill. Herbert Marcuse (1898-1979) has built his neo-Marxist theory of freedom by reverting to Hegel's concept of 'civil society'. Again, C.B. Macpherson (1911-87) has built his theory of democracy by reverting to Aristotle and J.S. Mill while rejecting Bentham's utilitarianism and the contemporary elitism of Schumpeter and Dahl.

LEGAL APPROACH

Legal approach stands for an attempt to understand politics in terms of law. It focuses its attention on the legal and constitutional framework in which different organs of government have to function, inquires into their respective legal position, their powers and the procedure which makes their actions legally valid. For instance, legal approach to Indian politics will proceed to analyse legal implications of various provisions of the Indian Constitution, duly documented by the decisions of the Supreme Court of India as well as by the opinions of legal luminaries, procedure of formation and legal position of the two Houses of the Indian Parliament and State legislatures, procedure of election or appointment, powers and position of the President, Prime Minister, Governors, Chief Ministers, Central and State Cabinets, etc., role and powers of the Supreme Court of India and High Courts, full legal implications of the federal set up, position of Fundamental Rights and Directive Principles of State Policy, etc. Similarly, legal approach to international politics will largely tend to analyse it in terms of the requirements of international law.

The legal approach may prove inadequate in understanding the complex political forces, processes and behaviour which might operate outside the legal-formal framework, yet it is not entirely insignificant. As Vernon Van Dyke has rightly observed:

> Nor is a legal approach to be disparaged. After all, both the procedures and the substance of political action at every level are often controlled by law. In the field of both domestic and international politics, law frequently prescribes the action to be taken in given contingencies; it also forbids action or fixes the limits of permissible action *(Political Science:* A Philosophical Analysis; 1960).

Moreover, every political process to become effective and stable must culminate in legal provisions whether it is an independence movement in a colonized country or an agitation for civil rights or certain concessions for any section of society. Besides, the study of constitutional law and international law, etc. in spite of its limited use in understanding politics, continues to play a pivotal role in the social and political life of almost every country.

INSTITUTIONAL APPROACH

Institutional approach is closely related to legal approach, yet it is different. Significantly, this approach does not solely bank on other disciplines—philosophy, history or law—for understanding politics. Amongst the traditional approaches, it alone gives independent identity to the systematic study of politics.

Traditionally, politics has been defined as the study of the state and government. Government itself is an institution, and its various organs, such as Parliament (legislature), Cabinet (executive), and Supreme Court (judiciary), etc. may also be recognized as institutions. Political parties—which exist independently—are also institutions in their own right. There are lots of other institutions in society, such as family, school, church, or club. A student of politics will be interested only in those institutions which have a direct bearing on politics. What is an institution?

In short, an institution is a set of offices and agencies arranged in a hierarchy, where each office or agency has certain functions and powers. Each office or agency is manned by persons with definite status and role; other persons also expect them to perform this role. The activities of an institution are not confined to its office-holders. For instance, ordinary voters who participate in the process of setting up a legislature through election are not themselves office-holders therein. As Vernon Van Dyke has aptly summed up:

> An institution is any persistent system of activities and expectations, or any stable pattern of group behaviour *(Political Science: A Philosophical Analysis;* 1960).

Accordingly, upholders of the institutional approach proceed to study the organization and functioning of government, its various organs, political parties and other institutions affecting politics. Classification of governments, starting from Aristotle (monarchy, tyranny, aristocracy, oligarchy, polity and democracy) to modern classification (democracy and dictatorship, parliamentary and presidential, unitary and federal, etc.), identification of levels of government (federal, state and local) as well as branches of government (executive, legislative, judicial), composition and powers of each of these and their inter-relationships (largely in legal terms), etc. are the chief concerns of this approach. It aims at giving an elaborate description of facts. Hence, it exemplifies a shift from normative to empirical approach, and from a historical to a contemporary concern within the sphere of traditional approaches. However, it relies heavily on description rather than explanation. Hence, it fails to qualify as a contemporary approach.

Other drawbacks of the institutional approach are: (*a*) with its preoccupation with the institutions, it neglected the individual; hence during the ascendancy of this approach, the study of voting behaviour and political attitudes of the individual was left to sociologists; (*b*) in the absence of overarching institutions governing international politics, it practically neglected the study of international politics; it confined its attention to international relations and description of the United Nations and its associated agencies, and left the study of international politics to historians and students of international law; (*c*) being concerned with the established institutions alone, it neglected the role of violence or threat of violence, political movements and agitations, war and revolutions, etc.; and finally, (*d*) it neglected the role of various informal groups and processes in shaping politics.

However, it should not be forgotten that institutions form a very important part of politics. Any discussion of politics without reference to the corresponding institutions will lead us nowhere. Moreover, in the present-day turmoil, particularly in the developing countries, constitution-making and institution-building is the order of the day. Institutional approach is inadequate in itself. But any other approach will also be incomplete without paying due attention to institutions.

[III]
CONTEMPORARY APPROACHES

Broadly speaking, contemporary approaches to the study of politics signify a departure from traditional approaches in two respects: (*a*) they attempt to establish a separate identity of political science by focusing on the real character of politics; and (*b*) they try to understand politics in totality, transcending its formal aspects and looking for those aspects of social life which influence and are influenced by it. Contemporary approaches are legion, and all of them may not fulfil these conditions. The following may be regarded as the most important: (*a*) behavioural approach; (*b*) post-behavioural approach; and (*c*) some important models of political analysis.

BEHAVIOURAL APPROACH

Behaviouralism, or the behavioural approach to the analysis and explanation of political phenomena, is particularly associated with the work of American political scientists after the Second World War (1939-45), but its origins may be traced back to the works of Graham Wallas *(Human Nature in Politics)* and Arthur Bentley *(The Process of Government),* both published as early as 1908. Both Wallas and Bentley were inclined to lay greater emphasis on the informal processes of politics and less on political institutions in isolation. Wallas sought to introduce a new realism in political studies in the light of the new findings of contemporary psychology. While classical economists—the champions of the *laissez-faire* doctrine—had treated man as a rational creature following his self-interest, the new psychology had revealed that man was not a rational creature in this sense and that his political actions were not totally guided by reason and self-interest. Human nature was too complex to be explained by simplistic utilitarian propositions. Wallas, therefore, insisted on exploring facts and evidence for understanding human nature and its manifestations in human behaviour. His chief message was that the political process could be understood only by analysing as to how people actually behaved in a political situation, not merely by speculating on how they should or would behave. Bentley, on the other hand, a pioneer of 'group approach' to politics, primarily sought not to describe political activity, but to provide for new tools of investigation. He was so much fascinated by the study of informal groups that he tended almost completely to ignore the formal political institutions. Greatly inspired by sociology, he proceeded to undertake a study of the roles of pressure groups, political parties, elections and public opinion in the political process.

Charles E. Merriam (1874-1953) was another pioneer of the behavioural approach. He is also famous as the founder of the Chicago School which made substantial contribution to the behavioural movement. In his article 'The Present State of the Study of Politics' published in *American Political Science Review*

(1921) and in his book *New Aspects of Politics* (1925), Merriam criticized contemporary political science for its lack of scientific rigour. He deprecated the work of historians as they had ignored the role of psychological, sociological and economic factors in human affairs. He argued that students of politics should make full use of recent advances in social sciences in order to develop interdisciplinary and scientific character of political science. He called for renewed scientific endeavour and emphasized the need for a 'policy science' by using quantitative techniques already developed in the fields of psychology and sociology. In his presidential address to the American Political Science Association (1925), Merriam exhorted political scientists to look at political behaviour as one of the essential objects of inquiry.

Apart from being an exponent of the scientific method for the study of politics, Merriam was also an ardent champion of democracy. In fact, he vigorously sought to put science into the service of democratic principles. He saw no inconsistency in promoting science and democracy together. William B. Munro ('Physics and Politics—An Old Analogy Revisited', *APSR;* 1927), another exponent of scientific method, however, argued that it was not a proper function of political scientists to teach democratic citizenship. Then G.E.G. Catlin, in his *Science and Method of Politics* (1927), advanced the case for a 'value-free' pure science. He treated 'power' as essence of politics and argued that analysis of 'power' should not be inclined in favour of any particular value-system. This view of politics as the science of power as well as a case for treating politics as a policy science was later developed thoroughly by Harold D. Lasswell (1902-78). His celebrated work *Politics: Who Gets What, When, How* (1936) proved to be a landmark in the empirical approach to politics as the study and analysis of power.

Despite these early attempts, behaviouralism in political science was systematically developed only after the Second World War, particularly through the writings of American political scientists. David B. Truman published his paper 'The Impact on Political Science of the Revolution in the Behavioural Sciences' in 1955. Robert Dahl's paper 'The Behavioural Approach in Political Science: Epitaph for a Monument to a Successful Protest' appeared in the *American Political Science Review* in 1961. Then Evron M. Kirkpatrick published his paper 'The Impact of the Behavioural Approach on Traditional Political Science' in 1962, and David Easton contributed his paper 'The Current Meaning of 'Behaviouralism' in Political Science' in 1967. Heinz Eulau's article on 'Political Behaviour' in the *International Encyclopedia of the Social Sciences,* published in 1968 was also an important contribution to the series. In a nutshell, behaviouralism stood for a shift of focus in the study of politics, from the formalism and normative orientations of the legalistic and philosophic schools to political behaviour, that is the behaviour of actual actors in the political field, such as power-holders, power-seekers as well as voters. Behaviouralism as such came to be understood as something wider than the study of political behaviour, yet political behaviour was its main focus. It would, therefore, be profitable to define 'political behaviour' at the outset. According to Geoffrey K. Roberts *(A Dictionary of Political Analysis;* 1971):

> Political behaviour, as an area of study within political science, is concerned with those aspects of human behaviour that take place within political contexts, that is within a state or other political community, for political purposes or with political motivation. Its focus is the individual person—as voter, leader, revolutionary, party member, opinion leader, etc.—rather than the group or the political system, but it necessarily takes account of the influences of the group on the individual's behaviour, the constraints of the system on the individual's opportunities for action, and the effects of the political culture on his attitudes and political habits.

Accordingly, the political scientists who undertook the study of political behaviour sought to account for the psychological and sociological influences on behaviour of the individual in a political situation. This involved the study of political processes and factors such as political socialization, political ideologies, political culture, political participation, political communication, leadership, decision-making, and even political violence. An understanding of most of these processes involved interdisciplinary and cross-disciplinary research. In any case, behaviouralism as a movement in political science did not remain confined to the study of individual-based political behaviour, but developed into a set of orientations, procedures and methods of analysis. In practice it embraced all that lends scientific character to modern political science.

Political Socialization

Political socialization refers to the process whereby an individual learns the political norms and beliefs, transmitted by the society from one generation to the next. Agencies of political socialization include family, peer groups, school, church, associations of various kinds, political parties and social movements, etc.

Political Ideology

Political ideology refers to a set of ideas and arguments used by any political organization to defend an existing or proposed system of distribution of power in society. These ideas are accepted to be true by their upholders without inquiring into the logical grounds of their validity.

Political Culture

Political culture refers to those aspects of the culture of a community — including its values, norms and beliefs — which lend legitimacy to its political institutions and ruling classes, and determine status of the individual vis-a-vis those institutions and classes.

Political Participation

Political participation refers to the process whereby individuals seek to take active part in the formation, articulation and implementation of public policies and decisions. In a wider sense, it includes the activities of politicians, public officials as well as ordinary citizens taking part in voting, party campaigning and community work. Various methods of protest against public decisions, indecision or inactivity are also regarded as the ways of political participation.

Political Communication

Political communication refers to the process whereby various groups of individuals communicate their demands, supports and protests to the political system, and government communicates necessary information, reports and decisions to the public. Media of mass communication (newspapers, radio, television, etc.) as well as public processions, shouting slogans, distributing leaflets and pamphlets, writing and sticking of posters on walls, submission of memoranda to high officials, etc. are the common instruments of political communication.

Political Violence

Political Violence includes rebellion, rioting, looting, sabotage, terrorism and physical conflicts between antagonistic groups within a state. It may include communal violence or violence between different racial, religious, regional or linguistic groups fighting for a larger share in public resources and power. Political violence is more likely to erupt in those countries where disparities of wealth and power seem to correspond to racial, religious, regional or linguistic distribution of population in society.

According to David Easton, the intellectual foundations of behaviouralism consist of eight major tenets:

- *Regularities:* It implies that there are discoverable uniformities in political behaviour which can be expressed in theory-like statements so as to provide for explanation and prediction of political phenomena.
- *Verification:* It requires that the validity of such theory-like statements must be testable, in principle, by reference to relevant behaviour.
- *Techniques:* It means that the means for acquiring and interpreting data should be examined self-consciouly, refined and validated for the purpose of observing, recording and analysing behaviour.
- *Quantification:* It is necessary because precision in the recording of data and statement of findings requires measurement which should be expressed in terms of actual quantities to facilitate proper analysis.
- *Values:* The behaviouralists drew a clear distinction between ethical

evaluation and empirical explanation, which were concerned with values and facts respectively. They insisted that objective scientific inquiry has to be value-free or value-neutral.

- *Systematization:* It stands for establishing close inter-relationship between theory and research, because research untutored by theory may prove trivial while theory unsupportable by data may turn out to be futile.
- *Pure Science:* It holds that the understanding and explanation of political behaviour is essential to utilize knowledge in the solution of urgent practical problems of society.
- *Integration:* It signifies integration of political science with other social sciences in order to evolve a comprehensive view of human affairs, to strengthen its validity and the generality of its own results.

Any political inquiry conducted according to these guidelines would be most conducive to generating reliable theory and scientific explanations. The behavioural movement had such a profound effect on political science that these tests became the rule of political inquiry.

Behaviouralism came to accord primacy to higher degree of reliability vis-a-vis higher degree of generality. It, therefore, focused on questions that could be answered reliably on the basis of the methods available. As Vernon Van Dyke has aptly illustrated: "The student who takes a behavioural approach is not likely to ask broad and vague questions like what caused the decline and fall of the Roman Empire... Nor is he likely to focus on ideologies or constitutions or laws or upon the organizational structure of institutions" *(Political Science: A Philosophical Analysis;* 1960). In short, behaviouralism focused on micro-level situations rather than attempting macro-level generalizations.

POST-BEHAVIOURAL REVOLUTION

By the mid-1960s behaviouralism gained a dominant position in the methodology of political science. However, its critics like Leo Strauss ('What is Political Philosophy?', *Journal of Politics;* 1957) had started arguing that the rise of behaviouralism was symptomatic of a crisis in political theory because of its failure to come to grips with normative issues. Sheldon Wolin ('Political Theory as a Vocation', *American Political Science Review;* 1969) declared that the preoccupation of political science with method signified an abdication of true vocation of political theory. Within the sphere of philosophy of science the publication of Thomas Kuhn's *The Structure of Scientific Revolutions* (1962) had promoted the view that significance of scientific method lies in its capacity of problem-solving and crisis-management, not in methodological sophistication. By the end of 1960s even the exponents of behaviouralism realized that its strict adherence to 'pure science' was responsible for its failure to attend to the pressing social and political issues of the period. In 1969, David Easton himself in his presidential address to the American Political Science Association, announced a new revolution in political science—'a post-behavioural revolution'—that represented a shift of focus from strict methodological issues to a greater concern with public responsibilities of the discipline and with political problems.

Relevance and action were the twin slogans of post-behaviouralism. It represented no complete departure from behaviouralism. Rather it stood for consolidating its gains and applying them for problem-solving and crisis-management. Easton emphatically drew the attention of contemporary political scientists to the impending threat of the nuclear bomb, inner conflicts within the US which might lead to civil war or dictatorship, and undeclared war in Vietnam which was perturbing moral consciousness the world over. He lamented that the behavioural political scientists were taking refuge in their 'ivory tower', seeking to perfect their methodology, as if they were not at all concerned with the outside world. Emphasizing the intellectuals' historical role in protecting the humane values of civilization, Easton warned that if they failed to play this role, they would be reduced to mere technicians or mechanics for tinkering with society. Reminding them of their responsibility to reshape society Easton concluded that scientists could adopt a rational interest in value construction and application without denying the validity of their science. Accordingly, post-behaviouralism seeks to reintroduce a concern for values and goals of social policy without relinquishing other tenets of the behavioural approach. In other words, whereas the behavioural approach had insisted on making political science a *pure science,* the post-behavioural approach sought to convert it into an *applied science*.

In the contemporary social science, the behavioural approach has shown increasing concern with solving the prevailing problems of society. In this way it has largely absorbed the 'post-behavioural' orientation within its scope.

Distinction between Behavioural and Post-Behavioural Approaches

The Issue	*Behavioural Approach*	*Post-Behavioural Approach*
Nature of Inquiry	Search for Pure Knowledge and Theory	Search for Applied Knowledge and Practice
Purpose of Inquiry	'Knowledge for Knowledge Sake'; Not Interested in Action	Relevance of Knowledge to satisfy social needs and Action for Problem-Solving
Focus of Study	• Micro-level Analysis; focus on small units • Process of Decision-Making	Macro-level Analysis; focus on the role of big units Content of the Decision
Attitude towards Values	Value-Neutral	Interested in the Choice of Values
Attitude towards Social Change	Interested in *Status Quo;* Not Interested in Social Change	Interested in Social Change for Solving Social Problems

[IV]
MODELS OF POLITICAL ANALYSIS

Political analysis is the product of the empirical-scientific orientation in the study of politics. In the classical tradition, Aristotle's classification of governments and Machiavelli's cost-benefit analysis of different techniques of leadership may be cited as earlier and rudimentary attempts at political analysis. However, political analysis in the real sense has flourished only in modern times, particularly with the adoption of scientific method in the study of politics. What is political analysis?

Political analysis involves several steps. We start with determining the nature of politics. David Easton's concept of politics as 'authoritative allocation of values' will serve as a suitable example. Politics is now everywhere recognized as a process. A process involves a set of interactions among its components. To proceed in the direction of political analysis, we must identify these components. This will guide us as to the relevant data which should be chosen for a proper understanding of politics. But how are these data inter-related? This will depend on our conception of the pattern of interaction of the components of the political process. So the next step is to arrange our data according to their inter-relationship as conceived by us so as to yield an explanation.

Now these two steps, *i.e.* determining the relevant data and evolving their suitable arrangement for yielding an explanation constitute a model of political analysis. Since such model is evolved at a conceptual level, it is possible to build several models of political analysis, depending upon our points of inquiry. Ideally, all explanations of a given situation derived through different models of political analysis should coincide, but this does not always happen.

Contemporary political science has evolved a large number of models of political analysis. Of these, the following are more important which could be chosen for a detailed description: systems analysis; structural-functional analysis; communications theory; and decision-making analysis. These models are associated with the liberal view of politics. Finally, Marxist analysis may be added to this list though it may lead to very different results.

SYSTEMS ANALYSIS

This is the pioneering model of political analysis. It conceives politics in terms of a political system. What is a system? As Robert Dahl has elucidated: "Any collection of elements that interact in some way with one another can be considered a system—a galaxy, a football team, a legislature, a political party" *(Modern Political Analysis;* 1991). For the purpose of analysis, elements of a system should be looked at in an abstract way rather than as concrete things. Hence, elements of a political system should not be seen as a group of individuals constituting a government or its organs, but as abstract elements interacting with each other in the sphere of politics.

The concept of political system in this sense was introduced by David Easton ('An Approach to the Analysis of Political Systems', *World Politics;* 1957) who is regarded the pioneer of systems analysis. The model of political system was fully developed by Easton in his *A Systems Analysis of Political Life* (1965). In short, Easton defined politics as the 'authoritative allocation of values' which broadly constitutes the political process. This does not take place in a closed circuit; its ends are connected with the social process. It is in this sense that the political system has been described as an open system. In other words, 'allocation of values' is made because there are corresponding 'demands' from the society or 'environment'; it becomes 'authoritative' because it gets 'supports' from the 'environment'. In David Easton's terminology, the 'political system' receives 'inputs' from the 'environment' in the form of 'demands' and 'supports'; it produces 'outputs' in the form of 'policies and decisions'. The 'outputs' flow back into the environment through a 'feedback' mechanism, giving rise to fresh 'demands', etc.

Easton's Model of Political System

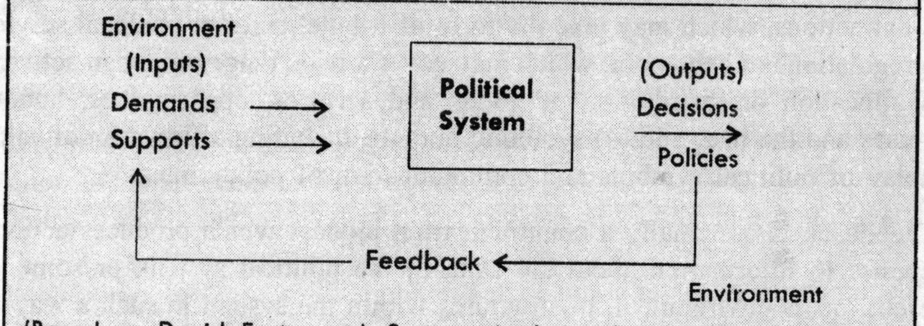

(Based on David Easton : *A Systems Analysis of Political Life; 1965*)

Easton has characterized demands as the raw materials out of which finished products called decisions are manufactured. He has described supports as the energy in the form of actions or orientations enabling the political system to convert the demands into authoritative decisions and policies. Demands may arise from any source—the people, politicians, administrators, opinion leaders and so on—depending on the nature of the regime. The extent of support is bound to vary—depending on the expectations of the people from their political system. Variability of support is bound to affect the destinies of the political authorities (often called governments), the regime (democratic, authoritarian, and the like), and the political community. Outputs are produced by the political system through special processes that ensure their acceptance as binding by most members of the society most of the time.

Easton has also given an elaborate classification of demands, supports and outputs which illustrates their nature thoroughly. Demands are sub-classified into four types: (1) demands for allocation of goods and services, such as wages and working conditions, educational opportunities, recreational facilities, roads and transportation, etc.; (2) demands for the regulation of behaviour, such as provision of public safety, controls over markets and rules pertaining to marriage, health and sanitation; (3) demands for participation in the political system, such as the right to vote, to hold office, to petition the government bodies and officials, and to form political associations; and (4) demands for communication and information, such as the affirmation of norms, the information regarding policy intent, and display of the majesty and power of the political system in times of foreign threats as well as on ceremonial occasions. Supports are also sub-classified into four types: (1) material supports, such as the payment of taxes and other levies, and rendering service in public interest, such as social work or military service; (2) obedience to law, rules and regulations; (3) participatory supports, such as voting, political discussion and other forms of political activity; and (4) paying attention to governmental communication, and display of deference or respect to public authority, symbols and ceremonials.

The outputs, which may be clubbed together as policies and decisions (a policy itself is a web of decisions), are again sub-classified into four categories: (1) extractions, which may take the form of tribute, taxes or personal services; (2) regulations of behaviour, which may cover a wide range of human activities; (3) allocation or distribution of goods and services, opportunities, honours, statuses and the like; and (4) symbolic outputs, including affirmation of values, display of political symbols and communication of policy intent.

Feedback is essentially a communication process which produces action in response to information about the state of the political system, or some part thereof, or its environment, to structures within the system in such a way that the future action of those structures is modified in consequence. The results of such modification may, in turn, produce further modifications, and so on. The feedback channel helps the political system in approaching its goals. It apprises the political system of the position of its goal, its own distance from the goal, and the changes in this distance brought about by its own performance, in response to information coming from the feedback process.

Under the normal circumstances, demands would serve as guide to the political system for determining its policies and goals, and supports will enable it to achieve its goals. It may be hoped that if the political system is capable of processing the demand-inputs effectively, support-inputs are bound to come forth from its environment. Feedback mechanism is expected to adjust outputs to inputs. However, maintaining a state of equilibrium in the political system is by no means a simple affair. Conversion of demands and supports into outputs in the shape of policies and decisions has to be regulated by a complex mechanism. Of the many demands made on the political system, some may be lost in transit without reaching the output stage. If there are too many demands, or too much insistence on particular type of demand, stress will arise and the channels will be overloaded. If so, various regulatory mechanisms will have to be applied to cope with the stress. In the first place, the structural mechanisms, such as pressure groups and political parties, will assume the role of 'gatekeepers' who will allow only legitimate demands to enter the political system. Secondly, cultural mechanisms will ensure that only right type of demands—which enjoy social approval—will be encouraged. Thirdly, communication channels can be increased to ensure a smooth flow of excessive demands into the system. Fourthly, demands may be controlled in the conversion process itself by the legislative, executive and administrative organs of government who are responsible for processing all demands. Should the stress reach a critical stage, and continue at that level for quite some time, changes in the authorities or even in the regime (such as through a revolution) might become inevitable. Failure to control the situation may even bring about eventual destruction of the system itself.

It is important to note that *Easton was the first to conceptualize political system as an 'information processing system'*. His framework of systems analysis was found very useful for the comparative analysis of diverse political units, such as modernized as well as developing polities. It has also been extensively used for an analysis of the international political system. Easton's model of political system has served as a starting point for Gabriel Almond's model of structural-functional analysis as also for Karl Deutsch's model of communications theory. However, it has been criticized for its inability in understanding the structure and function of political power as well as in analysing mass political behaviour, such as voting behaviour. In any case, it represents a substantial advance in the direction of constructing a theoretical framework from within the discipline of political science.

STRUCTURAL–FUNCTIONAL ANALYSIS

Like systems analysis, structural-functional analysis is based on the concept of political system. This model of political analysis has been more widely used in the sphere of comparative politics because it provides for standard categories for analysing different types of political systems. It originated in the sphere of social anthropology in the writings of Radcliffe-Brown and B. Malinowski. Then it was developed in the field of sociology by Talcott Parsons, Robert Merton and Marion Levy. Finally, Gabriel Almond and his associates developed it into a tool of political analysis.

Gabriel Almond and J.S. Coleman (*The Politics of the Developing Areas;* 1960) identified four characteristics of the political system: (*a*) all political systems have political structures; (*b*) the same functions are performed in all political systems with different frequencies and by different kinds of structures; (*c*) all political structures are multi-functional; and (*d*) all political systems are 'mixed' systems in the cultural sense, *i.e.* they are based in a culture which is always a mixture of the modern and the traditional.

This approach was further developed by Gabriel Almond and G.B. Powell in *Comparative Politics: A Developmental Approach* (1966). Almond and his associates argued that all political systems, regardless of their type, must perform a specific set of tasks if they are to remain in existence as systems in working order or in equilibrium, *i.e.* as 'ongoing systems'. These are the functional requirements of the system. With this assumption they sought to modify David Easton's model of the political system, suggesting that 'inputs' and 'outputs' recognized by Easton can best be understood as 'functions' or 'functional requisites' of a political system. They sought to redefine these inputs and outputs with a deeper understanding of the political process and proceeded to identify various structures corresponding to these functions, in order to evolve a 'structural-functional' framework. They conceded that in various political systems, these functions may be performed by different kinds of political structures and, sometimes, even by structures which are not overtly recognized as being primarily 'political'.

Accordingly, Almond and his associates discerned four input functions and three output functions. Input functions are: (1) Political socialization and recruitment; (2) Interest articulation; (3) Interest aggregation; and (4) Political communication. Output functions are: (1) Rule-making; (2) Rule-application; and (3) Rule-adjudication. Of these, output functions correspond to conventional governmental functions, which are performed by formal governmental organs, *viz.* legislature (rule-making), executive (rule-application) and judiciary (rule-adjudication). Almond has paid special attention to input functions which are performed by non-governmental structures or institutions. Although all structures are multi-functional, yet some structures are especially suited for specific functions.

Political socialization is the process whereby an individual acquires attitudes and orientations towards political phenomena; it also implies the process whereby society transmits political norms and beliefs from one generation to the next. *Recruitment* stands for the process whereby political groups enlist members for various important roles in the political process, either in addition to the existing members or as replacement for the acting members. Since political socialization prepares the individuals to assume various important roles in the social structure, it is instrumental to recruitment also. Family, school, neighbourhood and other primary groups are most suited to perform this function. *Interest articulation* implies the processes whereby opinions, attitudes, beliefs, preferences, etc. are converted into coherent demands on the political system. This function may be performed by various structures, but interest groups are most suited to perform this function. *Interest aggregation* is the process whereby various divergent interests are collated and translated into concrete demands of a very large section of society (preferably appealing to all sections of society), policy proposals and programmes of action, etc. Political parties are most suited to perform this function. Finally, *political communication* is the process whereby components of a political system, such as individuals, groups and institutions, transmit and receive information regarding the functioning of the political system. Mass media or the organizations controlling the media of mass communication are most suited to perform this function.

Model of Structural-Functional Analysis

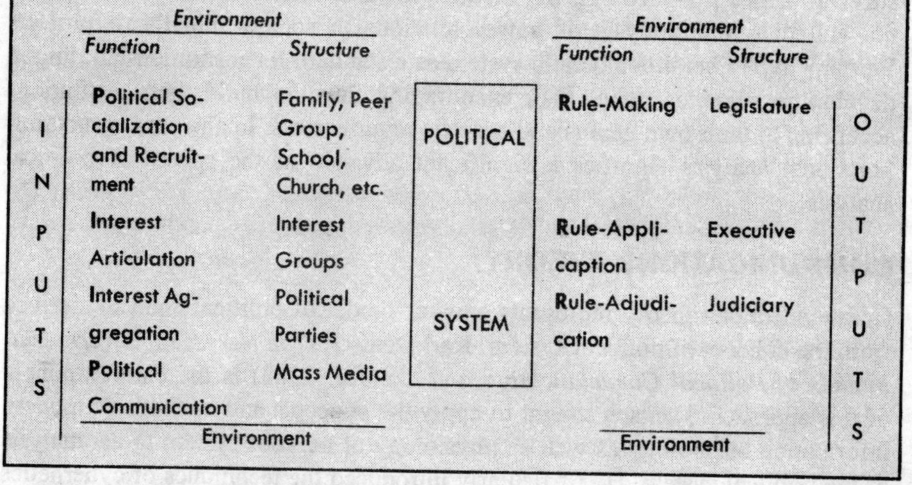

The structural-functional framework of political analysis has been particularly found useful for comparative politics. A developed political system is characterized by differentiation of structures for the performance of specific functions. In less developed political systems, functions of interest articulation, interest aggregation and political communication might be performed by some structures which have not taken a definite shape, but in a developed system growth of interest groups, political parties and mass media would be clearly discernible. Almond and Powell have identified two chief characteristics of development of political system, that is 'political development'. These are: (*a*) structural differentiation; and (*b*) secularization of culture. As they have elucidated: "A principal aspect of the development or transformation of the political system is ... *role differentiation,* or *structural differentiation.* By 'differentiation' we refer to the processes whereby roles change and become more specialized or more autonomous or whereby new types of roles are established or new structures and sub-systems emerge or are created" *(Comparative Politics: A Developmental Approach;* 1966). The underlying propensities of a political system, representing its psychological dimension, are compendiously described as *political culture.* Secularization of culture is concerned with this aspect of political system. As Almond and Powell have further observed: "The secularization of culture is the process whereby traditional orientations and attitudes give way to more dynamic decision-making processes involving the gathering of information, the evaluation of information, the laying out of alternative courses of action, the selection of a course of action from among these possible courses, and the means whereby one tests whether or not a given course of action is producing the consequences which were intended." These two criteria would enable us to measure the level of development of any given political system.

Structural-functional analysis has been criticized on various grounds. Firstly, it is alleged that this form of analysis is primarily concerned with a system's survival; hence it is ideologically inclined towards conservatism. Secondly, it is not suited to the analysis of power relations in society. Finally, it projects Western- type liberal-democratic system as a standard for institution-building in developing societies rather than encouraging them to build their institutions according to their own genius and specific requirements. In any case, structural-functional analysis signifies a significant advance in the sphere of political analysis.

COMMUNICATIONS THEORY

Communications theory represents another model of political analysis derived from the concept of political system. Karl Deutsch *(The Nerves of Government: Models of Political Communication and Control;* 1963) is the chief exponent of this approach. Deutsch sought to apply the concepts and methods of modern information technology as well as physiology of nervous system to an analysis of the political system. He particularly introduced the techniques of cybernetics to the sphere of political analysis. Cybernetics refers to the study of the operation of control and communication systems; it deals both with biological systems and man-made machinery. Deutsch declared that his work was concerned less with the bones or muscles of the body-politic than with its nerves—its channels of communication and decision.

Communications theory regards the function of communication as the centre of all political activity. An analysis of communications flowing from and flowing into political system would, therefore, be very helpful in the description, classification, analysis and explanation of the important aspects of political life. Deutsch argued that it might be profitable to look upon government somewhat less as a problem of power and somewhat more as a problem of steering, *i.e.* directing the course of its activity which is the main function of communication. He, therefore, regards political system as a 'network of communication channels'. It is largely a 'self-regulating' or 'self-controlling' system which evolves its own processes and mechanisms for the acquisition, collection, transmission, selection and the storage of information. As Morton R. Davies and Vaughan A. Lewis have aptly elucidated:

> The members of the political system come to acquire mechanisms for the transmission of messages and for the coordination and control of the channels of communication. The cohesion of a political system can be analysed in terms of the degree to which these coordination and control mechanisms continue to function properly—to adapt themselves, in the

context of the goals which they set, to the information which they receive from various sources; and even to modify the goals which they have set themselves *(Models of Political Systems;* 1971).

The problem of communication may be studied in three contexts: (*a*) communication within the political system; (*b*) communication between the political system and its environment; and (*c*) communication between two or more political systems. Its analysis involves the study of several components, including: (*a*) the structures meant for sending and receiving messages; (*b*) the channels used for the purpose of communication (along with their capacities and rates of utilization, expressed in terms of their load and load capacity, rate of flow, amount of lag and gain, *i.e.* delay or promptness in responding to the information that is received); (*c*) the processes of storage of information; (*d*) feedback mechanisms; (*e*) the codes and languages applied for the purpose of communication; and (*f*) the contents of the messages transmitted, etc.

Communication is by no means a smooth process. We must be very careful in detecting distortions. As James C. Charlesworth has pointed out: "The exponents of the *communicational* approach to political science emphasize the importance of distinguishing between what goes out from the source and what is exactly received at the other end. Which shall we examine—what a governmental agency says it says, or what the recipient says he hears?" *(Contemporary Political Analysis;* 1967). If the distortions could be corrected appropriately, lots of problems can be prevented or minimized. As Charlesworth has further observed: "In order to correct the distortion we must study the determinants of distortion. Hence, communications is a legitimate methodological segment of political science. This study is unfortunately not well developed, nor is it standardized or unified. If it were, we should have fewer industrial strikes, slum riots, university sit-ins, and crackpot picket lines" *(ibid.)*.

In political science, this approach is particularly useful for an analysis of the processes of bargaining, conflict-resolution, decision-making, evaluation of policies, estimating the impact of publicity and propaganda as well as for understanding the dynamics of international relations. However, this approach is hardly useful in the analysis of power structure of society, ideologies, allocation of resources, or in explaining the phenomena of violence and revolution, etc. Communications theory can, therefore, be commended for application only in a limited sphere of political science.

DECISION-MAKING ANALYSIS

Decision-making analysis denotes an attempt to understand politics as a process of arriving at decisions. It will be recalled that David Easton's original model of political system treats decisions and actions as outputs of the political system. In this sense, this approach is closely related to the concept of political system. Decision-making is a wider phenomenon. Exercise of any form of authority involves decision-making whether it is in the sphere of business, university-administration or family. In political science, however, we are concerned with those areas of decision-making which affect politics. In other words, here we are concerned with the process of arriving at public decisions. However, the scope of decision-making in political sphere itself is very wide. As Vernon Van Dyke has illustrated:

> Every actor is a decision-maker. Those acting for political parties decide which candidate to nominate. Voters decide whether to vote and for whom. Legislators decide which proposals to advance or support. Executives decide what legislation to seek, whether to sign or veto acts of the legislative body, precisely which steps to take in executing or administering the law, and what policies to pursue where action is left to their discretion *(Political Science: A Philosophical Analysis;* 1960).

In short, decision-making analysis is concerned with analysis of political systems, processes and behaviour in term of their decision-making mechanism and its functioning. It broadly involves the following:

(*a*) identification of the issues on which decisions are made;

(*b*) the structures involved in decision-making;

(*c*) the actors involved in decision-making (this may involve study of personality, if necessary);

(*d*) the alternative courses of action or options that were considered before making a choice;

(*e*) the factors influencing the choice of the decision-makers, *i.e.* their range of preferences vis-à-vis the utilities attached to each of the alternatives;

(*f*) any external factors, pressures or constraints which influenced their decision; and

(*g*) the outcome of the decision including its political costs.

Under normal circumstances, it is assumed that the decision-makers are capable of rational calculation (*i.e.* cost-benefit analysis) and that they are fully conscious of their goals so that they select the most efficient or feasible means of attaining these goals. However, if there is any departure from this course, *e.g.* if a decision is a product of routinized behaviour or irrational attitude on the part of some actors, social-psychological reasons thereof must be investigated and recorded.

Decision-making analysis does not conform to a single pattern. It may follow one of the several prevalent models. Some important models include:

(*a*) the models dealing with the identification of variables of stages involved in the decision-making processes, as used in the works of Richard Synder and Harold Lasswell;

(*b*) the models based on analogies between economic and political decision-making involving notions of maximizing advantage from the decision, as used in the works of Anthony Downs, J.M. Buchanan and G. Tullock; and

(*c*) the game theory which involves quantification of the results of decision strategies in certain types of competitive situation, *i.e.* a situation of conflict or bargaining in which it is assumed that each player will seek his maximum advantage under conditions of rationality.

Decision-making analysis essentially follows interdisciplinary approach by drawing substantially on psychology, sociology, administrative theory and organization theory. It also seeks to relate its findings to the work of other social scientists in the field of decision-making in non-political situations, with a view to evolving a general theory of decision-making. However, such general theory is not yet adequately developed.

Some exponents of decision-making analysis do not confine themselves to an analysis of particular decisions, and proceed to undertake studies of socio-economic background of decision-makers, *e.g.* legislators, administrators, ministers and even of voters. Some scholars tend to go into their styles of decision-making also. Some of them focus on the role of communications in decision-making.

Decision-making analysis can be applied to a wide range of situations involving local, regional, national as well as international politics. There, too, it may cover the study of a large variety of actors, *e.g.* voters, elites, functionaries of political parties, legislators, judges, government officials as well as officials of international organizations. It may adopt different models of analysis according to the needs of each situation.

[V] MARXIAN ANALYSIS

Marxian analysis deals with a wide range of social phenomena—their past, present and future. Politics figures therein only incidentally. It may, therefore, be called political analysis by proxy. Alex Callinicos has significantly observed: "Marxism denies that politics is a persisting feature of every form of society. Furthermore, it claims that politics, where it does exist, cannot be studied in isolation from the rest of society. Finally, Marxism, insofar as it is a practical programme as well as a body of theoretical analysis, seeks the *abolition* of politics. These claims are obviously incompatible with the notion of an autonomous discipline of Politics" ('Marxism and Politics' in *What is Politics? The Activity and its Study,* edited by Adrian Leftwich; 1984). According to Marxist point of view, politics is not a fundamental activity of human beings, and political system is not an autonomous structure as held by liberal models of political analysis. Politics is only a part of superstructure.

Marxian analysis starts with a distinction between 'base' (or 'substructure') and 'superstructure'. This building-like metaphor is used to postulate that the economic structure of society (which represents the base) is responsible for creating and transforming its social structure, including its legal and political structure, religion and morals, etc. (which represents the superstructure). Marx expressed this idea in his Preface to *A Contribution to the Critique of Political Economy* (1859), as follows:

> In the social production of their life, men enter into definite relations that are indispensable and independent of their will, relations of production which correspond to a definite stage of development of their material productive forces. The sum total of these relations of production constitutes the economic structure of society, the real foundation on which rises a legal and political superstructure and to which correspond definite forms of social consciousness. The mode of production of material life conditions the social, political and intellectual life process in general.

This means that the political system, as a part of superstructure, is not autonomous, that it does not grow out of itself, but emerges on the foundation of the economic structure of society. The economic structure or the mode of production itself changes with the development of forces of production (*i.e.* the means of production and labour power). This would bring about corresponding changes in the political system and other aspects of superstructure. Since the political system is neither independent nor autonomous, no useful purpose will be served by undertaking analysis of political system *per se*.

Marxism (particularly classical Marxism), therefore, insists on an analysis of the economic structure of society, historical stages of its development and the corresponding class structure prevailing at each of these stages (which is reflected in the 'relations of production') in order to understand the character of the political system. At each stage of historical development, society is divided into two antagonistic classes. The owners of private property or the major means of production rise to the position of 'dominant class' whereas those living solely on their labour on the terms dictated by the former constitute 'dependent class'. As long as the major means of production continue to be privately owned, the division of society into dominant and dependent classes cannot be eliminated, nor their class conflict can ever be resolved. Politics must always be traced back to its 'hidden basis' in the class struggle. Since politics arises from class struggle, it is historically a transient phenomenon. Different types of states merely reflect the different forms of class domination. As Marx and Engels observed: "Political power, properly so called, is merely the organized power of one class for oppressing another" *(Communist Manifesto;* 1848). Politics is the process through which antagonistic classes struggle to obtain, retain or influence state power. Thus, under capitalism, politics of the capitalist class involves their strategy for exploitation of the working class while politics of the working class implies their effort for organizing themselves to overthrow the capitalist system. In a nutshell, Marxism speaks of five stages of historical development, including one prehistorical stage.

Marxian Analysis of Historical Stages

Historical Stage	*Mode of Production*	*Class Structure*
Primitive Communism	Hunting, fishing, food-gathering, etc.	Classes not yet emerged
Slave System	Animal husbandry, domestic agriculture and crafts	Masters and slaves
Feudal System	Large-scale agriculture	Landlords and serfs
Capitalist System	Large-scale industry	Capitalists and workers
Socialist System	-do-	Workers in power and the former capitalists under subjection

It hopes that once genuine socialist system is established and there is no distortion in its working, common ownership of major means of production will eventually lead to abolition of classes; state and political power will become redundant; and politics itself will disappear. Society will then enter the phase of communism; it will become *a classless and stateless society where authority will be exercised without resort to power, and administration will be carried on without the state machinery.*

Marx, Engels and Lenin argued that political systems should be compared and contrasted with reference to their respective class structures. We should not be misled by their superficial similarities or differences. Illustrating his point from his contemporary experience, Marx pointed out that the laws and state system in North America and Prussia were based on similar system of property ownership, so these should be placed in the same category although apparently North America was a republic, and Prussia was a monarchy.

Under this approach, there is practically no scope of independent political analysis. However, neo-Marxists have realized that superstructure is by no means a weak structure, entirely dependent on the base. In capitalist systems, superstructure could be so strong that it may serve to strengthen the base itself. Hence, it needs independent analysis. Antonio Gramsci (1891-1937), an Italian Marxist and forerunner of neo-Marxism, concedes relative autonomy of the superstructure. He has particularly evolved a Marxian model of analysis of capitalist society. Gramsci identified two components of its *Structures of domination*: (*a*) *Structures of legitimation;* and (*b*) *Structures of coercion.* The structures of legitimation are provided by the civil society which is closer to the 'base' (the economic mode of production). It largely includes the family, school, church and other primary groups like neighbourhood and peer groups, which familiarize the citizens with the rules of behaviour and teach them to show natural respect to the authority of the ruling classes. These structures lend legitimacy to the rule of the capitalist class so that even injustice involved in this rule would give the impression of justice. They enable the ruling class to establish its *hegemony;* people are led to believe as if they are being ruled with their consent. On the other hand, the structures of coercion are provided by the governmental organization. Gramsci observed that the capitalist society largely depends on the efficiency of its structures of legitimation for its stability. It is only when the civil society fails to prevent dissent that the political society is required to resort to its structures of coercion, including police, courts and prisons.

Gramsci's Model of Analysis of Capitalist Society

Capitalist Society
(Structures of Domination)

Structures of Legitimation	Structures of Coercion
Civil Society (Family, School, Church and other primary groups)	Governmental Organization (All organs of exercising power over citizens, including police, courts and prisons)
Based on Consent	Based on Force

Hegemony

According to Antonio Gramsci (1891-1937), Italian Marxist, hegemony refers to a web of beliefs and institutional as well as social relations which serve as instruments of domination in society. In the capitalist society, family, school, church and other primary groups (e.g. neighbourhood and peer groups), play a leading role in creating consent which keeps the system going. Use of force is resorted to only when the instruments of consent fail to work.

Ralph Miliband *(The State in Capitalist Society: The Analysis of the Western System of Power;* 1969) has largely used this framework which exemplifies an attempt towards Marxian political analysis.

Later, Louis Althusser, French neo-Marxist (*For Marx;* 1965), argued that the base and superstructure are so closely intertwined that it is not logical to consider one of them, *viz.* the base as the prime mover of all social change. In some cases, revolution may begin from any part of the superstructure, *e.g.* politics, law, religion, culture, art and literature, etc. which would spread to the whole social structure although the economic factor would ultimately play the most effective role in this process.

Broadly speaking, we can identify three major models of Marxian analysis in contemporary political theory: Classical model; Cultural-Hegemonic model; and Structuralist model. They represent different notions about the relation between base and superstructure, and the corresponding strategies of revolution, as shown in the following chart.

Models of Marxian Analysis

The Issue	*Classical Model*	*Cultural-Hegemonic Model*	*Structuralist Model*
Exponents	Marx, Engels, Lenin	Gramsci, Poulantazs Mao Zedong	Louis Althusser
Relation between Base and superstructure	Superstructure is wholly dependent on Base	Superstructure is relatively autonomous	Base and Superstructure are interdependent
Strategy of Revolution	Start revolution in the Base; Superstructure would be automatically transformed	Start revolution in the Base, but continue the process in the Superstructure also	Start revolution either in the Base or any part of the Superstructure (e.g. law, literature, folklore, art forms, religious precepts, etc.). It would percolate to the whole set of Base-Superstructure complex

5

Interdisciplinary Perspective on Political Science

THE TERM 'DISCIPLINE' refers to a branch of learning, a field or subject of study. Thus, history, political science, economics, linguistics, anthropology, physics, chemistry, mathematics, botany, etc. are known as different disciplines. Systematic studies of the institutions and functioning of human society, man's behaviour in society and the interpersonal relationships of individuals as members of society are called *social sciences.* Thus political science, economics, sociology, social psychology, cultural anthropology, etc. are *social sciences.* Some of the disciplines embrace some features of the physical or natural sciences as well as social sciences. For instance, physical geography, physical anthropology and clinical psychology belong to the physical sciences while human geography, social or cultural anthropology and social psychology obviously fall in the domain of social sciences.

[I] THE INTERDISCIPLINARY APPROACH

When we rely on more than one discipline for the study of a given problem, or when there is a tendency to draw on or contribute to more than one discipline, our approach is called *interdisciplinary.* This approach can obviously be followed in the case of disciplines dealing with some common problems or with different aspects of the same or similar phenomena. The social sciences constitute one such group where interdisciplinary approach would be found most suitable for the study of their common problems.

The interdisciplinary approach helps us to evolve a broader perspective and thus enables us to understand problems more thoroughly and more fruitfully. The study of politics as a *social process* provides ample scope for an interdisciplinary approach. This implies: (*a*) making use of the findings, theories and models of other social sciences in understanding the political phenomenon; (*b*) verification of the theories and findings of political science from the data and theories of other social sciences; and (*c*) developing a broader perspective about political life with a view to making contribution to other social sciences. It should, however, be kept in mind that expanding the scope of our study should be purposeful and well-conceived. In other words, while entering the sphere of the other social sciences, we should not deviate from our main focus. In the present context, any reference to the problems of economics, sociology, psychology or anthropology should be made with the definite purpose of understanding the problems of politics, not at random. For instance, if we start the study of labour-management relations or the psychology of crowd behaviour in a given situation, we should undertake such studies only to analyse their impact on politics, not to understand those problems for their own sake.

GENESIS OF THE INTERDISCIPLINARY APPROACH

The interdisciplinary approach denotes a recent trend in political science. This may, of course, be traced in a rudimentary form in the traditional study of politics. For instance, Plato, ancient Greek philosopher, in his search for rulers for an 'ideal state' made it a point that the structure of the family and the nature of education would deeply affect the character and activities of those holding political office. Aristotle, another ancient Greek philosopher, demonstrated a causal relation between the distribution of wealth and status in communities and the type of political regime they had. In mid-eighteenth century, Charles de Montesquieu (1689-1755), a French philosopher, inquired into social-psychological foundations of different forms of government. However, these earlier studies were not marked by a deeper analysis of the forces shaping the course of events. Marx (1818-83) and Engels (1820-95), German philosophers, were probably the first to develop a new approach in social sciences in mid-nineteenth century, which could be called a systematic interdisciplinary approach. They located the primary source of political behaviour in socio-economic factors, *viz*. the level of technological development, mode of material production and the prevailing class structure. Then liberal thinkers were also inclined to inquire into the interlinkages between social, cultural, economic and political processes. Modern liberal political scientists have persistently been trying to demonstrate that the study of the political process necessitates an understanding of various social factors.

CHARACTERISTICS OF THE INTERDISCIPLINARY APPROACH

When we undertake the study of politics as a *social process* and define the political system as an 'open system' or a system of interactions, the interdisciplinary approach becomes imperative. In other words, when we assume that the political system receives 'inputs' from the social system or environment, and produces 'outputs' which re-enter the environment through the 'feedback' channel, it becomes necessary to widen the scope of our study so as to understand those aspects of the social process which affect the process of politics and are affected by it.

Product of Empirical Orientation

The empirical method stands for reliance on factual information, observation or direct sense-experience (*i.e.* the experience based on sight, sound, smell, taste and touch) as opposed to pure speculation. Empirical orientation in the study of politics is a relatively recent phenomenon. Otherwise, politics is one of the oldest disciplines of the Western world. Aristotle called it the 'master science' to demonstrate its crucial role in the ordering of various relationships within human society. The traditional study of politics was, however, characterized by its close link with philosophy. Other social sciences, such as anthropology, sociology, economics and psychology spun off from their parent discipline—philosophy—towards the end of the nineteenth century in the wake of empirical orientation in their respective spheres. Political science, in this respect, was a relatively late-starter. However, the empirical orientation in political science was accompanied by an understanding of the close link between political science and other social sciences.

Traditional political science was founded on ethics or moral philosophy. Its chief problem was to determine the norms of public life, and to evolve institutions according to those norms. It largely relied on the normative approach which may be distinguished from the empirical approach. The empirical approach is concerned with *facts*; it is descriptive; it deals with the *real*. On the other hand, the normative approach is concerned with *values;* it is prescriptive; it deals with the *ideal*. In other words, the empirical approach is concerned with what *is* there; the normative approach is concerned with what *ought* to be done. The chief requisites of the empirical approach may be described as follows: (*a*) it deals with observable facts and data; (*b*) it aims at explanation, that is it seeks to establish a correlation between different variables, to explore the cause-and-effect relationship, and to arrive at possible generalizations; and finally, (*c*) it tends to make predictions; that is when certain data and the precise relationship between different variables are known, the result could be predicted and verified.

The empirical orientation in political science led to the realization that the real world of politics could not be understood through images of an ideal state, nor merely in terms of formal institutions which may not conform to their declared objectives, in actual practice. It set a new trend of understanding politics as a process which takes place within the larger framework of the social system. Since the empirical method was first developed in other social sciences, such as economics, sociology, anthropology, psychology, etc. political science was attracted towards other social sciences not only to learn their methodology, but also to find out how far their data, theories and models could help in understanding the political phenomenon.

Focus on Political Behaviour and Systems Analysis

The empirical orientation in political science was responsible for the shift in emphasis from political institutions to political behaviour and political system. Firstly, it was realized that politics could be better understood in terms of the behaviour of the participants, namely the electorate, legislators, bureaucrats, executive and judicial authorities, and so on. In other words, political analysis involved not a mere description of ideas and institutions, but an analysis of the behaviour of the people—the individuals, groups of various types whether they belonged to particular structures of the government or were outside it, the *elite*, etc. This necessitated reliance on an interdisciplinary approach. As Heinz Eulau, in his article on 'Political Behaviour' in the *International Encyclopaedia of the Social Sciences* (1968), has elaborated: "As man's political behaviour is only one aspect of his total behaviour as a social being, political behaviour analysis must be interdisciplinary; it cannot neglect the wider context in which political action occurs. It is bound, therefore, to consider the possible effects of social, cultural and personal factors on political behaviour."

In the second place, the introduction of systems analysis in political science has also given an impetus to the interdisciplinary approach. Here an attempt is made to understand politics as a process in terms of the 'political system'. Political system is essentially regarded as a *sub-system* within the ambit of the larger *social system*. In other words, the political system does not operate independently or in isolation. The formal organs of the government—the legislature, the executive and the judiciary—do not produce their decisions on their own initiative or at their own will, but in response to the *demands* emanating from the social system, and these decisions in turn have their impact on the social system. When this framework of analysis is adopted, it becomes necessary to understand the economic, cultural, psychological and sociological aspects of the social organization in order to appreciate the full import of the political process.

Use of Data of Other Social Sciences

The interdisciplinary approach treats society as a totality whose various aspects are closely interrelated. Political science undertakes the study of the political aspect of society for which the data provided by other social sciences prove relevant and useful in various ways. For instance, you may require data on the rate of economic growth, distribution of national income, patterns of ownership of material wealth, educational levels and percentage of literacy of the population, religious and cultural attitudes of the people, their family structures, professional distribution, rural-urban ratio, etc. in order to ascertain whether a particular form of government (such as democracy) will be sustained by a given community or not. The political scientists' interest in *political socialization* and *political culture* has inspired them to draw heavily from the data of psychology and sociology; their interest in *political development* has increased their reliance on the data provided by sociology and economics; their interest in *political communication* has brought them nearer to social psychology. As Seymour Martin Lipset, in his Introduction to *Politics and the Social Sciences* (1969), has illustrated:

> The political scientist interested in political development has learned that he cannot treat his topic without looking for the conditions of social mobilization; men cannot become citizens in a political sense without changes in their values and personality orientations... Politics will be different in caste and non-caste societies. It will vary among systems which have different concepts of kinship ties, and the nature of class and status relationships in various traditional societies will affect the possibilities for acceptance of a legal-rational political order.

Use of Theories and Models of Other Social Sciences

The interdisciplinary orientation has also encouraged political scientists to make an abundant use of the theories and models evolved by other social sciences. For instance, the *elite* theory (that in every society, irrespective of its forms of social and political institutions, a small group of the chosen few always assumes a dominant position in relation to the rest of the community) was first systematically developed by Pareto (1848-1923), Mosca (1858-1941) and Michels (1876-1936) in the field of sociology. It was then applied to the analysis of political institutions, leadership and group behaviour, as also for giving new interpretations of democracy. Similarly, the Marxian framework of 'base and superstructure' (which postulates that legal and political structures, religion, morals, ideas and institutions in any society are shaped by the prevailing mode of material production) was first evolved in the field of economics and sociology, and then adopted as a tool of political analysis.

Some contemporary approaches to the study of politics in fact originated in other social sciences. David Easton's concept of the political system is derived from the concept of the social system originally developed in the field of sociology. The structural-functional approach was originally developed in the field of cultural anthropology by Malinowski and Radcliffe-Brown, then adopted in sociology by Talcott Parsons, and subsequently introduced in political science by Almond and Powell. Similarly, Harold Lasswell's model of the 'problem-solving' approach was derived from psychology. Understanding of politics as a process of bargaining is based on the theories of competition (*e.g.* perfect competition and monopolistic competition) originally evolved in the field of economics. Schumpeter and Anthony Downs have sought to analyse democratic politics using the economist's model of the open market.

Thus, the use of theories and models of other social sciences in the realm of political science has substantially contributed to its development.

[II]
INTERFACE BETWEEN POLITICAL SCIENCE AND OTHER RELEVANT DISCIPLINES

In the present context, it would be interesting to illustrate the relevance of interdisciplinary approach in the study of politics with reference to its interface with other important disciplines.

INTERFACE WITH HISTORY

The effect of interface between history and the study of politics may be seen in two important areas: (*a*) history is used as a rich storehouse of data for an understanding and interpretation of political phenomena, a comparative study of political situations and verification of hypotheses about politics; and (*b*) when history gives us not only an account of events but also cause-and-effect relationships, or rather, laws of historical development (such as Marx's materialist interpretation of history), this knowledge can be used for understanding the course of politics in a given situation.

Some traditional writers have placed history and political science in a very close relationship. Thus, John Seeley (1834-95) observes: "History without political science has no fruit; political science without history has no root!" Edward Augustus Freeman (1823-92) has gone to the extent of saying: "History is past politics, politics is present history." Today, such statements appear to be an oversimplification of a complex issue. In fact, the expanding horizons of political science have given it an independent status and identity. It uses historical material only selectively, although frequently. Present events often have their roots in the past which cannot be ignored. For instance, any study of the Indian political system must start with its historical antecedents; and the study of international politics must be based on the historical background. Similarly, many historical accounts need to be reconstructed to bring out the significance of various events in the light of political theory, such as the role of various classes including the *elites,* levels of politicization and the impact of changes on the economic life of society.

It is significant that unlike its traditional form, political science today is deeply concerned with the socio-economic foundations of political phenomena. Happily, there is a corresponding change in the outlook of modern historians with the increasing realization of the importance of socio-economic factors behind historical events and developments. In other words, the modern approach to history as well as political science is not confined to the 'great' deeds of kings and princes, their battles, victories, expansion and consolidation of empires, defeats, disintegration and downfall. Due importance is now being paid to the condition and role of the masses in the making of history as well as the shaping of politics. This simultaneous change of outlook has strengthened the age-old relationship between history and political science.

In short, political science cannot claim to evolve a foolproof theory unless it is substantiated and verified by historical data, both in terms of rule and exception. If political theory is derived from mere speculation, visionary perspective or limited observation, it is bound to lack scientific precision and thus crumble.

INTERFACE WITH GEOGRAPHY

Geography refers to a branch of learning that studies the composition of earth's surface, its various forms, such as land, waterways, oceans, mountains, mines, forests, deserts, etc. as well as their climatic and environment conditions. While physical features of these areas are studied under physical geography, the economic, social and political structures of the populated parts of the earth are largely studied under human geography.

Some political thinkers have particularly dwelled on the impact of geographical conditions on the political life of human communities. Aristotle, ancient Greek philosopher, argued that in his contemporary world, Greeks alone were endowed with the competence to evolve the institution of citizenship because of their typical geographical situation. There was little scope of this competence in the very cold regions of Persia and the North where people could hardly manage the means of their survival. On the other hand, the people of hot regions were indolent who would accept despotic rule in order to escape from hard work. In other words, politics and citizenship could flourish only in temperate regions of the world; there was no scope of engaging in politics for the peoples of very cold or hot regions. Then in early modern times, Charles de Montesquieu (1689-1755), French philosopher, sought to develop a sociological theory of government and law. He observed that their structure and operation were dependent on the physical conditions of the people, such as climate and soil. In more recent times, Henry Thomas Buckle (1821-62), English historian, in his unfinished *History of Civilization* (1861), contended that climate, soil, food and the aspects of nature are the primary causes of intellectual progress—the first three determine the accumulation and distribution of wealth, and the last one determines the accumulation and distribution of thought.

Interface between the studies of geography and politics has led to the evolution of two subdisciplines. The students of geography have evolved a new branch of learning—the 'political geography' where different regions of the world (countries, islands, waterways, forests, mountains, deserts, etc.) are identified in terms of nations occupying (or exercising their sovereignty over) those regions. On the other hand, the students of politics have evolved another branch of learning—the 'geopolitics' which inquires into the impact of geography of each country over its politics. While the influence of geography and politics on each other may be conceded, it would not be advisable to subscribe to 'geographical determinism' in the study of politics, or to the primacy of politics in the area of geographical studies.

Geopolitics

Geopolitics refers to a branch of learning which inquires into the impact of geography including the economic geography and demography of a country on its politics, particularly its foreign policy. It also inquires into the need of additional natural resources and additional space for its rising population and the prospects of extending its territory towards sea, mountain or other natural borders. All these factors help to understand the history, present situation and future trends of politics of different nations.

Some thinkers concede supreme importance of geography in a country's foreign policy. They argue that different nations may raise as many questions about their history as they like, but they can neither change nor question the facts concerning their geography.

Geographical Determinism

Geographical determinism refers to the view that people's physical features, their behaviour, temperament, character and culture are shaped by the geographical setting and climate conditions of the area where they are born and brought up.

Like all deterministic theories, this theory cannot be accepted because of its overemphasis on a single cause, and belittlement of other important factors that shape human character and culture.

INTERFACE WITH ECONOMICS

Economics is primarily concerned with analysing the factors which affect human behaviour in the process of material production, distribution and exchange. It inquires into the factors which affect decisions about investment or use of economically relevant resources—primarily capital, labour and goods. A closer analysis, however, reveals that these decisions are greatly affected by 'non-economic factors', such as cultural values, personality, political needs, and considerations of status.

Economics, in fact, started its early career in the eighteenth century as *political economy* which stood for the study and practice of the management of government and the nation. In late nineteenth century, it sought its independence from political theory and became increasingly occupied with price and market behaviour, under the influence of the *laissez-faire* doctrine. But the experience of the following decades revealed that an unrestrained economic system led to socially disastrous consequences—wide economic disparities, mounting exploitation of underprivileged sections, growing injustice and consequent friction.

This necessitated regulation of economic activity and subordination of economics to public control. The result is the renewed mutual interest between economics and political science.

Political theory today is primarily concerned with the conflicting demands of various groups and classes within a community or between different nations in the international sphere. These demands, though articulated in various forms, are largely the economic demands. No political system can sustain itself unless it demonstrates its ability to cope with the conflicting demands by evolving a somewhat stable equilibrium, harmony or reconciliation. This requires a deeper understanding of economic forces and factors. Policy-decisions or planning by the state—from the control of foreign trade to the regulation of the internal economic life of the community—will be devoid of essence unless the underlying economic issues are properly sorted out and resolved satisfactorily. The 'welfare state', 'service state' or even socialist state of today claims to take care of the economic security of citizens by providing for full employment, a reasonable standard of living, nutrition and health, etc. Developing nations are particularly faced with the challenge of acute and widespread poverty. Politics cannot deliver the goods until it is able to tackle the economic problem effectively. According to Marxian theory, too, all politics is shaped by economic forces. Thus, an adequate knowledge of economics becomes essential for the understanding and practice of politics. The interface between economics and politics has given rise to modern political economy.

Political Economy

Traditional political economy was concerned with the analysis of revenue and expenditure of the state which distinguished it from the management of domestic economy.

Modern political economy deals with political aspects of economic policy-making so that a social policy should prove not only economically efficient but also politically acceptable. In a broader sense, it focuses on those concepts and issues which are the common concern of economics and politics. Examples of such concepts are: demands, costs, allocation of resources, utility optimization, etc. Examples of such issues are: impact of economic factors on political life; impact of political decisions on economic life, etc. It also includes the use of economic models (e.g. rational choice theory) for the study of political behaviour. Marxist political economy focuses on the relation between mode of production and various social formations (e.g. slave-owning society, feudal society, capitalist society and socialist society).

INTERFACE WITH SOCIOLOGY

Sociology is chiefly concerned with the behaviour of men in an associative process. It inquires into how institutions, stabilized systems of expectations and actions fulfil the varying needs of man in society, particularly in a complex society. It, therefore, includes within its domain almost every aspect of human behaviour. Early sociologists, both in Europe and America, in fact, showed considerable interest in politics, as they could not ignore the role of political institutions as well as the process of formation of political attitudes and group norms which comprised important components of social institutions and social behaviour. The famous sociologists like Max Weber (1864-1920), Robert Michels (1876-1936), Vilfredo Pareto (1848-1923) and Emile Durkheim (1858-1917) turned to political analysis as a part of their sociological inquiry. Arther Bentley (1870-1957), who was trained as a sociologist in Europe, eventually turned out to be a major intellectual force in political science in America. Franklin Giddings (1855-1931), another American sociologist of repute, encouraged his students to undertake empirical studies of voting behaviour in the early 1920s.

The application of various concepts and methods of sociology to the study of political behaviour and institutions has given rise to a new venture called 'political sociology'. In fact, the practitioners of political sociology not only seek to explain political behaviour but also apply the analyses of bureaucratic structures developed in the works of Max Weber and Robert Michels to a variety of institutional structures, such as governmental agencies, trade unions, political parties, and even economic institutions.

The practice of politics involves taking public decisions. Any such decisions, to be effective, must take into account the social motivations of relevant groups. An inquiry into value-orientations, attitudes, habits, beliefs and prejudices of the people becomes indispensable to ascertain the possible response and chances of success of any social measure. Sociology proves quite helpful in this venture. In fact, the study of politics today extends its scope beyond formal procedures and institutions for which reliance on sociology becomes essential. In short, the discipline of political sociology thrives on the contributions from sociology as well as political science.

Political Sociology

Political sociology refers to a branch of learning which examines political institutions, processes and ideologies in the light of corresponding social structures, processes and modes of thought. It also examines the impact of political domination and decisions on social life. It treats political system as a subsystem within social system and inquires into their interrelationship.

In a broader sense, political sociology focuses on those concepts and issues which are the common concern of sociology and politics. Examples of such concepts and issues are: political socialization, political culture, political participation, social basis of political behaviour, political ideologies, political consensus and cleavage, power, authority and legitimacy, patterns of political leadership, etc.

INTERFACE WITH ANTHROPOLOGY

Anthropology refers to a scientific discipline which undertakes a comparative study of the course of development of human race from its origin to the present stage. It inquires into all aspects of physical features, social organization, language, culture, etc. of the human being from a scientific perspective. Political anthropology was originally evolved as a branch of social anthropology which inquired into the primitive forms of authority, government and law. It gives us insights for understanding the functioning of these institutions in modern society.

Political Anthropology

Political anthropology refers to a branch of learning which inquires into the ways of performance of political functions in primitive and tribal communities. In most of these communities, formal political structures are not found in a developed form. So we proceed to analyse their social arrangements and cultural traditions through which the superior members of the community exercise their authority over ordinary members. Then we try to understnad the general development of political structures on the basis of this information.

It is interesting to recall that the model of structural-functional analysis in the realm of political science originated in the sphere of social anthropolgy in the writings of B. Malinowski ('The Group and the Individual in Functional Analysis', *American Journal of Sociology;* 1939). and A.R. Radcliffe-Brown (*Structure and Function in Primitive Society;* 1952). Then it was developed in the field of sociology by Talcott Parsons, Robert Merton and Marion Levy. Finally, Gabriel Almond and his associates developed it into a tool of political analysis.

INTERFACE WITH PSYCHOLOGY

Psychology is primarily interested in learning the motives of human behaviour and the causes of variations in individual and group behaviour. Some human actions are, of course, the product of man's mental make-up as such. But some of his actions are also shaped by the pattern of man's participation in varying social situations. One of the key sources of personality formation and of individual behaviour is seen in the pattern of his interaction with other individuals in a given social setting. Psychology, therefore, also inquires into the effects of different group involvements on individual behaviour. This has given rise to a special branch of psychology, namely social psychology.

An inquiry into the formation of attitudes has inspired the psychologists to examine political values and behaviour. The growth of totalitarian political movements in the thirties and forties of the twentieth century aroused interest in the study of the 'authoritarian personality', which involved application of insights gained from psycho-analytic theory and social psychological methods to understanding extremist political appeals. Similar orientations influenced the work of Harold Lasswell (1902-78) and his disciples in their study of the influence of psychological factors on the appeal of extremist movements particularly, and on political behaviour generally.

Besides, the study of politics involves an interest in the process of formation and expression of public opinion, patterns of leadership including charismatic leadership, impact of propaganda and the role of mass communication in inculcating political culture. Social psychology proves particularly helpful in understanding these important aspects of the political process. The interface between psychology and politics has given rise to political psychology which is an important branch of social psychology.

Political Psychology

Political psychology refers to a branch of learning which uses the models and techniques of psychology for analysing psychological aspects of political behaviour. It may also be used for influencing political behaviour of a group. It may be regarded as a branch of social psychology which focuses on political aspect of social life. Its subject-matter may include: relation between individual's personality and his political behaviour; sources of similarities and dissimilarities between political attitudes; psychological bases of political learning, political socialization and leadership styles; techniques and impact of political propaganda, etc.

INTERFACE WITH PHILOSOPHY

Traditional study of politics was based on philosophy. Philosophy is primarily concerned with an inquiry into the essence of reality, limits of knowledge, nature of truth, relation between man and universe, purpose of the universe, the foundations of moral values and beauty, and so on. Philosophy makes use of empirical data, but it seeks clarification of the conceptual problems which may lie beyond the limits of empirical knowledge in all branches of learning. It is an attempt at the investigation of the substantive aspects of nature, man, society and politics. When it touches the problems of politics, it is identified as political philosophy.

Philosophy is sometimes distinguished from science on the ground that science exclusively relies on empirical method, *i.e.* the method based on sense-experience (the experience gained through sight, sound, smell, taste, and touch) whereas philosophy uses transcendental method, *i.e.* the method based on speculation about what is beyond our sense-experience; science is descriptive whereas philosophy is critical and evaluative. However, it should not be forgotten that science itself has grown from the pursuit of philosophy. Science not only owes its origin to philosophy, it derives its validity from philosophy itself. Auguste Comte (1798-1857), French philosopher, equated science with 'positive philosophy'. It marks the final stage in the development of knowledge—from theological to metaphysical, and then to the positive stage. Comte recognized sociology as the 'mother social science' which was based on the development of 'positive philosophy'.

With the growing craze for the use of scientific method in the study of politics in modern times, it became fashionable to distinguish 'political science' from 'political philosophy'. Rise of behaviouralism in 1950s and 1960s was particularly responsible for this attitude. However, since early 1970s with the advent of 'post-behaviouralism' and the revival of interest in theory of justice and other related principles (liberty, equality, community, etc.), political philosophy received a renewed prominence. Now scientific and behavioural studies of politics are undertaken to find facts and devise tools for achieving the goals of public policy whereas these goals are largely determined with the help of political philosophy.

Political Philosophy

Political philosophy refers to a branch of learning which is primarily concerned with moral and substantive dimensions of politics. Its central problems include the pursuit of good life, questions pertaining to norms and values, good and evil, virtue and vice, means and ends, right and wrong, and visions of an ideal state and society. Political philosophy inquires into the foundations of political life, grounds of political obligation, and moral worthiness of different political systems. It makes use of philosophical and historical method in determining the goals of public life. A major part of political philosophy coincides with moral and social philosophy.

INTERFACE WITH LAW

Early students of political science focused their attention on the 'state' which was envisaged as a mechanism of 'law-making', 'law-enforcement' and 'law-adjudication'. Recent scholars have sought to replace the concept of the 'state' by that of 'political system' which receives certain inputs from its evnironment and produces certain outputs which flow back into the environment. These outputs are largely recognized as 'rule-making', 'rule-application' and 'rule-adjudication'. In actual practice, 'rule' is understood to be a synonymous of law.

Theoretical foundations of law are studied under legal philosophy which largely coincides with jurisprudence. Legal philosophy is closely linked with political philosophy. Most of the important concepts of political philosophy, such as liberty, equality, rights, justice, etc. must be understood properly for a profound knowledge of legal philosophy.

Legal Philosophy

Legal philosophy or philosophy of law refers to a branch of learning mainly concerned with the nature and sources of law, criteria of its effectiveness and its role in social progress. It also inquires into the purpose of law and determines as to what laws are better than others; what laws should be obeyed or resisted. It further inquires as to how human nature and social temper need to be expressed and regulated through law. Since religion and custom also play an important role in regulating society, legal philosophy inquires into relation between religion, custom and law. Since law is concerned with dispensing justice to individuals and other entities, legal philosophy also inquires into nature, types, procedure and substance of justice.

Some political philosophers believe that law exists before the formation of the state itself. The state is simply concerned with discovering and declaring law for an effective regulation of the social organization. Others think that political decisions are taken by a government, but they cannot become effective until these are translated into legal provisions and enforced through legal mechanism. Again, some writers believe that political decisions are the product of the demands and other inputs flowing from the social environment. At times, new demands are articulated through social movements. In any case, they reach their logical conclusion only when the decisions taken in response to these demands are enshrined in law, and implemented through legal and political mechanism.

Some legal philosophers tend to see a close link between the conception of law and political philosophy. Ronald Dworkin (*Taking Rights Seriously;* 1977) argued that the nature of law cannot be understood in terms of a structure of rules. In difficult cases, judges have to rely on certain 'principles' for reaching a decision. These principles are by no means 'extra-legal' criteria since they are used by judges as part of law. Validity of a principle is to be sought from the realm of *political theory* rather than from the rationale of legal system itself. The constitutional standards and doctrines adopted by judges while invoking different principles are, therefore, subject to criticism like the problems of political theory.

CONCLUSION

Interdisciplinary approach to the study of politics is a modern approach which marks a departure from the classical approach. The classical approach, typified by Aristotle's description of politics as the 'master science' failed to distinguish between normative and empirical aspects of the study of politics. Although it was Aristotle himself who originally identified 'politics' as an independent discipline, yet he could not discern political phenomenon from other aspects of man's social life. In Aristotle's times all knowledge was covered by philosophy, and Aristotle only sought to distinguish 'political philosophy' from other branches of philosophy. It was only in the nineteenth century that different aspects of man's social life became independent subjects of empirical study as distinct from their philosophical foundations. Accordingly, psychology, sociology, economics, political science, etc. emerged as independent scientific disciplines.

The interdisciplinary approach in social sciences is of recent origin which assumed special importance in the latter part of the twentieth century. It does not seek to merge all social sciences into a single 'master science'. On the contrary, it insists that the results of our inquiry in any sphere should be based on and verified from the findings of all relevant social sciences. Thus, political science should not only make use of data, theories and models of other social sciences, but should also make a suitable contribution to an understanding of those disciplines.

Moreover, some approaches to the study of politics cover a limited range of inquiry by relying on a single discipline. Thus philosophical, historical, legal, economic, sociological, psychological and geographical approaches turn out to be partial approaches. On the contrary, the interdisciplinary approach seeks to overcome this shortcoming by relying on all other relevant disciplines for the purpose of evolving an integrated view of the subject.

> **While I am interested both in economics and in philosophy, the union of my interests in the two fields far exceeds their intersection.**
>
> **Amartya Sen**

6

Concept of the State

[I]

NATURE AND SIGNIFICANCE OF THE STATE

Concept of the state has figured as the central theme of traditional political theory. R.G. Gettel (*Political Science;* 1949) defined political science as 'the science of the state', while J.W. Garner (*Political Science and Government;* 1928) claimed that 'political science begins and ends with the state'. In modern political theory, significance of the concept of the state has been fluctuating. Some exponents of the behavioural approach in political science have even suggested abandoning the concept of the state altogether. Their main objection is that this concept does not help in understanding political reality or the political process, because (*a*) the term 'state' refers to a formal concept while real politics transcends the formal organization of the state; (*b*) the 'state' is usually conceived in terms of the 'ends' of the state which drags us to the realm of moral philosophy, far removed from the real world of politics; and (*c*) the concept of the state postulates a particular type of organization which excludes top organizations of certain societies, real or imaginary, and thus introduces the idea of 'pre-state' societies and 'stateless' societies. This leads to the assumption that political organization is not a universal phenomenon. David Easton, in his *Political System—An Inquiry into the State of Political Science* (1953), observed:

> One person sees the state as the embodiment of the moral spirit, its concrete expression; another, as the instrument of exploitation used by one class against others. One author defines it as simply an aspect of society, distinguishable from it only analytically; another, as simply a synonym for government; and still another, as a separate and unique association among a large number of other associations such as the church, trade unions, and similar voluntary groups.

After dwelling on these ambiguities in some detail Easton came to the conclusion that the word 'state' 'ought to be abandoned entirely'.

It is important to note that distaste for the term 'state' was confined to some exponents of liberal political theory, especially to some American political scientists. Marxist political theory continued to use the term 'state' to refer to a specific form of political organization. The terms 'slave-owning state', 'feudal state', 'capitalist state', 'socialist/communist state', as well as 'pre-state society' and 'stateless society' are the current coins of Marxist political theory. Even the empirically-oriented political scientists of the liberal tradition used the term 'state-building', especially in the context of developing societies, which signified a renewed interest in the concept of the 'state' as an institutional and constitutional mechanism. Then in the 1980s, attention swung back to the state, as exemplified by T. Skocpol, 'Bringing the State Back In' (*Bringing the State Back in: Strategies of Analysis in Current Research,* edited by P. Evans, D. Rueschemeyer and T. Skocpol; 1985). However, in contrast to the earlier concept of the state as an institutional structure, it was redefined as an active agent of shaping and reshaping society. It is thus evident that, in spite of some initial suspicions and objections, the concept of the state never became entirely redundant for the study of politics. What is, then, meant by the term 'state'?

MEANING OF THE STATE

It is significant that though some sort of political organization has existed since ancient times, such as Greek city-states and the Roman empire, yet the concept of the 'state' as such is comparatively modern. The contemporary concept of the state owes its origin to Machiavelli (1469-1527), an Italian philosopher, who expressed this idea in early sixteenth century as 'the power which has authority over men' (*The Prince;* 1513). This was an important idea because it describes the nature of the state, not the end of the state which was a question of political philosophy rather than political sociology or political science. This peculiar feature of the state has been the focus of attention of many recent thinkers.

Max Weber (1864-1920), a famous German sociologist, sought to evolve a 'sociological' definition of the state (1920):

> Sociologically, the state cannot be defined in terms of its ends... Ultimately, one can define the modern state sociologically only in terms of the specific *means* peculiar to it, as to every political association, namely the use of physical force (From *Max Weber,* tr. and ed. by H.H. Gerth and C. Wright Mills; 1946).

From this standpoint, Weber arrives at the following definition which is widely acknowledged in modern political theory: "A state is a human community that (successfully) claims the *monopoly of the legitimate use of physical force* within a given territory."

R.M. MacIver, an American sociologist, in his famous work *The Modern*

State (1926), sought to distinguish the state from other kinds of associations in that it embraces the whole of people in a specific territory and it has the special function of maintaining social order. It performs this function through its agent, the government 'which speaks with the voice of law'. Similarly, R.M. MacIver and C.H. Page (*Society: An Introductory Analysis;* 1950) observed: "The state is distinguished from all other associations by its exclusive investment with the final power of coercion." Harold J. Laski, in *An Introduction to Politics* (1931), similarly points out:

> Whereas all other associations are voluntary in character, and can bind the individual only as he chooses membership of them, once he is a resident of some given state, legally he has no choice but to obey its commands. The state, so to say, is the crowning-point of the modern social edifice, and it is in its supremacy over all other forms of social grouping that its special nature is to be found.

Association

Association refers to a human organization formed for the fulfilment of certain common objectives of its members which motivate them to come together, and work together.

Frederick M. Watkins *(International Encyclopaedia of the Social Sciences;* 1968) defines the state as 'a geographically delimited segment of human society united by common obedience to a single sovereign'. Watkins lays special emphasis on the element of sovereignty—the characteristic of the supreme law-making authority whose decisions are final. The supremacy of the commands of the state is an essential element which distinguishes it from all other associations of men. Geoffrey K. Roberts (*A Dictionary of Political Analysis;* 1971) tried to evolve a working definition of the state as:

> A territorial area in which a population is governed by a set of political authorities, and which successfully claims the compliance of the citizenry for its laws, and is able to secure such compliance by its monopolistic control of legitimate force.

ELEMENTS OF THE STATE

In the light of the various definitions of the state, it is customary to identify the state by its constituent elements which include: population, territory, government and sovereignty.

Population

The state is a human institution. The population is, therefore, an essential element of the state. However, the population can constitute a state only when it is united by the condition of interdependence, consciousness of common interest, and general regard for a set of common rules of behaviour and institutions.

The size of population for constituting a state cannot be fixed, yet it is always better that such population is self-sufficient to meet all the needs of life. If it is required to procure any goods or services from other states, normally it should be able to pay for them, although the possibility of foreign aid, as a temporary measure, cannot be ruled out. In any case, economic self-sufficiency is essential for the stability of a state.

The population of a state need not belong to a single race, religion, language or culture. A homogeneous population is no longer considered an essential feature of the modern state. The modern state claims to reconcile the interests of various groups of its citizens.

Territory

Territory is another essential element of a state. Other associations either exist within the state or they extend their sphere to several states; they do not need separate territory. But the state must possess a territory where its authority is accepted without dispute or challenge.

A state comes into existence only when its population is settled in a fixed territory. Friedrich Engels, in his *The Origin of the Family, Private Property and the State* (1884), notes that the formation of the state is accompanied by a division of population according to territory. In the pre-state society when people live as nomadic tribes, moving from one place to another in search of food, the members of the tribe are held together by the ties of kinship. With the formation of the state, citizens are allowed to exercise their rights and duties wherever they settle, irrespective of gens and tribes. The organization of citizens according to locality is the common feature of all states.

Some writers, like John Seeley (1834-95), hold that a fixed territory is not an essential aspect of a state. The nomadic tribes, who do not possess fixed territory, do constitute a state. This view is, however, no longer held valid. The nomadic tribes do have the institution of authority, or even government with custom-based law, but not a state. Political sociologists concede the existence of a 'political system' in such communities, but their organization still does not qualify to be a state. Moreover, the modern state is not a matter of internal organization; it needs international recognition as well, so as to enjoy its rights and perform its duties as a member of the comity of nations. International law regards possession of a fixed territory as the essential attribute of the state. Demarcation of physical boundaries is, therefore, essential for establishing the real identity of a state.

The territory of a state includes the land, water and air-space within its boundary. It also extends usually to a distance of three miles into the sea from its coast; this area is known as territorial waters, which may be sought to be extended further in times of war.

Territory embodies the sphere of sovereignty of the state. Territory contains natural resources for the sustenance of the population of the state. Territory provides for a sense of security and immense opportunities for a fuller life to its residents; it is an object of sentimental attachment—people love and worship their motherland; they are prepared to make supreme sacrifices for the protection and maintenance of the territorial integrity of their state. The feeling of patriotism—the sense of belonging to a state—binds the people of different races, with diverse religions, languages and cultures, by the thread of national unity and mutual cooperation.

Like population, the size of the territory of a state cannot be fixed. Territory is a geographical entity—an area of land, usually separated from other areas by sea, mountains or other big natural barriers. Sometimes territories are demarcated mainly on a political basis rather than on a geographical basis. In such cases, the peoples' sense of identification with a particular state becomes the basis of territorial demarcation. Reallocation of territories can bring about merger or alteration of the existing states or emergence of new states.

Government

Government is still another essential element of the state. According to J.W. Garner (*Political Science and Government;* 1928), "Government is the agency or machinery through which common policies are determined and by which common affairs are regulated and common interests promoted." If the state represents an abstract concept, government is its concrete form. In other words, authority of the state is exercised by government; functions of the state are performed by government. Laws of the state are made, declared and enforced by the legislative and executive organs of government; justice is dispensed by the judicial organ of government. Government is responsible for the maintenance of law and order and for the provision of common services—defence, issue of currency, foreign relations, roads, bridges, and even transport, communications, water, electricity, health and education, etc. and it is entitled to levy taxes for the provision of all such services. Without government, the people are a chaotic mass of disjointed particles, without common aims, common interests or a common organization.

A citizen has to deal with government of the state; any transaction between different states, including war, takes place through the medium of their governments.

However, government and state should not be treated as co-terminous. Governments may rise and fall without disturbing identity of the state, so long as they are formed and dissolved according to the established conventions, procedure or constitution of the state. But a state will lose its identity if it is suppressed by an alien power so much so that the established procedure of forming a government is also suspended. When the people of a state lose their right to have a government according to the established procedure, *i.e.* a legitimate government enjoying customary respect and obedience of the people, the state is reduced to a colony of the imperial power which suppressed it.

Sovereignty

Finally, sovereignty also constitutes an essential element of the state. Sovereignty denotes the supreme or ultimate power of the state to make laws or take political decisions—establishing public goals, fixing priorities and resolving conflicts—as also enforcing such laws and decisions by the use of legitimate force. In fact, sovereignty denotes the final authority of the state over its population and its territory. This authority may be exercised by the government of the day, but it essentially belongs to the state from which it is derived by the government.

It is by virtue of its sovereignty that a state declares—through the agency of the government—its laws and decisions and issues commands which are binding on all citizens, claims obedience thereto, and punishes the offenders. It is also by virtue of its sovereignty that a state similarly deals independently with other states.

Commands of the state are treated as superior to those of any other association or institution, even to the dictates of social custom or conscience of the individual, because sovereignty is the sole preserve of the state. As Max Weber (1920) points out:

> The right to use physical force is ascribed to other institutions or to individuals only to the extent to which the state permits it. The state is considered the sole source of the 'right' to use violence (From *Max Weber*; tr. and ed. by H.H. Gerth and C. Wright Mills; 1946).

Other associations are either voluntary or based on custom or necessity. The right to use legitimate coercion in its own right is the exclusive prerogative of the state.

A state continues to exist so long as it is armed with sovereignty. If a state loses its sovereignty because of internal revolt or external aggression, the result is anarchy and disappearance of the state as such. Some writers regard 'international recognition' as an essential element of the state. This denotes formal recognition of the sovereignty of the state over a given territory and population by other states. International recognition, however, is the outcome of the sovereignty of the state, not a condition of its existence. When a new state, like Bangladesh, comes into existence, it may be recognized by some states immediately while other states may withhold their recognition for quite a long time. Much depends on the foreign policy of a state whether to recognize the new state immediately or to defer it. USA had withheld recognition of the new states of USSR and People's Republic of China for decades after they came into existence, but they did exist as states. Hence, international recognition is only incidental to the sovereignty of the state, not a condition of its existence.

[II]
THE STATE AND OTHER ASSOCIATIONS

STATE AND SOCIETY

The term 'state' is sometimes used synonymously with 'society'. However, such usage arises from confusion—intentional or unintentional. A distinction between state and society is desirable, not only for scientific precision but also for saving individual from absolutist, authoritarian and totalitarian rule.

The state is usually described as 'society politically organized'. Society is an association of human beings which fulfils all their needs of life—from cradle to grave. The state fulfils their particular need of political organization—it subjects them to binding laws and decisions to provide for order and security, and common services. When a society is capable of performing these functions under the direction of a supreme decision-making authority, only then does it qualify for being a state. Society binds men into multifarious relationships—all such relationships do not fall in the domain of a state. Social relationships are usually determined by necessity, custom, courtesy, morality, mutual understanding, agreement or even contract; political relations are mainly determined by command and obedience. Social relations cover a large variety of subjects, to meet all the needs of human life—physical, emotional, intellectual, spiritual, and so on.

Society may coincide with the state, especially when society takes the form of a nation. Thus, Indian society and the Indian state refer to the association of the same set of persons. But that is not always the case. There can be a society within the state, such as a village community. Social relationships can extend beyond the state also. Thus, you can have friends, relatives, acquaintances, sympathizers, admirers, clients, customers or even colleagues beyond the national frontiers of your state. They belong to your society, but not to your state. Then, there can be a society without a state. Primitive tribes who constitute society need not constitute a state. Even the groups of hunters, root-diggers and food-gatherers of a primitive type form a society though they are not aware of the idea of the state.

The state is formed out of society. So society is a primary association. It is society which chooses the pattern of its political grouping. States may be created, altered or dissolved, but society goes on for ever. Men can live without a state, but not without a society. That is why man is described as a social animal by nature. Growth of the state is an attribute of civilization, whose form is subject to change with the advance of civilization. The state depends on society for its existence, not *vice versa.* Thus, R.M. MacIver (*The Modern State;* 1926) observed:

> There are social forms like the family or the church or the club, which owe neither their origin nor their inspiration to the state; and social forces like custom or competition, which the state may protect or modify, but certainly does not create; and social motives like friendship or jealousy, which establish relationships too intimate and personal to be controlled by the great engine of the state ... The state in a word regulates the outstanding external relationships of men in society.

Thus, man owes much more to society than what he owes to the state. But when state and society are identified and man's obligations towards society are attributed to the state, it leads to socially disastrous consequences—complete subordination of man to the authority of government, unrestrained by any control mechanism.

STATE AND CIVIL SOCIETY

Originally, the terms 'civil society' and 'political society' were used as coterminous. Thus, the term 'civil society' was applied synonymously with 'state'. But under the complex conditions of present-day society, it is necessary to recognize the distinctive features of civil society.

Initially, the ancient Roman thinker Marcus Tullius Cicero (106-43 B.C.) used the term 'civil society' in the sense of the state in the first century B.C. But in his view it was not merely the external structure of the state. It stood for a society whose members lived together as citizens, abided by civil laws and led a civilized, cultured and dignified life. In this sense, the barbarian communities did not qualify to be described as civil societies.

Seventeenth-century English philosopher John Locke (1632-1704) equated civil society with political society. He observed that when people relinquish the state of nature and set up a government for the protection of their natural right to 'life, liberty and property', they enter into civil society. Thus, civil society is a means to establish discipline, order and security for the human community. Eighteenth-century French philosopher Jean-Jaques Rousseau (1712-78) also treated 'civil society' and 'political society' as coterminous. It provides for legal equality of all citizens who thus become equal in the eye of law in spite of their natural differences.

State of Nature

State of nature refers to the hypothetical condition in which people live before the formation of the state.

German philosopher G.W.F. Hegel (1770-1831) sought to distinguish 'civil society' from the state which were based in 'universal egoism' and 'universal altruism' respectively. In Hegel's view, civil society represented an organization in which an individual dealt with all other individuals (apart from the members of his family) as means to serve his self-interest. It is the sphere of economic activities where an individual tries to know the needs of others and to satisfy them in order to satisfy his own needs. Another German philosopher Karl Marx (1818-83) accepted Hegel's description of civil society, but he did not accept Hegel's distinction between civil society and the state. Marx believed that in actual practice civil society represented the state itself. It recognized individual as a citizen and conceded equality of all individuals in the eye of law. But since the economic power in the contemporary civil society was in the hands of capitalist class, law also served the interests of this class.

Antonio Gramsci (1891-1937), Italian Marxist, identified two levels of the superstructure of capitalist society: (*a*) civil society which was nearer the base; and (*b*) political society which exercised overall control. Civil society includes family, school, church and other primary groups like neighbourhood, peer groups, etc. which transmit capitalist value-system to the new generation; political society comprises governmental organization including police, judiciary, prisons, etc. Civil society embodies 'structures of legitimation'; political society embodies 'structures of coercion'. Together they form 'structures of domination'. Capitalist society largely depends on the efficiency of the institutions of civil society for its stability.

Base and Superstructure

The terms 'base' and 'superstructure' are used in Marxist theory to describe the relation between economic structure of society and other aspects of social life. In this building-like metaphor, mode of production (*i.e.* the economic structure of society) constitutes the base, while legal and political structure, religion, morals, and other forms of social consciousness constitute the superstructure. It is believed that any change in the base results in corresponding changes in the superstructure.

Herbert Marcuse (1898-1979), Neo-Marxist philosopher in America, argued that Hegel's distinction between 'civil society' and the 'state' was particularly significant for an analysis of the problems of contemporary society. He noted that under the modern capitalism civil society had eclipsed the state whereas under the modern communism the state had eclipsed civil society. We must secure independence of both institutions in order to restore civil liberties of the citizens.

In short, distinction between the state and civil society must be maintained in order to prevent authoritarianism. In the contemporary discourse, the term 'civil society' is also used to describe the 'intermediary' associations between individual (or family) and the state. It is the product of 'freedom of association'. It is the bedrock of civil liberties. It serves as a channel of communication between individuals and the state and functions as a shock-absorber in the event of mounting tension between individuals and the state.

Civil Liberties

Civil liberties refer to the legal instruments of protection of the individual from arbitrary acts of government. These include personal freedom, freedom of movement, freedom of thought and expression, faith and worship, freedom of association, right to fair trial, equality before the law, etc.

Distinction between state and civil society may also be drawn in terms of their salient features as they operate in the contemporary world. The state is identified by its unified, formal structure comprising different organs of power, particularly legislature, executive and judiciary. On the other hand, civil society is comprised of loose organizations of citizens voluntarily pursuing public interest. The state is armed with supreme legal authority, *i.e.* sovereignty; civil society enjoys no formal, legal authority; at best, it enjoys moral authority over citizens. Then the state is empowered to exercise compulsory jurisdiction over its citizens and territory; civil society does not exercise compulsory jurisdiction anywhere; it largely depends on its ability of motivation and inspiration. The state is responsible for the maintenance of law and order as well as protection of its citizens from internal and external offences, natural and other calamities; civil society voluntarily undertakes protection of common interest of citizens by mobilizing them, pooling their resources, and exerting influence on government organs.

Distinction Between the State and Civil Society

The Issue	*Characteristics of*	
	The State	*Civil Society*
Structure	Formal, unified structure comprising identifiable organs of power—legislature, executive, judiciary	Comprises loose organizations of citizens voluntarily pursuing public interest
Authority	Armed with supreme legal authority, *i.e.* sovereignty	Enjoys no formal, legal authority; at best, it enjoys moral authority over citizens
Jurisdiction	Compulsory jurisdiction over its citizens and territory	No compulsory jurisdiction anywhere; it largely depends on its ability of motivation and inspiration
Functions	Maintenance of law and order; protection of citizens from internal and external offences, natural and other calamities	Protection of the common interest of citizens by mobilizing them, pooling their resources, and exerting influence on government organs
Resources	Huge resources at its disposal—ownership of national wealth, taxation, public debt, etc.	No definite assets or sources of income; it has to create its own resources through mobilizing subscriptions, grants and donations, etc.
Occurence	Universal; some form of political organization is found in all societies	It appears only in relatively advanced societies where citizens have become adequately conscious of their rights, duties and the common interest

Besides, the state has huge resources at its disposal, *e.g.* ownership of national wealth, power of taxation and raising public debt, etc. but civil society has no definite assets or sources of income; it has to create its own resources through mobilizing subscriptions, grants and donations, etc. Finally, the existence of the state is almost universal; some form of political organization is found in all modern societies. However, civil society comes into existence only in relatively advanced societies where citizens have become adequately conscious of their rights, duties and the common interest.

STATE AND GOVERNMENT

Government is regarded as an essential element of the state. In actual practice, the state is represented by the government. Governments exercise all authority and functions on behalf of the state. However, the terms 'state' and 'government' should not be used synonymously. 'State' represents a wider and more stable entity than 'government'. As R.M. MacIver (*The Web of Government;* 1965) has elucidated:

> When we speak of the state, we mean the organization, of which government is the administrative organ. Every social organization must have a focus of administration, an agency by which its policies are given specific character and translated into action. But the organization is greater than the organ. In this sense, the state is greater and more inclusive than government. A state has a constitution, a code of laws, a way of setting up its government, a body of citizens. When we think of this whole structure, we think of the state.

Thus, so long as a state maintains its identity and independence, governments may be formed and dissolved according to the established procedure without affecting the character of the state. But a state itself may lose its identity when it is suppressed and conquered by an alien power and its constitution or the established procedure of forming a legitimate government is suspended. The subjugated people may, however, retain or revive their feeling of national solidarity and strive to re-establish their state in due course.

The state serves as a symbol of unity of the people. The image of the state inspires unity among the people and provides them with an identity as a nation. It arouses national pride and a spirit of sacrifice among the people. Government only represents a working arrangement to carry out functions of the state. Government commands our obedience; the state commands our loyalty. Government may be good or bad, efficient or inefficient, but the state will continue to be a symbol of our national greatness. We may criticize or condemn the government, and still acclaim the greatness of our state.

It is, however, essential that our duties and obligations towards the state should be determined by the character of the government it creates. If the government loses its credibility, it should either be replaced according to the established procedure, or the credibility of the state itself will be eroded. The government should be subjected to constant watch so that it conforms to the image of the state as the protector and promoter of our common interests. Any theory which does not provide for a concrete control mechanism over the government is bound to have disastrous consequences.

The idealist theory tends to ignore the distinction between state and government. It creates an image of the perfect state. Hegel eulogized the state, especially the nation-state, as the 'march of God on earth'! This theory demands complete subordination of man to the authority and command of the state, without ensuring whether the actual government which makes such demands, conforms to the image of the ideal state or not.

The liberal-democratic theory is more rational in this respect. It treats the state as a product of the 'will of society', an instrument of 'conflict-resolution' and of securing the common interest; then it authorizes society to constitute a government by free choice, and demands that the government should be responsible to the people, and should work with the continuous consent of the people. Any political theory which creates a truly constitutional government cannot be ignorant of the fallibility of government. It must recognize the distinction between the state and government.

Marxist theory treats government as agency of the state. It attributes any imperfection of government to the state itself. Accordingly, so long as society is divided into dominant and dependent classes, any government is bound to serve as an instrument of the dominant class. Thus, Marxist theory regards the state itself as an instrument of class exploitation, and advocates transformation, and ultimate withering away, of the state in order to restore 'authority' to a classless society.

STATE AND NATION

The modern state usually takes the form of a nation-state. The frontiers of the state are called national frontiers; the interest of the state is described as national interest; the character of the people of a state is referred to as its national character. Relations between different states are known as international relations.

At the outset, a nation may be distinguished from nationality. Nationality usually refers to a set of people inspired by a feeling of unity based on common race, language, religion, culture, geographical compactness, common political aspirations and historical development. Most of these factors are based on birth and provide little scope for expanding the horizons of social relationships. Feelings of nationality separate one set of people from other similar sets. Sometimes this is accompanied by a sense of one's own superiority, or a sense of disdain for others which may lead to tensions, wars and other disastrous consequences. In any case, the feeling of nationality grows from a relatively narrow base.

Some writers tend to identify a nation by the same characteristics as those of a nationality, and then advocate a separate state for each nationality. This view is no longer held valid. A nation grows on a much wider base. It refers to people living in a defined territory, inspired by a sense of unity, common political aspirations, common interests, common history and common destiny though they may belong to different nationalities. In other words, groups of people of different races, with diverse religions, languages and cultures, etc. may live together although spread over different regions of a vast territory; they may feel united as citizens of the same state, owing their undivided allegiance to that state. Thus, nationhood transcends the divisive features of people, and extends to the permanent residents of a state. Members of a nation, of course, distinguish themselves from other nations. They may sometimes be prejudiced against other peoples. Yet a logical outcome of the idea of a nation postulales equality among nations, their co-existence and cooperation. Since 1920, the principle of national self-determination has been almost universally accepted which has led to the establishment of nation-states, and rapid development of international law to regulate relations between nation-states.

National Self-Determination

National self-determination refers to the principle that each nation has the right to be independent and to choose a suitable form of government for itself. At the end of the First World War (1914-18), Woodrow Wilson (1856-1924) conceived of it primarily as a criterion for the break-up of the empires defeated in the war, *i.e.* Austro-Hungarian, German and Ottoman empires. Around this time, V.I. Lenin (1870-1924) conceived of this principle essentially as the ground for granting independence to dependent nations from colonial and imperial domination.

After the Second World War (1939-45), the United Nations upheld this principle through various international documents. Thus, UN General Assembly resolution on the independence of colonial peoples (1960), two UN covenants on human rights (1966), UN General Assembly Declaration on Friendly Relations among States (1970) and the Final Act of the Conference for Security and Cooperation in Europe (1975) have gradually transformed it into a general legal principle of the international community.

The developing countries, *i.e.* the countries of Asia, Africa and Latin America who had won their independence from colonial and imperial domination, and sought to consolidate their independence after the Second World War (1939-45), are faced today with the gigantic task of nation-building. Most of them evolved a national sentiment during their struggle for independence, but disruptive tendencies started to emerge after they achieved their independence. Nation-building involves inculcating a feeling of unity among diverse linguistic, religious and cultural groups, and the process of their integration into a compact entity. The attempt is, however, bound to remain elusive unless they contain their widening economic disparities and free themselves completely from the foul play of neo-colonial powers who continue to exploit them despite their political independence.

[III]
RISE AND GROWTH OF MODERN NATION-STATE

The modern state is largely identified as the nation-state. The state has acquired its present form through a long historical process extending over thousands of years. The state itself was the product of the interplay of several factors, including kinship, religion, property, war, technical development, and political consciousness. Family was the first institution to emerge from the state of savagery, which brought some sense of attachment, obligation, order and security in the life of man. Originally, man's family was traced from the mother which gave rise to the matrilineal family. This, in due course, gave way to patrilineal and patriarchal family where a person's family was traced from father and the family was placed under the rule of the father; woman was reduced to being the property of man. The family gave rise to a larger social organization. Initially, kinship or blood-relationship provided a strong tie for people to live together and to fulfil their needs through the division of labour. In due course, some consistent patterns of behaviour and relationships of domination and subordination emerged. Social life came to be regulated by custom and authority. This eventually led to the evolution of the state.

Sociologists have generally identified the following forms of state in the course of its historical evolution—the tribal state; the Oriental empire; Greek city-state; Roman world empire; the feudal state; and, finally, modern nation-state.

THE TRIBAL STATE

The earliest form of tribal organization of authority—based on command and obedience relationship—is described as the tribal state. The tribal states were usually small in size. These were governed by chiefs, often assisted by advisory councils. Some of them were nomadic (hence not qualifying as 'states'); others were permanently settled in definite areas. While the main purpose of their existence was the preservation of internal order and the waging of aggressive or defensive war, they often retained strong traces of common birth, common religion, and common economic interests. The aborigines of Australia represent this type. The tribes of the Western hemisphere, before they came into contact with Europe, also belonged to this category.

The nomenclature 'tribal state' is, however, controversial. Many authors, including Engels, hold that some forms of tribal society did have the institution of authority, but they did not possess characteristics of the state in the proper sense of the term. Such societies have been described as pre-state societies. In any case, they represent a primitive form of social organization which was later developed into the state.

THE ORIENTAL EMPIRE

In course of time, population increased; new techniques of production were evolved and new sources of natural bounty were discovered. A warm climate, fertile soil, abundance of water and sunlight and vast areas free from geographical barriers helped men to accumulate wealth and to evolve new forms of social organization. In the fertile valleys of the Nile, the Euphrates, the Ganges, the Yellow River, and Yangtze, which are called the 'cradles of civilization', wealth accumulated and cities arose. Such areas, furnishing abundant food with little effort, attracted surrounding peoples belonging to different kinship groups. This was followed by their conflict and intermingling which eventually resulted in the creation of the state.

The increased prosperity led to the development of the art of war and conquest of territories. As the stronger groups won over the weaker ones, the inhabitants of these valleys were bound together into the empires of Egypt, Babylon, Assyria, India, and China. These empires were not strongly centralized, but were made up of subordinate units, practically autonomous in local affairs, yet under central supervision, obliged to furnish soldiers and to pay tribute.

The early advance of civilization was, therefore, marked by oppression and exploitation. In the frequent wars of conquests, the victors became masters, the vanquished slaves, with resultant social differences, castes and despotism. The rulers became supreme in collusion with a class of priests who became guardians of religion. The subjects were relegated to slavery and debasement. An elaborate network of officials was created by the ruling classes to fortify their authority, but the large size of empires eroded central authority, led to local revolts and external invasions, and consequent disintegration of these empires.

GREEK CITY-STATE

As civilization spread to the region around the Aegean and the Mediterranean, new geographical forms gave rise to new forms of social organization. Europe is a peninsula where land is broken by the sea into small units permitting communication, but making invasion from Asia difficult in those days. The peculiar location of Greece led to the evolution of a new form of political organization in the ancient days. The mountains and the sea divided this area into numerous valleys and islands. These could be easily defended, yet, because of the sea, these were not isolated. In contrast to the uniformity of Asia, the variety and moderation of nature in Greece developed a different mental attitude and genius. Here, small communities were settled in secluded valleys, guarded by mountains and the sea, yet in constant contact with the outside world through their harbours. Quite naturally, they evolved their political organization into city-states.

Greek city-states were free from the despotism that fettered the earlier empires. The small size of the state provided for closer relations between government and the citizen. Earlier forms of democracy, therefore, evolved in these city-states. However, their population was divided into freemen and slaves. Over two-third of the population was comprised of the slaves who had no rights of citizenship. The prominent city-states were Athens, Sparta, Orinth, Argos, Thebes, and Attica. Sparta is known for its perfect discipline while Athens provided an ideal platform for direct democracy.

Greek city-states disintegrated due to mutual rivalry, frequent wars between themselves and external invasion, first from Macedon, then from Rome.

ROMAN WORLD EMPIRE

After the downfall of Greek city-states, the main line of political development passed westward to Rome. In due course, Rome became the centre of civilization. It was situated in the centre of Europe, at the head of navigation of the only important river. The various settlements on the neighbouring hills were soon united with Rome by conquest or by federation. This led to the fusion of various types of people. Thus, in Rome the rigid fetters of custom were broken earlier than usual. Relations of various tribes were governed by compromise or treaty which paved the way for the growth of Rome's wonderful system of law. The process of conquest culminated in the formation of Empire.

The Roman empire evolved a well-knit political organization. Monarchy was replaced by aristocracy of birth and wealth. Though the population was still divided into patricians and plebeians, yet the plebeians enjoyed greater privileges than the Greek slaves. Internal dissensions were largely averted by extending citizenship. Assemblies were widened. However, the power of wealthy aristocrats increased with the expansion of empire. Religious sanction was added to the authority of the emperor which led to the concentration and centralization of authority. The result was the suppression of individual freedom; the institutions of democracy and local self-government disappeared. The strong empire eventually disintegrated under its own weight.

THE FEUDAL STATE

After the decline and fall of the Roman empire, central authority was eroded. In the Medieval Age which began in the fifth century of the Christian era, powers began to be exercised by feudal chiefs, *i.e.* the landlords holding big estates. This led to the formation of a hierarchical political organization with the king as the supreme lord at the top, and serfs at the bottom. In fact, the king exercised only superficial control as the lord over the feudal vassals who enjoyed the real power within their domain. The serfs were landless peasants, obliged to pass on a very major share of their produce to their feudal lords. Thus, society still remained divided into the exploiter and exploited classes—the lords and the serfs respectively.

With the erosion of the authority of kings, the Christian church emerged as another symbol of authority. The Pope emerged as the head of the Holy Roman Empire. By the beginning of the fourteenth century, when Popes were using their authority arbitrarily, the authority of the church was challenged and power of monarchy restored. On the other hand, the advent of the industrial revolution in mid-eighteenth century brought about a change in the mode of material production, leading to the emergence of a new industrial-merchant class, requiring large numbers of workers for the new industries. All these factors led to the dissolution of the feudal system and the emergence of a new state-system.

MODERN NATION-STATE

With the dissolution of the feudal system and erosion of the authority of the church, new individualism appeared which demanded greater freedom for man. A new political system was needed in accordance with the new ideas and new conditions. This took the form of the nation-state. As population became stationary and common interests developed, it became increasingly evident that new states would, in general, follow geographic and ethnic lines. Bonds of nationality and language, strengthened by natural boundaries, grouped the feudal fragments into more and more permanent combinations. This process led to the emergence of France, Spain, England, Switzerland, the Netherlands, Russia, and, later, Germany and Italy as the nation-states. This separation of territories into distinct states, each with its own national spirit, destroyed the idea of a common superior and paved the way for the rise of international law and the modern theory of sovereignty and legal equality of states.

The earlier nation-states were largely monarchies. However, since the eighteenth century, there has been a slow transition from absolute monarchy to constitutional monarchy and democracy in large parts of Europe. In some countries, such as England, the transition to democracy was relatively peaceful, while in France it was brought about by a violent revolution. In any case, with the growth and expansion of democracy, the principles of liberty, equality, popular sovereignty and rule of law came to be established as the principles of government in a large part of Europe.

The process of formation of modern nation-state started in Europe as early as the sixteenth century. However, European nations did not seek to extend this principle to all mankind. The industrial revolution and the emergence of a new industrial-merchant class in European countries opened up new avenues of prosperity for these people. But, at the same time, they required new sources of raw material, cheap labour and new markets for consumption of their industrial products. This led them to adopt the policy of colonialism which implied the exploration of new territories and expansion of their colonial net to the countries of Asia, Africa and Latin America, with the obvious intention of exploiting the natural and human resources of these countries. Though the colonial powers sought to exalt their own role in the garb of such phrases as the 'whiteman's burden', yet they indulged in the maximum possible exploitation of the subject peoples. Thus, nineteenth-century Europe is characterized by a strange paradox—a nation-state with liberty, equality and rule of law at home, and imperialistic exploitation abroad.

Colonialism

Colonialism refers to the practice under which a nation-state, after consolidating its national power, extends its domination over territories and peoples of other countries for exploiting their natural and human resources. The colonial power establishes its own administration in the subject country and takes all resources thereof under its own control.

Whiteman's Burden

Whiteman's burden refers to the argument advanced by the champions of British imperialism that nature had assigned the white races—particularly the British people—the sacred task of spreading enlightenment among the ignorant non-white people and rule over them for their benefit.

Political consciousness and national movements started emerging in the subject peoples in early twentieth century, especially after the First World War (1914-18) although in India, national movement had started in the nineteenth century. Besides, people in some countries were otherwise suffering under despotic rule. Political aspirations of the oppressed peoples of different countries brought about two important changes in the twentieth century: (*a*) socialist revolutions inspired by Marxist ideology, first in Russia (1917), and later in China (1949) and other countries; and (*b*) attainment of independence by the peoples of Asia and Africa from their colonial rulers, especially after the Second World War (1939-45), such as India, Pakistan, Burma (Myanmar), Egypt, Nigeria, Algeria, Ghana, Fiji, Vietnam, Indonesia, Libya, Syria, Zimbabwe and Namibia. These new nations along with Latin American countries are collectively described as the 'Third World' or the developing nations. Their social, economic and political life was shattered during the colonial rule; and they are now faced with the gigantic task of development, challenge of poverty and disruptive forces within, largely because of the exploitation of the masses by their ruling classes, sometimes in collusion with foreign powers. A large number of these nations were subjected to military dictatorship and oppression.

Marxian socialism, which brought about socialist systems in the world, advocated a world-wide organization of workers. Initially, it did not subscribe to the idea of confining workers' movements to national boundaries. However, harsh realities of human nature and practical necessity forced the peoples of the socialist states to accept and perpetuate their position as nation-states. A large number of socialist states have since relinquished socialism and are now heading towards liberalization as independent nation-states. Similarly, the new nations of the Third World have also stabilized as nation-states.

The stability of the nation-state system has led to the vast development of international law and international organizations (like the United Nations and its specialized agencies) to regulate the behaviour of nation-states, international transactions, to ensure collaboration in the development of science and technology, art, literature and culture as also to tackle global problems like prevention of atmospheric pollution, sharing of rare but essential resources, saving humanity from injustice, and so on.

However, exploitation in the international sphere continues in many new, subtle forms, such as neo-colonialism. The new nations require machinery and know-how from advanced nations to build up their own industrial-technological base. They get these things at the expense of their rare and valuable resources, and thus they are increasingly impoverished. The pattern of import-export of developing nations reveals how cheap they sell their own material and labour involved in their products, and how expensively they acquire the material and labour involved in the products of foreign nations! Even foreign aid to the developing nations has become a source of their exploitation. Besides, large numbers of talented persons from the developing nations, highly educated and trained in their own countries at huge public expense, migrate every year to serve the advanced nations. These are highly complex problems which need to be sorted out and tackled in order to save humanity from mounting exploitation and injustice.

Neo-Colonialism

Neo-colonialism refers to the practice under which an advanced nation does not maintain its political domination in a foreign territory, but taking advantage of its superior position in organization of trade and industry, uses the resources of a developing nation as a source of cheap labour and raw materials as well as a big market of its own products. It is a subtle method of economic exploitation of developing nations by the developed nations.

[IV]
NATIONALISM AND INTERNATIONALISM

The concept of nation-state is the focus of two conflicting ideologies, *viz.* nationalism and internationalism. Nationalism denotes a sentiment as well as an ideology. As a sentiment, it refers to an individual's attachment to his nation.

A nationalist in this sense accords primacy to his national interest over all other interests. As an ideology, nationalism postulates that the structure of a state or its political organization should be founded on nationhood. In other words, each nation should constitute an independent state; and each state should represent a particular nation. The people who identify themselves as a natural community, and claim to be the members of a nation must live under a political system of their own choice; they should enjoy an equal status with other nations in the world community; and no nation should be kept under the domination or supremacy of any other nation.

If the members of a community regard themselves as a nation, they can create or invent some elements of nationhood in order to strengthen their national sentiment. For example, they can evolve their 'national language', adopt a 'national flag', 'national anthem' and other symbols of national identity like national tree, national flower, national fruit, national bird, national animal, national river, etc., declare national festivals, build memorials of 'national heroes' before whom the entire nation bows its head; and they can inspire the members of the nation through popular songs, paintings and statues depicting heroic episodes of their national history.

If a community has evolved national consciousness but its territory is occupied by a colonial or imperial power, it can organize itself for the struggle of independence. It is called 'national movement'. In short, nationalism pays highest importance to one's loyalty and commitment to one's nation.

On the other hand, internationalism does not regard nation-state as the centre of political organization, nor it accepts nation as the object of individual's undivided loyalty. It insists that mankind should evolve larger organizations in order to achieve some great objectives. Broadly speaking, we may discern two streams of internationalism: (*a*) international communism; and (*b*) a principle of international organization. International communism is associated with the teachings of Marx (1818-83) and Engels (1820-95). In *Communist Manifesto* (1848), they observed that workers have no country of their own. They exhorted workers of the world to unite to bring about a socialist revolution all over the world. In their view, socialist revolution was necessary for the emancipation of humanity. This could not be confined to the boundaries of a particular nation.

As a principle of international politics, internationalism implies that in view of the growing contact between different parts of the world, a nation-state is no longer capable of fulfilling all the needs of its members, not to speak of mankind as such. Hence, peoples of different nation-states should form larger international organizations and cooperate to serve the common interest of mankind. In the case of a clash between national interest and universal human interest, human interest should be given precedence. In this sense, internationalism repudiates the idea of 'my country, right or wrong'. It insists that each nation-state should accept reasonable restraints on its sovereignty in the interests of world peace, collective security and observance of international law.

It is important to note that an earlier version of internationalism believed in international cooperation in military, commercial, educational and cultural spheres in the mutual interest of the nations concerned. But the United Nations called for international cooperation in order to maintain world peace and to eradicate hunger, disease, illiteracy and superstition from various parts of the world. In the contemporary world, the problems of environmental pollution, terrorism and drug-trafficking have assumed global dimensions. Internationalists should come forward to muster vigorous international cooperation in order to fight against these evils on the global scale.

[V]
CURRENT CRISIS OF THE NATION-STATE

In the history of mankind, various types of state systems were evolved in different ages, but none of them could provide for enduring peace and security to people. Greek city-states were fighting against each other. Roman empire was able to control peoples of different races but it failed to arouse a sense of social solidarity among them. In the medieval age, the Pope and the Emperor wanted to create a universal system on the basis of religious unity, but when different countries became aware of their national identities, the medieval empire was dissolved.

Today, nation-state is also facing a similar problem. It has proved more efficient than the medieval empire to provide mankind with security and happiness, but under the changed conditions it seems unable to perform this function. With the beginning of the twenty-first century, search for a new form of organization has begun which should be able to fulfil hopes and aspirations of humanity. But there is no certainty about the future form of the state.

In the modern age, nation and state are generally regarded as concominant, but many examples will prove otherwise. Some communities are scattered over different parts of the world who entertain a sense of unity on the basis of common race, common culture, common language and common religion and profess national consciousness on that ground, but they are unable to organize themselves as a single state. For example, the Kurds are scattered over Iraq, Iran and Turkey although they recognize themselves as one nation.

Then there are states in which different ethnic groups live together but they have not been able to assimilate themselves into one nation. Countries like Lebanon and Cyprus remained afflicted with civil wars for very long. Former USSR, Yugoslavia, Czechoslovakia and Ethiopia have split into a number of separate states due to such disruptive tendencies.

Many people have migrated to other countries in search of opportunities for advancement, and have become naturalized citizens of those countries. But they are so deeply attached to the language, culture, faith and customs of the countries of their origin that they are prepared to make sacrifices for the welfare of those countries. For example the Chinese who have settled abroad are still making substantial contribution to the advancement of China.

One major function of a nation-state is to provide for security to its residents. But due to the invention of lethal weapons and probability of their use by other countries, no nation-state has remained capable of providing full security to its residents. Thus if a country resorts to a nuclear attack on others with the help of advanced missiles, it would prove disastrous to humanity far and wide. Further, it would cause so much atmospheric pollution that no part of the globe is likely to be spared by its effect.

Even otherwise the atmospheric pollution caused by the disposal of the industrial waste is not confined to the boundaries of nation-states. Again, the increasing consumption of petrol and diesel by the advanced nations is responsible for causing immense harm to the global atmosphere. Cutting of forests and mountains for fuel, timber, limestone or hydro-electric power projects in any country causes soil erosion. Its cumulative effect results in distortion of weather cycle and consequent danger of global warming.

Global Warming

Global warming refers to the process involving extraordinary rise in earth's temperature due to increasing atmospheric pollution. This pollution results from the increasing consumption of petrol and diesel and soil erosion due to cutting of forests and mountains. It is feared that it will give rise to climate change, the melting of polar ice and consequent rise in sea-level.

Then information revolution all over the world has practically eliminated the distance between different countries in the matter of communication. Telephone, internet, e-mail, fax, etc. enable us to send a message or a copy of any document or picture from one corner of the world to another at the speed of light. With the help of satellite, television programmes can be transmitted and watched in all parts of the world simultaneously. Any important event occurring in any part of the world is reported so fast and so vividly in all other parts that nothing remains unknown. The increasing intimacy of the people all over the world has converted it into a 'global village'.

Unprecedented advancement of the means of transport and communication has paved the way for globalization of economy. Even criminals, drug traffickers and terrorists are making full use of the advanced means of transport and communication. The situation calls for a global effort to deal with the global problems. In this scenario, nation-state will have to play a new role for which it should concede necessary adjustment in its authority and sovereignty.

[VI]
CONTEMPORARY TRENDS IN ADVANCED INDUSTRIAL COUNTRIES AND THE THIRD WORLD

The contemporary world was politically divided into three major parts: the first world (Western capitalist countries plus Japan, Australia and New Zealand; often including Israel and South Africa); the second world (Communist states of Eastern and Central Europe, led by the former Soviet Union); and the third world (the newly independent, developing countries of Asia, Africa and Latin America). While the first world and the second world were engaged in the 'cold war', third world countries preferred to remain 'non-aligned' in order to focus on their development and also to contain the intensity of the prevailing 'cold war'.

Cold War

Cold war refers to the period of intense ideological conflict between capitalist and socialist nations since the end of Second World War (1945) till the collapse of socialist systems in Eastern Europe and Soviet Union (1991). During this period major capitalist and socialist nations had formed their respective military alliances which were termed as *power blocs*. There was no armed conflict between the two blocs, but a vigorous propaganda against each other was in full swing. Each of them wanted to demonstrate supremacy of its ideology and to enlist its following in the rest of the world. In international politics, this queer conflict created immense tension and threatened the world peace.

The term 'Cold War' in this sense was popularized by an American columnist, Walter Lippmann (1889-1974).

With the dissolution of the second world around 1991, and the consequent end of the 'cold war', this division became partly outdated. However, the third world still maintained its identity with a more vigorous focus on development. Its identity was reinforced by an alternative division of the world on economic basis which was in vogue along with its political division. The economic division of the world recognized two broad categories: the developed world and the developing world, sometimes identified as North-South divide. The concept of the developing world coincided with the third world. Indeed, the aggregate of the developing countries continued to be described as the third world even in the context of economic division of the world. With the increasing importance of economic power in the world politics, the economic division of the world has become more significant.

TRENDS IN ADVANCED INDUSTRIAL COUNTRIES

Western writers have been trying to demonstrate that the course of development in advanced industrial countries is determined by the level of their industrialization and consequent modernization, and not by their ideological commitment. This meant that the Western democracies and the communist states would follow a similar course of development. Max Weber (1864-1920), German sociologist, had observed in early twentieth century that all modern societies were prone to developing a 'legal-rational' model of bureaucracy. By the mid of the twentieth century, James Burnham (1907-87) tried to show (*Managerial Revolution;* 1942) that the rise of a new class of managers was common to capitalist, communist and mixed economies. This symbolized the shift of power from the legal owner of the means of production to the effective manager. Burnham declared that the war of 1939 (the Second World War) was the first great war of managerial society as the war of 1914 (the First World War) was the last great war of capitalist society.

Several economists and economic historians in 1960s postulated similar patterns of development in all industrial societies in spite of differences in their ideologies. Of these, W.W. Rostow (*The Stages of Economic Growth;* 1960), J.K. Galbraith (*The New industrial State;* 1964), and Simon Kuznets (*Economic Growth and Structure;* 1965) are particularly important. They argued that economic growth constitutes a uniform process involving definite stages of growth in all industrial economies irrespective of their adherence to diverse political ideologies. In other words, all industrializing societies are governed by a uniform 'logic' underlying this process. These may be identified by a number of common characteristics, *e.g.* the demand to utilize technology efficiently; the increasing specialization of tasks; the necessity of a highly skilled and educated manpower; an increasing ratio of workers in industrial and service sectors in relation to the agricultural sector; the growing significance of material incentives; evolution of more complex organizational structures; and the emergence of similar patterns of management, planning and policy objectives.

Then a host of sociologists also sought to identify common tendencies of development in all 'modernizing' societies. Thus, Marion J. Levy, Jr. (*Modernization and the Structure of Society;* 1966) and Talcott Parsons (*The System of Modern Societies;* 1971) asserted that universal structural constraints involved in the process of industrialization lead to the development of certain common characteristics in different types of societies. These include urbanization, expanding educational systems, similar occupational prestige and mobility patterns, falling birth and death rates, widespread electronic communication networks, etc. Advanced industrial societies are further characterized by the dominance of scientific rationalism over superstition, universalism over particularism, individualism over collectivism, standards of achievement over nepotism, and the dominance of a state that defines rights and obligations, extension of citizenship, increased political participation, and the expansion of individual liberties.

Critics point out that most of these characteristics focus on the Western model of development. The theory of universal characteristics of developed societies underplays the role of cultural and ideological factors as well as the strength of leadership prevailing in different types of political systems. It would be futile to look for these characteristics in the course of progress made in socialist countries and the third world. This theory is largely designed to project 'market society model' as a universal model of development which would work to the advantage of Western democracies at the expense of other countries.

Incidentally, the concept of 'post-industrial society', developed by Daniel Bell (*The Coming of Post-Industrial Society: A Venture in Social Forecasting;* 1974) gives a vivid picture of the most highly developed states in the Western world. Bell himself is a votary of the 'end of ideology' thesis which holds that the character of social-economic organization of a country at the advanced stage of industrial growth is determined by the level of its industrial development, and not by the prevailing ideology. His description of 'post-industrial society' throws many hints about the possible course of development in many countries beyond Western democracies.

In order to contrast a 'post-industrial society' with an 'industrial society', Bell observes that in an industrial society, corporation is the chief economic and social institution, and work is machine-oriented which leads to conflict between capital and labour. On the other hand, in a post-industrial society, corporation has a less central place, work relations are more people-oriented, and a lesser proportion of the labcur force works in industry than in services. In such a society, scientific and technical *elites* play prominent role; universities, research institutes and knowledge in general are held in high esteem; merit rather than property is the principle of social stratification; group competition replaces class warfare; and the social structure has a more rational and efficient basis. The economic function is subordinated to the political order because the government is responsible for planning. Experts and the bureaucracy play a leading role in such planning, and the state intervenes in the economy for a broad variety of reasons. This trend challenges some aspects of democracy and constitutes a danger to individual rights.

In a nutshell, advanced industrial societies in the contemporary world are distinguished by the expansion of service sector. More people are now employed in hotels, restaurants, shops, motor garages, transport and tourism, communication, entertainment and advertising jobs, etc. than those in factories. The business becomes more people-oriented. Government planning and regulation is extended to every part of public life. This may provide for some protection to ordinary people, but it may also involve strict vigilance on individual's life and some restriction on his freedom.

TRENDS IN THE THIRD WORLD

The third world largely comprises developing countries. Mostly they are situated in Asia, Africa and Latin America. They achieved their independence from colonial domination at various points of time after the Second World War

(1939-45), although Latin American countries had attained formal independence in early nineteenth century. They were at different levels of 'underdevelopment' at the time of their respective independence. Different countries made progress at different rates. They are now at different levels of 'development'.

Most of the third world countries remained politically 'non-aligned' in the era of the 'cold war', but most of them have now been economically 'linked' with the developed world, thanks to the all-pervading process of 'globalization'. Some countries had independently adopted socialist path without seeking alignment with the second world. The collapse of socialism in the Eastern Europe and the former Soviet Union (1989-91) had a profound impact on their mode of thought. Thus, Albania, Yugoslavia, Mongolia and Yemen relinquished socialist systems on their own. China, Vietnam, North Korea and Cuba have retained socialist system as modified by adopting some features of market society. China—the largest and the most important among them—has shown keen interest in the process of liberalization and globalization.

China gained independence in 1949 and emerged as a big communist power. It did not join the communist camp, nor took interest in the 'non-aligned' movement. It always proclaimed itself to be a part of the third world although non-aligned nations viewed this claim with suspicion. It is true that China did not qualify as a superpower, yet as a country with one billion people—largest in any country of the world, bountiful natural resources, and nuclear hardware is, by any standard, a great power. Incidentally, India and Pakistan have also become nuclear powers although Pakistan's economic condition remains deplorable.

Economic division of the world was sought to be formalized by the Report of the Willy Brandt Commission, entitled *North-South: A Program for Survival* (1980). It introduced the idea of division of the world into two hemispheres: North, which was economically more advanced; and South, which was less developed. This division paved the way for evolving more meaningful relation between rich and poor countries. Issues like North-South dialogue and South-South cooperation came into prominence in pursuance of this idea. However, technically this division was not found correct. There are some well-to-do nations, like Australia and New Zealand, and even South Africa, *south* of the equator; and some poor nations, like India and the rest of South Asia (Pakistan, Bangladesh, Nepal, Sri Lanka, Bhutan, Maldives and Afghanistan), most of South-East Asia, the Caribbean, Central America, and the northern region of South America are in the *north*.

Now with the disintegration of the second world, and further disintegration of some members of the former second world, like Yugoslavia and Czechoslovakia, the category of poor countries is no longer confined to the third world. Again, there is a wide variety of levels of development. Some Middle Eastern countries have a higher per capita income than does the United

States. Then the first generation of countries like Taiwan, the Republic of Korea (South Korea), Singapore and Hong Kong (the 'Four Dragons') had penetrated Japanese and Western markets; and the second generation of these newly industrializing economies is likely to excel in the competition. (Of these, Hong Kong has merged with China since 1997). On the other end of the spectrum, sub-Saharan Africa is the most marginalized region of the world.

On political side, a large number of third world countries came under military rule because of their political, administrative and economic instability. It has been superseded by popular rule in most of those countries. At one time, most of Latin American countries were under military rule. But in late 1990s, democracy had been established in the entire region. However, in 2000, there were attempts at military *coups* in Ecuador and Venezuela which failed due to public apathy and international opposition. In Africa, Nigeria had a pretty long history of military rule. It returned to civilian rule in 1999. In Asia, Pakistan returned to military rule in 1999 followed by democratic elections in 2002. Military rulers in Myanmar (Burma) have been constantly evading handing over power to people's elected representatives. However, after a half century of military dictatorship, it started moving to democracy since 2012, but the army still lurks heavily in the shadows. Since early 2011, there have been mass uprisings in West Asia against rampant political corruption harboured by the autocratic rulers. By the end of 2011, old authoritarian regimes were smashed in Tunisia, Egypt and Libya, although establishment of full-fledged democracy in these countries may take some time. Syria is still in the grip of people's struggle against violation of human rights by a tyrannical regime.

Finally, ethnic bias and fundamentalist attitude, combined with the widespread frustration of the youth on economic front in several parts of the third world, have given rise to terrorism at a large scale, threatening many parts of the world. Destruction of the World Trade Centre at New York in 2001, involving hundreds of casualties, was one of the most heinous acts of terrorism. Third world countries will not only have to solve their economic problems but also ensure an end to exploitation of vulnerable sections of people both at national and international levels.

[VII]
SIGNIFICANCE OF CIVIL SOCIETY

In contemporary discourse, the term 'civil society' is used in two senses. In one sense, civil society comprises the social institutions like school, church, club, and other similar groups of citizens which serve as structures of legitimation of the state. These institutions largely lend support to the state. This meaning of civil society corresponds to Gramsci's view of its role in sustaining the capitalist system. In the second sense, civil society stands for a set of public interest organizations set up by some conscious citizens which make various demands on the state or launch social movements to mobilize ordinary citizens on the way to social reform. The state must respond promptly to their demands in order to ensure smooth functioning of society. The role of civil society in this sense has assumed special significance in recent years.

Present-day concept of civil society closely corresponds to Tocqueville's view on the role of 'intermediary voluntary associations'. Alexis de Tocqueville (1805-59), a French philosopher, in his celebrated work *Democracy in America* (1835-40), argued that with the dissolution of aristocracy in Europe, an alternative for the pluralist dispersion of power was urgently needed. In the medieval Europe, there were three centres of power: Clergy, Nobility and Commoners. Of these, Clergy and Nobility enjoyed substantial powers in their respective fields. Commoners could also make their voice heard at the decision-making level because of their large numbers. But with the coming of democracy, old centres of power had been destroyed. Power was now concentrating in the hands of majority. This led to the danger of 'tyranny of majority'.

> **When a nation abolishes aristocracy, centralization follows as a matter of course.**
>
> **Alexis de Tocqueville, *The Ancien Regime* (1856)**

In order to protect the freedom of citizens, Tocqueville suggested that a vigorous system of voluntary associations could act as counterweights to the state power. They could crystallize and publicize opinions and interests which would otherwise go unheard. Moreover, these associations could stimulate collective self-help rather than reliance on state initiative. They could draw people into cooperative ventures, breaking down their social isolation and making them aware of their wider social responsibilities. They could function as 'schools of democracy', instilling habits of civic virtue and public spirit into their members. In short, these associations would serve as an effective instrument of defence of individual liberty and encourage close cooperation between the citizens to solve their common problems. Tocqueville was an ardent champion of freedom of association. He earnestly hoped that free political parties and a free press would prove to be most effective among these voluntary associations. In the contemporary context, various humanitarian groups and non-governmental organizations (NGOs) could be added to this list.

> **What is understood by republican government in the United States is the slow and quiet action of society upon itself.**
>
> **Alexis de Tocqueville, *Democracy in America* (1835-40)**

Civil society is now regarded as an important organ of democratic society. It includes a wide range of associations and social movements which provide ample opportunities to the citizens to develop their capacities and express their varying interests and diverse identities. It creates an atmosphere where the citizens are able to enjoy some level of autonomy or independence from government control or influence. It promotes a moral sense of obligation among the citizens and motivates them to participate in civic causes. It discourages their dependence on the government for the solution of their common problems. Thus it serves as the true source of democratization.

In recent political discourse, the concept of civil society has been further refined. Jean L. Cohen and Andrew Arato, in their essay *Civil Society and Political Theory* (1992), have defined civil society as an area of public activity distinct from both the state and the market. This area involves a range of groups and associations, including families. In this sense, civil society is regarded to be essential for a healthy democratic society. It permits participation and communicative interaction of individuals. Cohen and Arato have argued that this field of social life is designed to supplement the political institutions of representative democracy rather than serve as a replacement thereof.

Paul Hirst, a British academic, in *Associative Democracy: New Forms of Economic and Social Governance* (1994), has visualized civil society as a set of voluntary associations which would be the primary bases of democracy. He has evolved a model of democracy in which self-governing associations would perform public functions. This arrangement would not only reduce the burden on the centralized state, but also curtail its power. According to this scheme, the associations of civil society would only supplement the representative democracy rather than replace it. However, the goals of democracy would be achieved primarily through these associations rather than through the centralized state. The role of the state would be reduced to supervising and regulating the voluntary associations of civil society.

Robert Putnam, an American social scientist, in his article 'Bowling Alone: America's Declining Social Capital' in *The Global Resurgence of Democracy,* edited by Larry Diamond and Marc F. Plattner (1998), has suggested that the associations of civil society can create 'social capital', *i.e.* a set of social practices which involve civic engagement and ideas of reciprocity. Putnam firmly believes that such a network of civic involvement is necessary for an effective democracy. However, he laments that in the past two or three decades the Americans have forgotten 'the art of pursuing in common the objects of common desires', which was recognized and admired by Alexis de Tocqueville. Putnam has pointed out that the present-day American society is characterized by a reduction in citizens' activity in the associations of civil society, with a consequent decline in the quality of American democracy.

In short, civil society is now regarded as the central theme of democratic debate. It is also viewed as a device of democratic action against the old-style communist systems that sought to monopolize all political power in the hands of one-party state. Indeed the communist governments in Eastern Europe had demobilized civil society so that rulers could directly control the individual. In 1960s and 1970s, it was realized that the institutions of civil society could not only be used to strengthen the authority of the ruling class, but the opposition could also use this device to promote its own viewpoint. Where the authority of the ruling class could not be challenged at the political level, there the hegemony of the rulers could be undermined through manipulation of education and culture.

In late 1970s and 1980s, the device of civil society was widely used in East European socialist countries as a weapon against the all-encompassing claims of the totalitarian state. The Solidarity movement in Poland sought to build up the institutions of civil society as a 'parallel society' with a view to safeguarding the interests of workers. In Bulgaria, an environmental group called *'Ecoglasnost'* raised the issue of the wanton destruction of natural resources and the appalling pollution in industrial centres. Since these centres were functioning under government control, *Ecoglasnost* proved to be an effective organ of civil society as the anti-government movement in Bulgaria. After the successful revolutions of 1989 throughout the Eastern Europe, the concept of civil society gained immense popularity. Western intellectuals also found the concept of civil society as instrumental to the revival of citizen participation in public affairs in democratic societies where it had recently declined. In fact, 'civil society movement' in the recent decades has emerged as an ally of 'new social movements'.

Totalitarian State

Totalitarian state is a state that seeks to regulate and control all aspects of life of its citizens—whether public or private. In other words, it seeks to direct all political, economic, social-cultural and intellectual activities of people towards fulfilling certain aims which are determined by the state itself. No citizen has the right or opportunity to oppose or criticize the state, or to propose any new aim.

New Social Movements

New social movements refer to a diverse set of popular movements in the contemporary world that are devoted to humanist objectives, and marked by a departure from the conventional methods of political organization and action. In advanced capitalist societies, these movements have centred around feminist, ecological, peace and anti-nuclear issues. In Africa, Asia and Latin America they have focused on wider issues including women's and human rights, environmental and social issues, and uplift of the downtrodden. New social movements seek to empower the common people and mobilize the institutions of civil society towards the achievement of their common goals without involving the state.

It is now increasingly realized that civil society can prove to be an effective instrument to counter the citizens' indifference towards their civic duties. Today the people seldom participate in political discussion; they are hardly interested in a well-reasoned criticism of the government. Under the circumstances, civil society movement can motivate them to take active interest in public affairs and freely articulate their opinions. This will strengthen democracy. The intellectuals of today wish to establish a vast network of voluntary associations, which would be independent from the state as well as from trade and industry. It is significant that such associations can flourish only in a democratic set-up where people have complete freedom of speech, association and assembly.

Civil society movement demands that the conduct of public affairs should not be allowed to be concentrated in the hands of bureaucracy. Instead the citizen participation in these affairs should be fully encouraged. Civil society alone can provide the people with a forum where they can articulate their criticism of government policy and action. Thus, civil society would prove to be an effective instrument of removing economic inequalities and securing social justice.

> **Civil society connotes those areas of social life—the domestic world, the economic sphere, cultural activities and political interaction—which are organized by private or voluntary arrangements between individuals and groups outside the *direct* control of the state.**
>
> **David Held, *Political Theory and the Modern State* (1989)**

A CRITICAL APPRAISAL

Some observers view civil society as an area where citizens are able to enjoy some level of autonomy or independence from the government. It is expected to promote an active citizenry to adopt a moral sense of obligation and participate in civic causes. When people are encouraged to form multiple voluntary associations, they have the opportunity to express themselves along with the competing viewpoints and perspectives. They can also find effective solution of their common problems through these associations. For cxample, after the 1985 Mexico City earthquake, the urban poor worked through neighbourhood organizations to force the government and the World Bank to alter their recovery plans. Similar civic action groups have been formed to fight crime and corruption in Mexico and Nigeria. In Nigeria, groups of youngmen known as 'area boys' have played an active role in handling civic problems. They have a widespread approval from the people who are fed up with government inaction.

However, civil society movement is not an unmixed blessing. Does it promote democracy at all levels? Some observers point out that some organs of civil society are themselves afflicted by *elitist* or *oligarchic* tendencies. Some self-styled civil society activists try to mobilize people after popular slogans, only to gain undue importance and wide publicity in the media. Then some manifestations of civil society itself can take highly 'uncivil' forms. For example, activities of the groups like Carapintada military leaders in Argentina, and the Inkatha in South Africa indicate the proliferation of 'uncivil movements' that promote exclusion and violence as a means of competing for and gaining power within a democratic system. Such groups use democratic language, institutions and strategies for achieving their undemocratic ends. In short, the enlightened groups within the civil society should not only keep a vigil over the state and its bureaucracy, they should also ensure that any group trying to fulfil its sinister designs by pretending to be the part of civil society, is not allowed to destroy the spirit of democracy.

Elitism

Elitism refers to a theory of organization which holds that the chosen few—endowed with extraordinary talent and the qualities of leadership—should exercise all decision-making power.

Oligarchy

Oligarchy refers to a pattern of organization in which the chosen few exercise all power, largely by means of their manipulative skills.

7

Concept of Sovereignty

[I] MEANING OF SOVEREIGNTY

WHAT IS SOVEREIGNTY?

Sovereignty is regarded as an essential element of the state. The term 'sovereignty' is derived from the Latin word *superanus* meaning supreme. In the present context, sovereignty refers to supremacy or supreme power of the state. In what sense is the state regarded supreme or superior to other associations?

At the outset, it may be noted that sovereignty is primarily a legal concept. It denotes supremacy of the state primarily in the legal sphere. J.W. Garner, in his *Introduction to Political Science* (1910), had defined sovereignty as that 'characteristic of the state by virtue of which it cannot be legally bound except by its own will or limited by any other power than itself'. All classical definitions of sovereignty focus on supremacy of the state in the legal sense. All objections about sovereignty arise when this concept is shifted from the legal and juristic domain to other spheres such as moral, political, and sociological.

The basic idea is that the sovereign—be it a monarch, chief executive or an assembly—is able to declare law, issue commands and take political decisions (*i.e.* determining public goals and their priorities) which are binding on all individuals and associations within its jurisdiction. The sovereign commands physical force to punish those who ignore or disobey his orders or decisions. He issues laws, commands and decisions at his own will, not with the approval or consent of any other individual or association. Sovereignty, in its pure form, is more befitting a monarch than an assembly or a constitutional set-up but in actual practice we may refer to sovereignty of Parliament or sovereignty of the People of a state so long as it is accepted as a universal characteristic of the state. Moreover, supreme legal authority of the state can best be established through the concept of sovereignty itself.

In fact, sovereignty arms the state with supreme legal authority in both internal and external spheres. Internally, it establishes supremacy of the state over all individuals and associations as well as the territory under its control; externally, it upholds independence of the state from the control or interference of any other state or any other agency in the conduct of its international relations. Theoretically, each sovereign state is equal to every other in international law, regardless of its population, area or economic resources. The United Nations Charter states that the United Nations 'is based on the principle of the sovereign equality of all its Members' and recognizes a sphere of 'domestic jurisdiction' which is to be reserved to each member state.

International Law

International law refers to a set of general principles and specific rules which are duly recognized by the members of the international community in their dealing with each other. International law is primarily concerned with the regulation of their mutual relations, peaceful settlement of their disputes, and the rights of belligerent as well as neutral nations during the times of war.

Since the concept of sovereignty attributes supreme power to the will of the sovereign, it is by nature an absolute, unlimited and perpetual power. This may, however, *not* be interpreted as an *arbitrary* power. The absolute power implied by sovereignty is not intended to be exercised without reason or without invoking one's conscience or sense of justice or without regard to prevalent customs, social values, ideals or necessity of the common interest or public interest. Due regard to all these factors has to be given, otherwise the legitimacy and authority of the sovereign power will be rapidly eroded and sovereignty may eventually be lost. The idea behind the absolute nature of sovereignty is that, legally speaking, the sovereign is not obliged to consult or seek the approval of any other individual or group whether a particular decision, command or law is right or wrong. He is empowered to decide all such issues at his own will and discretion, and his decisions will be binding on all unless he himself chooses to revoke them.

Legitmacy

Legitimacy refers to the quality of an act or arrangement which is regarded as lawful by those affected by it. In other words, they regard it reasonable and beneficial for themselves as well as for the larger society.

HISTORICAL DEVELOPMENT

In fact, the modern theory of the state was perfected only when the concept of sovereignty was introduced into it. Jean Bodin, a French writer of the sixteenth century, was the first to formulate the concept of sovereignty systematically. Although in ancient days Aristotle had talked of supreme power located in different bodies according to the form of government, he had not given the idea of sovereignty because, in his view, the power of the ruler or ruling body was restricted by law which existed above them. Conditions in the Middle Ages were not favourable to the development of the concept of sovereignty because the emperor's power was limited on the one side by the rights of the feudal lords, and on the other side by the claims of the Pope to superior authority. The idea of sovereignty made its appearance with the dawn of the modern period. Towards the end of the medieval period a number of causes combined to create new political ideas. The feudal nobles were weakened by the Crusades and by their own quarrels. Commerce and the growth of towns destroyed their monopoly of wealth; new methods of warfare destroyed their military supremacy. Taking advantage of their weakness, the king increased his power and importance until he became supreme in the state.

Besides, the ruling monarchs of national states like England and France had achieved a degree of unification and centralization of authority never attained before, so that they freed themselves from the control of the Pope as well. Thus, the ground had been prepared for the development of the theory of sovereignty. Jean Bodin, who held Henry III, King of France, in highest esteem, became the chief exponent of this theory.

JEAN BODIN

Jean Bodin (1530-96), French philosopher, defined sovereignty as 'the absolute and perpetual power of commanding in a state', as the 'supreme power over citizens and subjects unrestrained by law'. Thus, Bodin places the sovereign above law, because he himself is the source of law. This view marked a significant departure from the medieval outlook. The medieval world conceived law as part of the universal and eternal order. Kings, councils and judges who enforced law were themselves under law. They were not empowered to create it. It could only be discovered by a study of custom and precedent. The idea of the state as a source of law was alien to medieval thought.

Bodin sought to reverse this position by making the sovereign himself the source of all law. Defining the state as an aggregation of families and their common possessions ruled by a sovereign power and by reason, Bodin argued that in every independent community governed by law there must be some authority, whether residing in one person or several, whereby the laws themselves are established and from which they proceed.

Bodin treated the sovereign above law but not above duty and moral responsibility. He imposed two important limitations on the powers of the sovereign: (*a*) firstly, there are some fundamental laws (such as, the Salic law of France, which excluded females from dynastic succession); the sovereign could not lawfully abrogate such laws; and (*b*) secondly, private property, being granted by the natural law or the law of nature, was inviolable; therefore, the sovereign could not tax his subjects without their consent.

> **Natural Law**
>
> Natural law refers to a set of rules of good conduct which exist independently of conventional law. These are directly derived from nature which can be discovered through moral intuition and by the application of human faculty of reasoning. Champions of natural law regard it as the source of all law as also superior to any other law.

HUGO GROTIUS

After about half a century of Bodin's enunciation of the theory of sovereignty, Hugo Grotius (1583-1645), Dutch jurist, widely known as the father of international law, made an important contribution to the concept of sovereignty. He brought out the implications of sovereignty of the state in the international sphere, *i.e.* independence of the sovereign state from foreign control. Grotius sought to build a system of international law on two distinct foundations: (*a*) Nations are subject to natural law or 'the dictate of right reason' in the same manner as citizens because the society of nations is formed on the same fundamental moral principles which guide the behaviour of men in society; and (*b*) Grotius recognized a 'voluntary' law of nations based upon their free consent, whether explicit as expressed in treaties and conventions, or implicit as expressed in usages and customs.

Thus, Grotius, like Bodin, attributed moral responsibility to sovereignty, but he extended it to the external sphere also. In the second place, he made it clear that nations respected international law not because it curtailed their sovereignty, but because they voluntarily chose to do so, of their free consent. In this way, Grotius introduced the idea of external sovereignty to the existing idea of internal sovereignty, and thus gave it a fuller shape.

THOMAS HOBBES

In the seventeenth century, Thomas Hobbes (1588-1679), English political thinker, further developed the concept of sovereignty. As an exponent of the theory of the social contract, Hobbes argued that the state was the product of the will of the people. Sovereignty is an attribute of the state; its character is determined by the terms of the social contract.

As men emerge from the state of nature—characterized by law of the jungle—and form a state to attain order, peace and security, they create a sovereign for this purpose. They surrender all their natural rights—the right of the stronger to oppress the weaker—to the sovereign. The surrender is complete, final and irrevocable. How can they ask for restoration of their natural rights once they have become civilized men! Defying the authority of the sovereign would mean reversion to the state of nature, the state of anarchy, law of the jungle, where the stronger will be free to oppress the weaker. Hobbes, therefore, places authority of the sovereign beyond challenge.

Hobbes's chief contribution to the theory of sovereignty consists in adding an element of legitimacy to authority of the sovereign, because be held: (*a*) that the sovereign is the product of the will of the people; and (*b*) that the sovereign enjoys his supreme authority for its functional value, that is by virtue of providing order, peace and security in place of anarchy and oppression.

John Locke (1632-1704), another English exponent of the theory of the social contract, did not concede absolute sovereignty of the state. He thought that the supreme power in society was held by the people which came into existence before the formation of the state. The natural rights comprising the right to life, liberty and property were retained by the people and the state was created for the protection of these vital rights. Ruler or government could not possess the power to abrogate these rights.

JEAN-JACQUES ROUSSEAU

In the eighteenth century, Jean-Jacques Rousseau (1712-78), French exponent of the theory of the social contract, made an important contribution to the theory of sovereignty, by introducing the doctrine of popular sovereignty. While Hobbes had created a sovereign apart from the people, Rousseau made the people themselves sovereign. In his opinion, the social contract was concluded between the people in their individual capacity on the one hand, and the people in their corporate capacity on the other. According to this line of argument, when people surrender their natural liberty in their individual capacity, sovereignty is retained by the people themselves in their corporate capacity, represented by the *general will*, while their *actual will* is subordinated to their *real will*. Rousseau, therefore, suggested that sovereignty belongs to the people; it could be exercised only in an assembly of the whole people. Government is but an agent of the *general will* which reigns supreme. In other words, a government cannot logically claim to hold sovereignty. Rousseau maintained that sovereignty is absolute and unlimited because the supreme direction and control of the *general will* is accepted by the people unconditionally in the interests of their freedom. Rousseau believed that man's freedom lies in obeying the dictates of the *general will* even if he feels constrained. That is why he quipped that 'man can be forced to be free'.

> **General Will**
>
> According to Jean-Jaques Rousseau (1712-78), French philosopher, the *general will* refers to the point of convergence of the real will of all members of a community. It reflects the true good of each individual as well as the common good of the whole community. Man realizes his freedom by submitting his particular will to the direction of the *general will*.

JEREMY BENTHAM

Jeremy Bentham (1748-1832), famous English Utilitarian, argued that sovereignty was not limited by law, but was subject to moral limitations. Bentham maintained that sovereignty was limited by the possibility of resistance, and there were conditions under which resistance was morally justified. He, therefore, insisted that the sovereign should justify his authority by useful legislation with the object of promoting the *greatest happiness of the greatest numbers.*

JOHN AUSTIN

In the nineteenth century, the legal notion of sovereignty was brought to its logical conclusion by John Austin (1790-1859), English jurist. He is regarded as the greatest exponent of the *monistic* theory of sovereignty. In his *Province of Jurisprudence Determined* (1832), Austin observed:

> If a determinate human superior, not in the habit of obedience to a like superior, receives habitual obedience from the bulk of a given society, that determinate superior is sovereign in that society, and that society (including the superior) is a society political and independent.

Austin's theory of sovereignty was influenced by the then prevailing conditions in England. The early Utilitarians had sought to remove the anomalies of the common law by subordinating it to a superior law which consisted in the universal and permanent dictates of natural reason; the state could neither ignore nor abrogate that superior law. Repudiating these arguments, Austin advanced his theory of *positive law* which expressed the will of the legal sovereign of the state and hence not bound by the dictates of *natural law* or any other superior law. Austin sought to define law as the command of the sovereign, obliging the subjects to do or refrain from doing, certain acts; failure to obey the law being visited by penalty. Thus, he identified the following characteristics of law: (*a*) It must emanate from a determinate source, that is the sovereign, to be clearly located in the state; (*b*) it must be the expression of the command of the sovereign; and (*c*) it must be backed by sanctions. In other words, disobedience to law must be punishable.

Positive Law

Positive law refers to the law that expresses the will of the sovereign, and that is duly enacted by a legislative body and recognized by the judiciary. Positive law is binding on all those coming within its jurisdiction, and its violation is effectively met with punishment. Positive law is judged by its legal validity, and not by its conformity to morals, customs or conventions unless these are enshrined in the body of law itself.

These characteristics are peculiar to the positive law of the state, not to be found in natural law, custom or religious commandments. Thus, natural law, or for that matter any superior law, is not law in the proper sense of the term. Accordingly, in case a positive law enforced by the state comes into conflict with the natural law or religious commandments, etc., the former must prevail. In this way Austin established supremacy of the power, authority and commands of the sovereign beyond doubt. He maintained that any rights of the citizens, including the right to property, were nothing but concessions granted by the sovereign. The subjects could have no legal right against the state.

By establishing a single source of all positive law, Austin put forward a *monistic* view of law, state and sovereignty. It is significant that Austin's theory solely dwells on the *legal* character of sovereignty; it does not repudiate moral or social limitations on the power of the state. He does not declare the state as a 'perfect embodiment of reason' as the idealist theory had maintained. Austin is an exponent of absolute and unlimited sovereignty purely from the *legal* or *formal* point of view. He admits that sovereign authority habitually observes fundamental moral principles though not legally bound by any external authority. He does not envisage an irresponsible sovereign, but holds that the sovereign cannot be formally made responsible to any authority similar to himself; his authority is legally superior to all individuals and groups within his jurisdiction.

[II] CHARACTERISTICS OF SOVEREIGNTY

Viewed as a purely legal concept, sovereignty may be identified by the following characteristics—absoluteness, permanence, universality, inalienability and indivisibility.

ABSOLUTENESS

Jean Bodin, the first exponent of sovereignty, said: 'Sovereignty is the absolute and perpetual power... of commanding in a state'. Sovereignty is regarded as absolute because it cannot be limited or restricted by any superior power or authority. The will of the sovereign reigns supreme in the state. The sovereign may, of his own will, pay due regard to moral principles, customs and traditions or public opinion, but he is not responsible to any authority—individual or group—similar or superior to himself. Similarly, the sovereign may pay due regard to international law by his free consent, not because he is obliged to obey the commands of any superior state or international organization.

Absoluteness of sovereignty is the logical outcome of its legal character, which may not hold good in the political sphere, nor would it govern the non-legal actions of the individuals and groups within the state.

PERMANENCE

Permanence of sovereignty is the corollary of its absoluteness. Bodin describes sovereignty as perpetual power because, 'if power be held only for a certain time (it does not matter how long a time), it is not a sovereign power, and he who holds it for that time is not a sovereign'.

In order to understand the permanence of sovereignty, it is necessary to distinguish between the state and government. Theoretically, sovereignty belongs to the state. Governments may bc formed and dissolved according to the established procedure, but the continuity of the state will not be affected by such changes. As such, sovereignty endures as long as the state maintains its independence. The quality of permanence should not be interpreted to mean that sovereignty is eternal. On the other hand, if a state loses its independence and is placed under the suzerainty of another state, its sovereignty is also lost.

UNIVERSALITY

Sovereignty is a universal, all-pervasive or all-comprehensive quality in the sense that it extends to all individuals, groups, areas and things within the jurisdiction of the state. If a state grants immunity or ex-territoriality to any category of persons, especially foreign heads of states, U.N. officials, foreign envoys, ambassadors, their staff, residence and vehicles, etc., it is because of its free consent, not because of any external obligation or restriction. In other words, it is a matter of international courtesy, not of compulsion. This concession can be withdrawn at any moment at the will of the sovereign.

International associations and multinational corporations operating within the territories of different states are also subject to the sovereignty of the respective states.

INALIENABILITY

As an essential element of the state, sovereignty cannot be transferred or given away without destroying the state itself. As Lieber has put it: "Sovereignty can no more be alienated than a tree can alienate its right to sprout or a man can transfer his life and personality without self-destruction." When a state cedes a portion of its territory to another state, the ceding state is not wholly destroyed. But from the point of view of the ceded portion, the original state no longer exists, and sovereignty of a new state comes into existence. This also proves that the sovereignty of a state over any area is not transferred but replaced by another state.

According to Hobbes, when people emerge from the state of nature, they create a sovereign. It is not a case of sovereignty being transferred from people to the sovereign, because in the state of nature sovereignty did not exist at all. When Locke postulates surrender of some of the natural rights of the people to the state on the condition that their fundamental natural rights to 'life, liberty, and property' shall be protected, it is not a question of transfer of sovereignty, because the people themselves remain supreme throughout, in spite of the formation of the state. In Rousseau's system of thought sovereignty is throughout held by the *general will,* although powers may be delegated to the government; hence, sovereignty proves to be inalienable.

INDIVISIBILITY

As sovereignty is an absolute power, it cannot be divided between or shared by different sets of individuals or groups. In every state, sovereignty must be vested in a single body, legally competent to issue the final commands. Division of sovereignty is bound to give rise to inconsistent, conflicting and ambiguous commands. This condition is not compatible with the very concept of sovereignty. In other words, a divided sovereignty is a contradiction in terms.

The principle of the federal state is usually cited as an exception to this characteristic of sovereignty. Federalism involves the allocation of powers between the federal (central or union) government and state governments which are regarded as independent and coordinate in their respective spheres. A.L. Lowell, an American writer, argued that 'there can exist within the same territories two sovereigns issuing commands to the same subjects touching different matters'. The Supreme Court of America also declared in one case that 'the United States are sovereign as to all the powers of government actually surrendered by the states, while each state in the union is sovereign as to all powers reserved'. We, in India, are no less familiar with federal government. We have legislatures and cabinets in the states besides the Union Parliament and the Cabinet. The subjects of legislation are divided into the Union List, State List and Concurrent List. Unlike the USA, however, in India the Union and the States are governed by a single constitution and residuary subjects of legislation are assigned to the Union. The main features of federal states in other countries are more or less similar.

This paradox can be resolved by making a distinction between 'sovereignty' and 'power' in the legal sense. Power emanates from sovereignty. Sovereignty rests in the state; power is assigned to the government. Sovereignty is supposed to be exercised by the state; power is exercised by the different organs of government—legislative, executive and judicial. The pattern of exercise of power depends on the nature of organization of the government. We describe states as 'unitary' and 'federal' because of different patterns of organization of their governments. Properly speaking, these are the forms of government, not the forms of state. In a unitary government, power is divided between a single set of legislature, executive and judiciary. On the other hand, a federal government involves various sets of such organs. Thus, the federal system represents an extension of the principle of division of powers between the organs of the federal and state governments. All of them combined together constitute a single state with a single sovereignty—absolute, perpetual, all-pervasive, inalienable and indivisible. The division of powers can be evolved or altered from time to time but sovereignty remains intact so long as the state maintains its independent existence. In the international sphere, too, the state continues to be regarded as one entity—single and indivisible—whatever its form of government and consequent division of powers.

It is again important to note that all these characteristics are peculiar to the legal notion of sovereignty. They are best represented by an absolute monarchy. In the actual working of the state—especially in the case of a democratic, federal, pluralist and constitutional government—it becomes extremely difficult to discover the seat or real character of sovereignty.

[III]
ASPECTS OF SOVEREIGNTY

Sovereignty is primarily a legal concept. However, in actual practice, sovereignty may take different forms under different conditions which are described as different aspects of sovereignty.

TITULAR SOVEREIGNTY

In constitutional monarchies, such as England and Japan, the Queen, the King or the Emperor is officially referred to as the sovereign. Such a ruler is only a nominal or titular head of state, without any real powers which are vested in different organs of the government according to the constitution of the state. This form of sovereignty is, therefore, called titular sovereignty.

DE JURE AND *DE FACTO* SOVEREIGNTY

In the case of revolutions, that is a successful overthrow of the existing regime in a state through unconstitutional means—that is not by the established procedure of replacing the existing government—a distinction arises between the formal and actual position. Thus, till such time as the new sovereign is legally established and recognized, there may exist two sovereigns—one in the legal sense who has lost his real powers; the other in the factual sense who has not yet been legally established. Under such circumstances, the legal or formal sovereign is said to retain *de jure* sovereignty while the actual sovereign comes to hold *de facto* sovereignty. This state of affairs can only continue temporarily because it is marked by uncertainty, confusion and irregularity. Some historical examples of the emergence of *de Jacto* sovereignty are—the authority exercised by Cromwell (1653-58) in England, by Napoleon (1799-1804) in France, and the Bolshevist group in Russia after 1917. The military dictatorships of the present-day world, established after a *coup d'etat,* also represent *de facto* sovereignty until they evolve suitable means to legitimize their authority. *De facto* sovereignty is so described because in actual practice its commands are obeyed by the people, either because of sheer force or a strong following among the people.

Some writers, including John Austin, refuse to draw a distinction between *de jure* and *de facto* sovereignty. They argue that adjectives like 'lawful' and 'unlawful' cannot be applied to the term sovereignty as it becomes meaningless without legal sanction. It would, therefore, be more logical if the terms *de facto* and *de jure* are applied only to government, not to sovereignty. The *de jure* sovereignty alone is sovereignty in the real sense of the term. The so-called *de facto* sovereignty remains inconsequential until it achieves the status of *de jure* sovereignty.

A CRITICAL APPRAISAL

The concept of sovereignty was evolved to bring the theory of the modern state to its logical conclusion. It sought to free the modern state from obligations towards other social institutions, particularly the authority of feudal lords and the papacy, and to establish the dignity of the state in the international sphere. Thus, the theory of sovereignty proclaimed the monopoly of the state in deciding public policy and declaring the law that binds all citizens in unequivocal terms. It instituted the nation-state as an independent entity in the international sphere, not bound by any organization superior to itself. In short, sovereignty armed the state with supreme authority in its internal as well as external affairs.

As a legal notion, sovereignty constitutes an essential element of the legal character of the state. In fact, the state cannot perform its function of regulating the life of its citizens unless it is equipped with supreme authority. The logic of the legal character of sovereignty postulates that it has to be absolute, permanent, universal, inalienable and indivisible. In the legal sphere, therefore, sovereignty cannot be held responsible to any human superior. When we say that the sovereign is not bound by any moral principles or international obligations except at his own will, it is only intended to emphasize that the sovereign cannot be subordinated to any other human agency for interpretation of such obligations.

But in the sphere of actual practice, all authority postulates responsibility. Sovereignty, being supreme authority, postulates highest responsibility. Theoretically, we may evolve the image of a perfect sovereign and thus justify him exercising supreme authority. But in the real world, sovereignty has to be vested in human beings who, being mortals, are as imperfect as any other human beings. When the authority of a mortal human sovereign is proclaimed to be absolute, perpetual, beyond any responsibility or obligation, it leads to socially disastrous consequences—the most cruel and degenerate forms of autocracy, tyranny and authoritarianism, untold oppression inside the state and more destructive wars outside.

To straighten the issue. it is imperative to draw a distinction between the state and the government so that sovereignty is always regarded as an attribute of the state—conceived as an abstract idea—while the government consisting of human beings, whatever their wisdom or excellence of character, is only assigned definite powers, to be exercised through an established procedure with inbuilt checks and safeguards. This is necessary so that no organ of the government is able to become omnipotent. This would imply a *departure from the original concept of sovereignty* which sought to vest sovereignty in a 'determinate person or body of persons'. This would mean a constitutional government. Only this kind of government can be expected to function in a responsible manner and deliver the goods, especially in the present age of democracy when the people are claimed to be the real sovereign—'the sovereign without crown'.

Constitutional Government

Constitutional government refers to a type of government in which powers of governance (legislative, executive and judicial powers) are exercised by those who are appointed through the prescribed procedure, in a prescribed manner and under regular legal and political restraints as provided by a constitution. A constitution in this context denotes a set of rules, procedures, practices and conventions which prescribe structures, functions, powers and responsibilities of different organs of government, the procedure of their formation, working and dissolution; relation between the state and its citizens, etc.

Constitutional government is characterized by the supremacy of law which implies that both public authorities and citizens are equally subject to law and the constitution; all citizens are entitled to equal protection of the laws and they have free access to political and judicial channels for communicating their demands and the redressal of their grievances. In short, a constitutional government stands for a limited, responsive and responsible government. Its principal objective is to secure liberty and justice for the people.

[IV] CONCEPT OF POPULAR SOVEREIGNTY

WHAT IS POPULAR SOVEREIGNTY?

Sovereignty is primarily a legal concept. The legal sovereign is supposed to be absolute and omnipotent, functioning solely according to his own judgement and will—right or wrong. He can ignore and override any other considerations—prescriptions of divine law or natural law, principles of morality, dictates of public opinion, etc. According to the classical theory, legal sovereignty is vested in the 'determinate person or body of persons'. It is definitely organized, precise and recognized as the source of law. It represents the will of the state and its commands are legally binding. Its disobedience is visited by penalties. It is the source of all rights in society. It is absolute, unlimited and supreme.

In the political sphere, the concept of legal sovereignty is fit for application to absolute monarchy. It is significant that Jean Bodin and John Austin—the chief exponents of legal sovereignty—had built their theories in the context of absolute monarchies. This sort of situation does not create problems of inconsistency between theory and practice. However, as we move to other forms of government, we are faced with the dilemma of reconciling the idea of legal sovereignty with the actual powers of the sovereign body. That is why A.C. Dicey (*An Introduction to the Study of the Law of Constitution*; 1885) observes: "Behind the sovereign which the lawyer recognizes there is another sovereign to whom the legal sovereign must bow." This another sovereign is described by Dicey as the political sovereign.

Absolute Monarchy

Absolute monarchy refers to a form of government in which all powers of governance are held by a single person — king, queen, or any other royal personage who reigns over the country. Powers of the ruler are not bounded by any rival source of authority, such as custom, precedent, natural law, divine law, common law or judicial interpretations of law. The ruler exercises absolute powers by virtue of his personal authority or his own interpretation of custom, natural law or divine law, etc. This system is opposed to the concept of constitutional government.

When political sovereign comprises all members of a community, *i.e.* the people, the idea of its supreme legal authority is expressed as 'popular sovereignty'. In other words, the idea of popular sovereignty regards people as the source of all authority in the state. In its view, the organs of state which exercise supreme power of law-making, law-enforcement and adjudication, draw their legitimacy from the will of the people. It does not rely on any superior law–natural law, religious commandments or any other authority—to ascertain what is right or wrong. It does not look for any source of 'superior reason' apart from the mind of the people. Thus, it regards people themselves, in their corporate capacity, as the embodiment of reason, the best judges of right and wrong, and hence the real source of supreme authority. This doctrine comprises the cornerstone of the classical theory of democracy.

HISTORICAL DEVELOPMENT

Jean-Jaques Rousseau (1712-78) is regarded the chief exponent of the doctrine of popular sovereignty. However, its early indications may be found in ancient as well as medieval political thought. Marcus Tullius Cicero (106-43 B.C.), ancient Roman philosopher, postulated that the ultimate source of political authority may be traced to the aggregate people of a state. However, when Roman Empire became very powerful, it was conceded that will of the Emperor was the source of validity of law.

Medieval European thought regarded God as the source of all authority. Pope was his representative on earth. In the final phase of the medieval age, Marsiglio of Padua (1275-1343), Italian philosopher, sought to challenge the absolute authority of Pope in order to restore the authority of the people. In the medieval

Europe, it was believed that temporal rulers should submit themselves to papacy not only in ecclesiastical matters but also in temporal matters. On the contrary, Marsiglio in his *Defensor Pacis* (1324) tried to prove that papacy and clergy should submit themselves to the whole people not only in temporal matters but also in spiritual matters. Marsiglio described the principle of supreme authority of the people as 'republicanism'. He argued that the powers of the priesthood should be confined to the administration of the sacraments and the teaching of divine law, but even in these functions priests should be regulated and controlled by the people and their elected government. He held that the priesthood itself should be elected by the people of each community rather than being appointed by Pope who was chosen by an oligarchy. The principle of legitimacy required that Pope himself should be elected by the whole of Christendom.

In early modern age, Johannes Althusius (1557-1638), German jurist, also indicated the idea of popular sovereignty in his own way. He conceived of sovereignty as the supreme power of performing those acts which are necessary for the material and spiritual welfare of the members of a state. In his view, the state is the product of a contract or consent of the people. Hence, the state must exercise sovereignty to secure welfare of its members. In essence, sovereignty resides in all the members of a state although it may be exercised by a particular body from time to time. Since people themselves cannot perform the functions of the state directly, they delegate these functions to their representatives. Still the final authority implied by sovereignty remains with the people themselves. In other words, the rulers in a democracy are required to function under the ultimate control of the people.

ROUSSEAU'S CONCEPT OF THE GENERAL WILL

Rousseau's concept of the general will gives best expression to the idea of popular sovereignty. Thomas Hobbes (1588-1679) had created a sovereign authority apart from the people. Rousseau created a sovereign out of the people themselves. Hobbes made sovereignty an instrument of serving self-interest of the individual; Rousseau made it an instrument of serving the common good. Rousseau justified his doctrine of popular sovereignty on moral grounds.

At the outset it may be noted that Rousseau's idea of the will cannot be separated from thought. He makes a distinction between the will of the individual, *i.e.* the *particular will* and the will of the community, *i.e.* the *general will.* Particular will may either be inclined towards general will, or it may turn against it. When an individual is motivated by his momentary self-interest disregarding the interest of others, he is acting against the general will. It is called his 'actual will'. For example, when an individual wants to jump red light on a crossing, he is acting on actual will. On the contrary, when he decides to follow all traffic rules strictly, he tends to act in the common interest, *i.e.* according to the general will; then he is acting on his 'real will'. In other words, real will involves 'self-discipline' in the interest of the community. It also serves the individual's real and long-term interest which cannot be separated from the common interest. Actual will reflects an individual's lower self; real will reflects his higher self.

When different individuals act on their actual will, their interests would clash with each other because everybody would be acting on his momentary self-interest. It may be followed by disastrous consequences. For instance, when people want to jump red light on a crossing, it may result in accident. But when they act on their real will, there is little possibility of their clash. When all are self-disciplined, there will be a smooth flow of traffic. It will ensure safety of one and all. When an individual is acting on actual will, he is not only acting against the interest of the community, but also acting against his own real interest, or against his true 'freedom'. When he is prevented from acting in that way, he may feel constrained, but he is not being deprived of his 'freedom' in the real sense of the term. That is why Rousseau quips: "A man can be forced to be free." When people act on their actual will, they are bound to have differences. But when they act on their real will, their differences would disappear. They would start thinking alike. As the proverb goes: "All wise men think alike." General will is, therefore, harmonious. It reflects the real will of all members of the community. It is described as the point of convergence of the real will of all members of the community.

Genesis of the General Will

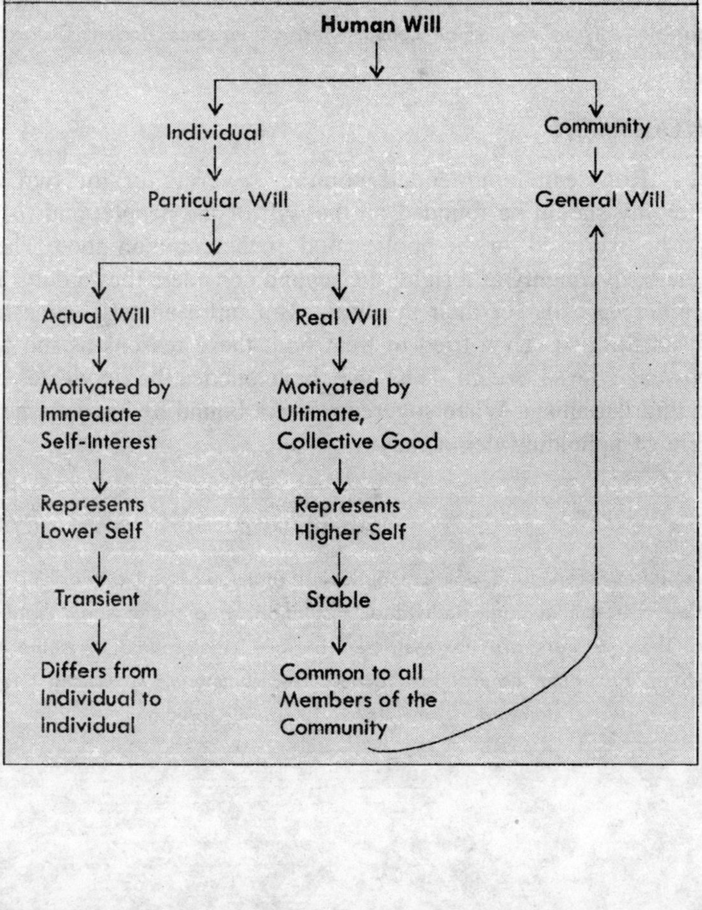

Rousseau's concept of popular sovereignty stands for the supreme authority of the general will in a society. Since general will is reflected in the higher self of each member of the community, it is morally superior to any other expression of will. Sovereignty of the general will would ensure the rule of the right reason in society which would be constantly devoted to the common good. General will is elevated to the position of an absolute, unlimited and inalienable sovereignty because it reflects the common will of all right-thinking people.

The concept of popular sovereignty does not rely on any principle of higher law, *e.g.* natural law, divine law or divine revelation, but regards the organized power of the people as the source of all reason to determine what is right or wrong. It therefore embodies the best expression of the principle of classical democracy. However, it is suitable only for a small and uniform community, preferably for 'direct democracy' as Rousseau himself conceded. In the contemporary large and complex societies where 'representative democracy' is inevitable, it can only be accepted for its symbolic significance.

Direct Democracy

Direct democracy refers to a system of governance in which all public decisions are taken by the general body of citizens at their regular meetings. It is feasible only in very small communities, as in some ancient Greek city-states.

CONCLUSION

Indeed, Rousseau commended popular sovereignty for two reasons: (*a*) Sovereignty should be founded on the will of the people; and (*b*) Sovereignty should be exercised for the public good or the common good. The first reason considers sovereignty as a right; the second considers it as a duty. The principle of democracy calls for their synthesis. But unfortunately, some thinkers have confused the two. They tried to treat both these reasons as the foundation of the power of the sovereign. Thus, they have opened the floodgates of absolutism and authoritarianism. When sovereign is not bound by his duty, he is no longer capable of upholding democracy.

Absolutism

Absolutism refers to a political outlook that requires all powers of governance to be vested in a single individual, institution, or a set of some rigid standards, etc. These powers are not restricted by any rival source of authority, such as custom, precedent, natural law, divine law, common law, judicial interpretations of law, public demand or the force of public opinion.

Authoritarianism

Authoritarianism refers to a political outlook or attitude that requires everybody or everything to conform to an established order enshrined in customary practices or a set of beliefs. It subordinates all concerned to a person or a group which is regarded as the guardian of that order.

In practical politics, distinction must be drawn between the 'state' and 'government'. The principle of popular sovereignty may be invoked to concede sovereignty of the state which is an abstract entity. But government is comprised of human beings who are fallible in spite of their best education and training. If sovereignty is attributed to government, even if it is elected by the people, the possibility of its misuse cannot be ruled out. As Aristotle had warned: 'power and virtue cannot coexist.' Democracy can function only with a 'constitutional government' which implies the existence of effective checks on the power-holders.

Again, Rousseau has not drawn a clear distinction between 'will' and 'reason'. Reason is mainly concerned with the questions of 'right' and 'wrong'. Will is supposed to be neutral. Reason deals with complex questions which are subject to prolonged debate. Will is a simple matter which can be ascertained empirically. It is the crux of liberal theory. The questions of 'superior will' and 'inferior will' drag it into the field of reason. Thus it enters the realm of idealist theory which is often invoked in support of absolutism. In short, Rousseau's philosophy must be taken with a note of caution.

Idealist Theory

Idealist theory refers to the theory of state chiefly advanced by G.W.F. Hegel (1770-1831), German philosopher, which eulogizes the state as embodiment of *Reason* and holds that individual's freedom lies in accepting the dictates of the ideal state. This theory proves disastrous when an existing government is allowed to exercise authority of the ideal state without questioning the character of the persons who form that particular government.

8

Pluralist Theory of Sovereignty

THE CLASSICAL THEORY OF sovereignty, as enunciated by various thinkers from Jean Bodin (1530-96) to John Austin (1790-1859), largely dealt with the legal character of sovereignty. It held sovereignty as absolute, perpetual, universal, inalienable and indivisible. It envisaged a single sovereign in the state—a person or a body of persons. It is, therefore, described as the *monistic* theory of sovereignty.

When this monistic theory is applied to the political field, it gives rise to many problems. In the political sphere, the state is represented by government which claims sovereignty on behalf of the state. When the relationship between individual and the state is defined in terms of sovereignty, it postulates the *unlimited* authority of the state over individual which implies *unlimited* political obligation. In other words, the idea of the supreme, absolute and unlimited authority of the state reduces individuals to the status of dumb-driven cattle who have to follow the dictates of the state. In actual practice, these dictates are issued by the government consisting of human beings who may be wise or foolish, benevolent or selfish, virtuous or vicious—but in no case perfect, divine and infallible. Thus, the theory of sovereignty in the political sphere implies complete subordination of one set of individuals to another set of similar individuals. The pluralist theory of sovereignty seeks to resolve this dilemma.

[I]
GENESIS OF THE PLURALIST THEORY

The form of sovereignty as developed from Jean Bodin to John Austin was generally regarded as an essential attribute of the modern state till the nineteenth century. Accordingly, it was almost universally admitted that the state is superior to all other human associations in society because sovereignty is exclusive to the state. This implied supreme legal authority of the state. In essence, it coincided with the organic theory of the state which glorified the state as the fountain of all moral and social values. The juristic theory went to the extent of evolving a juristic *personality* of the state.

Organic Theory of the State

In this metaphorical expression, the state is compared to an organism or a living body, and individuals are regarded as its organs. An individual separated from the state loses his existence and identity like an organ severed from the body.

However, the socialists—especially, Marx and Engels—had demonstrated in the nineteenth century itself, how the economic interests of the dominant class exclusively determined the policy of the state. The rise of capitalism combined with the theory of the absolute state posed a real threat to freedom in society. Many a thinker expressed serious concern at this state of affairs.

J.N. Figgis (*Churches in the Modern State;* 1913) saw clearly that the ascendance of the absolute state in his own day was directly linked to 'the horror of that very economic and industrial oppression which is the distinctive gift of modern capitalism to history'. Besides, in the twentieth century, there was an all-round development of social sciences which promoted new theories regarding the nature of the state. Modern psychology exploded the myth of the personality of the state which was earlier used to exalt the state and its sovereignty. Modern sociology, again, demonstrated that law is the product of prevailing social conditions, not an expression of the commands of the sovereign. This led several modern thinkers to realize that the state is only a partial manifestation of the social nature of man, with a defined sphere of activity. It cannot be treated as an all-comprehensive institution encompassing all aspects of the social life of man as the classical theory of sovereignty had postulated. This gave rise to the pluralistic theory which launched a systematic attack on the doctrine of state-sovereignty.

In short, the pluralist theory sought to redefine the nature of the state as one of the several associations of human beings operating in society to secure the multifarious interests of individuals. In view of this, it envisaged a new role for the state as an arbiter over conflicting claims of different associations. It also repudiated the exclusive and absolute claim of the state to individual's allegiance; it insisted that the state should compete with other human associations to establish its claim to superior authority.

It is significant that the pluralist challenge to state-sovereignty coincided with the conditions created by the First World War (1914-18). During war-time the state required its citizens to sacrifice everything—including their near and dear ones, even their own lives—for the sake of the state. The people did make untold sacrifices, yet this state of affairs prompted an inquiry into whether the state was logically entitled to make such enormous demands. There were men, known as 'conscientious objectors', who claimed that their conscience urged them to oppose bloody war as a means of settling human disputes. Moreover, the policy of war was determined by the men in power who were as imperfect and fallible as any other human beings. A little folly on their part could escalate war and bring untold suffering to the citizens of the state. How, then, could the absolute authority of the state be taken for granted?

Harold J. Laski (*A Grammar of Politics;* 1938) enumerated two important factors which prompted the pluralist attack on sovereignty of the state:

(*a*) In the first place, the state claimed legal omnipotence; and it claimed the allegiance of its citizens on the ground that it represented the total interest of the society within its territorial jurisdiction. The pluralists pointed out that legal omnipotence was a purely formal concept often invalid in fact; and they argued that however majestic and powerful, the state in fact was only one of many associations in society, that, in experience, there were always limits to powers, and these were set by the relation between the purpose the state sought to fulfil and the judgement made by men of that purpose;

(*b*) In the second place, the pluralist doctrine was derived from the realization that the state's claim to pre-eminence always means, in fact, the sovereignty of a government composed of fallible men whose intentions alone are not a sufficient justification for so vast a claim. There went into the making of pluralism an historic analysis derived from the conflict between churches and the state, between trade unions and the state, between, as in the case of the conscientious objector to military service, the individual and the state.

[II]
MAIN TENETS OF THE PLURALIST THEORY

The pluralist attack on sovereignty was inspired by the doctrine of political pluralism. According to *A Dictionary of the Social Sciences* (ed. Julius Gould and William L. Kolb; 1964), 'political pluralism refers to those doctrines... which assert that certain groups in society (*e.g.* family, church, union, local government) embody important social values prior to and independent of their authorization or approval by the state'. So the pluralist theory of sovereignty proceeds from the idea of the pluralistic nature of society.

THE PLURALISTIC NATURE OF SOCIETY

The pluralist theory represents a shift in focus from the legal to the sociological character of the state. It recognizes the role of several associations in society, formed by men in pursuance of their multifarious interests. Some of these associations have been in existence prior to the origin of the state itself; some of them exist independent of the state, that is they are neither created, nor sponsored, nor maintained, nor even regulated by the state. Sociologically speaking, the state is but one of these associations, standing side-by-side with them, not above them. Such associations include the church and other religious organizations, trade unions, cooperative societies and chambers of commerce, and so many voluntary associations devoted to education, cultural and scientific pursuits. All these associations embody some social value, means of satisfying some needs and other worthwhile pursuits.

Association

Association refers to a human organization formed for the fulfilment of certain common objectives of its members which motivates them to come together and work together.

Pluralists hold that it is morally preferable for individuals to be associated politically with a wide range of associations in pursuance of their specific interests. These groups provide them an opportunity to make use of their creative abilities and to seek self-fulfilment in various spheres of life. No outside agency, not least the state, should interfere in their functioning unless their activities are required to be regulated in the interest of public order, public safety or public morality.

ROLE OF THE STATE AS COORDINATOR

When there are several associations in society to take care of the varied interests of individuals and for the fulfilment of their personality, what is then the nature and role of the state? According to the pluralist standpoint, the state does not exist above these associations. In fact, the state, as the society politically organized, cannot be conceived as distinct from these associations. To be sure, *the state itself is an association of associations.* As an association coordinates the activities of its members, so the state co-ordinates the activities of these associations in society. It is a means of resolving the conflicting claims of these associations, by evolving a common basis of their functioning, not by imposing its own will or regulations upon them, but by harmonizing and coordinating their several interests so as to secure the 'common good', the 'common interest', or the 'public interest'. This role of the state is essential for the maintenance of order in society.

It is significant that the pluralist theory seeks to curtail or limit the absolute authority of the state as against the theory of state-sovereignty. It does not seek to abolish the state itself as anarchists do. The pluralists postulate some recognized functions of the state. For instance, the functions of maintaining internal order and security, defence from external enemies and enforcement of voluntary contracts should be left to the state unless a contract is deemed to be void on moral grounds.

THE STATE MUST JUSTIFY ITS CLAIM TO AUTHORITY

As the state is only one of the associations in society intended to serve the interests of society, its claim to superior authority cannot be taken for granted. The state enjoys a privileged position in the sense that its jurisdiction is compulsory over all individuals and associations within its fold. It is equipped with coercive powers so that it can punish those who ignore or defy its commands. These characteristics do not automatically establish the superior authority of the state. On the other hand, they postulate a higher moral responsibility on the state. The pluralists require the state to justify the exercise of its special powers.

The state, as an association of associations, is required to secure the 'common interest' or the 'public interest' by harmonizing the interests of all associations operating in society. Some of the associations might be more organized and more vocal than others; some of the vulnerable sections in society might be devoid of any organization. Some of the interests might be well-represented in the assemblies, or impressed upon the state through various investigatory commissions, through special delegations, or through mass movements, demonstrations and rallies; others might be dormant and hardly noticed. Theoretically, the state is expected to ensure that all interests are given due weightage while seeking their coordination in pursuance of the common interest. The state, as an arbiter of conflicting claims, must demonstrate that it is not dominated by any special interest or 'vested interests' while exercising its authority; otherwise it would betray the confidence reposed in it. As Benn and Peters (*Social Principles and the Democratic State;* 1975) have asserted: "The state must not be allowed to fall into the hands of men concerned only for the interest of a limited group. It must be sensitive to all, without succumbing to anyone or any limited coalition of interests."

This is the most delicate and difficult task of the state. It will be recalled that even the Marxian attack on the state is based on the argument that the capitalist state and its predecessors have been the instruments of serving the interests of the dominant class at the expense of the dependent class!

DECENTRALIZATION OF AUTHORITY

The pluralists do not extend unconditional support to the sovereign authority of the state. They do not accept the state as a *Leviathan* (a sea-monster who is capable to overpower all sea-creatures) as imagined by Thomas Hobbes (1588-1679). They repudiate monopoly of the state on the allegiance of all individuals. They demand that the state should justify its claims to allegiance on moral grounds. They argue that expansion of the authority of the state undermines democracy and liberty of the individual and that concentration of authority in the state erodes administrative efficiency. The complexity of the economic and political relations of the modern world cannot be dealt with by a monolithic view of the state. They, therefore, contend that the management and control of society should be shared by several associations in proportion to their contribution to the social good.

The pluralist theory, therefore, advocates reorganization of the state through a set of institutions guaranteeing its effective limitations, such as workers' and consumers' unions, which should serve as countervailing powers in the state.

[III] EXPONENTS OF THE PLURALIST THEORY

The doctrine of political pluralism was developed by a number of social and political thinkers from Europe and America. Emile Durkheim (1858-1917)—a French sociologist, Otto von Gierke (1841-1913)—a German political theorist, F.W. Maitland (1850-1906)—an English legal historian, and G.D.H. Cole (1889-1959)—an English economist are regarded as the forerunners of the pluralist theory. Gierke and Maitland enunciated the theory of the real personality of groups which became the focus of attention of many a later pluralist. According to the Gierke-Maitland thesis, as outlined in Gierke's *Political Theories of the Middle Age,* translated with an Introduction by Maitland (1900), each group in society possesses a real personality and will, and it plays a distinctive role in the process of law-making. The state, of course, plays the principal role in this sphere, but it is by no means exclusive. In other words, law is not made by the state alone; several social groups make their own contribution to this process. These social groups enjoy certain privileges and create certain obligations independent of the state's formal sanction.

Exponents of the pluralist theory include Léon Duguit—French legal luminary, Hugo Krabbe—a Dutch jurist, Harold J. Laski, Ernest Barker, and A.D. Lindsay—English political thinkers, and Robert M. MacIver—an American sociologist. Of these, Laski and MacIver are the most outstanding.

LÉON DUGUIT

Léon Duguit (1859-1928), French legal philosopher, in his celebrated work *Treatise on Constitutional Law* (1921-25), argues that laws are not an expression of the commands of an absolute sovereign. They are the conditions of *social solidarity,* that is manifested in the interdependence of men in society. In other words, laws embody those fundamental rules which sustain the social life of men. They are obligatory not because they are the commands of a 'determinate human superior', as the classical theory of sovereignty maintains, but because their observance is crucial to the functioning of human society. Accordingly, laws exist even before the origin of the state itself; they are by no means a product of the state. The state itself is an instrument of securing *social solidarity.*

Duguit, therefore, subordinates the state to the rules of *social solidarity* which find expression in the form of laws. He, therefore, argues that *'public service' rather than sovereignty is the essential characteristic of the state.* Thus, Duguit rejects the theory of absolute sovereignty and makes the state responsible to society. He is not primarily interested in the political importance of the social groups within the state. Rather, he insists that administrative actions should be subjected to judicial limitations.

HUGO KRABBE

Hugo Krabbe (1857-1936), a Dutch jurist, proceeds to distinguish between law and the state, and argues that law is independent of and superior to the state. Thus, sovereignty is an attribute of law, not of the state. Krabbe holds that law does not emanate from *social solidarity,* but from a *sense of right* of the majority of the community constituting the state. In his *The Idea of the Modern State* (1922), Krabbe asserts that the essence of the state is to be found in the operation of legal relations, not in the operation of relations between the strong and the weak. Krabbe's theory of the state rejects the idea that power is an essential feature of the state. In his view, the state is essentially a legal community— a portion of mankind having its own independent body of legal relations. The purpose of the state is to reconcile conflicting interests within the community in conformity with the values embodied in the law.

A.D. LINDSAY

A.D. Lindsay (1879-1952), English political philosopher, in his 'The State in Recent Political Theory' (*Political Quarterly;* 1914), accepts the theory of the real personality of associations of human beings and argues that the state is only one of the numerous associations each of which possesses a corporate personality of its own. Many other associations, being smaller than the state, are more homogeneous and represent a closer community of interests. If they are permitted to act autonomously, they are likely to attract the deeper loyalties of their members, and prove themselves to be more effective agencies of social coordination than the state itself. Lindsay, therefore, insists that each one of these associations should be given greater authority and initiative, so much so that they should be allowed to legislate for themselves. Thus, Lindsay pleads for breaking the monopoly of the state in law-making and advocates decentralization of legislative powers to the several associations in society.

ERNEST BARKER

Ernest Barker (1874-1960), English political philosopher, on the other hand, rejects the concept of the 'real personality' of the group, although he admits the juristic claim that the permanent groups within society existed prior to the state and that each of them has a corporate character and functions of its own.

In his *Political Thought in England from Herbert Spencer to the Present Day* (1915), Barker observes: "We see the state less as an association of individuals in a common life; we see it more as an association of individuals, already united in various groups for a further and more embracing common purpose."

Barker argues that the state should necessarily adjust the relations of associations to itself, to other associations and to their own members in order to maintain the integrity of its own scheme to preserve the equality of associations before law and to protect individuals from the possible tyranny of the group. Thus, he views the state as an association of associations, a community of communities, and an agency for harmonizing the interests of the groups as well as of individuals.

HAROLD J. LASKI

Harold J. Laski (1893-1950), a brilliant English thinker, is the most ardent champion of the pluralist theory of sovereignty. He is a prolific writer and his views on this subject lie scattered in a large number of his works—*Authority in the Mordern State* (1919); *The Foundations of Sovereignty and Other Essays* (1922); A *Grammar of Politics* (1925/1938); *An Introduction to Politics* (1931); *Studies in Law and Politics* (1932); *The State in Theory and Practice* (1935); *Reflections on the Revolution of Our Time* (1943), etc. Though very brilliant, he has not been very consistent in his formulations. After adjusting his pluralist position between liberalism and Marxism, he ultimately emerged as an exponent of positive liberalism—a combination of liberalism and socialism. In his scheme of the reorganization of the state on the basis of democratization of power, Laski comes out as an ardent pluralist.

In the early phase of his political thought, that is in the 1920s, Laski advanced vigorous criticism of the theory of state sovereignty, and held that this theory would pass like the theory of the divine right of kings which had had its day. He thought of sovereignty as nothing more than a legal fiction and a barren concept. But, in a later phase, that is in the 1930s, Laski began to evolve a balanced view of pluralism—identifying the points of its strength and weakness, and then he conceded the importance of sovereignty as an essential element of state-power, though he viewed the state itself as an agency for regulating class-relations in society, while he himself preferred a classless society.

Attack on Absolute Sovereignty

In his A *Grammar of Politics* (1938), Laski proceeds to scrutinize the theory of sovereignty from three aspects and discovers its weaknesses everywhere. In the first place, historical analysis of the state repudiates the idea of absolute sovereignty. He accepts Sir Henry Maine's (1822-88) criticism of Austin and shows how custom and tradition substantially limit the exercise of sovereign power. These are not legal checks imposed by some determinate human superior, nor do they operate with the express or tacit consent of the sovereign himself. The deference which even omnipotent monarchs and sultans have to show to custom, is a political need, a dictate of prudence and expediency. Besides these limitations in the internal sphere, sovereignty is also subject to limitations in the external sphere. Here Laski finds the claims of absolute sovereignty incompatible with the interests of humanity. As he observes: "In a creative civilization what is important is not the historical accident of separate States, but the scientific fact of world-interdependence. The real unit of allegiance is the world. The real obligation of obedience is to the total interest of our fellow-men" (*A Grammar of Politics;* 1938).

In the second place, the theory of absolute sovereignty fails as a theory of law. Here Laski accepts Dicey's (1835-1922) distinction between legal and popular sovereignty as a proof of the absurdity of Austin's definition of sovereignty as determinate and indivisible. He proceeds to show how even the idea of popular sovereignty is not workable. In Laski's own words, "everyone knows that to regard the King-in-Parliament as a sovereign body in the Austinian sense is absurd. No Parliament would dare to disenfranchise the Roman Catholics or to prohibit the existence of trade unions. If it made the attempt, it would cease to be a Parliament. That is to say that in practice legally unlimited power turns out to be power exercised under conditions fairly well known to each generation."

Finally, the theory of sovereignty does not hold good in the analysis of a political organization. Laski cites the case of the federal state, particularly of the United States, to show that the location of sovereignty—as envisaged by Austin—is very difficult in the case of such political organizations.

Distinction between the State and Government

Laski dwells on the distinction between the state and government to demonstrate the inadequacy of the theory of absolute and unlimited sovereignty. He points out that, in actual practice, the so-called sovereign powers of the state are claimed by the government, that is a body of persons issuing orders and enforcing obedience thereto. In the exercise of these powers, the government can never be allowed to become absolute and irresponsible. In his *The State in Theory and Practice* (1935), Laski observed that government is but the agent of the state:

> It exists to carry out the purpose of the state. It is not itself the supreme coercive power; it is simply the mechanism of administration which gives effect to the purpose of that power. It is not, we are told, sovereign in the sense in which the state is sovereign; its competence is defined by such authority as the state may choose to confer upon it; and if it oversteps that authority it may, where such provision exists, be called to account.

Pointing to the dangers of conferring absolute powers on government, Laski further observes:

Every government is composed of fallible men. They may deliberately exploit the authority they possess for their own selfish purposes. They may, with the best intentions, but quite unreasonably, mistake the private interest of a few for the well-being of the whole community. They may be ignorant of the position they confront, or be incompetent in handling it. Circumstances such as these have occurred in every political society at some period of its history. The value of the distinction between state and government is the possibility it offers of creating institutional mechanisms for changing the agents of the state, that is the government, when the latter shows itself inadequate to its responsibilities.

Moral Grounds of Allegiance

In *The Foundations of Sovereignty* (1922), Laski argues that the state is only one among many forms of human associations and, as compared with other associations, it has no superior claims to an individual's allegiance. He argues that the state has no right to the allegiance of an individual save insofar as his conscience gives assent. His point is that to demand unquestioning obedience to the orders of the sovereign authority without giving the individual the right to judge for himself their moral adequacy is morally wrong; it stunts the growth of his moral personality. In his *A Grammar of Politics* (1938), Laski argues that the larger functions of the state postulate larger responsibility as well. The state can justify its existence only as a 'public service corporation':

> The State differs from every other association in that it is, in the first place, an association in which membership is compulsory. It is, in the second place, essentially territorial in nature ... The State controls the level at which men are to live as men. It is, in administrative terms, a government whose activities are shaped by the common needs of its members. To satisfy those common needs, it must control other associations to the degree that secures from them the service such needs require.

In other words, the state must justify exercise of its social authority by ensuring an effective coordination of functions of other human associations in the best public interest. Its claim to the allegiance of individuals will rest on the efficient performance of its functions.

Laski tries to demostrate the pluralistic character of the state on the basis of the pluralistic character of society itself. He observes that society is not a uniform organization of all citizens. Citizens organize themselves into several associations according to their specific interests and these associations in turn organize themselves into society. Thus society is an association of associations, or a federation of various interest groups. This principle should form the basis of authority of the state. So Laski declares: "... because society is federal, authority must be federal also" (*A Grammar of Politics;* 1938). In other words, the state should exercise its authority over the various interest groups which constitute it.

But each interest group should in turn exercise its authority over its members.

Thus Laski insists that sovereignty in the state should be shared by many groups according to the respective value of the functions of each group. The state should perform its coordinating function, but it has no right to omnipotence. The power of the state should become coordinative instead of being hierarchical, and authority should become federal instead of being absolute and indivisible. Laski's plea to make authority federal is the cornerstone of his pluralist doctrine. Its logical conclusion may be found in his concept of the democratization of power.

Democratization of Power

In his pluralist fervour, Laski feels deeply concerned about the undemocratic control of industry and politics by the economic overlords in society—a characteristic feature of capitalist civilization. In his *Reflections on the Revolution of Our Time* (1943), Laski most eloquently declares:

> In modern society, the large industrial corporations are controlled by a caste of economic directors, mainly remarkable for their skill in financial manipulation, who are masters alike of their shareholders and of the consumers and are not seldom in a position to hold even the states to ransom. Their power is as massive in volume as it has largely been irresponsible in operation. We have reached a stage in historical evolution where either their power must be subordinated to the interest of the community or the interest of the community will be a tragic pseudonym for their power.

This state of affairs cannot be transformed, Laski feels, unless the vital instruments of production are owned and controlled by the community. But he immediately shifts from this socialist solution to an alternative scheme of democratization of power—a pluralist solution. Laski identifies four bases of economic power—the supply of capital and credit; the ownership and control of land; control of the import and export trades; and, finally, control of transport, fuel and power. Socialization of these vital resources will avert concentration of economic power in society and start the process of the democratization of power.

ROBERT M. MACIVER

Robert M. MacIver (1882-1970), American sociologist, has developed his pluralistic theory in his two outstanding works: *The Modern State* (1926) and *The Web of Government* (1947/1965). MacIver takes a sociological view of the state and traces its evolution from primitive social structures to its modern form. In this process he rejects the theory of absolute sovereignty and vindicates the pluralist view of the state.

Supremacy of Law

As the outset, MacIver identifies the state as one of several human associations. The state is distinguished from other associations because it gives expression to law, not because it is characterized by sovereignty. MacIver has advanced three arguments against the doctrine of sovereignty: (*a*) In the first place, the concept of the *general will,* as formulated by Rousseau (1712-78) and Green (1836-82), is sometimes invoked as the basis of sovereignty. But it is difficult to discover the existence of the general will in the state. There are many persons in the state who differ from the prevalent will in the state. The states of the past included vast numbers of aliens and slaves apart from the citizens whose will could not be reconciled with the so-called will of the state. Besides, the state appears as an upholder of custom and, therefore, loyalty to the state in such a case is derived from men's regard for custom, not for the state itself; (*b*) Secondly, even in a democratic state, it is very difficult to locate the ultimate sovereign. There is no homogeneous will of the people. Majority and minority opinions exist simultaneously. One government is replaced by another; will seems to go on changing; policy also changes therewith; and (c) Finally, power in the state is always exercised by a political government. Limits to the power of government are set by the constitution over which government has no direct control. The stability of the authority of government depends on its legitimacy for which it must conform to the prevalent traditions and social values.

MacIver, therefore, argues that the state is subject to the supremacy of law which exists apart from the state. Thus he observes:

> It is not the office but the instrument, not sovereignty but the law and the constitution that wear the legitimate armour of might. The government has power as the guardian of the constitution, as the executor of law, not in its own right. Outside the realm of law its use of force is as irreducible to principle as that of any strong man armed. To law, therefore, we must turn, and not to sovereignty as such, if we are to attain a true definition of the state (*The Modern State;* 1926).

Law, in this sense, cannot be regarded as an expression of the will of the state. The state does not create law. Law exists prior to the state; the state only grasps it and gives it a definite expression in the form of its statutes. In other words, the state only codifies law, or modifies its form; it cannot make or remake it. As MacIver points out: "The state can no more reconstitute at any time the law as a whole than a man can remake his body." MacIver agrees with Hugo Krabbe that the authority of law is greater than the authority of the state.

Basis of Authority

As the state is one of several human associations, the basis of authority of the state cannot be different from that of other associations or corporations. MacIver asserts: "Every association of any magnitude has grades of authority and control analogous to those of the state" (*The Modern State*). A business corporation has a body of shareholders who are united in the will and interest to uphold the corporation. The shareholders must choose a board of directors, but neither on the choice nor on the policy of the board are they likely to be unanimous. In the sphere of the state, the will of the people—which is nothing more than the dominant will or the majority will—is analogous to the will of the shareholders and government is analogous to the board of directors. The state, accordingly, derives its authority from the will of the majority of the people, not in its own right.

A corporation is recognized by law; it entails certain rights and obligations. The state is similar to other corporations in this sense also. It is recognized by law, and has its definite rights and obligations. What is, then, the relation of the state to other corporate entities—the human associations whose right it recognizes and defines?

According to MacIver, the state

> gives them a special status defining their privileges and responsibilities. The state does not create the corporation but only regulates its legal character... The association, such as a professional group or a body of believers, exists apart from and prior to the state's act of recognition. The state cannot, for the most part, either make or unmake it ... The great associations are as native to the soil of society as the state itself. The state can scarcely even decide whether it will or will not recognize them.

How can the state fulfil the function of control and coordination of human associations unless it enjoys supremacy over them? Does it imply that, while other associations cater to the partial interests of men, the state is the guardian and agent of the universal interests of men?

MacIver's answer to these questions comprises the essence of his pluralist position. He argues that the state does not regulate the internal affairs of other associations; it does not and cannot determine their purposes or, for the most part, their methods. It does not treat them as its own agencies or instruments. The state comes into the picture only when the interests of one group encroach on another. In other words, the state acts only in order to resolve the conflicting interests of various associations in society. The state cannot impose its own will on human associations for the protection of the 'common interest'. In MacIver's own words, the state

> stands for the common interest; but only so far as the common interest is sufficiently unified to admit of political expression, and only so far as it is sufficiently externalized to admit of legal regulation. True, it stands for the common interest; but not for the whole of the common interest

> ...The common interest is no simple objective, attainable in its entirety by an inclusive authority. The partial interests of a thousand associations, cultural and economic, are also parts of the common interest.

Even if the state claims to be the protector of the common interest, it cannot demand superior authority on this account. Other associations may cater to less extensive interests of men, yet they may attract their deeper loyalties because they are more intimate and more closely bound with the traditions and beliefs of groups. As MacIver further observes: "On this account the doctrine of absolute sovereignty, if actually practised in the states of today with all their diversities of culture, would be fatal to the harmony of social life."

Initially, MacIver seems to hold that the state should not use its authority to regulate the internal affairs of any other human association. But in the later part of his life, he sought to introduce a note of caution in this matter. In a subsequent edition of *The Web of Government* (1965), MacIver makes a distinction between two types of organizations: those which serve the emotional and cultural interests of men and cannot be regulated by the state; and those which serve the economic interests of different groups, and have to be regulated to serve the common interest. As he points out:

> There are schools and styles in every form of art, in every field of cultural expression. The followers of any one ... take delight in their own, in the difference itself. Religions may alike proclaim the brotherhood of man or the fatherhood of God, but each has its own conception of the fatherhood. To coordinate them all into one would be to destroy their characteristic qualities, to drain them of their vitality.

On the other hand, the associations formed to serve the economic interests of various groups cannot be treated on similar lines. As MacIver argues:

> Economic activities, for example, cannot be left to the free arbitrament of individuals and groups without serious interference with public order. Thus, an employer cannot lower the wages of his employees below the prevailing rate ... extend the hours of labour without doing harm to his fellow employers as well as to his employees ... No more can a man rightly claim to use his property in any way that seems good to him. His property not only is the fruit of the cooperative labour of many men but also it is the potential if not the actual source of the livelihood of others. If he neglects it, lets it run to waste or ruin, or actually destroys it he is injuring his fellows.

Recognition of this distinction between the two types of associations provides a profounder basis to MacIver's pluralist theory.

A CRITICAL APPRAISAL

The pluralist theory of sovereignty is important because it deals with the problem of sovereignty in the political sphere. It is significant that the classical theory of sovereignty was developed by several thinkers from Jean Bodin to John Austin as a purely legal concept. These thinkers were generally conscious of the moral responsibility of the sovereign, but they did not recognize any human superior whose advice or approval would be necessary for the sovereign. This position could be upheld so long as sovereignty was nothing more than a legal notion.

But once the theory of absolute and unlimited sovereignty is accepted, the distinction between the state and government is soon forgotten or ignored and absolute powers are claimed by a government in the name of the state, paving the way for autocracy and tyranny. It is, therefore, quite expedient that the implications of sovereignty in the political sphere are worked out and spelled out so that sound principles of politics and government could be evolved. This is precisely the field where the pluralist theory has made an important contribution.

The exponents of the pluralist theory have elaborated the limitations on the authority of the state—in practice, on the authority of government. Some of the pluralists, like A.D. Lindsay and Robert M. MacIver, have even regarded other associations as objects of deeper individual loyalties than the state. Harold J. Laski has used the pluralist model especially to curb the concentration of economic power—a baneful product of capitalism. MacIver has, of course, made an important point by prescribing different roles of the state with regard to the cultural and emotional groups on the one hand, and economic interest groups on the other.

There are, however, some dangers inherent in the pluralist theory. When interest groups become the centre of individual loyalty, so much so that some groups attract deeper loyalty than the state itself, there is a danger that some groups might become unduly powerful; they may dictate unjust terms to society because of this power. For instance, the unions of those performing essential services, such as mechanics, engineers, doctors, dispensers, drivers, and even sweepers, may be able to exert undue pressure on the authorities because they can disrupt normal social life, while teachers, artists, scientists, etc. may not be able to press for their just and genuine demands. Moreover, some categories of persons, such as traders and workers, are usually more organized and vocal than other categories, such as consumers. The pluralist model of government, in such cases, implies pre-eminence of the interests of dominant groups over those of the vulnerable sections of society.

Under the circumstances, the responsibility for protecting the common interest devolves on the state. The state should act as an agency for harmonizing the conflicting claims of different interest groups—because some groups might be unduly eloquent in advancing their claims while others might not be even conscious of their interests, not to speak of properly organizing and articulating their genuine demands. The state should, therefore, determine the requirements of the common interest in admitting the respective claims of the various interest groups.

Again, with the ascendancy of big corporations in the modern state, the position of other groups has considerably weakened. The giant corporations have in fact eclipsed other social groups as regards their influence on the policy-making process. Under such circumstances, public policy can hardly be regarded as an end-product of mutual adjustment of group interests. In order to restore the rightful place of smaller groups vis-a-vis the bigger ones, the state must play an effective role in curbing the powers and influence of the more powerful organs, particularly the big corporations. This would call for a stronger base for the state sovereignty than what the pluralist theory might concede.

9

Contemporary Challenges to Sovereignty

CONVENTIONAL THEORY OF sovereignty upholds supreme legal authority of the state in internal as well as external sphere. In recent years this theory was challenged from both sides: (*a*) Internal challenge to sovereignty of the state came from the growing authority of various groups and associations who claimed allegiance from their members within the state. This was manifested in the pluralist theory of sovereignty; and (*b*) External challenge to sovereignty came from international environment which threatened autonomy of the nation-state. The process of globalization further aggravated the situation. Here we shall focus on the external challenges to the sovereignty of the nation-state.

[I]
LEGACY OF IMPERIALISM

IMPERIALISM AND COLONIALISM

Imperialism has a long history. Apparently it has wound up, but the forces involved in its expansion continue to work in subtle and disguised forms. Originally, imperialism meant the formation of an empire, that is bringing several countries under the control of one supreme authority. In this sense, it has existed since ancient times. In modern times, it found a new expression in the form of 'colonialism'. Edward Said (*Culture and Imperialism;* 1993) has aptly drawn *distinction between the two terms:* "Imperialism means the practice, the theory, and the attitudes of a dominating metropolitan centre ruling a distant territory" whereas "colonialism, which is almost always a consequence of imperialism, is the implanting of settlements on distant territory." In actual practice, however, the term 'imperialism' is used more comprehensively. It includes various expressions of 'colonialism' also.

Modem forms of imperialism are the product of expansion of trade and industry in several countries of Europe. For example, in the eighteenth and nineteenth centuries, Britain, France, Belgium, Netherlands, Spain and Portugal, among others, sought to set up their colonies in a number of countries in Africa, Asia and America for the expansion of their trade and industry after their own national consolidation. They started exploiting the natural and human resources of those countries to strengthen their own economies. Champions of imperialism usually argue that they seek to extend the benefit of civilization to the 'uncivilized' people. Indeed it is an attempt to attribute moral dignity to the pursuit of their self-interest.

J.A. Hobson (*Imperialism;* 1902), English economist, defined imperialism as a search for 'captive market'. He argued that imperialism was the direct result of the expanding forces of modern capitalism. He held that the maldistribution of wealth in a capitalist society created a desire to spread markets beyond its own territory in search of profit. In his view, imperialism was a method of exploitation. Then V.I. Lenin (*Imperialism: The Highest Stage of Capitalism;* 1916), a Russian Marxist and Revolutionary, argued that imperialism was an economic necessity of capitalist economy. Accordingly, when capital accumulates to such an extent that it cannot at all find profitable use in the main capitalist countries, they are forced to look abroad for profitable outlets. Lenin identified three driving forces behind the imperialist expansion: search for new spheres of investment, new markets, and new sources of raw materials. Foreign trade allows capitalists to secure a higher rate of return than that available at home. Overseas investment opens up new sources of labour and markets, and allows access to raw materials at extremely cheaper rates.

Captive Market

Captive market refers to a market where consumers are constrained to purchase necessary goods from a single or the very few suppliers. So they have practically no choice to select from a variety of products or to buy the necessary goods at competitive or reasonable rates. On the other hand, the suppliers have the opportunity to extract maximum profits.

Lenin described the 'division of nations into oppressor and oppressed' as the 'essence of imperialism'. Although Lenin exhorted all oppressed nations to unite against their oppressors and overthrow them, yet his message could not go beyond Russian Revolution (1917) at that time. However, the oppressed nations gradually became aware of the nature of their exploitation by their colonial masters and they launched their struggle for independence individually. As a result, the process of 'decolonization' began after the Second World War (1939-45) when colonial rulers began to concede independence to their subject countries. India was the first to gain independence in 1947.

ADVENT OF NEO-COLONIALISM

However, the exploitation of the former colonies of Asia, Africa and Latin America did not stop with the achievement of their independence. The former imperialist powers acquired new, subtle means of exploiting the former colonies which are compendiously described as 'neo-colonialism'. In short, *neo-colonialism refers to the strategy of a colonial power which does not maintain its political domination in a foreign territory, but continues its economic exploitation by using it as a source of cheap labour and raw materials as well as a big market for its industrial products.* The new nations or the developing countries, with their vast size and population and low level of industrial development, remain the chief source of supply of raw materials and labour-intensive products for the developed world. But the price levels for such products are largely dictated by the rich countries until they can organize themselves into a semi-cartel like the Organization of the Petroleum Exporting Countries (OPEC) (founded in 1960). For other products, such organizations simply do not exist.

In the absence of sufficient capital and technical expertise required for their industrialization, the developing countries are forced to make use of their resources in labour-intensive industries with a low margin of profit. On the other hand, developed countries make use of their resources in capital-intensive and technology-intensive industries with a high margin of profit. Thus, international trade continuously operates to the disadvantage of the developing countries. The victims of neo-colonialism hardly find a way to solve their problems of poverty, unemployment and technological backwardness or to stop their exploitation. Thus for long Chile, Brazil, Panama and other Latin American countries served as the source of cheap raw materials and cheap labour for the industries of the United States. Similarly, the Asian countries like Taiwan, Malaysia and Philippines used to serve as backyards for the Japanese industries.

Then developed countries invest their capital in the developing countries through Multinational Corporations (MNCs) which manufacture and market a variety of consumer goods within those countries and earn huge profits for the countries of their origin. This gives them an opportunity to make use of cheap labour as well as raw materials of the developing countries for their own advantage. Again, the developing countries also serve as the provider of cheap labour for the production of components in consumer goods assembled elsewhere where requisite expertise is available. Often the poorer countries lack the expertise or investment capital to benefit from the marketing of finished products, but they can provide the labour for factories owned and built by companies based in richer countries. In some cases, the MNCs tend to locate their 'dirty' industries in the developing countries, taking advantage of their less strict environmental controls. The disaster at the Union Carbide plant at Bhopal (India) in 1984 is the case in point. Then the dumping of toxic wastes in Africa by the industries of the advanced nations could be cited as another example of this tendency. Moreover, the highly skilled manpower of the developing countries like doctors, engineers and other professionals, produced at a high public cost, is sometimes directly transferred to the developed world for want of adequate career opportunities in their own countries. This phenomenon is called 'brain drain'.

The term 'neo-colonialism' was coined by the first President of independent Ghana, Kwame Nkrumah (1909-72) in his essay *Neo-colonialism: The Last Stage of Imperialism* (1965). This work follows the style and line of argument of Lenin's *Imperialism: The Highest Stage of Capitalism* (1916). Nkrumah argued that although countries like Ghana had technically achieved independence, the ex-colonial powers and newly emerging superpowers such as the United States continued to play a decisive role in their economic affairs through international monetary bodies, and through the fixing of prices on world markets, multinational corporations and cartels and a variety of educational and cultural institutions. In Nkrumah's view, neo-colonialism was more injurious and more difficult to detect than the conventional form of colonialism.

In a nutshell, the legacy of imperialism still continues to afflict the developing countries who have gained formal political independence. A developing country which declares itself to be a 'sovereign, democratic republic' may still feel constrained by the forces of neo-colonialism.

[II]
ROLE OF THE POWER BLOCS

Another factor that remained a source of constraint on the sovereignty of the developing countries was the emergence of the power blocs after the Second World War (1939-45). However, these countries decided to fight against this constraint and largely maintained their independence throughout.

GENESIS OF THE POWER BLOCS

After the Second World War, a large part of the world was divided into two big ideological camps. Of these one was the capitalist camp led by the United States; another was the communist camp led by the Soviet Union (the then USSR). The United States as well as the Soviet Union was capable of facing any big power with its large military might and nuclear weapons. Hence, each of them was recognized as a 'superpower'. Thus, each ideological camp was led by a superpower.

Both the superpowers had formed their respective military alliances. The chief military alliance of the capitalist camp was North Atlantic Treaty Organization (NATO) which was founded in 1949. Its leading members were the United States, the United Kingdom, France, Belgium, Netherlands, Luxemberg, Denmark, Norway, Iceland, Portugal, Italy, West Germany (Federal Republic of Germany) and Canada. The chief military alliance of the communist camp was Warsaw Pact which was founded in 1955. Its members included the USSR, Albania (which left it in 1968), Bulgaria, Czechoslovakia, East Germany (German Democratic Republic), Hungary, Poland and Rumania.

Since both these camps sought to dominate the world with their huge power apparatus, these were termed as the *'power blocs'*. But each of them wanted to demonstrate the supremacy of its ideology and to enlist its following in the rest of the world. There was no armed conflict between the two groups, but a vigorous propaganda against each other was in full swing. In international politics, this queer conflict was described as the *'Cold War'* which created immense tension and threatened the world peace. The term 'Cold War' in this sense was popularized by the American columnist Walter Lippmann (1889-1974).

The emergence of the power blocs coincided with the decline of imperialism. A large number of countries of Asia and Africa gained their independence after the Second World War (1939-45) and established their identity as the new nation-states. The countries of Latin America, who had formally gained their independence in early nineteenth century, also joined them. These countries had remained underdeveloped during the long period of foreign domination. They were chiefly interested in maintaining their independence and securing their social and economic development. Together they were described as the 'third world' at the instance of the French economist and demographer Alfred Sauvy (1898-1990). Fortunately, some of these countries had distinguished world leaders with a great vision. So most of these countries, under the able leadership of Nehru (of India), Nasser (of Egypt) and Tito (of Yugoslavia) adopted the policy of remaining away from the power blocs. This policy was termed as 'non-alignment'. Eventually, non-alignment became a distinctive feature of the third world.

Gradually, non-alignment evolved into a movement as well as a common forum for the new nations. Its aims included the opposition to colonialism and neo-colonialism all over the world, to promote disarmament for the maintenance of world peace, to promote cooperation between the developing countries and to form organizations to look after their common interests in the field of trade and industry, technological development, education and information, etc. They particularly tried to dispel the tension between the two power blocs and to build a bridge of understanding between the two.

IMPACT OF THE POWER BLOCS

The emergence of the power blocs posed a new threat to the sovereignty of the nation-state. In the past, any state could manage its defence by organizing its military power and by entering into alliance with other friendly states. But when the superpowers created very big military alliances, with their own nuclear weapons and Intercontinental Ballistic Missiles (ICBMs), no nation-state remained capable of providing for an effective security of its citizens by conventional means. Under the circumstances, each nation-state felt constrained to rely on either superpower and to join its camp. This meant compromising one's independence and bowing to the commands of a superpower. When the new nations decided to maintain their independence through the policy of non-alignment, they really had a tough time, facing criticism, pressures and threats from both side. But eventually this came to stay.

However, since the early 1990s, there has been a radical change in the position of the power blocs. The reforms initiated by Mikhail Gorbachev in the Soviet Union in 1985 encouraged free flow of information, social and political debates, decentralization of economy and review of foreign policy in the communist camp. This led to the relaxation of the Soviet Union's control over the communist nations of Eastern Europe, and eventual collapse of the communist system in most of these countries by 1991. This marked the dissolution of the one power bloc led by the former USSR and consequent end of the 'cold war'. The Wall of Berlin between East and West Germany was demolished, and Warsaw Pact also became redundant. However, North Atlantic Treaty Organization (NATO) is still going strong. From military angle, only one power bloc is left now. However, *the substantive base of domination in the contemporary world has been shifting from military power to economic power,* spread over various centres. Besides, the use of superior technology has led to the spreading of environmental pollution all over the world, and linking of all parts of the world by an effective communication network. In short, the process of 'globalization' has emerged as a new challenge to the sovereignty of the nation-state.

[III]
PROCESS OF GLOBALIZATION

PRIMACY OF ECONOMIC ISSUES

The emerging problems of global concern and magnitude call for global solution. These problems may touch many areas but primarily they are centred around economic issues. For many years, the superpowers and their allies focused on the predominance of military power, and paid only secondary importance to the economic issues. For most of the 1950s, 1960s and early 1970s, lethal weapons in possession of a nation were regarded the symbols of its power; its economic assets and liabilities were not regarded so significant. However, in late 1970s and 1980s economic issues began to acquire greater importance in international politics.

Now it was increasingly realized that the economies of major powers were linked with the world economy. For instance, it was discovered that the United States, Western Europe and Japan had become dependent on foreign sources of energy and other non-fuel mineral resources. Then, Japan had emerged as a major international economic actor whereas the United States was reduced from the world's greatest creditor nation to the world's greatest debtor nation. The Soviet Union and Eastern European states conceded that they too had immense budget deficits. Western Europe decided to create a single European Common Market. Third world countries were groaning under a heavy debt burden, and its large segments were still wanting in economic development. The centre of international economic growth had shifted to the Western Pacific. And a large part of the world had been transformed into a single financial market, thanks to the development of electronic banking.

Increasing importance of economic issues in world politics became evident in so many other areas also. Thus, when Iraq conquered Kuwait in 1990, many countries feared that their economies would be hard hit by Iraq's control of a large part of the world's oil reserves. Again, the economies of various nations were so interlinked that they seemed to comprise a world economy. This may be illustrated by some examples. An aircraft built in America flew Japanese businessmen to Indonesia to secure oil for Japanese industries. French financiers used the same aircraft to track their investments in stock markets in London, New York, Tokyo and Hong Kong. When American consumers purchased less expensive East Asian textile products, U.S. textile manufacturers were forced to lay off workers. Then in order to strengthen their position in the textile market, American entrepreneurs sought to invest in high-technology West German textile machines. These machines were purchased with the money that was deposited by Saudi princes in Italian banks.

Interlinkages between the economies of various nations may be illustrated further. When Japanese manufacturers lower the prices of various electronic gadgets, the prices of VCRs, TVs and microwave ovens fall in America. Nuclear accident at Chernobyl in the former USSR (1986) gave rise to the fear that its radiation had contaminated the food chain over half a world. When terrorists destroyed World Trade Centre in America (2001), whole world was shocked while watching its live telecast on TV. When famine sweeps Africa, TV viewers around the world are touched by the tragedy. Burning of forests in Indonesia brings climate change in whole South East Asia. News of a hole in the Earth's ozone layer over Antarctica comes as a warning of global disaster for the chemical industries world over.

Under the circumstances, it is natural to ask: if all nation-states have become interdependent in their economic relations, environmentally and even emotionally, how can a particular nation claim absolute sovereignty in its external relations? What is the duty of developed nations towards promoting economic growth in the developing societies? At what point the issues of national importance end and those of international importance begin? How can needy nations lay hands on those essential and rare resources which are the exclusive monopoly of the few nations? Which nations are responsible to control worldwide terrorism, drug-trafficking and environmental degradation? The concept of external sovereignty of nation-state will have to be revised suitably in order to deal with such situations.

It is important to note that in the era of military supremacy, submission from other countries is obtained through coercion or threat of coercion. But in the era of economic supremacy, submission is apparently obtained through consent as in an open market, although some countries may be driven by economic necessity to accept some onerous terms and conditions.

GLOBALIZATION AS A CONSCIOUS POLICY

When globalization became inevitable, many nations of the world thought of finding out its beneficial aspects and adopting it as a conscious policy. This also coincided with the increasing popularity of 'liberalization' and 'privatization' in many parts of the world. Way back in 1980s, governments of USA and UK decided to reduce their liability of public welfare in order to contain the rising burden on public exchequer. The crisis which engulfed Eastern European socialist economies towards the end of this decade and their eventual collapse in early 1990s proved that state-sponsored development could not sustain an economy for long. Then third-world countries also realized that the expansion of welfare services at the expense of the tax-payer had failed to serve its purpose due to bureaucratic inefficiency and corruption. Increasing tax-burden on able and industrious sections led to the loss of incentive and consequent decline of output. Again, the mounting demands of subsidies could not be met with the available resources. So liberalization became order of the day.

Liberalization

Liberalization refers to the policy of removal or relaxation of government control or restriction on economic activity of the people with a view to maximizing its efficiency. It seeks to reduce the state's liability towards welfare of the individuals and promote incentive-based rewards rather than dependence on various subsidies.

Privatization

Privatization refers to the policy of transferring government ownership and control of any sector of economy to private ownership and control in order to improve the standard of its management and to prevent loss to the public exchequer.

Policy of globalization represents a logical conclusion of the policy of liberalization and privatization. This policy also became popular since 1980s. It holds that economic efficiency can be increased further if economic activity is allowed to benefit from the resources available at the global scale. It encourages the utilization of capital and machinery available in one part of the world, raw materials in another part, labour in still another part for the process of production and search of markets for the final product all over the world. Its objectives include the minimization of cost of a product, enhancement of its quality, and the maximization of profit from its marketing.

Globalization encourages the expansion of multinational corporations (MNCs), because they are best-suited to mobilize capital and other resources including managerial skills. It promotes the expansion of transport and communication network, because that is the primary condition of its operation. It distributes standard goods and services to every nook and cranny of the world and thus introduces uniform style of living and uniform ways of entertainment. Finally, it contributes to the development of a global culture which is expected to create greater understanding among different peoples of the world.

> **Globalization has changed us into a company that searches the world, not just to sell or to source, but to find intellectual capital — the world's best talents and greatest ideas.**
>
> **Jack Welch**

A CRITICAL APPRAISAL

Some writers eulogize globalization as a boon for humanity. They argue that now national boundaries do not stand in the way of progress of an individual or a community, thanks to globalization. Men have gained access to the treasure of knowledge and culture which is the product of genius all over the world. Now local communities have the opportunity to benefit from technology, information services and markets available anywhere in the world. Finally, globalization has created awareness regarding global environment all over the world, and different nations have come to recognize global problems as a matter of their individual and collective responsibility.

Others condemn globalization as a bane for a large part of the world. They believe that globalization is a device to maintain domination of the developed countries of the West over the developing countries. They regard it an expression of neo-colonialism. They argue that Western culture is being projected as global culture through the so-called globalization, and thereby the cultural heritage of the East is being eroded. Besides, local economies are being made subservient to Western economies by linking them with each other in the name of globalization.

Critics of globalization assert that global culture and global economy have not come into existence in the course of natural evolution, but they have been invented by the capitalist nations to serve their self-interest. Underdeveloped countries are being entrapped by projecting the inevitability of globalization. Some critics allege that for the developing countries, globalization implies the acceptance of terms and conditions dictated by International Monetary Fund

(IMF), World Bank and other Western-dominated agencies which result in benefiting a tiny class within the country at the expense of the large majority.

Some Requisites of Globalization

Structural Adjustment

A process closely linked with globalization. It implies reforms that enhance productive potential and facilitate improvement in economic performance and standard of living. International Monetary Fund (IMF) provides assistance on concessional terms to low-income countries to enable them to carry out such reforms. These largely include: (*a*) Measures that eliminate inefficiency in the use of resources and allow more rapid adjustment to technological innovations and changes in relative prices; and (*b*) Measures to increase output potential by adding to productive resources (such as capital and labour) or by raising overall productivity.

Regional Economic Integration

The process whereby groups of certain countries seek to eliminate the artificial barriers in the way of international trade and competition. This is largely accomplished by (*a*) Preferential Trade Agreement; (*b*) Free Trade Area; (*c*) Customs Union; (*d*) Common Market; and (*e*) Economic Union. This process gives an impetus to globalization.

Again, some writers strive to strike a balance between the merits and demerits of globalization. They concede that globalization has failed to eradicate poverty from the world or reduce economic disparities. It has caused environmental degradation, prompted intolerance, encouraged militarism, disintegrated communities and worsened the condition of subordinate groups. But it should not be forgotten that globalization has raised real per capita income in the world to three times since 1945; it has reduced the ratio of the extremely poor in world population to a half; it has created awareness regarding environment, and congenial conditions for disarmament. It has brought the condition of subordinate groups to limelight and inspired them to form their global organizations for their emancipation. It has also liberated them from the ideological domination of their local communities and enabled them to fight for their legitimate rights.

> We must ensure that the global market is embedded in broadly shared values and practices that reflect global social needs, and that all the world's people share the benefits of globalization.
>
> Kofi Annan (Seventh Secretary-General of the United Nations)

On the whole, any attempt to stop the process of globalization in the present day scenario would be futile. We must seriously analyse its beneficial and harmful aspects and devise suitable ways and means to maximize its benefits for humanity and prevent its damaging effects. Scholars of international relations have evolved diverse perspectives for the analysis of globalization. Of these, the following are particularly important: (*a*) Realist perspective; (*b*) Liberal perspective; and (*c*) Radical perspective.

Perspectives on Globalization

Realist Perspective

Globalization does not alter the existing territorial division of world into nation-states. It increases interdependence of different societies and economies but it does not interfere with the state-system. It does not transcend state sovereignty, nor the struggle for political power between states.

Liberal Perspective

Globalization has transformed world politics by replacing states as central actors by a myriad of other groups and organizations whose importance differs according to the issue-area concerned. With the help of revolution in technology and communications interlinking economies of different nations, it has introduced a new international division of labour, bringing greater efficiency, choice and prosperity.

Radical Perspective

Globalization is nothing but the latest stage in the development of international capitalism. Above all it is a Western-led phenomenon which further deepens the existing divide between the metropolitan and peripheral economies. At best it is an instrument of neo-colonialism.

It is worth-noting that the realist perspective attempts to project an objective view of globalization, but it largely evades its critical evaluation from the viewpoint of developing nations. The liberal perspective seems to be biased in favour of advanced nations while the radical perspective sees it as a source of injustice towards developing nations. Resistance to globalization largely comes from the radical circles. Instead of rejecting it altogether, the developing nations must resist only those aspects of globalization which can be proved to imply injustice towards their economy or polity. They should also try to take advantage of the new opportunities of economic development thrown open to them by the process of globalization.

10

Diverse Perspectives on the State

CONCEPT OF THE state comprises the core of political thought. Political thought has been defined as 'thought about the state, its structure, its nature, and its purpose'. There is a long tradition of political thought. Several political thinkers and schools of thought have developed ideas about the nature and purpose of the state according to different points of view. When new ideas appeared, old ideas were criticized or modified. In the realm of political philosophy it is not necessary that old ideas be dead before the new ideas become acceptable. Unlike the principles of natural sciences (such as physics, chemistry and biology), the old and new principles of political theory exist simultaneously, claiming their rightful place. None of the current political ideas can claim absolute authority or validity. Their merits and demerits need constant examination before arriving at any consistent conclusions.

An acquaintance with the diverse perspectives on the state would equip us with valuable insights for dealing with public affairs. Of these, the following may be treated as particularly important: (*a*) Organic theory of the state; (*b*) Mechanistic Theory of the State; (*c*) Liberal-individualist perspective; (*d*) Welfare State perspective; (*e*) Class perspective; (*f*) Communitarian perspective; (*g*) Post-colonial perspective; (*h*) Gandhian perspective; (*i*) Feminist perspective; and (*j*) Pluralist perspective. Our purpose should be to bring out complexity of the problem, and not to pronounce any final verdict. Political theory can only provide provisional solution or a working formula in the light of our understanding of a given situation, but debate must go on as and when a new genius enters the fray.

[1] ORGANIC THEORY OF THE STATE

The organic (or organismic) theory of the state represents the earliest thinking about the nature of the state although it has received some new interpretations in recent times. In a nutshell, this theory compares the state with an *organism* or a living body, and the individuals with its organs. This has two obvious implications. In the first place, since the existence and worth of the organs depend on the existence of the organism, so the existence and worth of individuals depend on the existence of the state. Secondly, different organs are fit to perform different functions within the organism—some of them are naturally superior to others. Likewise, different groups and classes in society are naturally fit to perform different functions—some are destined to enjoy a superior position in relation to others in the interests of the entire society.

THE STATE AS A NATURAL INSTITUTION

Organic theory of the state regards the state as a natural institution. According to this view, you cannot imagine the existence of man as man, that is as a civilized being, without the existence of the state. Thus, ancient Greeks held the view that the state comes into existence for the sake of life, and continues for the sake of good life. In other words, the existence of the state is an essential condition of the existence of man as a civilized being. That is why Aristotle held that man by nature is a 'political animal'. One who lives without the state is, in Aristotle's view, either a beast or a god. The state is so fundamental to human existence that Aristotle declared in his typical style: *'State is prior to man'*. This is not intended to describe a historical fact, but to make a logical point since you cannot think of man *as such* (that is one who is neither *subhuman* nor *superhuman)* without thinking of the state, as you cannot think of an organ without thinking of its position in an organism. Thus, Aristotle *(Politics,* Book I) describes the relation between the individual and the state as follows:

> The State is by nature clearly prior to the family and to the individual, since the whole is of necessity prior to the part; for example, if the whole body be destroyed there will be no foot or hand, except in an equivocal sense, as we might speak of a stone hand; for when destroyed the hand will be not better than that... The proof that the State is a creation of nature and prior to the individual is that the individual, when isolated, is not self-sufficing; and therefore he is like a part in relation to the whole. But he who is unable to live in society, or who has no need because he is sufficient for himself, must be either a beast or a god.

The view of the state as a natural institution was challenged by the scientific revolution of the seventeenth century which advanced the 'mechanistic' theory of the state. However, towards the end of the eighteenth century and throughout the nineteenth century men became dissatisfied with the mechanistic theory which looked upon individuals as spare parts of a machine. This led to a renewed interest in the organic theory of the state for a meaningful explanation of the relation between individual and the state. Edmund Burke (1729-97), the chief exponent of conservatism, argued that the state was the product of a process of historical growth which he often likened to the growth of a living organism. Like an organism, Burke argued, the state could not survive its dissection; it was also greater and more complex than any of the parts which made it up. Then with the development of 'nationalism', the state was portrayed as the embodiment of the nation and an object of worship. This idea served as the basis of the idealist theory. G.W.F. Hegel (1770-1831), a German philosopher, was the most eloquent champion of this view who declared: 'State is march of God on earth.'

The modern theory of evolution gave a new impetus to likening the state with biological phenomena. Thus, the organic theory of the state received a new fillip from the contributions of the *biological school* of political theory, which flourished in the nineteenth century. The pioneers of this school likened the development of political institutions with the growth of living beings towards higher forms of life as manifested in the increasing differentiation of parts. The metaphor was stretched to such a degree that they sometimes drew strange parallels between the state and natural man. They spoke of the 'tissues of the State', of its systems of nutrition and circulation, of organs within it fulfilling specifically the functions of brain, nerves, fibres, heart, muscles, even stomach and nose. Bluntschli (1801-81) went to the extent of saying that the state was the masculine sex while the Church was feminine.

THE STATE AS AN ETHICAL INSTITUTION

The second implication of the saying that 'the State comes into existence for the sake of life and continues for the sake of good life' is that the state is an instrument of good life. In other words, living in a state enables man not only survive but also secure an excellent life. Accordingly, the state has a moralizing effect on the life of man so that, by performing his duties and enjoying his rights as a citizen of the state, man is able to achieve moral excellence. Thus, the organic theory views the state as an ethical institution.

The ethical foundations of the state, as envisaged by the organic theory, rest on the differentiation of functions. Aristotle, like any other champion of the organic theory, believes in the natural differences between the capabilities of different individuals. He declares in clear terms: "From the hour of birth some men are marked out for subjection and others for rule." Thus, some are destined to be masters and others to be slaves. In this way Aristotle treats slavery as a natural institution, and defends it on the grounds that the masters are endowed with a high degree of virtue which can be preserved by enjoying the *leisure* while the slaves can benefit from that virtue by serving their masters. Thus, the institution of slavery is supposed to secure the good life both for the masters and the slaves.

An important contribution to the theory of the state as an ethical institution was made by the modern *biological school* of political theory. Drawing a clear distinction between the organic view and the mechanistic view of the state, the exponents of the biological school identified three essential characteristics of an organism:

(*a*) In the first place, there is an intrinsic relationship between the parts and the whole. Thus, unlike the part of a machine, the part of an organism has no existence apart from its position within that organism. For instance, a wheel retains its essential character as a wheel whether it is fitted in a machine or taken out, while a hand loses its character as a hand as soon as it is separated from the body;

(*b*) Secondly, an organism shows organic unity of its parts and it tends to grow from within. In a machine, old parts can be replaced by the new, but an organism cannot be altered by substituting new parts for old, yet it can transform itself gradually through natural growth; and finally,

(*c*) An organism exists as an end-in-itself while a machine is, at best, a means to an end which exists outside itself.

The exponents of the biological school maintained that the state possesses all the three characteristics of an organism and, therefore, it should be regarded as organic in nature. Thus, they recognized an intrinsic relation between man and the state. As an organism is the real source of life and energy for its parts, so the state is the spring of good life for its citizens. Some writers even claimed that the state represents the developed form of the rational nature of man, and therefore eulogized the state as a 'Moral Organism', 'Super-organism', and an 'Organism of Organisms'. Some of them attributed personality to the state and glorified it as a 'Real Person' or a 'Super Person'. As distinct organs of an organism, such as hands, feet or teeth, can have no real interest of their own apart from the interest of the organism itself, so the interests of individuals could not be distinguished from the interest of the state. Thus, the champions of the organic theory claimed that individuals could have any rights within the state but they could never have any rights against the state. True freedom of the individual lies in obedience to the laws of the state.

A CRITICAL ESTIMATE

Indeed, the organic theory of the state has been in vogue since ancient times. It was challenged by the mechanistic theory in the seventeenth century, but its revival in the nineteenth century is an ample proof of its strength. The organic theory views the state as the greatest institution which helps man achieve the highest development of his potential. However, in spite of some merit, the weaknesses of the organic theory are quite striking.

Subordination of Man to the State

In this theory, man is completely overshadowed by the state. His personality is not only subordinated but submerged in the personality of the state. In this scheme, man is treated as no more than a conduit pipe for the divine energy, as a passive creature for whom things must be done, not as a being who finds fulfilment in positive activity. The individual is not allowed to take a stand at the instance of his own conscience because he cannot rise above his predetermined position within the framework of the state.

The organic theory, in fact, visualizes the attributes of an 'ideal' state and prescribes relations between man and the state accordingly. In actual practice, however, the state is represented by a set of men exercising the powers and functions of the state. Now there is no mechanism to ensure that these men will display the same degree of wisdom, sincerity and responsibility as attributed to an 'ideal' state.

Thus, in its actual working, the organic theory subjects men to the authority of state officials—legislators, ministers, judges, bureaucrats, military commanders, etc.—who may be as imperfect as their subjects, if not more than they are. At times state officials may take decisions according to their narrow selfish interests. Disastrous decisions may be taken at whim of the decision-makers displaying their utter lack of vision. If the authority of such decisions is considered absolute and beyond challenge, and if all citizens are required to sacrifice everything in the name of the state, such decisions are bound to destroy the state itself. The experiences of the Nazi and Fascist regimes in Germany and Italy respectively during the period between the two World Wars offer a striking example of such an eventuality.

Distorted View of Freedom

The organic theory postulates that man can have no rights against the state, and thus leaves no safeguards for his liberty. In fact, it reduces the liberty of the individual to obedience to the commands of the state. It ignores the distinction between the state and society while determining the extent of the authority of the state. Robert M. MacIver (*The Web of Government;* 1965) has, therefore, rightly observed:

> If we do not distinguish society, with its countless uncentralized relationships and activities, from the state, with its specific centrally coordinated activities, we are on the dangerous road to totalitarianism. Then we shall demand that men surrender themselves, their all, to the state—which means that government becomes the complete master of men.

This sort of queer logic has been invoked by several thinkers and statesmen for a complete suppression of man's freedom. As MacIver has further pointed out:

> This is the road Rousseau opened up when he spoke of 'forcing men to be free'. This is the road Fichte and Hegel prepared, making them the

forerunners of the ruinous and finally nihilistic doctrine of Fascists and Nazis. This is the road that under the signs of liberty and unity invites men to the concentration camp and the death of the creative spirit.

Nihilism

Nihilism refers to an outlook that harbours negative attitude towards everything. For a nihilist, nothing is worth believing, worth protecting or worth respecting. He holds no purpose in life; no allegiance to anyone.

Denial of Equality

The organic theory of the state is essentially undemocratic. Following the analogy of the organism it argues that since the toes cannot dictate to the brain, so there is no question of representation of the ordinary people to the seat of authority. Thus, wisdom and authority become the monopoly of the chosen few and the masses are alienated from the process of decision-making. This is a clever device for preserving the inequality of status and opportunity on the pretext of supposed ethical principles. Such arguments have been frequently advanced by all those who have vested interests in the prevailing injustice in society whether they have been justifying slavery, racial supremacy, imperialism or any other form of discriminatory practice. There is no scientific evidence of any fundamental differences in the excellence of different categories of people. Most differences in the excellence of people in any sphere of life are the product of the socio-economic arrangements. Educational development, economic opportunities, adequate health-care and cultural participation, wherever provided, have always helped develop their excellence which was never recognized by the champions of the organic theory of the state.

[II]
MECHANISTIC THEORY OF THE STATE: IDEA OF THE SOCIAL CONTRACT

Mechanistic theory of the state, as distinguished from *organic theory of the state,* arose in a particular historical setting when several factors contributed to its development. The growth of the physical sciences in seventeenth century Europe tended to transform men's ideas about society and the state. It was now argued that since 'nature' itself behaved like a machine, governed by universal laws to be discovered by observation and reason, so society and the state should also be understood as mechanisms. Thus, the social order came to be understood as a part of the 'natural order' and any *interference* with the spontaneous adjustment between individuals was thought to be detrimental to the smooth functioning of the social order. This idea of 'non-interference' highly suited the interests and aptitudes of the new middle class—the merchants and the industrialists who flourished in those days in the climate of a 'free market' society. The philosophy of liberalism emerged against this background, which sought to protect the social and economic interests of this class.

Liberalism

Liberalism refers to a principle of politics which regards 'liberty' or 'freedom' of individual as the first and foremost goal of public policy. Liberty, in this sense, implies 'liberation' from restraints, particularly from the restraints imposed by an authoritarian state. This principle was evolved in the West in late seventeenth century in order to liquidate feudal privileges of the land-owning class and to create favourable conditions for the new entrepreneurial class to enable them to contribute to social progress.

This new perspective on the state was particularly strengthened from two sides: (*a*) the exponents of the 'social contract' sought to trace the origin of the state in a way that fitted into liberal mode of thought; and (*b*) the exponents of modern economics made a strong case for *laissez-faire* individualism which confirmed liberal-individualist view of the state.

THEORY OF THE SOCIAL CONTRACT

The theory of the social contract presents a typical version of the origin of the state from the liberal point of view. This theory treats the state as the product of the mutual agreement of men, created with a definite purpose, to serve certain social needs.

The liberal theory originated from the mechanistic concept of the state although some later thinkers, like T.H. Green (1836-82) and H.J. Laski (1893-1950) joined the liberal stream without subscribing to the mechanistic concept. In short, the mechanistic theory treats the state as an artificial contrivance. It postulates deliberate efforts behind the formation of the state. This implies the possibility of two life-patterns—one before the origin of the state, the other after the creation of the state. According to this theory, the state is not a natural institution, but an artificial device or instrument invented by men for their mutual benefit; it is intended to serve the interests of all individuals or all sections of society. It regards the state as the product of the will of society; hence, it is an expression of the 'common will'.

The idea of the creation of the state through a contract is found in a rudimentary form in ancient thought of both the East and the West. Kautilya's *Arthashastra* makes a pointed reference to it while some ancient Greek sophists described the state as an outcome of the contract between men. Some traces of this theory are also found in ancient Roman law. But all these references should not be taken to mean that the theory of the social contract flourished in ancient times. On the contrary, this theory was systematically formulated at a particular point of European history, in order to drop a curtain on the values of the feudal system and to introduce the new values of the capitalist system.

> **Feudalism**
>
> Feudalism refers to the system of economic, political and social organization which flourished in the medieval Europe. Economically it was based on large-scale agriculture where social status of different sections of society was determined by land tenure. Land was held by various ranks of landlords in return for homage and military service to be rendered to the king. It was tilled by serfs who were obliged to render labour services and dues to the landlords. All sections of society including clerics, soldiers, administrators and toilers were tied to each other by mutual obligations. With the advent of Industrial Revolution in the mid of the eighteenth century, it became necessary to break this system to ensure freedom of the new entrepreneurial class as well as the new working class.

EXPONENTS OF THE THEORY

Thomas Hobbes (1588-1679), John Locke (1632-1704) and Jean-Jacques Rousseau (1712-78) are regarded as the main exponents of the theory of the social contract. Of these, Hobbes and Locke are from England while Rousseau belongs to France. This theory held the field in Europe in the seventeenth and eighteenth centuries. Some later thinkers, such as Immanuel Kant (1724-1804), Herbert Spencer (1820-1903), John Rawls (1921-2002) and Robert Nozick (1938-2002) made use of this theory to elaborate their own systems of thought.

Hobbes was a tutor to William Cavendish, the son of Earl of Devonshire. He sought to justify the absolute power of the sovereign in his famous work *Leviathan* (1651). He condemned the Civil War of 1642 as he saw in it the forces of disintegration. He sought to establish the absolute sovereignty of the state as an essential condition of social solidarity.

Locke, on the other hand, sought to justify the Glorious Revolution of 1688. He was an ardent advocate of constitutional monarchy. In his *Two Treatises of Civil Government* (1690), Locke argued that if the monarch ever behaved in a despotic manner, the people had the right to remove him from authority. Brought up in the tradition of British conservatism, Locke was not the sworn enemy of monarchy, but he sought to establish it 'in the consent of the people'.

> **Glorious Revolution**
>
> In the history of England, Glorious Revolution refers to the momentous event of 1688 when King James II was dethroned. In his place, his daughter Mary and her husband William of Orange were enthroned. James was an absolutist; Mary and William accepted the condition of ruling with the advice of Parliament. In this bloodless revolution, an absolute monarchy in England was replaced by a constitutional monarchy.

Rousseau had no such particular purpose to serve. Yet he was a brilliant writer whose ideas not only inspired poets and men of letters but induced the revolutionary upsurge that shook the French polity to its foundations. He is regarded as the source of inspiration of the great French Revolution (1789).

OUTLINE OF THE THEORY

Social contract theory of the origin of the state implies that there was a time when men lived or would have lived without any recognized civil law, without the state. This stage or life-pattern of men is described as the 'state of nature'. Then the state was created through the voluntary agreement of all individuals who constitute the state. Hobbes, Locke and Rousseau have drawn different pictures of the 'state of nature', the 'terms of the contract' and the character of sovereignty which came into existence as a consequence of the birth of the state. It is important to note here that the whole theory of the social contract is based on speculation. It seeks to trace the origin of the state through logic, not through historical or scientific evidence. Locke refers to a historical fact to illustrate this point: the Mayflower Compact (1620)—an agreement drawn by the passengers aboard the 'Mayflower' (the ship) designed to unify the enterprising Europeans who intended to settle in the newly found American continent. In any case, the historical reference used as an illustration is no evidence of its historical character.

THE STATE OF NATURE

The state of nature envisaged how men live or would have lived without the authority of civil law, state or political control. At this stage, there is no industry, no systematic production. Men live not only close to nature, they have to depend on the bounty of nature for their survival. Their behaviour is largely governed by their inner impulses, unrestrained by civil law, although a 'natural law' is supposed to have existed at this stage. Men have no recognized rights, although they enjoy some 'natural rights'. As all these conditions are determined by logic or particular line of argument, not on the basis of any scientific evidence, they do not lead to any uniform conclusion. Different authors have, therefore, given different versions of the state of nature, etc.

HOBBES

Hobbes draws a gloomy picture of the state of nature. This is a natural corollary of his concept of human nature. Hobbes postulates that man is selfish by nature; self-interest is the mainspring of human action. Men are moved to action not by intellect or reason, but by their appetites, desires and passions. In the absence of law and justice, the state of nature is characterized by a perpetual struggle, ceaseless conflict and constant warfare. In Hobbes's own forceful words, the life of man at this stage is 'solitary, poor, nasty, brutish and short'; 'every man is enemy to every man'. In pursuance of his own pleasure, man wants power over others; but as the physical and mental powers of natural men are nearly alike, nobody is able to overpower the other. Hence, men stand in natural fear of each other. It is a state of total insecurity.

In such a state there is no room for industry. 'Might is right' is the order of the day. Men are free to take what they can, and to rob whomsoever they can. There is no law to prevent oppression or to contain the 'law of the jungle'. It is a state of absolute anarchy. Hobbes is quite clear that he is not describing a historical fact, but only trying to demonstrate what would happen if there were no settled government for any length of time.

Hobbes argues that there can be no morality or consciousness of duty or obligation in the state of nature, because these are possible only after the establishment of law and government. Natural rights are, therefore, nothing more than the natural powers of men, used to oppress others. At best, natural liberty is nothing but 'the liberty each man hath to preserve his own life'. This urge for 'self-preservation' is embodied in the law of nature or natural law. This conforms to the rules of prudence and expediency. It is natural law which prompts men to abandon the state of nature and to establish law and government. It consists in the rules of self-preservation, particularly as follows: (*a*) Everybody should aim at securing peace; (*b*) Men should be willing, in concert with others, to give up their natural rights; (*c*) Men should keep their contracts; and finally, (*d*) Men should show gratitude or return beneficence for beneficence. Thus, the requirement of self-preservation itself created a sense of duty in the minds of men which prompts them to form the state.

LOCKE

Locke draws an entirely different picture of the state of nature. In his view, it is not a state of constant warfare. On the contrary, it is a state of 'peace, goodwill, mutual assistance and preservation'. It is a state of liberty, not a state of licence. The majority of people at this stage obey the law of nature, that is the law of inward morality. Men are by nature rational beings, impelled by their inner nature to treat humanity—whether in their own person or in that of any other person—in every case as an end, never as a means only. But still, there are a few persons who set aside the rules of morality in pursuance of their self-interest. In the absence of any established authority in the state of nature, it becomes very difficult to deal with such offenders. If men become judges of their own case, justice would not be secured. In this respect, the state of nature proves to be inconvenient. In order to rectify this defect, men abandon the state of nature and enter into civil or political society by means of a contract.

Natural law, according to Locke, consists in the rules of morality implanted in the human conscience. Natural rights consist in the 'perfect freedom and equality' of every man 'not only to preserve his property, that is his life, liberty and estate, against the injuries and attempts of other men, but to be judge of, and punish the breaches of natural law' committed by others. When men enter into political society, they surrender their natural rights to be judges in case of breaches of law. This power is now vested in the community instead of individuals. But they still retain their natural rights to 'life, liberty and property'.

Locke's picture of the state of nature is, again, hypothetical, not a historical account. As W.T. Jones (*Masters of Political Thought, Vol.* 2; 1971) has elucidated:

> Locke means by the natural law ... a rule for human behaviour only, and one which is not a description of how men do behave, but a statement of how they ought to behave. Hence by his state of nature, paradoxically enough, Locke primarily means something which is *not* natural or historical ... By saying, for instance, that in a state of nature men are free and equal he does not merely mean that there was a time in the past when men were, in fact, free and equal; he means rather to assert that they ought to be free and equal.

ROUSSEAU

Rousseau, in his *Discourse on Inequality* (1755), paints a fascinating picture of the state of nature. He describes natural man as a 'noble savage', living a life of idyllic blissfulness and primitive simplicity. He states that men in the state of nature are equal, self-sufficient and contented. But with the rise of civilization, inequalities raise their head. With the development of arts and science, private property comes into existence with the consequent division of labour. This necessitates the establishment of civil society. The state is thus an evil; its formation becomes necessary due to inequalities among men. Here Rousseau seems to anticipate Marx as regards the origin of the state.

However, in his later work *The Social Contract* (1762), Rousseau takes a modified view of the civil state. He seeks to justify its existence, not as a manifestation of inequalities in society but as an instrument for the protection of liberty. In his opening sentence of *The Social Contract,* Rousseau strikes a different note: 'Man is born free, but he is everywhere in chains.' He seems to make the point that the civil state has deprived man of his natural liberty. But he immediately proceeds to 'ignore this question' and attempt a justification of this 'change'. He seeks justification of authority in the natural agreement among men. So he observes: "Since no man has a natural authority over other men, and since might never makes right, it follows that agreements are the basis for all legitimate authority among men." When men abandon the state of nature to enter into civil society through the social contract, their loss is handsomely compensated. As Rousseau asserts, what man loses by the social contract is his natural liberty and unlimited right to all which attracts him and which he can obtain; what he gains is civil liberty and the property of what he possesses.

TERMS OF THE CONTRACT

Corresponding to their notions of the state of nature, natural law and natural rights, Hobbes, Locke and Rousseau have given different interpretations of the terms of the social contract.

HOBBES

Hobbes postulates a single contract by which men abandon the state of nature and establish society and state together. Through this historical fiction he tries to convey a philosophical truth—that the government does not rest on sheer force; it rests on the will of the people.

The social contract, according to Hobbes, is concluded among the people themselves who emerge from the state of nature. The sovereign is not a party to the contract. According to Hobbes's logic, the sovereign did not exist before the conclusion of the contract—he comes into existence as a result of this contract, hence he cannot be a party to the contract. It is a contract of each with all and of all with each, to set up a sovereign authority. By this contract every man gave up his natural rights and powers to a 'common power' who would 'keep them in awe' and give them security. Men entered into the social contract to set up a ruler, as if every man should say to every man: "I authorize and give up my right of governing myself to this man, or to this assembly of men, on this condition, that thou give up thy right to him, and authorize all his actions in like manner."

Thus the social contract brings a sovereign into existence who enjoys supreme and absolute authority. All men in society, apart from the sovereign himself, become his subjects. All natural rights of men are surrendered to the sovereign once and for all. The powers conferred on him cannot be withdrawn, because if men chose to revive their natural rights, they would revert into the state of nature, characterized by anarchy and total insecurity. Hobbes, therefore, does not admit people's right to revolt or revolution. On this basis, he condemned the English civil war of 1642.

> **English Civil War**
>
> **In British history, Civil War refers to the horrific war (1642-49) between Royalists (supporters of absolute powers of King Charles I) and Parliamentarians (champions of the overriding powers of the Parliament). In this long-drawn war, the Royalists were defeated, and Charles I was executed at the behest of the Parliamentary army in 1649.**

Since, according to Hobbes, the state and society come into existence together through a single contract, repudiation of the contract would result not only in the overthrow of the government but the disintegration of society itself. That is why Hobbes treats sovereignty as absolute, indivisible and inalienable. He creates unlimited political obligation.

Hobbes's theory of the social contract would appear flawless only if a perfect and infallible person or assembly could be found and established as sovereign. But how can imperfect mortals justify the exercise of such a universal and absolute authority in the real world? Hobbes cleverly evades this fundamental question.

LOCKE

Locke tries to overcome this difficulty by postulating several stages of the contract. As Jeremy Waldron has elucidated: "Contract and consent have three stages in Locke's description: first, men must agree unanimously to come together as a community and pool their natural powers so that they can act together to uphold one another's rights; second, the members of this community must agree by a majority vote to set up legislative and other institutions; third, the owners of property in a society must agree, either personally or through their representatives, to whatever taxes are imposed on the people" (*The Blackwell Encyclopaedia of Political Thought,* edited by David Miller; 1987). This theory of several stages of the contract marks a clear departure from Hobbes's position. Hobbes postulates that society and state are formed together; they are dissolved together. On the contrary, Locke believes that society and state were created in different steps: creation of society is the primary step; setting up of the government is a secondary step. So, if the government is dissolved, society does not disintegrate. Order will be restored by setting up another government in its place.

In Locke's system of thought the nature of government resembles a 'trust'. In other words, a government, like a trust, is bound to act within the terms of its constitution. By drawing a distinction between the process of formation of society and state, Locke places government under the control of society. This leaves no scope for absolutism. As Waldron has significantly observed: "Absolutism of the kind Thomas Hobbes envisaged is ruled out on the grounds that people hold their natural rights to life and liberty as a sort of trust from God and therefore cannot transfer them to the arbitrary power of another. Since government is set up to protect property and other rights and not to undermine them, the government may not take or redistribute property without consent" (*ibid.*)!

While Hobbes creates absolute sovereignty, Locke evolves a constitutional government. Hobbes postulates an unconditional surrender of natural liberty to the sovereign, because in his system of thought natural liberty is the source of constant conflict and consequent anarchy. Locke postulates conditional and partial surrender of natural rights, because some natural rights are fundamental; they cannot be given up because they are the cornerstone of human freedom.

According to Locke, people give up their natural right to 'judge of and punish the offenders of natural law' in their own case or in the case of other persons. This right is now vested in the community, the 'common power' or the government which assumes the role of 'umpire'. But this right is surrendered on the condition that their rights to 'life, liberty and property' will be protected and kept intact. Society retains the authority to watch whether the government is exercising its powers strictly in accordance with the terms of the contract or not.

This implies: (*a*) in the first place, that government must govern with the 'consent of the people'. It is the people who are endowed with the faculty of 'reason'—conscience, sense of morality, knowledge of right and wrong. Government is created by the will of the people, but as an artificial device it cannot embody 'superior reason'; and (*b*) secondly, if in any case the government falters from its duty, the people have the right to overthrow that government and set up another government in its place. Thus, Locke recognizes the people's right to revolution. It is on this basis that he justifies the 'bloodless' or 'Glorious' revolution of 1688, which had led to the flight of James II from England and the establishment of William and Mary on the throne.

It is significant that Locke treats 'right to property' as a fundamental natural right which cannot be surrendered to the government. He proceeds on the assumption that property consists in one's 'fruit of labour'. Locke argues that when an individual mixes his labour with natural resources, this act is sufficient to establish his exclusive right on the product which does not depend on the consent of other people. Locke's theory of taxation is also based on his notion of the citizen's right to property. He postulates that the government should take only what is necessary to carry on its business. It has no power to take anything more without the owner's consent.

ROUSSEAU

Rousseau, like Hobbes, postulates a single contract, and thereby creates absolute, indivisible and inalienable sovereignty. But Rousseau distinguishes himself as an exponent of popular sovereignty. Sovereignty, according to Rousseau, is not vested in a ruler apart from society itself as Hobbes had assumed; instead, it is vested in the people themselves. When people enter into the social contract, they relinquish their natural rights in their individual capacity; they surrender these rights to their collective whole. Thus, what they lose in their individual capacity, they get back in their corporate capacity, in improved form. No one is a loser in the bargain. Everybody is a gainer, because when any one is attacked, society as a whole comes to his rescue. Sovereignty is indivisible, yet it is shared by each member of the civil society. In Rousseau's own words: "Each of us puts his person and all his power in common under the supreme direction of the *general will,* and in our corporate capacity we receive each member as an indivisible part of the whole."

> **General Will**
>
> **According to Jean-Jaques Rousseau (*The Social Contract;* 1762) the *general will* refers to the point of convergence of the real will of all members of a community. It reflects the true good of each individual as well as the common good of the whole community. Sovereignty of the *general will* constitutes the foundation of popular sovereignty.**

The creation of popular sovereignty by vesting it in the *general will* is a unique contribution of Rousseau which laid the foundations of modern democracy. As Robert M. MacIver (*The Modern State;* 1926) has elucidated:

> The secret of Rousseau's doctrine is found in the substitution, for a sovereign of *the* sovereign. His sovereign is the 'general will', and he is perfectly ready to apply to it all the sweeping attributes which Hobbes delivers to his 'one man or assembly of men'. It too is one and indivisible, inerrant, indestructible, omnipotent.

Rousseau, of course, maintains that liberty in the state of nature is a great boon. But in due course of time, when population multiplies and the treasures of nature start depleting, it is no longer possible for men to enjoy natural liberty as before. In other words, natural liberty is now threatened because of the changed circumstances. When the gifts of nature no longer sustain men, they have to consolidate their own powers to save themselves. They, therefore, create civil society to maintain their freedom. As MacIver has observed:

> The precarious liberty of the state of nature is well lost for the assured and enlarged liberty of the social order. The idea that law was not merely consistent with liberty, not merely a possible guardian of it, but the very form of its realization, was of profound importance for the true interpretation of the state. It gave a new and most significant setting to the problem of political obligation. For Rousseau that problem solves itself when government is vested in the true sovereign, the 'general will'. When that is attained, then 'each, coalescing with all, may nevertheless obey only himself, and remain as free as before' (*ibid.*).
>
> (Political Obligation = the grounds and extent of individual's obligation to obey law and the commands of political authority.)

In other words, when man acts in the state against his own will under the direction of the *general will,* he is not losing his freedom. In fact, the constraint imposed by the *general will* is instrumental for securing his larger and ultimate freedom, which reconciles freedom of each with freedom of all. Thus, Rousseau, in his typical style, postulates a condition when 'man can be forced to be free'.

The concept of the *general will* is the heart of Rousseau's doctrine, which must be distinguished from other types of human will. As Patrick Riley has elucidated: "Rousseau himself insists that 'the general will is always right', that it is 'the will that one has as a citizen'—when one thinks of the common good and not of one's own particular will as a private person" (*The Blackwell Encyclopaedia of Political Thought,* edited by David Miller; 1987). Subsequent writers have used the distinction between actual will and real will in order to explicate Rousseau's distinction between particular will and general will. The existence of these two types of will is the source of conflict within the mind of man. Actual will is motivated by his immediate, selfish interest. Real will is motivated by his ultimate, collective good. Actual will is reflected in his 'lower self'; real will is reflected in his 'higher self'. Actual will prompts him towards gratification of his desires; real will induces him to acts of reason. Actual will is transient, unstable and inconsistent; it changes from moment to moment. Real will is stable, constant, consistent and determinate. Man's freedom consists in overcoming his actual will and following the direction of the real will. Real will expresses his true freedom. It subordinates man's self-interest to the interests of the community—common interest or common good—which is shared by each and all.

But individual by himself is imperfect. At times he may not be able to discriminate between his actual and real will. This dilemma is resolved by the transition from the 'particular' to the *'general' will.* The *general will* harmonizes the interests of each with those of all. It is neither a 'compromise' nor the common denominator, but the point of convergence of the real will of all—an expression of the highest in every man. It is the spirit of citizenship in its concrete shape. Man's particular will may push him to a state of confusion; but the *general will* always shows him the right way.

Following this line of argument, Rousseau travels much ahead of his original position. He starts with describing civil society as an expression of *'superior will'* but ends up with treating it as an expression of *'superior reason'*. He starts with the mechanistic view of the state but ends up with the organic view of the state. He starts as an ardent liberal but ends up as an ardent idealist. *Rousseau was the most brilliant writer of his time* but he is also most confusing. *Liberals and idealists adore him alike; they also condemn him alike.*

Idealism

As a philosophical doctrine, idealism regards 'idea' or 'consciousness' as the essence of the universe, and treats all social institutions as the manifestation of the prevailing idea. It recognizes dynamic character of the idea, and holds that the idea keeps on moving ahead in the direction of a perfect moral order. As a political outlook, idealism calls for identification of a perfect moral order and requires the individual to abide by the dictates of that moral order.

A CRITICAL APPRAISAL

Social contract theory of the origin of the state has been described as 'bad history, bad logic and bad philosophy'. It has been subjected to searching criticism from various angles.

David Hume (1711-76) argued that government was not created through a deliberate decision of the people. It arose because people realized that it was to their advantage to support any authority that enforced the rules of justice effectively. Hence, the idea of the social contract as depicted by Hobbes, Locke and others was both historically improbable and philosophically unnecessary to explain allegiance. As Roger Scruton has elucidated: "Hume attacked the doctrine of the social contract, arguing that the criterion of tacit consent is inapplicable, most people being inevitably constrained by cultural, linguistic and habitual ties to stay where they are, whatever the government that should exert jurisdiction over them" (A *Dictionary of Political Thought;* 1982).

The theory of the social contract is not founded on any historical evidence. When we trace the origin of an institution like the state, it is not proper to rely on mere fiction, like that of the social contract. There is no historical validity of the assumption that men originally lived in a so-called state of nature, and then they thought of creating political institutions by mutual agreement to establish order and security. The Mayflower Compact of 1620 is often cited to show the possibility of a social contract. It was a statement drawn by English emigrants to America travelling by the ship *Mayflower:* "We do solemnly and mutually, in the presence of God and one another, covenant and combine ourselves together into a civil body-politic for our better ordering and preservation." This historical illustration, however, cannot be treated as an evidence of the historical character of the social contract. Even the illustration is not adequate. The Mayflower Compact was drawn up by men who were already familiar with government; they were not emerging from a state of nature as the exponents of social contract theory have postulated.

In the second place, Sir Henry Maine's historical research on early political institutions has found no evidence to show that social and political organization owes its origin to any deliberate contract among men. According to Maine's theory, the movement has been from one of 'status' to one of 'contract'. Thus, in primitive society, membership of a social group determined the status of an individual. The idea of the contract emerged with the dawn of the modern era, when the individual could change his status through a free contract.

To shift the modern idea of the contract to the earliest times is, therefore, a bad logic. The idea of the contract is an individualist idea; it makes the will of the individual the basis for political authority. Primitive man was not at all aware of this idea. Life of the primitive man was largely governed by custom at the various levels of groupings—family, clan, phratry, tribe, gen, etc. Law, sovereignty and political institutions grew from this process in a very slow and gradual manner, not by a compact of freely contracting individuals.

Moreover, a contract, in order to be valid, requires the force or sanction of the state, which exists above and apart from the contracting parties. The so-called social contract had no such sanction behind it, because it precedes the establishment of the state itself.

Again, the theory of the social contract postulates the existence of natural liberty and natural rights in the state of nature, that is before the formation of the state. This does not stand up to logic. Rights are the product of a developed social consciousness which are enforced by the institutionalized law. How could natural rights have existed in the earliest stage when political awareness and institutionalized law were totally absent? Edmund Burke (1729-97) argued that the social contract, if it could be said to exist at all, certainly marked the surrender of natural rights.

Exponents of the Social Contract: Comparative Study

The Issue	*Hobbes's View*	*Locke's View*	*Rousseau's View*
Human Nature	Selfish and Cruel	Rational Being	Simple and Innocent ('noble savage')
State of Nature	War of every-one against everyone	State of Peace, Good Will, Mutual Assistance and Preservation	State of 'idyllic blissfulness'
Natural Rights	Natural powers to oppress others + natural urge for self-preservation	Right to life Liberty and property	Natural Liberty to fulfil all needs from the natural world as long as there is natural abundance
Purpose of the Contract	Creation of an all-powerful Sovere-ign who would contral everyone and protect every one	Setting up a Government that would protect natural rights of men and punish the offenders	When the scarcity situation arises, civil society must be formed to provide security of property earned by people's own labour
Terms of the Social Contract	Every man gives up his natural rights and powers to a 'common power' who would keep them in awe and give them security	Men agree to pool their natural power and uphold one another's rights; they give up the right to be the judge in their own case	All Individuals surrender their natural liberty to the power of the community that provides them civil liberty; what they lose as individuals, gain back as as members of the community
Nature of the Sovereignty	Supreme and Absolute Sovereignty	Limited Sovereignty — Government as a Trust of the Community	Absolute, Indivisible and and Inalienable Sovereignty of the General Will
Revelant Political Theory	Absolutism; no scope for right to resistance	Constitutionalism; people's right to revolution conceded	Popular Sovereignty; right to resistance not necessary

From the philosophical point of view, it is not fair to treat any contract as eternally binding on all generations. Tom Paine (1737-1809) criticized the theory of the social contract from this viewpoint and declared it a dead weight on the wheel of progress. He asserted: "Every age and generation must be as free to act for itself in all cases as the age and generations which preceded it". It is significant that the idea of the freedom of contract, which was regarded as sacrosanct from the seventeenth century to the nineteenth century, is no longer upheld by progressive thinkers of the modern age.

The theory of the social contract tries to demonstrate that the state is the product of the will of all individuals comprising the state. It establishes the state as an instrument of harmonizing the interests of all individuals and all sections of society. But, in any society, particularly in modern capitalist society, some dominant sections or the chosen few are so well-organized and vocal that they become self-styled representatives of the will of society, and seek to justify their authority on this ground. The complex problem of social inequality and injustice needs a more searching analysis. It cannot be solved through a simplistic formula of the 'social contract'.

It is significant that the theory of the social contract was advanced at a juncture when the system of feudal relations was giving way to the norms of market society, which laid the foundations of the capitalist system. The relations of the feudal society are determined by tradition; those of the capitalist society are determined by contract. The doctrine of the social contract played a historical role by providing for a theoretical justification for the new pattern of human relations necessitated by the emergence of the capitalist society.

[III]
LIBERAL-INDIVIDUALIST PERSPECTIVE

THEORY OF *LAISSEZ-FAIRE* INDIVIDUALISM

Theory of *laissez-faire* individualism was developed by classical liberalism or negative liberalism, which started taking shape in the eighteenth century and was systematically formulated in the nineteenth century. It placed individual at the centre of its philosophy. It sought to argue that individual is endowed with the faculty of 'reason' which enables him to find what is most conducive to his interests. Classical liberalism, therefore, advocated individual's right to freedom of trade, freedom of contract, freedom to bargain and freedom of enterprise. It postulated private property as the condition of progress, because property was viewed as a product of individual's labour, ingenuity and enterprise. Since all freedoms of the individual ensued from the element of 'reason', they were regarded valuable for society. The profit motive of the individuals and their open competition were, therefore, regarded as 'functional' and, hence, conducive to social progress. The function of the government was to protect individual's freedom or liberty, to enforce contracts, to guarantee peaceful employment of property and to provide the external conditions of law and order.

With its emphasis on individual as the centre of importance, classical liberalism advocated the policy of *laissez-faire,* a French term which means 'leave alone'. It signified non-intervention by the state in the economic activities of individuals. This phrase was in common usage in mercantile and industrial circles in nineteenth century England, and in other parts of the world, to express a belief in the freedom of industry and economic activity from state interference. *Laissez-faire* individualism refers to an aspect of liberal political theory which regards property rights of the individual as a necessary condition of liberty, and seeks to set definite and circumscribed limits on the regulatory powers vested in the government over social and economic processes. This theory dubs the state a 'necessary evil': it is evil because it imposes regulations and restricts the freedom of the individual, yet it is necessary because, without its regulation, freedom of the individual cannot be safeguarded.

EXPONENTS OF THE THEORY

The exponents of *laissez-faire* individualism include Adam Smith (1723-90), Jeremy Bentham (1748-1832), James Mill (1773-1836) and Herbert Spencer (1820-1903), British economists and political thinkers. Besides, John Stuart Mill (1806-73), the famous English economist and political thinker, made an important contribution to the theory of *laissez-faire* individualism, but the development of his thought marks the transition from negative liberalism to positive liberalism, and thereby he made a unique contribution to liberal theory.

ADAM SMITH

Adam Smith was a Scotsman. He is regarded as the father of the science of economics. His famous work, *Inquiry into the Nature and Causes of the Wealth of Nations* (1776), became an important source of the ideas and policies in favour of *laissez-faire* individualism.

Influence of Physiocrats

Smith was deeply influenced by the *Physiocrats*—a French school of economic thought which flourished during the eighteenth century. The Physiocrats who were inspired by Rousseau's early thought, believed in the goodness and bounty of nature and the goodness of man 'as he came from the bosom of nature'. In their view, government should always strive to conform to nature. So long as men do not interfere with each other's liberty and do not combine among themselves in order to encroach upon the liberty of others, governments should leave them free to find their own salvation. Criminals, mad men, and monopolists should be eliminated. The state should not interfere in the activities of normal and law-abiding citizens. From this followed the doctrine of free trade between nations on grounds of both justice and economy. For, the greater the competition, the more will each strive to economize on the cost of his labour to the general advantage.

Adam Smith learned a lot from the Physiocrats, but he sought to eliminate their errors and to develop those ideas which suited his own thinking. He rejected the leading idea of the Physiocrats that agriculture was the sole source of the wealth produced. He held the view that commerce and industry, as well as agriculture, were the source of wealth. His main objective was to find out which policy of the state would be conducive to increasing the wealth of a nation and to promoting national prosperity.

Concept of Economic Man

Smith asserted that everyone has a natural propensity to trade. If given a free rein, this tendency would stimulate economic activity, resulting in an increase in the production of goods. The profit motive is a natural instinct which inspires every trader in his activity. The selfish motive of the enterpriser is, nevertheless, conducive to promotion of the general good. It harmonizes with national prosperity, thereby benefiting all—government, business and labour.

Nineteenth century critics of orthodox economic theory have used the term *'economic man'* to deprecate this view of human nature. They have accused Adam Smith and other classical economists of having grossly distorted the true nature of man by assuming that, in a capitalist system, virtually all economic activity must be motivated by purely selfish considerations, and thus giving prominence to baser motives at the expense of the higher values of life. The classical economists, including Adam Smith, no doubt stressed on the importance of self-interest in the field of economic behaviour. But Adam Smith never gave a blanket endorsement to the idea of beneficence of self-interest. Yet he was convinced that self-interest frequently played an essentially beneficent role in economic affairs, for in the pursuit of his own interests, man on occasion was 'led by an invisible hand to promote an end which was no part of his intention'.

Capitalism

Capitalism refers to an economic system of the modern age largely based on industrial mode of production where means of social production (land, buildings, mines, forests, machinery and capital), distribution and exchange are owned by private entrepreneurs, a large number of workers are employed on wages at the market rate, and economic activity is primarily devoted to private profit. Here workers are free to work anywhere according to their skills and capabilities as well as market demand.

Smith argued that the selfish individual, while working within the framework of competition, would unwittingly promote the welfare of society despite his exclusive concern with furthering his own interests. It is significant that Smith's formulation in this respect came to occupy a central place in orthodox economic theory, and was soon refined through the instrumentality of hedonistic psychology which regarded considerations of pleasure and pain as the prime movers of human behaviour. Many prominent economists of the nineteenth century, including the Utilitarians—Jeremy Bentham and his followers accepted this view of man. They regarded man as a highly rational creature who persistently endeavoured by means of the hedonistic calculus, to maximize pleasure and minimize pain.

Concept of Natural Liberty

In accordance with his concept of man, Adam Smith postulated a system of 'natural liberty'—implying perfect freedom of commerce and industry—in order to promote national prosperity. He emphasized the key role of businessman in the economic life of a nation. He argued that businessman knows his own interests far better than any government can tell him. In order to enable the businessman to pursue his interests most effectively, which would automatically contribute to national prosperity, the only wise policy for a government to follow is *laissez-faire*. Thus, in his *Wealth of Nations* (1776), Adam Smith defined the system of 'natural liberty' as follows:

> Everyman, as long as he does not violate the laws of justice, is left perfectly free to pursue his own interest in his own way, and to bring both his industry and capital into competition with those of any other man or order of men. The sovereign is completely discharged from...the duty of superintending the industry of the private people, and of directing it towards the employments most suitable to the interest of the society.

Functions of Government

According to this system of 'natural liberty', the role of government is confined to three duties of great importance: (*a*) defence of the nation against foreign aggression; (*b*) protection of every member of society, as far as possible, from injustice or oppression of every other member thereof, *i.e.* establishing an exact administration of justice; and (*c*) erection and maintenance of public works and running certain public institutions which could not be undertaken by an individual or a small number of individuals because the profit accruing from their maintenance would never repay the expenditure involved.

Adam Smith, therefore, advocated the abolition of restrictions imposed on commerce and industry by the government in pursuance of the policy of mercantilism. Likewise, he urged that all producers should be free to compete in a free market: to sell their goods, their services and their labour at prices determined by market competition. In this 'obvious and simple system of natural liberty' there would exist the freedom of enterprise, the freedom of trade between nations, the freedom of contract between buyer and seller as well as between employer and worker.

> **Mercantilism**
>
> Mercantilism refers to an economic theory prevailing in seventeenth century and early eighteenth century Europe which held that a nation's power was dependent on national prosperity. National prosperity could be enhanced by maximizing exports and minimizing imports. A nation should import cheap raw materials and export expensive finished goods. Mercantilism upheld the state's intervention in economy for the protection of indigenous industries. It recommended lowering of wages to keep the prices of its products quite low in the world market.

JEREMY BENTHAM

Bentham made an important contribution to the theory of *laissez-faire* individualism as a great exponent of Utilitarianism. Utilitarianism stands for the revival of the classical hedonism of Epicurus. This implied that man's behaviour should be governed by the consideration of advancement of pleasure and avoidance of pain. This theory was adapted by Bentham to the conditions of eighteenth and nineteenth century Europe to prove its relevance.

Concept of Utility

Bentham and his followers argued that the concepts of absolute rights, absolute sovereignty and absolute justice had no relevance to the realities of social life. There was only one absolute standard of regulation of human affairs, *viz.* that of absolute expediency. Political institutions and public policies should, therefore, not be rated as good or bad in relation to some visionary and arbitrary concepts of human rights and obligations; they should be judged by their fruits. These thinkers held that the satisfaction of individual should furnish the yardstick of *utility,* and when a decision is to be taken for the whole society, the controlling principle should be the *'greatest happiness of the greatest number'*.

Bentham interpreted happiness as the balance of pleasure over pain derived from a thing or a course of action. Thus, he postulated: 'Nature has placed mankind under the governance of two sovereign masters, *pain and pleasure*'. Taking it to be an incontrovertible fact of human psychology, Bentham and his illustrious follower, James Mill, held that men always desire only pleasure and are averse only to pain. If they desire any other thing, it is only because they have learnt by experience that these things bring pleasure and avert pain. They defined the *utility* of a thing or action as its tendency to produce pleasure and to avert pain. Accordingly, they defined right action as the one most likely to give the greatest balance of pleasure over pain to the persons liable to be affected by it. Thus, Bentham postulated that pleasure and pain were susceptible to measurement. He repudiated any qualitative differences between different kinds of pleasure, and focused on their quantitative differences. Bentham's attitude on this issue was satirically expressed in the famous saying: "Quantity of pleasure being equal, pushpin is as good as poetry." Bentham even laid down certain criteria for measuring pleasure and pain, known as the 'hedonistic calculus' or 'felicific calculus'. The criteria for measurement of pleasure included:

1. *intensity* (how strong is its feeling?);
2. *duration* (how long it lasts?);
3. *certainty* (how certain we feel to have it?);
4. *proximity* or *propinquity* (how near it is to us, *i.e.* how early we can have it?);
5. *fecundity* (does it also produce other types of pleasure?);
6. *purity* (no pain is mixed with it); and
7. *extent* (how many people are affected by it?).

Of these the first six criteria are meant to judge the utility of a thing or action for the individual while the seventh criterion *(extent)* is relevant to judging public policy as expressed in the principle of 'greatest happiness of the greatest number'.

Principles of Legislation

Bentham rejected the ideology of natural rights and the social contract, yet he subscribed to the sovereignty of 'reason' and proceeded to find a formula for the application of reason to human affairs which should be free from the pitfalls of metaphysical abstraction. He repudiated the theory of the *general will* as something transcending the will of the individual, and defined the interest of the community as the sum total of the interests of the several members who compose it. Thus, he accorded a central place to individual on questions relating to public policy or legislation. He defined the interest of the individual as something which tends to increase the sum total of his pleasures, or to diminish the sum total of his pains. The interest of the community could likewise be discovered by aggregating the interests of all individuals who composed it. Pleasure or happiness should not be taken as a shadowy attribute of some *superperson,* called a social organism, but must find actual expression in the lives and in the experience of definite individuals. With this principle as the guiding star, the legislator is required but to calculate the pleasurable or painful consequences of an action, actual or proposed, and he would know whether it was right or wrong, sound or unsound. Bentham postulated this principle as the sole criterion of determining the 'greatest happiness of the greatest number' which would serve as a guide to all public policy and legislation.

Bentham insisted that in calculating pleasure and pain for the purpose of determining public policy, each individual should be treated as one unit and that none should be given special consideration: 'each to count as one, and no one for more than one'. Thus he asserted the necessity of treating all men as equals. He did not base his doctrine of equality on 'natural law'. Instead, he proceeded on his original assumption: men were born to be happy—that is the plain dictate of experience. Since freedom is essential to happiness, men are entitled to freedom. But equal freedom of each individual postulates 'equality'; therefore, man's liberty must be limited and conditioned by the ultimate test of general welfare. Bentham showed that 'equality' was a political good, because it was the only practical way of dealing with large numbers of people. By placing equal importance on the happiness of all individuals, Bentham sought to curb the legislators' tendency of ignoring happiness of the people in pursuance of their own moral standards or in promoting happiness of their own choice.

Critics point out that in practice Bentham's philosophy tends to marginalize the individual, as his formula of 'greatest happiness of the greatest number' aims to maximize happiness of the collectivity, ignoring the share of particular individuals.

Functions of Government

Bentham, of course, treated the state as an instrument devised by man for the promotion of happiness of the community, yet he did not contemplate any wide scope of state activity. Believing that men are moved to act solely by the desire for pleasure and the avoidance of pain, and that each individual is the best judge of his own interests, Bentham and his followers came to the conclusion that *main function of the state is legislation,* and that the chief objective of legislation is to remove all institutional restrictions on the free actions of individuals. Individual himself is capable of exercising moral judgement; the state cannot improve character of the people. The state should restrict its sphere of activity to restraining individuals from indulging in activities which affect the general happiness adversely. *Punishment of offenders is another important function of the state.* The state should not interfere in the activities of law-abiding citizens who are the best judges of right and wrong, moral and immoral. In this way, Bentham also upheld the doctrine of *laissez-faire* individualism.

JAMES MILL

James Mill was a close associate and follower of Jeremy Bentham. He played an important role in propagating Bentham's Utilitarianism as well as his principles of law, administration, education and psychology. He founded his 'philosophical radicalism' on the basis of Bentham's Utilitarianism, and led a radical-reformist movement which aimed at extension of franchise and representation of the interests of the working class in British Parliament. Besides Bentham's Utilitarianism, James Mill undertook an intensive study of Hobbes's individualism and Adam Smith's classical political economy. He is well-known for popularizing the views of his favourite thinkers rather than for advancing an original doctrine.

After analysing the prevailing institutions of England, particularly the aristocratic government, legal system and mercantilist economy, he came to the conclusion that these institutions obstructed the way to 'the greatest happiness of the greatest number'. In his *Essays on Government* (1825), he commended democratic government as good government which sought to work for the benefit of the citizens. He argued that aristocratic government is motivated by self-interest which promotes corruption. This can be prevented by instituting a representative government based on universal suffrage, secret ballot and periodic elections. James Mill particularly liked the middle rank, and hoped that when democratic institutions are established, the people would follow their footsteps.

HERBERT SPENCER

Sociological foundation of *laissez-faire* individualism was provided by Herbert Spencer, an English political thinker, in his works *Social Statics* (1850), *The Man versus the State* (1884), and *The Principles of Ethics* (1892-93). Starting from an idea of universal evolution, Spencer postulated the tendency of all things to ultimate equilibrium and the consequent tendency of all things to transform themselves by a process of evolution in order to attain this equilibrium. Accordingly, individual tends to equilibrate himself with his social environment by adaptation, and by inheritance of that adaptation, until he attains, in a perfect equilibrium, *the blessedness of final anarchy*. In this process of evolution, the state has a very limited role to play, and that is the function of protection—administration of the law of equal freedom. Spencer treated the state as a 'joint-stock protection company for mutual assurance'. It should not assume any other function, nor otherwise interfere with the process of natural evolution.

Thus, Spencer argued that the state should not undertake public health, nor give the poor any relief because that would defeat the operation of the law of natural selection. Spencer subscribed to the principle of the 'struggle for existence' and 'survival of the fittest' as a guiding principle of social evolution. He, therefore, argued that if 'family ethics' (*i.e.* the rule of diverting common resources towards maintenance of the weak) was applied to the state, it would retard progress by giving the weakling more than he deserved and perpetuating an undeserving life. Thus, Spencer stretched the concept of negative liberty to such an extreme that he considered elimination of the weak in the struggle for existence as part of the process of social progress.

Natural Selection

Natural selection is a corollary of Charles Darwin's (1809-82) theory of biological evolution which upholds the twin principles of 'struggle for existence' and 'survival of the fittest'. Accordingly, natural selection refers to the process whereby the nature selects only fit creatures to survive and eliminates the unfit ones. Herbert Spencer (1820-1903), English philosopher, recommended the model of natural selection for social organization. In his view, this held the key to social progress. So Spencer favoured a purely competitive society where the state had to play a very limited role, that is to provide for protection and enforcement of contracts. He argued that the state should not undertake public health, nor give any relief to the poor because that would defeat the operation of the law of natural selection.

RECENT DEVELOPMENTS

In the past few decades, the theory of *laissez-faire* liberalism was revived with a new vigour. It sought new grounds of keeping the state away from interference in the market forces. It is variously described as *neo-liberalism, neo-classical liberalism,* or *libertarianism.*

It is interesting to recall that towards the end of the nineteenth century and the beginning of the twentieth century, liberalism tended to accommodate some tenets of socialist and idealist thought, which was responsible for the emergence of the theory of 'welfare state'. Thus negative liberalism of the eighteenth century had given way to positive liberalism by the first half of the twentieth century. The liberalism of T.H. Green (1836-82), L.T Hobhouse (1864-1929) and Harold J. Laski (1893-1950) conceded positive role of the state in regulating economic system in the interests of the poor and deprived sections of society. The principle of liberty was sought to accommodate the principles of equality and justice within the liberal frame of thought.

However, during the second half of the twentieth century, some thinkers in the liberal tradition found the theory of 'welfare state' to be inimical to individual liberty, and sought to revive the original concern of this tradition with *laissez-faire* philosophy. Their thought is an important component of contemporary liberal theory. It is described as 'libertarianism' in order to indicate its renewed concern with 'liberty' and to distinguish it from the recent trend towards positive liberalism. In a nutshell, libertarianism upholds full autonomy and freedom of the individual; it seeks his 'liberation' from all institutions which tend to restrict his vision of the world, including the institutions of religion, family and customs of social conformity apart from political institutions. Philosophically, it repudiates the deterministic outlook of human life, and maintains that the human personality, character, thought and actions cannot be construed as an outcome of his circumstances. In other words, it treats man as the maker of his destiny. It is, therefore, hostile to all social and legal restrictions on an individual's freedom of action. In the political sphere, libertarianism particularly insists that man's economic activity must be actively liberated from all restrictions to enable him to achieve true progress and prosperity.

Drawing inspiration from the 'natural rights' theory of John Locke, libertarianism holds that certain rights of the individual which precede his political life, are indefeasible and these cannot be surrendered in favour of the collectivity. It particularly defends the right to acquire and hold property and the freedom of contract. These rights are by no means the product of the state itself, hence the state cannot be allowed to intervene for any artificial balancing of rights. It even condemns taxation of the rich for the benefit of the poor. It argues that taxation for welfare of certain sections of society involves the forced transfer of fruit of one man's labour to another, which serves as a disincentive to individual. On the contrary, if all individuals are free from state compulsion, they will put their best into the system. In effect this means that *laissez-faire* capitalism is most conducive to social progress.

An extreme form of libertarianism holds that all government is illegitimate; hence it comes closer to 'anarchism'. However, while anarchists project a vision of society wherein use of force would become redundant, extreme-libertarians look forward to the establishment of a system in which function of protection would be assigned to private protective agencies. On the other hand, moderate-libertarians concede that government may legitimately engage in police protection and enforcement of contracts for which civil as well as criminal courts might be established. In addition, it may undertake national defence, but nothing beyond these functions. Thus they uphold, at best, a 'nightwatchman state'. The amount of taxation, they hold, should be restricted to serve these purposes only.

The chief exponents of libertarianism include F.A. Hayek (1899-1992), Isaiah Berlin (1909-97), Milton Friedman (1912-2006) and Robert Nozick (1938-2002). Thus Robert Nozick, in his *Anarchy, State and Utopia* (1974), following Locke's method argues that individuals do have certain rights in the state of nature. They would hire protective agencies for their property holdings. The dominant protective agency, having *de facto* monopoly of force in a given territory, would emerge as a 'state-like entity'. Accordingly, the state has no legitimate powers beyond the functions of protection, justice and defence; it is not authorized to engage in redistributive transfers among the citizens who were originally its clients. Hence, 'welfare state' is ruled out. Nozick holds that acquisition or transfer of property without force or fraud is just. The right to property is derived from the fact that an individual is 'entitled' to it. It is not necessary to prove that he morally deserves it. He is 'entitled' to acquire and hold property either through mixing his labour with nature, by virtue of just acquisition of an unowned property or by receiving property from someone who has just initial title to it. Legal rights are, therefore, the product of voluntary exchanges. Nozick argues that inequalities at the level of production and voluntary transfers should not be sought to be rectified at the level of distribution. However, if there is only one source of water in a desert, nobody should be allowed to monopolize it. Nozick attempts to demonstrate that a libertarian society, which allows all individuals and groups to shape their life according to their wishes, fulfils the most plausible definition of a utopian social order.

[IV]
WELFARE STATE PERSPECTIVE

TRANSITION TO POSITIVE LIBERALISM

Liberal theory which stood for negative liberalism in its early phase, was transformed into positive liberalism in its later phase. Positive liberalism promoted the idea of the welfare state, as it pleaded for positive role of the state in securing welfare of its citizens, particularly of their vulnerable sections.

Welfare State

Welfare state refers to a state that safeguards liberty of its citizens, and also undertakes regulation of free market economy in order to safeguard the interests of vulnerable sections like peasants, workers and consumers. It resorts to differential taxation of different strata of society according to their ability to pay, and mobilizes necessary resources to provide for the supply of essential goods and services (like food, clothing, shelter, health care, elementary education and recreation, etc. to various social strata according to their ability to pay). Further, it undertakes the protection of cultural heritage including monuments, museums, libraries, art galleries, botanical gardens and zoological parks, etc. Then it also promotes higher education and scientific research, etc. to step up intellectual and cultural development of society. In short, welfare state is concerned with all aspects of welfare of its citizens, apart from the maintenance of law and order.

Negative liberalism had sought to establish free-market society which promoted capitalism. The success of capitalism in the nineteenth century demonstrated that the free-market society created large inequalities among human beings and caused oppression of the vulnerable sections—peasants, workers, consumers, etc. With the enormous growth of the labour force in industrial cities, freedom of contract in practice meant freedom for factory-owners to hire and fire their workers to maximize their profits with the consequent insecurity and suffering of the workers. Freedom of trade was not restricted to commodities—labour was also treated as a commodity. The result was the inhuman condition of the workers, child labour, slum housing, and free sale of poisoned meat, bad gin and other things injurious to health. When freedom of enterprise was interpreted as the total absence of regulation on business and industry, it brought disastrous consequences for the bulk of society, not the greatest happiness of the greatest number held so dear by the classical economists.

Classical liberals had sought to justify a free-market society on the basis of the 'equality' of individuals. Bentham had argued that in aggregating individual utilities, each individual was to count as one. He had sought to justify the liberal state as the state most calculated to maximize utilities—security of life, freedom of individual movement, security of property, etc. He had also postulated that a free-market society enabled each individual to maximize his own utility, and therefore brought everyone into productive relations which would thus maximize the aggregate utility of society. But in this process he was caught in a dilemma—to reconcile theoretical equality with practical inequality. As C.B. Macpherson, in his *Democratic Theory—Essays in Retrieval* (1973), has aptly illustrated:

> Bentham was clear that the market must be left to determine the allocation of the material product among the individuals who contributed to it by their labour or land or capital, although he saw that this would mean

> persistent inequality. He acknowledged, indeed, that there was a case for equality of wealth or income. This followed from the principle of diminishing utility—the principle that a second loaf of bread doesn't give a hungry man as much satisfaction as the first loaf, or more generally that the more you have of anything the less the utility to you of any increment. Given this principle, and given that each individual's satisfaction was to count as one, it followed that the aggregate utility of the whole society would be greatest if everyone had equal amounts of wealth.

Bentham tried to escape from this dilemma by introducing another element—the criterion of productivity—and decided the case in favour of inequality. As Macpherson has further elucidated:

> As soon as Bentham had thus demonstrated the case for equality, he argued that it had to yield to the case for productivity. Without security for unequal property, there would be no incentive to capital accumulation, and without capital accumulation there would be practically no productivity. Besides, without a large labour force whose incentive was fear of starvation, the market could not maximize productivity (*ibid.*).

However, subsequent liberal thinkers could not escape from this dilemma so easily. The working class was not only increasing in size, its condition was also deteriorating. Its voice could not be suppressed any longer. The socialists were incessantly pressing for a solution of the problems of the working class. The liberals were also forced to realize that their insistence on freedom and human rights had created conditions of oppression in society. They must resolve the contradictions of the liberal theory—as evidenced by the oppressive character of the capitalist system—otherwise the whole edifice would tumble down. As a result, the tenets of the liberal theory were revised towards the last quarter of the nineteenth century and this process of revision went on during the twentieth century.

EXPONENTS OF POSITIVE LIBERALISM

John Stuart Mill (1806-73) was the first prominent liberal thinker who started with a defence of *laissez-faire* individualism, but on realizing its weaknesses in the light of new socio-economic realities, he proceeded to modify it. In the event he turned out to be a pioneer of positive liberalism. After Mill, Thomas Hill Green (1836-82) and L.T. Hobhouse (1864-1929), both English political thinkers, made important contributions to the theory of positive liberalism. Green and Hobhouse insisted on a positive role of the state in removing social inequalities, and they stated their case eloquently and convincingly. Subsequently in early twentieth century, Harold J. Laski (1893-1950), English political thinker, and Robert M. MacIver (1882-1970), American sociologist, sought to provide new foundations for the liberal theory—a pluralistic base in lieu of its hitherto individualistic base which was not found to be strong enough.

JOHN STUART MILL

J.S. Mill is the most brilliant of nineteenth-century liberal thinkers. He played an important role in drawing a distinction between the political and economic spheres, and in working out the implications of liberal theory in these spheres. Thus, while in the political sphere he proved himself to be a strong supporter of constitutional and representative government, in the economic sphere he was inclined towards social justice; so he laid the foundations of the 'welfare state'. In this way, Mill gave a positive direction to liberal theory.

> **Social Justice**
>
> Social justice refers to a social policy which seeks to prevent concentration of valuable resources of the community (wealth, prestige and power) in the hands of the chosen few, and to create a social order which will enable the deprived and underprivileged sections of society to gain a respectable share thereof by virtue of their ability, effort and need.

Revision of Utilitarianism

Mill was brought up in the Utilitarian tradition of Bentham; he was also an ardent champion of individualism. As C.E.M. Joad, in his *Introduction to Modern Political Theory* (1924), has elucidated:

> Mill, in common with other Utilitarian thinkers... insists on regarding every political question in terms of the happiness or unhappiness of human beings, and not... in terms of an abstraction such as the General Will or the personality of the State. While conceding, therefore, the contention of the Absolutists that since the State is a natural growth or organism, it is only in the State that the individual can enjoy the fullest happiness of which his nature is capable, he goes on to point out that this admission does not mean that the State does not exist for the happiness of individuals. He then proceeds to draw the conclusion that it is the business of Government actively to promote the happiness of individuals, and that, if it fails in this respect, it must give way to some other form of social organization that succeeds.

Mill agreed with Bentham in identifying happiness with pleasure and unhappiness with pain. But he disagreed with Bentham's view that happiness could be measured by quantitative differences of pleasures, not by qualitative differences. Mill maintained that some pleasures were qualitatively superior to others. He believed that the quality of pleasure was no less important than its quantity. Mill's view on this issue was expressed in these powerful words: "It is better to be a human being dissatisfied than a pig satisfied: better to be Socrates dissatisfied than a fool satisfied." Mill's attitude on this issue implied a departure from Bentham's position on the method of aggregation and maximization of pleasure, happiness or utility. As C.B. Macpherson, in his

Democratic Theory—Essays in Retrieval (1973), has observed:

> Mill revolted against Bentham's material maximizing criterion of the social good. He could not agree that all pleasures were equal, nor that the market distributed them fairly. He held that men were capable of something better than the money-grubbing and starvation-avoiding existence to which Benthamism condemned them. He rejected the maximization of indifferent utilities as the criterion of social good, and put in its place the maximum *development* and use of human capacities—moral, intellectual, aesthetic, as well as material productive capacities.

In Defence of Liberty

Mill is an ardent champion of liberty. He insists on liberty of thought and expression as well as liberty of conduct. He defends liberty of thought and expression on two important grounds. In the first place, he argues that it is useful to society. He asserts that rational knowledge is the basis of social progress, and the only way of confirming and extending true knowledge is to submit all ideas, old and new, to the test of free discussion and debate. As C.E.M. Joad, in his *Introduction to Modern Political Theory* (1924), has observed:

> Mill's essay *On Liberty* is perhaps the most famous vindication of freedom of thought, and the most powerful plea for the toleration of opinions we fail to understand, in the whole of literature. He insisted upon the extension of this freedom to 'cranks', on the ground that, while nine cranks out of ten are harmless idiots, the tenth is of greater value to mankind than all the normal men who seek to suppress him.

In the second place, Mill advocates liberty of thought and expression on the ground of human dignity. As Isaac Kramnick and F.M. Watkins, in *The Age of Ideology—Political Thought, 1750 to the Present* (1979), have elaborated:

> Quite apart from the question of social utility, he tried to show that individual self-determination is a basic human right, indispensable to the development of any sort of moral responsibility. No line of thought or action, objectively true and useful though it may be, is morally significant unless it is followed, freely and consciously, as a matter of personal conviction. Without liberty to choose between conflicting claims, a human being loses his or her rightful dignity as a moral and rational being.

On the liberty of conduct, Mill takes another line of argument. He draws a distinction between two types of actions of men: 'self-regarding actions' and 'other-regarding actions'. Proceeding on these premises, Mill advocates complete freedom of conduct for the individual in all matters not affecting the community, *i.e.* in the case of 'self-regarding actions'. However, in the case of 'other-regarding actions', *i.e.* in matters which do affect the community, Mill conceded the right of the community to coerce the individual if his conduct is prejudicial to its welfare. Thus, Mill defends complete freedom of conduct for the individual unless it adversely affects the community. But the state could also interfere in the self-regarding action if it was thought to be injurious to individual himself. Thus the state would be perfectly justified in preventing a man from crossing a bridge which was known to be unsafe. Ernest Barker, in his *Principles of Social and Political Theory* (1951), has severely criticized Mill for separating the conduct of individual into two parts—one which concerns others, and the other which merely concerns himself. Barker observes:

> We cannot separate two different compartments of individual conduct; but we can separate the sphere of Society from that of the State. Because we cannot separate our individual conduct into two different compartments, and because we are bound to regard the whole of our conduct as concerning others no less than ourselves, we have to admit that the whole of our conduct is controllable—*so far as the criterion of its concerning others is the criterion of judgement.*

Barker suggests an alternative division of the conduct of individuals into 'the sphere of voluntary action, proceeding by the method of free cooperation' which should be left to society, and 'the sphere of uniform and regulated action, based, in the last resort, on the method of compulsory enforcement', which should be left to the state. Barker, in fact, has tried to shift liberal theory from an individualistic to a pluralistic base.

Positive Role of the State

Mill's distinction between 'self-regarding actions' and 'other-regarding actions' of the individual should, however, be appreciated in the historical perspective. It meant a clear departure from the early *laissez-faire* individualism which had tried to place most of the behaviour of the individual beyond regulation, in order to vindicate the 'free market society'. Mill was making an attempt to define a sphere where an individual's behaviour could be regulated in the interests of society. Thus he was contemplating a positive role for the state in securing community welfare even if it implied curbing the liberty of the individual to some extent. In his mature years, Mill definitely moved beyond traditional liberalism. Indeed, it was in pursuance of his liberal values that Mill sought to lay the foundations of a more humane society as against the one provided by nineteenth century capitalism.

In the first edition of his *Principles of Political Economy* (1848), Mill had attacked Socialism, but in its last edition (1866), he revised his views on the right to property as he realized its implications as the basis of the capitalist system. He argued that the right to property was not absolute or sacrosanct, and went to the extent of advocating considerable restrictions on the rights of inheritance and bequest. He maintained that the right to property in land was not sacrosanct because no man made the land; it was the original inheritance of all mankind. Rent was the effect of natural monopoly—not a product of an individual's effort: it was a fit subject for taxation. He argued that incomes of landlords continued to increase without any effort, risk or sacrifice on their part. Hence, if the state appropriated the increase of their wealth or a part thereof for diverting it to the use of the community, it was no violation of the principles on which the right to private property was founded or justified. The landlords had no claim to accession of such riches on the general principle of social justice. Mill argued that these additional riches should properly be diverted to the welfare of their real authors, that is the working class who were the real producers of wealth from the land.

This approach to the problem of taxation and the limitation of the right to property paved the way for a new line of thinking. This was developed by later liberal thinkers who thoroughly rejected the tenets of *laissez-faire* individualism. For example, L.T Hobhouse, in his *Liberalism* (1911), presented a brilliant analysis of the basis of property and the case for its taxation on these lines:

> The basis of property is social... The prosperous businessman who thinks that he has made his fortune entirely by self-help does not pause to consider what single step he could have taken on the road to his success but for the ordered tranquility which has made commercial development possible, the security by road, and rail, and sea, the masses of skilled labour, and the sum of intelligence which civilization has placed at his disposal, the very demand for the goods which he produces which the general progress of the world has created, the inventions which he uses as a matter of course and which have been built up by the collective effort of generations of men of science and organizers of industry. If he dug to the foundations of his fortune he would recognize that, as it is society that maintains and guarantees his possessions, so also it is society which is an indispensable partner in its original creation.

Recognizing this social basis of property, Hobhouse proceeds to discover the true basis of the theory of taxation. Thus, he observes:

> The true function of taxation is to secure to society the element in wealth that is of social origin, or more broadly, all that does not owe its origin to the efforts of living individuals. When taxation, based on these principles, is utilized to secure healthy conditions of existence to the mass of people, it is clear that this is no case of robbing Peter to pay Paul (*ibid*.).

Thus, the idea of social origin of property and its corresponding responsibility towards society, as originally conceived by Mill, foreshadowed the rise of positive liberalism of the later era.

THOMAS HILL GREEN

T.H. Green is another outstanding exponent of positive liberalism. He sought to revise liberal theory of the state under the influence of idealist theory, derived from the teachings of Rousseau, Kant and Hegel.

Concept of Moral Freedom

At the outset, Green recognizes 'moral freedom' as the distinctive quality of man. He proceeds to distinguish between negative and positive freedom. Negative freedom consists in the satisfaction of one's desires, acting according to one's own choice or sweet will. It is the sphere where man enjoys being left alone. On the other hand, positive freedom consists in acting according to reason, achieving self-realization or self-perfection. True liberty or positive freedom of man, therefore, consists in the act of 'good will', whereby man identifies himself with his ideal self or character. Ernest Barker, in his *Political Thought in England—1848 to 1914* (1928), has elucidated Green's concept of liberty as follows:

> Liberty can only be liberty for this good will: it can only be liberty for the pursuit of the objects which such a will presents to itself. Liberty is therefore no negative absence of restraint, any more than beauty is the absence of ugliness. It is 'a positive power of doing or enjoying something worth doing or enjoying'.

Theory of Rights

Exercise of true liberty, according to Green, postulates rights. Rights do not emanate from any transcendental law as Locke had imagined, but they emanate from the moral character of man himself. Under a system of rights, each individual recognizes in his fellow, and each claims from his fellow, that he shall recognize in him the power of pursuing ideal objects. Since each individual is a moral being, and in this respect all individuals are alike, it follows that the ideal objects of all are the common objects. In other words, rights imply the opportunity to pursue ideal objects; and since these are the common objects of all men, theoretically there is no question of a clash between the rights of different individuals.

Since rights exist within a social system, Green argues that there can be no unrecognized rights. Whose recognition do they need? Green concedes that all rights are not legal rights only. He draws a clear distinction between the state and society and holds that rights are not dependent on recognition by the state; they need recognition by *the moral consciousness of the community.* The consciousness of the community signifies an eternal consciousness. Human consciousness or consciousness of the ideal self is but a part of that eternal consciousness, not of the mechanical order of nature. Therefore, man can pursue his moral end and attain self-realization only in a social community, not in isolation. Thus, Green is concerned not with legal rights, but with ideal rights. These rights can be realized in society when society is properly organized on the basis of 'good will'. As Barker has observed with regard to Green's concept of rights:

> The rights of which Green speaks are relative to morality rather than law; and the recognition of which he speaks is recognition by a common moral consciousness rather than by a legislature. The rights are relative to morality, in the sense that they are the conditions of the attainment of the moral end; and the recognition is given by the moral consciousness, because it knows that they are the necessary conditions of its own satisfaction (*ibid.*).

Role of the State

The moral consciousness emanating from society—which impels men to pursue ideal objects—is also responsible for the creation of the state. In other words, the state is the product of moral consciousness. According to Green's line of argument, human consciousness postulates liberty; liberty involves rights; rights demand the state. The state is, therefore, *an instrument of perfection* as the liberal theory holds; it is not an embodiment of perfection—as the idealist theory claims. The state owes its origin to the social nature of men; genuine human personality is essentially a social phenomenon. It is inconceivable that n isolated natural man should be a moral agent. Man exercises his moral reedom within the social organization, for which he needs rights. But rights are maintained by the state; hence the state serves as an essential foothold for exercising moral freedom.

It is important to note that Green favours subordinating individual to the community as Rousseau and Hegel had maintained. He also insists on duty of the citizen to follow the *general will* and devote himself to the common good. But he does not treat the state and society as coterminous. This marks his departure from the idealist tradition. Again, he adheres to the liberal tradition by insisting on individual's rights. In his view, state recognizes and maintains rights but it is not the very source of rights. The real authority behind rights is the moral consciousness of the community. The state must obey that authority. Thus positive law can be criticized and improved upon in the light of the state's ideal purpose: the moral perfection of men.

Green exalts society or the community as the primary and eternal source of moral consciousness. The state is something secondary, a means or an instrument. The state, therefore, cannot serve the end of moral freedom directly, but it can create favourable conditions for the exercise of moral freedom. The state and its law can regulate only the external order of society. As Barker has elucidated:

> The supreme limitation on the State lies in its own essence. Its function is essentially, Green conceives, a negative function. It is limited to the removal of the obstructions that hamper human capacity when it seeks to do 'things worth doing'. The state has no positive moral function of

> making its members better: it has the negative moral function of removing the obstacles which prevent them from making themselves better (*Political Thought in England 1848 to 1914;* 1928).

In other words, the function of government is to maintain conditions of life in which morality shall be possible. Morality consists in the disinterested performance of self-imposed duties, not in obeying the commands of the state.

Green tends to describe the function of the state as *negative,* only to distinguish it from the *positive* function of the community as the source of moral consciousness. He is by no means a champion of negative liberalism. When compared to *laissez-faire* liberalism, Green is definitely an exponent of positive liberalism. The state's function of removing obstacles in the way of men's pursuit of ideal objects is a *positive* function. His conception of the state as an agent for moral development led him to favour the intervention of the state to secure the welfare of citizens. That is why he argued that the state is entitled to make education compulsory.

Right to Property

As a defender of rights, Green upholds the right to property as a means of realizing a will *potentially* directed to the social good. On this ground he even defends property in capital. Barker has summed up Green's views on 'property in capital' as follows:

> There is nothing in its essence which is anti-social. On the contrary, it is constantly being distributed through the community in wages to labourers and in profits to those who are engaged in exchange; nor is there anything in the fact that labourers are hired in masses by capitalists to prevent them from being, on a small scale, capitalists themselves. On the same ground of potential social value, Green also defends inequality of property (*ibid.*).

Green argues that the freedom of the individual postulates freedom to acquire and possess material goods according to one's potentiality to contribute to the social good. The social good requires that different individuals should fill different positions in the social whole. Hence, differences in property are 'functional' from the point of view of the social good, which should be recognized by the social conscience.

But on this point—the question of the inequality of property—Green is faced with a dilemma. When the right to property creates conditions under which some men take an unduly large share and others are prevented from acquiring property as a means of their 'self-realization', this right becomes an obstacle in the exercise of moral freedom by the many. Thus, Green proceeds to realize the malady of the capitalist system which created such conditions. But he locates its origin in the system of 'landed property' as it existed in England, of which he disapproved. As Barker has elucidated:

> Such property, he held, is unique. It is unique in that it is limited: 'the capital gained by one is not taken from another, but one man cannot acquire more land without others having less'. It is unique in that it is the basis on which the whole tower of modern society rests: 'from it alone can be derived the materials necessary for any industry: on it men must find house-room; over it they must pass in communicating with each other' (*ibid.*).

Thus, Green tends to blame the feudal system of the past for all the evils of the present capitalist system—the plight of the proletariat and suppression of their moral freedom. As Barker has noted: "It is thus to the system of landed property that Green seems inclined to assign the creation of a proletariat, neither holding nor acquiring property."

Green, of course, made a significant contribution to liberal political theory by discovering the moral foundations of social life, and by subordinating the state to the will of society which alone embodies moral consciousness. But he made a great mistake in locating the ills of the capitalist system. As C.B. Macpherson, in his *Democratic Theory—Essays in Retrieval* (1973), has observed:

> Green recognized that the existence of a proletariat—his own word—was inconsistent with the rationale of private property, which required that everybody should have enough property, over and above a bare subsistence, to enable him to develop and perfect himself. But he had so little insight into the nature of capitalism that he could attribute the existence of a proletariat not to the nature of capitalist enterprise but to the continuing effect of an original forcible seizure of land in feudal times, and subsequent 'unrestricted landlordism'. By putting the blame on feudalism, and on the continuing rights of unproductive landowners, he exempted capitalism from responsibility for the condition of the bulk of the people.

HAROLD J. LASKI

Laski further developed the liberal theory of the state in the light of his experience of the momentous events which shook the world in the first half of the twentieth century. He witnessed the First World War (1914-18), the Socialist Revolution in Russia (1917), the formation of the League of Nations (1920), the rise of fascism in Italy (1919-20), the Great Depression in Europe (1929), etc. which profoundly influenced his thinking. He was deeply concerned with the crisis of capitalism, yet he saw no promise in the outcome of the socialist revolution. In the event, he sought to achieve the socialist goal through the mechanism of liberal democracy. He was so critical of the capitalist system and its underlying principles that at times he advocated the abolition of the right to property which was the mainstay of the capitalist system. But he was so deeply attached to liberal democratic values that ultimately he agreed to make necessary changes in the capitalist system so that it would serve as an instrument of social justice.

In his *State in Theory and Practice* (1935), Laski talks of the 'breakdown of capitalism' under the conditions of mature capitalism. He observes: "The test of an economic system is . . . the test of its capacity to exploit to the full all the potentialities of its productive power. Judged by that test, it is surely not illegitimate to speak of a 'breakdown' of capitalism both in England and the United States." Illustrating his point from the conditions then prevailing in England, Laski notes that "with two million unemployed; devastated economic areas like South Wales and the North East Coast; the staple export trades, like cotton and coal, iron and steel and shipping, announcing that they verge on bankruptcy;... a situation like this, with a government in office which proclaims its faith in the necessity of private enterprise, may fairly be described quite soberly as a breakdown."

Again, in his *Reflections on the Revolution of Our Time* (1943), Laski strongly deprecated the undemocratic control of industry and politics by the economic overlords—an outcome of the capitalist system—as follows:

> In modern society, large industrial corporations are controlled by a caste of economic directors, mainly remarkable for their skill in financial manipulation, who are masters alike of their shareholders and of the consumer, and are not seldom in a position to hold even the states to ransom. Their power is as massive in volume as it has largely been irresponsible in operation. We have reached a stage in historical evolution where either their power must be subordinated to the interest of the community or the interest of the community will be a tragic pseudonym for their power.

These and many other observations made by Laski demonstrate that he was deeply concerned with the possibility of disaster for mankind unless the capitalist system was suitably transformed.

Laski, however, did not approve of doctrinaire communism or the repetition of the Russian Revolution for the emancipation of mankind. He insisted on the unity of the working class, but hoped that they could achieve their goal within the framework of a liberal democracy. In fact, he saw no inherent contradiction between the goals of Marxian socialism and the method of political democracy.

Laski, therefore, proceeded to identify certain *positive* characteristics and tendencies of the 'modern state' which held some promise for the underprivileged sections. Thus, in his *State in Theory and Practice* (1935), Laski observed:

> There is hardly a function of social welfare undertaken by governments today which is not an effort to provide the poor with some, at least, of the amenities that the rich are able to provide for themselves ... The state . . . seeks to convince its citizens that its action is unbiased by organizing

> for them the material conditions of an adequate life, and especially for those of its citizens who cannot afford these conditions for themselves.

Illustrating the range of such services provided by the state since 1919, Laski proceeds: "Health, education, housing, social insurance, the regulation of hours and wages in industry, the control of factory conditions, the provision of meals for poor school children, are only outstanding examples of the range. . . We may say that it is the outcome of a profounder social conscience."

Laski is so deeply impressed by this softening attitude of the liberal state that he rejects the Marxist interpretation of the state as a class-instrument. Thus, in a subsequent paragraph, Laski comments:

> No modern state would subordinate human rights to the interests of property; this is shown by the whole character of modern legislation. When the state concerns itself with the quality of our food, the protection of child welfare, the safeguarding of the unemployed against industrial insecurity, the provision of educational opportunity—all of these services provided at the expense of the taxpayers—it is rhetorical exaggeration to regard it as a class-instrument.

It is precisely here that Laski looks for justification of the liberal state. He is not fascinated by the Marxist vision of a 'stateless' society. He undoubtedly insists on a clear distinction between the state and society and warns against vesting society's authority in the agency of the state, which in actual practice is represented by a band of officials—fallible human beings. Yet he pays rich tributes to the institution of the state. In his *A Grammar of Politics* (1938), Laski affirms: "The State is the keystone of the social arch. It moulds the form and substance of the myriad human lives with whose destinies it is charged." As a true liberal, however, Laski does not take the state as such to be an embodiment of perfection, as the idealist theory of Hegel had held. On the contrary, Laski pins his faith on the perfectibility of the state. In other words, he hopes that if the state is made to fulfil certain functions, it can become an instrument of perfection of mankind. In his *State in Theory and Practice* (1935), Laski spells out the criterion for testing the state as follows:

> The claim of the state to obedience... rests upon its will and ability to secure to its citizens the maximum satisfaction of their wants. To present this claim as valid there must be an absence of bias in the performance of this function. Where the effort of the state is seriously perverted to the interest of some special group within the society it controls, sooner or later revolution is likely to occur.

Thus, Laski postulates that the state is not *essentially* an instrument of class power or class domination or class exploitation. If any such state exists in the real world, it represents a perverted form of the state. Any state can be made to serve the interests of humanity, and if that is ensured, revolution can be averted. In his *A Grammar of Politics* (1938), Laski has presented an elaborate scheme for transforming the political and economic organization of society, with special reference to England. In the political sphere, he attempts at a refinement of the mechanism of liberal democracy; in the economic sphere he pleads to tone down the rigours of the capitalist system by making it welfare-oriented. He does not advocate total abolition of the capitalist system, probably because he thinks that retention of liberal democracy must imply continuation of some features of the capitalist system. He does not envisage 'anything like the disappearance of private enterprise'. Yet he hopes to eliminate the 'enormous economic disparities of the present system'. Thus he proceeds:

> Men will still be able to make fortunes; but, especially in the period of transition, they will be subject to heavy taxation upon income, and still heavier duties upon their estates at death. For it must be emphasized that to establish a system of rights involves expenditure by the State; and, particularly in the epoch of change, the wealth devoted to that purpose must largely be derived from the taxation of wealthy men. That is one of the unavoidable privileges of the rich.

In short, Laski seeks to transform the capitalist state by the democratization of economic power, that is by ensuring larger public control over vital instruments of production and distribution, reducing enormous economic disparities by a progressive system of taxation and establishing a democratic state increasingly concerned with the welfare of its citizens.

ROBERT M. MACIVER

Robert M. MacIver is another twentieth-century exponent of positive liberalism. With a strong sociological background, MacIver traces the evolution of the state from primitive social structures to its fuller development as a modern democratic state.

As regards the origin and nature of the state, MacIver rejects social contract theory formulated by the early exponents of the liberal theory. He tends to agree with T.H. Green who made a careful distinction between the sphere of law and that of morality, although MacIver differs from Green in making all rights, ethical as well as political, depend on social recognition. However, he approves of Green's distinction between the state and society. Thus, in his *The Modern State* (1926), MacIver observes:

> Green made a careful distinction between the sphere of law and that of morality . . . Political obligations can and should be enforced, whereas moral duties cannot: unless the latter express the free will of a moral being they lose their character. Political law therefore exists simply for the removal of obstacles in the way of free moral activity within society. It creates the order within which that freedom can exist. Hence the state has a limited sphere and cannot be identified with the whole activity of society.

It is society which meets all the needs of human personality. Men seek to serve their varied interests through several associations. The state is only one of such associations.

A number of associations have existed in society even before the formation of the state. Many activities of the present-day associations do not fall within the sphere of state-regulation. The state is not superior to all other associations in the moral sense, although it may claim superior authority as an instrument of law. Law itself exists above the state, but it is declared and enforced by the state. In MacIver's own words: "The government has power as the guardian of the constitution, as the executor of law, not in its own right." The state does not create law of its own will; law exists prior to the state; the state grasps it and gives it a definite shape. But since law is bound to act through external sanction, the state should refrain from touching those activities of the associations which are not to be judged by the external conduct of men, but by the spirit behind their conduct. Thus, according to MacIver, "The whole creative side of human thought and endeavour, including religion and morality in its proper sense, are outside the sphere of the state. Its place is determined by the fact that law is an instrument of limited range. The state should only, if it is true to its own nature, enforce those acts the doing of which, from whatever motive, is necessary for the good life within society."

MacIver, therefore, holds that the state does not regulate the internal affairs of other human associations. It cannot determine their purpose, nor their methods for the most part. The state comes into the picture only when the interests of one group encroach upon another. The state acts only in order to resolve the conflicting claims of different social groups. The state is not entitled to impose its own will on any human association for the protection of the 'common interest'. It can only harmonize different social interests originally expressed through human associations. In his *The Web of Government* (1965), MacIver argues that the state should not undertake regulation of those organizations which are formed to serve the emotional and cultural interests of men, but those serving economic interests of different groups cannot be left to make mutual adjustment, even if there is no visible conflict between them. Thus, the relations between employer and worker, landlord and tenant, trader and consumer, etc. essentially come within the purview of state regulation, whereas religious, artistic and cultural activities must remain beyond the jurisdiction of the state.

MacIver sought to base the authority of the state on the functions it performs. The state is subservient to society; it derives its authority from society for which it fulfils certain conditions. The state neither serves all interests of men in society, nor does it command their undivided loyalty. The sphere of the state is not coextensive with that of society. Society is an all-comprehensive institution which serves all the interests of individuals—material, intellectual, emotional, moral, spiritual, etc.—through its network of associations. The state is only one of such associations, meant to serve definite interests—its authority is limited like its obligations. The powers and prerogatives of the state are dependent on the services rendered by it. MacIver has, therefore, advanced the theory of the 'service state'. He tends to keep its authority within definite limits. As he observes in *The Modern State* (1926):

> The state... commands only because it serves; it owns only because it owes. It creates rights not as the lordly dispenser of gifts, but as the agent of society for the creation of rights. The servant is not greater than his master. As other rights are relative to function and are recognized as limited by it, so too the rights of the state *should* be. It has the function of guaranteeing rights.

The society or community thrives on the unity or solidarity of men. This unity is derived from the feeling and experience of the common interest. It is upheld by the common ways which serve them all. When the 'community of interests' is stronger than the 'division' or clash of interests, social solidarity and social organizations are likely to be highly developed. Perfection of the social organization is reflected in the perfection of the state. Accordingly, the state plays a crucial role in the social life of men. As MacIver himself points out:

> All the business of life is rendered possible by its aid, and all who live along it must contribute to its upkeep. It is the basis of all social communications. Therefore, whatever else a man may be, he must be a member, or at least a subject, of the state.

The state is a symbol of the great achievements of civilization. It can prove to be an effective organ of attaining social unity and solidarity, and this particular function distinguishes it from all other human associations. In the words of MacIver, although the state is but one among the great associations, yet its own peculiar function is no other than that of giving a form of unity to the whole system of social relationships. It can achieve this end, as successfully as other associations achieve their ends, without arrogating to itself again that omnicompetence which it has vainly sought to establish.

MacIver is convinced that only a democratic state can perform the unifying function most effectively. He argues that the modern democratic state has distinguished itself from its earlier forms. Thus, he observes:

> The state can act... as a unifying agent, but only in so far as it has itself undergone evolution towards democracy. For this reason we regard democracy as the form of the state proper, for only under democratic conditions can it achieve this proper function, this function, in other words, which it and it alone is capable of performing.

The evolution of the democratic state—the state as an instrument of reconciliation of diverse interests and resolution of conflicts, the state as an agent of social solidarity—is a unique achievement of modern civilization which marks a departure from its historical forms. Historically, the interest of the state has been identified with that of the ruling class—military or landed oligarchy, or later plutocracy. The modern democratic state, on the contrary, stands not for the interests of a particular class, but to serve the interests of all society. That is precisely the true function of the liberal state.

This line of argument shows that MacIver has no apprehension of the evils of the capitalist system as long as democratic mechanism of the state is kept intact. Some recent champions of the liberal state have even tried to demonstrate that under the capitalist system of production actual power has shifted from the hands of the capitalist class to some other groups, such as a 'managerial class' as James Burnham (1907-87) has maintained, or to a variety of power *elites*, as C. Wright Mills (1916-62) has pointed out.

The great merit of the liberal theory of the state lies in evolving institutions and procedures for a constitutional government. Its tragedy is that it is often invoked in order to justify the capitalist system, with its inherent contradictions—the conditions of dominance and dependence it creates in the economic sphere, in spite of its policy of social welfare and incremental change. The needs of social justice demand a thorough transformation of the economic system as well. It is for the genius of the present-day world to evolve more effective structures to secure social justice.

[V]
CLASS PERSPECTIVE

Class perspective on the state is associated with Marxism. It is different from the mechanistic theory as well as from the organic theory. It treats the state neither as a 'natural institution' nor as an 'ethical institution' as the organic theory has held. It, of course, treats the state as an artificial device. But unlike the mechanistic theory, it treats the state neither as a manifestation of the will of the people, nor as an instrument of reconciliation of conflicting interests.

Marxism

Marxism refers to a set of political and economic principles enunciated by Karl Marx (1818-83) and Friedrich Engels (1820-95) in order to lay scientific foundations of socialism. It seeks to understand the problems of human society through historical analysis, and treats history as a process of conflict between antagonistic forces and classes. This conflict arises from the faults in the mode of production in which one class comes to gain ownership and control of the means of social production and compels the other class to work on the terms and conditions dictated by the former. This conflict reaches its peak in the age of capitalism when it can be resolved only through a revolutionary overthrow of capitalism, placing all means of social production (land, buildings, mines, forests, machinery and capital, etc.) under social ownership and control, enforcing universal labour and ensuring full development of the forces of production.

According to the class theory, the state comes into existence when society is divided into two antagonistic classes, one owning the means of social production and the other being constrained to live by its labour. In other words, it is the emergence of 'private property' that divides society into two conflicting classes. Those owning the means of social production acquire the power to dominate the other class not only in the economic sphere but in all spheres of life.

THE STATE AS AN INSTRUMENT OF THE DOMINANT CLASS

With the emergence of 'private property', society is divided into 'dominant' and 'dependent' classes. The dominant class, in order to maintain its stronghold on economic power, invents a new form of power—political power. The state is the embodiment of political power. It is, therefore, essentially subservient to economic power. Thus, according to the class theory, the state neither originates in the will of the people, nor does it stand for the benefit of all society, but is an instrument devised by a dominant class for its own benefit. It is imposed on society from above to serve the interests of a particular class. The state has not existed from eternity. It came into existence at a particular stage of historical development. It is a product of the conscious effort of the dominant class which first acquires the means of production and thereafter political power. The state is, therefore, by no means a natural institution as the organic theory had maintained.

Unlike the organic theory, again, the class theory makes a clear distinction between the state and society. Society and the state do not come into existence together. The class theory treats society as a natural institution, and the state as an artificial device. In other words, man is by nature a social animal, but not a 'political animal' as Aristotle had assumed. Society is a natural institution because it is an essential condition for the production of material goods which are indispensable for the survival of man. Production is the most important of all human activities. Since men in association produce more than men in isolation, society is a natural means of securing the necessities of life. The forms of production at any given stage of social development determine the pattern of social relations. Under 'primitive communism', when the state has not yet made its appearance, means of production are meagre and communally owned. At this earliest stage, there is no private property; hence society is not divided into antagonistic classes.

At a later stage, when the means of production are somewhat developed, that is when the hunting, fishing and food-gathering economy is replaced by an economy based on animal husbandry, domestic agriculture and small industry, there is 'surplus production' which is cornered by a class owning the major means of production. As a result, 'dominant' and 'dependent' classes come into existence. The structure of society is always determined by the prevalent form of production. The hand-mill gives you society with the feudal lord; the steam-mill gives you society with the industrial capitalist. The attitudes and outlook of society—the forms of its legal, political and intellectual relations as well as religious and social institutions—are determined by the material conditions of life. Whatever the form of the state, it is invariably an instrument of the dominant class.

THE STATE AS AN INSTRUMENT OF CLASS EXPLOITATION

The dominant class uses the machinery of the state to serve its own interests which involve the exploitation of the dependent class. The state is, therefore, an instrument of oppression and exploitation—an embodiment of injustice. It does not rest on moral foundations as the organic theory believes. It is not even an instrument of harmonizing the diverse interests of various individuals or groups as the mechanistic theory claims. Instead of being a means of conflict-resolution, the state, according to the class theory, is a device for the suppression of class conflict. It maintains order in society not because it is able to secure the willing obedience of its subjects, but because it uses its coercive power to secure compliance from the dependent class. The state also uses its 'ideological power' to create an illusion of 'consent' of the governed as also to offer moral justification for its existence.

Ideological Power

Ideological power refers to the power derived from one's ability to secure popular support for a particular ideology, that is the set of ideas accepted to be true by their upholders without inquiring into the basis of their validity. Ruling classes in any state strive to gain ideological power by convincing the people that their authority conforms to the accepted ideas regarding 'the best system of government'.

The pioneers of the class theory of the state—Marx, Engels and Lenin—have made it amply clear that the state is but an instrument of class rule and exploitation. Marx and Engels, in their famous *Communist Manifesto* (1848), observed: "Political power, properly to called, is merely the organized power of one class for oppressing another." Engels, in his *Socialism—Utopian and Scientific* (1880), confirmed: "The State is an organization of the particular class which was *pro-tempore* the exploiting class." Again, in his *The Origin of the Family, Private Property and the State* (1884), Engels illustrated: "The state of antiquity was above all the state of the slave-owners for the purpose of holding down the slaves, as the feudal state was the organ of the nobility for holding down the peasant serfs and bondsmen, and the modern representative state is an instrument of exploitation of wage labour by capital." Then Lenin, in his *The State and Revolution* (1917), elaborated: "According to Marx, the State is an organ of class *rule,* an organ for the oppression of one class by another; it is the creation of 'order', which legalizes and perpetuates this oppression by moderating the conflict between the classes."

Since the class theory views the state as an embodiment of social injustice, it looks forward to the emancipation of mankind in a classless and stateless society. Historical forces till the establishment of capitalism have introduced changes in the form of the state—from slave-owning to feudal to capitalist state—but they have failed to transform the class character of the state itself. This is to be achieved by a socialist revolution by which the 'proletariat' (propertyless workers) would expropriate the 'bourgeoisie' (capitalists) and 'socialize' the major means of production. The state would still be retained as an instrument of 'class exploitation', but the hitherto 'dominant' and 'dependent' classes would change their positions. In other words, the socialist state ('dictatorship of the proletariat') would use the state apparatus for the suppression of the former capitalists. When all remnants of capitalism are cleared, work is made compulsory for everyone, and the forces of production are fully developed, society would become classless, and the state would become redundant. This would result in the 'withering away' of the state. Thus, a classless and stateless society would come into existence which would be characterized by 'cooperation' instead of conflict, 'equality' instead of domination, and 'justice' instead of oppression and exploitation of one class by another.

A CRITICAL ESTIMATE

The chief contribution of class theory of the state lies in discovering and demonstrating the role of economic forces in shaping history. The earlier historians had hardly paid attention to this role. By focusing on this role, Marx opened up new possibilities of historical writing. In fact, class theory of the state was a very powerful attack on the complacency of social thinkers who held that the state existed for the benefit of all social groups, and that the different conditions of the rich and the poor were of their own making. Class theory sought to trace the roots of social injustice in the conditions created by the social system itself although it claimed to be an instrument of the 'common good' and justice. This theory demonstrated that the poverty of the masses is the outcome of their oppression and exploitation by the property-owners. It has also shown how the conditions of this injustice could be terminated by a proletarian revolution which would pave the way for the emergence of a classless and stateless society. However, the class theory, too, is not free from weaknesses, which need examination.

No Rigid Class Division in Society

Critics of class theory of the state have pointed out that classes are not fixed and rigidly maintained blocks within society as this theory assumes. Liberal thinkers have pointed to the constant process of social mobility—changing status of men and women by dint of their talents, effort and changing market demand. The class theory holds that under the capitalist system there will be a sharp polarization in which the 'middle class' will eventually disappear. Some liberal researchers have, however, shown that under the capitalist system the size of the middle class has actually been steadily expanding, without any symptoms of its disappearance. Some thinkers have advanced alternative theories. For instance, James Burnham (*The Managerial Revolution;* 1941), attempted to demonstrate that at the advanced stage of capitalism power had, in fact, shifted from the hands of capitalists to a new managerial class—a phenomenon never envisaged by the class theory of the state.

Capitalism with a Human Face

Champions of capitalism argue that twentieth-century capitalism was different from nineteenth-century capitalism when Marxism emerged. These thinkers claim that capitalism had transformed itself by adopting the model of 'welfare state', whereby it had become an instrument of social justice. The extensive labour legislation, a progressive system of taxation and elaborate provision of common social services, especially for the needy sections, are cited as the glowing examples of capitalism with a human face. It is claimed that with the mitigation of the rigours of capitalism, class-conflict and revolutionary spirit are becoming irrelevant and outdated.

No Signs of Classless Society in the Socialist Countries

It is alleged that in the (former) USSR and the People's Republic of China, where socialist revolutions along Marxist lines had taken place, there were no indications of the emergence of a classless and stateless society. On the contrary, the state-apparatus in the socialist countries proved to be much more repressive than that in liberal democracies, and their social set-up was characterized by a pyramid of power, instead of moving towards classlessness. M. Djilas (1911-95), a Yugoslav thinker, in his *The New Class* (1957), pointed out that although major property holdings in the Soviet Union and Eastern Europe had been abolished, those who held senior positions in state administration and in the Communist Party had emerged as a new privileged class, relegating the idea of a classless society to the background. Many thinkers even termed the class theory of the state as 'utopian' although this theory itself was advanced to repudiate 'utopian socialism' of the nineteenth century by 'scientific socialism'. As the later developments have shown, the popular protest against administrative excesses and corruption eventually led to the winding up of communism in the Soviet Union as well as in Eastern Europe.

In fact, class theory of the state is now being revised by its champions. It is now being increasingly realized that instead of looking for a rigid class division in the present-day society, it would be more fruitful to look for the different 'structures of domination' as well as 'forms of domination', and launch a systematic attack on such structures and forms in order to restore freedom, equality and justice in society.

RECENT DEVELOPMENTS

Marx and Engels regarded the mode of production as the 'base', and the 'state' as a part of the 'superstructure'. Accordingly, the state was hardly worthy of independent analysis. Moreover, the capitalist state was identified as the source of clash between the interests of the *bourgeoisie* (the owners of the means of social production who constituted the dominant class) and the *proletariat* (the propertyless workers who formed the dependent class). The state could not represent the 'common interest' as no such interest could exist in the capitalist society. As stated in the *Communist Manifesto* (1848): "The executive of the modern state is but a committee for managing the common affairs of the whole *bourgeoisie.*" However, Marx and Engels threw little light on the mechanism by which the dominant class controls the state power. Max Weber (1864-1920), a liberal thinker, rejected Marx's economic determinism and sought to demonstrate the autonomy of state power (*The Theory of Economic and Social Organization;* 1922). Weber argued that the state had powerful resources of its own. It enjoyed exclusive control over legitimate use of force in society which was not accessible to private interests. It maintained a strong organization in the form of bureaucracy which could formulate, implement and monitor the policies of the state. The state power, therefore, could not be reduced to an instrument of class interests.

Base and Superstructure

The terms 'base' and 'superstructure' are used in Marxist theory to explain the relation between economic structure of society and other aspects of social life. In this building-like metaphor, mode of production (*i.e.* the economic structure of society) comprises base or foundation (also called substructure) of society. It conditions the forms of state and various aspects of social consciousness which belong to superstructure. Superstructure includes legal and political structure, religion, morals, social practices and other expressions of culture. In the course of social development, changes in the mode of production give rise to corresponding changes in all parts of the superstructure.

Classical Marxism treats superstructure as wholly dependent on the base. Neo-Marxists sought to redefine this relationship in different ways. Some writers like Antonio Gramsci (1891-1937) and Nicos Poulantzas (1936-79) conceded relative autonomy of the superstructure in the capitalist society whereas others like Louis Althusser (1918-90) upheld interdependence of base and superstructure.

Antonio Gramsci (1891-1937), Italian Marxist, was the first to concede relative autonomy of the state in the tradition of Marxist thought. Gramsci made a clear distinction between two levels of superstructure: (*a*) *political society* which represented state power and relied on *force* for exercising its domination; and (*b*) *civil society* which was closer to the base and relied on *consent* for exercising its domination. Gramsci pointed out that the *structures of domination* in the culture of the capitalist society comprised of two elements: (*a*) the *structures of coercion* which belonged to the realm of political society; and (*b*) the *structures of legitimation* which belonged to the realm of civil society. Gramsci paid special attention to the functioning of civil society which was exemplified in the institutions of family, school and church, etc. These institutions familiarized the individual with the rules of behaviour and inculcated a natural deference to the authority of the ruling class. While political society or 'the state' exercised 'direct domination' or command through the institution of 'juridical' government, civil society exercised 'hegemony' throughout society which represented a web of beliefs and institutional as well as social relations. In effect, civil society legitimized the rule of the *bourgeoisie* so that nobody would challenge its supremacy. Capitalist society largely depends on the efficiency of these institutions for its stability. It is only when civil society fails to prevent dissent that political society is required to resort to coercion.

Ralph Miliband (1924-94) and Nicos Poulantzas (1936-79) are other Marxist thinkers who have expressed conflicting views on the relative autonomy of the state. Miliband (*The State in Capitalist Society;* 1969) has accepted the unity of state power and class power. His view is described as *'instrumentalist theory of the state'*. He adheres to classical Marxist position that the state is invariably an instrument of class power. He has argued that class character of the capitalist state is perpetuated by: (1) the middle class or upper class background of the state officials; (2) the economic power of the capitalist class; and (3) the inherent desire of the politicians and bureaucrats to continue the existing economic system on which their own position depends. Poulantzas, on the other hand, has drawn a clear distinction between the position of the capitalist class and the state power (*Political Power and Social Classes;* 1973). His view is described as *'structuralist theory of the state'*. He has conceded the relative autonomy of the state. He has argued that class domination is not automatically translated into state power and the state cannot properly be regarded simply as the instrument of a class. The state enhances its legitimacy by invoking authority of 'the people'. The capitalist class enhances its legitimacy by dissociating itself from state repression. Relative autonomy of the state helps in improving its economic performance on the one hand, and promoting capitalist interests on the other. Rejecting Miliband's concept of the unity of class and state power, Poulantzas treats the state itself as an arena of class struggle.

It may be questioned whether overemphasis on the autonomy of state power, as distinguished from the power of the dominant class, does not amount to departure from the original tenets of Marxism!

[VI]
COMMUNITARIAN PERSPECTIVE

Communitarian perspective on the state indicates a recent mode of thought. It marks departure from the philosophy of liberalism because it places the relation between individual and society in a new perspective. It is based on the philosophy of communitarianism which contradicts many assumptions of the liberal theory. Liberal theory implied an 'unencumbered self' detached from pre-existing social forms, as exemplified by the concept of 'possessive individualism'. The term 'possessive individualism' was coined by C.B. Macpherson in his notable work *The Political Theory of Possessive Individualism: Hobbes to Locke* (1962) to describe the main assumption underlying modern liberal theory. According to this view, 'individual is the sole proprietor of his own person or capacities for which he owes nothing to society'. Such a view denies his commitment to other individuals, traditions, practices and conceptions of the good. It holds that self is prior to its ends. It is fully competent to choose its ends as well as its roles and dispositions.

In contrast to this 'atomistic' view of individual, communitarianism advances the concept of the 'situated self', as constituted by his social roles, practices and situations. In other words, communitarianism holds that an agent's identity is constituted by specific commitments to his social situation. While liberalism insists on 'liberty' of individual, his interests and rights, communitarianism focuses on his social identity and upholds acceptance of 'authority' because it expresses our common will or reflects our common identity, our shared values and beliefs. It is significant to note that the atomistic view of society held by liberalism led to the erosion of the sense of responsibility and the moral standards attached thereto. Communitarianism seeks to restore that sense of responsibility and reconstruct moral standards on that basis.

While liberalism chiefly draws on the ideas of Adam Smith, John Locke and Jeremy Bentham, communitarianism is inspired by the ideas of Aristotle, J.J. Rousseau, G.W.F. Hegel and T.H. Green. While contemporary exponents of liberalism or 'libertarianism' include Isaiah Berlin, F.A. Hayek, Milton Friedman and Robert Nozick, contemporary sources of communitarianism may be found in the views of Michael Oakeshott (1901-90) and Hannah Arendt (1906-75). Its present-day exponents include Alasdair MacIntyre (*After Virtue;* 1981), Michael Sandel (*Liberalism and the Limits of Justice;* 1982), Charles Taylor (*Hegel,* 1975; *Sources of the Self,* 1989) and Michael Walzer (*Spheres of Justice;* 1983). MacIntyre constructs an idea of the narrative self: a notion of personal identity that comes from the web of social and communal bonds. He argues that 'individuality' owes its origin to the framework of an established community; it cannot be the product of an individual's choice.

Broadly speaking, communitarians have attacked the liberal mode of thought on the ground that it is too focused on the importance of individual liberty, and insufficiently appreciative of the way in which human beings require a place in a well-functioning community in order to flourish. The term 'community' stands for a form of society whose members are informed by the 'community spirit' or 'a sense of community'. It denotes a 'network of relationships' which are characterized by intimacy and durability. It may be distinguished from 'association' which is based on impersonal and contractual relations. Liberal theory equates society with 'association', whereas communitarian theory equates society with 'community' to determine the nature and extent of social obligation. Communitarians argue that an individual cannot ensure full development of his personality unless he is committed to the spirit of community towards his fellow-beings.

Liberals believe that each person should define and seek his own 'good' within a political structure which defines and enforces what is 'right'. On the other hand, communitarians hold that a political structure has an important role to define what is 'right' as well as 'good' and to help the citizens to seek the good. Liberals define the 'common good' as a sum total of the good of all individuals which is exemplified by the reconciliation of their conflicting interests. On the contrary, communitarians define the 'common good' as a uniform entity where the good of all individuals would converge. They believe that government should strive to create a well-functioning society which would enable all citizens to achieve a good life by participating in its functioning. However, like liberals, communitarians also subscribe to democratic form of government.

Communitarians insist that each of us, as an individual, develops an identity, talents and pursuits in life only as a member of the community and by sharing in its corporate life. Political life should, therefore, focus on the rights of the community, not on those of individual. MacIntyre *(After Virtue;* 1981) ridicules the liberals' concept of individual as an 'autonomous moral agent', disconnected from the social fabric. He argues that individuals flourish only within an atmosphere of 'socially established cooperative human activity'. The state must promote and protect this activity and thereby encourage the development of human excellence. MacIntyre and other communitarians believe that if the state treats individuals as disconnected beings and lets them loose to realize their rights (as liberals seem to wish), the result would be social disintegration and moral disaster. Such disaster has already become visible in modern liberal states as evident in the prevalence of crime and violence, the breakdown of the family, and the rampant drug abuse.

Michael Sandel *(Liberalism and the Limits of Justice;* 1982) attacked John Rawls's *A Theory of Justice* (1971) for his conception of rational negotiators deliberating as the disconnected and disembodied individuals in the so-called 'original position' who have come together to find out the principles of justice.

It is a typical representation of the liberal attitude which tries to understand human beings independently of all activities, desires, ideas, roles and pursuits that characterize human lives in actual society. Sandel observes that after subtracting all these characteristics, nothing is left of the person whom we want to understand. Sandel asserts that the person can only be understood in the context of his 'embeddedness' in a particular time, place and culture. Only with this understanding, a political theory can generate laws, institutions and practices that would be genuinely good for us and conducive to a fully just society. This alone will create a 'deeper commonality' which will be informed by 'shared self-understanding' as well as affection.

Michael Walzer *(Spheres of Justice;* 1983) has sought to reconstruct the liberal approach to justice—as the problem of determining suitable criteria of distribution—by introducing a communitarian approach to this problem. Walzer has argued that the criteria of distribution should correspond to the 'spheres' in which distribution is being considered, so that, for instance, economic justice will be different from political justice. According to Walzer, each sphere of justice will have its own right reason (or relevant reasons) for distribution of the good that it distributes. Thus the spheres of politics, or health, or education, should not be contaminated by the domination of money, for money properly rules in the sphere of commodities; the sphere of office should not (beyond a certain limited point) be contaminated by nepotism, which belongs to the sphere of kinship and love; the sphere of kinship should not be contaminated by male domination. The market properly conceived as the place for the distribution of various social goods on a reasonable basis should be free for all. As the dominance of money (above all) is incompatible with the integrity of politics, merit, kinship, etc., so the dominance of money in all these spheres must finally disappear. Walzer's vision of a new social order comprehends the appropriate arrangements of a decentralized democratic socialism: a strong welfare state run, in part at least, by local and amateur officials; a constrained market; an open and demystified civil service; independent public schools; the sharing of hard work and free time; the protection of religious and familial life; a system of public honouring and dishonouring free from all considerations of rank and class; workers' control of companies and factories; a politics of parties, movements, meetings and public debate.

Charles Taylor *(Philosophical Papers;* 1985), a brilliant spokesman of communitarianism, has echoed MacIntyre's attack on the liberal conception of human beings as autonomous choosers. He rejects 'atomistic' concept of individuals which focuses on their 'will' and sets aside the complexities of the human personality. Taylor asserts that if human beings want their genuine development, they must acknowledge first that they are situated in a society. Some feminist writers and religious thinkers have also confirmed that real communities cannot be created out of an aggregate of 'freely choosing adults'.

Distinction Between Liberal and Communitarian Perspectives

The Issue	*Liberal Perspective*	*Communitarian Perspective*
Chief Concern	Freedom and legal equality of individuals	Values of community life
Individual's Position	Individual can discover and and pursue his good by means of Reason independently of the cultural traditions and social roles prevailing in his society.	Individual can discover and pursue his good only in the context of the cultural traditions and social rules prevailing in his society because his good is an integral part of the common good
Nature of Reason	Reason is inherent in the individual for which he is not indebted to society	Reason is derived from the concerns, beliefs, goals, aspirations and traditions embedded social life of the individual; it cannot exist in a vacuum
Role of the State	In order to promote freedom and equality of people the State should rely on democratic organization and inculcate the spirit of toleration among people so that nobody interferes in their pursuit of individual good	The State should use democratic organization to facilitate the emergence of the good that comprehends the good of all citizens and which must be pursued by all. It should exercise its power and authority to maintain the prevailing cultural traditions and social roles which are necessary for the realization of the common good
Basis of Legitimacy	The political society should establish its legitimacy in the eyes of individual persons	The political society should establish its legitimacy in the eyes of the society as a whole, not in the eyes of individual persons

The difficulty with communitarianism is that in spite of its strong ethical base, it has no mechanism to ensure that its principles will be adopted as the general rules of behaviour. In a nutshell, *communitarianism represents a strong moral philosophy, but it does not provide for an equally strong political philosophy.*

[VII]
POST-COLONIAL PERSPECTIVE

Post-colonial perspective on the state does not embody any new theory of the state. Nevertheless it enables us to understand some new aspects of state-system which are not covered by the conventional theories. In short, *post-colonial perspective denotes an attempt to analyse the problems of the newly independent nations, particularly against the background of their relations with colonial and neo-colonial powers.*

Post-colonial perspective on the state must be based on the experience of post-colonial societies themselves, *i.e.* the societies who gained their independence from colonial domination recently (from the mid of the twentieth century onwards) and who aspire to develop themselves into strong nations. Why they remained underdeveloped? Why they were subjugated by Western nations? Why they are still unable to develop themselves? Even after their independence from colonial powers, why they continue to be exploited by neo-colonial powers? How can they solve their problems?

Colonial Powers

Colonial powers refer to those Western nations (e.g. Britain, France, Belgium, Spain, Portugal, etc.) which became powerful by establishing their domination and administration in a large part of Africa, Asia and Latin America during the eighteenth, nineteenth and early twentieth centuries and exploiting their natural as well as human resources.

Neo-colonial Powers

Neo-colonial powers refer to those developed nations of the West who continue to exploit the newly independent countries of Africa, Asia and Latin America in late twentieth century through international trade, conditional aid, investment in multinational corporations (MNCs), military intervention, cultural domination and transfer of pollution, etc.

An analysis of the history of colonialism, the impact of colonial domination, the forces which promoted national movements and the consequences of the process of decolonization would throw light on the general pattern of domination in the international sphere, which is crucial to an understanding of state-system. It shows, at the outset, that West European nations who had achieved national consolidation by the seventeenth century set out to achieve their modernization through industrialization and urbanization as they already had the benefit of scientific discoveries and inventions. They needed cheap raw materials, cheap labour and vast areas of operation. They found countries of Africa, Asia and Latin America as their easy prey. These countries were rich in natural resources and labour force but they had little advantage of modern education or national solidarity. Some of these countries had inherited great civilizations of ancient times which had been shattered during the medieval age. For instance, India and Egypt were known for their magnificent past, but they hardly had the potential of national consolidation or their modernization in the mid of the eighteenth century. Thus, a large part of Africa, Asia and Latin America fell prey to colonial domination.

This shows that enterprising people, after their national consolidation, seek to set up political domination over other countries whom they identify as their targets of exploitation. After establishing their political domination and administration in those countries, they project their own culture as superior to the native culture and try to win admiration, respect and loyalty of the native people. They even claim to be performing the task of civilizing the so-called uncivilized people whom they continue to exploit. They also try to create institutions and *elites* within the native people who would help them in carrying on their administration.

Thus, colonial rulers propagated the idea that Europe was the centre of all progress and modernity. It was superior to other regions of the world in terms of history, language, literature and technology. Its culture, art, political structures and social conventions were claimed to be so superior that they would have a civilizing effect on the colonized people. Even racial superiority of Europeans over other people was asserted. Champions of colonialism claimed that they were fulfilling the noble responsibility of extending the benefits of civilization to 'primitive' people as exemplified by the notion of 'whiteman's burden'. They make these claims in such a forceful and convincing style that many of the colonized people hardly suspect their intentions.

Colonial powers do promote education, industry, transport, communication, etc. and create administrative and political structures in the colonized territories, and thereby contribute to their progress. But all these measures are deliberately designed to facilitate and stabilize their rule. Macaulay's infamous 1835 Minute on Indian Education had proposed the deliberate creation in India of a class of 'brown whitemen' educated to value European culture above their own. Indian Railways, posts and telegraphs, schools, colleges, universities, hospitals, etc. were created to strengthen the British administration.

It is also true that the educational and administrative structures created by the colonial powers promote an awareness and consciousness among the colonized people. They remove their lethargy, dispel superstitions, and prompt them to think in a rational manner. They create an urge for social reform in their mind, which is sometimes reinforced by the revival of their past glory and a sense of protest against their exploitation by the colonial powers. All these factors often give rise to national movement which may culminate in the struggle for independence. When a colonial power is unable to contain this struggle, it may choose to hand over power to the local *elite* with the hope to have their support after their departure. Moreover, when a colonial power has already taken full advantage of its long rule, its further maintenance may seem to be a costly affair. So it may 'grant' independence to the colonized territory and switch over to new forms of exploitation by neo-colonial methods.

It may further be conceded that political independence of the colonized people does not necessarily mean an end to their adherence to the values cherished by their colonial rulers. In many cases, these values may persist, along with political, economic and cultural models of the colonial regime, even after independence. In the contemporary scenario, some of these values and models have become a part of global culture which are being reinforced through the process of 'globalization'.

The new nations or the developing countries, which comprise the bulk of the 'third world', are faced with the gigantic task of nation-building and state-building. Many of these countries have not naturally evolved as nations, but they represent the territorial and administrative divisions made by the colonial powers for their administrative convenience. With their large size, vast population and cultural multiplicity the tasks of nation-building and state-building in these countries are quite challenging. Nation-building stands for the process by which people transfer their commitment and loyalty from smaller tribes, villages or petty principalities to the larger central political system. It involves developing a sense of community among the people within the jurisdiction of a political system and provides for a sense of identification, a common object of their allegiance, an emotional bond and social solidarity. It gives them a national identity cutting across their group loyalties based on religion, race, caste, language, region, culture, occupation, etc.

State-building, on the other hand, implies a process whereby a common centre of power is evolved in order to establish law and order throughout the state and to extend the defensive and welfare services of the state to each and every part of its territory. Nation-building and state-building are complementary activities. When people of all categories are sure to benefit from the protective and welfare services provided by the state, they are likely to focus their allegiance to the state and give precedence to national interest over their sectarian interests. Conversely, if all people owe their allegiance to one central authority, the state will find it easier to extend its protective and welfare services to all parts of its territory.

Task of nation-building is often sought to be accomplished or facilitated by the adoption of national symbols like national flag, national emblem, national anthem, national song, national calendar, national flower, national bird, national animal, national tree, national river, as well as national festivals, etc. This may be reinforced by popularization of national heroes—new and old. At times, glorification of some mythological characters may be added to this effort, but this may create some problems in multi-religious countries. Fortification of secular values is necessary in multi-communal countries like India. Problems of mass poverty, illiteracy, unemployment, ill-health, housing, etc. must also be tackled effectively, otherwise nothing would prove effective in creating a sense of community and fellow-feeling.

In fact, the process of nation-building in these countries had been started by their distinguished leaders during the course of their national movement and struggle for independence. These men of high calibre and character were able to mobilize the masses and create social harmony within large sections of the population. They had instilled a hope in the people that the dawn of independence would usher in a new era. It was expected that with the liquidation of foreign domination, post-colonial state would become an instrument of fulfilling needs and aspirations of the masses.

However, actual happenings largely belied these hopes. Independence was followed by the multiplication of demands from a myriad of sections of people. Bureaucracy, particularly the police, inherited from the colonial regime was used to oppression of the people. It proved extremely difficult to make it sympathetic towards people. Again, with the gradual disappearance of national stalwarts, new generations of political leadership hardly matched their calibre and character. Politics became a game of enlisting support of narrow sectional interests and negotiating for a share of power in government. The result is overall deterioration of national life. However, new generations of non-political, brilliant professional *elites* in the post-colonial societies have contributed significantly to national prosperity and have created widespread awareness of democratic and human rights as well as the needs of social justice.

[VIII]
GANDHIAN PERSPECTIVE

Gandhian perspective on the state is based on the social and political thought of Mahatma Gandhi (M.K. Gandhi) (1869-1948). Gandhi was an Indian moral philosopher whose thought is scattered in a large number of notes and pamphlets as well as in his *Autobiography* (*My Experiments With Truth;* 1929). He did not produce any treatise containing a systematic exposition of his thought. His perspective on the state will have to be gleaned from his relevant observations on this subject.

NATURE OF THE STATE

Gandhi was a champion of non-violence or *ahimsa* which deprecates all types of coercion. He believed that state was a manifestation of power and law which were based on coercion. State is inclined to impose its own will on individuals with the help of an elaborate machinery of police force, law-courts, prisons and military power. It suppresses an individual's individuality as it tries to cast all individuals into a uniform mould. It destroys his sense of self-reliance and stunts his personality. It deprives him of his freedom and obstructs the progress of human society.

Gandhi observed that modern state was more powerful than ancient and medieval states as it was more organized and more centralized. Power of the state was concentrated in the hands of the few who did not hesitate to misuse it. In Gandhi's view, individual is endowed with soul, but state is a soulless machine. State's acts are devoid of human sensitivity. State goes by rules and regulations. Those who enforce these rules do not feel any moral responsibility.

Indeed, Gandhi condemned political power on moral ground, and not on historical or economic grounds. He was convinced that if non-violence or *ahimsa* could be adopted as a universal principle of human behaviour, political power as well as state would become redundant. The result would be an 'enlightened anarchy'. So Gandhi wrote in *Young India* (1931):

> To me political power is not an end but one of the means of enabling people to better their condition in every department of life through national representatives. If national life becomes so perfect as to become self-regulated, no representation becomes necessary. There is then a state of enlightened anarchy. In such a State everyone is his own ruler. He rules himself in such a manner that he is never a hindrance to his neighbour. In the ideal State, therefore, there is no political power because there is no State. But the ideal is never fully realized in life. Hence the classical statement of Thoreau that that government is best which governs the least.

In this respect, Gandhi was a follower of Count Leo Tolstoy (1828-1910) who was a religious minded pacific anarchist. Tolstoy was inspired by his faith in Christianity; Gandhi found the basis of this philosophy through his faith in Hinduism *(sanatana dharma),* although he taught equal respect for all religions. Both Tolstoy and Gandhi accorded precedence to spiritual bliss over material satisfaction. Both attacked private property as it enabled the few to lead a luxurious life by exploiting the labour of large numbers. Gandhi did not agree with some other anarchists like P.J. Proudhon (1809-65), Mikhail Bakunin (1814-76) and Peter Kropotkin (1842-1921) who regarded religion as a hindrance to human development.

GANDHI AND MARX

Like Marx (1818-83), Gandhi also believed in classless and stateless society for the emancipation of mankind. But he interpreted it quite differently. For Marx, classes represented the division of society into *haves* and *have-nots, i.e.* the owners and non-owners of private property. Marx anticipated the emergence of a classless society through a violent revolution in which capitalists would be overthrown and labour would become compulsory for every able-bodied person. For Gandhi, class distinction arose from a mental outlook which regarded one type of work (*e.g.* physical labour) as inferior to another type (*e.g.* mental labour). Gandhi commended 'dignity of labour' (particularly, physical labour) as the key to a classless society. He prescribed 'bread labour' for everybody which implied 'the recognition of the necessity of some physical exertion even for mental workers, so that they may be performing some productive function in a spirit of service to the community'.

Marx suggested social ownership of means of social production for the creation of a classless society. Gandhi enunciated the principle of 'trusteeship' which required the 'change of heart' of capitalists to regard their business and industry as a 'trust' of the people, and not as their private possessions. Marx saw the state as an instrument of the dominant class, and hoped that in a classless society, state and political power would become redundant; hence a 'stateless' society would come into existence. Marx wanted full development of technology and forces of production so that everybody's needs could be satisfied. On the contrary, Gandhi wanted replacement of huge machinery by human labour to provide for jobs to the teeming millions, limiting one's needs to the minimum and elevation of human character so that external force to regulate their behaviour would become unnecessary; hence a 'stateless' society would become a reality. Marx deprecated religion as 'opium of the people' and wanted to eliminate its role in society; Gandhi saw religion as a moralizing force and wanted to secure its due place in society. Marx professed 'scientific socialism'; Gandhi professed 'moral individualism'.

Moral Individualism

Moral individualism refers to a philosophical principle which regards individual as an end-in-itself, endowed with 'dignity'. Accordingly, no human being can be treated as a means to serve an end which lies beyond his conscious existence; no worldly thing can be treated as more valuable than a human being; and no human being can accept an obligation except at his own free will.

CONCEPT OF *SWARAJ*

Gandhi's concept of *Swaraj* confirms his firm commitment to moral individualism. The term *'swaraj'* literally means 'self-rule', 'self-government', 'self determination' or 'independence'. This term became popular during India's struggle for independence. Gandhi sought to expand its meaning and scope.

Gandhi argued that *swaraj* did not simply mean political independence from the foreign rule; it also implied the idea of cultural and moral independence. If a country is politically independent but culturally dependent on others for choosing its course of action, it would be devoid of *swaraj*. *Swaraj* does not close the doors of learning from others, but it requires confidence in one's own potential and decisions. Gandhi thought of *swaraj* as a system in which all people will have a natural affinity with their country and they will readily collaborate in the task of nation-building.

Swaraj or self-government rules out people's dependence on government. This applies even to their own government. Thus, Gandhi wrote in *Young India* (1925):

> Self-government means continuous effort to be independent of government control, whether it is foreign government or whether it is national. *Swaraj* government will be a sorry affair if people look up to it for the regulation of every detail of life.

Gandhi's concept of *swaraj* also exemplifies his vision of a true democracy. Under this system, people will not merely have the right to elect their representatives, but they will become capable of checking any abuse of authority. As Gandhi wrote in *Young India* (1925):

> Real *Swaraj* will come not by the acquisition of authority by a few but by the acquisition of the capacity by all to resist authority when it is abused. In other words, *swaraj* is to be obtained by educating the masses to a sense of their capacity to regulate and control authority.

For Gandhi, the idea of *swaraj* was not confined to the political goal of securing independence from foreign yoke. It also implied moral regeneration of the individual himself—the process of 'self-control', 'self-discipline' and 'self-purification' which must continue even after the independence. As Gandhi himself observed:

> I am not interested in freeing India merely from the English yoke. I am bent upon freeing India from any yoke whatsoever. I have no desire to exchange 'king log for king stork'. Hence for me the movement of *swaraj* is a movement of self-purification
>
> (*Selections from Gandhi* by Nirmal Kumar Bose; 1948).

Gandhi sought to demonstrate that individual self-government, *i.e.* self-control or self-mastery, was as important as political self-government itself. Thus he wrote in his *Autobiography (My Experiments With Truth;* 1929):

> Self-government depends entirely upon our own internal strength, upon our ability to fight against the heaviest odds. Indeed, self-government which does not require that continuous striving to attain it and to sustain it, is not worth the name. I have therefore endeavoured to show both in word and deed that political self-government—that is self-government for a large number of men and women—is no better than individual self-government, and therefore, it is to be attained by precisely the same means that are required for individual self-government or self-rule.

As a votary of purity of means as well as ends, Gandhi tried to assert that we must rely on non-violence or *ahimsa* for the attainment of political self-government as well as individual self-government.

Gandhi elaborately dwells on the principle of non-violence or *ahimsa* as the way to transform individual character and also as the guiding principle of political struggle. He demonstrates the superiority of non-violence over violence 'at least in the majority of the cases'. He asserts that the force of love and pity is infinitely greater than the force of arms. The principle of non-violence (*ahimsa*) is founded on soul-force (*atmabal*) while violence was founded on body-force (*sharirbal*). The qualities of soul-force are akin to love-force (*prembal*), compassion-force (*dayabal*), the force acquired by self-suffering (*tapobal*) and moral force (*nitibal*). All these forces become operative when mind is able to control itself and the passions. An individual endowed with these forces would be naturally inclined to adopt the technique of non-violent resistance (*satyagraha*) as his method of political struggle.

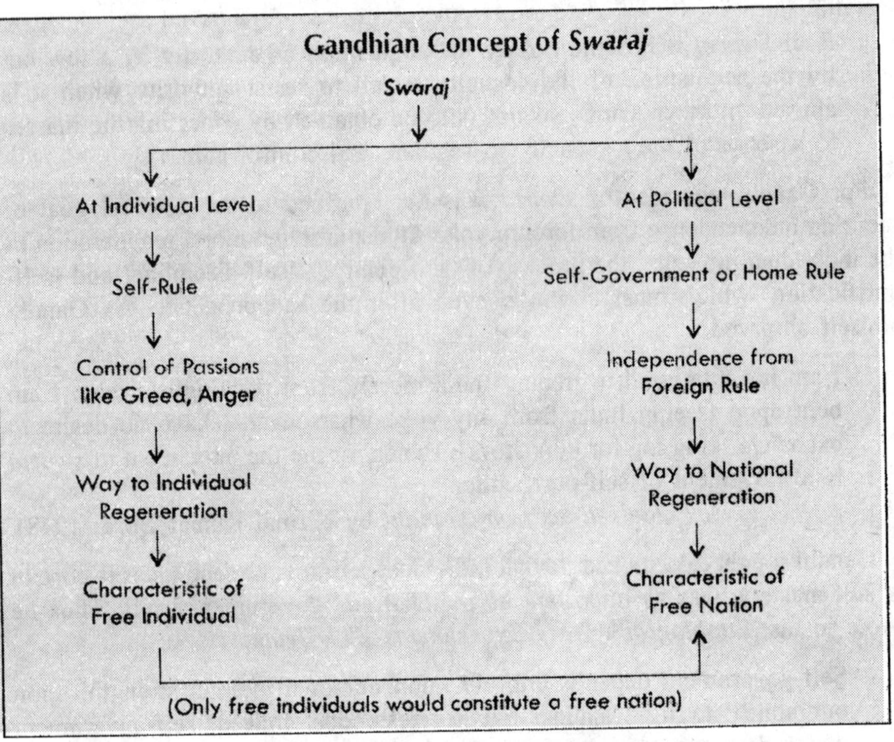

[IX]
FEMINIST PERSPECTIVE

Feminist perspective is primarily concerned with the inferior status of women as a characteristic of the state system. It focuses on two crucial aspects of the nature of the state: (*a*) State as an instrument of regulation of the public sphere; and (*b*) State as an instrument of power. As regards regulation of the public sphere, feminists argue that the dominance of man over woman is not confined to the public sphere; it extends to all aspects of her life including the most intimate relations like sexual relations. In order to secure justice to woman, the sphere of purely personal relations between man and woman will also have to be regulated. Hence feminists insist on redefining the term 'political' in this context. This idea is expressed in the slogan: 'the personal is political'. Kate Millett (1934-2017), noted American feminist, in *Sexual Politics* (1971), sought to redefine politics as "power-structured relationships, arrangements whereby one group of persons is controlled by another". Her study of some well-known romantic writers revealed that power, not eroticism or sexual passion, was their real subject, and the urge to dominate was at issue in their every written sexual encounter.

Again, in the public sphere, state and politics are concerned with the conflict over the distribution of scarce resources, including contests for control of state apparatus and its policies. Here too, women constitute a deprived section. For centuries they have been deprived of the right to property and right to vote. State is identified as a key actor in meeting the demands of women like protection from male violence, greater reproductive rights (*i.e.* the right to have children as per their choice), changes in family and employment law, provision of pension benefits and other welfare schemes.

As regards the role of the state as instrument of power, feminists have tried to demonstrate how male power becomes embedded in different branches of the state apparatus and in the state policies. Zillah Eisenstein, in her noted work *The Radical Future of Liberal Feminism* (1981), has argued that the liberal state represents itself as fully autonomous so that all positions therein are equally open to all players, including women. Such a state is not bothered to ascertain the actual share of power enjoyed by women. Socialist feminists have attacked the liberal state on many grounds: welfare policies of Western capitalist state tend to increase women's dependence on men within the capitalist mode of production; the state seeks to free women's labour for exploitation in the labour market; and it tends to serve men's interests by maintaining women's unpaid labour in the home.

According to feminists, women constitute a deprived section in all parts of the world. In the post-colonial states (*i.e.* the newly independent states of the third world), women's lives are less often touched by state regulation because of the poor implementation of the state welfare provisions. Besides, women often become victims of state violence in this part of the world. Again, in the formerly socialist states of Eastern Europe, the state was associated with 'forced emancipation' which implied the employment of women in strenuous jobs, not suited to their capability and temperament.

The widespread exclusion of women from state power has still wider implications. It has caused environmental degradation as women by nature are nature-friendly vis-à-vis men. Moreover, men take pride in showing their valour in warfare while women are peace-loving by nature. With the exclusion of women from power, the state tends to build its strength on military power. This results in mounting tension among nations and the lack of active cooperation among them for securing the interests of entire mankind.

[X]
PLURALIST PERSPECTIVE

Pluralist perspective portrays the state as a mechanism designed to serve the interests of various groups simultaneously. It has descriptive as well as normative overtones. On the descriptive side, it deals with the working of a democratic state in the contemporary world. On the normative side, it prescribes that wherever the interests of some influential sections in society get undue prominence at the expense of other sections, the situation should be suitably rectified.

A pluralist state repudiates a single centre of power in society. In other words, it is characterized by multiple centres of power. Such a state does not hold supreme power. It must act as an impartial arbitrator between the claims of several social groups for the allocation of the scarce resources of the community. Further, it must justify its authority by proving to be the guardian of justice in society. Only a democratic state, which provides the right to freedom of association to its citizens, would be capable of evolving into a pluralist state. This right would enable the citizens to form independent associations for pursuing their specific interests as well as their common interest. In due course, these associations would become powerful enough to counterbalance the power of the state. *The set of associations formed to pursue the larger interest of the community constitute 'civil society'.* In the contemporary world, civil society is regarded the bulwark of democratic order.

Civil Society

Civil society includes a wide range of voluntary associations of citizens which tend to motivate them to participate in civic causes and to solve their common problems through collective self-help rather than reliance on state initiative. It serves as a medium of crystallizing and publicizing their opinions and interests which would otherwise go unheard. It draws people into cooperative ventures, breaking down their social isolation and making them aware of their wider social responsibilities. Thus it serves as the true source of democratization. In common parlance, civil society acts as an intermediary between the state and citizens.

An authoritarian state does not allow the formation of independent associations of citizens. If some strong associations of citizens happen to emerge in an authoritarian state, that state is likely to give way to a democratic system. For instance, the rise of Solidarity (an independent union of workers) in Poland in 1980 and the emergence of environmental groups and such other associations in the Eastern Europe in 1980s culminated in the collapse of authoritarian regimes in that region.

Movement towards pluralism began in early twentieth century as a protest against the doctrine of state sovereignty. Léon Duguit (1859-1928), a French legal theorist, contested the idea of sovereignty solely resting with the state. Harold J. Laski (1893-1950), an English political thinker, and Robert M. MacIver (1882-1970), an American sociologist, made a fervent appeal for treating the various social groups as different centres of power in society. They argued that the state should compete with these groups for winning the loyalty of citizens by serving their interests more effectively.

Contemporary concept of the pluralist state was evolved in a different direction. Robert Dahl and Charles Lindblom's *Politics, Economics and Welfare* (1953) and Robert Dahl's *A Preface to Democratic Theory* (1956) and *Who Governs?* (1961) are regarded as landmarks in the evolution of the theory of pluralist state. They tried to demonstrate that a democratic society was marked by a widespread distribution of political resources, and that different interests prevailed in different political disputes and at different times. Dahl and Lindblom described their model of a working democracy as 'polyarchy'. This implied a situation in which power is not centralized but dispersed among numerous interests and groups. The role of government in such a situation is little more than that of an honest broker in the middle. N. Polsby in his essay *Community, Power and Political Theory* (1963) went a step further and asserted that in such a situation at the bottom *nobody* really dominates.

The concept of pluralist state in this sense implies that all groups would bargain on equal footing, which is not the case in actual practice. Moreover, some groups may lack internal democracy so much so that the dominant personalities in those groups may project their own will as the will of the whole group. As a result the real interests of the members of those groups might be relegated to the background. These points were later conceded by the exponents of the pluralist theory. Thus, Charles Lindblom in *Politics and Markets* (1977) admitted that business and property enjoyed a privileged position in the market-dominated polyarchies of the West, which enabled them to exercise undemocratic control of society. Then Robert Dahl in *Dilemmas of Pluralist Democracy* (1982) conceded that pluralism cannot be treated as an open competition between truly equal political forces. In order to reduce the inequalities of these forces, Dahl recommended those policies which would promote redistribution of power in society. Thus, the descriptive and normative sides of the pluralist perspective on the state come very close to each other.

11

Grounds and Limits of Political Obligation

THE PROBLEM OF political obligation is one of the most prominent issues of political philosophy. It is primarily concerned with the question: how far, when and why an individual is obliged to obey law and the commands of political authority. This may be accompanied by such duties of the citizen as payment of taxes, political participation and voting, jury service and military duty, etc. which are necessary for the maintenance of political institutions. Broadly speaking, these duties are regarded as part of the individual's political obligation. Political philosophy inquires into the logical and moral grounds of political obligation so as to determine its proper scope and limits. This question is so complex that it is not possible to find its definite answer which would be universally acceptable. However, an inquiry into different viewpoints expressed in this behalf can enlighten us in finding an answer to this problem in a particular context.

[I]
THEORIES OF UNLIMITED OBLIGATION

THE DOCTRINE OF *FORCE MAJEURE*

Force Majeure means superior strength, an irresistible compulsion or coercion. The doctrine of *force majeure*, therefore, regards the superior strength of the state as the source of political obligation. According to this view, the state is so powerful that the individual has no option but to obey its laws and commands, whether he likes them or not. In this sense, political obligation is based on the fear of punishment or other unpleasant consequences which would follow from disobedience of law. This view of political obligation identifies the state or government as the embodiment of political authority; its invincible power as the source of its authority. Since individual is too weak to challenge the authority of the state, his political obligation is unlimited.

The difficulty with this theory is that it is not based on any moral ground. It simply invokes the dubious rule of 'might is right'. It does not allow the individual to inquire whether a law is right or wrong; it does not care to secure his willing obedience. It does not permit the individual to resist any law or command which could be wrong in his judgement. It creates a ground of obedience which is akin to surrender under the threat of an armed robber rather than following the advice of a doctor in the interest of individual's own health. With these characteristics, it could hardly be treated as a sound theory of political obligation.

DIVINE RIGHT THEORY

The theory of divine right of Kings holds that the authority of the sovereign is derived from God; hence obedience to the state is as imperative as obedience to God. The early hints of this theory are found in ancient Indian political thought. In Europe, this theory was developed during the ascendancy of monarchy. Its chief exponent was Robert Filmer (1588-1653). In the recent times, this theory was upheld in pre-communist Tibet and some tribal kingdoms. It is seldom invoked in the modem state.

Since God's will is binding on all mortals, this theory upholds an unlimited political obligation. It establishes political obligation on religious rather than moral ground. If a King turns out to be a tyrant, people have to obey him as a punishment for their sin. James I of England (1566-1625) sought to justify his tyrannical rule precisely on this ground.

Some writers equate the divine right theory with 'charismatic authority'. This comparison is not well-founded. Charismatic authority is the characteristic of political leaders who command obedience of their followers because of their mystical, personal qualities which may or may not be accompanied by invoking their divine origin. Moreover, charismatic authority is purely personal which may vanish with the disappearance of the person holding such qualities. But divine right theory concedes inheritance of the same authority. It is, therefore, akin to 'traditional authority' rather than charismatic authority.

Since this theory denies any right of the individual to exercise his judgement about right and wrong and to resist any wrong law or command, this too can hardly be treated as a genuine theory of political obligation.

CONSERVATIVE VIEW

Adherents of conservatism uphold obedience to the state or political authority for practical reasons. David Hume (1711-76) argued that the advantages of obedience to any type of political authority outweigh the disadvantages of having no government at all. He, therefore, upheld unconditional political obligation in view of practical utility of a government. Edmund Burke (1729-97) similarly argued that politics was a matter of 'prudence and practicability'. Defending the case for social continuity, he contended that revolution is evil, not only because it involves violence and destruction, but also because it results in misuse of power by those who manage to capture it. Burke ruled out extreme versions of reform because they destroy the social fabric without providing for the mechanism of its repair. In his view, "society is far too complex a system to be tinkered with. A people's constitution is the result of many minds in many ages. It is no simple, no superficial thing, nor to be estimated by superficial understandings...A society is a delicate organism, developing and adapting itself to circumstances. To interfere with any major institution would start a chain of repercussions throughout the whole system, with results no man could foresee."

Conservatism

Conservatism refers to a political outlook that promotes respect for the long-standing social practices, and insists on maintaining those institutions which have stood the test of time. When change is inevitable or it has already taken place, conservatives will attempt to moderate it with a view to ensuring minimum disturbance in the existing order. David Hume (1711-76), a Scottish philosopher, and Edmund Burke (1729-97), an Irish statesman, are regarded the chief exponents of conservatism.

Michael Oakeshott (1901-90), a contemporary conservative, defined politics as the 'pursuit of intimations of the traditions of behaviour'. According to him, the aims of a political association lie within the community itself which must be discovered, rather than imported from speculative philosophy. Political activity is neither a product of contract nor of any mutuality of purpose. It is akin to the model of informal conversation which develops by its internal logic, rather than a discourse on a well-thought out subject. Political obligation, then, is a diffuse obligation, like an obligation arising out of friendship which does not follow any fixed pattern, nor emanates from any conditions of a contract. Thus, political obligation is incidental to the political activity which arises from the normal social life, rather than from the pursuit of any transcendental objectives. In a nutshell, the conservative view of political obligation is based on legitimacy rather than on consent or morality.

[II] THEORIES OF LIMITED OBLIGATION

PRINCIPLE OF CONSENT

Some theories regard individual's consent as the proper source of political obligation. According to this view, 'man is born free'; he can be expected to obey a ruler only with his consent. In other words, a government can exercise its power only with an explicit or implicit consent of its citizens. Some thinkers argue that if an individual accepts the protection of the prevailing system through abiding by its rules, his tacit consent may be taken for granted. Others hold that mere acceptance of a legitimate authority is not sufficient to explain the source of political obligation: it must be proved that people themselves created that authority with their consent. The theory of the 'social contract' represents the best formulation of this viewpoint.

The chief exponents of the theory of the social contract are: Thomas Hobbes (1588-1679), John Locke (1632-1704), and Jean-Jaques Rousseau (1712-78). These thinkers have postulated a 'state of nature', that is a hypothetical stage before the creation of political authority. Social contract represents the method of arriving at agreement for setting up the state; it marks a transition from the state of nature to civil society. The terms of the contract define the grounds and limits of political obligation.

Hobbes equates men in the state of nature with wild animals. In his view, man's life in the state of nature was 'solitary, poor, nasty, brutish and short'. It was a state of war of each against all, and hence fraught with insecurity. Men entered into covenant to translate their urge for self-preservation into reality. Hence, they surrendered all their natural rights to the newly created political authority—the sovereign. This surrender was final and irrevocable, because any departure from this position would result in the reversion to the state of nature. Although Hobbes postulates an unlimited political obligation, yet it is solely based on consent not imposed from above. That is why Hobbes contends that "a conqueror acquires dominion only if his vassals are understood to have tacitly promised obedience".

Locke's picture of the state of nature is not so gloomy. He argues that man is by nature a rational creature who is generally inclined to follow the rules of morality. Hence, the state of nature was a state of 'peace, good will, mutual assistance and preservation'. Civil society was established by mutual consent of the people, only to deal with the few law-breakers who could not be allowed to be the judge in their own case. Under the social contract, man surrenders the right to be the judge in his own case to the state which is entrusted with the task of protection of his natural right to 'life, liberty and property'. Government is, therefore, created as a trust which can be dissolved if it fails to perform this function. Accordingly, Locke upholds a limited political obligation and concedes individual's right to resistance and revolution.

Rousseau has painted a fascinating picture of the state of nature, as a state of idyllic blissfulness—when man was close to nature and enjoyed the beauty and bounty of nature without any restriction. But in due course the increasing size of population and the consequent scarcity of goods brought a sense of insecurity among men when 'natural liberty' ceased to be a source of constant happiness. This led to a conflict between individual's actual will (motivated by his immediate self-interest) and real will (motivated by his ultimate good which coincided with the good of the community). In order to overcome this difficulty, men entered into the social contract by placing themselves under the direction and control of the 'general will' which represented the convergence of the real will of all members of the community. Thus, natural liberty was replaced by 'civil liberty' which provided for an effective security of their possessions. Rousseau, therefore, postulated absolute sovereignty and unlimited political obligation. However, this obligation is not owed to any external authority; it is addressed to the general will of the community of which the individual himself is a part. In other words, it embodies consent of the individual to subordinate his 'lower self' to his 'higher self'. This subordination is not inimical to his true freedom even if he feels the pinch of suppression of his 'lower self'. That is why Rousseau quipped: 'man can be forced to be free'.

General Will

According to Jean-Jaques Rousseau (1712-78), a French philosopher, the *general will* refers to the point of convergence of the real will of all members of a community. It reflects the ultimate good of each individual as well as the common good of the whole community. Rousseau believed that man would realize his true freedom by submitting his particular will to the direction of the *general will.*

Among the exponents of the social contract, Locke alone postulates a conditional consent; hence he clearly creates a limited political obligation. Hobbes and Rousseau postulate unconditional consent and absolute sovereignty. They seem to create an unlimited political obligation. But since this obligation is based on their consent, and it is intended to serve their interest, it cannot be treated as unlimited in the real sense. Hobbes creates a powerful state structure—symbolized by *Leviathan* (a sea monster) who dominates all others. He provides for no mechanism to curb the state if the actual sovereign turns out to be tyrannical. Rousseau, too, creates an equally powerful sovereign, but it does not stand above the community. Theoretically this is all right, but in actual practice sovereignty will be exercised by a government consisting of a group of persons who might project their selfish and foolish designs as the expression of the general will. Rousseau, of course, favoured small communities governed by direct democracy where such a situation would not arise. But this is not practicable in modern times. So Rousseau's solution does not show us the way to prevent the abuse of force by government. In fact, the whole idea of consent, given once for all, is not a sound basis of political obligation. A government based on consent must be dependent on the continuous consent of a vigilant electorate, to be renewed and re-expressed at regular intervals. In this light Locke's formulation of the social contract may be treated to be on the sound footing.

MORALIST VIEW

Moralist view of political obligation is a double-edged sword. It can be invoked for vindicating limited as well as unlimited obligation. Morality is based on our sense of right and wrong, which impels us to do what is right, and to avoid what is wrong . We attain knowledge of the rules of morality from our inner self—our conscience. We obey these rules of our own volition. We regard these rules as the mainstay of our social system. We respect others' person and property because we expect them to respect our own person and property. We try to maintain public order because it is beneficial for ourselves as well as others. Ideally, laws and commands of public authority should conform to the principles of morality. If they do, we will certainly respect them. As Keith Hyams has significantly observed:

> The law forbids us to steal, to murder, to rape, and to do a number of other things that most of us would not dream of doing anyway, even if the law were not to exist. So it looks as though much of the law simply tells us to do, or not to do, things that we already think we should or should not do out of an independent sense of right and wrong. Perhaps, then, our duty to obey the law amounts to nothing more than a duty to obey the rules of morality, which distinguish right from wrong ('Political Authority and Obligation', *Issues in Political Theory,* ed. by Catriona McKinnon; 2008).

Accordingly, when the provisions of law coincide with the rules of morality and receive our spontaneous approval, then we feel naturally obliged to obey law and the commands of public authority. This argument can be invoked to vindicate unlimited political obligation.

On the contrary, if a particular law or a command of public authority does not coincide with our moral judgement, we are not obliged to obey it. In other words, if a law compels someone to act against his conscience, a clash may arise between legal obligation and moral obligation. For example, if a worker is morally committed to a trade union which has given a call for strike but the strike has been legally banned, he will have to face the consequences of acting against law if he chooses to honour his moral commitment.

Thus, from the moralist point of view, individual's obligation to obey political authority is conditional, and not absolutc. This argumcnt can bc invoked to vindicate limited political obligation. As Keith Hyams has illustrated:

> This argument only requires obedience to just laws. The citizens of Nazi Germany or present-day Burma, for example, would not be required to obey the oppressive laws imposed by their governments. But even liberal democracies tend to do a lot more than just enforce the basic rules of morality...Disagreements about the roles of justice and equality in morality have implications for the permissibility of redistributive taxation (*ibid.*).

When citizens realize that an existing or a proposed law or administrative action is wrong, they may decide to defy it. They may even launch a systematic campaign to oppose it, not to speak of obeying it against their conscience. This point was further developed by the idealist view of political obligation.

IDEALIST VIEW

The idealist school of thought originally created an unconditional and unlimited obligation, but later it was modified to admit a note of caution. G.W.F. Hegel (1770-1831), famous exponent of idealism, eulogized the state as 'the incarnation of divine reason' and the 'march of God on earth'. He argued that when individual obeys the state, he essentially follows divine reason and thereby exercises his freedom. Hegel, therefore, postulated an unlimited political obligation without drawing a clear distinction between the state (which was an abstract entity) and government (which consisted of a group of fallible persons exercising actual authority). It is unfortunate that fascist regimes invoked Hegel's argument to demand unconditional obedience from their citizens and led them to the path of untold disaster.

> **Fascism**
>
> Fascism refers to an anti-democratic theory advanced by Benito Mussolini (1883-1945), Italian dictator, which eulogized nation-state as the supreme moral authority. It exhorted people to set aside all rules, conventions and legal limitations, and religiously follow the dictates of their leader in pursuit of national glorification.

It was T.H. Green (1836-82) in the idealist tradition who declared that government cannot claim an unconditional obedience of its citizens. Green argued that individual owes his allegiance to society, not to the state or government. Accordingly, the organized power of society should be recognized as political authority for the purpose of determining political obligation. Green's concept of political obligation is based on his concept of the 'common good'. He pointed out that it is society, not the state, which is the pivot of the common good.

Green's view of human nature is sharply opposed to the utilitarian view. Whereas utilitarians treat the human being as a pleasure-seeking animal, Green holds that human beings do not seek pleasure as such. The rational basis of human activity is will or reason, not desire or passion. As self-conscious beings, men and women wish to realize the good which they grasp along with other members of the community. According to Green, human beings do not identify their self-interest as distinctly as they identify the common good. Common good not only comprehends the good of all members of the community, but their conceptions of the common good are also identical. In his *Lectures on the Principles of Political Obligation* (1882), Green argued that the state itself is obliged to promote the common good as conceived by its citizens, and that individual is obliged to obey only those laws which will promote the common good. If individuals think that they will serve the cause of the common good by defying any command of the state, their political obligation does not prevent them from such defiance.

According to Green, it is the consciousness of the common good which prompts human beings to accept their duties. They tend to sacrifice their self-interest for the sake of the common good for they realize that they can attain self-realization only as members of the community, not as separate individuals. The question of priority between the individual and the community is irrelevant because individuals have no existence outside the community, and no community can exist without its constituent individuals. The true basis of the community lies in each individual treating every other individual as an end-in-itself, because each member of the community is recognized as capable of pursuing ideal objects. The true object of politics as well as of morality is to improve the moral character of individuals. This should be the criterion of evaluation of any institution or law. In other words, each institution or law should enable the citizens to exercise their good will and reason in the conduct of their affairs. It is the moral nature of human being which postulates his freedom. Freedom requires all members of the community to have equal opportunity of self-development. It is the duty of the state to create such conditions that are conducive to human freedom. Green points out that law can force the individual to perform certain acts, but these would be external acts only. No law can make them moral because morality is dependent on something freely willed. In Green's words, 'Will, nor force, is the basis of the state'.

Thus, Green's view of political obligation banks on the moral nature and capacity of human beings. It reduces the state to an instrument of securing the common good as conceived and defined by its citizens. By recognizing the organized power of the community rather than the state as the object of political obligation, Green rules out the claim of any government to demand unconditional obedience from its citizens. Likewise, Harold J. Laski (1893-1950) ruled out unconditional obedience to any government by drawing a distinction between the state and government. He argued that if a government claims allegiance of human beings, it will have to compete with other human associations in securing their highest welfare.

[III]
THEORIES AGAINST POLITICAL OBLIGATION

MARXIST VIEW

According to the Marxist view, the state is by no means the organized power of the community. It is indeed the organized power of the dominant class—

particularly the class owning the major means of production. Its purpose is not the general welfare, but helping the strong competitors to increase their wealth and power by exploiting the weak competitors as well as the dependent class. In a class-divided society, individual can have no political obligation towards the state. At best, an individual can have any obligation towards society, provided it is a classless and stateless society. Till such a society comes into existence, we can only think of worker's obligation towards the working class. Under the capitalist system, where enemies of the working class are in power, the worker has obligation 'against the state'. It requires him to show solidarity with the working class in order to create a strong organization for revolution against the capitalist regime.

Classless and Stateless Society

According to Marxism, classless and stateless society refers to the highest stage of social development. At this stage, the division of society into antagonistic classes disappears as all means of social production are placed under common ownership and every able-bodied person voluntarily becomes a worker. The state which used to serve the interests of the class owning the means of social production, becomes redundant at this stage; so it 'withers away'.

ANARCHIST VIEW

Anarchist view of political obligation is based on the philosophy of anarchism. It advocates the abolition of all organized authority as well as the state mechanism in order to build a society wherein all human beings shall freely and spontaneously adjust with each other without requiring an external force to regulate their relations. It, therefore, upholds negative political obligation. Anarchists like P.J. Proudhon (1809-65) and Peter Kropotkin (1842-1921) argued that all governmental authority is illegitimate because the state is indeed a coercive institution, which is suited only to a corrupt and unjust society. The individual is only obliged to uphold justice. So he is obliged to resist the state and devote himself to building a new system where all members of society will spontaneously cooperate with each other.

Anarchism

Anarchism refers to a political outlook which holds that society should be organized without coercive power of the state. In its view, government is an unnecessary evil. Men are benign by nature. Society is a natural institution. Men are capable of organizing themselves into a just society through voluntary cooperation, but they are corrupted by the intervention of the coercive power of the state. Anarchists reject all forms of authority, including authority of the state, that interfere with the spontaneous associations and actions of individuals.

It is important to note that Marxian and Gandhian views, as upholders of stateless society, come closer to the anarchist view of political obligation.

[IV]
GANDHIAN PERSPECTIVE

Mahatma Gandhi (1869-1948), Indian social philosopher and activist, recognized severe limits of political obligation, as his principle of 'civil disobedience' indicates. Civil disobedience implies the act of deliberately disobeying an unjust authority and breaking an unjust law. The duty of civil disobedience to an unjust law is the counterpart of the duty of civil obedience to a just law. Civil disobedience may be resorted to as a protest against an unjust policy of government or in order to draw attention of the government to a demand for political reform.

The term 'civil disobedience' was originally coined by an American writer—Henry David Thoreau (1817-62), who published an essay in 1848 to explain why he had refused to pay taxes to the state for several years for which he had to undergo imprisonment. Thoreau argued that people must register their protest against any injustice perpetrated by their own government. Harold J. Laski has cited the case of 'conscientious objectors' to military service during the period of the First World War (1914-18), who had to undergo punishment for refusing to render military service as they believed in peaceful solution of all human disputes.

Mahatma Gandhi sought to combine the principle of civil disobedience with his principle of non-violent struggle and *satyagraha* (the principle of insistence on truth) during India's struggle for independence. Gandhi set a practical example of civil disobedience when he led the march to the seashore in 1930 to defy the ban on making salt by the Indians. This ban was imposed by the British colonial rulers which was thought to be unjust by Gandhi and his followers. Gandhi firmly believed that civil disobedience was based on a profound respect for law in general; only unjust law should be broken—that, too, when all methods of persuasion and petition for withdrawal of such law had been tried and had failed. The act of civil disobedience should be performed non-violently and in full public view; and penalties entailed by this act should be accepted willingly.

> Disobedience to be civil must be sincere, respectful, restrained, never defiant, must be based upon some well-understood principle, must not be capricious and above all, must have no ill-will or hatred behind it.
>
> Mahatma Gandhi (*Young India:* 1920)

It is again important that the true object of civil obedience is 'change of heart' of the authorities concerned. This should be resorted to only against a tyrannical regime, foreign rule or unjust government. If a government generally maintains the citizens' rights and it can be influenced through democratic method, resort to civil disobedience will not be necessary. Finally, civil disobedience should not be resorted to for pressing the demands of any particular section against the general or public interest.

> People in a democracy should be satisfied with drawing the Government's attention to mistakes, if any. They could remove the Government if they wished to. But they should not obstruct them by agitating against them. Ours is not a foreign Government having a mighty army and navy to support them. They have to derive their strength from the people.
>
> Mahatma Gandhi (*Delhi Diary;* 1948)

CONCLUSION

Political obligation is a complex issue. Its grounds and limits have to be considered very carefully before conceding it. At the outset, it is necessary to realize that the individual owes political obligation to political authority. An idealistic view of political authority may involve a serious departure from the realistic position. Rousseau postulated political obligation to the 'general will'; Hegel projected a divine image of 'the state' as the object of political obligation; and Green suggested political obligation towards the 'organized power of society' as distinguished from the state. But how do we encounter these abstract entities in real life? Philosophically, we may owe political obligation to any ideal object, but in actual life such obligation is always demanded by a band of government officials which must be considered with utmost caution. As Laski has succinctly pointed out: "The state's claim to preeminence always means, in fact, the sovereignty of a government composed of fallible men whose intentions alone are not a sufficient justification for so vast a claim" (*A Grammar of Politics;* 1938).

It is important to remember that government is only an external agency; a good government is the product of human ingenuity. However, the power of reasoning is still retained by human beings themselves; it cannot be transferred to the instrument created by them. So the individual himself or herself remains the best judge as to whether a law is just or not. At the same time, no single individual can become wiser than all others. So when a law or government order is thought to be unjust, there should be full public debate and discussion on the issue, and the decision to oppose or resist it should be taken when public opinion on that issue has been largely crystallized and mobilized. Some sectional interests or opinions may still differ, and efforts should be made to understand and analyse all points of view for arriving at a consensus. It is also necessary to realize that the failure of government to fulfil all our aspirations should not be treated as a sufficient ground of resistance, because such failure could be the outcome of paucity of resources, enormity of the problem or genuine priority of claims of others. For instance, a government should not be resisted because it failed to provide for full employment, universal education and medical care, etc. since no government on earth is expected to solve all our problems. Then, before resorting to extreme measures like direct action, strike, picketing, hunger strike or courting arrest in large numbers, all constitutional means and methods should be tried fairly.

Finally, it is essential to see that the resistance should not be taken too far. As Burke had warned, resistance is the medicine of the constitution, not its daily bread. Reform should be undertaken to achieve a definite objective, and the situation should be reviewed and a further programme chalked out after fulfilment of that objective. If major issues are resolved, minor issues could be left to take care of themselves. Revolution is not ruled out, but it should be undertaken as a long-term programme, not as a sudden overthrow of the system. A. Appadorai (*The Substance of Politics;* 1975) has rightly suggested: "While the conscientious individual who leads the resistance may often be motivated by the highest moral purpose, he must remember that he may be followed by others less conscientious who may take advantage of the opportunity to gain their selfish ends." If change is accompanied by chaos and confusion, the situation is most likely to be exploited by anti-social elements. If old order is destroyed indiscriminately without leaving the foundations for the construction of a new order, the result would be disastrous, because, to destroy is easy, to reconstruct is difficult.

12

Concept of Law

LAW IS THE characteristic of a situation where an object or individual behaves uniformly under specific conditions, indicating regularities of behaviour. Law is responsible for all orderliness in the universe and society. To understand the nature of law, it is essential at the outset to distinguish between two types of law: (*a*) Descriptive (or Scientific) Law; and (*b*) Prescriptive (or Stipulative) Law. Descriptive or scientific law exists and operates in the universe, independently of our will. We can only discover it, but cannot alter it nor escape from it. No external agency is required to enforce it. Since it is beyond our control, its test is 'true' or 'false'. The terms 'right' or 'wrong' may be applied in its case only in the factual sense, as alternatives of 'true' or 'false', and not to invoke any moral standards. In any case, we can apply our knowledge of scientific law to serve human purposes. The examples of descriptive or scientific law are: 'law of gravitation' (in physics) and 'law of diminishing returns' (in economics). These laws can be applied for making mechanical devices or improving industrial production. A scientific law can be challenged or redefined only by a new scientific discovery and a proof supported by experimentation. On the other hand, prescriptive law determines what an individual should or should not do under specified conditions. Each organization makes some rules for its members which are binding on them. These rules are enforced by sanctions, so that any deviation or departure from these rules makes one liable to punishment, denial of some benefit or privilege. The existence of an organization is dependent on observance of such rules. The set of such rules applicable to the larger society or community comes in the category of prescriptive law.

Prescriptive law is, therefore, man-made law, adopted by human society for regulating its behaviour, although it may be based on some forceful considerations, such as long-standing custom, 'human conscience', the prevailing level of social consciousness or dominant public opinion. However, this can be changed according to our needs and mode of thinking. For instance, a penal code which prescribes punishment for various types of offences represents the prescriptive law. Since this type of law can be altered according to our sense of justice, its test is 'right' or 'wrong' in the moral sense. But when applied objectively, say, by lawyers and law-courts, its test is 'valid' or 'invalid' although some doctrines of fairness, reasonableness, due process, etc. may be invoked in its interpretation. In other words, the 'letter of law' may be supplemented by the 'spirit of law' during the course of its interpretation and in the process of adjudication. In political science and all other social sciences as well as jurisprudence, the term 'law' is throughout applied to indicate prescriptive law, unless otherwise indicated by the context.

[I] NATURE OF LAW

The nature of law has been described differently by different schools of thought in view of different applications of this term. The principal schools of thought as prevalent in the Western tradition are: (*a*) Natural Law School; (*b*) Analytical Jurisprudence; (*c*) Historical Jurisprudence; and (*d*) Sociological Jurisprudence.

NATURAL LAW SCHOOL

This school of thought sees law as representing binding obligations arising from the moral sphere. It holds that positive law or enactment draws its sanctity or authority from a higher law, 'the law of nature' or 'natural law' which exists independently of our will, and which can be discovered by the human faculty of reasoning. It is, however, different from scientific law because its character is normative rather than positive. It postulates the existence of a universal system of 'justice' or 'right' as distinct from human enactments and rules.

> **Positive Law**
>
> Positive law refers to the law that expresses the will of the sovereign. Usually it is duly enacted by a legislative body and recognized by the judiciary. It is binding on all those coming within its jurisdiction, and its violation is effectively met with punishment. Positive law is judged by its legal validity, and not by its conformity to morals, customs or conventions unless these are enshrined in the body of law itself.

This view of law has been prevalent in the West since ancient times, particularly since stoic philosophers (c. 300 B.C.). In Roman jurisprudence, it was recognized as a standard against which all civil law should be judged. In the medieval times, it was equated with divine law. In the eighteenth century, it was developed, particularly by Immanuel Kant (1724-1804), as an objective standard to which all rational nature should conform. In the contemporary world, it is particularly invoked in the arguments concerning universal human rights.

ANALYTICAL JURISPRUDENCE

Analytical jurisprudence or 'Legal Positivism' regards 'positive law' as the only real law. It owes its origin to thc Anglo-Amcrican lcgal tradition which flourished in the nineteenth century. It sees all law as a positive and direct command of a competent authority, enforceable by effective sanctions. It focuses on the nature of law in the technical sense of the term, as distinguished from its conception as a moral standard. It denies the status of law to the rules that are based on a body of conventions or expectations, without the presence of a proper authority to enforce them effectively, such as 'international law', which is largely based on international courtesy and mutual understanding between the civilized nations. It rejects the 'natural law' doctrine as unscientific, grounded on mythical entity, and rooted in confusion between law and morality. John Austin (1790-1859), an English jurist, is regarded the chief exponent of this school of thought, who tried to discover the key doctrines and ideas underlying a formal legal system.

International Law

International law refers to a set of general principles and specific rules which are duly recognized by the members of the international community in their dealing with each other. International law is primarily concerned with the regulation of their mutual relations, peaceful settlement of their disputes, and the rights of belligerent as well as neutral nations during the times of war.

Austin defined law as a command of the sovereign person or body, as promulgated in a particular political society. He argued that 'international law' was not law in the real sense because it was neither promulgated by a sovereign, nor enforced by a political superior. At best, international law could be described as an expression of 'positive morality' as distinguished from 'positive law'. Subsequent thinkers in this tradition sought to modify Austin's formulations as regards the criteria of validity of positive law. Hans Kelsen, in his *General Theory of Law and State* (1961), argued that validity of law is derived from its proper promulgation as well as from its conformity to a 'basic norm'. Kelsen postulated a hierarchy of norms to which sanctions are attached. The lower-level norms derive their validity from higher-level norms so that there is a basic norm at the top of this hierarchy to which entire legal system must conform. In spite of his insistence on the normative character of law, Kelsen remains a positivist because he separates the questions of morality and moral obligation from those of legal validity and legal obligation.

> **Norms**
>
> In sociology, the norm refers to a standard or the shared expectation of behaviour that is considered culturally desirable or appropriate. Norms of a society are regarded almost as prescriptive as the prevalent rules and regulations, although they do not enjoy the formal status of rules. For example, looking after one's parents in the old age would be a norm though there might be no law to enforce this obligation.

H.A.L. Hart, another major thinker of this school, in his *Concept of Law* (1961) argued that Austin's conception of law as based on coercive order was too narrow as it was largely derived from the model of criminal law. If viewed in proper perspective, the scope of law is not restricted to the acts of command and punishment. While criminal laws embody a set of coercive orders, civil laws and procedure cannot be compared to it as they also provide for certain private arrangements, such as contracts, marriages and wills. Different types of law serve different purposes. Besides punishing offenders, laws may distribute benefits and regulate various organizations. Hart equates law with rules which determine duties, obligations, rights and powers and also provide for the procedure of law-making and its amendment. Hart also rejects Kelsen's conception of the 'basic norm', as based on misunderstanding. He argues that the standard of validity of a rule cannot exist in a vacuum. It is derived from the social fact rather than from a hierarchy of norms standing within the legal system. For instance, an act may be lawful in terms of English law, but not so in terms of French law. Hence, norms of legal validity are indeed rooted in a social system, not in the legal system itself.

Ronald Dworkin rejected Hart's conception of law as a structure of rules and sought to reformulate the conception of law by introducing the role of 'principles' in a legal system. In *Taking Rights Seriously* (1977), Dworkin argued that Hart's model cannot be applied to the analysis of all aspects of a legal system, particularly in the context of disputed cases where application of rules does not give a clear answer. In difficult cases, judges have to rely on certain 'principles' for reaching a decision. These principles are by no means 'extra-legal' criteria as they are used by judges as part of law. An outstanding example of this situation is the principle which holds that a man should not benefit from his own wrong. This principle was invoked to prevent a murderer benefiting from his victim's will. Positivists, who conceive of a legal system exclusively in terms of rules, have no answer to deal with such a situation. Pointing to the distinction between rules and principles, Dworkin observed that rules are precise and their applications can be specified whereas principles are not so precise and different principles may conflict with each other. Judges have the discretion to choose a befitting principle for reaching a decision in a particular case. It is by no means an easy task. Moreover, principles can be invoked only to suggest reasons or justifications for the decision, but the decision itself cannot be derived from the application of a principle. Different principles are independent of each other. Unlike norms behind the rules, they cannot be arranged in a hierarchy so as to indicate primacy of one principle over another. Validity of a principle is to be sought from the realm of *political theory* rather than from the rationale of legal system itself. The constitutional standards and doctrines adopted by judges by invoking different principles are, therefore, subject to criticism like the problems of political theory.

In a nutshell, critics of legal positivism have tried to highlight inadequacies of positive law by pointing to the cases which cannot be solved with the help of positive law alone. Kelsen refers to 'basic norm' of the legal system; Hart points to the 'structure of rules'; and Dworkin introduces reliance on 'principles' as essential complements of positive law. All of them point to the complexity of the nature of law which cannot be understood from its apparent form only.

HISTORICAL JURISPRUDENCE

Historical jurisprudence or 'Legal Evolutionism' believes in tracing the essence of legal ideas and institutions to their historical roots. According to this view, legal evolution is the outcome of the play of social forces. Its chief exponents include F.C. Savigny (1779-1861), German jurist, and Henry Maine (1822-88), British jurist. Savigny (*On the Vocation of Our Age for Legislation and Jurisprudence;* 1814) identified law as the expression of the *spirit* of a particular people—their race as well as culture. He, therefore, recognized custom as the fundamental form of law because it originated in the life of the people. Legislation was merely a device of translating popular consciousness into enactments.

Henry Maine (*Ancient Law: Its Connection with the Early History of Society and Its Relation to Moral Ideals;* 1861) rejected Savigny's approach to law as a heritage of a particular people. Instead he sought to evolve a general framework in order to explain the evolution of law and legal ideas in universal terms. From a comparative analysis of the evolution of legal institutions in different societies, Maine came to the conclusion that progressive societies are characterized by a 'movement from status to contract'. In short, according to historical school, law has no fixed content. Change in social institutions and awareness brings about corresponding changes in the substance of law.

SOCIOLOGICAL JURISPRUDENCE

The exponents of this school include Ludwig Gumplowicz (1838-1909), Léon Duguit (1859-1928), Hugo Krabbe (1857-1936), Roscoe Pound (1870-1964) and Harold J. Laski (1893-1950). In sharp contrast to the analytical jurisprudence, sociological school holds that the state is not the source of law; it is only an agency to impute legal value to the rules which already exist in society to take care of social interests. Law is, therefore, not only prior to the state but also superior to the state. However, law has a unique importance in society as an instrument of solving social problems and achieving social progress. Thus,

Roscoe Pound *(The Spirit of the Common Law;* 1921) insists on assessment of law according to the defined social purpose. In order to achieve social progress, law should be open to interpretation and revision in the light of changing levels of social consciousness. Pound holds that the proper function of law is 'social engineering'.

In a nutshell, according to sociological school, substance of law is to be determined with reference to the social purpose which it is designed to serve. While the historical school tends to discover the essence of law from the social institutions of the past, the sociological school largely seeks its significance in our vision of the future.

[II]
SOURCES OF LAW

In a technical sense, law is the command of the state, recognized by various organs of the state, and enforced by sanctions. In this sense, the state is apparently the source of all law. However, the state does not make law by itself, at its own will. Pluralists like R.M. MacIver (1882-1970) believe that law existed even before the emergence of the state; the state does not create law but only declares it. In what forms does law exist, apart from its formal enactment and application? An inquiry into these questions will lead us to the sources of law.

CUSTOM

Social usage or custom is the oldest and most important expression of law. Social life of human beings was regulated by custom long before the emergence of the state. Custom represents those modes of behaviour which were found suitable after trial for a long time, and which were stabilized and accepted as standard forms of behaviour. Human beings came to treat them as binding rules. Those who violated these rules were ridiculed, deprived of certain privileges of social life including normal social intercourse, or punished so much so that they could be exterminated or executed.

We have many customs which were neither created nor inspired by the state. For example, institutions of marriage and family, based on custom, are certainly prior to the state. State may make laws to regulate these institutions with the changing needs and levels of consciousness. Similarly, rules of economic transaction were derived from social usage which eventually became the subject of elaborate legislation. Common Law of England is based on custom which is recognized by law-courts as valid as law itself.

RELIGION

In primitive communities, custom and religion were intertwined. Religion determined not only the modes of worship but also a good deal of custom regulating social life. In a traditional society, the close links between the priest and the king are an ample proof of close relations between religion and politics. Ancient Roman law is largely grounded in a set of religious rules. Ancient Indian codes of law cannot be distinguished from scriptures. Hindus and Muslims in India even today have their separate personal laws based on their religious beliefs and practices, particularly for regulating marriage and inheritance.

SCIENTIFIC COMMENTARIES

Several publicists and eminent jurists have written treatises giving interpretation of the substance of law prevailing in different countries. In these works, they have raised questions on which the law is either silent, or vague, or uncertain. They have advanced their well-built arguments and proofs to deal with such situations. They have expressed their opinions so effectively and convincingly that these are treated as authentic as law itself. It is true that very few of such treatises have won due recognition, yet they constitute an important source of law. In England, opinions of Edward Coke (1552-1634) and William Blackstone (1723-80) are treated as authoritative as law; in America, works of Joseph Story (1779-1845) and James Kent (1763-1847) enjoy similar status. The opinions of these scholars are recognized even by law-courts for arriving at their decisions. Many eminent jurists have written elaborate commentaries on Indian constitutional law; one or two of them might be recognized as authoritative, in due course.

ADJUDICATION

In most countries, judicial decisions and verdicts are accompanied by the explication of such principles or interpretations of law which serve as precedents for future decisions. The case law of England and Supreme Court decisions in America and India are the case in point. Where law is silent, vague or uncertain, judges may express their opinions to deal with such situations, with well-built arguments and proofs. At times they tend to expand the scope of law by giving it new interpretations according to the changing needs of time, and thus make their own contribution to the existing body of law.

EQUITY

Equity, like adjudication, is another form of judge-made law. Whereas adjudication involves interpretation and application of the existing law, equity breaks a new ground. Where existing law is inadequate, judges may use their common sense, or their own understanding of fairness to give relief to a disadvantaged party. Equity is derived from the principles of natural justice rather than from the letter or the spirit of law. Equity was used in ancient Roman law. In the modern age, equity is often invoked in the cases involving law of contract.

Natural Justice

Natural justice refers to a set of those principles of justice which belong to the unwritten part of law. These principles are invoked when the judges act according to their own 'sense of justice'. On the procedural side, natural justice largely requires as follows: no man shall be the judge in his own cause; both sides shall be heard; the judge shall give full consideration to the case and exclude all irrelevant considerations from his mind while reaching a decision; like cases shall be decided alike; not only shall justice be done but it shall be seen to be done; and finally, judgement shall include not only the bare decision, but the reasons which lead to it.

On the substantive side, natural justice permits the judges to invoke human values to give relief to a disadvantaged party. In this sphere, natural justice comes closer to social justice.

Social Justice

Social justice refers to a social policy which seeks to prevent concentration of valuable resources of the community or mankind (wealth, prestige and power) in the hands of the chosen few, and to create a social order which will enable the deprived and underprivileged sections to gain a respectable share thereof by virtue of their ability, effort and need.

In the judicial process, the principle of social justice is largely invoked to mitigate undue hardship to the underprivileged and disadvantaged party to a case.

LEGISLATION

Finally, legislation may be included in this list, although it refers to the process of law-making rather than a source of law. With the rise of democracy, popularly elected assemblies enact a large number of measures which continuously supplement the existing body of law.

[III]
SPHERE OF LOW

LAW AND MORALITY

Technically speaking, law is the product of a prescribed procedure. It is valid only if it is properly enacted and recognized. Morality, on the other hand, is based on the sense of rightness and justice. Ideally speaking, laws should be made in conformity with the principles of morality. However, in actual practice, law and morality may take different courses. If law compels someone to act against one's conscience, a clash may arise between legal obligation and moral obligation. For example, if a worker is morally committed to a trade union which has given a call for strike but the strike has been legally banned, one will have to face the consequences of acting against law if one chooses to honour one's moral commitment.

Law is concerned with the external actions of man, and not with his inner motives. Morality springs from one's conscience which may or may not be translated into overt acts. Thus envy, ingratitude and hypocrisy are morally wrong but these will not be legally punished until they result in such actions that are legally wrong. Morality imposes certain duties on man towards other human beings and various parts of his environment which may not be legally enforceable. Law can prevent us from certain immoral acts, but it cannot make us moral. Morality can be inculcated only through proper education and a congenial cultural environment. Again, it is morality which makes us law-abiding citizens.

> When men are pure, laws are useless; when men are corrupt, laws are broken.
>
> *Benjamin Disraeli* (1804-81)

Sanction behind law is force. If law is not observed out of moral conviction, it may be observed out of fear of punishment. Departure from law will be met with punishment; departure from morality will be followed by the prick of conscience, social disapproval and loss of reputation.

Law is relatively clear and consistent; moral standards may at times be disputed or doubtful—these may change with time and place. Changes in law may be preceded or followed by the corresponding changes in moral consciousness. Some moral beliefs as well as social practices could be based on superstition or outmoded thought, and law may take a lead in social reform. For instance, the idea of abolition of child marriage, widow-burning, untouchability or bonded labour was first conceived by a few reformers, but it created larger moral awareness when it was translated into concrete law.

Some laws are morally neutral in their apparent form, adopted as a matter of convenience for the maintenance of public order. For instance, traffic laws may direct us to keep to the left or to the right. They are morally neutral as long as they are equally applicable to all. However, observance of such laws is also inspired by our moral sense, that is equal concern for the convenience and safety of all road-users.

Since our social life is practically regulated by law, it is imperative that laws should be adjusted with the changes in our moral consciousness. Otherwise, laws will prove to be tyrannical. Such laws will not only be frequently violated but the whole system of law will be overthrown.

LAW AND LIBERTY

Liberty or freedom is formally defined as 'absence of restraint'. Law, on the other hand, imposes restraints on certain activities of individuals. Does law, then, curtail liberty or can it be reconciled with liberty? It is a complex issue. It is possible that a tyrannical state may make tyrannical laws and destroy liberty of individuals. However, under democratic and welfare state purpose of law is to protect and promote liberty. How does law perform this function?

When liberty is accepted as a universal principle, it is imperative that liberty of one individual does not endanger the liberty of another individual. This necessitates restriction on liberty of individual so as to allow equal liberty to all. Law is precisely the means of imposing such restriction. D.D. Raphael, in his *Problems of Political Philosophy* (1976), has significantly observed: "Law restricts liberty in requiring us to do things that we might otherwise not want to do, and in requiring us to refrain from actions that we might otherwise want to do. The restrictions upon liberty imposed by the law may be intended to protect the liberty of others (or sometimes of oneself) which would be impeded by the behaviour that the law restricts, or alternatively the restrictions of law may be intended to promote other values than liberty... For either of these reasons the restrictions of law may be desirable, indeed essential." Raphael has identified four spheres in which restrictions imposed by law on individual's liberty can be considered as rational: (*a*) Crime; (*b*) Civil Disputes; (*c*) Economic Control; and (*d*) Provision of Social Welfare.

In the Sphere of Crime

Those acts of individuals which are deemed to be a threat to the liberty and safety of other individuals (or their own safety) are declared offence under the law, for which punishment is prescribed. The law concerning such acts is called 'criminal law'. For instance, violation of traffic rules is a crime because it jeopardizes safety of the road-users. Theft, causing physical injury, rape, and murder are other examples of crime which are punishable under the law. Besides, the acts which might harm the individual himself and his family may also be declared cognizable offences and punishable under the law. Examples of such acts include alcoholism, drug-addiction, and attempt to suicide.

> **Cognizable Offence**
>
> Cognizable offence refers to an act that would be perceived as contrary to law of the land; hence capable of being dealt with in a court of law.
>
> In India, cognizable offence refers to an act against which police is empowered to register an FIR (First Information Report), arrest the accused, and produce the results of its investigations before a competent court of law.

In the Sphere of Civil Disputes

The law relating to private rights of individuals and disputes between them is called 'civil law'. The term 'individuals' in the present context comprehends 'corporate bodies' also. For instance, if an individual causes damage to another's property due to negligence, he is required to pay damages, and not to undergo punishment. If somebody violates a contract or a husband harasses his wife, the aggrieved party can have recourse to civil law. Compensation for causing defamation can be claimed in a civil law court under the law of tort. In certain cases, a matter of civil law may become so grave that it becomes a subject of criminal law. Examples of such cases are fraud, misappropriation and criminal breach of trust for which a report can be lodged in a police station. Similarly, if rash driving results in killing somebody, it is to be dealt with under the criminal law.

Law of Tort

Law of tort implies a body of rights, obligations, and remedies that are applied by courts in civil proceedings to provide relief for persons who have suffered harm from the wrongful acts of others. This law is mainly concerned with providing compensation for personal injury or property damage caused by negligence, defamation, intimidation, etc. However, any loss suffered due to breach of a contract is normally dealt with under law of contract, and not under law of tort.

In the Sphere of Economic Control

Modern state regulates a lot of economic activities and this necessitates certain restrictions on individuals and groups. For instance, the state determines minimum wages of workers, regulates payment of dearness allowance, specifies conditions of work and various types of compensations payable to the workers. Employers are bound by the labour laws governing these matters. Besides, law may declare some functions as essential services and ban strikes in the concerned sector. Laws governing quality control, weights and measures, prevention of adulteration and other measures for protection of the interests of consumers may also be cited as examples of economic control.

In the Sphere of Social Welfare

The rise of welfare state has tremendously expanded the sphere of legal regulation. It provides for taxation of relatively rich sections for the provision of schools, hospitals, cheaper transport and housing, etc. for the relatively poor sections as well as for the common services. Similarly, entrepreneurs may be encouraged or even obliged to set up industries in backward areas to ensure development of those areas. Broadly speaking, the law in this sphere is used as an instrument of social justice.

CONCLUSION

The conflicting claims of law and liberty as well as those of law and morality can be reconciled only when it can be proved that the restrictions imposed by law are based on logical or rational grounds, that is they are intended to broaden the scope of liberty or to improve the moral standards of society on the whole.

[IV]
SUPREMACY OF LAW

In the civilized world, supremacy of law is sought to be established either through the principle of rule of law, or through due process of law.

RULE OF LAW

Rule of law denotes a principle of governance which requires the following conditions to be fulfilled: (*a*) Law of the land should be properly notified so that the citizens know as to how it will effect them; (*b*) Laws should be *general* in form so that they are uniformly applicable to all the citizens; there should be no separate laws for any specific category of the people; (*c*) No law should be applicable with retrospective effect; and finally, (*d*) Power of governance should be exercised strictly in accordance with the procedures, principles and restraints provided in the body of law, and not on any other basis.

The main thrust of the rule of law is that government should not be arbitrary, but should be conducted through the procedures authorized by legislation and passed in proper form; citizens should be punished for breaches of law and for nothing else; and official status should not protect a person from the operation of legal sanctions, if he has broken the law. A.V. Dicey (1835-1922), eminent British jurist, in his *Introduction to the Study of the Law of the Constitution* (1885), termed the rule of law the governing principle of the British constitution. According to him, it stands for 'equality before the law' which implied equal subjection of all classes—including the officials—to ordinary law of the land, administered by ordinary law-courts. This was the distinctive feature of the British legal system as distinguished from the French legal system. Under the French legal system disputes between officials and subjects were dealt with by a special division of the judicial system, while in England they were dealt with by ordinary law-courts concerned with disputes between subject and subject. Officials in England did not enjoy immunity from law as enjoyed by foreign diplomats.

However, Dicey's reference to French legal system should not be interpreted to mean that the French maintain an 'administrative law' which is not the part of their ordinary law. In fact, French administrative law is very much the part of their legal system which is the basis of its validity. It would be wrong to say that French civil and criminal law is the part of their ordinary law, but their administrative law does not fall in this category. The only distinctive feature of the French is that in France the disputes between officials and ordinary citizens are dealt with by a specialized branch of their judicial system, whereas such disputes in England are dealt with by ordinary law-courts. The precise distinction between the two lies in their respective judicial organization, and not between the nature of their legal systems.

Rule of law in England also implies that since there is no provision of 'constitutional guarantee' of the rights of the citizens (because of its unwritten constitution), the remedies, benefits and liberties provided in their ordinary law are the foundation of their constitutional system. Dicey's critics argue that the rule of law simply regulates the legal procedure; it is silent as regards the content of law. It has no mechanism to contain the unlimited sovereignty of the British Parliament. If the Parliament enacts an unjust or discriminatory law, it cannot be remedied by the rule of law. However, this criticism is based on a very narrow interpretation of Dicey's thought. Dicey himself pointed out that the true meaning of this principle can be understood by carefully examining the manner in which the law of England deals with the right to personal freedom, freedom of discussion, public meetings, martial law, collection and expenditure of public revenue and the responsibility of ministers. Thus, the essence of the rule of law lies in the provision of legal protection of individual rights. It is true that the unrestricted sovereignty of the British Parliament provides for no scope of 'constitutional guarantees', yet this sovereignty is controlled by constitutional conventions which make the legal sovereign accountable to the political sovereign, that is the electorate.

Truly speaking, the term 'rule of law' comprehends those devices of limited government which are adopted for the protection of rights of the citizens. In other democratic countries where written constitutions have been adopted, such as the United States and India, civil rights are protected by constitutional guarantees. These rights represent a concrete expression of the tenets underlying the wider interpretation of the rule of law.

In common parlance, rule of law requires that laws should be definite and unambiguous, clearly notified and made known to everybody, and equally applicable to all. But it does not imply identical rights and duties of all citizens. This may be illustrated by the case of traffic regulation. Every road-user is governed by the same law, but it does not rule out streamlining of traffic according to the nature, size and speed of each vehicle. Here rule of law requires that every road-user should be fully aware as to which side or lane he or she should take, how to give way to faster traffic, how to overtake slower traffic, where one is allowed to turn, slow down or stop, and so on. It may even give priority to police vehicles, ambulance, fire service vehicles and other emergency services over the rest of the traffic provided they display proper signs of warning, and make necessary announcements to this effect.

DUE PROCESS OF LAW

In the United States, the counterpart of the English principle of the rule of law is known as the 'due process of law'. This provision was inserted in the American Constitution through the Fifth Amendment of the Constitution (1791) which reads: "No person shall...be deprived of life, liberty or property, without due process of law." This principle is largely applied in two important spheres of individual's rights: (*a*) In the procedural sphere, it requires that where individual's rights are dependent on the order established by the state, these should be exercised in accordance with fixed rules and procedures; and (*b*) In the sphere of substantive rights, it gives due recognition to individual's basic personal and civil liberties. For example, in the procedural sphere the state may require the individual to obtain a licence for driving a vehicle which contains all the conditions on which this licence is issued. But in the sphere of substantive rights, the state cannot ask the individual to obtain a similar licence to exercise his right to worship. Right to worship is individual's substantive right for which no procedure can be prescribed by the state.

In the sphere of criminal law, the due process implies that an accused is entitled to a fair trial, that is he shall be given an opportunity to see that the charges framed against him are determined by proper legal procedure, an opportunity to prepare his defence, the right to counsel, the right to submit evidence and cross-examine, and to get impartial judgement, etc. This principle has now been extended to cover civil proceedings between individuals and decision-making administrative agencies involving denial of any benefits or rights to individuals.

13

Concept of Power

[I]

NATURE AND SIGNIFICANCE OF POWER

SIGNIFICANCE OF POWER

'Power' may be regarded as one of the central concepts of political science. It is said that the concept of power holds the same status in the realm of political science as held by the concept of money in the realm of economics. The focus on power emancipates the study of politics from the status of an appendage to the study of philosophy or history or law. It also transcends the realm of formal institutions to focus on the real motives and objectives of human beings which lie behind all political activity and institution-building.

During the early phase of development of modern political science, Frederick Watkins had observed: "The proper scope of political science is not the study of the state or of any other specific institutional complex, but the investigation of all associations insofar as they can be shown to exemplify the problem of power" (*The State as a Concept of Political Science;* 1934). This view was confirmed by William A. Robson who suggested: "It is with power in society that political science is primarily concerned—its nature, basis, processes, scope and results...The 'focus of interest' of the political scientist is clear and unambiguous; it centres on the struggle to gain or retain power, to exercise power or influence over others, or to resist that exercise" (*The University Teaching of Social Sciences: Political Science;* 1954).

In fact, the significance of power in the political phenomenon was brought out by the traditional thinkers like Machiavelli (1469-1527), Hobbes (1588-1679) and Nietzche (1844-1900) as well as by modern writers like Max Weber, Catlin, Merriam, Lasswell, Kaplan, Watkins, Trietschke and Morgenthau. The exponents of the 'power' view of politics focus on the study of 'the acquisition, maintenance and loss of power'. Harold Lasswell and Abraham Kaplan *(Power and Society;* 1950) defined political science as 'the study of the shaping and sharing of power'. Max Weber's definition of politics also implies a focus on power in the context of national as well as international politics: "Politics is the struggle for power or the influencing of those in power, and embraces the struggle between states as well as between organized groups within the state" (cited in G.E.G. Catlin, *Systematic Politics;* 1965). Similarly, Michael Curtis (*Comparative Government and Politics;* 1978) observed: "Politics is organized dispute about power and its use, involving choice among competing values, ideas, persons, interests and demands." Elucidating the scope of the study of politics, Curtis continues: "The study of politics is concerned with the description and analysis of the manner in which power is obtained, exercised and controlled, the purposes for which it is used, the manner in which decisions are made, factors which influence the making of those decisions and the context in which those decisions take place." If power is so important for the study of politics, what is meant by power?

MEANING OF POWER

Bertrand Russell (*Power: A New Social Analysis;* 1938) defined power as 'the production of intended effects'. In other words, power denotes the ability of a person to fulfil his desires or to achieve his objectives. In common parlance, the term 'power' may be used in multifarious contexts. For instance, we talk of the power of man over nature or material things, and the power of man over man. Most of the theorists of power, including Russell, prefer to restrict its use to 'power over human beings'. H.V. Wiseman (*Political Systems: Some Sociological Approaches;* 1966) defined power as 'the ability to get one's wishes carried out despite opposition'. Stephen L. Wasby (*Political Science—The Discipline and its Dimensions;* 1972) similarly observed: "Power is generally thought to involve bringing about of an action by someone against the will or desire of another." Then, Robert Dahl (*Modern Political Analysis;* 1991) described power as a kind of influence; it is exercised 'when compliance is attained by creating the prospect of severe sanctions for non-compliance'.

All these definitions give prominence to that aspect of power which is exercised by a man or a group over an 'unwilling' lot. They are, therefore, one-sided. Power, to be effective and stable, often takes the character of 'authority' which also comprehends legitimacy; that is the capacity to secure willing obedience. Use of force or coercion or sanctions may be resorted to only when legitimacy fails to work. It is authority which ensures social acceptance and effective implementation of rules, policies and decisions.

It is, therefore, necessary to understand the precise relationship between power, authority and legitimacy.

[II]
POWER, AUTHORITY AND LEGITIMACY

> Authority = Power + Legitimacy

Authority consists of two important components: Power and Legitimacy. Legitimacy of an act or arrangement implies that the members of society treat that arrangement as beneficial to society as well as to themselves. So they willingly tend to abide by it. Power alone involves capacity to get a decision obeyed by others against their will. Robert M. MacIver (*The Web of Government;* 1965) aptly defined power as 'the capacity in any relationship to command the service or compliance of others'. Power may involve the use of 'force', but service or compliance of others will best be obtained when they regard the command as 'right', 'good' or 'beneficial'. Power, to be effective and stable, must be accompanied by the capacity to secure willing obedience. Use of force or coercion or sanctions may be resorted to only when legitimacy fails to work. *If we think of power as a naked sword, authority may be envisaged as a sword in its scabbard.* While power is based on fear or force, legitimacy is based on respect and willing compliance. In any case, power and legitimacy play complementary roles in securing obedience to the commands of authority. No authority would function effectively in the absence of adequate instruments of power.

> You can go a long way with a smile. You can go a lot further with a smile and a gun.
>
> Al Capone

Power relation in society may be expressed in terms of command and obedience. If command is based on genuine motivation, it may result in willing obedience. In such case, power is accompanied by legitimacy, obedience is rendered with consent, and the power relation in question takes the form of authority. On the contrary, if command is based on coercion or threat of punishment, obedience comes from fear, and the power relation takes the form of tyranny which would eventually lead to rebellion. So legitimacy is the best instrument to ensure effective and enduring use of power. Most people will follow rules habitually if these are regarded to be legitimate. *Legitimacy, like beauty, lies in the eye of the beholder.*

> **Legitimacy**
>
> Legitimacy refers to the quality of an act or arrangement which is regarded as lawful by those affected by it. In other words, they regard it reasonable and beneficial for themselves as well as for the larger society.

Manifestations of Power

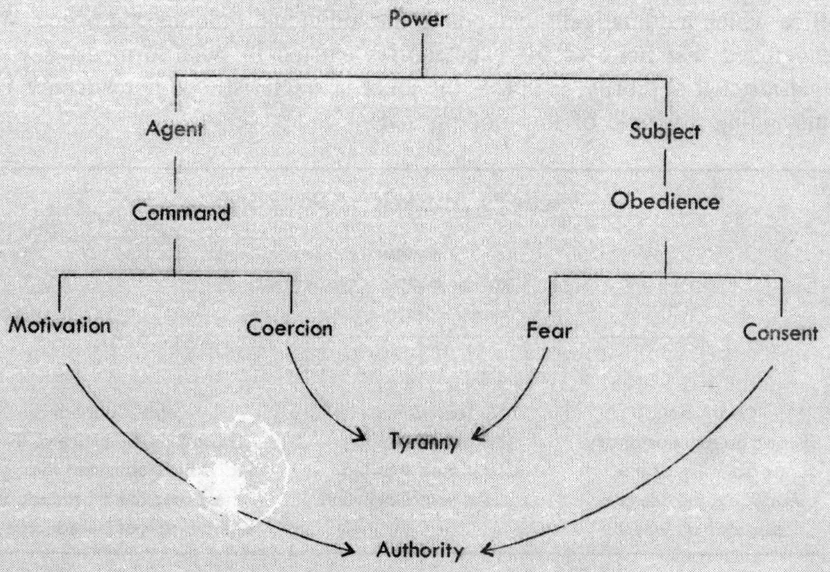

Power exercised through Motivation+Obedience rendered by Consent are manifested in Authority.

Power exercised through Coercion+Obedience rendered out of Fear are manifested in Tyranny.

Tyranny

Tyranny refers to a situation in which people are forced to live or work under very unpleasant or harsh conditions as they are obliged to submit to the arbitrary will of their master. In politics, tyranny is manifested in an unjust and cruel rule where ruler or ruling group is armed with absolute power, and it tends to terrify or oppress the people in order to secure obedience to its arbitrary commands.

Max Weber (1864-1920), German sociologist, identified three prominent types of authority. In the first place, *charismatic authority* grows out of personal charm or extraordinary 'gift of grace' of the leader, whether in the religious or in political sphere. In the religious sphere, it is exemplified by Jesus Christ. In the political sphere, it may include the examples of Oliver Cromwell (1599-1658) in England, Adolf Hitler (1889-1945) in Germany, and Mahatma Gandhi (1869-1948) in India.

Secondly, *traditional authority* implies the right to rule as established by tradition, such as in the case of hereditary or dynastic rule. Finally, *legal-rational authority* is founded on the sanctity of a political or administrative office held by an individual, that is where he is appointed through the prescribed procedure, such as merit-based selection, promotion, election, rotation or nomination. It is not based on the personal characteristics of the individual holding an office. In other words, legal-rational authority is attached to an office which automatically extends to the individual holding that office. Weber recognized that none of these categories existed in pure form. In any case, legal-rational authority, which is the chief characteristic of bureaucracy, is the outstanding attribute of the modern state.

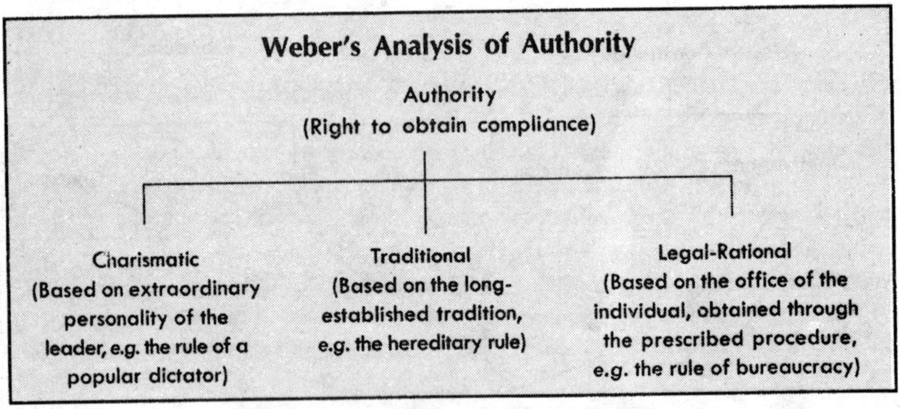

[III]
DIFFERENT FORMS OF POWER

Social Analysis of power cannot be confined to the realm of 'political power'. Economic and ideological forms of power should also be taken into account as they play an important role as the support-bases of political power. It is, therefore, necessary to distinguish between these three major forms of power.

POLITICAL POWER

According to Alan Ball (*Modern Politics and Government;* 1988), "The concept of political power. . . is a key concept in the study of politics for if politics is the resolution of conflict, the distribution of power within a political community determines how the conflict is to be resolved, and whether the resolution is to be effectively observed by all parties." In order to identify the nature of political power, it is essential, at the outset, to distinguish between the *formal* and *informal* organs of such power. Legislature, Executive and Judiciary are the traditionally recognized organs of power in a state; they represent the formal organs. The obedience secured by these organs, backed by sanctions, is an important form of political power. Executive and Legislature, taken together, make laws, policies and decisions regulating the allocation of values in a society. They impose taxes and use a vast machinery for the collection of taxes. They issue licences, permits, and regulate a large variety of citizens' actions, such as keeping vehicles and arms, running certain businesses, maintaining the quality of products, working conditions of the labour, building of houses, etc. There is police to catch hold of offenders, courts to try the offenders and settle disputes, and prisons to punish the convicts. Then military is meant to deal with foreign aggressors. In short, formal organs of political power play an effective role in a given territory.

Informal organs of political power not only take the form of political parties in power and in opposition, but also a large number of pressure groups, public opinion, popular movements, etc. Thus, political power is not the sole prerogative of the formal organs of the state but these organs themselves are responsive to the 'inputs' received from the 'environment'. This may be illustrated with reference to three cases: (*i*) in independent states, public opinion, popular movements and organized interests directly influence the decision-making; in democracies, the ruling party is bound to seek a fresh mandate from the people at regular intervals; (*ii*) in the colonies, dependencies and dictatorships, the struggle for independence and strong popular movements are sooner or later able to secure not only substantial concessions but even to win their independence; and (*iii*) in the international sphere, organized groups of nations do exercise their influence on the 'authoritative allocation of values'. The constant pressure exercised by 'third world' countries on the superpowers to change their economic and foreign policies is a case in point.

ECONOMIC POWER

Economic power is the power derived from the possession of material things, especially the major means of production and distribution. It is a potent factor behind politics. For instance, big landlords, industrial tycoons and business magnates are able to influence public decisions regarding the fixation of priorities in the economic development in a liberal democracy. In India itself the organized economic interests have been able to secure priority of colour TV for the urban rich, over drinking water for the rural poor.

The possessors of economic power in a liberal democracy exercise their influence on politics in several ways. Their pressure groups are stronger, more organized and more vocal. For instance, in India, the chambers of commerce and industry are very strong, the workers' unions are not as strong, peasants' unions are less strong and consumers' organizations are the weakest lot. The major newspapers and TV channels are owned by a handful of big business houses who take full advantage of these media to promote opinion which suits their interests. Besides, the big business houses extend a large amount of financial help to political parties, often clandestinely, and to the candidates seeking elections. The recipients of such help play a dual game—they pay lip-service to the interests of the masses but are secretly committed to safeguarding the interests of their financiers.

IDEOLOGICAL POWER

Ideological power provides a more subtle base of political power. The ideas upheld and promoted by the ruling classes in a given society regarding the 'best system of government' constitute political ideology. Ideology may be defined as 'a systematic set of arguments and beliefs used to justify an existing or desired social order' (Joseph Dunner, ed., *Dictionary of Political Science;* 1965). An outstanding feature of political ideology is that it provides legitimacy to the ruling classes and helps them maintain their stronghold on political power. When people are made to believe that a particular system of government is the best system, they will not be inclined to challenge the authority of the ruling classes. When people have learnt to respect their laws, the need for coercion to secure their obedience would be eliminated or, at any rate, minimized.

Political ideology involves not only a set of beliefs, it is always action-oriented. It puts forward a 'cause' for which people are prepared not only to fight but to make a lot of sacrifices. As Alan Ball (*Modern Politics and Government;* 1988) has elaborated: "Individuals are prepared to fight for causes, often realistically hopeless causes, or to undergo ill-treatment and torture in the belief that some political values are superior to others." Ideology is often devoid of reason. It picks up certain convenient formulae and elevates them to the level of 'absolute truth' by exploiting people's sentiments. Thus, some ideas are held sacrosanct by a particular group while others remain indifferent or even disdainful towards those very ideas.

Ideological power represents the manipulative power of the dominant classes which holds sway on the thinking and emotions of the people. Ideology even creates an illusion of 'consent'. Under an ideological spell, the people express their approval to the rule of particular persons and policies. They are led to believe that they are being governed with their 'consent' while they actually continue to be governed according to the designs of the dominant classes. Marx and Engels (*The German Ideology;* 1846) had noted that 'the ideas of the ruling class are in every epoch the ruling ideas'. According to them, the class which owns the means of material production in any society also controls the means of mental production. Antonio Gramsci (1891-1937), an Italian Marxist, gave the concept of 'hegemony' to explain the phenomenon of ideological domination, particularly of the capitalist class, in the contemporary society. Hegemony, in this sense, denotes a form of rule where power is apparently exercised with the consent of the ruled.

Hegemony

According to Antonio Gramsci (1891-1937), Italian thinker, hegemony refers to the ability of the ruling classes to create a web of beliefs and institutional as well as social relations which are projected as acceptable to all parts of society. Hegemony is an outstanding characteristic of capitalist society where family, school, church and other primary groups play a leading role in creating consent; it keeps the system going. Use of force is resorted to only when the instruments of consent fail to work.

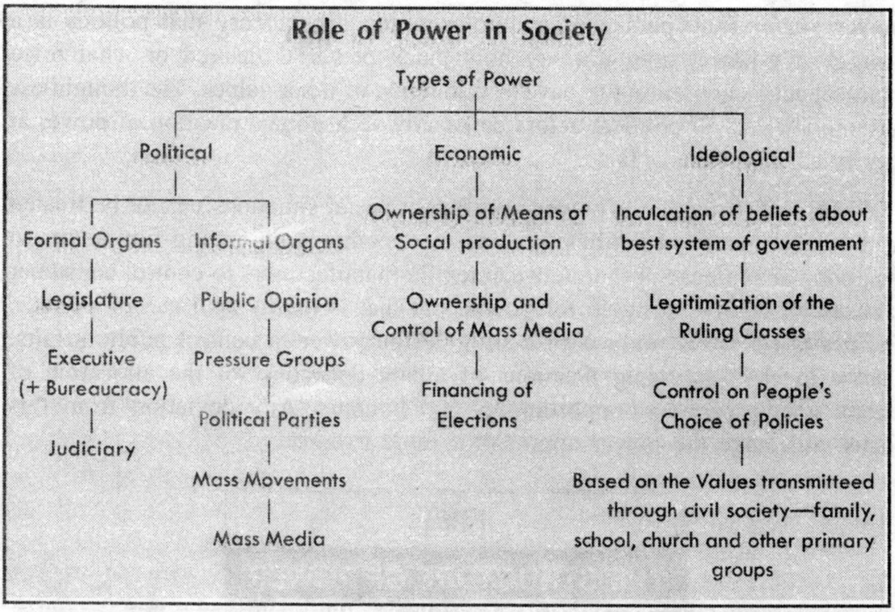

According to Gramsci, the spiritual and cultural supremacy of the ruling class in the capitalist state was accomplished through the manipulation of 'civil society', particularly through the mechanism of socialization, such as family, school, church and other primary groups. Gramsci's concept of 'hegemony' also explains why the working-class parties have only achieved a relatively moderate degree of success in the open competition for political power in the capitalist countries. Gramsci, therefore, asserted that revolution in the economic sphere was not enough to end the capitalist domination. It was necessary to reinforce revolution in the cultural sphere in order to achieve this end.

A CRITICAL APPRAISAL

The chief merit of the power approach lies in its ability to identify the motive force operating behind politics. Moreover, it can be applied to an analysis of domestic as well as international politics. However, this approach suffers from several drawbacks. In the first place, it lacks precision. As Vernon Van Dyke has elucidated: "Power is said to derive from sources ranging from tacitly accepted rules of politeness to the possession of spaceships; and it is said to manifest itself in situations ranging from a request that the salt be passed at the dining table to a situation in which states are exchanging all-out thermonuclear blows" (*Political Science—A Philosophical Analysis;* 1960). This sort of imprecision in the concept of power itself defies any classification or quantification of data for the purpose of political analysis.

Secondly, this approach seeks to reduce all politics to a struggle for power, and ignores other important purposes for which men have recourse to politics. As Dyke has further elaborated: "Political actors rarely, if ever, struggle for power alone. They pursue other purposes, too. The theory that politics is a struggle for power does not say how much power is desired or what price political actors are willing to pay for it in terms of other values. The thoughtless assumption that all political actors constantly seek a maximization of power at any price is obviously false."

Finally, all struggle for power in different social situations cannot be treated as a subject-matter of politics. For instance, competition among film-actors to win popular applause or that between textile-manufacturers to control consumer choices do involve struggle for power, but that is hardly an issue of politics. Politics is concerned only with a struggle for power to control public affairs, that is to have access to positions of taking decisions for the allocation of public goods, services, opportunities and honours. Any deviation from this focus will make the power approach a futile exercise.

[IV]
THE STRUCTURE OF POWER

> All men would be tyrants if they could.
>
> *Abigail Adams* (1776)

The student of politics is chiefly concerned with identifying the centres of power in a given society or in an international setting and relating them to the mode of authoritative allocation of values prevailing in that setting. This approach to the study of politics is a typically modern approach. It should not be confused with the traditional approach which recognized a threefold division of the 'powers' of a government—legislative, executive and judicial—and tried to describe them according to the formal constitution of a given country. The modern approach marks a departure from the traditional one as it implies a shift in focus from the formal organization to the informal one. In other words, we are no longer satisfied by learning as to 'who rules a country according to its constitution'; we want to know and identify the categories of people who actually wield power although the constitution guarantees 'equality of status and opportunity'. Political power in a country is always rooted in its socio-economic and ideological structures. It is, therefore, essential to discover the real sources and centres of power in society in order to understand its politics.

Can we identify such groups in a society out of which one group has constantly exercised power over another group? Different schools of thought have offered different answers to this question. Marxist school of thought views the situation in 'class perspective'. Elitist school of thought holds that an *elite* always dominates the masses. Then feminist school of thought tends to analyse the situation in 'gender perspective'. Finally, pluralist theory upholds 'group perspective' on power which tries to show that several groups in society have their own share in the exercise of power.

[V] CLASS PERSPECTIVE

CLASS AS THE SOURCE OF POWER

Class perspective on power was developed by Marx (1818-83) and Engels (1820-95) in the mid of the nineteenth century. According to this theory, political power is the product of economic power. In other words, the tree of political power grows on the roots of economic power; the edifice of political power is raised on the foundation of economic power. Economic power is vested in the ownership of means of social production. From the dawn of civilization, society was divided into two antagonistic classes—haves and have-nots—on the basis of ownership and non-ownership of the means of social production. In the ancient society, these classes were represented by masters and slaves; in the medieval society, by lords and serfs; and in modern capitalist society, by capitalists and workers.

> **Means of Social Production**
>
> Means of social production refer to the means by which material production is carried out for the larger society. In the modern society, these include land, mines, forests, buildings, capital, machinery, organization and labour. When society is divided into classes, all means except labour are owned by the dominant class: labour alone is retained by the dependent class.

This theory recognized 'class' as the organizing category for exercising power in society. Those who managed to grab ownership of the means of social production organized themselves into the 'dominant class', and forced the rest of society to do hard work on the terms and conditions determined by the market situation. This part of society was reduced to 'dependent class'. Thus, the society was divided into two antagonistic classes whose interests could never be reconciled. The dominant class resorted to intense exploitation of the dependent class in order to strengthen its power and position.

> The history of all hitherto existing society is the history of class struggles.
>
> Marx and Engels
> (Communist Manifesto; 1848)

In any case, the conditions prevailing in the past ages did not permit or enable the dependent class to organize itself fully so as to enter the phase of a decisive class struggle. It was only under capitalism that the working class found an opportunity to build its strong organization to fight against its oppressors. In ancient slave-owning society, the slaves were scattered to distant households with little communication among themselves. In medieval feudal society, the serfs were similarly scattered to distant agricultural estates. But in modern capitalist society, the conditions of industrial production led to the concentration of workers in big cities with strong communication between themselves. They became not only conscious of their strength but also of their common enemy—the capitalist class which exploited them so intensely. Marx and Engels believed that the overthrow of the capitalist class was not only imminent but also inevitable. Marx and Engels (*Communist Manifesto;* 1848) gave a clarion call: "Workers of all countries, unite!" Its concluding part reads: "The Communists. . . openly declare that their ends can be attained only by the forcible overthrow of all existing social conditions. Let the ruling classes tremble at a Communistic revolution. The proletarians have nothing to lose but their chains. They have a world to win."

This doctrine of class struggle was strongly endorsed by Lenin (1870-1924), Rosa Luxemberg (1871-1919), Mao Zedong (1893-1976) and other leading Marxists. However, Antonio Gramsci (1891-1937), an Italian Marxist of early twentieth century, introduced the concept of 'hegemony' to explain the subtle sources of capitalist domination. It added a new dimension to the strategy to fight against capitalism in contemporary society.

Capitalism

Capitalism refers to an economic system of the modern age, largely based on industrial production where means of social production (land, buildings, mines, forests, machinery and capital), distribution and exchange are owned by private entrepreneurs, a large number of workers are employed on wages at the market rate, and economic activity is primarily devoted to private profit.

Bourgeoisie

Bourgeoisie refers to the class comprising the owners of means of social production, distribution and exchange under capitalism: the capitalist class.

Proletariat

Proletariat refers to the class comprising the propertyless workers under capitalism: the working class.

Socialism

Socialism refers to an economic system of the modern age, largely based on industrial production where means of social production (land, buildings, mines, forests, machinery and capital), distribution and exchange are placed under social ownership and control, and economic activity is primarily devoted to fulfilment of social needs.

Exponents of Marxism believed that the class struggle led by the working class would culminate in a socialist revolution. This would mean overthrow of capitalism and setting up a new economic and political system in which all means of social production would be placed under social ownership and control. During the socialist phase, work would be made compulsory for every able-bodied person and efforts will be made for fuller development of the forces of production. This would eventually result in the emergence of communist society which would be a 'classless' society. With the abolition of the division of society into dominant and dependent classes, the use of power will become redundant.

POWER AND HEGEMONY

Antonio Gramsci (1891-1937) admired the Bolshevik Revolution (1917) of Russia as a victory of the will power over economic conditions. But he also warned that this strategy would not be suitable under the conditions prevailing in Western society where the working class had come to accept the existing arrangements. He set aside certain assumptions of classical Marxism and produced a new analysis of the capitalist state.

Gramsci noted that the real source of strength of the ruling classes in the West is manifested in their spiritual and cultural supremacy. These classes manage to inculcate their value system in the mind of their people through the institutions of the civil society. Gramsci particularly focused on the structures of domination in the culture of the capitalist society.

The conventional Marxist theory had held that economic mode of production of any society constituted its base while its legal and political structure and various expressions of its social consciousness including religion, morals, social custom and practices constituted its superstructure. It believed that the character of the superstructure was determined by the prevailing character of its base. During the course of social development, the changes in the base led to the corresponding changes in the superstructure. So it focused on changes in the base; the superstructure was not regarded to deserve an independent analysis. Gramsci did not accept this position. He suggested that the superstructure of contemporary Western society had attained some degree of autonomy; hence its analysis was also necessary.

> Gramsci... scorned the idea that socialism would arise, inevitably, from the ashes of a doomed capitalism, he ... pleaded with Marxists to end their obsession with economics and pay more attention to the realm of culture.
>
> Joseph V. Femia

Gramsci particularly focused on the structures of domination in the culture of the capitalist society. He identified two levels of its superstructure:

(*a*) *Political Society* or *State* which resorts to coercion to maintain its domination. The whole organization of government comes within its purview. The structures associated with this part of superstructure are called 'structures of coercion';

(*b*) *Civil Society* which resorts to obtaining consent of the citizens to maintain its domination. This part of the superstructure is closer to the base and it is relatively autonomous. The structures associated with this part are called 'structures of legitimation'. Gramsci pays special importance to this part of the superstructure.

According to Gramsci, the institutions of civil society—family, school and church familiarize the citizens with the rules of behaviour and teach them to show natural respect to the authority of the ruling classes. These structures lend legitimacy to the rule of the capitalist class so that even injustice involved in this rule would carry the impression of justice. That is why these are called 'structures of legitimation'. They enable the capitalist society to function in such a manner that the ruling classes seem to be ruling with the consent of the people. *When the power is apparently exercised with the consent of its subject, it is called 'hegemony'.*

Gramsci's Analysis of Hegemony in Capitalist Society

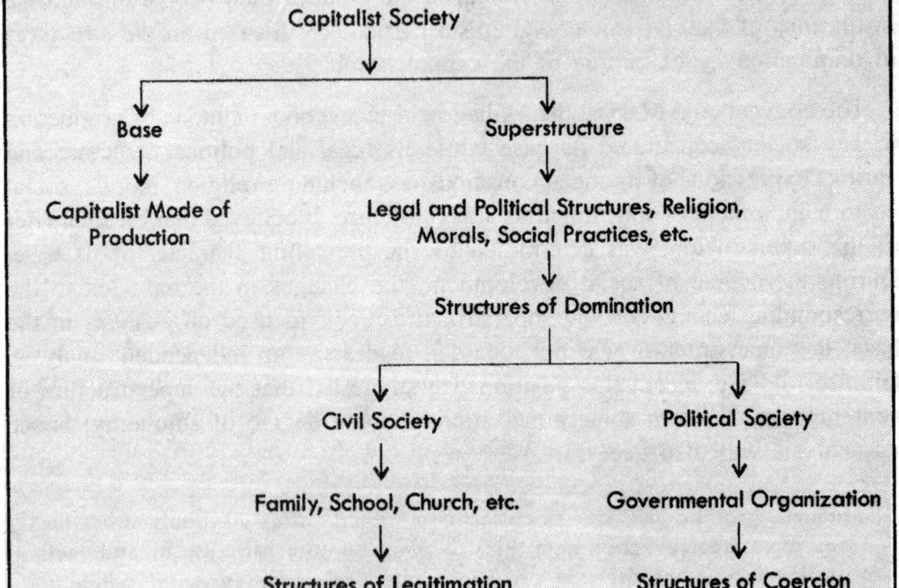

Gramsci points out that the 'structures of legitimation' within the capitalist society usually prevent any challenge to its authority. Capitalist society largely depends on the efficiency of these structures for its stability. It is only when civil society fails to prevent dissent that political society is required to make use of its structures of coercion, including police, courts and prisons.

This analysis leads us to the conclusion that the strategy of communist movement should not be confined to the overthrow of the capitalist class but it should make a dent in the value system that sustains the capitalist rule. This value system is likely to persist through the institutions of civil society even under socialist mode of production. Fresh efforts will have to be made to transform the culture of that society by inculcating socialist values in the minds of the people. According to Gramsci, it would be futile to hope that true socialism would automatically emerge from the ashes of capitalism.

Gramsci tried to convince the Marxists that they should emerge from the spell of economics and continue their ideological warfare in the field of culture, art and literature, and philosophical debates. The revolutionaries must infiltrate the autonomous institutions of civil society and create a new mass consciousness informed by the socialist value system.

Gramsci was primarily a humanist. He was opposed to any type of tyranny. He did not want to use revolution in order to set up a coercive state, but wanted to democratize all institutions. In fact, he sought to replace the state by a regulated society where all decisions would be made through consensus, and not by means of coercion.

[VI]
ELITE THEORY

Elite theory of power was advanced in early twentieth century by three famous sociologists: Pareto, Mosca and Michels. The term *'elite'* as a category of sociological analysis was introduced by Pareto while the idea associated with this theory was floated earlier by Mosca.

The term *'elite'* was derived from the French where it meant to be something excellent. Accordingly, the *elite* theory tends to divide society into 'excellent' and 'ordinary' people who are placed in different positions. So, like class theory, *elite* theory accepts a broad division of society into dominant and dependent groups. But unlike class theory, *elite* theory treats this division as somewhat natural and functional. It regards competence and aptitude (and not the emergence of private property) to be responsible for this division. Again, while class theory held that the division of society into dominant and dependent classes could be set aside through a socialist revolution, *elite* theory sees little prospects of a thorough-going change in this position.

Vilfredo Pareto (1848-1923), an Italian sociologist, in his *The Mind and Society* (1915-19), used the term *'elite'* to indicate a superior social group, *i.e.* a group of people who show highest ability in their field of activity whatever its nature might be. It was a minority group which took all major decisions in society. The other part of society which fell short of this level of ability was termed as mass of the people, or 'masses'. Masses are characterized by the lack of qualities of leadership as well as the fear from responsibility. They feel that in public life it would be safe to follow the *elite*.

Within the *elite* Pareto distinguished between 'governing *elite*' and 'non-governing *elite*'. 'Governing *elite*' is one that wields power for the time being while 'non-governing *elite*' constantly endeavours to replace it by showing greater ability and excellence. In short, behaviour of the *elite* is characterized by a constant competition between governing and non-governing *elites*. This results in what is called 'circulation of *elites*'. In any case, masses have no chance of entering the ranks of *elites*.

Pareto's Model of Circulation of *Elites*

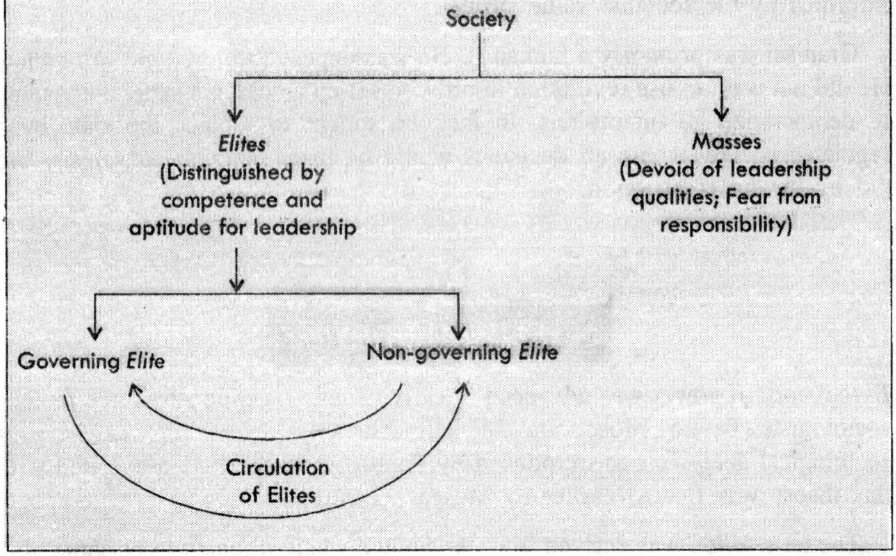

Apart from intelligence and talent, Pareto also recognizes courage and cunning as the qualities of the *elite*. He observes that 'the lions' (who are distinguished by their courage) are more suited to the maintenance of *status quo* under stable conditions, while 'the foxes' (who are distinguished by their cunning) are adaptive and innovative and cope better during periods of change.

Gaetano Mosca (1858-1941) was also an Italian sociologist. In his noted work *The Ruling Class* (1896), he postulated that the people are necessarily divided into two groups: the rulers and the ruled. The ruling class controls most of the wealth, power and prestige in society. The ruled are not competent to replace it. Whatever form of government might be adopted, it is always this minority which exercises all power in society. Mosca defined ruling class as a political class that represents the interests of the important and influential groups, especially in a parliamentary democracy. In any case, the ruling class tends to invoke moral and legal principles in order to win consent of the ruled.

While Pareto regards intelligence and talent as the outstanding qualities of *elite*, Mosca's ruling class was distinguished by its capacity of organization. Of the two Italian elitists, Mosca is more democratic. He believed that leadership could emerge at all levels including the grass-root level. Each stratum of society has the potential of producing good organizers for itself. They need not look for outsiders for their guidance and control.

Mosca argued that the dominance of the ruling class was essential to provide for proper organization of the unorganized majority. Members of the ruling minority always enjoy a high degree of esteem in the eyes of the people because of their outstanding qualities. Mosca also held that a constant competition between the upper and lower strata of society led to something like the 'circulation of *elites*'.

While class theory held that the division of society into classes was based on exploitation, *elite* theory believed that the division of society into *elite* and masses was functional. They compensate each other in sustaining the social organization. This division does not give rise to any injustice in society. Hence, the masses need not rise in revolt against the ruling class. Under this system, social change, if any, would be confined to the 'circulation of *elites*'. In this process, an outmoded *elite* may be replaced by a more dynamic *elite*, but masses will have no opportunity to come to power.

Robert Michels (1876-1936), a German sociologist, made important contribution to the development of the *elite* theory. In his famous work *Political Parties: A Sociological Study of the Oligarchical Tendencies of Modern Democracy* (1911), Michels propounded his 'Iron Law of Oligarchy'. He proceeded to demonstrate that every organization—whatever its original aims—is eventually reduced to 'oligarchy', that is the rule of the chosen few who tend to use their authority in self-interest. He held that majority of human beings are apathetic, indolent and slavish. They are permanently incapable of self-government. So they have to bank upon their leaders for pursuing their social objectives. Trade unions, political parties and other organizations are the vehicles of such leadership.

Michels points out that any organization may be set up with democratic aims, but as the organization grows in size and complexity, its management is left to the professional experts. In due course these experts or leaders become indispensable for the organization. They use their manipulative skills, including oratory, persuation and playing upon sentiments of the people in order to perpetuate themselves in power. They become so prominent by virtue of their expertise and experience that it becomes very difficult to replace them at periodical re-election. In exercising their undisputed power, they set aside the original aims of the organization. The growth of oligarchy in every organization is so inevitable as if this process is governed by an 'iron law'.

This 'iron law of oligarchy' rules out the possibility of 'circulation *of elites'* as envisaged by Pareto and Mosca. It belies all hopes of democracy in any society or organization. All forms of government are also destined to be reduced to oligarchy. However, critics of Michels' iron law of oligarchy point out that this law cannot be uniformly applied to all organizations. Members of some organizations could be more vigilant, vocal and assertive than those of others. Again, some organizations by their nature could be more democratic than others. For example, political parties may offer more options to their members than trade unions. In any case, Michels' observations could serve as a warning to those who sincerely believe in democratization of institutions. This view was subsequently applied to the practical situations by some leading sociologists.

Oligarchy

Oligarchy refers to a pattern of organization in which a small group of the chosen few makes all decisions largely in its own interest, mostly by means of its manipulative skills. This group is also called oligarchy.

Max Weber (1864-1920), German sociologist, inspired by this theory came to reject the prevalent definition of democracy as 'government by the people'. He sought to redefine democracy as 'a competition for political leadership'. In his essay on 'Socialism' (1918), Weber emphatically pointed to the relative independence of political power from social classes. He argued that if socialism is sought to be established through a socialist revolution, it was destined to become the dictatorship of officials rather than the dictatorship of proletariat as envisaged by the Marxist theory. Weber asserted that the inequality of political power is in no way diminished or eliminated by the abolition of classes. In other words, even in the so-called 'classless society' all power was bound to be concentrated in the hands of the chosen few. A democratic form of government was preferable because it provided for an open competition for political leadership. This model of democracy was adopted and further developed by Joseph Schumpeter (1883-1950), American economist and social thinker.

C. Wright Mills (1916-62), American sociologist, presented a new version of the *elite* theory in his famous work *The Power Elite* (1956). He preferred the term 'power *elite'* to 'ruling class'. While Marxian concept of the 'ruling class' implied that an economic class would exercise all political power in society, Mills' concept of 'power *elite'* implied a combination of several groups who exercised all power by virtue of their high status in all important spheres of social life. It signified an inner circle of power-holders in modern American society.

Mills observed that modern American society was ruled by a set of three loosely interlocking groups who had come to occupy the pivotal positions of power: the captains of industry, military leaders and prominent politicians. These three groups, taken together, constituted the 'power *elite*'. They not only share their cultural and psychological orientations, but also often share their social origins. In other words, the top groups in economic, military and political organizations in the United States were linked by ties of family and friendship and shared common social backgrounds.

According to Mills, the power *elites* do not owe their power to fulfilling social demands. They themselves are capable of creating such demands. They occupy the strategic command posts within the social structure. The power *elite* constitute a self-conscious class whose members help each other on the basis of mutual understanding, tolerance and cooperation in order to strengthen each other's power and position. They project their image of high moral character only with a view to commanding respect in society, but they are scarcely sensitive to their moral or social responsibility.

[VII]
GENDER PERSPECTIVE

Gender perspective on power is represented by the feminist theory. It recognizes the division of society into two broad groups on the basis of gender: men and women who were biologically (and also perhaps psychologically) fit to perform different functions. This division was created by nature for sustaining the human race and to enable the human beings to build up an excellent civilization and culture, but it is society which placed men and women in dominant and dependent positions respectively. Feminists demand a thorough-going change in this arrangement and wish to liberate women from the undue dominance of men.

The age-old and universal dominance of man over woman is manifested in the *concept of patriarchy.* Friedrich Engels, in his *The Origin of the Family, Private Property and the State* (1884), observed that in the antiquity when the institution of marriage was not invented, lineage of a person could be reckoned only through the female line. Consequently, women as mothers were treated with a high degree of consideration and respect. The transition to monogamy, in due course, where the woman belongs exclusively to one man, implied the erosion of that respect. In Engles' own words: "The overthrow of mother right was the *world-historic defeat of the female sex.* The man seized the reins in the house also, the woman was degraded, enthralled, the slave of the man's lust, a mere instrument for breeding children ...The first effect of the sole rule of the men that was now established is shown in. . . the patriarchal family."

Literally, patriarchy means 'rule of the father'. The term was originally used to describe the social organization based on the authority of male heads of households. In the contemporary usage, it has come to mean male domination in general. It is now used to describe a social system in which men dominate, oppress and exploit women. It comprehends the various ways in which men exercise power over women. Broadly speaking, the social relations involving reproduction, violence, sexuality (including the use of pornography) and work culture are identified as parts of the patriarchal system.

Modern theories of patriarchy postulate that there is a fundamental division of interests between most men and most women as a result of social structuring of gender relations. Some writers focus on biological differences between men and women as the basis of patriarchy. For instance, they point out that men show their greater physical strength in warfare, and women are constrained by nature to perform an elaborate role in the reproductive function. Others see sexuality as an instrument of control of women by men. Still others focus on male violence as the basis of this control. Again, some feminists have asserted that men benefit from women's labour, both as unpaid house-work and as poorly paid work in the labour market.

Feminist sociologists have broadly given three types of account of patriarchy. In the first place, those influenced by the work of the French psychoanalysts and structuralists have argued that a society's culture is dominated by the symbols of male origin. According to the second account, patriarchy is essentially based on the household in which men dominate women economically, sexually and culturally. This view treats marriage contract as a labour contract through which women exchange unpaid domestic services for their upkeep. Finally, Marxist feminists argue that patriarchy and capitalism support each other. Within the household, men take the benefit of women's unpaid domestic labour, and thus relieve their employer—the capitalist of the liability to pay for that labour. Outside the home, women are segregated to perform some specific jobs for which very low wages are paid. In fact, all these accounts focus on different aspects of women's exploitation in society and they should be read together to draw a full picture of the situation.

The extent of economic exploitation of women in contemporary society is amply reflected in a United Nations Report (1980). It reads: "Women constitute half the world's population, perform nearly two-thirds of its work hours, receive one-tenth of the world's income, and own less than one-hundredth of the world's property." Present-day situation in this matter is not very different from the forgoing description. In other spheres of life, *e.g.* cultural and social spheres, similar data to show the extent of exploitation of women by men might not be available, but a general awareness about this exploitation led to strong protests manifested in Women Liberation Movement which emerged in the United States since the early 1970s. Soon this movement also spread to Europe and other parts of the world. This movement focused on equal rights and status for women in a male-dominated society. Some prominent organizations associated with this movement were: National Organization for Women (NOW), Boston's

Bread and Roses, Berkeley Women's Liberation Group, Women's Radical Action Project, Women's Equity Action League (WEAL), National Women's Political Caucus (NWPC), etc.

Broadly speaking, Women Liberation Movement demanded truly equal treatment of men and women. It required that many of society's myths, values and beliefs concerning status and role of women in society should be fundamentally reassessed and changed. These changes must embrace the patterns of work and family life, social behaviour, decision-making, politics, religion and education. Even the more personal and private domain of sexuality needed to be redefined. These demands led to a widespread debate on diverse issues concerning women. These include day-care facilities for children, the development of a non-sexist vocabulary (*e.g.* the term 'chairman' should be replaced by 'chairperson'), and the representation of women and their roles in the mass media, including advertising. These debates have not only led to the enactment of new laws in some countries, but also to the worldwide acceptance of new norms protecting dignity of women.

In India, some important legislation concerning the protection of women include: the Immoral Traffic (Prevention) Act, 1956; Dowry Prohibition Act, 1961; Indecent Representation of Women (Prohibition) Act, 1986; the Commission of *Sati* (Prevention) Act, 1987; Hindu Succesion (Amendment) Act, 2005 (which gives equal rights to daughters in joint family property); and Protection of Women from Domestic Violence Act, 2005.

[VIII]
GROUP PERSPECTIVE

Group perspective on power corresponds to pluralist theory. Whereas class perspective, *elite* perspective and gender perspective on power maintain that the exercise of power divides the society into two broad categories—dominant and dependent groups, pluralist theory of power does not subscribe to this view. According to this theory, power in society is not concentrated in a single group, but it is dispersed amongst a wide variety of social groups. These groups are largely autonomous and almost independent centres of decision. Organizations of workers, peasants, traders, industrialists, consumers, etc. could be cited as examples of such groups in the contemporary society. These groups cannot be classified into dominant and dependent groups. They have their share of power in their respective spheres of operation.

Since these groups are more or less interdependent within the social organization, they tend to balance each other's power. Public decisions are largely the outcome of this equilibrium. The pluralist theory gives a description of actual distribution of power in society as well as its justification. This theory is based on the philosophy of pluralism which upholds a political system suited to a pluralist society. Pluralist society is that society in which power and authority are not concentrated in a particular group but they are spread to various centres of decision-making.

Pluralism

Pluralism refers to a political outlook that gives due importance to the diverse interests and viewpoints in society. It tends to promote the emergence of several centres of power and authority, rather than accepting the state as the sole controller of people's actions.

The present form of pluralist society represents a modern arrangement, but early hints of this arrangement can be traced to medieval Europe. In that age, monarchy and church regulated different spheres of human life while craft corporations and feudal lords commanded obedience from their subjects in their respective spheres of authority. But this system cannot be likened to the modern version of pluralist society. In fact, medieval society was characterized by several competing centres of power and legitimacy which simultaneously demanded loyalty from the same set of persons. Their social and political life was intertwined. However, modern pluralist society does not seek to mix up social life of citizens with their political life. It encourages them to form autonomous groups. These groups are not required to compete with the authority of the state. They are designed to serve as intermediary bodies between individuals and the state. They seek to convey the sentiments of their members to government and try to influence the process of policy-formation and decision-making.

In a pluralist society, individuals may be divided into several competing groups according to their status and interests, but politically they continue to be the members of the same community. They owe allegiance to the same state. They are governed by the same law and public policy. They enjoy equal rights as citizens. Hence, pluralist society represents a social system which provides for the coexistence of a variety of social customs, cultural traits and religious beliefs. They participate in the political process under uniform political institutions.

French writer Alexis de Tocqueville (1805-59) observed that the absence of intermediary groups in France was responsible for the French Revolution (1789) whereas the United States was able to maintain democracy due to the presence of such groups. Tocqueville suggested that in order to protect democracy, these intermediary groups should be kept free from state interference. However, modern pluralists insist that these groups should be allowed to exercise their influence on government in the process of policy-formation and government should also seek cooperation of these groups in the process of decision-making.

Contemporary pluralist theory appeared in the 1950s, particularly with the publication of Robert Dahl and Charles Lindblom's *Politics, Economics and Welfare* (1953), Robert Dahl's *A Preface to Democratic Theory* (1956) and *Who Governs?* (1961). It was based on the assumption that there was a widespread distribution of political resources, and that different interests prevailed in different political disputes and at different times. Dahl's model of democracy, described as 'polyarchy', postulated that society is controlled by a set of competing interest groups, with the government functioning as little more than an honest broker in the middle. Then N. Polsby, in his *Community, Power and Political Theory* (1963), pointed to an unspoken notion in pluralist research that at bottom nobody dominates.

Interest Groups

In a liberal democracy, interest groups refer to groups of people who organize themselves for pursuing their specific, collective interest. They try to serve their interests through obtaining the support of public opinion by publicizing their viewpoint widely, and pleading to government to mould its policy to suit their interest. Examples of interest groups are: trade unions, lawyers associations and chambers of commerce and industry.

Critics point out that pluralism focuses only on the decision-making process. It overlooks those issues on which no decision could be taken though some of those issues might be very important. Moreover, even if different groups bargain on equal footing, some groups may lack internal democracy. As a result, leaders or spokespersons of those groups may play a dominant role. Steven Lukes, in his *Power: A Radical View* (1974), has pointed to a 'third dimension of power'. It implies that power-holders can so manipulate the wants of others that their *real interests* are suppressed.

These points of criticism have led to some modification in the pluralist theory in its later phase of development. Thus Charles Lindblom, in his *Politics and Markets* (1977), conceded that there is a privileged position of business in the market-dominated polyarchies of the West; that they are controlled undemocratically by business and property. Robert Dahl, in his *Dilemmas of Pluralist Democracy* (1982), conceded that pluralism cannot be treated as an open competition between truly equal political forces. In order to reduce the inequalities of these forces, Dahl has recommended those policies which would promote redistribution of power in society.

In a nutshell, the subtle forms of domination existing within certain groups and the predominant position of some groups in society should not be ignored while using group perspective for the analysis of power in society.

Comparative Perspective on Power				
The Issue	*Class Perspective*	*Elite Perspective*	*Gender Perspective*	*Group Perspective*
Relevant Theory	Marxist Theory	*Elite* Theory	Feminist Theory	Pluralist Theory
Nature of Division of Society	Haves and Have-nots	*Elite* and Masses	Men and Women	Several Autonomous Interest-Groups
Basis of the Division	Ownership of Private Property	Competence of the few	Biological Differences	Diversity of Interests
Role of the Power-holders	Exploitation	Organization and Ledership	Exploitation	Mutual Bargaining
Prospects of Change	Yes	No	Yes	Not Needed
Instruments of Change	Socialist Revolution	Not Needed	Women's Liberation Movement	Not Needed

[IX]
CONSTRUCTIVE VIEW OF POWER

The conventional view of power is largely concerned with the status of a dominant person or group (the 'agent' of power) *vis-à-vis* its dependent person or group (the 'subject' of power). In this situation the agent treats himself as an end, and his subject as a means to that end. Now, if we decide to equip the subject with some power, what would be the result? What type of power would be required for the subject? Does he only need the power of 'retaliation'? Does he need the power to free himself from subjection? Or does he need the power to improve his condition and secure his independent development?

This distinction between two types of power is often described as 'power over' and 'power to'. Thus, the conventional view of power was primarily concerned with 'power' (of the agent) 'over' (his subject). This view cannot be set aside in any meaningful analysis of power. However, the modern view insists on including in this analysis the concept of 'power' (of the subject) 'to' (achieve a goal of his own choice). When we insist on 'empowerment' of vulnerable sections (*e.g.* empowerment of women or of the poor), we, in fact, demand to equip them with 'power to' resist their oppressors and gain an opportunity and ability to utilize their capacities for self-development. Some contemporary thinkers have paid due attention to the analysis of this type of power also. Of these, Hannah Arendt, C.B. Macpherson and Mahatma Gandhi are most important.

Hannah Arendt (1906-75), modern American philosopher (who was originally a German Jew), distinguished between 'violence' and 'power' to arrive at a constructive view of power. In her view, when rulers use force to fulfil their design against the wishes of the people, it may be called 'violence'. On the other hand, power essentially belongs to the people. Analysis of power in society is not concerned with the question: 'Who rules whom?' It has nothing to do with 'command-obedience relationship'. Hannah views political institutions as 'manifestations and materializations of power'. In other words, when people act according to the principles of power, their achievements take the form of political institutions.

In her notable work *On Violence* (1969), Hannah Arendt gives some hints of her very complex concept of power. She suggests that power is 'not the property of an individual'. It 'corresponds to the human ability not just to act but to act in concert'. She believes that power relations are essentially cooperative. Power in this sense belongs to a group and remains in existence only so long as the group holds together. Power is the quality of individuals acting and speaking together. While the outcome of their power may be retained in the shape of various political institutions, power itself cannot be stored or held in possession.

These characteristics of power give us a clue to the further distinction between violence and power. Arendt holds that power keeps the public realm together; violence threatens its existence. Here we must distinguish between the 'public realm' and the 'state'. When people voluntarily behave in such a way that they create congenial conditions for each other, they create the public realm. When they are forced to behave in a particular way by an external agency, they are under the state. According to Arendt, power is the quality of the people constituting the public realm; violence is the property of the state which is used against the people. Violence relies on the instruments of its application; hence it can be held in possession. Arendt warns: "Where genuine power is absent, violence may emerge to fill the gap."

In Arendt's terminology, 'authority' and 'power' also belong to different spheres of action. Authority is linked with command-obedience relationship; it gives rise to a hierarchical order. It is based on violence; hence it corresponds to the sphere of the state. On the other hand, power belongs to the people; it creates an egalitarian order. It is based on consensus and persuation; hence it corresponds to the public realm. In Arendt's view, only power but never violence can create legitimate authority. Again she warns: "Violence can destroy power; it is utterly incapable of creating it."

The public character of power and its significance was brilliantly brought out by Hannah Arendt in her essay *On Public Happiness* (1970). Illustrating her position from the American experiment in democracy, she observed that the fundamental assumption underlying popular political participation in that country was "that no one could be called happy without his share in public happiness, that no one could be called free without his experience in public freedom, and that no one could be called either happy or free without participating, and having a share, in public power" (*The Frontiers of Political Theory,* ed. by Henry Kariel; 1970).

In a nutshell, Arendt's concept of power condemns the use of force or violence by the state and exhorts the people to cooperate in order to create and sustain a social order that would be conducive to their common happiness and freedom.

Hannah Arendt's Analysis of Power

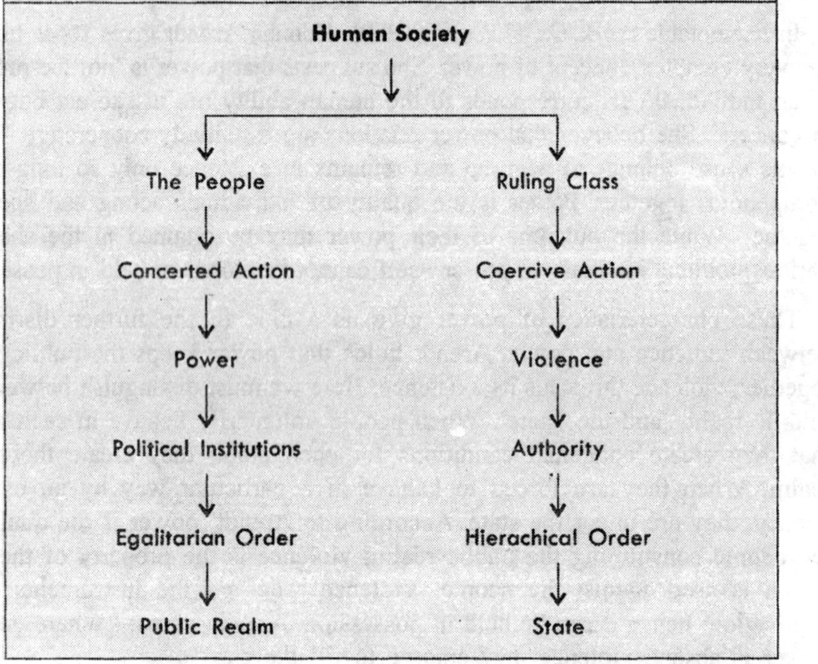

> Action, as distinguished from fabrication, is never possible in isolation; to be isolated is to be deprived of the capacity to act.
>
> ... ...
>
> Under conditions of tyranny it is far easier to act than to think.
>
> ... ...
>
> There are no dangerous thoughts; thinking itself is dangerous.
>
> Hannah Arendt

C.B. Macpherson (1911-87), a political philosopher from Canada, has given a fuller analysis of power in his *Democratic Theory—Essays in Retrieval* (1973). He makes a distinction between two components of power: *extractive power* and *developmental power.* Extractive power represents the familiar concept of power, *viz.* a person's ability to use others' capacities to serve his own purpose or 'power over' others. It implies the ability to extract benefits from others. It is interesting to note that the Western tradition of political thought from Machiavelli (1469-1527) to James Mill (1773-1836) has broadly focused on this concept of power. This attitude was not a product of intellectual carelessness but it was a factual description of power relations in a market society.

Developmental power, on the other hand, denotes a person's ability to use his own capacities for the fulfilment of his self-appointed goals. The use of extractive power in modern capitalist society is exemplified by the power of owners of land and capital. By virtue of this ownership, they can buy and use the manual and intellectual capacities of others for their own benefit. The workers and ordinary people who do not own land and capital or other means of social production, would be benefited only if they win developmental power for themselves.

It is important to note that Macpherson not only introduced the concept of developmental power, he also paid special attention to elaborate it. Thus, developmental power of a person enables him to develop his truly human capacities. Some examples of such capacities are: capacity for rational understanding, for moral judgement and action, for aesthetic or artistic activity, for love and friendship and, of course, the capacity for materially productive labour. The concept of developmental power is based on the moralist view of human nature. While the utilitarian view considers man simply as a consumer of material things or utilities, the moralist view regards him as a *doer* and *creator*. It requires that he should not face any impediments or constraints while using his human capacities to achieve his objectives.

Macpherson points to three impediments to the maximization of a person's developmental power: (*a*) lack of adequate means of life; (*b*) lack of access to the means of labour; and (*c*) lack of protection against invasion by others. The problems created by the scarcity of the means of life and the scarcity of the means of labour are technological and material as well as cultural and ideological. Macpherson is quite convinced that these problems cannot be resolved within the framework of a market society based on capitalist social relations. He suggests that the solution to these problems can be found in a new system which would combine the protection of civil liberties with a socialist mode of production. Only then individual would be able to make full use of his developmental power and thereby achieve his 'creative freedom'.

Macpherson's Analysis of Power

The Issue	*Utilitarian View*	*Moralist View*
Concept of Human Nature	As a Consumer	As a Doer and Creator
Goal of Human Life	Maximization of Utilities	Maximization of Powers
Requisite Type of Power	Extractive Power	Developmental Power.
Consequence of the Use of Power	Satisfaction of Material Wants	Creative Freedom

Mahatma Gandhi (1869-1948), an Indian social philosopher, also reflected on the situation involving the use of power. Gandhi did not write a treatise containing his social thought, yet his scattered thoughts on various social issues are quite significant.

In the present context, Gandhi's insistence on 'power to the people' is very important. When *Swaraj* (independence + self-government) was set to be the goal of independence movement of India, Gandhi wrote in *Young India* (1925):

> Real *Swaraj* will come not by the acquisition of authority by a few but by the acquisition of the capacity by all to resist authority when it is abused. In other words, *Swaraj* is to be obtained by educating the masses to a sense of their capacity to regulate and control authority.

Here, Gandhi sought to define power from the point of view of the ruled. It implied that the rulers should never gain or exercise absolute power over the ruled. If the ruled felt that their rulers were becoming too powerful, they would use their moral power to challenge the authority of the rulers. They could stand up in protest, launch social movements and exert moral pressure on the rulers to change their way of working. Thus power of the ruled would be akin to performing the 'Socratic function of speaking truth to power'.

[X]
POSTMODERN PERSPECTIVE

Postmodern perspective on power is based on the theory of postmodernism. Postmodernism stands for a late twentieth-century movement in philosophy, art and literary criticism which extends to various forms of social theory including political theory. Its philosophical foundations correspond to the stand taken by Friedrich Nietzsche (1844-1900), a German philosopher who believed that there is no truth, only a plethora of interpretations. Accordingly, there is no objective reality, only a plurality of perspectives. Similarly, there is no genuine distinction between right and wrong, only expressions of power relations. In others words, *those in power determine what is right, good or beautiful; anything not conforming to this standard is considered to be wrong* or substandard. Influential works on postmodernism include Jean-Francois Lyotard's *Postmodern Condition* (1979/1984) and Richard Rorty's *Contingency, Irony and Solidarity* (1989).

Broadly speaking, postmodernism implies that the structure of 'privilege' and 'power' pervades the entire social system. It operates in the field of our language as well as our social life. Its implications in our language have been brought out by Jaques Derrida (1930-2004), a French philosopher in his celebrated work *Of Grammatology* (1976) wherein he has outlined his concept of 'Deconstruction'. Its functioning in our social life has been amply demonstrated by Michael Focault (1926-84), another French philosopher, in his notable work *Power/Knowledge* (1980).

> **Deconstruction**
>
> Deconstruction stands for an approach to understanding the meaning of words not as representing some concrete reality or truth, but by contrasting them with their opposite concepts which they seek to suppress. Jaques Derrida (1930-2004), French philosopher, is regarded the chief exponent of this approach. Accordingly, the word *masculine* does not denote some concrete reality; its meaning can be understood only through an intellectual process, called *deconstruction,* that is by contrasting it with the word *feminine* which refers to the subordinate position. Similarly, the word *transcendental* would be meaningful only in relation to *empirical;* and the word *sacred,* only in relation to *profane.* In each case, one category is regarded as culturally superior in relation to another.

Focault—another exponent of postmodern perspective on power—has made an important contribution to political theory by challenging many traditional assumptions. He has argued that political theory and discourse continue to assume a paradigm of power derived from premodern experience. Old paradigm of power, dating from eighteenth century, conceived power as the repressive force. It is embodied in the rules which prescribe as to what is allowed and what is forbidden. However, *the new concept of power operates through disciplinary norms rather than through command-and-obedience relationship.* In the modern regime, the rulers and their agents do not reach out from a centre to control unruly subjects through fear. Instead, people are now ruled through social institutions which rise up from the ground and reach out to people through various social channels. These institutions set up disciplinary norms and make people conform to the prevailing standards of reason, order and good taste. *Power is now exercised through several institutions that organize and manage people in a complex division of labour. These institutions include not only schools, offices, police departments and prisons, but also hospitals, clinics and many welfare organizations.*

In a nutshell, postmodernist perspective on power regards the prevalent norms of truth, beauty and morality as unacceptable, because they simply reflect the mode of thinking of power-holders in society. Accordingly, there can be no objective criteria for determining the nature of truth, beauty and morality. It holds that any expression made at any particular time cannot be treated as 'modern' because the concept of 'modernity' has been constantly changing. No particular description of the real can be treated as finally true. Different descriptions thereof can be equally true or false. Different cultural expressions cannot be placed in the categories of 'high' and 'low' cultures.

Postmodernism seeks to establish sociological linkages between higher and lower values with the distribution of power in society. Accordingly, power-holders in society are held in high esteem so that their culture is regarded morally superior to that of the 'powerless'. However, this view cannot be accepted as a plea to demolish the philosophical distinction between higher and lower values which comprises the very foundation of human civilization.

14

Concept of Citizenship

[I]
NATURE OF CITIZENSHIP

WHAT IS CITIZENSHIP?

Citizenship refers to the status of an individual as a full and responsible member of a political community. Thus citizen is a person who owes allegiance to the state and in turn receives protection from the state. He must fulfil his duties and obligations towards the state as the state grants him civil, political and social rights. Hence, citizenship implies two-way relationship between individual and the state.

Genesis of Citizenship

(Two-way relationship between Individual and the State)

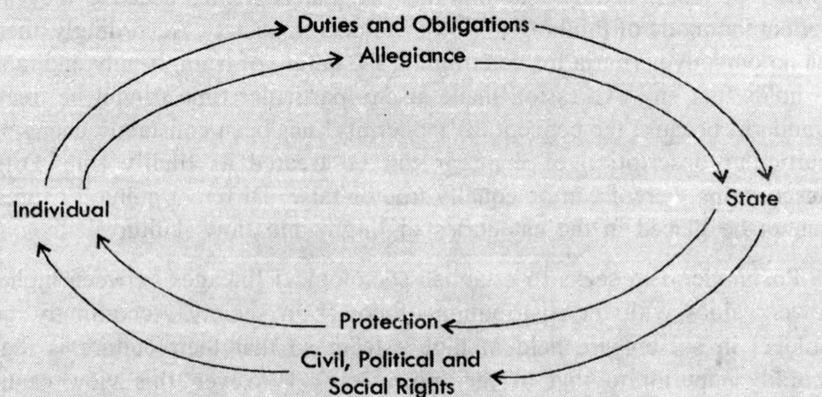

In order to understand the significance of citizenship, *distinction* must be drawn *between* a *'subject' and* a *'citizen'*. A subject is usually subservient to the state where the right to rule is reserved for a privileged class. But citizens themselves constitute the state. Citizenship is the product of a community where the right to rule is decided by a prescribed procedure which expresses the will of the general body of its members. While ascertaining their will, nobody is discriminated on grounds of race, religion, gender, place of birth, etc. T.H. Marshall, in his *Citizenship and Social Class* (1950), observed that citizenship implies full membership of a community: those who possess this status are equal with respect to the rights and duties associated with it. Marshall adds that different societies will attach different rights and duties to the status of citizen, for there is no universal principle which determines necessary rights and duties of citizenship in general.

It is possible that some groups of the citizens of a state are not satisfied with their existing rights. These persons are regarded to be citizens of their state only in a formal sense of the term. But they do not enjoy substantive citizenship as some of the rights of citizenship are denied to them in actual practice. These groups can resort to a social movement for the restoration of their rights. This movement may combine conventional forms of political participation, such as voting, pressure group tactics and lobbying with unconventional political activities, such as protests, sit-ins, demonstrations and rallies. Examples of some of such citizens movements are: abolitionist movement and civil rights movements of America, working class movements of Europe, and *adivasi* (tribal) and *dalit* (depressed classes) movements of India.

Indeed, the original concept of citizenship exclusively focused on the sense of duty where the question of rights was relegated to the background. But in the contemporary society, citizenship is primarily concerned with certain rights. In this scheme, duties of the individual are accepted only as long as they are considered to be essential for the maintenance of those rights.

HISTORICAL DEVELOPMENT

The idea of citizenship in its early form is found in ancient Greek and Roman state systems. It is worth noting that the form of ancient Greek community was entirely different from the present-day political community of democratic nation-states. In a modern democratic state, all members of a community are regarded as its citizens. But in ancient Greek city-states, very few inhabitants (about ten percent) enjoyed the status of 'freemen' who were treated as full citizens. These citizens were equal among themselves as regards their rights. There was no discrimination between the rich and the poor among freemen. The rest of the community comprised of slaves, women and aliens who had no rights of citizenship. That is why Aristotle regarded citizenship as a privilege of the ruling class. In this sense, citizenship stood for effective participation in the exercise of power.

In any case, in ancient Greek political tradition, this privilege of the ruling class was also regarded to be the part of their duty. All 'citizens' were expected to perform this duty in order to secure good life for themselves as well as for the 'non-citizens'.

After the decline of Greek city-states, a new definition of citizenship was evolved in the 'Roman Empire'. Initially there, too, citizenship was confined to power-holders. Later it was extended to the ordinary people and those vanquished in war. Thus, diverse types of people came within the ambit of citizenship. Only the people of lowest rank and women were excluded from the benefit of citizenship. However, different categories of 'citizens' were entitled to different types of rights—a practice that does not fit into the modern concept of citizenship. Roman practice was different from the Greek, as citizen was no longer defined to be the protector of law but as one who was under the protection of the laws.

During the medieval Europe, political authority was eclipsed by ecclesiastical authority. Temporal citizenship was no longer considered to be important. In the fifteenth and sixteenth centuries, with the advent of modern thought, the idea of citizenship again occupied the centre-stage in Italian republics. Niccolo Machiavelli (1469-1527), famous Italian thinker, gave a new lease of life to this idea. In seventeenth-century England, James Harrington (1611-77), and John Milton (1608-74) redefined the idea. Harrington drew a picture of an ideal system of the future which would be an 'empire of the laws, not of men'. The exponents of the Glorious Revolution (1688) of England particularly popularized the idea of citizenship. In the eighteenth century, this idea became very popular during the days of American Revolution (1776).

The idea of citizenship reached its zenith with the French Revolution (1789) and the consequent Declaration of Rights of Man and Citizen. This Declaration echoes the views of Jean-Jaques Rousseau (1712-78). Rousseau, in his *Social Contract* (1762), wrote that citizen is a free and autonomous person. He is entitled to participate in all those decisions which are binding on all citizens. On seeing the rise of commercial society in Europe, Rousseau realized that the clash between the common good and the private interests was inevitable. This clash would undermine the social unity. Rousseau deliberately gave prominence to the common good over private interests.

In the nineteenth century, the ascendancy of liberalism gave rise to market relations which promoted a new notion of citizenship. Now the idea of natural rights came to be regarded as the basis of citizenship. The idea of natural rights in this sense was advanced by John Locke (1632-1704) in England. Locke had argued that the 'right to life, liberty and property' was the mainstay of natural rights. The citizens set up the state for the protection of these rights. If the state fails to protect these rights, the individual would be free to exercise his 'right to resistance' against the state. Under the influence of these views, citizenship came to be regarded as indicative of 'rights against the state'. In any case, this notion of 'negative rights' made a significant contribution to the development of liberal-democratic societies. Eventually, the notion of 'positive rights' was evolved in these societies which brought the idea of citizenship to its logical conclusion. In a nutshell, 'absence of restraint' on certain activities of the individual within the state constitutes his 'negative rights'. On the other hand, when the state extends its support to individual in his self-development, it constitutes his 'positive rights'.

[II]
COMPONENTS OF CITIZENSHIP: CIVIL, POLITICAL AND SOCIAL RIGHTS

In the present-day society, substantive citizenship is defined in terms of three important components: civil, political and social rights. T.H. Marshall, in his *Citizenship and Social Class* (1950), analysed the concept of citizenship in an evolutionary perspective. He identified three stages of development of the rights associated with citizenship in England since the eighteenth century. At the first stage, civil rights (constituting *civil citizenship)* were evolved in the eighteenth century. These included: equality before the law, liberty of the person, freedom of speech, thought and faith, the right to own property and conclude contracts. At the second stage, political rights (constituting *political citizenship*) were evolved in the nineteenth century. These included: the right to take part in elections, the right to serve in bodies invested with political authority, whether legislatures or cabinets. Finally, at the third stage, social rights (constituting *social citizenship)* were developed in the twentieth century. These included: the right to a certain standard of economic and social welfare, the right to a full share in the social heritage. Four sets of public institutions were equipped to take care of these three types of rights: the courts, representative political bodies, the social services and schools. The courts protect the civil rights of the citizens; representative political bodies protect their political rights; social services and schools provide for their social rights. In short, the evolution of citizenship was completed with the development of welfare state.

Evolution of Substantive Citizenship in England (Marshall's Analysis)

Period of Development	*Form of Citizenship*	*Nature of Rights*	*Protective Institutions*
Eighteenth Century	Civil Citizenship	Civil Rights	Courts
Nineteenth Century	Political Citizenship	Political Rights	Representative Institutions
Twentieth Century	Social Citizenship	Social Rights	Social Services and Schools

Welfare State

Welfare state refers to a state that safeguards liberty of its citizens and also provides for various types of social services for them, e.g. social security (financial assistance in the case of loss of job or any other source of income, death of the bread-winner, prolonged illness or physical disability or any other calamity), free education, public health, poor relief, supply of essential goods and services like foodgrains, milk, fuel and transport to the needy at subsidized rates. It undertakes the protection of cultural heritage including monuments, museums, libraries, art galleries, botanical gardens and zoological parks, etc. It also promotes higher education and scientific research, etc. to step up intellectual and cultural development of society. It makes use of public resources and taxation of the relatively rich to provide for a vast network of social services and social security.

These components of citizenship, *viz.* civil, political and social rights have to be developed in each state that claims to be humane and progressive. The scope of these rights can be elaborated further keeping in view the logic behind them.

An effective provision of civil rights requires that the benefit of these rights should be extended equally to minorities and majorities. In other words, while making provision of these rights, no discrimination should be made between different citizens on racial, religious, linguistic, gender or any other similar ground. If any group, particularly a minority group, faces such discrimination, it can resort to a civil rights movement to secure restoration of these rights. For instance, the American Negroes (the black citizens) had to resort to such movement. They had to fight for the enforcement of those rights which existed in law but denied to them in actual practice. The American Supreme Court had allowed them unrestricted use of public property and unrestricted entry into public institutions way back in 1954. But they had to endure a prolonged struggle for the enforcement of these rights throughout the United States. As a result of their mass movement, Civil Rights Act was passed in 1964 forbidding racial discrimination in employment, education, or accommodation.

Similarly, an effective provision of political rights requires that all citizens should be eligible to gain political office through a prescribed procedure; ordinary people should be able to elect the rulers of their choice, to replace the unwanted rulers, to influence public decisions, to criticize public policies, decisions and actions, and to offer alternative policies and programmes. In communist countries (like the People's Republic of China and the former USSR), political power remained the monopoly of one party—the Communist Party. They held regular elections, but the ruling party had the exclusive right to nominate candidates. Ordinary people in these countries indeed had no choice, nor the capacity to replace the power-holders. So the citizens did not have political rights in the true sense of the term, although they dubbed their system a 'people's republic'. In 1989 when thousands of students demonstrated at Tiananman Square in China's capital city, demanding their democratic rights, they were declared to be rebels and many of them were shot dead.

Finally, social rights of citizens are largely provided in a welfare state. In nineteenth-century Europe, the functions of state were largely confined to the maintenance of law and order. It was dubbed a 'nightwatchman state'. It was regarded to be an instrument of safeguarding property of its citizens. Its power of taxation was largely determined by the needs of performing this function. The idea of welfare state originated in Germany in the nineteenth century itself as a programme of 'social insurance' (1883) under Prince Bismarck (1815-98). It was adopted in England in early twentieth century as national compulsory health insurance (1911). It reached its zenith with the publication of Beveridge Report (1942). This report pronounced the objective of the state to tackle the five great evils: *Want, Disease, Ignorance, Squalor* and *Idleness.* Special attention was paid to the provision of financial assistance to the citizens in case of unemployment, sickness and old age. Beveridge Report is regarded as the foundation of the system of welfare state. The implementation of this report turned England into a model welfare state.

It is important to note that in England various components of citizenship developed in a logical order. Hence, the structure of citizenship in England can serve as a model for other countries. Initially, the evolution of civil rights in England created an atmosphere which paved the way for the evolution of democracy. Democracy secured political rights of the citizens which enabled them to participate in public life and to influence public decisions. This led to the evolution of welfare state which secured their social rights. On the other hand, the concept of citizenship in the United States hardly developed beyond the provision of civil rights. Even their implementation was not extended to all citizens. Hence, the women as well as the black Americans had to resort to mass movements for the enforcement of their civil rights.

It is again worth noting that after the Second World War (1939-45), the concept of citizenship developed in different directions in Eastern and Western parts of Europe. In Western Europe, initially civil and political rights were established under liberal-democratic systems. Subsequently, social rights were introduced under welfare state system in order to curb the inegalitarian tendencies of the capitalist economy. But in Eastern Europe, initially elaborate provision of social and economic rights of citizens was made under communist dictatorships, and their civil and political rights were heavily curtailed. From 1989, the citizens of these countries (Hungary, Poland, East Germany, Czechoslovakia, Bulgaria, Rumania and Russia) launched widespread anti-establishment movements in support of their demand for basic civil and political rights, which led to the collapse of communist systems by 1991.

[III]
THEORIES OF CITIZENSHIP

In the contemporary political discourse, several theories have been advanced regarding the logical basis and the proper scope of citizenship. Of these, five theories are particularly important: (*a*) liberal theory; (*b*) libertarian theory; (*c*) communitarian theory; (*d*) Marxist theory; and (*e*) pluralist theory.

LIBERAL THEORY OF CITIZENSHIP

According to this theory, civil rights constitute the foundation of citizenship. These rights reach their logical conclusion through an evolutionary process in which political and social rights come into existence. Since this theory believes in the evolution of the rights associated with citizenship, it is also described as *'unilinear'* or *'evolutionary theory of citizenship'*. T.H. Marshall is regarded the chief exponent of this theory. In his *Citizenship and Social Class* (1950), Marshall observed that citizenship prescribes equal rights and duties, liberties and constraints, powers and responsibilities for different individuals. Under citizenship, the individuals come together to decide the terms of their association. The idea of citizenship runs counter to the idea of class division of society. A social class promotes inequality between different individuals on the basis of ownership of property, level of education and the structure of economy, but citizenship tends to bestow equal status upon them.

Citing the example of modern England, Marshall has shown that the idea of citizenship begins with the provision of civil rights, and proceeds further by giving rise to political and social rights respectively. When it is fully developed, the individual no longer remains dependent on the market system. So citizenship in its fully developed form leads to redistribution of goods and services, benefits and burdens. In this form, it embodies the idea of social justice. Thus, when some people fail to provide for health care, education or housing for their family, then as citizens they are entitled to state assistance.

> **Social Justice**
>
> Social justice refers to a social policy which seeks to prevent concentration of valuable resources of the community (wealth, prestige and power) in the hands of the chosen few, and to create a social order which will enable the deprived and the underprivileged sections to gain a respectable share thereof by virtue of their ability, effort and need.

Since citizenship assures a share to all individuals in the common heritage of the community, it creates in them a bond of allegiance to that community.

This aspect of citizenship strengthens their sense of duty.

Critics argue that this theory is too optimistic. Redistribution of benefits and burdens for the provision of social rights involves taxation of some sections to benefit others. Nothing comes free. If someone gets something free, someone else must be paying for it. To maintain goodwill and solidarity in society, it is necessary that taxpayers are not subjected to undue burden and heartburn. It is a really difficult task.

LIBERTARIAN THEORY OF CITIZENSHIP

This theory regards citizenship as the product of free choice and contract among individuals. It considers 'market society' as a suitable model of civic life. Robert Nozick is the chief exponent of this theory. In his *Anarchy, State and Utopia* (1974), Nozick observed that individuals resort to private activity, market exchange and voluntary association in order to realize their values, beliefs and preferences. The need of citizenship arises because some of the necessary goods and services cannot be obtained in this manner. For this, public provision becomes necessary. In this sense, citizen means a rational consumer of public goods.

Nozick likens the state to a large enterprise, and citizens as its customers or clients. Men hire protective institutions for the protection of their right to property. State proves to be the most efficient among all protective institutions. It enjoys monopoly of use of force in a given territory.

Critics point out that free-market-based individualism does not provide for adequate foundation of social solidarity. This model of citizenship would lead to sharp disputes and intense clash of interests within society. For instance, if we adopt this concept of citizenship, such questions would arise: why should those who do not avail themselves of the services of government hospitals or government schools be forced to pay for them? And why should those who do not own property be forced to pay for the maintenance of the huge police force largely meant to protect private property? Again, why should those who do not love their country be forced to pay for the maintenance of the huge military force?

This argument may be extended to hold that the people should avail themselves of the services of private insurance companies, not of state, for necessary assistance in old age, theft, accident and other unforeseen calamities. In this way, by and by government would become redundant and the idea of citizenship would become irrelevant.

COMMUNITARIAN THEORY OF CITIZENSHIP

As against the libertarian theory, the communitarian or *'republican theory of citizenship'* insists on a strong bond of affinity between individual and the state. This conception of citizenship conceives the citizen as someone who plays an active role in shaping the future direction of his or her society through political debate and decision-making. In other words, the distinctive feature of citizenship is 'citizen participation'. The exponents of this theory include Hannah Arendt (*The Human Condition;* 1958), Michael Walzer (*Spheres of justice;* 1983), and Benjamin Barber (*Strong Democracy;* 1984).

The main tenet of this theory is that a citizen should identify himself with the community of which he is a member, and take active part in its political life. Then only he can contribute substantially to the realization of the common good. In other words, an individual can become a citizen of a community in the true sense of the term by assimilating himself with the culture, traditions, beliefs and sentiments of that community.

Critics argue that this model of citizenship would only be suitable to a small, homogeneous society with common traditions as existed in the fourth century B.C. at Athens and fifteenth century Florence. Jean-Jaques Rousseau had evolved his concept of the 'general will' in his celebrated work *The Social Contract* (1762), keeping in view the image of such society. General will represented a point where real will of all the members of a community was supposed to converge. This is not feasible in the very large and complex society of today. In contemporary society, broad issues of consensus may be discovered through a widespread debate, but it would not be possible to identify the existence of the 'general will' which pervades the entire community.

MARXIST THEORY OF CITIZENSHIP

Marxist theory sees citizenship as the product of class conflict. According to this view, citizenship is founded on those rights which a class happens to win for itself after suppressing the rights of its antagonistic class. Anthony Giddens is the chief exponent of this theory. In his two important Works *A Contemporary Critique of Historical Materialism* (1981) and *Profiles and Critiques of Social Theory* (1982), Giddens has sought to contradict Marshall's view in order to vindicate the Marxist view of citizenship. He has particularly raised three issues:

(1) Marshall treats the development of citizenship as if it were something that unfolded in phases according to some inner logic within the modern world. Giddens finds this account an oversimplification of the role of politics and the state, as if the whole process was supported and buttressed by 'the beneficent hand of the state'. Giddens argues that the underprivileged have achieved their citizenship in substantial degree only through struggle; they succeeded to tilt the balance of power in their favour only during the times of war, particularly during the period of world war;

(2) According to Marshall, development of citizenship has taken place in a unilinear manner. Giddens disagrees with him on this point. He argues that it was the product of various social movements. The varying strength of these movements led to variations in the benefits conceded to the underprivileged. Erosion of welfare rights of the poor during 1970s and 1980s, particularly under Margaret Thatcher (in England) and Ronald Reagon (in the United States), are the cases in point; and

(3) Marshall identified three types of rights associated with citizenship: civil, political and social rights. He held that these rights belong to a single category. On the contrary, Giddens identifies two types of citizenship rights which belong to different categories:

(*a*) Individual freedom and equality before the law signify those civil rights which were largely won by the emergent bourgeoisie through their struggle against the feudal privileges. These rights helped to consolidate industrial capitalism and modern representative state; and

(*b*) Economic civil rights signify those rights for which working-class and trade-union activists fought against bourgeois system of power. These include workers' right to form their union, expand its activities, right to bargaining and right to strike. These rights sought to challenge the dominance of the capitalist system.

Class Conflict

In Marxist theory, class conflict refers to the constant conflict between dominant and dependent classes which began with the emergence of private property. The dominant class comprised the owners of means of social production. The dependent class which thrives on its labour power, is oppressed and exploited by the dominant class. The antagonistic interests of these classes cannot be reconciled. The class conflict is bound to continue until the abolition of private property through a socialist revolution, and the consequent emergence of a classless society.

Bourgeoisie

In Marxist theory, the term bourgeoisie stands for the class of modern capitalists, owners of the means of social production and employers of wage labour.

According to Giddens, development of citizenship and modern democracy began in late sixteenth century with the expansion of state sovereignty and administrative build-up. This paved the way for the extension of the state's capacity for surveillance which implied the collection and storing of information about members of society. This type of supervision increased the state's dependence on cooperative forms of social relations. It was no longer possible for the modern state to manage its affairs by force alone. More opportunities were generated for subordinate groups to influence their rulers. Giddens has termed this phenomenon as 'two-way' expansion of power.

In his later work *The Nation State and Violence* (1985), Giddens has conceded that contemporary capitalism is different from nineteenth-century capitalism. Labour movements have played a prominent role in its transformation. In most of the capitalist countries of today, 'welfare capitalism' has come into existence which safeguards the civil rights of the working class. These civil rights have helped to consolidate industrial capitalist system. Thus, Giddens has departed from the original tenets of Marxism and has come round the view that citizenship rights can be maintained within the structure of liberal democracy.

PLURALIST THEORY OF CITIZENSHIP

Pluralist theory of citizenship treats the development of citizenship as a complex and multi-dimensional process. Accordingly, it cannot be attributed to a single cause. In order to understand it, we must pay attention to the role of diverse factors that are responsible for its development.

David Held, in his *Political Theory and the Modern, State* (1989), observed that from the ancient world to the present day, citizenship meant a reciprocal relationship between individual and community. In other words, individual is entitled to certain rights against the community; he also owes certain duties to the community. Thus, rights and duties are interdependent; they are two sides of the same coin. An individual's rights imply duties of others; his duties imply rights of others. Essence of citizenship lies in participation in the life of the community.

> **The true source of rights is duty. If we all discharge our duties, rights will not be far to seek.**
>
> **Mahatma Gandhi**

It would be misleading to regard citizenship only as an outcome of evolution or a product of class conflict. As Held has elucidated: "Citizenship is about involvement of people in the community in which they live; and people have been barred from citizenship on grounds of gender, race and age among many other factors. To analyse citizenship as if it were a matter of the inclusion or exclusion of social classes is to eclipse from the view a variety of dimensions of social life which have been central to the struggle over citizenship" (*Political Theory and the Modern State;* 1989).

Pluralist theory insists on inquiring into all types of discrimination against people, whether on grounds of gender, race, religion, property, education, occupation or age. In the contemporary world, so many social movements have been launched against different types of social discrimination. These include feminist movement, black movement, religious reform movements, workers' movement, children rights movements, *dalit* movement, *adivasi* movement and ecological movement, among others. Pluralist theory recommends that the problem of citizenship should be analysed in the context of all these movements. Since these movements are steadily spreading to new directions, analysis of citizenship becomes a subject of continuous research.

Pluralist theory does not provide for any fixed framework for the analysis of the problem of citizenship. It largely deals with the ever-expanding scope of this problem in the contemporary scenario. The theory itself is in the process of formation. The direction for its advancement was indicated by B.S. Turner (*Citizenship and Capitalism: The Debate over Reformism;* 1986).

Comparative Perspective on Citizenship

The Issue	*Liberal Perspective*	*Libertarian Perspective*	*Communitarian Perspective*	*Marxist Perspective*	*Pluralist Perspective*
Nature of citizens	Individuals Negotiating the Terms of their Association	Rational Consumers of Public Goods	Active Participants in Pursuit of the Common Good	Members of a Class Fighting for their Rights against the Dominant Class	Diverse Groups Fighting Against Discrimination on Various Grounds
Model of their organization	Welfare State	Competitive Market Society	Close-Knit Community	Workers' State	Pluralist Society
Goal of citizenship	Citizens' Welfare	Provision of Necessary Public Goods	The Common Good	Workers' Rights	Coexistence without Discrimination
Method of goal-attainment	Rational Allocation of Benefits and Burdens	Paying the State for its Services	Citizens' Participation	Class Conflict	Diverse Social Movements
Exponents	T. H. Marshall	Robert Nozick	Hannah Arendt, Michael Walzer, Benjamin Barber	Anthony Giddens	B.S. Turner

[IV]
NATURE OF DEMOCRATIC CITIZENSHIP

In the present-day world, citizenship is sought to be extended to all the members of a nation-state without discrimination on grounds of race, region, religion or sex, etc. This attitude brings it closer to the idea of democracy which seeks to establish legal and political equality among all sections. Ancient Greeks had equated democracy with the rule of the many who lacked education, culture and wealth. They, therefore, sought to confine citizenship to those who had the right to take public decisions by virtue of their superior knowledge, education, ability and excellence. Then ancient Romans sought to modify this view as they maintained that the democratic popular will could actually give greater power to a state. Bernard Crick has succintly expressed their view as follows. "Good laws to protect all are not good enough unless subjects become active citizens making their own laws collectively" ('Politics as a Form of Rule: Politics, Citizenship and Democracy' in *What is Politics?*, edited by Adrian Leftwich; 2004). This argument was based on the view of man as an active individual, a maker and shaper of things, not just a law-abiding, well-behaved acceptor or subject of a traditional order.

In modern times, a new view of democracy in relation to citizenship emerged in eighteenth-century Europe. It originated in the writings of Jean-Jaques Rousseau (1712-78), followed by the French Revolution (1789). It held that everyone, regardless of education or property, had a right to make his or her will felt in matters of public policy and the state. Rousseau's concept of the general will postulated that the common good was better understood by well-meaning, simple, unselfish and ordinary people from their own experience and conscience rather than by the over-educated elite living in artificial surroudings of high society who tended to elevate their biased understanding of things to the pedestal of 'Reason'—the only source of knowledge of truth! Since this view eulogized the wisdom of ordinary people, it could profitably be invoked to secure the liberation of a class or a nation, whether from oppression, ignorance or superstition. But as Bernard Crick has pointed out, the upholders of this view in eighteenth-and-nineteenth-centuries Europe who cared so much for liberty, did not call themselves democrats at all; rather they called themselves constitutionalists or civic republicans. Rousseau's faith in popular sovereignty did not match with the idea of representative government.

French Revolution

In European history, French Revolution refers to the culmination of the series of violent political and social upheavals in France (1789-99) caused by the revolt of the middle classes against the prevalent regime. It resulted in the overthrow of King Louis XVI, the end of monarchy a long with the supremacy of nobility and clergy, followed by the establishment of popular sovereignty.

General Will

According to Jean-Jaques Rousseau (*The Social Contract*; 1762), *the general will* refers to the point of convergence of the real will of all members of a community. It reflects the true interest of each individual as well as the common interest of the whole community. Sovereignty of the general will constitutes the foundation of popular sovereignty.

Popular Sovereignty

The idea of popular sovereignty is based on the view that ordinary people are the real source of sovereignty, that is the supreme legal authority of a state. Jean-Jaques Rousseau (1712-78), French philosopher, sought to locate sovereignty in *the general will* which represents the point of convergence of the real will of all members of a community. Real will is the will which directs them towards the attainment of good of each of them. Since their good lies in the common course of action, their real will directs them to the fulfilment of the same objectives.

Civic Republicanism

Civic republicanism refers to a political outlook which holds that individual freedom can only be achieved through political participation. At the outset, this principle concedes the necessary interdependence of human beings. It follows that in the face of mutual vulnerability, we share a common fate. Political participation is the key to determining that common fate, and making concerted effort to secure a meaningful freedom for all of us.

Finally, the close linkage between democracy and citizenship appeared in American constitution (1787), many new constitutions of nineteenth-century Europe and South America as well as in the new West German constitution, Japanese constitution and Indian constitution which were framed after the Second World War (1939-45). Bernard Crick has identified the outcome of these constitutions as "the democratic notion that everyone must mutually respect the equal rights of fellow citizens within a regulatory legal order that defines, protects and limits those rights". It represents a fusion of the idea of power of the people and the idea of legally guaranteed individual rights. In Crick's view, these two ideas could be combined, nevertheless they are distinct ideas. There are instances of highly intolerant democracies where rights are secondary; there are also instances of reasonably tolerant democracies where majorities cannot overturn the rights of individuals or minorities. In any case, the idea of democratic citizenship still suffers from many handicaps, in theory as well as in practice. A setback for this idea came in the form of elitist theory of democracy which was challenged by C.B. Macpherson (1911-87), Canadian political philosopher.

Elitist theory of democracy implies that citizen participation is not a necessary condition of democracy. Thus, for Joseph Schumpeter (1883-1950), running of government and framing of public policies is the task of professional politicians; the role of ordinary citizens is confined to voting for the politicians, the political parties and the programmes of their choice at the time of periodic elections. In other words, modern democracy is primarily the rule of politicians in which ordinary citizens play a very limited role at regular intervals. Robert Dahl's (1915-2014) pluralist theory of democracy also reconciles with a low level of citizen participation. C. B. Macpherson (*Democratic Theory—Essays in Retrieval;* 1973) observed that Schumpter-Dahl axis treats democracy a mechanism designed to maintain an equilibrium. It conceives of democracy as a competition between two or more elite groups for the power to govern the whole society, requiring only a low level of citizen participation. In Macpherson's view, it is a distorted view where democracy is reduced from a humanist aspiration to a market equilibrium system.

In the realm of practice, Crick observes that England is less democratic than the United States of America. But as Robert Putnam in his noted work *Bowling Alone: The Collapse and Revival of American Community* (2000) has pointed out, even in the United States today there is now too little citizenship or positive participation in politics in the republican tradition of the early American Republic. Putnam laments that in thc past two or three decades the Americans have forgotten the art of pursuing in common the objects of common desires which was admired by Alexis de Tocquville (1805-59) in his celebrated work *Democracy in America* (1835-40). The reduction in citizens' activity in the associations of civil society had led to the decline in the quality of American democracy.

Civil Society

Civil society includes a wide range of voluntary associations of citizens which tend to motivate them to participate in civic causes and to solve common problems through collective self-help rather than reliance on state initiative. It serves as a medium of crystallizing and publicizing their opinions and interests which would otherwise go unheard. It draws people into cooperative ventures, breaking down their social isolation and making them aware of their wider social responsibilities. Thus, it serves as the true source of democratization.

In common parlance, good citizenship demands a strong civic sense on the part of citizens. What is civic sense? It implies a sense of responsibility on the part of the citizen for maintaing a clean and well-ordered society where all citizens feel safe and comfortable. A citizen endowed with civic sense would always be prepared to suffer himself instead of causing inconvenience, disturbance or loss to others. He will accord priority to his duties over his rights. However, the wider concept of citizenship embodies a comprehensive system of rights and duties.

Bernard Crick has drawn a distinction between *passive citizenship and active citizenship* which would throw more light on the problem of democratic citizenship. In this sense, passive citizenship may be found in many autocratic systems, *e.g.* some African, South-East and East Asian States or in the Middle East. Under such regime, a citizen would excerise his rights as well as duties under the prevailing laws and practices, but he has no control over the formation or functioning of government. He is simply a law-abiding citizen who cannot express his opinion or articulate his demand against the power-holders.

Autocracy

Autocracy refers to a system of governance where a single person (who may also claim to be acting on behalf of a group or party) would exercise absolute power in an arbitrary manner. There may exist certain laws, conventions and even a constitution but in the absence of any effective mechanism to enforce their provisions, the autocratic ruler would set aside all of them at his will and function as an all-powerful authority. Examples of autocrats include the Czars of Russia before the Russian Revolution (1917), Stalin (1879-1953), Hitler (1889-1945), etc.

On the other hand, active citizenship is to be found only in democratic states. An active citizen would not only exercise his rights and duties under the existing laws but participate in choosing public functionaries and articute his opinions and demands against the prevailing allocation of values. Bernard Crick has particularly focused on the following rights of citizens in this category: "free speech, the election of public officers and the right to combine together to change things, big and small; or to prevent undesired changes".

According to Crick, a passive citizen can be a 'good citizen'; so one can be a good citizen in an autocratic state. One can be a good citizen in a democratic state also, without being an 'active citizen'. He would obey the law, pay taxes, drive carefully and cause minimum offence to others by his behaviour. To become an active citizen, the minimum that he can do is to cast his vote at the time of election. But to be an active citizen in the real sense, he will have to do a lot more. He will feel concerned with the common cause of the people, make others aware of that cause, combine and cooperate with them to serve that cause, raise voice against the neglect of public issues and alert public officials to do their duty. Education for citizenship calls for learning this role of citizens. As Crick has aptly educidated: "For citizenship surely involves public discussion about whether laws work badly, or whether they are unjust and how they can be changed. Young people need an education that helps them become, by both knowledge and experience, politically literate." Active citizenship largely emanates from moral sensibility which, in turn, comes from political understanding.

Bernard Crick's concept of 'active citizenship' holds the key to all essentials of 'democratic citizenship'. In order to bring out the significance of active citizenship in democratic societies (that is the democratic citizenship), he has drawn a parallel between economic theory and political theory. So he observed:

> Just as economics is concerned with price, that in a world of finite resources everything we want is at the cost of something else (or of others), so political theory is concerned with decision-making and persuation: an assertion that, except in times of emergency, societies are best governed politically, not autocratically, that is by public persuasion and publicized compromises among competing values and interests, not by coercion, force or fraud.

CONCLUSION

Democratic citizenship stands for a model of democracy which holds that the maintenance of free institutions depends on a high level of popular participation in public affairs. It may be justified as a practical necessity as well as a moral and civic duty of citizens. It is intended to introduce an element of full-fledged political participation to make up for the deficiencies of the prevalent model of representative democracy. The idea of democratic citizenship, therefore, comes very close to the concept of participatory democracy.

Concept of participatory democracy regards people's political participation as the basic principle of democracy. In short, *political participation denotes the active involvement of individuals and groups in the governmental processes effecting their lives.* In other words, when citizens themselves play an active role in the process of formulation and implementation of public policies and decisions, their activity is called political participation. Conventional mode of political participation includes voting, contesting for public office, campaigning for a political party or contributing to the management of a community project like public safety, cleanliness drive, or the maintenance of a public park, etc. Interestingly, an act of opposition or public protest also involves political participation. For example, signing a petition, attending a peaceful demonstration, joining a protest march, procession or demonstration against a public authority, or forming a human chain, etc. come within the purview of political participation. Indeed, the various acts of public protest in a non-democratic set-up, like passive resistance, civil disobedience and *satyagraha,* also qualify as political participation. They are the manifestation of a strong awareness of public interest.

Passive Resistance

Passive resistance refers to a method of peaceful protest against an unjust law or order. It may involve picketing at a prominent place where the law or order in question is sought to be enforced; ceremonial march; holding public meetings, shouting slogans without causing provocation, distributing posters and literature, etc.

Civil Disobedience

Civil disobedience refers to an open and intentional act of breaking an unjust law and undergoing the prescribed punishment in order to draw public attention to an issue of public importance. It also includes the formal violation of prohibitory orders and courting arrest, etc. for a similar purpose.

Satyagraha

Satyagraha refers to a technique of fighting against injustice. This technique was evolved by Mahatma Gandhi (1869- 1948), Indian social philosopher and political activist. Literally it means insistence on truth. Gandhi defined it as the use of 'soul force' or 'truth force' against various forms of brute force. He sought to use this method particularly in three areas which represented stark embodiment of injustice: (*a*) Racial discrimination in South Africa against Indians and black races; (*b*) British rule in India which had suppressed the freedom and culture of Indians; and (*c*) Ugly social practices then prevailing in Indian society (such as untouchability, communal prejudice and hatred, etc.)

Gandhi showed the way to use 'soul force' against brute force through 'self-suffering' that would secure 'change of heart' of the opponent who would then be forced to depart from the path of injustice. In *Hind Swaraj* (1910), Gandhi defined *Satyagraha* as "a method of securing rights by personal suffering: it is the reverse of resistance by arms. When I refuse to do a thing that is repugnant to my conscience, I use soul force. It involves sacrifice of self".

Present-day champions of participatory democracy argue that representative democracy gives little opportunity to its citizens for any significant participation in the decision-making process. Consequently, under the prevailing system, electorates have so little knowledge and understanding of political problems; voters are so indifferent to voting; political representatives are so averse to public accountability; and corruption and abuse of power are so rampant in the whole administration! If people are properly motivated by the spirit of democratic citizenship, they will be inclined to discuss public issues elaborately, keep a strict watch on the activities of politicians, and they shall be able to prevent the corruption and abuse of power. Hence, citizen participation is not only a necessary condition of good society, but it is an essential part of good society.

[V]
CRITIQUES OF CITIZENSHIP

In the contemporary world, it is being widely argued that the prevalent concept of citizenship does not provide for adequate rights for all parts of society. In this context, two types of critiques are particularly important: (*a*) the feminist critique; and (*b*) the subaltern critique.

THE FEMINIST CRITIQUE

> If a test of civilization be sought, none can be so sure as the condition of the half of society over which the other half has power.
>
> Harriet Martineau (1837)

Feminist critics of citizenship argue that even after getting full citizenship in law, women continue to suffer from subjection in their social life. From 1960s and 1970s, the status of women in society and politics has become a centre of attention. Earlier it was usually thought that after establishing legal equality of men and women, women were not left with any issue of complaint. After extension of the right-to-vote to women, some studies of voting behaviour were produced. It was found that women's participation in voting was lower in comparison to men. To explain this situation, it was argued that women were largely interested in private and domestic affairs; they were less interested in politics and public affairs and probably they had no time to attend to these matters.

However, when the size of family began to shrink and more and more women took up jobs, the above explanation regarding women's sphere of interest was no longer held to be valid. Again, it was noticed that more and more women were taking part in voting, but their share at various levels of political authority had remained insignificant. While the electorates of various countries of the world had nearly fifty per cent women, their share at the level of political representation was far below that of men. However, women's share in legislatures of the world has been steadily increasing in the recent decades. In the Western countries, it has risen from less than ten per cent to an average of thirty per cent. In Scandinavian Countries (Sweden, Norway, Denmark), it ranges between about forty to forty-five per cent.

According to Grant Thornton International Business Report (2011), women currently hold twenty per cent of senior management positions globally, down from twentyfour per cent in 2009, and up just one per cent from 2004. Across the world, Thailand has the greatest percentage of women in senior management (45%), followed by Georgia (40%), Russia (36%), Hong Kong and the Philippines (both 35%). The countries with lowest percentages are India, the United Arab Emirates and Japan where less than ten per cent senior management positions are held by women.

In the sphere of international politics, the representation of women is still meagre. In November 1990, thirty-four Heads of Government of European countries gathered to sign the historic Charter of Paris for the New Europe. The gathering marked the end of the Cold War. In newspaper headlines, it was described as the 'end of an era'. But feminists ask: "Which era had come to an end?" In any case, it was not an end of the patriarchal era. In the group-photo of these thirty-four heads of government, only two women could be spotted after a thorough search. These were: Gro Brundtland, Prime Minister of Norway, and Margaret Thatcher, Prime Minister of Britain. Two days after this Conference, Mrs. Thatcher also resigned, and a man replaced her as Prime Minister. In this situation, what is the consequence of granting full citizenship to women if their representation in public life remains so negligible?

Happily, the situation has now improved on this front. Some outstanding women, all over the world, including the countries of Asia, Africa, Latin America, Europe, New Zealand and Canada, have held the positions of Prime Minister, President or similar category. Some women have been chosen for the prestigious Nobel Prize also. Then, some women have excellent record of performance in various important positions like those in legislatures, cabinets, bureaucracy, diplomacy, journalism, legal profession, fine arts, academics and scientific research, etc. This record is an ample proof of the potential of woman power. But it is no proof of opportunities open to women as their share in these positions continues to be far from satisfactory.

It has now been proved beyond doubt that the biological differences between man and woman do not account for the inferior status of women. The present status of women is chiefly the product of social arrangements. Women often spend most of their time in domestic work and in rearing the children. Most women do not get an opportunity to develop their own personality. They are made to believe that the proper sphere of their activity is within home and that they need not take interest in public life. From the beginning girls are taught to pay more attention to personal relations, not to personal success. Boys are taught to be firm, assertive and aggressive; girls are taught to be obedient, shy and submissive. Boys are encouraged to become doctors, engineers and lawyers; girls are encouraged to become school teachers, nurses or secretaries. In short, the experience gained by women in their own professional life does not help them to take up a political career.

> **Woman is shut up in a kitchen or in a boudoir, and astonishment is expressed that her horizon is limited. Her wings are clipped, and it is found deplorable that she cannot fly.**
>
> **Simone de Beauvoir (1908-86)**

Feminists, therefore, assert that until the condition of equal participation of women in public life is fulfilled, the concept of citizenship cannot be brought to its logical conclusion. In India, a beginning in this direction has been made by making reservation of one-third of the seats in *panchayats* for women. This will encourage women to join politics at grass-root level. By and by their representation at this level can be increased to one-half, and provision can also be made for their adequate representation in legislative assemblies and parliament. The opening up of vast opportunities of higher education would also prove to be instrumental to their larger representation in administration and high-profile professions. In this way, the idea of citizenship can be realized fully from the feminist point of view.

THE SUBALTERN CRITIQUE

The term 'subaltern' literally means someone 'of inferior rank'. In social life superior and inferior ranks are quite common. Their identification would be a simple matter. However, problem would arise when people are supposed to be equal as citizens in the legal-formal sense, but they are treated as superior and inferior in actual practice. Subaltern critique of citizenship deals with such situations.

The concept of 'subaltern' was introduced in social theory by Antonio Gramsci (1891-1937), an Italian Marxist, in his analysis of capitalist system. It was applied to those groups in society who were subject to the 'hegemony' of the ruling classes. Hegemony implied the ability of the ruling classes to create a web of beliefs and institutional as well as social relations which are projected as acceptable to all parts of society. In other words, it refers to the tactics adopted by the ruling class to convince the subject classes that their rule catered to the common interest. The subject classes were made to believe that they were being ruled with their consent.

Under the capitalist system, apparently equal rights were granted to all citizens. But in actual practice, capitalists performed the function of the ruling class. Peasants, workers and other subordinate groups who were denied access to 'hegemonic' power were described by Gramsci as 'subaltern' classes. Similarly, earlier historical stages had their own ruling classes and subaltern classes. Both types of classes played their role in building up human civilization. But history as a discipline focused on the role of the ruling classes, and ignored the role of the subaltern classes. Gramsci observed that this history was one-sided and incomplete. He insisted on an inquiry into the role of the subaltern classes to have an unbiased view of history. In other words, study of history should include the support extended by the subaltern classes to the ruling classes, the contribution made by the subaltern classes independently, and the organizations and movements started by the subaltern classes to oppose the ruling classes.

In contemporary social analysis, the scope of 'subaltern theory' has been considerably expanded. It is now conceded that all the groups who suffer from discrimination on any irrelevant grounds (that is the grounds which disregard their 'human' status) can be treated as subaltern groups. In a way, the treatment meted out to 'subaltern groups' is closely linked with the question of 'human rights'. Thus, any social group that is treated inferior to others on grounds of gender, age, vocation, class, caste, race, region, religion, language, culture, etc. comes within the purview of 'subaltern groups'. The members of these groups may be regarded as full-fledged citizens in the formal sense, but they may be looked down upon by the dominant groups because of some deep-rooted hatred, prejudices or even superstitions. The real causes of their inferior status lie elsewhere. They may have been deprived of opportunities to have education and other sources of enlightenment, to enter into modern professions, to participate in the common cultural heritage, or they may lack the means of their legal protection, of building up their organizations and raising their voice against the prevailing injustice, and so on. Enlightened sections of society must come to their rescue if the idea of citizenship has to be realized in the true sense of the term.

Until lions have their historians, tales of the hunt shall always glorify the hunters.

African Proverb

15

Concept of Human Rights

[I]
NATURE OF HUMAN RIGHTS

Human rights are those rights to which an individual is entitled by virtue of his status as a human being. While civil, political and social-economic rights are dependent on an individual's status as a citizen of a particular state, his human rights are not determined by this condition. Thus the scope of human rights is very wide. They set the standards for the provision and expansion of civil, political and social-economic rights. Again, *where an individual's civil, political and social-economic rights are exhausted, he can still hope to get some relief under the umbrella of human rights.* For instance, a foreigner, a refugee, a prisoner-of-war or a proclaimed offender may have been left without ordinary rights, yet the beneficent hand of human rights will not be withdrawn from over his head.

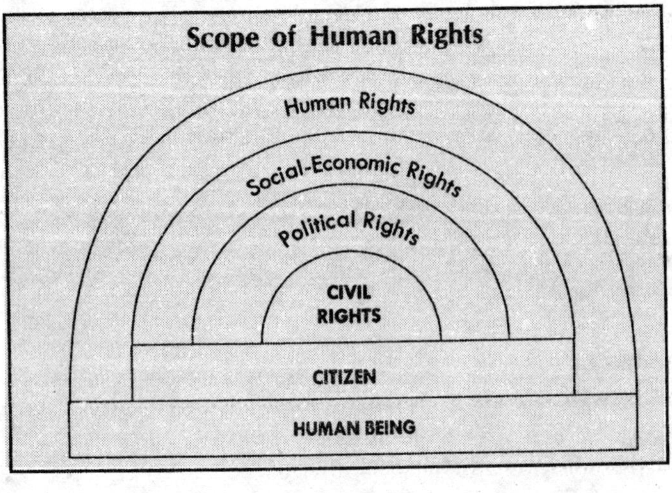

Human rights constitute the very source of all rights of human beings. They embody the scheme of ideal rights. They provide for moral foundation of any system of rights. In a way, they are akin to the concept of justice. As the idea of justice determines the principles on which law should be based, so the idea of human rights sets the standards on which all other rights should be based. Moreover, when ordinary rights are reinterpreted in the light of human rights, they enter the ever-expanding domain of human welfare. For instance, the right to life in this context may be interpreted to include the right to live on uncontaminated land, to breathe in clean air and to consume clean water; and government may be held responsible to satisfy these conditions. Nevertheless, human rights can only be realized as 'rights'. In other words, human rights, like any other rights, have to be enforced by a state or an international tribunal which should be capable of enforcing them. Anybody who claims any human rights must prove himself to be law-abiding and must submit himself to law for appropriate justice. In order to understand the true character of human rights, it would be worthwhile to inquire into the nature of rights as such.

[II]
CONCEPT OF RIGHTS

MEANING OF RIGHTS

The idea of rights provides for an essential tool of analysis of the relations between individual and the state. The state claims authority over individual, but when the state is viewed as an instrument of society, it is essential that authority of the state is made to depend on the function it performs. In other words, when the state is regarded as a means and the individual as the end, the state cannot be armed with absolute authority over individual. If the state claims authority, individual must claim rights. Individual owes allegiance to the state and obeys its commands because the state serves his interests. What does individual claim from the state? An answer to this question will elucidate the concept of rights.

Rights essentially belong to the sphere of conflicting claims between individual and the state. Any political theory which holds that an individual cannot have rights 'against the state' is no theory of rights. It is important to note that *the benefits which flow automatically from the existence of the state do not constitute rights.* Rights come into the picture only when authority of the state is sought to be limited, or when individuals and their groups demand a positive role of the state to secure better conditions of life. Thus, Thomas Hobbes (1588-1679), J.J. Rousseau (1712-78), and G.W.F. Hegel (1770-1831) may have paid rich tributes to the state, in their own ways, for creating congenial conditions for the happiness of men, but they have failed to evolve any concept of rights.

Absence of rights makes the happiness of individuals depend on the chance benevolence of the powers-that-be. If there are no rights of individuals to curb the authority of the government and to prescribe functions of the government, the state assumes unbridled power. It may soon degenerate into absolutism, authoritarianism, despotism and tyranny. Glorification of the state, without an in-built mechanism to curb authority of the state, means complete subordination of individual to the ruler or the ruling groups, thereby opening the floodgates of corruption, oppression, exploitation and injustice.

The concept of rights or 'human rights', therefore, originates from the voice of protest against oppression perpetrated by the dominant groups in society. Rights are meant to safeguard the individual from the irresponsible and arbitrary use of power by the ruling class. As Robert M. MacIver, in his Preface to *Great Expressions of Human Rights* (1951), significantly observed:

> Over most parts of the earth and throughout the major range of recorded history the masses of men have lived in a condition of misery and oppression. Nearly everywhere small dominating groups acquired the techniques of power and used them to keep in subjection their fellowmen... In every age the voice of protest has been heard. In every age the vision of human liberation has been glimpsed.

In modern times, this vision of human liberation has been developed into the concept of human rights. These rights are no longer expressed merely as certain demands. On the other hand, they are sought to be enshrined in the structure of the constitution so as to prevent the government from using its power in an arbitrary and irresponsible manner. As MacIver has further noted: "The cry for human rights now becomes more than exhortation or protest. It becomes the precise demand for the legal and constitutional embodiment of specific claims to liberties, and then to opportunities" (*ibid.*).

In a nutshell, *rights consist in claims of individuals which seek to restrict arbitrary power of the state and which are required to be secured through legal and constitutional mechanisms. In addition, these may include some benefits which the state may extend to its citizens to improve the quality of their life.*

NEGATIVE AND POSITIVE RIGHTS

The concept of rights is a dynamic concept. With the development of social consciousness, rights are subjected to continual review and redefinition. It is interesting to note that rights are always demanded and even granted as the 'rights of man'. But their beneficiaries are usually those classes which articulate this demand, because they formulate the demands of rights in a manner best suited and calculated to serve their own interests. However, with the spread of modern consciousness, the concept of rights has been modified in two important directions. It is now admitted that: (*a*) the advantages of rights should not be confined to a tiny class which is placed in a privileged position by virtue of its money and manipulative power; and that (*b*) rights should not be confined to delimiting the sphere of state activity and authority, but should also prescribe the functions and responsibility of the state so as to make them beneficial to the bulk of society. This trend indicates a shift of focus from *negative* to *positive* rights.

Negative rights suggest the sphere where the state is not permitted to enter. They suggest the sphere of freedom of individual which shall not be encroached by the state. Positive rights, on the other hand, prescribe the responsibility of the state in securing rights of individuals. They require the state to take positive measures for the protection of the weaker and vulnerable sections or those placed in a vulnerable position. In fact, the negative and positive rights should be treated as parts of a *continuum,* not as distinct entities.

Continuum

Continuum refers to a logical device for representing a range of variables which fall between two opposites. It is based on the assumption that though the two opposites are situated on extreme positions like the two ends of a straight line, yet they are directly linked with each other so that they provide easy access from one extreme to the other.

Broadly speaking, negative rights indicate as to which acts of the individual shall not be restricted by the state. Thus, 'freedom of thought and expression' implies that the state shall not impose any restriction on individual's thought and expression. So it comes in the category of negative rights. But if we say that the state shall provide universal education to promote its citizens' faculty of thought and expression, it will be described as their positive right. In short, positive rights indicate the responsibility of the state to improve the life of its citizens and to help them in their self-development. For example, right to medical care, right to work, right to legal aid, etc. also qualify as positive rights. *A capitalist state gives precedence to negative rights while a socialist state gives precedence to positive rights. A welfare state aims at combining negative rights with positive rights as far as feasible.*

[III]
CONVENTIONAL THEORIES OF RIGHTS

Conventional theories of rights seek to identify the basis on which the familiar rights of human beings are founded. Of these the following are particularly important: (*a*) theory of natural rights; (*b*) theory of moral rights; (*c*) theory of legal rights; (*d*) historical theory of rights; and (*e*) social-welfare theory of rights.

THEORY OF NATURAL RIGHTS

Theory of natural rights represents an early expression of the liberal perspective on rights. It was very popular in seventeenth and eighteenth century political thought. It treats the rights of man as a corollary of natural law. In other words, these rights are not granted by the state, but they come from the very nature of man, his own intrinsic being. This theory was broadly developed on two important bases—the contractual basis and the teleological basis.

> **Natural Law**
>
> Natural law refers to a set of rules of good conduct which exist independently of conventional law. These are directly derived from nature which can be discovered through moral intuition and by the application of human faculty of reasoning. Champions of natural law regard it as superior to any other law.

Contractual Basis

In the first place, the theory of natural rights is based on liberal theory of the origin of the state from the 'social contract'. According to this theory, certain rights were enjoyed by man in the 'state of nature', that is before the formation of civil society itself. These comprise the natural rights of man, which must be respected and protected by the state.

Among the exponents of the social contract theory, John Locke (1632-1704) is the most ardent champion of natural rights. Locke gave a new turn to the social contract theory which was introduced by Thomas Hobbes (1588-1679). Hobbes draws a gloomy picture of the state of nature and deprecates natural rights as the freedom of the stronger to oppress the weaker. He, therefore, postulates an unconditional surrender of natural rights when civil society is formed. Jean-Jaques Rousseau (1712-78), another exponent of the social contract theory, depicted natural rights in a different light. Rousseau draws a fascinating picture of the state of nature and glorifies natural rights. Nevertheless, he postulates that these rights become irrelevant in civil society. They are, therefore, surrendered as the price of civil rights. In effect, both Hobbes and Rousseau do not think that natural rights would be maintained by the state.

Locke, however, postulates that man surrendered only some of his natural rights, particularly the right to be the judge of his own acts, on the condition that his fundamental natural rights, *viz.* the rights to 'life, liberty and property' shall be protected by the state. If the state failed to maintain these rights, man had the right to overthrow government and to set up a new government in its place. Thus, it was Locke who tried to demonstrate how natural rights—that is the rights derived from the state of nature—constitute the basis of the principles of governance.

Teleological Basis

Teleology means the doctrine of the final causes. It refers to the view that any developments in human life are the product of the purpose or design that is served by them. The teleological view of rights, therefore, seeks to relate the rights of man with the purpose of human life. These rights do not depend on any institutional arrangements, but ensue from the very nature of man and serve the purpose of his life. These are, therefore, natural rights.

Tom Paine (1737-1809), in his *Rights of Man* (1791), enunciated the theory of natural rights on teleological basis. Paine rejected the doctrine of the social contract as it was 'eternally binding, and hence a clog on the wheel of progress'. He insisted that every generation should be free to think and act for itself. But rights to 'liberty, property, security and resistance of oppression', which are the proud possessions of man in a civil society, derive their sanction from the natural rights 'pre-existing in the individual'.

EVALUATION

The theory of natural rights played an important role in modern history. It served as a source of inspiration for the American and French Revolutions. The American Declaration of Independence (1776) expressed this idea as follows:

> We hold these truths to be self-evident, that all men are created equal, that they are endowed by their Creator with certain inalienable Rights, that among these are Life, Liberty and the pursuit of Happiness. That to secure these rights, Governments are instituted among Men, deriving their just powers from the consent of the governed. That whenever any Form of Government becomes destructive of these ends, it is the Right of the People to alter or to abolish it, and to institute new Government, laying its foundation on such principles and organizing its powers in such form, as to them shall seem most likely to effect their Safety and Happiness.

Similarly, the French Declaration of the Rights of Man and of the Citizen (1789) expressed the idea as under:

> Men are born and remain free and equal in rights. Social distinctions can be based only upon public utility...
>
> The aim of every political association is the preservation of natural and imprescriptible rights of man. These rights are liberty, property, security and resistance to oppression.

However, in spite of the historical significance of natural rights theory, it remains an ambiguous theory. The doctrine of natural rights was put forward at a historical juncture with a view to securing favourable conditions for a 'free market society'. Hence, natural rights were interpreted in such a manner that they could be instrumental to its establishment. It follows that 'natural rights' can be interpreted in order to uphold the values of the particular class which invokes these rights. Natural rights are claimed to be eternal and immutable. But, in actual practice, they are capable of immense variations. Aristotle saw 'slavery' as natural, as he said: "From their hour of birth some men are marked out for subjection, and others for rule." This view is no longer upheld. Some people treat man as 'naturally superior to woman'; others treat them 'equal by nature'. The right to property was for long treated as a 'natural right', but this view was radically modified under the influence of socialist thought. In short, the concept of natural rights is a subjective concept. Their character depends on the views and values of the class which grasps, interprets and articulates them. In any case, natural rights constitute an essential element of logic. Any class which rises against some prevailing injustice, may invoke 'natural rights' to prove as to 'what stands to reason'. Natural rights comprise a dynamic concept; there can be no 'fixed' natural rights. Their interpretation depends on the nature and degree of the prevailing social consciousness.

It is because of these limitations that 'natural rights' are now rarely invoked for building up a rational system of rights in contemporary society. Modern states as well as international organizations and movements widely invoke 'human rights', instead of natural rights, to determine their policy objectives or goals. Human rights are based on recognition of 'human dignity' which cannot be exchanged for any type of substantive benefit. A broad consensus is found in society about the contents of human rights. A series of international declarations and conventions concerning human rights have substantially contributed to the formation of this consensus.

THEORY OF MORAL RIGHTS

Like theory of natural rights, theory of moral rights emanates from the dictates of human Reason. It particularly relies on human being's sense of right and wrong, good and evil, etc. Accordingly, rights should conform to what is right or good (*i.e.* conducive to well-being) for all human beings. Moral rights are based on the accepted morals in society. Collins Cobuild English Language Dictionary defines morals as "principles and values based on what a person or society believes are right, proper or acceptable ways of behaving". The sense of right ensues from human conscience. In spite of some cultural variations regarding the conceptions of right and wrong, good and evil, etc., it may be hoped that ultimately all human beings would think alike on moral questions. Different societies may follow different customs, laws and practices, yet the same moral rights are likely to be recognized in all societies, particularly in all modern societies.

It is important to note that moral standards or norms have to be recognized as superior to custom or law because law itself must be judged by those standards. In other words, they set the end that the law ought to serve. In fact, moral principles provide for the starting point of law. As Morris Ginsberg (*On Justice in Society;* 1965) has significantly observed:

> There is a moral element in all law as soon as the notion emerges that no one ought to be a judge in his own cause and methods are provided for settling disputes by reference to general rules without the use of force by the parties concerned...Moral factors gain in strength in the course of social development and legislation comes more and more to rely on fact-finding inquiries and scrutiny of the ends which the law ought to serve.

Exponents of the theory of moral rights sought to build this theory on teleological basis as done by some exponents of the theory of natural rights. Immanuel Kant (1724-1804), German philosopher, sought to build a bridge connecting the moral realm to the political-legal realm. He argued that Reason is the distinctive feature of man and of human agency. It impels him to treat himself and all other persons as ends, and not as means only. If all persons had a good will, then they would respect all others as ends—indeed as members of a 'kingdom of ends'. But such conditions are not present in nature, hence political community becomes necessary to aid the man to ascend towards Reason. That is how political-legal realm comes into existence which should be responsible to protect moral rights of man.

T.H. Green (1836-82), English philosopher, also sought to build his theory of moral rights on the teleological basis. Green argues that the rights of man do not emanate from a transcendental law as Locke had maintained, but they come from the moral character of man himself. Each individual, impelled by his moral consciousness, tends to seek ideal objects. Since all individuals share the same moral consciousness, their ideal objects are common objects. Thus, when they form a state, all individuals agree to recognize each other's claim to pursue their ideal objects. Green undoubtedly holds that rights depend on recognition, but their recognition is granted by the moral consciousness of the community—which is shared by all individuals—not by the state. In fact, Green is concerned with ideal rights, not with legal rights. Ideal rights derive their sanction from the inherent moral propensity of man, not from the 'force' of the state.

Transcendental Law

Transcedental law refers to the law which cannot be grasped by ordinary people through their practical experience or by anyone through the sense-experience (*i.e.* the experience gained through sight, sound, smell, taste and touch).

EVALUATION

Adherents of moral rights theory believe in the convergence of law and morality. For example, Ronald Dworkin (*Taking Rights Seriously;* 1977) held that in the sphere of rights, separation between law and morality was impossible. He argued that law ought to 'take rights seriously'. Rights trump other considerations such as community welfare. Individual rights are seriously compromised if in a hard case a judge takes decision on personal opinion, intuition, or the exercise of his strong discretion. In that case, rights may simply be subordinated to the interests of the community.

In his another well-known work *Law's Empire* (1986), Dworkin projected his vision of 'law as integrity' which combined the goals of descriptive theory and normative theory. He argued that a judge should not try to give voice to his own moral or political convictions, but as an author in a chain of the common law. Dworkin's account of the judicial function requires the judge to treat the law as if it were a seamless web. There is no law beyond the law which comprehends the principles of morality. Indeed law and morality are inextricably intertwined. Pragmatists who find justification for state coercion in the justice or efficiency or any other virtue, fail to take rights seriously. They treat rights as instruments of some other virtue. They fail to realize the independent existence of rights. For them rights are simply a means by which to make life better.

Drawing a distinction between principles and policies, Dworkin observes that principles describe rights; policies describe goals. But rights are trumps. They have a 'threshold weight' against community goals. They should not be squashed by a competing community goal. Dworkin contends that in difficult cases, where application of rules does not give a clear answer, judges have to rely on certain principles for reaching a decision. These principles are by no means 'extra-legal' criteria as they are used by judges as part of law. Illustrating the nature of principles, Dworkin refers to the observation that 'a man should not benefit from his own wrong'. This principle was invoked by the New York Court to rule that a murderer could not be allowed to benefit from his victim's will.

On the other hand, critics of moral rights theory argue that moral rights, like natural rights, are purely hypothetical and not concrete rights. They argue that the so-called moral rights denote mere expectations of people which cannot be termed as their rights in the real sense of the term. Drawing a distinction between law and morality, Joseph Raz (*The Authority of Law;* 1979) argued that the law is autonomous; we can identify its content without recourse to morality. Then, champions of moral relativism constitute another group opposed to moral rights. They contend that there are no fixed morals for all societies at all times. Hence, moral rights cannot be recognized as universal rights.

Moral Relativism

Moral relativism refers to the view that no moral principle or value system can be treated as universally right or acceptable. It holds that the validity of any moral principle can be established only with reference to a particular social or historical context.

It is true that social consciousness of human beings is constantly evolving.

Hence each generation in each society tends to redefine moral rights. In any case, the concept of moral rights cannot be abandoned because of their changing character. It may be hoped that modern consciousness would everywhere endorse the same set of moral rights as universal rights.

In short, legislative authority is primarily concerned with making 'law according to justice'; hence it is guided by morality. On the other hand, judicial authority is chiefly concerned with dispensing 'justice according to law' where morality takes a back seat. However, enlightened judges frequently invoke the principles of natural justice and social justice within the limitations imposed by the legal provisions; here they are guided by the prevailing moral consciousness of the community.

THEORY OF LEGAL RIGHTS

Theory of legal rights holds that all rights of man depend on the state for their existence. There can be no right in the proper sense of the term unless it is so recognized by the state. According to this theory, no rights are absolute, nor are any rights inherent in the nature of man as such. Rights are relative to the law of the land; hence they vary with time and space. Rights have no substance until they are guaranteed by the state. This implies: (*a*) in the first place, that there are no rights prior to the state, because they come into existence with the state itself; (*b*) secondly, it is the state which declares law and thereby guarantees and enforces rights—no rights can exist beyond the legal framework provided by the state; and (*c*) finally, as the law may change from time to time, the substance of rights also changes therewith—there can be no 'fixed' rights in any society, not to speak of eternal or universal rights.

Hobbes argued that the only fundamental right of the individual, *viz.* the right of 'self-preservation', is better maintained by the state than by the individual himself. Hence, man must depend on the state for the maintenance of his rights. He is free to do anything which is not restrained by the state. In other words, man can have no rights against the state.

Jeremy Bentham (1748-1832) is the greatest champion of the theory of legal rights. He rejects the doctrine of natural rights as unreal and ill-founded. In his *Principles of Legislation* (1789), Bentham observed:

> *Rights,* properly so called, are the creatures of *law* properly so called; real laws give birth to real rights. *Natural rights* are the creatures of natural law; they are a metaphor which derives its origin from another metaphor... What there is natural in man is means—faculties. But to call these means, these faculties, *natural rights* is again to put language in opposition to itself. For *rights* are established to insure the exercise of means and faculties. The right is the *guarantee;* the faculty is the thing guaranteed. How can we understand each other with a language which confounds under the same term things so different?

Bentham condemns natural rights as an invention of fanatics, which are dogmatic and unintelligible, devoid of reasoning. About their upholders, Bentham remarks: "Instead of examining laws by their effects, instead of judging them as good or as bad, they consider them in relation to these pretended natural rights; that is to say, they substitute for reasoning of experience the chimeras of their own imaginations."

(Chimera = an unrealistic idea or false imagination, exemplified by a mythological monster with the head of a lion, the body of a goat, and the tail of a serpent.)

It is thus evident that the theory of legal rights was advanced with a focus on political reality and to repudiate the imaginative character of natural rights theory.

EVALUATION

Harold J. Laski, in *his A Grammar of Politics* (1938), criticized the theory of legal rights as follows:

> So purely legalistic a view has nothing to contribute to an adequate political philosophy. A legal theory of rights will tell us what in fact the character of a State is; it will not tell us, save by the judgement we express upon some particular State, whether the rights there recognized are the rights which need recognition.

In other words, the theory of legal rights takes account of the factual position only; it takes note of what rights are legally recognized and guaranteed in a particular state. Political philosophy would like to inquire as to what rights must be recognized by the state according to the community's conception of justice. Political theory is interested in ascertaining what rights of men are essential for the fulfilment of the social purpose or human personality. How can we judge the character of a state unless we are able to evolve a conception of ideal rights which should be maintained by every state worth the name?

Ernest Barker, in his *Principles of Social and Political Theory* (1951), has beautifully described this dilemma about the nature of rights. He observes:

> Ideally a right will always be derived simultaneously from two sources, and will possess double quality: (1) the source of individual personality, and the quality of being a condition of its development; (2) the source of the State and its law, and the quality of being secured and guaranteed by the action of that law.

In actual practice, we may find a sort of right which is derived only from one of these sources, and therefore, possesses only one quality. Such a right does not qualify for being regarded as a full right. Barker prefers to call it a 'quasi-right'. Thus, he illustrates:

> We may have a quasi-right which has only the source of individual personality and the quality of being a condition of its development, such as the right of a slave to personal liberty in a slave-owning State; and equally, and conversely, we may have a quasi-right which has only the source of the State and its law and the quality of being secured and guaranteed by the action of that law, such as the right of a slave-owner in a slave-owning State to the enjoyment of property in persons.

Such a situation demonstrates the difference between the ideal and the actual position. The gulf between legal and ideal rights can be bridged by fixing responsibility of the state in securing ideal rights. Once ideal rights are conceived by the community through its moral consciousness, steps must be taken to secure legal sanction for those rights, otherwise such rights are bound to remain but in an empty form.

HISTORICAL THEORY OF RIGHTS

Historical theory of rights holds that rights are the product of a long historical process. They differ from state to state and from time to time because of the different levels of historical development of society. Rights grow out of custom which stabilized through usage in several generations.

This theory originated in eighteenth-century conservative political thought. Its upholders defended evolutionary change and deprecated revolution. At best, they supported a revolution inspired by the established order of society. Edmund Burke (1729-97), the greatest champion of historical theory of rights, criticized the French Revolution (1789), for it was provoked by a conception of abstract rights of man—liberty, equality, fraternity. On the contrary, he glorified the English Revolution (1688), which sought to reassert the customary rights that Englishmen had enjoyed from very early days and which had found expression in such documents as the Magna Carta (1215), the Petition of Right (1628), etc. The advocates of historical theory of rights eulogize the constitutional history of England as the story of the evolution of rights through a long historical process.

Conservatism

Conservatism refers to a political outlook that promotes respect for the long-standing social practices, and insists on maintaining those institutions which have stood the test of time. When change is inevitable or it has already taken place, conservatives will attempt to moderate it with a view to ensuring minimum disturbance in the existing order. David Hume (1711-76), a Scottish philosopher and Edmund Burke (1729-97), an Irish statesman, are regarded the chief exponents of conservatism.

EVALUATION

Historical theory of rights is important because it suggests that the state cannot create rights at its own will, nor is it required to follow abstract and subjective conceptions of natural rights. The state has only to recognize those rights of men which have already come into vogue through long-standing usage and custom.

But the difficulty with this theory is that it does not provide for any criterion to ensure that rights are based on a sense of justice. Many customs, evolved through a long historical process, involve injustice and the oppression of some vulnerable sections of society. If custom is to serve as the guiding star for the recognition of rights, the state and its law can hardly be made to serve as an instrument of social change. Slavery, infanticide and polygamy are established in many societies by custom. The customs *of sati, devadasi,* and untouchability are the familiar examples from recent and current Indian history which show how injustice could be perpetuated through the oppressive custom in which certain sections have vested interests! The state must ban such customs in order to ensure that rights become vehicles of justice, not of tyranny.

Custom of *Sati*

The practice of *Sati* refers to an outdated custom of orthodox Hindu society under which a widow was required to be burnt alive on the funeral pyre of her dead husband as a proof of her life-long chastity.

Custom of *Devadasi*

The practice of *Devadasi* refers to an outdated custom of some sections of orthodox Hindu society under which a young maiden was dedicated to a deity and she was not allowed to marry throughout her life. In practice, after gaining maturity she was forced to live as a dancer, entertainer and a sex-slave of the priest and the distinguished visitors of the temple.

Untouchability

Untouchability refers to a widespread practice of orthodox Hindu society under which certain outcaste Hindus were treated as untouchable by the caste Hindus; their touch was believed to pollute the caste Hindus; they were refused entry into temples, and were not allowed to use common wells, ponds, inns and other common services.

SOCIAL-WELFARE THEORY OF RIGHTS

Social-welfare theory of rights marks a departure from the conventional theories of rights. It seeks to set the standards on which rights should be founded although they would become operative only when translated into legal provisions.

This theory postulates that rights are, in essence, conditions of social welfare. The state should set aside all other considerations and recognize only such rights as are designed to promote social welfare. For example, the Utilitarian school of the nineteenth century, led by Bentham, had postulated the 'greatest happiness of the greatest number' as the sole criterion of legislation and recognition of rights. Among the contemporary advocates of social-welfare theory, Roscoe Pound (1870-1964) and Zechariah Chafee (1885-1957) are the most outstanding. Pound argues that interpretation of law should follow its defined social purpose. Chafee holds that law, custom, natural rights, etc. should all yield to what is socially useful or socially expedient. Rights should be determined by the 'balance of interests' under the prevailing social conditions.

Social-welfare theory seems to be quite reasonable because no theory of rights can be held valid until it serves the cause of social welfare. This theory eliminates the subjective, ambiguous, dogmatic and static criteria. But, again, this theory presents practical difficulties. The question is—who will define social welfare or social expediency? Usually it is an *elite*—a group of the chosen few who dominate in all spheres of social life, assume the power to interpret the requirements of social welfare. It will be recalled that Bentham's formula of the 'greatest happiness of the greatest number' was in effect invoked to create the rights suited to a 'free market society' which resulted in the oppression of the working class. The liberal theory of securing the 'balance of interests' is also invoked to uphold the capitalist system in spite of its oppressive mechanism. At best, social-welfare theory of rights is a relative theory, and its merit is dependent on the condition that it serves the cause of social justice so that the oppressed sections themselves hold the power and get the opportunity to define social welfare for determining the scheme of rights in a given society.

Social Justice

Social justice refers to a social policy which seeks to prevent concentration of valuable resources of the community (wealth, prestige and power) in the hands of the chosen few, and to create a social order which will enable the deprived and underprivileged sections to gain a respectable share thereof by virtue of their ability, effort and need.

Social-welfare theory of rights found a reasoned and elaborate expression in social-democratic perspective on rights.

[IV] SOCIAL-DEMOCRATIC PERSPECTIVE

Social-democratic perspective on rights seeks to achieve the objectives of individual liberty and social justice together. It is best represented by Laski's theory of Rights.

LASKI'S THEORY OF RIGHTS

Harold J. Laski (1893-1950) made an important observation on the significance of rights: "Every State is known by the rights that it maintains. Our method of judging its character lies, above all, in the contribution that it makes to the substance of man's happiness" (*A Grammar of Politics;* 1938). This was his favourable subject on which he reflected in a number of his works. Taking a creative view of politics, Laski has thoroughly investigated the moral foundations of rights which postulate a synthesis of liberal and socialist values within a democratic structure. In the event, he has evolved a theory of the 'service state' and produced a rather elaborate blue-print of a just society. Laski has reverted to the problem of rights in a number of his works, such as *Liberty in the Modern State* (1930/1949), *Democracy in Crisis* (1933), *The State in Theory and Practice* (1935), *Reflections on the Revolution of Our Time* (1943), *The Dilemma of Our Times* (1952), etc. Yet a comprehensive and systematic formulation of his theory of rights is found in his leading work *A Grammar of Politics* (1925/1938).

Synthesis of Liberal and Socialist Values

As a liberal thinker, Laski is a votary of liberty. In fact, it is his love of liberty which inspires him to take up the cause of social and economic equality, and he turns out to be an ardent champion of social justice. In this process, he attacks the foundations of the capitalist system, but rejects the Soviet-type socialist system for its suppression of liberty. He is convinced that the democratic structure can be effectively used to secure a synthesis of liberal and socialist values.

In his *The Dilemma of Our Times* (1952), Laski strongly argued that liberty, which is the essence of rights, is neither perfectly secure in a capitalist democracy like America, nor in a socialist dictatorship like Russia. It is the rigidness of the two systems which is responsible for crushing one or the other vital aspect of individual liberty. In his earlier work *Liberty in the Modern State* (1930/1949), Laski pointed out that the enthusiasts of Moscow and of Washington differ only in the object of their worship. In Russia, the suppression of liberty takes the form of resistance to the admission of incorrect 'bourgeois' notions; in America, liberty is suppressed in the name of inhibition of licence. The threat to liberty always comes from those privileged sections who are opposed to equalization of privileges. As Laski wrote: "A scrutiny of history... makes it plain that the right to liberty will always be challenged where its consequence is the equalization of some privilege which is not generally shared by men" (*Liberty in the Modern State;* 1930/1949). In his *Reflections on the Revolution of Our Time* (1943), Laski demonstrated that the liberal state, which claimed to safeguard liberty, in effect proved to be inadequate because of its denial of social equality. Thus, he observed:

> The liberal state, though it represented a definite gain in social freedom upon any previous social order, was in fact no more than the exchange of one privileged class for another. And its refusal to link political liberty with social equality had grave consequences. It brought into the control of authority a race of men... (who) equated effective economic demand with right. They argued that for the weaker to go to the wall was a law of nature to which we were disobedient at our peril.

In his *Grammar of Politics* (1938), Laski strongly attacked the inequalities prevailing in the modern state. As he asserted:

> The State...does not distribute equally the means—especially knowledge and economic power—to influence the policy that is adopted... The wealth of the community increases, but it does not in a critical way relieve their wants. Our knowledge increases by leaps and bounds; but those who have genuine access to the intellectual heritage of the race are still but a fragment of the people... The rule of the rich, whether of landed men or of those who owned industrial capital, has been devoted firstly to the accumulation of wealth, and secondly to preventing its diffusion.

In a subsequent paragraph, he declares this degree of social inequality to be intolerable:

> The contrast in the modern world between men and women who have never known a decent house, a decent meal, and clothing that barely protects them against the elements, and those who have never known what it is to have unsatiated a want that the possession of property can supply is an intolerable one.

Laski, therefore, pleads for establishing a 'service-state'—where industrial production is undertaken in order to meet the social needs, not for private profit. He is inclined to suggest a socialist solution:

> Either the State must control industrial power in the interest of its citizens, or industrial power will control the State in the interests of its possessors. The first need of the masses is to realize the right to adequate payment for their effort. The first principle, therefore, of industrial organization is a system of institutions directed to that end.

Moral Foundations of Rights

Laski, like T.H. Green (1836-82), erects his theory of rights on moral foundations. However, he is seriously concerned with the satisfaction of material needs of the masses. Laski is much ahead of Green in dealing with the maladies of the capitalist system. Thus, Laski holds that rights are not concessions granted by the state. On the contrary, they are superior to the state, because they provide for a standard to judge the state itself. He, therefore, proclaims:

> Rights, in fact, are those conditions of social life without which no man can seek, in general, to be himself at his best. For since the State exists to make possible that achievement, it is only by maintaining rights that its end may be secured. Rights, therefore, are prior to the State in the sense that, recognized or not, they are that from which its validity derives (*A Grammar of Politics;* 1938).

Laski's view marks a departure from some prevalent notions of rights. Rights are not historical in the sense that they have at some time won their recognition. But they are historical in the sense that they are demanded by a society at a certain level of its development. Rights are not natural in the sense that they can be compiled into a permanent and unchanging catalogue. But they are natural in the sense that they must demand their recognition according to the level of development of society. The contents of rights change with time and place.

The moral basis of rights postulates equal treatment of all citizens in the matter of securing their rights. As Laski suggests: "In any State the demands of each citizen for the fulfilment of his best self must be taken as of equal worth; and the utility of a right is therefore its value to all the members of the State" *(ibid.)*. Laski's insistence on equality is evident throughout his works. In his *State in Theory and Practice* (1935), Laski argues:

> The State... must postulate the equal claim of its citizens to the benefits which accrue from its exercise of power ...No small part of the history of political philosophy is occupied by elaborate attempts to prove that particular groups of men are unfit for the privileges of citizenship... Aristotle's defence of slavery, Locke's defence of the exclusion of Roman Catholics, Hitler's defence of the exclusion of the Jews, from citizenship, are all attempts to erect private possessions into universal principles of reason. None of them stands examination by a thinker who does not accept the particular emotional prejudice upon which they are based.

In his defence of equality, Laski tends to accommodate his liberal-individualist position with the requirements of public welfare. In his *Grammar of Politics* (1938), Laski admits the differentiation of rights, according to functions, provided that the elementary needs of each individual have been satisfied. As he observes:

> We build rights upon individual personality because, ultimately, the welfare of the community is built upon the happiness of the individual. I cannot have rights against the public welfare, for that, ultimately, is to give me rights against a welfare which is intimately and inseparably associated with my own.

Here, Laski, like T.H. Green and Robert M. MacIver, draws a distinction between the state and the community. One may have rights against the state, but not against the community which represents the common good. Moral authority of the state, as its claim to allegiance, is based on its devotion to the common good and its recognition of the claims of personality. In Laski's own words:

> Any social order which fails consistently to recognize the claims of personality is built upon a foundation of sand. Sooner or later it will provoke the dissent of those whose nature is frustrated by its policy. Its disasters will become their opportunity. For to deny the claims of right is to sacrifice the claim to allegiance. The State can exercise moral authority upon no other *basis* (*ibid.*).

Accordingly, rights, in Laski's view, are not the creature of law but the ideal objects of law itself. Thus, he maintains:

> A State... exists, it exerts authority, it claims allegiance, in order that those citizens may realize in their lives the best of which they are capable. To that end they have rights... Obviously, therefore, rights are not the creatures of law, but its condition precedent. They are that which law is seeking to realize. Institutions are, then, bad or good in proportion as they fail or succeed in the promotion of the purpose of rights (*ibid.*).

Rights and Duties

When rights are erected on moral foundations, they are essentially accompanied by duties. Laski carefully points to their correlation. As he argues:

> The possession of rights... does not mean the possession of claims that are empty of all duties... Our rights are not independent of society, but inherent in it... To provide for me the conditions which enable me to be my best self is to oblige me, at the same time, to seek to be my best self. To protect me against attack from others is to imply that I myself will desist from attacking others (*A Grammar of Politics;* 1938).

Rights are, therefore, correlative with duties or 'functions'. Man is entitled to rights to enable him to make his contribution to the social good. Function is implicit in right.

The concept of rights postulates that the state as well as the individual shall pursue the ideal objects of society. Accordingly, the duty of the individual is co-extensive with the duty of the state. If the state fails in its duty, it is the duty of the individual to resist the state. As Laski elucidates:

> My duty ... to the State is, above all, my duty to the ideal the actual State must seek to serve. There are, then, circumstances in which resistance to the State becomes an obligation if claims to right are to be given validity (*ibid.*).

Moreover, as the rights of man are subservient to the common good, it is his duty to contribute to the common good in exercise of his rights. Laski therefore urges: "Men must learn to subordinate their self-interest to the common welfare. The privileges of some must give way before the rights of all." Provision of rights and duties in this sense is not compatible with the division of society into privileged and underprivileged sections.

Social and Economic Rights

As a liberal thinker with strong socialist leanings, Laski is not satisfied with the provision of political liberty alone. In fact, Laski has produced an elaborate blueprint of a just society with a scheme of social, economic as well as political rights. He insists on the citizen's right to work as an essential means to earn his livelihood. As he points out: "The citizen has a right to work... To leave him without access to the means of existence is to deprive him of that which makes possible the realization of personality" *(ibid.)*. On the same principle, Laski demands provision of insurance against unemployment, although he is against parasitism. Laski also pleads for humane conditions of work and fair wages under the present industrial system of production. Besides, the workers should have a share and voice in industrial management in order to save them from the tyranny of capitalism. As Laski points out:

> Any theory of rights in the modern State... must realize that the institution of private property... leaves the control of the industrial machine to the owners of capital, and that individual freedom, as when the single handicraftsman worked for the master, is no longer possible. Obviously, in such a background, we must prevent that ownership of capital from degenerating into dictatorship (*ibid.*).

Then Laski advocates the citizen's right to such education as will fit him for the tasks of citizenship. Coming to political rights, he insists on the citizen's right to political power, with three derivative rights: right to franchise, right to be chosen as governor and right to be chosen for political office. Laski, as a true liberal, is an ardent champion of freedom of speech and expression, which should be extended to all the citizens. This implies the freedom of criticism of the government which is the cornerstone of democracy. As Laski argues: "A government can always learn more from the criticism of its opponents than from the eulogy of its supporters. To stifle that criticism is—at least ultimately—to prepare its own destruction" (*ibid.*).

As a positive liberal and being extremely conscious of the tyranny of the capitalist system, Laski has radical views on the right to property. Like all rights, it must be related to the function performed. As Laski suggests:

> If property must be possessed in order that a man may be his best self, the existence of such a right is clear. But it is also obvious that such a right is immediately susceptible to stringent limitations. Rights... are the correlative of functions. I have the right to property if what I own is,

broadly speaking, important for the service I perform (*ibid.*).

Right to property must be subordinated to the maintenance of common welfare. This right loses its moral justification the moment it becomes an instrument of power over others:

> I can never justly own if the result of my ownership is a power over the life of others. For if the personality of other men is directly subject to changes of my will, if their rights as citizens, in other words, become the creatures of this single right of mine, obviously they will soon cease to have any personality at all. No man, in such a background, has the right to own property beyond that extent which enables the decent satisfaction of impulse (*ibid.*).

In short, Laski's theory of rights seeks to evolve a synthesis of individual rights with common welfare.

CONCLUSION

Laski's theory of rights takes three essential aspects into consideration: interests of the individual; interests of the various groups through which his personality finds channels of expression; and interest of the community which is manifested in the outcome of the combined pressure of social forces. The individuals, or for that matter social groups cannot be left to define their own rights in a conflicting manner. It is the instrumentality of the state which resolves their conflict and regulates the behaviour of individuals and groups by common rules. So Laski concludes:

> We must live by common rules. We must build an organ which enforces and interprets those common rules. We must so build it that both group and individual are safeguarded in their freedom and their equality so far as institutions can provide a safeguard... There will always be either powerful individuals or powerful groups who make their way against other less apt to assertiveness. Our effort must be a search for the compromise which allows to the largest possible number a life that is worthy of our resources (*ibid.*).

Thus, Laski attempts the fusion of the liberal-individualist, liberal-pluralist and liberal-socialist theories. He tries to fit liberty and equality in a common scheme. His scheme is most fascinating. In any case, he comes to believe that the present liberal-capitalist system can somchow be remodeled so as to secure the ends of social justice. He presents elaborate plans for the decentralization and democratization of power—economic as well as political power. But the question is—who will tame the manipulators of power? Will they just be prepared to relinquish their privileged position on the fascinating prescriptions of an expert political scientist? How can a substantive social change be effected without strong pressure from the oppressed classes themselves? Laski's scheme needs to pass the test of political reality.

In any case, Laski has given valuable hints for the reorganization of society according to the principles of social justice. His ideas constitute important tenets of 'modem consciousness'. His views are thought-provoking and a source of inspiration for intellectuals. They can take up the cause of the oppressed and vulnerable sections with a view to working for the establishment of a just society.

Conventional Theories of Rights: Comparative Study

Basic Tenets	*Natural Rights Theory*	*Moral Rights Theory*	*Legal Rights Theory*	*Historical Rights Theory*
Based on the Primacy of	Natural Rights	Moral Rights	Legal Rights	Historical Rights
Sources of Rights	Natural law, *i.e.* the rules of good conduct, as discovered through Reason	Human beings' sense of right and wrong, good and evil, conventionally accepted by society	Positive law, *i.e.* the law duly enacted by the state, expressing its will	The product of historical process, recognized by society from time to time, stabilized through custom
Grounds of Justification	Rights ensue from the dictates of human Reason; validity of any rights can be accepted only when they conform to natural rights	Real rights can only be built on moral foundations; validity of law depends on its moral justification	No rights will be operative anywhere until they are sanctioned by law; natural or moral rights are abstract rights, not valid in practice	Conceptions of Rights change with the historical development; there can be no fixed rights for all times
Chief Exponents	John Locke (1632-1704); Tom Paine (1737-1809)	Immanuel Kant (1724-1804); T.H. Green (1836-82)	Jeremy Bentham (1748-1832)	Edmund Burke (1729-97)
Points of Criticism	Thinkers at different ages differ on what is natural; natural rights are abstract rights which cannot be operative unless sanctioned by law	Moral rights are only speculative; adherents of moral relativism argue that there are no fixed morals for all societies for all times.	Legal rights are only operative rights; political philosophy seeks to determine the principles on which rights should be based	Many customs and social practices involve social injustice and oppression; historical rights do not provide the standards on which rights should be founded

[V]
MARXIST PERSPECTIVE

Strictly speaking, there is no Marxist theory of rights. Exponents of Marxism have occasionally analysed the *principles of freedom, equality and justice* as the basis of social organization, not with reference to their implications as the 'rights of man'. In practice, however, socialist states have evolved elaborate schemes of rights which can be discussed in the context of the Marxist theory of rights.

CONCEPT OF RIGHTS

It will be recalled that the cause of the 'rights of man' was initially taken up by the exponents of the liberal-individualist theory in seventeenth and eighteenth century Europe. Marxist theory arose in the mid-nineteenth century when liberal-individualist rights had largely been established, but these mainly served as the foundation of the capitalist system. Marx (1818-83) and Engels (1820-95) realized that the so-called 'rights of man' had nothing to offer to man as such. These rights were designed to serve the interests of a particular class—the bourgeoisie, the capitalist class, the owners of the means of social production. These rights were secured by law, but law was nothing but a part of the superstructure raised on the foundation of the material conditions of life—the mode of production, determined by the prevalent property-relations in society. The state and its law could not escape the thrust of its class character. In other words, howsoever rich tributes may be paid to the dignity or rights of man under the liberal-capitalist system, the rights secured by it are bound to support a system of exploitation—exploitation of the common man, the worker, by the captains of business and industry. The liberal-individualist rights, ranging from the freedom of trade, freedom of contract, freedom of thought and expression to the 'right to vote', had, therefore, no substantive advantage for the common man so long as society was divided into antagonistic classes—dominant and dependent, oppressor and oppressed, exploiter and exploited classes.

Marxist theory even repudiates the liberal-individualist concept of man—an atomized and alienated individual, motivated by enlightened self-interest, a possessive individual, seeking to attain a special status and privileged position in society. This image of man perfectly fitted into the scheme of a 'free market society' which sought to glorify the 'exploits' of man. It was inclined to identify social interest with the sum total of the interests of different individuals and, in the event, established the hegemony of a handful of 'enterprising' individuals— rich in money and manipulative power. The liberal-individualist theory reduced the 'rational man' into an expert in the calculation of self-interest, and its pursuance at the expense of others.

On the other hand, Marxist theory sought to secure the freedom of man from these conditions of injustice and exploitation. It insisted on the sociable nature of man. In its view, man by nature tends to seek his fulfilment through a 'rational' social organization. A normal man does not aspire to 'distinguish' himself from society to attain a superior position, but to contribute to the good of society in a free and cooperative effort. This view of man is not conducive to any theory of rights of man apart from the rights of society itself.

RIGHTS UNDER THE CAPITALIST SYSTEM

Rights under the capitalist system are the product of the demand of equality raised by the new middle class—the bourgeoisie, the merchant-industrialist class—in the seventeenth century. This class invoked the principle of equality against the feudal system which blocked the development of productive forces of the emerging capitalist system. The exponents of the liberal theory saw the justification of the struggle for human rights in the social equality of all men. The demand for liberty, equality and fraternity became the watchword of the French Revolution (1789) in late eighteenth century.

But when this new middle class—the bourgeoisie—came to power, it refused to extend the principle of equality in substantive terms to the working class—the proletariat. As Engles, in his *Anti-Dühring* (1878), observed:

> This equality reduced itself to bourgeois equality before the law;...bourgeois property was proclaimed as one of the essential rights of man; and...the government of reason...came into being...as a democratic bourgeois republic. The great thinkers of the eighteenth century could, no more than their predecessors, go beyond the limits imposed upon them by their epoch.

In other words, the bourgeoisie sought to dilute the revolutionary content of the demand for social equality by preserving private property in the means of production, and thereby legalizing an exploitative system of social relationships.

Marx and Engels, however, appreciated the advantage of civil liberties and representative institutions evolved by the bourgeois democracy which enabled the working class to organize itself, to propagate its ideas and to learn the art of government. They, however, insisted on bringing the principles of freedom and equality to their logical conclusion, in replacing the capitalist system by the socialist system and ultimately bringing about a classless society.

RIGHTS UNDER THE SOCIALIST SYSTEM

According to Marxist theory, the socialist system—which is established by the proletariat after overthrowing the capitalists in a violent revolution and socialization of the major means of production—is much more conducive to establishing equality as a principle of social organization. But the socialist system itself is a transitional stage. Perfect equality and justice are possible only under communist society which is characterized by the abolition of classes and the 'withering away' of the state. The governing principle of communist society will be: 'from each according to his ability, to each according to his need'. But this is not practicable under the socialist system which is still stamped with birthmarks of the old society from whose womb it comes. Its governing principle, therefore, is not perfect equality, but a workable form of equality: 'from each according to his ability, to each according to his work'.

Now this principle is akin to that prevailing in the capitalist system, but different in some important respects. V.I. Lenin (1870-1924), in his *State and Revolution* (1917), admits that this principle embodies a 'bourgeois right' which implies inequality. Yet it marks an advance over the capitalist system:

> The first phase of communism... cannot yet provide justice and equality; differences, and unjust differences, in wealth will still persist, but the *exploitation* of man by man will have become impossible because it will be impossible to seize *the means of production*—the factories, machines, land, etc.—and make them private property... Marx shows the *course of development* of communist society, which is *compelled* to abolish at first *only* the 'injustice' of the means of production seized by individuals, and which is *unable* at once to eliminate the other injustice, which consists in the distribution of consumer goods 'according to the amount of labour performed' (and not according to needs).

Lenin, on the authority of Marx, calls it a defect of the socialist system, but treats it as inevitable because rights can never be higher than the economic structure of society and its cultural development conditioned thereby:

> And so, in the first phase of communist society (usually called socialism) 'bourgeois right' is *not* abolished in its entirety, but only in part, only in proportion to the economic revolution so far attained, *i.e.* only in respect of the means of production. 'Bourgeois right' recognizes them as the private property of individuals. Socialism converts them into *common* property. *To that extent*—and to that extent alone—'bourgeois right' disappears (*ibid.*).

It is significant that the socialist system, established in the USSR since 1917 under the stewardship of Lenin himself, had taken care to secure the social and economic rights of the citizens in the real sense, not in the formal sense. Their constitution of 1977 had substantially enlarged these rights. The citizens of the erstwhile USSR were guaranteed not only equality before the law, but also equal rights in all spheres of economic, political, social, and cultural life. Above all, they were entitled to the right to work, *i.e.* guaranteed employment and pay in accordance with the quantity and quality of their work, not below the state-established minimum, including the right to choose their trade or profession. They also had the right to rest and leisure, the right to health protection, and social security—including the right to maintenance in old age, in sickness, and in the event of complete or partial disability or loss of the breadwinner. Then they had the right to housing, right to education, right to enjoy cultural freedoms—freedom of scientific, technical and artistic work 'in accordance with the aims of building communism'. Theoretically, they were also entitled to freedom of speech, of the press, and of assembly, meetings, street processions and demonstrations, in accordance with the interests of the people and 'in order to strengthen and develop the socialist system'. They had the right to associate in public organizations that would promote their political activity and initiative, etc. 'in accordance with the aims of building communism'. They also had the right to profess or not to profess any religion, and to conduct religious worship, etc. In actual practice, however, no liberal-democratic rights were allowed to be exercised during the ascendancy of socialism.

The Soviet system was severely criticized for its suppression of freedom of opinion and protest. Western countries branded it a country behind the 'Iron Curtain'. The new rights granted to the citizens, especially the freedom of speech, assembly, association and demonstration, etc. were apparently conditional—as governed by the 'aim of building up communism'. The prerogative to judge whether a particular activity conformed to this aim or not, rested with the state especially the authorities of the Communist Party. It is only after the collapse of communism in the former Soviet Union (1991) that the liberal-democratic rights of citizens have been restored. Unfortunately, however, these changes were also accompanied by a sharp decline of social and economic rights.

The combination of liberal and socialist rights is a difficult task. Laski has tried to evolve a theoretical framework for such a combination. We, in India, have been trying to secure such a combination in practice. Many modern thinkers— Barker, MacIver and Macpherson—have been working on this theory. The elimination of injustice and exploitation in economic life without suppressing the liberal freedoms of people is a challenging task in the present-day world—for the political scientist as well as for the statesman.

[VI]

GENESIS OF HUMAN RIGHTS

The idea of human rights comprehends the whole range of rights of human beings. What is the source of this idea? Historical accounts or legal documents or anthropological data could be consulted to find out as to how different types of rights of human beings have been evolved over time. But these would hardly enlighten us about the real basis of human rights as such. In fact this idea emanates from the human concern with good and evil, right and wrong, etc. Among the conventional theories of rights, the idea of human rights comes close to the theory of moral rights because this theory is based on the principle of human dignity. In any case the conventional theory of moral rights could only be treated as an elementary approach. It will have to be developed fully in order to understand the precise basis of human rights.

The problem of human rights emerged as a matter of serious concern for the whole world after the Second World War (1939-45). During Nuremberg Trials (1946), some German Nazis were tried for 'crimes against humanity' apart from war crimes. The most barbarous and inhuman atrocities committed by the accused on the Jews of their country were termed 'crimes against humanity'. This action was based on the assumption that 'human rights' are valid by themselves; these are above the law of any nation; violation of these rights would be treated as 'crime against humanity'.

In 1948, the United Nations issued an elaborate list of human rights, known as 'Universal Declaration of Human Rights'. It advised its member-nations to give a wide publicity to these rights in their respective countries, particularly in schools and other educational institutions. This declaration is best suited to building up a free, democratic, welfare state. It embodies an excellent scheme of human rights.

[VII]
UNIVERSAL DECLARATION OF HUMAN RIGHTS

This declaration contains 30 articles, apart from its Preamble. Its Preamble states that the recognition of the inherent dignity and equality of all human beings and their inalienable rights is the foundation of freedom, justice and peace in the world. Disregard and contempt for human rights have resulted in barbarous acts which have outraged the conscience of mankind. The advent of a world in which human beings shall enjoy freedom of speech and belief in freedom from fear and want is the highest aspiration of the common people. If man is not to be compelled to have recourse, as a last resort, to rebellion against tyranny and oppression, it is essential that human rights should be protected by the rule of law.

Rule of Law

Rule of law refers to the principle which requires that the law of the land should be properly notified so that the citizens know as to how it will affect them; any action against an individual should be taken only under that law, and not on any other basis. Hence no one should be arbitrarily arrested, nor punished without a fair trial.

In order to promote the development of friendly relations between nations, the United Nations Charter (1945) reaffirmed the faith of its members in fundamental human rights, in the dignity and worth of the human person and in the equal rights of men and women. It was determined to promote social progress and universal respect for observance of human rights and fundamental freedoms.

At the outset, this declaration gives prominence to civil and political rights of human beings and legal protection thereof. Then it pays due importance to their social-economic rights. Finally, in order to strengthen the foundation of these rights, it highlights individual's duties towards the community.

Articles 1 and 2 focus on rational nature of all human beings and reaffirm faith in their dignity, freedom, equality and fraternity. They rule out any discrimination between them on grounds of race, colour, sex, language, religion, political or other opinion, national or social origin, property, birth or other type of status.

Articles 3 and 4 provide for everyone's right to life, liberty and security of person; prohibition of slavery, slave trade and servitude. Article 5 rules out torture, cruel, inhuman or degrading treatment or punishment to any person.

Articles 6 to 11 provide for equality before the law, equal protection against any discrimination, legal remedy, freedom from arbitrary arrest, detention or exile, and adherence to fair legal procedure in case a person is accused.

Article 12 rules out arbitrary interference with any individual's privacy, family, home or correspondence, and attacks upon his honour and reputation.

Articles 13 and 14 provide for the right to freedom of movement and residence and the right to seek asylum from persecution in other countries.

Article 15 provides for the right to a nationality; Article 16 for the right to marry and found a family with the free and full consent of the intending spouses; and Article 17 for the right to own property.

Articles 18, 19 and 20 provide for the right to freedom of thought, conscience and religion; the right to freedom of opinion and expression; and the right to freedom of peaceful assembly and association.

Article 21 provides for the right to take part in the government of one's country through one's chosen representatives and the right of equal access to public service. It also recommends that the will of the people, expressed in periodic and genuine elections, by universal and equal suffrage, by secret voting, shall be the basis of authority of government. In this way, this Article regards democratic form of government as an essential feature of human rights.

It is worth-noting that Articles 1 to 21 of the present declaration embody an elaborate scheme to provide for civil, political and legal rights of all human beings all over the world.

On the other hand, Articles 22 to 26 provide for social and economic rights of the individual. These include the right to social security, right to work, to free choice of employment, to just and favourable conditions of work, equal pay for equal work, just and favourable remuneration, right to form trade unions, right to rest and leisure, adequate standard of living, special care and assistance during motherhood and childhood, and right to education.

Article 27 provides for cultural rights including the right to participate freely in the cultural life of the community, to enjoy the arts and to share in scientific advancement and its benefits, and author's right to the protection of the moral and material interests resulting from his scientific, literary or artistic production.

Article 28 focuses on everyone's entitlement to a social and international order in which all these rights and freedoms can be fully realized. This article is concerned with the sphere of application of the rights in question.

Finally, Articles 29 and 30 focus on everyone's duties to the community to ensure full development of his personality. Any individual would be entitled to the aforesaid rights and freedoms on the condition of recognizing similar rights and freedoms of others and of meeting the just requirements of morality, public order and the general welfare in a democratic society. No state, group or person would have any right to engage in any activity involving the destruction of any of these rights and freedoms.

It is important to note that India, as an active member of the United Nations and as an ardent champion of human rights, has given due recognition to the contents of the Universal Declaration of Human Rights. This is manifested in various parts of the Indian Constitution (1950; as amended from time to time), including its Preamble, Fundamental Rights, Directive Principles of State Policy and Fundamental Duties. The Supreme Court of India has cited the Universal Declaration of Human Rights in some of its judgements from time to time in order to promote democratic spirit and social justice. Government of India has set up a National Human Rights Commission since 1993 in order to promote awareness about these rights and to ensure their protection. This Commission has been doing a commendable job since its inception.

Apart from the Universal Declaration of Human Rights, leading nations of the world have expressed their resolve to respect human rights through several international compacts. Of these, European Convention on Human Rights (1950), International Covenant on Civil and Political Rights (1966), International Covenant on Economic, Social and Cultural Rights (1966), American Convention on Human Rights (1969), Helsinki Accords (1975), and African Charter on Peoples' an Human Rights (1981) are particularly important. Besides, citizens of many countries have formed non-governmental organizations (NGOs) for the protection of ordinary people's human rights. For example, in India, we have 'People's Union for Civil Liberties' and 'People's Union for Democratic Rights' who have done a good work in this sphere. The most prominent non-political humanitarian organization 'Amnesty International', with headquarters in London, inquires into the cases of injustice due to political, religious and racial persecution the world over and submits its reports to the United Nations and the Council of Europe at regular intervals. Its reports get wide publicity in the mass media and generate awareness of human rights everywhere.

Evolution of Rights and the Corresponding Political Order

Primacy of the Relevant Category of Rights	*Corresponding Political Order*
Natural Rights	Nightwatchman State
Civil Rights	Constitutional Government
Political Rights	Democratic State
Social-Economic Rights	Welfare State
Human Rights	Humane World Order

[VIII]

SCOPE OF HUMAN RIGHTS

The concept of human rights is subject to continuous evolution. So it is not possible to indicate the full range of human rights. If we try to identify some broad categories of human rights, some of them would be overlapping each other. For the sake of convenience, we may discuss them under four headings: (*a*) Right to life; (*b*) Right to property; (*c*) Civil liberties and democratic rights; and (*d*) Social, economic and cultural rights. Substance of these rights must be interpreted with due regard to the need to maintain humane conditions of living and to protect human dignity.

RIGHT TO LIFE

It implies that an innocent person shall not be caught, detained, subjected to physical torture or death. Upto this point it is a negative right. With the growing consciousness of human rights, positive aspects of right to life are being increasingly highlighted. Accordingly, the state shall not only protect human life from the onslaught of various offenders and natural calamities within the country as well as foreign aggressors, but also provide for a clean and pollution-free atmosphere as well as uncontaminated land, and take care of public health. It will also save human life from starvation, disease and adverse weather conditions.

RIGHT TO PROPERTY

It implies the right to own material things acquired by an individual through legal means. The state must protect this right of the individual. This right is the foundation of security of one's fruit of labour, day-to-day comforts of life, and one's means of a decent livelihood. However, modern consciousness nowhere regards the right to property an absolute right. The property that enables a person to establish control over lives of others will always be subject to compulsory acquisition by the state for public purpose. Compensation for this acquisition would be determined by public authority in view of the needs of social justice.

CIVIL LIBERTIES AND DEMOCRATIC RIGHTS

The terms 'civil liberties' and 'democratic rights' are sometimes used interchangeably. It is believed that civil liberties can be effectively provided only under a democratic system which safeguards democratic rights of the individual. Again, at times the term 'democratic rights' is applied synonymously with 'human rights'. Although these three terms are closely interrelated, it would not be proper to use them loosely. At the outset, it may be realized that the term 'human rights' denotes a wide range of rights. It comprehends civil liberties, democratic rights, and a lot of other measures intended to maintain human dignity. Democratic rights broadly suggest a set of those rights which enable the individual, as a full citizen of his community, country or nation, to take part in public life, to elect government of his choice, to influence government decisions, and to acquire political office through the prescribed procedure. This is primarily the arena of political rights.

Civil liberties, on the other hand, belong to the arena of legal rights. It is true that civil liberties can be maintained most effectively under a democratic system. *Democratic system is a necessary but not a sufficient condition of maintaining civil liberties*. In any case, a democratic system would be deemed to be faulty if it fails to maintain civil liberties. In short, civil liberties are best secured by democratic rights; and democratic rights are in turn best secured by human rights. Besides, only a democratic government enables the citizens to protect their own freedom by electing new officials if the government infringes on their civil liberties. Then what is meant by civil liberties?

Broadly speaking, civil liberties include freedom of thought and expression, faith and worship, freedom of movement, freedom of association and assembly, the right to a fair trial and freedom of the person. Freedom of the person includes freedom from arbitrary search, arrest or detention. Similarly, freedom of thought and expression includes freedom of the press, and freedom to criticize the government. These rights and liberties are essential to protect the individual from arbitrary acts of government, and to enable him to enjoy his freedom in various spheres of life. In any case, these liberties must be exercised with a sense of responsibility and with due regard to the needs of maintaining similar liberties of others.

Relation Between Civil Liberties, Democratic Rights and Human Rights

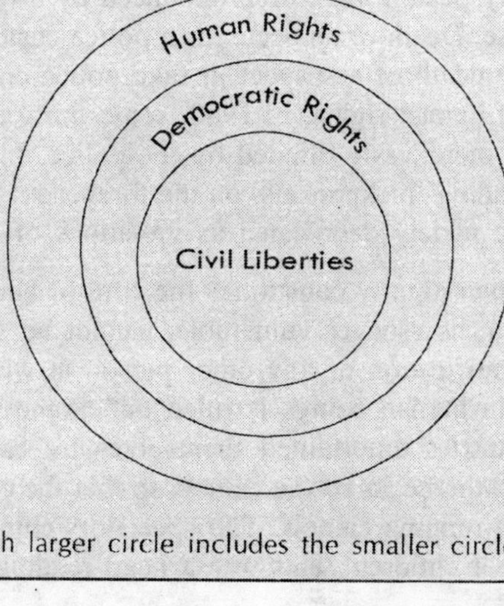

Each larger circle includes the smaller circle

It is important to note that the notion of freedom of the person (or personal freedom) and the right to a fair trial emanate from the concept of 'rule of law' (a principle of English constitutional practice), and the right to a fair trial is also a part of 'due process of law' (a principle of American constitutional practice). The concept of 'due process of law' holds that no person shall be deprived of life, liberty or property except in accordance with the explicit provisions of law and with due regard to his rights. Then 'rule of law' requires that the law of the land should be properly notified so that the citizens know as to how it will effect them; any action against an individual should be taken only under that law, and not on any other basis. Hence, no one should be arbitrarily arrested, nor punished without a fair trial.

The principle of human rights further requires that no arbitrary law should be enacted, and no one should be subjected to inhuman treatment under false pretence of legal action. Cases of undertrials languishing in jails for over a decade even without charges being framed against them involve a gross violation of human rights. No one should be subjected to extreme insult or torture for confession of a crime or disclosure of a secret. Even when someone's offence is proved, he should not be subjected to extremely cruel and disgraceful punishment. For instance, if a woman has committed a heinous crime, she should not be forced to a naked parade or outrage of her modesty as a measure of punishment. Such inhuman punishment would be degrading not only to that particular individual but to womanhood as such and to humanity at large. Similarly, when a criminal is awarded a death sentence, he should be subjected to a peaceful death, not to an extremely painful death like being burnt alive or being thrown into boiling oil. Such inhuman acts cannot be permitted in a legal system of a civilized society. On the same logic, the use of atomic, biological and chemical weapons in war is banned under international law as it brings untold suffering upon the population, and thereby violates human rights.

Punishment to any person must be pronounced by a judicial authority after a fair trial of the case. Death of an accused in police custody, rape of a woman in police custody or death of a suspect in fake police encounter are the most serious violations of human rights. In 1980, some thirty accused in Bhagalpur jail (in Bihar) were mercilessly blinded by the police. In 1994, Punjab police engraved a tattoo reading 'pickpockets' on the foreheads of some tribal women. Such incidents were widely deprecated as violations of human rights.

Protection of human dignity constitutes the core of human rights. It implies that a human person, howsoever vulnerable, cannot be subjected to inhuman treatment for the gratification of any other person at whatever price! So any type of trafficking in human beings is ruled out. Some years ago, some rich traders of gulf countries entertained themselves by camel race. They tied human children with the necks of the camels so that the crying children served as a spur to the fast-running camels. The spectators enjoyed this scene at the cost of innocent, poor children! This was a heart-rending case of violation of human rights. Similarly, child labour involving children of tender age working in strenuous and hazardous occupations also amounts to violation of human rights.

National Human Rights Commission of India has focused on some other aspects of the problem concerning the protection of human dignity. Apart from the need to reform police system, it has emphasized the need to reform administration of prisons and correctional institutions, the need to prevent the curse of prostitution, the curse of manual scavenging, starvation deaths, and the need to improve the health of expectant mothers to save future generations from physical and mental retardation. It is now widely accepted that cold-wave deaths as well as malnutrition deaths and diseases, particularly in India, involve the violation of human rights.

SOCIAL-ECONOMIC AND CULTURAL RIGHTS

These largely include the right to education, right to work, congenial conditions of work, rest and a reasonable level of living and health, social security and opportunity to participate in the cultural heritage of the community. These rights are the product of social consciousness of the present age. Provision of these rights is linked with the problem of social justice. It is a matter of debate whether such provision should be treated as a part of the scheme of human rights. It is argued that in a large number of third world countries, these rights cannot be protected for want of adequate resources. How can we treat them as rights if they cannot be secured in a sizable part of the world?

But it should not be forgotten that the concept of human rights is based on the idea of 'ideal' rights which express the goals of social life. If it is not feasible to provide these rights in some parts of the world today, their significance as human rights will not diminish on this ground. They can certainly serve as guiding principles of public policy. If a state cannot provide them for want of resources for the time being, these rights will show the way to its long-term goals.

CONCLUSION

In the contemporary world, the scope of human rights needs to be expanded further. The problems of protecting life and health in the present-day society have become more complex. The spread of terrorism, drug-trafficking and environmental pollution are now threatening the life of people. It is the duty of the state to save people from that threat. This duty of the state must be included in the list of human rights. Whereas the efforts of nation-states might have been sufficient to protect the traditional human rights, the new human rights can be maintained only through the global effort.

The increasing awareness of human rights in the contemporary world may be treated as a great achievement of our civilization. However, at times some wrong tendencies are encouraged in the name of human rights. For instance, sometimes human rights are invoked to shield hardened criminals and terrorists, and human rights of their victims are sought to be overlooked who have to suffer untold miseries due to their inhuman acts.

Again, many developed countries tend to impose restrictions on the import of goods from the developing countries under the pretence that human rights were violated in the process of manufacture of those goods, such as it involved child labour or prisoners' labour. Such grounds are advanced without ascertaining the truth.

When any type of injustice is sought to be promoted by invoking human rights, the real situation must be analysed with utmost caution and care.

[IX]
THEORIES OF HUMAN RIGHTS

If human rights are taken in a wider sense, *i.e.* as a means of protecting individual from onslaughts or atrocities of arbitrary power, there is hardly any dispute about their status. But if they are viewed as a tool in the hands of individual to safeguard the interests of a particular category of individuals or to maintain a particular type of social order, they are likely to receive different treatment from different schools of thought. These divergent views regarding the nature and status of rights or human rights may be called theories of human rights. Of these, liberal, libertarian, Marxist, communitarian and feminist theories are most important.

Liberal theory of rights, as expounded by John Locke (1632-1704), focuses on rights of individual against the state. Although Locke makes a distinction between society and state and sees no serious conflict between individual and society, his theory of rights deals with a possible conflict between individual and the state. He postulates that individuals form the state as a trust for the protection of their natural right to 'life, liberty and property'. If the state fails in this duty, individuals can resist it. If it still fails, they can dissolve it. In fact, Locke does not make a distinction between state and government. That is why society will not disintegrate with the dissolution of state or government. In short, liberal theory of rights treats individual as the end and state as the means.

Libertarian theory of rights, as expounded by Robert Nozick (1938-2002), gives more prominence to the individual. It maintains its faith in the natural rights of individual and treats the state as a private firm. Individuals 'hire' the state, chiefly for the protection of their property holdings. The state has no authority to engage in redistributive transfers among citizens who were originally its clients.

Marxist theory of rights, as expounded by Karl Marx (1818-83) and V.I.

Lenin (1870-1924), holds that the rights maintained by any society are the rights of its ruling class or dominant class at the expense of the dependent class. So the capitalist society protects the rights and interests of capitalists at the expense of the working class. Workers will have to overthrow capitalists and socialize the major means of production in order to create a new order that would protect the rights and interests of the working class.

Communitarian theory of rights, as advanced by Alasdair MacIntyre (1929-), focuses on individual's commitment to the community which represents the common good. This theory refuses to recognize independent interests or rights of the individual.

Finally, feminist theory as, represented by Shulamith Firestone (1945-) and Sheila Rowbotham (1943-), among others, insists on restoring the rights of women in a male-dominated society. It seeks to transform the prevalent system of rights which has been responsible for the subordination of women to men in all societies in all ages.

Comparative Perspective on Human Rights

The Issue	*Liberal Theory*	*Libertarian Theory*	*Marxist Theory*	*Communitarian Theory*	*Feminist Theory*
Status of Individual	Holder of Rights	Holder of Rights	Member of a Class	Integral Part of the Community	Varies with Gender
Nature of the Community	Aggregate of Individuals	Aggregate of Individuals	Divided into Dominant and Dependent Classes	Source of all Social Life	Sphere of Male Domination
Status of Authority	Subservient to Individual	Like a Private Service Agency	Instrument of Exploitation	Instrument of the Common Good	Instrument of Male Domination
Object of Commitment	Self-interest	Self-interest	Class interest	the Common Good	Women's Rights and Interests
Status of Rights	Most Prominent	Most Prominent	Instrument of Class Interest	Instrument of the Common Good	Instrument of Resisting Male Domination
Exponents	John Locke	Robert Nozick	Karl Marx, V.I. Lenin	Alasdair MacIntyre	S. Firestone, S. Rowbotham

[X]
THREE GENERATIONS OF RIGHTS

Concept of rights embodies a dynamic idea. As society becomes more concerned with individual's safety and development, list of the existing rights is suitably revised and enlarged so as to create favourable conditions to achieve these objectives. In the contemporary world, the list of rights thus recognized has become quite comprehensive. The ever-growing rights are now identified as three generations of rights: (*a*) First-generation rights include civil and political rights; (*b*) Second-generation rights include social and economic rights; and (*c*) Third-generation rights include the newly recognized human rights, such as cultural rights of minorities in a multicultural society or nation.

> **Multicultural Society**
>
> Multicultural society refers to a society wherein people belonging to different cultural groups live together as equal citizens. These groups must have freedom to preserve the salient features of their respective cultures (e.g. language, symbols of identity, religion, places of worship, custom, dress code, eating habits, styles of living, art and craft, etc.) within the larger society; none should be forced to assimilate into the dominant culture.

Besides these, third-generation rights are also regarded to include the rights enshrined in Article 28 of the Universal Declaration of Human Rights (1948). It reads: "Everyone is entitled to a social and international order in which the rights set forth in this Declaration can be fully realized." These 'solidarity' rights have been interpreted to include the rights to social and economic development, to participate in and benefit from the resources of the earth and space, scientific and technical information (which is particularly important for the developing nations), the right to healthy environment, peace and humanitarian disaster relief.

Identification of the three generations of rights suggests the sequence of the evolution of different categories of rights. However, these three generations will have to coexist to provide for a meaningful scheme of rights. It is important to note that the Universal Declaration of Human Rights comprehends all the three generations of rights although third-generation rights figure there only in a symbolic sense.

FIRST-GENERATION RIGHTS

First-generation rights comprise civil and political rights of the citizen including freedom of thought and expression, freedom of movement, freedom of association, religious freedom, etc. These rights are for the most part rights of the individual against government interference. The legislation providing for these rights requires government to do no more than simply restrain its own executive arm. Initially these rights were evolved in pursuance of the policy of liberalism. However, by and by they became an integral part of democratic rights of citizens and paved the way for evolution of the second-generation rights. For example, the courts in India sought to expand the scope of the right to life to include the right to health-care and clean atmosphere, both of which are second-generation rights.

> **Liberalism**
>
> Liberalism refers to a principle of politics which regards 'liberty' or 'freedom' of individual as the first and foremost goal of public policy. Liberty, in this sense, implies 'liberation' from restraints, particularly from the restraints imposed by an authoritarian state. This principle was evolved in the West in late seventeenth century in order to liquidate feudal privileges of the land-owning class and to create favourable conditions for the new entrepreneurial class to enable them to contribute to social progress.

SECOND-GENERATION RIGHTS

With the growing consciousness among disadvantaged sections and their sympathizers, it was realized that the first-generation rights were not sufficient to take care of all sections of society. Hence, some new rights were added to the list which required the state to play positive role in extending tangible help to the needy sections. These were termed as 'second-generation rights'. These included such provisions as right to education, right to work, right to medical care, right to housing, etc. which could be secured only through social welfare programmes and social legislation. Second-generation rights are best protected by a welfare state.

> **Social Legislation**
>
> Social legislation refers to the process of making laws giving relief to the poor, weaker and vulnerable sections of society. Examples of social legislation include the laws providing for special assistance to the orphans, the aged, the sick, the disabled and the unemployed etc. apart from Anti-Dowry laws, laws concerning abolition of prostitution, emancipation of the bonded labour, etc.

Second-generation rights have been recognized by many States through their Constitutions or International Covenants. For example, International Covenant on Economic, Social and Cultural Rights (1966) (which came in force from 1976) urges on the member states to "recognize the right of everyone to an adequate standard of living for himself and his family, including adequate food, clothing and housing, and to the continuous improvement of living conditions". Similarly, the Indian Constitution (1950) includes an elaborate part on Directive Principles of State Policy urging the State to secure welfare of the people. For example, Article 41 included in this part provides: "The State shall, within the limits of its economic capacity and development, make effective provision for securing the right or work, to education and to public assistance in cases of unemployment, old age, sickness and disablement, and in other cases of undeserved want."

In short, second-generation rights are given due recognition in a very large part of the world.

THIRD-GENERATION RIGHTS

Many nations of the world have a sizeable portion of cultural minorities due to historical reasons. Members of these minorities owe allegiance to the State, and they are regarded as equal citizens of the State. With the increasing demand of new talents in progressive countries, migration of foreign people to these countries in search of better opportunities and settling there permanently, more and more countries are having cultural minorities within their territories. Now these cultural minorities wish to maintain the salient features of their respective cultures (*e.g.* language, symbols of identity, religion, places of worship, custom, dress code, eating habits, style of living, art and craft, etc.) because of their sentimental attachment to their original cultures. They do not want to assimilate into the dominant culture but they wish to maintain their identity and autonomy in some respects. When these minorities are given the freedom and opportunity to preserve their cultural institutions and practices and to exercise some measure of political autonomy, their rights in this behalf are described as third-generation rights.

In short, third-generation rights in this sense refer to cultural rights of minorities in a large country to preserve their cultural institutions and practices. These do not imply mere absence of interference by the State (akin to the first-generation rights) but tangible protection and assistance in maintaining their cultural identity. Article 27 of International Covenant on Civil and Political Rights (1966) declares: "In those States in which ethnic, religious or linguistic minorities exist, persons belonging to such minorities shall not be denied the right, in community with the other members of their group, to enjoy their own culture, to profess and practise their own religion, or to use their own language." In the Indian Constitution (1950), Cultural and Educational Rights of minorities figure in the part concerning Fundamental Rights. Article 29 of the Constitution reads: "Any section of the citizens residing in the territory of India or any part thereof having a distinct language, script or culture of its own shall have the right to conserve the same." Article 30 recognizes the right of minorities to establish and administer their own educational institutions. It further provides: "The State shall not, in granting aid to educational institutions, discriminate against any educational institution on the ground that it is under the management of a minority, whether based on religion or language." The state is obliged to maintain communal harmony, ensure due respect of sacred books of various religious communities and full safety of their holy cities and places of worship.

Provision of third-generation rights is meant to infuse a sense of security among cultural minorities in a large country. It strengthens their allegiance and commitment to the nation. It promotes unity in diversity. Moreover, existence of the variety of cultures encourages various cultural groups to learn new languages, to study literature of those languages, adopt new art forms and learn new skills. To accomplish this task, people should be broad-minded enough to appreciate and adopt the ways of strangers. On the contrary, insistence on narrow cultural identities may sometimes prove inimical to democratic spirit. For example, *in India when people vote on the basis of caste, religion, language or region, many tainted politicians find their way to legislatures* so that law-breakers become law-makers. Sometimes minority groups insist on retaining certain outdated, irrational and unjust practices in the name of maintaining their identity and oppose any law intended to change those practices. So *the question of preservation of identity should be tackled with a note of caution.* The enlightened people of diverse cultural groups—whether in majority or minority—should come together to oppose unjust and irrational elements found in different cultures and encourage the evolution of a common culture incorporating the rich heritage of different languages, literature, styles of decency, art and craft, etc. That is precisely the requirement of a composite culture which encourages cooperation and collaboration between various communities and paves the way for social progress. In fact, the provision of third-generation rights in this sense reaches its logical conclusion in the evolution of a composite culture in a large and multicultural country like India.

Finally, third-generation rights seek to endow the individual with the benefits of world citizenship. It recognizes his right to a fair share in the resources of earth and space, right to healthy global environment, peace and humanitarian relief in case of natural disasters, and also an access to scientific and technical information which is the proud possession of all humanity.

Three Generations of Rights

First-Generation Rights	*Second-Generation Rights*	*Third-Generation Rights*
• Civil and Political Rights	• Social and Economic Rights	• Cultural Rights of Minorities
• Freedom of Movement, Association and Assembly	• Right to Health and Medical Care	• Full Safety of Sacred Books, Sacred Places and Places of Worship
• Personal Freedom (Freedom from Arbitrary Arrest and Right to Fair Trial)	• Right to Education and Information	• Environmental Rights (Right to Clean Air, Clean Earth, Clean Water, etc.)
• Religious Freedom (Freedom of Conscience)	• Right to Employment, Housing, etc.	• Right to Share the Common Heritage of Mankind

> The most certain test by which we judge whether a country is really free is the amount of security enjoyed by minorities.
>
> Lord Acton (1834-1902)

[XI]
DEBATE ON STATUS OF THE HUMAN RIGHTS

ISSUE OF THE DEBATE

Debate on the status of human rights revolves round this question: Do we have a scheme of human rights which are capable of universal application, or different societies need different sets of human rights? The main challenge to the universal character of human rights comes from the advocates of 'cultural relativism' who argue that human rights for any particular community should be based on its cultural values and practices, and not on any universal principles. Interestingly, some other objections to the universality of human rights—particularly those emanating from ideological differences—are also raised under the pretext of cultural differences.

The general concept of human rights is based on very noble and rational principles. In a nustshell, human rights stand for those rights of human beings which aim at the protection of human dignity and elimination of inhuman treatment to any person under any circumstances. These rights are extended to every human being by virtue of being a human being, not as a citizen of any particular state, nor as a member of any particular group. Where an individual's civil, political and social-economic rights are exhausted, he can still hope to get some relief under the umbrella of human rights. For instance, a foreigner, a refugee, a prisoner-of-war or a proclaimed offender may have been left without ordinary rights, yet the beneficent hand of human rights will not be withdrawn from over his head. No reasonable person will quarrel with this laudable idea of human rights.

However, in actual practice, lists of human rights are drawn in an eclectic manner. We try to make it as comprehensive as possible. Whatever rights seem to be beneficial for human beings from diverse sources of their origin, would find place in our list. If all of them could be adjusted in a single scheme, without inner contradictions, we will have an ideal scheme of human rights which could be commended for universal application. But this is not always possible. If we look at the list of human rights enshrined in the Universal Declaration of Human Rights issued by the United Nations in 1948, we find that it includes a vast variety of rights. Some of these rights may not be compatible with each other. For instance, it seeks to secure civil and political rights of individuals along with their social-economic rights. It is well known that the relative status of these two sets of rights corresponds to the distinction between liberal and socialist constitutions. In a liberal constitution, civil and political rights are given priority over social-economic rights which can be secured only marginally depending upon the resources of the state. On the other hand, in a socialist constitution (like that of the former USSR), social-economic rights are given priority over civil and political rights because they can be protected only marginally under a command economy. In India, we are quite familiar with this dilemma. In our Constitution (1950), we have separate provisions on Fundamental Rights (mainly dealing with Civil and Political Rights) and Directive Principles of State Policy (mainly concerned with Social-Economic Rights of citizens) with different legal status.

> **Command Economy**
>
> An economy where crucial economic processes are largely determined by government, and not by market forces. Government exercises its control over economy through a planning body which implements society's major economic goals. Such economy may be able to solve the problems of unemployment and idle capacity of industrial plants and take care of the basic economic needs of the community, but it may not be able to give wider choice to the citizens in the sphere of their economic and political aspirations.

Further, the Universal Declaration of Human Rights provides for the protection of civil liberties and democratic rights of citizens. While these rights are very important to ensure freedom of the individual, critics of these rights argue that they tend to create and sustain the institutions of liberal democracy and a market model of society which are not conducive to the values cherished by some societies, particularly some developing nations. That is where the argument concerning cultural relativism is usually invoked.

MEANING OF CULTURAL RELATIVISM

The theory of cultural relativism was evolved in the sphere of social anthropology in the context of studying various primitive societies. The exponents of this theory maintained that we cannot understand, interpret, or evaluate social and social-psychological phenomena meaningfully unless we realize the role of these phenomena against the background of the larger social and cultural system where they occur. The customs prevailing in a particular culture can be properly judged and evaluated only by considering the values associated with them, the needs satisfied by them, and their general relationship to other obligations, expectations and moral codes of the culture under study. It also means that when a Western scholar undertakes the study of a developing society, he should try to understand and evaluate it in terms of the beliefs and values rooted in its culture, and not in term of his own value-system. He should try to learn the language and symbols used in the society under study, and not interpret their behaviour in terms of his own language. As Allan G. Johnson has illustrated:

> Westerners may be aware that in Tibet brothers often share a single wife, but this awareness is unlikely to make them more tolerant of such practices in their own scoieties. Thus, the consequences produced by a culture

hold within that culture regardless of how differently things might be done elsewhere ('Cultural Relativism', *The Blackwell Dictionary of Sociology;* 1995).

The awareness generated by the idea of cultural relativism makes us broad-minded towards our own as well as others'culture. We become less blind and arrogant in relation to other societies, and less rigid and dogmatic in evaluating and changing our own attitudes. We are convinced that none of the ways of living observed by us is 'natural' or 'universal' or 'sacrosanct', but different societies may evolve different cultural patterns which may have their own merits (and demerits). It would enable a vegetarian to appreciate the life style of a non-vegetarian, and *vice versa.* It would enable fair-complexioned people to appreciate black aesthetics and social symbols. We can go a step further and try to understand the socio-economic causes behind certain cultural traits. Thus, we may realize that certain 'dirty' habits of a community are the outcome of its 'poverty'; its economic amelioration would be necessary in order to cultivate clean habits therein.

Black Aesthetics

Black aesthetics refers to the set of standards of beauty and art forms as prevalent in the culture of the black races. Historically, white races had managed to gain dominant position in the world; their standards of beauty and art were projected as universal standards. Now black races have not only achieved independence, they have also shown that they are no less intelligent, talented and competent, their aesthetic standards are no longer considered as inferior to those of the white races.

Some communities admire their traditional culture for certain positive features. For example, they may be proud of their style of 'simple living and high thinking', cooperative spirit and respect for elders, etc. It is alleged that the new scheme of human rights (described as 'universal human rights') seeks to promote individualism (based on the spirit of self-assertion and pursuit of self-interest), a competitive social order (based on market society model) and consumerism. This is bound to vitiate their culture and disturb their peace. Some critics deprecate the new scheme of human rights as an attempt at Westernization of the new nations. Some commentators argue that the new human rights promote greed among people which results not only in various types of social conflicts but also in environmental degradation. All such allegations must be thoroughly examined before accepting any of them.

A CRITIQUE OF HUMAN RIGHTS

Any critique of human rights should be based on an objective assessment of their merits and demerits. They cannot be set aside merely on the ground that they are 'alien' to our culture. It is true that the growing awareness of human rights has disturbed the existing equilibrium of many societies. We should try to find out whether this 'disturbance' is positive or negative. If it has smashed some superstitions, we should welcome it. If it has awakened some subdued sections of society and motivated them to fight against injustice, then too there is no reason to be fussy. It is possible that the awareness of human rights among the oppressed has annoyed certain vested interests who are now crying foul. If so, we should try to convince everybody that redistributive justice will pave the way for overall progress of society. If the cake is peacefully redistributed among a larger number, it is better than giving way to a mad scramble in which the cake itself might be destroyed.

On the other hand, if our culture had maintained some great values like cooperative spirit, regard for elders, hospitality, care of the destitutes, helpless and distressed people and so on, we should ensure that these values are not eroded with the arrival of human rights. There is no clash between old values and new rights provided we are sufficiently careful. Advocates of cultural relativism oppose human rights because they conflict with the prevailing cultural practices of different societies, as if those practices are 'sacrosanct'! In fact, human rights should be commended for accomplishing the abolition of many inhuman and illogical practices prevailing in some societies. For example, the practice of female genital mutilation was found in diferent cultures of Africa, Asia and South America. It is neither mandated by any religion, nor based on any apparent logic, but became a part of blind tradition. With the awareness of human rights, it was widely condemned by the international community as a violation of girls' and women's rights, and outlawed in some countries. The inhuman and retrograde practices of child sacrifice, infanticide and female foeticide are being strongly opposed by human rights activists. In India, the initiative taken by Raja Ram Mohan Roy (1772-1833) in seeking ban on widow-burning on the pyres of her dead husband (the practice of *sati*) may be regarded as a precursor to the philosophy of human rights.

In some cases, human rights were opposed as conflicting with religious beliefs. For example, in 1981, the Iranian representative to the United Nations contended that the Universal Declaration of Human Rights embodies "a secular understanding of the Judeo-Christian tradition", which could not be implemented by Muslims without trespassing the Islamic law. In early 1990s, the former Prime Ministers of Singapore (Lee Kuan Yew) and of Malaysia (Mahathir bin Mohammad) both claimed that Asian values were significantly different from Western values. They argued that Asian values included a sense of loyalty and a spirit of foregoing personal freedoms for the sake of social stability and prosperity, and therefore authoritarian government was more appropriate in Asia than democracy. Apparently, this view was strongly biased and partisan. It was countered by Mahathir's former deputy A. Ibrahim in 1994, who asserted: "To say that freedom is Western or un-Asian is to offend our traditions as well as our forefathers, who gave their lives in the struggles against tyranny and injustices." Again, in 2003, Singapore's opposition leader Chee Soon Juan contended that it is racist to assert that Asians do not want human rights.

Adherents of cultural relativism tend to ignore the fact that modern human rights are by no means rooted in Western culture; at best, they are rooted in Western political philosophy which marks a departure from Western culture itself. Most influential human rights thinkers like John Locke (1632-1704) and John Stuart Mill (1806-73) were born in a culture which violated human rights by running big Empires. The concept of human rights is new to all cultures, dating back no further than 1948 when the Universal Declaration of Human Rights was issued. This declaration was drafted by people drawn from many different cultures and traditions, including a US Roman Catholic, a Chinese Confucian philosopher, a French Zionist and a representative from the Arab League, among others, and drew upon advice from thinkers like Mahatma Gandhi.

Michael Ignatieff in his paper published in 2001 argued that opposition to human rights under the pretext of cultural relativism comes exclusively from those who commit human rights abuses because of their powerful position in particular cultures; their victims are the vulnerable sections within those cultures. In other words, the universal character of human rights is largely opposed by the vested interests, and not on strong logical grounds.

It is further important to note that the World Summit held in 2005 reaffirmed the international community's adherence to the principle of "the universal nature of human rights and freedoms... beyond question".

The original list of human rights provided in the Universal Declaration of Human Rights (1948) has now been expanded under several conventions, charters and protocols, etc. which reaffirm their universal character and sphere of application. The newly recognized human rights include: environmental rights; rights of future generations; lesbian, gay, bisexual and transgender rights; right to international trade; and right to water. In 2002, the United Nations Committee on Economic, Social and Cultural Rights recommended the access to water as a human right: "The human right to water is indispensable for leading a life in human dignity. It is a prerequisite for the realization of other human rights." It may be hoped that by and by a fair share of all nations in the rare resources of the earth and the atmosphere as well as in the knowledge-base of human civilization might be accepted as one of the principles of human rights.

16

Concept of Liberty

THE CONCEPT OF 'liberty' or 'freedom' denotes a very important principle of political philosophy. Liberty is sometimes regarded as the distinctive principle of liberalism, but freedom is acclaimed as a universal principle. Freedom is eulogized by liberal, idealist as well as Marxist theory. Nobody quarrels with freedom as an end, but different schools of thought differ on the means and mode of realizing freedom. Even the champions of absolutism, authoritarianism and slavery pay lip service to freedom, claiming that for ordinary men, submission to authority—regarded as the symbol of some sort of excellence—is the best way to realize freedom.

Champions of liberty have, however, always challenged the claims of the privileged classes to such excellence. The ideal of liberty has inspired many revolutionary struggles against despotism and foreign regimes. It is significant that the struggle for liberty is always informed by the spirit of equality. That is, when some oppressed sections rise against their oppressors—as in peasant revolts or national struggles of independence—they challenge the alleged superiority of their oppressors, demanding equality and justice on the universal principle of human equality.

[I]
NATURE OF LIBERTY

For a clearer view, the idea of liberty may be analysed in terms of (*a*) freedom as the quality of human being; and (*b*) freedom as the condition of human being.

FREEDOM AS THE QUALITY OF HUMAN BEING

When we consider freedom as the quality of human being, we assert that only a human being, as distinguished from other living beings, is capable of freedom.

Animals, birds and insects are governed by the rule of the 'struggle for existence' and 'survival of the fittest'—the fittest is the one physically strongest and cleverest. They have no 'aim of life' beyond mere existence. Man as *homo sapiens* has distinguished himself from other living beings as he claims to have an aim in his life. He has created the whole complex of institutions—civilization and culture—in pursuance of this aim. Animals are mere slaves of nature; man has largely learnt to tame, control and harness nature to serve his purpose of life. Freedom is the distinctive quality of man.

> **Every animal leaves traces of what it was; man alone leaves traces of what he creates.**
>
> **Jacob Bronowski (1973)**

In short, freedom as the quality of human being is manifested in man's capacity for obtaining scientific knowledge of inexorable laws of nature and applying them for the benefit of mankind. In the absence of such knowledge, human beings are bound to remain slaves of nature; their ignorance could prove disastrous for them. In other words, human being's ability to gain scientific knowledge is the source of their freedom.

FREEDOM AS THE CONDITION OF HUMAN BEING

When we consider freedom as the condition of human being, we enter the realm of liberty which is usually defined as 'absence of constraint'. Constraint or restraint may be internal as well as external. In politics, we are largely concerned with external restraint; in philosophy, we think of internal as well as external restraint. However, when we contemplate positive action by the state for 'the removal of a constraint', we return to the realm of politics. So the concept of liberty has very wide implications in the sphere of political philosophy.

We demand liberty for the human being (as a condition of life) because we treat him to be a rational creature. In this sense, liberty implies that when a human being applies his rational faculty and comes to know what is best for him (and also for society because as a rational being he cannot think of something which is good for him, and not for society), and he has the ability to achieve it, his activity should not be hindered by any external, unreasonable restraint. So far our demand is confined to the removal of external restraint; hence it is termed as *negative liberty.*

Now a man may not be free even if there is no external restraint. For example, when a person is suffering from physical pain or is mentally disturbed, he may not be able to do what he loves to do. Man is not only a rational creature, he is also a sensitive creature. He may feel constrained due to hunger, thirst or fatigue. So freedom in the widest sense requires that man should not feel any internal or external constraint. This means freedom from physical pain, disease, ignorance, fear or want. It is very difficult to look for such freedom in the real world. However, *we can judge a state by its performance in the sphere of minimizing all possible constraints in the life of its citizens.* In this respect, a state tends to secure *positive liberty* for its citizens.

Again, we wish to have freedom for man as a rational agent. A person under certain circumstances may depart from rational thinking and may forget the value of freedom. A slave may feel contented with his slavery. Some people may turn to be the slaves of superstitions, irrational customs and social practices. Some others may multiply their wants under strong peer pressure. Still others may be swayed by consumer culture; they may seek satisfaction from increasing consumption of material things, and may become indifferent to joys of nature. They may not be inclined to derive any pleasure from the treasures of literature, art and music which enable a man to rise above trivial wants. If a person is not free in the real sense, and still he is not keen to have freedom, efforts should be made to arouse his conscience and make him anxious to win his freedom.

> Servitude is of two kinds : slavery to domination from outside, and to one's own artificial needs.
>
> Mahatma Gandhi

> Slaves become so debased by their chains as to lose even the desire of breaking from them.
>
> Jean-Jaques Rousseau (*The Social Contract;* 1762)

CONCLUSION

However, despite the long history of man's civilization, he has not yet risen fully above the rule of the animal kingdom. So long as the elders, the more experienced, more learned, more competent, more prudent and more energetic men in society manage common affairs for the common good, men do not lose their freedom in obeying their commands. But in actual practice, it is mostly the selfish, strong and shrewd persons who managed to assume dominant positions and acquire special privileges in society. As a result, society was divided into privileged and underprivileged sections—the oppressor and the oppressed, the exploiter and the exploited, the dominant and dependent groups—because one set of men assumed power over the lives of others. The privileged classes have developed a vested interest in the existing order. They have sought to justify that order by stressing its virtues in order to establish the legitimacy of their dominant position. A typical example of this tendency may be found in Aristotle's defence of slavery. Aristotle argued that men differ from one another in their moral excellence; that the slaves were not full human beings, capable of virtue—they were merely 'living tools'. He suggested that slaves receive the benefit of virtue solely by serving their masters. He also argued that the system of slavery provided 'leisure' for the freemen which was essential for the exercise of virtue.

Thus, the privileged classes have always stood in defence of the *status quo*— no change in the existing situation. It is only when the subjugated sections rise in revolt against injustice and oppression that they challenge the special privileges of the dominant sections and raise the slogan of liberty to press their claim of equality. Liberty is, therefore, a force behind social change—it is the voice of the oppressed; it is the voice against injustice; it is the voice to reestablish human values as against the rules of the animal kingdom.

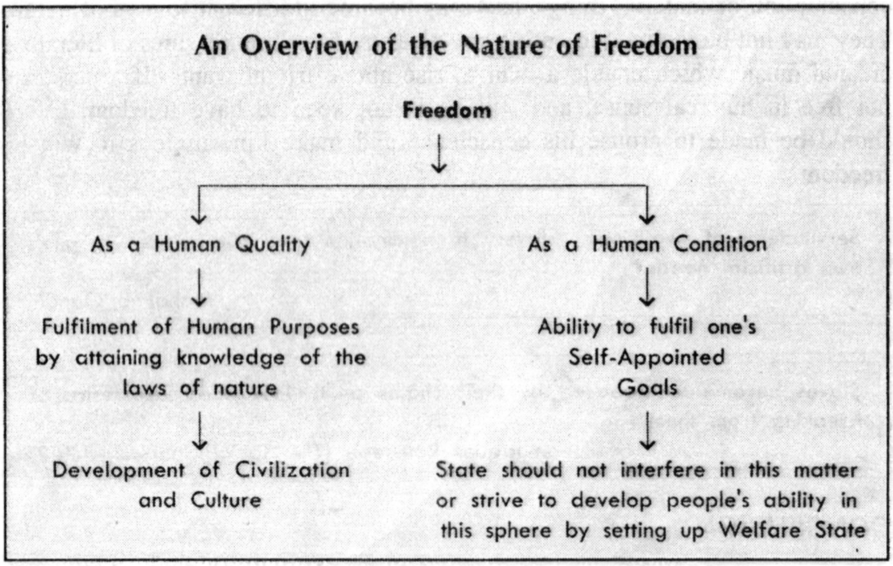

[II] SCOPE OF LIBERTY

The problem of liberty involves the adjustment of claims between individual and society (or community). The state comes into the picture because it is the instrument or agency for regulating their relations. If the claim of the individual is stretched to an extreme in utter disregard of the interest of society, liberty would be reduced to 'licence'. On the other hand, if liberty of the individual is increasingly restricted in the supposed interest of society, the result would be an unconditional submission to authority, hence the loss of liberty, amounting to tyranny. It is, therefore, essential to draw a distinction between liberty and licence on the one hand, and to fix the proper frontier between liberty and authority on the other.

Relation Between Liberty and Authority; Liberty and Licence

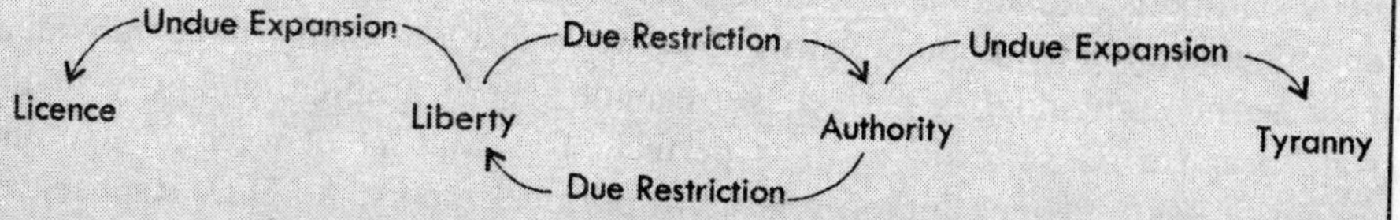

Liberty demands due restriction on Authority;
Authority demands due restriction on Liberty;
Undue expansion of Liberty results in Licence;
Undue expansion of Authority results in Tyranny.

(Tyranny = a cruel, unjust and oppressive rule of a person or a small group of people who exercise absolute power over everyone else within their jurisdiction.)

LIBERTY AND AUTHORITY

It is evident that liberty of the individual has to be restricted by a measure of equal liberty to be enjoyed by others. In other words, one man's liberty should not become an obstruction in the enjoyment of similar and equal liberty by others. As liberty is demanded for man as a 'rational being', it follows that liberty is meant to enable men to pursue 'rational objects' or 'ideal objects'. If they do so, each individual shall pursue his happiness in consonance with the happiness of society; and individual's good will become an integral part of the social good. In such a perfect state, no regulations would be necessary. But since, in the real world, individuals are not perfect—they are only capable of perfection—the regulation of liberty becomes necessary to safeguard liberty itself. As Ernest Barker (*Principles of Social and Political Theory;* 1951) has observed:

> Liberty within the State is thus a relative and regulated liberty: it is the greatest common measure of liberty which is possible for all, as determined and defined (1) by the need of each to enjoy similar and equal liberty with others; and (2) by the need of all to enjoy the specific liberty of realizing specific capacities.

This view of relative and regulated liberty does not dismiss or dilute the essence of liberty. On the contrary, it provides for a more substantive foundation thereof. As Barker has elucidated:

> A relative and regulated liberty, actually operative and enjoyed, is liberty greater in amount than absolute liberty could ever be—if indeed such liberty could ever exist, or ever amount to anything more than nothing at all (*ibid.*).

Regulation of liberty implies the recognition of authority of the state over the individual. If liberty of the individual cannot be permitted to be absolute, can we allow the authority of the state to become absolute? Thus, the conflict between liberty and authority is no less grave than the conflict between absolute and regulated liberty. In other words, if we deny absolute liberty to the individual because no individual is perfect, we cannot accord absolute authority to the state because no state on earth is perfect. The conflict between liberty and authority has remained a thorny issue in political theory. As D.D. Raphael, in his *Problems of Political Philosophy* (1976), has illustrated:

> Most political theorists recognize that individual liberty and State authority conflict with each other, and that a balance has to be struck between them and the values they represent. Some, like Hobbes, are prepared to say that liberty must be severely limited to make way for the benefits of State authority. Others, like Locke and J.S. Mill, think that State authority should be markedly limited so as to leave as much room as possible for liberty.

In any case, limitations on the authority of the state have to be laid down to make authority more meaningful with reference to its social purpose. A state may possess unlimited legal powers. For instance, the British Parliament is regarded as legally omnipotent. But in the real world, no state can afford to exercise unlimited powers. As Raphael has elucidated:

> No State has unlimited practical power to make any law that it pleases, even though it may possess unlimited legal power. A legislature that has any sense and that wants to remain in office will pay more regard to political than to legal possibilities, to what it can effectively do than to what it may legally do.

A state makes law; it has the power to enforce that law by coercion. In other words, the law is backed by sanctions; the state is free to use the methods of compulsion. However, compulsion comprises a physical weapon, not a moral weapon which would be not only more effective, but more conducive to the social purpose of state authority. Thus, state authority would be much more justified if it is backed by moral support and *legitimacy* instead of mere force. Legitimacy denotes the support extended by the people to the state and its law out of their moral beliefs and values.

Legitimacy

Legitimacy refers to the quality of an act or arrangement which is regarded as lawful by those affected by it. In other words, they regard it reasonable and beneficial for themselves as well as for the larger society.

Legitimacy comes from the people. A state is legitimate if people believe that it is necessary for them and that its actions are lawful and valuable to society. As long as its legitimacy is unquestioned, the state will rarely need to use force.

But if its legitimacy is widely questioned, the state is in a dangerous situation. A regime is in serious trouble if the people believe that its military is illegitimate, its police brutal, and its courts unfair. It may have power—the ability to get its orders obeyed despite widespread opposition—but it does not have authority rooted in legitimacy. Authority of the state or law would prove most effective only when most people accepted it on moral grounds. When most people recognized a moral obligation to obey law, they would be acting from a moral motive, and not under compulsion.

LIBERTY AND LICENCE

When liberty is interpreted as the absence or removal of all restraints on the actions of individual in utter disregard of the interest of other individuals, liberty degenerates into licence. Such a condition is not compatible with the maintenance of social order, nor with the maintenance of liberty itself. In that case, one man's liberty would become another's constraint or oppression; liberty of the strong would amount to the suppression of the weak; liberty of the wolf would amount to death of the innocent sheep; the large fish will be free to swallow the smaller one, and there would be a still larger fish to swallow the former. A thief's liberty to take away anybody's property would become a threat to everybody's security. A driver's freedom to drive at any speed in any direction at his own whim would endanger the life and liberty of all users of the road. Such a situation is obviously self-contradictory. It cannot be permitted in a civil society, otherwise it would defeat the very purpose of social organization.

If freedom is not to become a prerogative of a single individual, or for that matter of a group of individuals, it must be regulated in such a way that none shall use his freedom so as to destroy the freedom of others. As L.T. Hobhouse, in his *Elements of Social Justice* (1922), has pointed out: "The unchartered freedom of one would be the conditional servitude of all but one, and conversely a freedom to be enjoyed by all must impose some restraint upon all." Ernest Barker, in his *Principles of Social and Political Theory* (1951), has sought to apply this principle in the wider socio-economic context:

> The need of liberty for each is necessarily qualified and conditioned by the need of liberty for all... The liberty of the owner of capital to determine the conditions of work in the factory which he owns is a relative liberty which must be adjusted to the liberty of the worker to do his work under such conditions as leave him still a free agent and give him also a share in the determination of the conditions of work. Because the liberty of each is, thus, relative to that of others, and has to be adjusted to that of others, it must always be regulated; and indeed it would not exist unless it were regulated.

In a nutshell, for maintaining liberty in society in the real sense, it is necessary to maintain proper balance between liberty and authority so that it is not reduced to tyranny, and also to prescribe its proper limits so that it does not degenerate into licence.

[III]
DIMENSIONS OF LIBERTY

Liberty may formally be described as 'absence of restraint'. This means that in order to maintain liberty of the individual, the state should not impose any restraints on his activities in various spheres of life. What type of activities of the individual should remain unrestrained? 'Unrestrained' does not mean 'unregulated'. It simply implies that the activities in question should not be subjected to 'unreasonable restraints'. In order to identify the proper sphere of such activities, we may distinguish between civil, political and economic liberty of the individual.

CIVIL LIBERTY

Civil liberty, according to Barker (*Principles of Social and Political Theory*; 1951), is the liberty of man in the capacity of an individual person—his personal liberty. This consists in three somewhat differently expressed articles: (*a*) physical freedom from injury or threat to the life, health, and movement of the body; (*b*) intellectual freedom for the expression of thought and belief; and (*c*) practical freedom of a person to enter into mutual obligations with others in consideration of their mutual benefit—that is the freedom of contract.

Of these, the first article is almost non-controversial. Freedom of movement, etc. should not be restricted except in the interest of public safety, law and order which are themselves essential conditions of freedom. Physical injury, etc. should not be inflicted on anybody except as a punishment for a crime duly proved, and in accordance with the prescribed law and by the prescribed authority in this behalf. As for the second article concerning the freedom of thought and belief, various reasons may be advanced in its defence. J.S. Mill (1806-73), the most ardent champion of liberty, has brilliantly demonstrated the importance of this freedom from the point of view of the individual as well as for the society in his famous essay *On Liberty* (1859). The permanent interests of man as a progressive being, according to Mill, depend upon or at least can be furthered by the advancement of knowledge, which flourishes best in an atmosphere of free discussion. In order to direct social policy wisely, it is necessary that there should be freedom to criticize the existing institutions and to put forward unpopular opinions, no matter how offensive they may be to the prevailing attitudes:

> The peculiar evil of silencing the expression of an opinion is that it is robbing the human race—posterity as well as the existing generation—

> those who dissent from the opinion, still more than those who hold it. If the opinion is right, they are deprived of the opportunity of exchanging error for truth; if wrong, they lose, what is almost as great a benefit, the clearer perception and livelier impression of truth, produced by the collision with error.

The third article of civil liberty mentioned by Barker, *viz.* the freedom of contract, however, needs closer examination. It is generally conceded that people enjoy the freedom to enter into contracts for their mutual advantage, provided that no damage is inflicted on a third party. But the difficulty arises when this freedom is exploited by a stronger party in a bargain to impose very disadvantageous terms on the weaker party. L.T. Hobhouse, in his *Elements of Social Justice* (1922), therefore, insists on the initial equality of the contracting parties in this matter:

> Freedom of contract is insufficiently defined when it is regarded as consisting solely in the absence of control. Freedom of contract implies such a substantial equality between the parties as on the whole leaves to each a real choice between concluding and rejecting the bargain. Where no such equality exists, one party acts under a degree of compulsion.

Absolute freedom of contract, in an extreme case, may be used to allow a man, or even force him, to sell himself to slavery and thereby deprive him of his freedom in perpetuity. Modern judicial thinking, therefore, always views the freedom of contract as a right which should operate under reasonable limitations.

It is important to note that various elements of civil liberty are now clubbed together and described as 'civil liberties'. Protection of civil liberties is regarded an essential feature of liberal democracy.

Civil Liberties

Civil liberties refer to the legal instruments of protection of the individual from arbitrary acts of government. These include personal freedom, freedom of movement, freedom of thought and expression, faith and worship, freedom of association and assembly, right to fair trial, equality before the law, etc.

POLITICAL LIBERTY

Whereas a man enjoys civil liberty in the capacity of an individual person, he enjoys political liberty in the capacity of a citizen. To William Blackston (1723-80), political liberty meant the power of curbing government, from which it follows that he conceived of government as something external. But in modern democracy, where government is constituted by the people themselves, political liberty is "a liberty not of curbing government, but of constituting and controlling; constituting it by a general act of choice or election, in which we all freely share on the basis of universal suffrage;

controlling it by a general and continuous process of discussion, in which we all freely share according to our capacities" (Ernest Barker, *Principles of Social and Political Theory;* 1951).

This view of political liberty postulates the tangible right of the people to be represented in decision-making bodies, and to influence their decisions by freely articulating their views and opinions on issues of public policy. In effect, it is intended to ensure that the state shall be sensitive and responsible to the prevailing social consciousness.

In any case, mere provision of political liberty in this sense cannot be treated as adequate. Where elections are fought and won with the help of money and manipulative power, and where the media of mass communication are held in ownership or under strong influence of a privileged class, particularly by big business magnates, who exploit these instruments for earning more profits, mere political liberty can hardly secure real or substantive freedom for the people.

ECONOMIC LIBERTY

Economic liberty, broadly speaking, belongs to man in his capacity as a worker whether with hand or brain, engaged in some gainful occupation or service. In this sense, Barker suggests that economic liberty is implied in the articles of civil liberty already enumerated. In fact, however, economic liberty is a ticklish issue. It is capable of conflicting interpretations by conflicting parties: employer and worker, trader and consumer, landlord and tenant, etc. One party would interpret it as the freedom to secure maximum profit; the other would insist on reasonable terms, reasonable price and quality, reasonable rent, etc. Under such circumstances, if the stronger party is not curbed to safeguard the interests of the weaker party, the principle of liberty will be reduced to mockery. This is the sphere where the adjustment between the claims of liberty and equality becomes most essential. As R.H. Tawney, in his *Equality* (1938), has significantly observed:

> When liberty is construed, realistically, as implying not merely a minimum of civil and political rights, but the securities that the economically weak will not be at the mercy of the economically strong, and that the control of those aspects of economic life by which all are affected will be amenable, in the last resort, to the will of all, a large measure of equality, so far from being inimical to liberty, is essential to it.

In short, it is in the economic sphere that the claims of negative liberty and positive liberty come into direct conflict and confrontation. Unless social policy is geared to safeguard the interests of the vulnerable sections in this sphere, the application of the principle of liberty or freedom would be devoid of any content or substance.

[IV]
LIBERAL-INDIVIDUALIST VIEW OF LIBERTY

NEGATIVE AND POSITIVE LIBERTY: THE EARLY DEBATE

Liberal writers use the terms 'liberty' and 'freedom' synonymously. For them, liberty or freedom is the supreme value which must be the guiding principle of all public policy. It is generally the liberty of individual which they wish to protect, and it is defined as 'the absence of restraint' or 'the absence of constraint or coercion'. What types of constraints beset the man which are sought to be removed in pursuance of the principle of liberty or freedom?

To illustrate this point, we may refer to the *Atlantic Charter* (1941), a declaration of 'Four Freedoms', which was drawn up during the Second World War (1939-45) by President Roosevelt of the United States and Prime Minister Churchill of the United Kingdom to indicate their war aims. The four freedoms were: freedom of speech, freedom of worship, freedom from fear, freedom from want. Can we classify these four freedoms on the basis of some common features? D.D. Raphael, in his *Problems of Political Philosophy* (1976), has identified two pairs comprising these four freedoms:

> The first pair of freedoms specify two kinds of action which should be free or unrestrained; they answer the question, freedom to do what? 'Freedom of speech' is freedom to say what one likes. 'Freedom of worship' is freedom to practise whatever religion one chooses. The second pair of freedoms in the Atlantic Charter specify two kinds of restraint which should be removed or prevented: they answer the question, freedom from what? 'Freedom from fear' claims that men should not be prevented by fear from doing whatever they choose to do, fear of a Government with secret police such as the Nazis used, or fear of war and insecurity. 'Freedom from want' claims that men should not be prevented by want from doing what they would choose to do, want or poverty due to unemployment, the lack of living wage, or the inability to work because of sickness or old age.

It is significant that the two types of freedoms included in the said Charter of four freedoms have a much wider application than a statement of aims of the Second World War. They could be used to highlight the aims of public policy in a modern state, particularly a welfare state. The first type of freedoms, such as freedom of speech and freedom of worship, symbolize the *negative* aspect of liberty. They imply a negative role of the state, that is not to restrict the individual in pursuing his self-appointed goals. The second type of freedoms, such as freedom from fear and freedom from want, symbolize *the positive* aspect of liberty. They call for a positive role of the state, that is to remove certain impediments in the way of the individual in exercising his freedom.

Once this basic distinction between negative and positive aspects of liberty is recognized, the actual lists of freedoms falling under each category can be suitably enlarged. It is also essential to remember that these two types of freedom, namely *negative liberty* and *positive liberty,* are not opposed to each other. In fact, they are complementary; they are two sides of the same coin. They are incomplete without each other, although some thinkers accord primacy to one over the other.

It is also important to note that the struggle for liberty started in seventeenth century Europe with the rise of a new merchant-industrialist class which raised the demand of negative liberty, particularly in the economic sphere. It was intended to pave the way for the establishment of capitalism against the prevailing forces of feudalism. As Norman P. Barry, in his *An Introduction to Modern Political Theory* (1989), has elucidated: "The negative conception of liberty ...flourished at a time when individuals were struggling to be free from the unnecessary restraints of arbitrary government and when individual choice determined the allocation of resources. The main political axiom of the negative liberty doctrine was that 'everyone knows his own interest best' and that the state should not decide his ends and purposes." The champions of negative liberty not only believed in individual choice of resources and techniques, but also the choice of parties to deal with in their transactions. Thus, 'freedom of contract' was recognized as an essential requirement of liberty.

Henry Sidgwick (1838-1900) argued that a person who freely negotiated a contract, expressed his individual choice even if the terms were particularly onerous to him. The early liberals who stood for liberty in all spheres insisted that law must enforce all contracts (with some exceptions, such as in the case of contracts of slavery) since each individual was the best judge of his own interest, and he used his judgment before entering into any contract. The state was not allowed to impose its own conception of 'good' on the individuals in their mutual dealings. This idea of negative liberty led to the doctrine of *laissez-faire,* that is freedom from government interference in economic affairs. Hence, most of the advocates of negative liberty, such as Adam Smith (1723-90), Jeremy Bentham (1748-1832), James Mill (1773-1836), Henry Sidgwick (1838-1900) and Herbert Spencer (1820-1903), favoured the minimal state.

This liberal-individualist view of liberty was originally put forward by the spokesmen of the new middle class—the merchant-industrialist class which sought to establish a 'free market society' against the mercantile policies of the state. It was argued that, in an atmosphere of non-intervention, the interaction between self-interest of each individual would result in the promotion of social interest as a whole. The exponents of *laissez-faire* individualism saw society as an aggregate of atomized, alienated individuals, joined together by a bond of mechanical unity. Liberty was seen as the freedom of trade, freedom of enterprise, freedom of contract, a free competition of the market forces of supply and demand. The state was viewed as a negative state, a necessary evil, which was required not to interfere with the natural liberty of men, but only to maintain their liberty by protecting their person and property from the onslaught of other individuals.

Mercantile Policy

Mercantile policy refers to the policy which advocated state intervention in economy for the protection of indigenous industries to ensure import of cheap raw materials and export of expensive finished goods. These steps were thought to be necessary for enhancing national prosperity.

***Laissez-Faire* Individualism**

Laissez-faire individualism refers to a political outlook which holds that individual is endowed with the faculty of 'reason'. It enables him to find what is most conducive to his interest in a given situation. This outlook upholds 'non-intervention' of the state in the economic activities of individuals. It, therefore, advocates individual's right to freedom of trade, freedom of contract, freedom to bargain and freedom of enterprise.

The concept of negative liberty played an important historical role. It proved instrumental in the establishment of capitalist system in Europe. It released the forces of production which were blocked by the feudal system inherited from the Middle Ages. But by the middle of the nineteenth century, it became evident that the capitalist system supported by negative liberty had brought about miserable conditions for workers and consumers. The appalling disparities of wealth and power—mounting oppression, exploitation and injustice in society—amply demonstrated contradictions in this concept of liberty. Humanist writers, socialists, Marxists and positive liberals came forward to demand a new definition of liberty. They argued that the non-interventionist policy of the state, particularly in the economic sphere, was not compatible with liberty as a universal principle. The employer's freedom to hire and fire workers at his will in the face of a rapidly rising labour force in industrial cities had made a mockery of the freedom of contract; the workers were forced to live under constant insecurity and threat of unemployment, to work under uncongenial conditions, and to live a life of abject poverty at a sub-human level. The benefit of 'liberty' was now sought to be extended to the working class, largely because of the mounting pressure from the working class itself.

It was John Stuart Mill (1806-73) who introduced the conception of positive liberty and consequent transition from negative liberalism to positive liberalism. Mill started with a defence of *laissez-faire* individualism, but realizing its weaknesses in the light of the new socio-economic realities, he proceeded to modify it. Mill was the first prominent liberal thinker who realized that the working classes were being deprived of their due share in a capitalist economy based on *laissez-faire* individualism. He, therefore, sought to discover an area where state intervention could be justified. At the outset, he drew a distinction between two types of actions of men: 'self-regarding actions' whose effect was confined to the individual himself; and 'other-regarding actions' which affected others. Mill advocated complete freedom of conduct for the individual in the sphere of self-regarding actions unless he was proceeding on a self-destructive path due to ignorance. However, in the sphere of 'other-regarding actions' Mill conceded the right of the community to coerce the individual if his conduct was prejudicial to its welfare. Whether it is possible to draw a clear line of demarcation between 'self-regarding actions' and 'other-regarding actions' of the individual is beside the point. The real significance of making such a distinction lay in Mill's effort to define a sphere where an individual's behaviour could be regulated in the interests of the community. Thus, he was contemplating a positive role for the state in securing social welfare even if it implied curbing liberty of the individual to some extent. It was Mill who gave a sound theory of taxation, pleaded for the limitation of the right of inheritance, and insisted on state provision of education.

After J.S. Mill, T.H. Green (1836-82), L.T. Hobhouse (1864-1929) and H.J. Laski (1893-1950) further developed the positive concept of liberty. Green postulated a theory of rights and insisted on the positive role of the state in creating conditions under which men could effectively exercise their moral freedom. Hobhouse and Laski postulated that private property was no absolute right, and that the state must secure the welfare of the people—no matter if it is constrained to curtail economic liberty of the privileged few. In short, the idea of positive liberty reached its logical conclusion in the concept of the welfare state.

Welfare State

Welfare state refers to a state that safeguards liberty of its citizens and also provides various types of social services for them, e.g. social security (financial assistance in the case of loss of job or any other source of income, death of the bread-winner, prolonged illness or physical disability or any other calamity), free education, public health, poor relief, supply of essential goods and services like foodgrains, milk, fuel and transport to the needy at subsidized rates. It undertakes the protection of cultural heritage including monuments, museums, libraries, art galleries, botanical gardens and zoological parks, etc. It also promotes higher education and scientific research, etc. to step up intellectual and cultural development of society. It makes use of public resources and taxation of the relatively rich to provide for a vast network of social services.

THE CONTEMPORARY DEBATE

It is significant that political thought of the early exponents of positive liberty is associated with the theory of welfare state, which first flourished in England and then spread to other parts of the world. Positive liberty is now regarded as an essential complement of negative liberty in all modern states. However, some contemporary liberal thinkers, known as exponents of Libertarianism, have sought to lay renewed emphasis on negative liberty. Of these, Isaiah Berlin (1909-97), F.A. Hayek (1899-1992), Milton Friedman (1912-2006) and Robert Nozick (1938-2002) are the most prominent.

Libertarianism

Libertarianism refers to a contemporary principle of politics which seeks to remove all impediments in the way of individual's liberty as the basic principle of public policy. It rejects welfare state and treats free market society as an essential condition of liberty. It stands for minimum intervention of the State in mutual dealings of individuals.

Free Market Society

Free market society refers to a model of society where all social relationships are reduced to market relations, that is the relations between supplier and consumer. Accordingly, all individuals (or families) are expected to ascertain each other's needs and earn their living by fulfilling them. Thus, it cultivates respect for each other's abilities and achievements, and encourages their dealings for mutual advantage. However, since its organization is based on the cruel forces of demand and supply, it has little room for humane considerations or a sympathetic treatment towards disadvantaged people.

Views of Berlin

Isaiah Berlin, in his *Two Concepts of Liberty* (1958), sought to give a new turn to the distinction between negative liberty and positive liberty. According to Berlin, negative liberty of individual consists in not being prevented from attaining his goal by other human beings. On the other hand, positive liberty treats individual as his own master. In both cases liberty implies *an absence of restraint*. Political liberty belongs only to the sphere of negative liberty. In other words, the state can only secure negative liberty to the individual by ensuring that he is not prevented from choosing his course of action. On the other hand, positive liberty belongs to individual's own will and capacity which is beyond the scope of the state. If one cannot fly like an eagle or swim like a whale, one is by no means deprived of political liberty on this count. Similarly, if a man is too poor to afford something on which there is no legal ban—a loaf of bread, a journey round the world, recourse to law courts—he cannot complain that he has been deprived of political liberty. The capacity or incapacity to fulfil one's desires belongs to man himself; the state is not concerned with this sphere. Berlin has thus taken the position that the availability or non-availability of means is entirely an individual's own concern and that the state has no responsibility of making the required means available to him. Accordingly, the existing social inequalities cannot be questioned from the point of view of liberty. Berlin's position on this point is itself questionable.

On closer analysis, it becomes clear that Berlin has confused the two spheres of positive liberty, namely the moral sphere and the material sphere. In the moral sphere, Berlin's conception of positive liberty is very illuminating. Norman P. Barry, in his *An Introduction to Modern Political Theory* (1989), has elaborated Berlin's view as follows: "Positive liberty...does not interpret freedom as simply being left alone but as 'self-mastery'. The theory is a special theory of the self—the personality is divided into a higher and lower self and a person is free to the extent that his higher self, the source of his genuinely rational and long-term ends, is in command of his lower self, wherein lie his ephemeral and irrational desires. Thus, a person might be free in the sense of not being restrained by external forces but remain a slave to irrational appetites; as a drug-addict, an alcoholic or a compulsive gambler might be said to be unfree." It is obvious that in the moral sphere, a man may be deprived of his freedom due to lack of self-control, not due to coercion by other men. The state can do little to restore freedom to the individual in this sphere.

However, when we turn to the material sphere, enjoyment of positive freedom is hampered by different reasons. Here again, Berlin has confused the two types of disabilities. Just recall his illustrations: "If one cannot fly like an eagle or swim like a whale"—this disability is fundamentally different from the second one, that is "if a man is too poor to afford...a loaf of a bread, and...recourse to law courts." In the first case, Berlin is pointing to natural limitations, something that is *unalterable.* Hence, any complaint in this behalf would be untenable. In actual life, such disabilities are never sought to be overcome by political action. But in the second case, Berlin is referring to such disabilities as are the product of social arrangement that is *alterable* by political action. An urge for removal of such disabilities has led to several social and political movements, even revolutions, the world over. Lots of people are poor, backward and ignorant not because of their own failure, inability or negligence, but because of social injustice. The source of their plight may be traced to what may aptly be termed 'coercion by other individuals' where state intervention would be justified by Berlin's own standards. As B.C. Parekh, in his *Contemporary Political Thinkers* (1982), has significantly observed: "It is not clear what Berlin would say if an individual thought that his lack of means was the result of social arrangements and therefore, amounted to an interference by other men." C.B. Macpherson has criticized Berlin in his *Democratic Theory—Essays in Retrieval* (1973) on similar lines: "...the division Berlin makes between negative and positive liberty will not bear the weight he puts on it, ultimately because each of the two concepts is defined in a way which neglects or understates the role of those impediments..., namely, lack of access to the means of life and the means of labour...his negative liberty is, for that reason, too narrowly conceived, and... it is at bottom a mechanical, inertial concept of freedom which is fully appropriate only to a complete market society." In asserting positive liberty as the desire of the individual to be his own master, to be self-directed, to be moved by his own conscious purpose, Berlin saves the individual from the authoritarian claims of the idealist theory, and thus makes further contribution to the liberal-individualist theory. In any case, Berlin's concept of positive liberty does not correspond to positive liberals' concept of positive liberty.

> **Idealist Theory of Freedom**
>
> It refers to the theory of freedom chiefly advanced by G.W.F. Hegel (1770-1831) which eulogizes the state as embodiment of *Reason* and holds that individual's freedom lies in accepting the dictates of the ideal state. This theory proves disastrous when an existing government is equated with the state, and it is allowed to exercise the authority of the ideal state without questioning the character of the persons constituting that particular government.

The more logical distinction between negative liberty and positive liberty is one that focuses on the role of the state under different situations. According to this view, negative liberty consists in the 'absence of restraint', *i.e.* non-interference by the state in certain activities of the individual, to enable him to pursue his own happiness so long as he does not obstruct others in their similar freedom to pursue their happiness. Positive liberty, on the other hand, consists in extending the opportunity to the individual to pursue his happiness where he is obstructed in doing so for want of the means or capacity due to the prevailing socio-economic conditions. As S.I. Benn and R.S. Peters, in their *Social Principles and the Democratic State* (1975), have illustrated:

> If education is expensive and the parents are poor, it makes a mockery of freedom to say that one is free to educate one's children merely because there is no law or custom against it. Choice may *be formally* unlimited; there can be no freedom unless it is also *effectively* unlimited. To remove any hindrance to people doing what they want to do thus counts as an extension of freedom.

Any state regulation which seeks to reconcile the claims of liberty with opportunity, in fact, signifies the transition from negative liberty to positive liberty:

> To provide a cripple with an artificial leg, an ignorant man with education, an unemployed man with a job, all count as positive extensions of freedom. Legal compulsions are then a small price to pay for positive freedoms of this sort; for we yield a little only to receive back more. And the absolute goodness of freedom remains intact (*ibid.*).

It is significant that positive freedom in the present sense deals with the social dimension of freedom. In other words, negative liberty denotes an absence of restraint so that the state shall abstain from imposing 'unreasonable' restraints on the individual; positive liberty signifies removal of constraints which are the product of the social set-up and which are capable of being removed by making necessary changes in the social set-up. If a man is faced with the lack of capacity in the fulfilment of his desire, he will not make it a *political issue* until he is convinced that his incapacity emanates from the socio-economic conditions, and that it can be removed by making necessary changes in those conditions. If one cannot fly like an eagle or swim like a whale, one does not make it a political issue because one's incapacity in this matter is not a product of socio-economic conditions, nor can it be removed by altering the socio-economic conditions. But if one does not get a job, or adequate wages, or quality goods at a reasonable price, or essential supplies and services, or the opportunity for education, etc., one is convinced that these conditions are alterable by changes in social policy, and therefore, proceeds to demand a political solution of these problems.

To take another instance, some men are born white, some are born black. This is the outcome of some sort of natural order, not of socio-economic conditions. Men do not complain of it at the political level, nor do they demand that the black races should be converted into white, because they know that this condition is not alterable. But when society discriminates between white and black races, and denies the black certain privileges extended to the white men, the resentment by the black races is justified because this is seen as social injustice which can be set right by making necessary changes in social policy. In short, positive liberty implies the removal of only such constraints and provision of only such opportunities which can be accomplished through alteration of socio-economic conditions. As D.D. Raphael, in his *Problems of Political Philosophy* (1976), has elucidated:

> A man who is locked up in prison is not at liberty, because he is restrained by the action of other persons. And we may speak of freedom from want, or of freeing mankind from the scourge of cancer, when we mean that the impediments to which we refer, although not imposed by human action, are capable (we hope) of being removed by human action. But we should not say that a man is unfree because he is restrained by a natural impediment which cannot be removed by human action.

Views of Hayek

F.A. Hayek, in his *Constitution of Liberty* (1960), used the terms 'liberty' and 'freedom' interchangeably. He argued that *a man possesses liberty or freedom when he is not subject to coercion by the arbitrary will of another*. This is the essence of individual freedom which should not be confused with any other meaning of freedom. Hayek particularly sought to contrast individual freedom with three other meanings of freedom, which represent 'political freedom', 'inner freedom' and 'freedom as power' respectively. Political freedom allows participation of men in the choice of their government, in the process of legislation, and in the control of administration. This does not necessarily coincide with individual freedom. Thus, Hayek argues that a non-democratic order may be permissive and a democratic order may be restrictive;

hence, political freedom is neither a necessary nor a sufficient condition of individual freedom.

Then, inner freedom refers to the extent to which a person is guided in his actions by his own considered will rather than by momentary impulse or circumstance. It stands opposed not to coercion by others but to moral weakness or the influence of passing emotions. Hence, it is different from individual freedom. Finally, freedom as power signifies the power to satisfy our wishes, or the extent of the choice of alternatives open to us. There is a vital difference between non-interference with another's act and a person's effective power to act. A person may be able to do what he may not lawfully do, or unable to do what nobody is trying to prevent him from doing. Hence, freedom as power should not be confused with individual freedom.

Hayek insists on preserving the original meaning of the word 'freedom', enhancing its value by closely restricting its application. He argues that the cardinal value of liberty should not be exploited by the advocates of collectivism to justify large amounts of state intervention. If liberty is viewed as power, there is no end to the number of legislative measures which can be justified as extending the range of choice of persons, or their effective power to do whatever they may wish. The result could be the destruction of individual liberty in the name of a spurious notion of liberty. Hayek is not denying that the limited provision by government of skills and opportunities is desirable; he is only saying that *such enabling activities should not be represented as promoting freedom!*

Collectivism

Collectivism refers to a principle which holds that society should be organized on the basis of collective control of economic production and political decisions. Generally this control is to be exercised through state institutions. Collectivism is directly opposed to individualism. It is closely related to various forms of socialism, communism and syndicalism, etc.

In short, Hayek identifies freedom as 'freedom from constraints of the state' in the tradition of James Madison (1751-1836), Alexis de Tocqueville (1805-59) and Lord Acton (1834-1902). Hayek defines and defends liberalism as a doctrine which emphasizes the minimization of the coercive powers of government. He argues that the state should positively promote competition, and should undertake non-coercive service functions, as the market mechanism does not provide for all needs. *The state* should ensure minimum income to each individual or family, but *should not make market itself an instrument of distributive justice!* Dwelling on the antithesis between liberty and equality, Hayek argues that individuals differ greatly in their skills and abilities and this natural tendency towards inequality can be countered only by the authoritarian suppression of individual talents and aspirations. Thus, he observes:

> From the fact that people are very different it follows that, if we treat them equally, the result must be inequality in their actual position, and that the only way to place them in an equal position would be to treat them differently... The equality before the law which freedom requires leads to material inequality... The desire of making people more alike in their condition cannot be accepted in a free society as a justification for further and discriminatory coercion (*The Constitution of Liberty;* 1960).

In a nutshell, Hayek's argument against equality is based on two premises. In the first place, he assumes that liberty consists in 'absence of coercion' in the sphere of individual activity by other individuals or the state. Secondly, he observes that individuals differ in their talents and skills and their equality before the law (in consonance with the principle of liberty) is bound to create inequality in their actual position in terms of their material status. Hence, any attempt to create material equality among different individuals is bound to involve 'coercion' which would deprive them of their freedom.

Hayek's concern for freedom is so profound that he even tends to ignore the claim of 'equal freedom' for all individuals. He recognizes the value of individual freedom not so much from the standpoint of the individual as from that of society. For Hayek, acquisition and use of new knowledge is the key to social progress. An individual makes his contribution to progress through the cumulative growth of knowledge: "If there were omniscient men...there would be little case for liberty... Liberty is essential in order to leave room for the unforeseeable and unpredictable" (*ibid.*). The larger the sum total of human knowledge, the smaller the share each individual can absorb. Nobody is competent enough to pronounce a final word about human affairs. Submission to another's will is, therefore, disastrous. The value of any particular freedom is not to be judged by counting heads. The importance of freedom to do a particular thing has nothing to do with the number of people who want to do it. It is quite possible that the freedoms vital to social progress may not be widely sought. *Hayek, therefore, asserts that it is better that some should be free than none and better that many should have full freedom than that all should have a limited freedom!* Thus according to Hayek, the 'cake' of freedom is not to be divided on the basis of 'equal shares for all', but on the basis of each individual's contribution to progress. Since each individual has unknown potential of making contribution to progress, it is difficult to ascertain each individual's entitlement to different amounts of freedom! *Hayek's conclusions are not consistent with his own assumptions.* He begins with taking individual as the end and ends up by reducing him to a means!

Views of Friedman

Milton Friedman, in his *Capitalism and Freedom* (1962), sought to identify capitalism or a competitive market society as a necessary condition of freedom, which implies repudiation of equality for the sake of maintaining freedom. He defines freedom as 'the absence of coercion of a man by his fellow men', and argues that freedom of the individual, or perhaps of the family is the liberal's ultimate goal in judging social arrangements. He suggests that 'a free private enterprise exchange economy' or 'competitive capitalism' is both a direct component of freedom, and a necessary though not a sufficient condition of political freedom. Friedman's contempt for equality is inherent in his very concept of freedom. He argues that in order to maximize this freedom, governments should be allowed to handle only those matters which cannot be handled through the market at all, or can be handled only at so great a cost that the use of political channels may be preferable. Accordingly, government is required only to sustain and supplement the market society and nothing beyond that. As Macpherson has elucidated: "This would mean government moving out of almost all its welfare and regulatory functions. Controls on, or support of, any prices, wages, interest rates, rents, exports, imports, and amounts produced, would all have to go; so would present social security programmes, housing subsidy programmes, and the like" (*Democratic Theory — Essays in Retrieval;* 1973).

Macpherson has rightly pointed out that Friedman's view of the capitalist market economy—that it can co-ordinate economic activities without coercion—rests on an elementary conceptual error. Friedman fails to distinguish between simple exchange economy and capitalist economy—the latter being characterized by the separation of labour and capital. In a capitalist economy, labour force exists without its own sufficient capital, hence it has no choice in the market. Man needs creative freedom to put his labour into creative channels; he cannot remain idle like an animal or a machine. Capitalism obstructs his attempt to employ his labour creatively with a free choice as he is coerced by the market forces beyond his control. The only possibility of mitigation of this coercion lies in a regulatory welfare state which is opposed by Friedman. Hence, Friedman's concept of freedom is ill-conceived and partial.

> **What distinguishes the capitalist economy from the simple exchange economy is the separation of labour and capital, that is the existence of a labour force without its own sufficient capital and therefore without a choice as to whether to put its labour in the market or not.**
>
> **C. B. Macpherson (*Democratic Theory—Essays in Retrieval;* 1973)**

Views of Nozick

Robert Nozick is another prominent liberal who seeks to oppose the principle of equality in strong terms. In his *Anarchy, State and Utopia* (1974), Nozick tries to determine functions of the state on the basis of his theory of origin of the state. Following Locke's method, Nozick asserts that individuals have certain rights in the state of nature. They would hire protective associations for their property holdings. The dominant protective association would become the 'state'. Nozick maintains that the acquisition or transfer of property without force or fraud is just, but not otherwise. Rights are the product of voluntary exchanges. The state comes into existence for the performance of limited functions, particularly for the maintenance of property rights of the individuals. This leads to legitimacy of a minimal state which does not engage in redistributive transfers among citizens who were originally its clients. Inequalities at the level of production should not be sought to be rectified at the level of distribution.

However, if there is only one source of water in a desert, nobody should be allowed to monopolize it. But this restriction should not apply to the products of human effort and talents. Thus, he who discovers remedy of a fatal disease is entitled to demand any price for it. In this way, Nozick assumes that all inequalities of wealth and power are the product of individual differences in talents and efforts and that it would not be just to remove or reduce these inequalities by redistributive transfers. This is the familiar argument of those liberal-individualists who tend to ignore the role of differences in social status in the differential outputs of different individuals. This view does not correspond to the realities of the capitalist system and is, therefore, ill-founded.

Distinction Between Negative and Positive Liberty

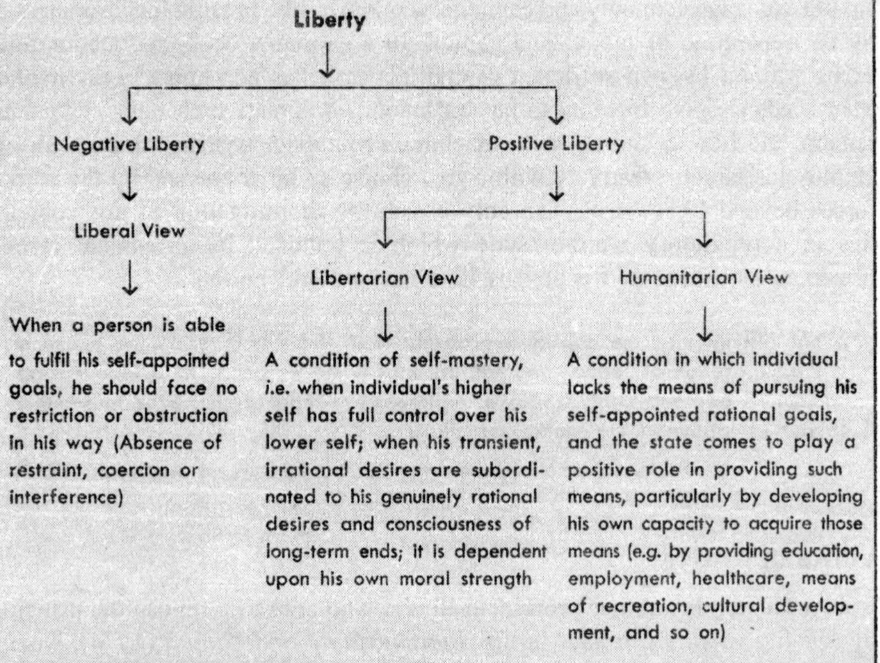

(Libertarians believe that the state can secure only negative liberty of the individual; acquisition of positive liberty is his own concern. On the other hand, moralists or humanitarians expect the state to secure positive liberty of the individual through its various welfare programmes.)

[V]
MARXIST CONCEPT OF FREEDOM

MARX AND ENGELS ON FREEDOM

Marxist concept of freedom is different from its liberal-individualist concept. It analyses freedom against the background of socio-economic conditions. According to the Marxist view, freedom is not something that an individual enjoys in isolation or by 'being left alone'. Marxism does not accept the theory of an atomized, alienated and possessive individual being capable of enjoying freedom. As Marx (1818-83) and Engels (1820-95), in their joint work *Holy Family* (1844), observed:

> The members of civil society are not atoms. The specific property of the atom is that is has no properties and is therefore not connected with beings outside it by any relations determined by its own natural necessity. The atom has no needs, it is self-sufficient; the world outside it is absolute vacuum, *i.e.* it is contentless, senseless, meaningless, just because the atom has *all* its fullness in itself. The egoistic individual in civil society may in his non-sensuous imagination and lifeless abstraction inflate himself to the size of an atom, *i.e.* to an unrelated, self-sufficient, wantless, absolutely full, blessed being.

Rejecting the atomistic view of the individual, Marx and Engels argue that the natural needs of man, the very conditions of his existence, bring him into a natural relation with other individuals and civil society comes into existence, which holds the individuals together.

Marxism does not accept the Utilitarian view that the common good can be derived from a mechanical aggregation of the good of different individuals. On the contrary, Marxism holds that the common good can be secured only by creating socio-economic conditions conducive to the enjoyment of freedom within society. These conditions involve access to the material means of satisfaction of wants and the opportunity for self-development. The key to freedom lies in establishing a rational system of production which will be based on the highest development of the forces of production, and provide the means for satisfaction of everybody's needs. As John Lewis, in his *Marxism and the Open Mind* (1976), has elucidated:

> For Marx, freedom means the ability to achieve the totality of human goods, satisfaction of aspirations, material and spiritual—fundamental to which is the mastery and rational control of the process of production of the material conditions of human life.

Utilitarianism

Utilitarianism refers to a school of thought founded by Jeremy Bentham (1748-1832), which treats pleasure and pain as the chief motive force behind all human actions. The balance of pleasure over pain derived from a thing or a course of action is termed as 'utility' which is the source of 'happiness'. According to this view, the guiding principle of public policy should be 'the greatest happiness of the greatest number' which represents the aggregate of happiness derived by individual members of society.

LEAP FROM NECESSITY TO FREEDOM

According to the Marxist view, capitalist system of production is not at all conducive to the conditions of human freedom. It is characterized by constraint or *necessity*. Necessity denotes the condition under which the life of man is governed by laws of nature, such as the law of gravitational force, which exist independently of man's will. Man can acquire scientific knowledge of these laws for his own benefit, but cannot change them at his will. As Engels, in his *Anti-Dühring* (1878), has elucidated:

> Necessity is *blind* only *in so far as it is not understood*... Freedom does not consist in any dream of independence from natural laws, but in the knowledge of these laws, and in the possibility this gives of systematically making them work towards definite ends.

This applies both to the laws of external nature and to the laws of our internal nature. As Engels has further observed:

> Freedom, therefore, consists in the control over ourselves and over external nature, a control founded on knowledge of natural necessity; it is, therefore, necessarily a product of historical development. The first men who separated themselves from the animal kingdom were in all essentials as unfree as the animals themselves, but each step forward in the field of culture was a step towards freedom.

The capitalist system has been facing continual crises because:

> society is suffocated beneath the weight of its own productive forces and products which it cannot use, and stands helpless, face to face with the absurd contradiction that the producers have nothing to consume, because consumers are wanting. The expansive force of the means of production bursts the bonds that the capitalist mode of production had imposed upon them. Their deliverance from these bonds is the one pre-condition for an unbroken, constantly-accelerated development of the productive forces, and therewith for a practically unlimited increase of production itself.

A scientific analysis of the forces of production reveals that only socialization of the means of production can help society to tide over this crisis which would usher in a new era of freedom. As Engels has elaborated:

> Man's own social organization, hitherto confronting him as a necessity imposed by nature and history, now becomes the result of his own free action. The extraneous objective forces that have hitherto governed history pass under the control of man himself. Only from that time will man himself, with full consciousness, make his own history—only from that time will the social causes set in movement by him have, in the main and in a constantly growing measure, the results intended by him. It is *humanity's leap from the kingdom of necessity to the kingdom of freedom.*

A similar focus on freedom is to be found in the picture of the future communist society as depicted by Marx and Engels in the *Communist Manifesto* (1848):

> When, in the course of development, class distinctions have disappeared, and all production has been concentrated in the hands of a vast association of the whole nation, the public power will lose its political character... In place of the old bourgeois society, with its classes and class antagonisms, we shall have an association, in which *the free development of each is the condition for the free development of all.*

HUMANIST BASIS OF FREEDOM

Marx, in his *Economic and Philosophic Manuscripts* (1844)—which were discovered and published as late as 1932—laid down the ethical basis of socialism and humanist foundations of freedom. He severely criticized capitalism for its dehumanizing effect. Marx demonstrated that the capitalist system deformed the productive activity of man and caused his alienation in several ways. Accordingly, the alienation of man in contemporary society was an outcome of the system of commodity production, division of labour, private ownership, market economy, monetization of exchange and similar features of the capitalist system. Marx identified four levels of alienation: (*a*) In the first place, man is alienated from his own product and from his work process, because the worker plays no part in deciding what to produce and how to produce; (*b*) Secondly, man is alienated from nature—his work does not give him a sense of satisfaction as a creative worker; under mechanization, the work tends to become increasingly routinized and monotonous; (*c*) In the third place, man is alienated from other men through the competitive character of the economic system which forces everyone to live at someone else's expense and divides society into irreconcilable class interests; and (*d*) Finally, man is alienated from himself because the *realm of necessity* dominates his life and reduces him to the level of animal existence, leaving no room for the taste of literature, art and cultural heritage. Thus, capitalism subordinates all human faculties and qualities to the conditions created by the private ownership of capital and property. The capitalist himself, no less than the worker, becomes a slave to the tyrannical rule of money.

Capitalism

Capitalism refers to an economic system of the modern age, largely based on industrial production, where means of social production (land, buildings, mines, forests, machinery and capital), distribution and exchange are owned by private entrepreneurs, a large number of workers are employed on wages at the market rate, and economic activity is primarily devoted to private profit. Here workers are free to work anywhere according to their skills and capacities as well as market demand.

Socialism

Socialism refers to an economic system of the modern age, largely based on industrial production in which the means of social production (land, buildings, mines, forests, machinery and capital), distribution and exchange are placed under social ownership and control, and economic activity is primarily devoted to the fulfilment of social needs. Here work is compulsory for every able-bodied person, and the state takes care of deploying all natural and human resources for the social benefit.

Alienation

Alienation refers to a state of mind in which individual is isolated from the significant aspects of his social existence or from the creative aspects of his own personality.

Deliverance from this bondage is only to be found in the realization that society is a creation by which man attains a fuller measure of freedom, which is obstructed by the peculiar conditions created by the private property, and these conditions exist in their worst form under the capitalist system. Its remedy may be found in a socialist revolution which will enable society to restore human values and inaugurate a new era of freedom. As Engels, in his *Anti-Dühring* (1878), has elucidated:

> By this act, the proletariat frees the means of production from the character of capital they have thus far borne, and gives their socialized character complete freedom to work itself out. Socialized production upon a predetermined plan becomes henceforth possible. The development of production makes the existence of different classes of society thenceforth an anachronism. In proportion as anarchy in social production vanishes, the political authority of the state dies out. Man, at last the master of his own form of social organization, becomes at the same time the lord over nature, his own master—free.

In short, while the liberal-individualist theory of freedom concedes that freedom of man can be secured with minor adjustments within the capitalist system, Marxist theory seeks to replace the capitalist system by socialist system in order to secure the conditions of freedom.

MARCUSE'S CONCEPT OF ONE-DIMENSIONAL MAN

Herbert Marcuse (1898-1979), who claimed to be a Marxist, gave a brilliant analysis of the problem of freedom in contemporary Western society. Orthodox Marxists as well as structural Marxists have been insisting on a scientific and economic interpretation of Marxism. In contrast, Marcuse, like many other exponents of the humanist stream of Neo-Marxism, underlined the subjective, critical and humanist dimension of Marxism. He rejected Soviet Marxism as a distorted version of Marxism and sought to revive the original, humanist interpretation of Marxism as a tool of analysis as well as an instrument of social change.

Neo-Marxism

Neo-Marxism refers to a set of those principles which seek to review the conditions prevailing in the contemporary world in the light of basic tenets of Marxism. Humanist stream of Neo-Marxism does not recognize the 'mode of production' as the sole determinant of social change, but undertakes an analysis of the subtle forms of dominance and dependence at various levels of contemporary society—such as economic, political, cultural and psychological levels—and tries to work out the way to human emancipation.

In his *One-Dimensional Man: Studies in the Ideology of Advanced Industrial Society* (1964), Marcuse dwelled on the theme of alienation in contemporary Western society. He gave a penetrating critique of capitalism as regards its impact on human freedom. According to him, capitalism exercises monopolistic control not only on production and distribution, it also creates the desire and demand for commodities through a clever manipulation of the mass media. The result is a widespread craze for consumer goods which develops into a distorted second nature of man. Consumer capitalism renders the oppressed sections insensitive to their original discontent, by stimulating their trivial, material desires which can be easily satisfied. Under the spell of gratification of these trivial desires, the genuine urge for freedom disappears. Against this background, the alienated human beings become unaware of their alienation. Under the circumstances, they should first be awakened to realize their condition of alienation in order to arouse their urge for freedom.

In *Eros and Civilization* (1966), Marcuse furnished a blueprint of society where alienation will be removed and freedom will be restored. It will be a democratic community where work will become play, and necessary labour will be organized in harmony with liberated, and authentic, individual needs. Discontinuance of repressive performance will eliminate surplus repression, thus freeing the person from alienated labour. Marcuse concludes with an optimistic note that the Western society has already evolved a technology which is geared to meet most of the human needs. It is sufficient to enable men to live in freedom and dignity. Once they understand the necessary conditions of freedom, they can transcend the era of violence and anarchy and build a new society where freedom will reign supreme.

Marcuse's view concerning the possibility of happiness has been criticized on many grounds. Some critics believe that human needs are endless; gap between aspiration and achievement will never allow human beings to attain happiness. Then who would bring about revolution? Marcuse has no faith in the revolutionary potential of the proletariat. He pins his hopes on the marginal elite of unbrainwashed students and radically dispossessed members of the poorest classes. Some critics argue that after denying the revolutionary potential of the proletariat, Marcuse loses his claim to be called a Marxist!

[VI]
FREEDOM AS EMANCIPATION

It is important to note that libertarians and humanitarians have conceived positive freedom in different ways. Isaiah Berlin, a prominent libertarian, identified positive freedom as 'self-mastery': a person is free when he controls his own life, rather than being an instrument of someone else's will. David Miller has identified three elements of Berlin's conception of positive freedom: (*a*) Freedom as power or capacity to act in certain ways, as contrasted with the mere absence of interference; (*b*) Freedom as rational self-direction, the condition in which a person's life is governed by rational desires as opposed to the desires that he just as a matter of fact has; and (*c*) Freedom as collective self-determination, the condition where each person plays his part in controlling his social environment through democratic institutions (*Liberty,* 'Introduction' to his edited book; 1991).

Humanitarians

Humanitarians are those persons who believe in showing compassion towards humanity, particularly towards the helpless, oppressed and suffering people. Humanitarians are largely inclined to work for the welfare of the downtrodden.

Like Berlin, all libertarians maintain that the role of the state should be confined to securing negative freedom of the individual. They argue that if the state becomes the guardian of positive freedom (in the sense as perceived by them), it would imply moral superiority of the so-called enlightened group which runs the state, and thereby pave the way to totalitariansim. People would then be prompted to subordinate their actual liberty to the supreme value of the 'higher liberty'. Norman Barry (*An Introduction to Modern Political Theory;* 1989) has aptly expressed this view as follows: "The route to totalitarianism is plainly laid out when the higher purposes of the individual are made equivalent to those of collectivities such as classes, nations and races."

> **Totalitarianism**
>
> Totalitarianism refers to a system of governance in which the state seeks to regulate and control all aspects of life of its citizens—whether public or private. In other words, it seeks to direct all political, economic, social-cultural and intellectual activities of people towards fulfilling certain aims which are determined by the state itself. No citizen has the right or opportunity to criticize the state, or to propose any new aim.

On the contrary, humanitarians conceive positive freedom differently. For them, liberty or freedom lies not in the condition of 'being left alone', but in a positive action by the state to 'liberate' people who are oppressed or deprived of necessary means of exercising their freedom. In short, libertarians largely seek freedom primarily for those who are competent, resourceful and capable of taking decisions while humanitarians demand freedom for those who are disadvantaged, oppressed and placed in unfavourable condition. That is why humanitarians tend to equate freedom with 'emancipation'.

IDEA OF EMANCIPATION

What is 'emancipation'? According to *Collins Cobuild English Language Dictionary,* "To emanicpate someone means to free them from social, political or legal restrictions that are considered to be degrading or unnecessary, or from having to do degrading work." We are quite familiar with emancipation of slaves. Slaves were the people who were totally deprived of their freedom. A slave was legally the property of his master, like goods and animals. His master had full right on his life. His master could take any service from him. A slave owned nothing. Any labour done by the slave would become the property of his master. The master could sell or gift his slave to others. The practice of slavery was widespread in many parts of the world in ancient times. Emancipation of a slave meant that he would cease to be the legal property of another, and would live according to his free will.

In medieval times, slavery was largely replaced by serfdom. Serf worked as a peasant and cultivated land which was owned by the landlord. He received a small, fixed share of the produce as a return of his toil. Serf had some freedom in comparison to a slave. He could have his family and his belongings, but he could not leave his duty without permission of his lord. If land was sold to another person, his lord would change, but he would continue to serve there on the same terms and conditions. In this case, emancipation of a serf would mean giving him the freedom to leave his place and earn living by his labour in the open market. This would relieve him of all traditional obligations attached to his status.

In modern times, all workers (whether at a factory, office, shop or household) are legally free though they may be under some constraints due to market conditions. Marx and his followers talked of 'emancipation' of workers from the constraints of the capitalist system. They, therefore, called for overthrow of capitalism to secure workers' emancipation. *Communist Manifesto (1848)* exhorted 'Workers of all Countries' to 'Unite' for they had 'nothing to lose but their chains'. They had 'a world to win'. Marxists hoped that a forcible overthrow of capitalism by the organization of the working class would be followed by the transition to socialism, and eventually to communism. This final transition would mark the leap from 'the kingdom of necessity' to 'the kingdom of freedom'. In short, in all cases emancipation implies the act of 'liberation' of people from different types of oppressive conditions. For humanitarians, the substance of freedom lies in the act of emancipation.

In contemporary world, we talk of 'emancipation' of women. Apparently women are not placed in bondage comparable to that of slaves, serfs, industrial workers, etc. Still they have been subjected to many forms of legal, social and moral bondage which are the source of their oppression. Removal of this bondage would set them free and open vast opportunities of their social and cultural development. That is precisely the goal of their emancipation. Besides many subaltern groups in contemporary society are also awaiting their emancipaton in this sense.

Subaltern Groups

Subaltern groups refer to those sections of society who are more-or-less permanently placed in subordinate or inferior position because of various constraints inherent in the social structure. These are exploited, oppressed and marginalized groups who are forced to live at mere subsistence level or even at sub-human level because a lion's share of social resources and political power is cornered by a tiny, privileged class. Restoring rights of the subaltern groups is the chief concern of social justice.

Social Justice

Social justice refers to a social policy which seeks to prevent concentration of valuable resources of the community (wealth, prestige and power) in the hands of the chosen few, and to create a social order which will enable the deprived and the underprivileged sections to gain a respectable share thereof by virtue of their ability, effort and need.

Next step in the direction of 'freedom as emancipation' may be identified as a condition in which freedom would become an instrument of 'development' of the individual. This may be termed as 'developmental view of freedom', as exemplified by Macpherson's concept of creative freedom, and Amartya Sen's view of development as freedom.

[VII]
FREEDOM AS DEVELOPMENT

The idea of freedom as development is opposed to the libertarian view of freedom which conceives freedom as 'absence of restraint' or as 'being left alone'. The libertarian view is designed to benefit those fortunate people (the rich and the strong) who are placed in an advantageous position in a competitive situation. This interpretation of freedom does not favour the unfortunate lot (the poor or the weaker) who might be left to suffer in such a situation. On the contrary, the idea of 'freedom as development' contemplates a situation in which the disadvantaged sections of society would be able to improve the quality of their life by means of their talents and efforts. This view does not invoke mercy of the rich towards the poor; it seeks to protect everybody's dignity and self-esteem while pursuing the course of self-development. The idea of freedom as development finds adequate expression in the philosophy of two prominent social thinkers: C.B. Macpherson and Amartya Sen.

MACPHERSON'S CONCEPT OF CREATIVE FREEDOM

C.B. Macpherson (1911-87), Canadian political philosopher, does not claim to be a Marxist, yet he is one of the acute critics of capitalism. Norman Barry (*An Introduction to Modern Political Theory;* 1989) calls him a neo-Marxist. In his celebrated work *Democratic Theory —Essays in Retrieval* (1973), Macpherson argues that Western democratic theory is characterized by two basic principles: (*a*) maximization of utilities; and (*b*) maximization of powers. Under the first principle, man is recognized as a consumer of utilities, that is essentially as a bundle of appetites demanding satisfaction from society. The second principle is derived from J.S. Mill's revision of orthodox utilitarianism. It is an ethical principle which treats man as a doer and creator, demanding development and application of his uniquely human capacities. Essence of freedom lies in fully realizing his creative faculties. Real freedom can be exercised through *developmental power,* as distinguished from *extractive power.* This may be termed as 'moralist view' of power.

Making a distinction between the two components of power, Macpherson observes: Extractive power represents the familiar concept of power, *viz.* a person's ability to use others' capacities to serve his own propose, that is 'power over' others. It implies the ability to extract benefits from others. It is interesting to note that the Western tradition of political thought from Machiavelli (1469-1527) to James Mill (1773-1836) has broadly focused on this concept of power. This attitude was not a product of intellectual carelessness but it was a factual description of power relations in a market society.

Developmental power, on the other hand, denotes a person's ability to use his own capacities for the fulfilment of his self-appointed goals. The use of extractive power in the modern society is exemplified by the power of owners of land and capital. By virtue of this ownership they can buy and use the manual and intellectual capacities of others for their own benefit. The workers and ordinary people who do not own land and capital or other means of production would be benefited only if they win developmental power for themselves.

It is important to note that Macpherson not only introduced the concept of developmental power, he also paid special attention to elaborate it. Thus, developmental power of a person enables him to develop his truly human capacities. Some examples of such capacities are: capacity for rational understanding, for moral judgement and action, for aesthetic or artistic activity, for love and friendship and, of course, the capacity for materially productive labour. The concept of developmental power treats a person as a *doer* and *creator*. It requires that he should not face any impediments or constraints while using his human capacities to achieve his objectives.

Macpherson enumerates three impediments to the maximization of a person's developmental power: (*a*) lack of adequate means of life; (*b*) lack of access to the means of labour; and (*c*) lack of protection against invasion by others. The problems created by the scarcity of the means of life and the scarcity of the means of labour are technological and material as well as cultural and ideological. Macpherson is quite convinced that these problems cannot be resolved within the framework of a market society based on capitalist social relations. He suggests that the solution to these problems can be found in a new system which would combine the protection of civil liberties with a socialist mode of production. Only then individual would be able to make full use of his developmental power and thereby achieve his 'creative freedom'.

Macpherson on the Genesis of Creative Freedom

The Issue	*Utilitarian View*	*Moralist View*
Concept of Human Nature	As a Consumer	As a *Doer* and *Creator*
Goal of Human Life	Maximization of Utilities	Maximization of Powers
Requisite Type of Power	Extractive Power	Developmental Power
Consequence of the Use of Power	Satisfaction of Material Wants	Creative Freedom

Macpherson argued that in the capitalist market society, developmental power of the poor sections is negligible; their extractive power is nil. On the contrary, the owners of land and capital wield immense power to exploit the manual and intellectual power of the non-owners. In other words, the poor who are constrained to sell their capabilities according to the needs of the market, have little opportunity for maximization of their developmental power. Their developmental power—which is the key to one's creative freedom—is continuously eroded in such a society. Macpherson concludes: "It is in the welfare-state variety of capitalism ... that there is a certain amount of checking of economic power by the political power" (*Democratic Theory—Essays in Retrieval;* 1973).

AMARTYA SEN'S CONCEPT OF DEVELOPMENT-ORIENTED FREEDOM

Amartya Sen, contemporary Indian economist and social philosopher, has made significant contribution in the field of welfare economics. Initially, Sen (*Quality of Life,* edited by Martha C. Nussbaum and Amartya Sen; 1993) sought to promote 'capabilities approach' to champion the cause of everybody's share in the process and fruits of development. This approach insists on allocation of various goods and other benefits according to differential human capabilities of its beneficiaries. For example, here disabled persons (like physically challenged, visually challenged or otherwise handicapped persons) are redefined as 'differently abled' persons. An attempt is made to identify the residual abilities of each person and their value in enriching the social life. Now each person is given adequate additional resources to enable him or her to develop those capabilities so that he or she is able to lead a respectable social life, and to attain a common level of welfare. The impact of this approach is reflected in the United Nations Development Programme which adopted certain 'Capability Indicators' at the instance of Amartya Sen. However, critics of 'capabilities approach' seem to argue that identification of such capabilities is sometimes rooted in the cultural bias of its adherents. For example, they may tend to replace the model of 'simple living and high thinking' by the life-style of 'consumer culture'. In any case, this flaw can be overcome by associating culturally enlightened scholars from diverse backgrounds in the process of identification of socially valuable capabilities. Possibility of this flaw does not warrant that the 'capabilities approach' should be abandoned altogether.

Subsequently, Amartya Sen (*Development as Freedom;* 2000) sought to focus on the close interlinkages between the ideals of freedom and development. Drawing our attention to the value of freedom, Sen quoted eighteenth-century poet William Cowper who observed:

> *Freedom has a thousand charms to show,*
> *That slaves howe'er contented, never know.*

Sen laments that in the contemporary world of unprecedented opulence, millions of people living in rich as well as poor countries are still unfree. It is true that the twentieth century has established democratic and participatory governance as the preeminent model of political organization. Ideals of human rights and political liberty are now universally accepted. People live much longer, on an average than ever before. Different regions of the globe are now closely linked; this was never possible in the past. This has happened not only in the fields of trade, commerce and communication, but the interaction between ideas and ideals is also spreading all over the globe.

However, a vast section of humanity all over the world is still deprived of enlightenment as well as prosperity. Technically these people are not slaves, yet they are denied elementary freedom and remain imprisoned in one way or another by economic poverty, social deprivation, political tyranny or cultural authoritarianism. Incidentally, Sen refers to many new as well as old problems which have plagued the contemporary world. These include persistence of poverty and unfulfilled elementary needs, occurrence of famines and widespread hunger, violation of elementary political freedoms as well as basic liberties, extensive neglect of the interests of women and their immense potential to contribute to the social good, the worsening threat to our environment which is endangering the sustainability of our economic and social lives. Many of these deprivations, in one form or the other, are visible in rich as well as poor countries.

The main purpose of development is to extend the benefit of freedom and to spread its 'thousand charms' to the unfree citizens. Sen persuasively argues that freedom is the ultimate goal of social and economic arrangements, and the most efficient means of realizing general welfare. Sen concedes that social institutions like markets, political parties, legislatures, the judiciary and the media contribute to development by enhancing individual freedom; these are in turn sustained by social values. In this way, Sen attempts to link values, institutions, development and freedom in an elegant analytical framework. In his view, the possibility of individual's freedom depends on a positive answer to the following question: "What is the relation between our collective economic wealth and our ability to live as we would like?"

This approach views the expansion of freedom as the primary end as well as the principal means of development. Development in this sense refers to the removal of various types of unfreedoms that leave people with little choice and little opportunity of exercising their potential combined with their faculty of reason. We must distinguish between two important aspects of human freedom: (*a*) Freedom as the pre-eminent objective of development; and (*b*) Effectiveness of particular kinds of freedom to promote other kinds of freedoms. For example, there is a strong evidence that economic and political freedoms help to reinforce one another. It is wrong to consider them as hostile to one another. Similarly, social opportunities of education and healthcare, which may require public action, complement individual opportunities of economic and political participation;

they also help to foster our own initiative in overcoming our respective deprivations.

Critics point out that in ultimate analysis, Sen confines himself to the economic criterion as the sole measure of individual's well-being as well as freedom. However, it should not be forgotten that apart from economic poverty Sen emphatically refers to social deprivation, political tyranny and cultural authoritarianism as potent impediments to individual's freedom. Hence, in Sen's view, political and cultural factors, apart from economic factor, comprise significant criteria of freedom. In short, Sen equates freedom with 'social justice' in the broader sense, as applicable to social, political, cultural as well as economic spheres of individual's life, and also as applicable in national as well as international spheres.

Social Deprivation

Social deprivation refers to the condition in which a particular social unit (such as a class, caste, creed, race, gender or otherwise indentifiable group) is deprived of a respectable status irrespective of its merit, effort or the value of its contribution to the social good. For example, in the Indian caste system, lowest castes were the victims of social deprivation; women all over the world have been denied their due place in the social system; black and other coloured people have been deprived of equal rights in many countries of the world. Social deprivation presents a glaring example of social injustice.

Political Tyranny

Political tyranny refers to a situation in which state machinery is widely used to create oppressive conditions for the people. Broadly speaking, state machinery includes legislative, executive and judicial organs of the state. Hence under political tyranny laws are largely unfair and arbitrary, police and bureaucracy tend to disgrace and terrify the people to get their commands obeyed, and courts are seldom prepared to give relief to the oppressed.

Cultural Authoritarianism

In a multicultural society, cultural authoritarianism refers to the tendency of the dominant cultural group to project its culture as the most virtuous, dignified and prestigious, with a view to persuading other cultural groups to despise their own culture and emulate the ways of the dominant culture.

CONCLUSION

As we proceed to analyse the problem of libety or freedom in various contexts, its complexity is gradually revealed to us. At the outset, when liberty is defined as 'absence of restraint', it seems to be a simple matter. This was the earliest definition put forward by the classical liberalism. According to this view, the state may impose certain restraints on the individual only in order to maintain public order and security and to ensure enforcement of contracts. Liberty is seen as an area where the state has no interference. It is argued that in order to allow maximum liberty to the individual, the state should restrict itself to minimum functions which are most essential. Market forces (like 'invisible hand of the market' —Adam Smith's pharse) are seen as the natural regulatory mechanism for the mutual adjustment of civilized individuals who generally know and abide by the rules of the game. This was precisely the view upheld by *laissez-faire* individualism.

Subsequently, it was realized that market is not a smooth and humane agency for the adjustment of human relations, that the individual is not deprived of his freedom only because of the restraints imposed by the state, but he suffers from a large number of constraints including those emanating from the vagaries of blind market forces. A welfare state with a vast network of regulations was, therefore, seen as a necessary instrument of freedom.

In due course, more and more direct or indirect, apparent or subtle sources of constraint, coercion and domination were detected by different thinkers and schools of thought which curtailed freedom of the individual at different levels. It was realized that in many cases the state could practically do nothing in tackling these sources of constraint. Marxists saw the state itself as an instrument of 'dominant class' and envisaged 'withering away of the state' as the way to human freedom and emancipation. Libertarians like Berlin contended that the state could guarantee 'negative liberty' alone; that the individual himself was responsible for winning or losing his 'positive freedom'. On the other hand, neo-Marxist thinkers like Marcuse held that necessary means of freedom were already available in contemporary Western society; that the individual was deprived of his freedom as he became a slave to technology and consumer capitalism; that a genuine urge for emancipation will go a long way in establishing a new social order where freedom will reign supreme.

In a nutshell, the quest for freedom is a continuous process. Although freedom is sought for the individual, yet it cannot be enjoyed by the individual in isolation. Genuine freedom—or maximum possible freedom—can be attained only in a congenial social order where (on the lines of Marx's phraseology) 'free development of each will be the condition for free development of all'.

17

Concept of Equality

EQUALITY, LIKE LIBERTY, is a prominent political ideal of the present-day world. The French Revolution (1789) was fought for 'liberty, equality, fraternity'. Liberty and equality, taken together, describe the conditions of human emancipation. They constitute the voice of the oppressed, the voice against injustice, and the voice for changing unfair social conditions. Liberty and equality, in this sense, may be interpreted as complementary principles. In some other contexts, they may appear to be mutually contradictory. It is, therefore, essential to understand the nature and essence of equality in order to determine its proper relationship with the principle of liberty and justice.

[I]
IDEA OF EQUALITY

The problem of equality and inequality has figured in political thought since earliest times. Aristotle, for instance, discovered that 'inequality' was a cause of rebellion in many a state. He defined justice as 'treating equals equally and unequals unequally'. This was a typical statement in that it insisted on recognition and maintenance of existing inequalities in society—between master and slave, between rich and poor, between morally superior and morally inferior, and so on. Modern idea of equality, on the contrary, seeks reduction in inequalities insofar as they can be proved to be unjust according to the prevailing social consciousness.

EQUALITY AS A STATEMENT OF RIGHT, NOT OF FACT

At the outset, it is essential to note that the modern idea of equality is derived from the theory of rights. Equality is a *prescriptive term,* not a *descriptive* one. We argue that men *must be* treated as equal, not that they are in fact equal. We, of course, advance some logic in support of our claim to human equality. For instance, we postulate that man *as such* is a rational being; he is endowed with the faculty of 'reason'; all men are created equal by God. Or we argue that the physical, emotional and intellectual needs of all men are similar; hence all are *entitled* to equal rights. We do not say that all men are equal in their physical or mental capacities, beauty and talents, etc. Sometimes we dwell on physical attributes to press our claim, such as when we argue that men may differ in the colour of their skin, but they are all similar in the colour of their blood, hence they should be treated equally. Nature has not made different persons with different elements. A drug does not discriminate between the Jew and the Gentile while showing its effect. Blood group of the black may match with that of the white whereas it may not match in the case of two whites or two blacks. The black may donate his eye or kidney to the white to restore his lost vision or to give him a new lease of life. In short, the distinction between different races is not ordained by nature. Thus, we tend to establish some fundamental equality among men—equality as a fact—to press their claim of equality as a right. The grounds on which the claim of equality of all human beings is sought to be founded or established, are compendiously described as *foundational equality*.

Sometimes it is argued that the idea of equality does not derive its support from nature, as the idea of liberty does, hence it is not based on reason. For instance, it is stated that nature has created all things unequal, right from the sun and the moon, sky and earth, mountains and oceans, plants and trees, birds and animals to men and women, older and younger, stronger and weaker, wiser and stupid, and so on. Hence, the principle of equality nowhere holds good. Why should it be imposed against the scheme of the nature itself? Such arguments come in very handy to those who wish to preserve their privileged position. They are quite apprehensive of the idea of equality because they believe that liberty enables men to acquire unlimited wealth, power and prestige while equality seeks to diminish their achievements. They even try to demonstrate that any measure to limit their liberty, in the interest of equality, will rob society of its valuable assets, and that the idea of equality should be thoroughly abandoned in the interest of society!

This line of argument is, however, based on a distorted concept of liberty. Freedom in society can serve as a valid rule only when it is interpreted as 'equal freedom' of all, not otherwise. Absolute liberty will only result in the liberty of the strong and the clever to oppress the weak and the simple. If liberty is not to degenerate into license, it must be qualified by equality. In other words, I can enjoy my freedom only to the extent that it does not infringe on the similar and equal freedom of others. Now, this principle cannot be restricted to the legal sphere; it must be extended to the political, social and economic spheres also. As R.H. Tawney, in his classic *work Equality* (1938), has observed:

> If liberty means...that every individual shall be free, according to his opportunities, to indulge without limit his appetite... it is clearly incompatible, not only with economic and social, but with civil and political, equality,

which also prevent the strong exploiting to the full the advantages of their strength... But freedom for the pike is death for the minnows. It is possible that equality is contrasted, not with liberty, but only with a particular interpretation of it.

Accordingly, the introduction of equality is not intended to dilute the content of liberty but to make it more relevant and substantive. If the principle of equality is invoked to prevent some section of society from acquiring unlimited money, power or prestige, it is only intended to restrict the element of 'exploitation' so that other sections of society are not deprived of their due share in these advantages. Equality aims at widening the base of social benefits lest these benefits are cornered by a small and vocal minority impoverishing the rest of the community.

Exploitation

Exploitation refers to a form of social oppression in which one party takes undue advantage of the vulnerable position of another party. The stronger party uses the physical and mental capacities—resources, talents and skills, etc.—of its victim for its own profit or gratification of its own desires.

It is, therefore, evident that liberty and equality, as human rights, do not emanate from very different sources. On the contrary, they are based on the same logic, and they are intended to serve the same social purpose.

EQUALITY AS A MODERN IDEA

Equality in the present sense, *i.e.* as a principle of correcting the unjust inequalities in society, is a typically modern idea. There is no doubt that large inequalities of wealth, prestige and power have always remained a prominent and almost universal feature of social structure throughout human history. But as Tom Bottomore, in his *Classes in Modem Society* (1965), has demonstrated:

> During the greater part of human history this inequality among men has been generally accepted as an unalterable fact. Ancient and medieval writers, when they touch upon the subject of the social hierarchy, always tended to provide a rationalization and justification of the established order, very often in terms of a religious doctrine concerning the origin of social ranks...Only in modern times and particularly since the American and French Revolutions, has social class, as a stark embodiment of the principle of inequality, become an object of scientific study, and at the same time of widespread condemnation in terms of new social doctrines.

In other words, traditional thinkers took the phenomenon of social inequality as something divinely ordained. They sought to demonstrate that man could lead an ideal life according to his predetermined status. This mode of thought was quite natural to slave-owning society, feudal society and caste-based society which were not used to scientific reasoning. They took social order, like natural order, as something not capable of change by human design or effort.

However, with the dawn of the scientific age when men learned to control natural forces after obtaining rational and empirical knowledge of nature, they also sought to gain rational knowledge of social structures. Many a thinker sought to discover the real foundations of social inequalities, and subjected them to a rational analysis. In other words, social thinkers of the modern age were led to inquire: (*a*) how far the existing inequalities in society were the product of the social arrangement and, could therefore be altered by making corresponding changes in the social structure; and (*b*) how far those social inequalities, which were thus alterable, could be upheld by reason. The main thrust of this line of thinking was to pave the way for removing such social inequalities as were not 'reasonable', and which were also 'removable' by human effort.

EQUALITY AS AN IDEA OF SOCIAL CHANGE

Scientific thinking about the social structure led to the demand for social change. Jean-Jaques Rousseau, in his *Discourse on the Origin of Inequality* (1755), drew an important distinction between the two types of inequalities found in social life: *natural* inequality and *conventional* inequality. Natural or physical inequality, as a statement of fact, consists in the differences of age, health, bodily strength and qualities of mind and soul. Conventional inequality, on the other hand, consists in the different privileges that some men enjoy to the exclusion of others, such as inequalities of wealth, prestige and power. It follows that one form of inequality is not dependent upon human choice, being more or less ordained by nature. The other form of inequality is largely man-made; it emanates from the social order more or less deliberately designed by men themselves. Recognition of conventional inequality provides for ample scope to review the basis of social distinctions and to restructure social relations according to the new concepts of social justice. Thus, the French Declaration of the Rights of Man and the Citizen (1789), which was inspired by Rousseau's revolutionary ideas, recorded: "Men are born and remain free and equal in rights. Social distinctions can be based only upon public utility."

It is significant that with the advance of scientific knowledge and technology, more and more areas of natural inequality are coming within the 'alterable' sphere. We know that health and bodily strength can be considerably improved by proper nutrition, and mental make-up can be considerably developed by proper education and training. Even physical deformities and mental handicaps can be prevented by timely care, protection and treatment, so much so that an individual's appearance is amenable to plastic surgery and the skill of the beautician! The availability of these benefits to any individual is again dependent on his socio-economic status and the technological development of the society in which he lives. It is becoming increasingly clear that a large part of humanity is being deprived of the benefits of modern civilization largely because of the prevailing social distinctions and inequalities, not because of some divinely ordained system.

Thus, the demand for equality is always raised as a demand for social change, that is changes in that part of the social structure which is found to be 'alterable' as well as unjust. As John Rees, in his *Equality* (1971), has elucidated:

> It is when men, or some of them, see certain...inequalities as unjust and alterable that equality as an ideal becomes a potent force in political life... Before an inequality can become the object of criticism and regarded as unjust it would seem to be a necessary condition that it should be alterable... But by no means all alterable inequalities are thought to be unjust for, making due allowance for the variety of standpoints as to what constitutes injustice, there are some inequalities which are accepted as socially useful, not to say beneficial.

If nature has imposed the burden of child-bearing on women, some may consider it unjust but nobody would make it a political issue because this aspect of natural inequality between the sexes is unalterable. If some are more beautiful, talented or energetic than others, and thus enjoy more importance, this would not be resented in society unless the more gifted persons employ their natural qualities to exploit others. So long as authority and division of labour are based on rational grounds, inequality of status and position does not become objectionable. The relation between teacher and student, doctor and patient, traffic-controller and road-user, etc. may involve some sort of dominance and subordination, but so long as authority is exercised in the general interest, inequality is not at issue.

EQUALITY DOES NOT IMPLY LITERAL EQUALITY

Inequality becomes a ground of complaint and resentment only when it is thought to be unjust. To be sure, equality demands a progressive reduction of inequalities where they are thought to be unreasonable; it does not imply literal equalization. In other words, inequality in society may be thought to be 'reasonable' or 'unreasonable', according to the prevalent idea of justice. According to the prevalent view of ancient slave-owning society, medieval feudal society and early capitalist society, inequality between master and slave, lord and serf, capitalist and worker was regarded reasonable. But with the development of the modern view of social justice, especially the socialist view, this inequality was regarded unjust and unreasonable, and hence challenged. Marx (1818-83) and Engels (1820-95) have amply demonstrated that the division of society into classes—capitalists and workers, bourgeoisie and proletariat, haves and have-nots—involves 'exploitation' and that this is prejudicial to the development of conditions of human happiness.

Social Justice

Social justice refers to a social policy which seeks to prevent concentration of valuable resources of the community (wealth, prestige and power) in the hands of the chosen few, and to create a social order which will enable the deprived and the underprivileged sections to gain a respectable share thereof by virtue of their ability, effort and need.

The ideal of equality does not contemplate that all material goods, entire national income or all educational opportunities available in society should be equally distributed among all members of society. It rather means that men, who are different in their physical and mental capacities, aptitudes and skills, talents and energies, should be given equal opportunities for the development of their personal qualities and capacities, in the shape of material goods, comforts, education, training, etc.

R.H. Tawney, in his powerful book on *Equality* (1938), argued that opponents of equlity sought to contradict a view of equality which was not maintained by its defenders. Egalitarians did not believe in abolishing all differences in incomes so as to ensure 'equal shares for all'. They only aimed at the pooling of the surplus resources of the nation's income by means of taxation so as to create the conditions of well-being for all members of society. By opposing the case for 'equalization of all incomes', anti-egalitarians are 'bombarding a position which no one occupies'.

The principles on which just distribution of goods, services, honours, etc. is sought to be determined, are compendiously described as *distributive equality.* It concedes that men differ not only in their talents and efforts, they also differ in their needs. However, all human beings have similar basic needs. State or society must take care of these basic needs of everybody. It should also take care of the specific needs of certain disadvantaged sections, *e.g.* physically challenged, sick or other types of vulnerable people. In short, distributive equality aims to create 'equality of opportunity', but it does not favour 'equality of outcome'. The idea of distributive equality comes very near to that of social justice. *While foundational equality seeks to establish equality of all human beings in the moral sense, distributive equality seeks to establish equality in moral as well as material sense.* Foundational equality refers to a pretty old idea which was originally expressed in the realm of Religion. But distributive equality embodies a modern idea which was initially expressed in the spheres of Law and Politics, and then extended to all spheres of social life, including economic and psychological spheres.

Inequality has the natural and necessary effect... of materializing our upper class, vulgarizing our middle class, and brutalizing our lower class.

Matthew Arnold (1822-88)

Distinction Between Foundational and Distributive Equality

Equality

Foundational Equality	Distributive Equality
All human beings are equal to each other	Society should treat its members more equally
In the moral sense	In the moral as well as material sense
A pretty old idea originally expressed in Religion	A modern idea initially expressed in Law and Politics and then extended to all spheres of social life

[II]
EQUALITY OF OPPORTUNITY

> **All of us do not have equal talent, but all of us should have an equal opportunity to develop our talents.**
>
> **John F. Kennedy (1963)**

Equality of opportunity is an important tenet of egalitarianism. Egalitarians hold that all human beings have equal social and political rights. Egalitarianism regards equality as the basic principle of public policy. It implies that no rational grounds have to be stated while conceding equal opportunities, equal rights and equal benefits to different individuals; justification must be given only when inequality or discrimination among them is sought to be introduced or maintained.

Promoting equality among human beings is by no means a simple task. At the outset, it is necessary to distinguish between *equality of outcome* and *equality of opportunity.* Equality of outcome is the goal of hard-core egalitarians. It implies equal distribution of rewards, such as income, wealth and other social goods. Since men differ not only in their social and family backgrounds but also in their talents and efforts, equal distribution of rewards disregarding these differences will involve injustice apart from killing incentive among the more competent and industrious. This would result in lesser production and lower level of excellence. Lesser production means lesser distribution even when it is equal! If we fail to prevent general impoverishment of society, adherence to the principle of literal equality will hardly give any relief to the poor. This line of argument impels us to surrender the goal of 'equality of outcome' in favour of 'equality of opportunity'.

Now the principle of equality of opportunity may be applied in two distinct situations: (*a*) Competitive situation; and (*b*) Non-competitive situation. In a competitive situation, equality of opportunity implies access to a scarce good or a prize (*e.g.* in the case of coming first in a race or an examination). In a non-competitive situation, it implies equal access to essential goods and services plus a good of one's choice, depending upon one's ability and effort. Success in any field of excellence like music, art, culture, academics, law, engineering or medicine is the case in point.

In a competitive situation, all competitors should be placed in identical or near-identical situation. For example, all players in a game start from equally favourable or unfavourable conditions; all should pass a test to prove that none has taken a drug or any other stimulant. In a non-competitive situation, all participants should get a minimum support plus 'separate but equal' facilities to prove their worth. Equality of opportunity in a competitive situation is fit for market society or meritocracy. On the other hand, equality of opportunity in a non-competitive situation is fit for a moderate egalitarian society or the 'community of equals'.

Market Society

Market society refers to a model of society where all social relationships are reduced to market relations, that is the relations between supplier and consumer. Accordingly, all individuals (or families) are expected to ascertain each other's needs and earn their living by fulfilling them. Thus, it cultivates respect for each other's dealings for mutual advantage. However, since its organization is based on the cruel forces of demand and supply, it has little room for human considerations or sympathetic treatment towards disadvantaged people.

Meritocracy

Meritocracy refers to a hypothetical system of social organization in which highest positions are assigned to the wisest, most talented and highly educated members of society. This term was introduced by Michael Young in his noted work *The Rise of Meritorcacy* (1961). He argued that under the modern technocracy in America, the practice of distribution of high offices on the basis of political loyalty and service was giving way to the rising demand of merit. He held that the provision of equal opportunities on the basis of merit was bound to deprive the lower classes of competent leadership. On the other hand, the meritorious in any field would get instant recognition. As a result, the social distance between upper and lower classes would be widened. This system would prove particularly oppressive to the ordinary, weaker and disadvantaged sections of society.

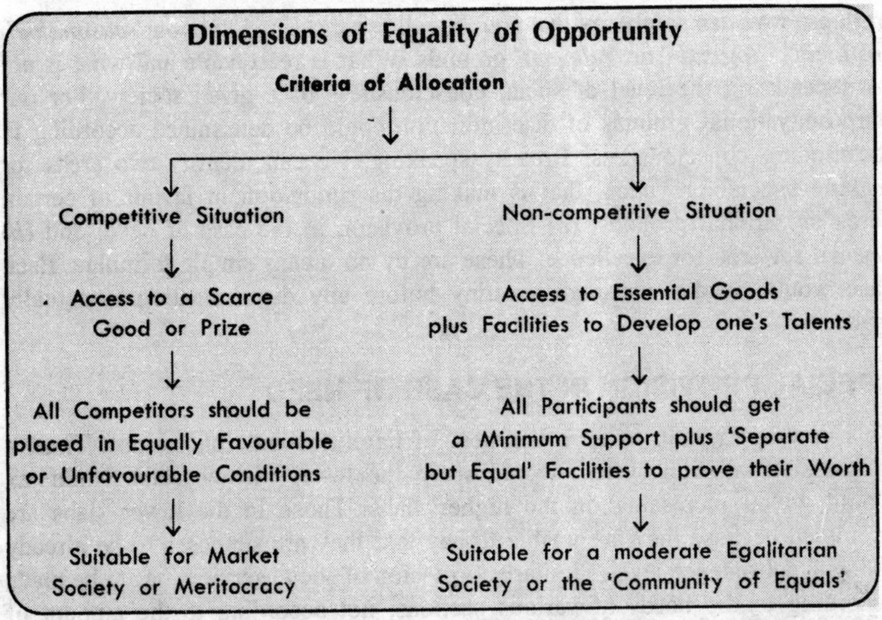

Advocates of equality of opportunity argue that government's task is to create equal opportunities for its citizens; it is for each individual to decide whether to use an opportunity or neglect it! Even when a citizen chooses to use the opportunity, his achievement would depend on his talent and effort. In any case, *equality opportunity is seldom likely to result in equality of outcome.*

In short, equality of opportunity calls for creating conditions in which everyone has the same starting point, or equal life chances. It seeks to reduce the impact of inequalities attached to social, cultural and economic backgrounds of various persons but agrees to giving them differential rewards according to their differential talents, skills and efforts. This again is quite difficult in practice. Those who had a poor start in life because of long-standing social inequalities will have to be given some special concession, such as exemption from fees, relaxation of age-limit and reservation of seats or posts, etc. Further, effective steps will have to be taken by the state and society to ensure educational and cultural development of the disadvantaged sections apart from promoting their material well-being. In this way, equality of opportunity calls for extending the process of 'equalizing' to the roots of our social structure.

[III]
RATIONAL GROUNDS OF DISCRIMINATION

If equality does not imply literal equality in distribution of rights and advantages, it is bound to accept discrimination on certain grounds. What are those grounds? Since we defend the principle of equality on the basis of 'reason', or 'logic', we can safely say that equality allows discrimination on *'reasonable'*, *'rational'*, *'logical'*, or *'relevant'* grounds. What is reasonable and what is not so depends on the level of social consciousness of a given society. For our purpose, rational grounds of discrimination could be determined according to the modern consciousness. Broadly speaking, we can identify two areas for making special provision, that is making discrimination in favour of certain cases on rational grounds: (*a*) Special provision in the case of need; and (*b*) Special rewards for excellence. These are by no means simple formulae. Each case would need a thorough scrutiny before any discrimination is actually made.

SPECIAL PROVISION IN THE CASE OF NEED

This may apply both to apportionment of liabilities and concessions. Thus, a progressive taxation system would spare the lower income slabs while tax would go on increasing on the higher slabs. Those in the lower slabs are exempted because they are unable to pay tax; they are supposed to be already living at subsistence level. Similarly, provision of social services has to be made according to the needs of various sections, not according to the amount of taxes that they pay for the financing of these services. Thus, the benefit of cheap transport, postal services (*e.g.* ordinary post card), schools, hospitals, libraries, places of entertainment, etc. may largely be availed by those who pay very little towards their financing. Scholarships may be given on merit-cum-means basis (in fact, merit would be secondary criterion; means would be the first consideration).

Public funds would be kept readily available to rush aid to the victims of fire, flood, famine, earthquake, epidemic, war or crime, etc. The state is obliged to provide for uneconomic roads, and other essential supplies and services, such as transport services, water, electricity and fuel, foodgrains, milk, vegetables, etc. at subsidized rates in order to meet the genuine needs of the community. Reservation of jobs and other advantages for the disadvantaged and weaker sections, such as women, the handicapped, the Scheduled Castes and Scheduled Tribes, etc. largely conforms to this criterion.

SPECIAL REWARD FOR EXCELLENCE

The doctrine of equality is sometimes dubbed 'philosophy of poverty', not only because it tends to serve the cause of the poor but also because it tends to impoverish society in its standards of excellence. Thus, David Hume (1711-76) had argued that equality would endanger the virtues of 'art, care and industry' and instead of preventing want in a few, it would lead to the impoverishment of the entire community. Such a view is based either on a misunderstanding or misrepresentation of the principle of equality. Such apprehensions about the impact of equality stem from its interpretation as literal equalization of rewards irrespective of talents, efforts and even needs of various individuals. A rational view of equality does not accept this position. In fact, faith in equality neither implies equalization of results nor disrespect of excellence.

Special provision for excellence is itself a basic tenet of the principle of equality. It comes into play when basic 'needs' have been largely met, and special talents and efforts are to be given special rewards *provided they are beneficial to society.* Let us take the example of an orchestra group. It is quite possible that we may get an 'equal' or 'near equal' performance of each artist by giving finest instruments to the less skilled and very ordinary instruments to the finest players. A similar equality may be obtained by giving very good books to the students of low calibre and ordinary books to the most brilliant; or by giving excellent clothes to the plain-featured girls, and ordinary clothes to the most beautiful girls! But is such equality desirable, not to speak of reasonable? Such a ridiculous interpretation of equality can be expected only from its opponents, not from its supporters. Equality is meant to create conditions where talents would not rot, where special efforts would not go waste. A rational interpretation of equality would insist that, after making necessary provision for the basic needs, best musical instruments should be given to the best players, best books to the best students, and best clothes to the best girls. This criterion should not be taken as unconditional acceptance of the 'market society model'. We have made an important proviso that *such excellence should be beneficial* to *society.* A market society eulogizes 'private profit' as the highest virtue, and allows 'manipulators' to earn largest profits for their private consumption at the expense of the vulnerable sections of society. The principle of excellence, on the contrary, postulates a situation in which the service rendered to society becomes the sole criterion of distinction and special reward which is conducive to promoting the spirit of fraternity.

[IV]
DEBATE ON REVERSE DISCRIMINATION

If the principle of equality is interpreted to concede discrimination in favour of some deprived sections, this would not go unchallenged. In the United States, this issue has given rise to a debate on 'reverse discrimination'. It means that when favoured treatment is accorded to the 'hitherto deprived sections', particularly to blacks and women, others have a ground to complain that they are being deprived of equality of opportunity. In other words, discrimination in favour of the deprived sections results in discrimination against the general category. When some sections are entitled to a privileged access to job opportunities and higher education or professional training, it involves reverse discrimination towards other sections. It is argued that if equality means 'removal of discrimination', there is no justification for turning the existing discriminatory practice on the basis of race and sex in the reverse direction.

Some of the champions of 'affirmative action' for the deprived sections argue that since blacks and women were deprived of adequate opportunities of their development in the past, they should now be compensated for the loss. Others contend that preferential treatment for these sections will help in fulfilling the objective of equality. For instance, an increase in the number of black doctors and lawyers would establish their real equality with the whites. Still others claim that since the opportunities of advancement in social life are so scarce, these should be allocated not merely on the grounds of 'merit' but also on the basis of 'need'. The need of the deprived sections is so pressing that if they have the minimum required qualifications, they should be given preferential treatment in the allocation of jobs and educational opportunities to enable them to escape the tough competition.

Affirmative Action

Affirmative action refers to a public policy which accords special concession in matters of admission to sought-after courses of education and training, appointments, promotions, housing, health-care, etc. to those who were deprived of adequate opportunities in an open competition, particularly due to some discriminatory practices of the past. Affirmative action is meant to compensate the relevant sections (e.g. women, blacks, backward communities, etc.) for the injustice meted out to them in the past.

Among the opponents of 'affirmative action', the champions of neo-conservatism hold that the principle of equality in society can only be applied in the sphere of 'equality of opportunity'. An attempt to establish 'equality of outcome' by affirmative action would be disastrous because it would erode the spontaneous respect for merit and authority which is the foundation of social stability and progress. Others argue that such affirmative action is inimical to procedural justice. If blacks and women *collectively* get favoured treatment over whites and men, rather than *individually* as deprived persons, it is quite likely that rich and socially advantaged blacks and women—who happen to be the opinion leaders of these categories of persons—get preference over poor and underprivileged whites and men. It is also argued that whites and men of the present generation are not responsible for the injustice meted out to the older generation of blacks and women. To penalize them for no fault of theirs is tantamount to departure from substantive justice. Finally, some opponents of affirmative action contend that personal dignity and self-respect are the cornerstone of the philosophy of equality. If a person knows that his or her position is the reward of preferential treatment rather than his or her merit, it will hurt his or her self-esteem and give rise to a feeling of inferiority.

In India, the issue of 'reverse discrimination' is not raised as loudly as in America, because Indian society is particularly sympathetic towards the deprived sections. But here, too, the problem of identification of deserving cases is quite ticklish. In a country affected by widespread poverty and acute scarcity, there is always the danger that the more alert and vocal sections of the so-called backward classes might corner all the benefits meant for the deprived sections. In order to remedy this situation, the Supreme Court of India ruled in 1992 that the 'creamy layers' among the backward classes should be excluded from the benefits of reservation meant for these classes so that they accrue to the genuine and deserving cases only. The Supreme Court also ruled that total reservation for all eligible categories should not exceed 50 per cent, otherwise it would result in 'reverse discrimination'. Again, in order to save the new generation from utter frustration and lack of incentive, it is strongly felt in some quarters that the backward classes should be provided with adequate opportunities of educational and professional development whereafter they should be obliged to compete with the general category. Indeed, the question of reverse discrimination demands a very cautious solution.

Creamy Layer

Creamy layer refers to that part of a backward community which is relatively advanced and well-off. This part is sought to be excluded from the concessions meant for the backward community in question so that the benefits so provided are diverted to the really deserving cases.

[v]
DIMENSIONS OF EQUALITY

FORMAL AND SUBSTANTIVE EQUALITY

When we try to apply the principle of equality to various spheres of social life, we come across many forms of equality. Recognition of these forms or dimensions of equality may be considered as an attempt to understand the implications of the same principle from different angles. At the outset, we may distinguish between formal equality and substantive equality. When we join a queue and wait for our turn, all are governed by the same rule: 'First come, first served'. In this respect, all are treated equally. It is the manifestation of formal equality. Those joining the queue or waiting for their turn are not discriminated on any other ground like their social or economic status, race or religion, etc.

But when ladies, senior citizens or the physically challenged are allowed to form a separate queue to help them to get quicker service, the general rule is relaxed in favour of the needy, weaker or vulnerable sections. This step marks the transition from the sphere of formal equality to substantive equality. In short, formal equality implies the absence of discrimination in making the sought-after things available to all citizens whereas substantive equality tends to help the weaker and deprived sections to have those things with lesser effort or at a lesser cost. When the facilities of education, medical care, travel and entertainment are open to all, *i.e.* anybody can avail himself of these facilities if he can pay for them, this would amount to formal equality. But if the state gives fee concession, scholarships or other incentives to the poor and deprived sections to enable them to take advantage of these facilities, this would be termed as substantive equality.

Broadly speaking, legal as well as political equality comes within the purview of formal equality, although the provision of legal aid to the poor and needy sections would be a step in the direction of substantive equality. On the other hand, social and economic equality is intended to meet the requirements of substantive equality.

LEGAL EQUALITY

The principle of equality was first put forward as the demand for legal equality, that is the grant of equal legal status to all individuals in society irrespective of their birth, physical and mental capacities, or other differences. Jean-Jaques Rousseau, in his *Social Contract* (1762), observed that extension of legal equality to all citizens was the primary characteristic of civil society. As he wrote:

> It is that instead of destroying natural equality, the fundamental pact substitutes a moral and lawful equality for the physical inequality which nature imposed upon men, so that, although unequal in strength or intellect, they all become equal by convention and legal right.

The idea of legal equality thus emanates from moral considerations and serves as the basis of equal rights of men. Ernest Barker, in his *Principles of Social and Political Theory* (1951), argued:

> The State which vests us with legal personalities,...or 'masks', vests us all with equal masks, partly because it simply cannot distinguish our differences even if it would...but ultimately for the far deeper reason that we all matter equally before the law, whatever our differences may be... The principle of Equality accordingly means that whatever conditions are guaranteed to me, in the form of rights, shall also, and in the same measure, be guaranteed to others, and that whatever rights are given to others shall also be given to me.

Legal equality, which is taken for granted today, was, in fact, won after a prolonged struggle in human history. Ancient societies usually did not even entertain the idea of legal equality. For instance, *Manusmriti,* ancient Hindu scripture and statute-book, prescribed different grades of punishment for the same offence according to the caste of the offender: the lower the caste, the harsher the punishment. On the civil side, it prescribed different rates of interest chargeable from borrowers: the higher the caste, the lower the rate of interest. Similarly, Aristotle, ancient Greek philosopher, recommended differential punishments for the same offence for freemen and slaves, on the alleged ground that the slave was less sensitive to punishment! Barker has given an elaborate description of the struggle for legal equality, with instances from recent history. He observed:

> There was a long reign of legal inequality. Down to 1772, the slave was denied any legal capacity on English soil; he was not a person in the eye of the law, and he had no share in the enjoyment of rights... Under the laws regulating the suffrage, down to the year 1918, a person in receipt of poor relief was similarly condemned to an inferior degree of legal capacity by being denied the right of voting along with and on the same terms as others... Under the common law relating to property, married women, down to 1870, were destitute of legal capacity for ownership;... under the laws regulating the suffrage all women, down to 1918, were without any legal capacity for exercising a vote (*Principles of Social and Political Theory;* 1951).

The principle of legal equality, or equality before the law, comprises the foundation of legal justice in the present-day world. J.R. Lucas, in his *Principles of Politics* (1976), observed:

> Equality before the law does not guarantee equal treatment by the law but equal access to the law, and consideration only of those factors laid down by the law as relevant. Nobody is so lowly as not to have recourse to the courts, nobody is so mighty as not to have to answer to the courts: anybody can invoke the courts' aid, everybody must render them obedience: and the courts will decide disputes, after hearing arguments on both sides, fairly and impartially, without fear or favour.

In short, legal equality implies equal subjection of all citizens to the law and equal protection of the laws for all citizens.

However, legal equality by itself is no guarantee of justice in a society inflicted by extremes of wealth and poverty, as in India. Equality before the law can secure equal benefit of the law for all citizens only when all citizens can equally afford to approach the courts of law for restoration of their rights or recompense of any injury inflicted on them. So long as legal costs remain exorbitant, legal procedures remain too intricate and economic disparities among various sections of the population remain too wide, it is doubtful whether formal equality before the law is going to secure justice for all citizens. Harold J. Laski, in his *State in Theory and Practice* (1935), had significantly observed:

> Nor must we forget the fact that wealth is a decisive factor in the power to take advantage of the opportunities the law affords its citizens to protect their rights. The ability to undertake an action in the courts, even with the provision made for legal aid to the poor, remains a grim financial question, and, on the civil side of the law, with its massive hierarchy of

> appeals, the advantage is solidly with the rich...as a general rule, the ablest lawyers will be at the service of those only who are able to afford them.

We, in India, are quite familiar with this drawback of legal equality. The irony of the situation is that, whereas an innocent poor is hardly able to defend himself in a court of law, smugglers, black-marketeers, profiteers, adulterators and other anti-social elements manage to engage the best brains to defend them in the law-courts!

Lucas has also warned: "Justice is not served if the case of one party is incompetently presented and that of the other, superbly well by the best barrister that money can buy" (*The Principles of Politics;* 1976). Under the circumstances, a great responsibility devolves on the judges who must view the cases in their proper socio-economic perspective. Provision of legal aid can also be somewhat helpful, within certain limitations. As Lucas further observed:

> We rely heavily on our judges to discover the real merits of the case in spite of the differing abilities of counsel. But we rightly ensure by means of Legal Aid that equal access to the courts is at least not an empty Equality, and that nobody is denied a hearing through inarticulateness or poverty.

The matter does not end here. The judges are guided by their own social philosophy, which is again a product of socio-economic conditions. It is true that the rich are able to hire the services of the most competent lawyers, and that the most successful lawyers, and judges too, usually come from the upper strata of society who are likely to be naturally inclined to safeguard the interests of the rich out of their conviction. Here, again, what Laski had observed in the context of England applies to India as well. In his *Parliamentary Government in England* (1938), Laski observed:

> Our judges are recruited from the ranks of successful lawyers; and, overwhelmingly, our system makes the successful lawyer a man who has spent the major part of his life in serving the interests of property. He comes, therefore, almost unconsciously, to accept the assumptions of the economic system in being, and to adopt, without examination, the legal doctrines evolved for the protection of those interests.

It is, therefore, evident that although legal equality represents an important achievement of the modern state, it is not adequate without suitable changes in our socio-economic structure.

POLITICAL EQUALITY

Political equality denotes the equality of political rights of citizens. It implies the right to be represented in decision-making bodies on an equal footing, *i.e.* on 'one man, one vote' basis. It also postulates that nobody will be barred from holding political office on grounds of religion, race, caste, sex, or place of birth, etc. This, in turn, means that there will be no privileged classes in society entitled to rule, and that the rulers will not accord any special consideration to the will or interests of any particular individual or group in society. The doctrine of political equality is derived from the general belief that man as such is a rational being, capable of political judgement irrespective of his physical and mental capacities, education and wealth, etc. It also proceeds from the assumption that when equal political rights are extended to all men, they will be able to give best expression to the common good and to prevail upon policy-makers to adjust public policy to the requirements of the common good.

The demand for political equality originated along with that of legal equality—they were undifferentiated in the beginning. As D.D. Raphael has observed: "The French Revolutionaries, in demanding equality, were demanding a removal of arbitrary privilege, such as that which confined political rights to the rich and the well-born" (*Problems of Political Philosophy;* 1976). In a later phase of development of liberal theory, political equality came to be identified more and more with the democratic rights of people and universalization of franchise, equal freedom to hold and express political opinions without fear or favour, and equal right to form associations to influence political decisions.

Political equality started as a progressive idea. It led to the establishment of democracy in the Western world. This was, however, found to be inadequate by the masses whose hopes and aspirations were belied by the prevailing socio-economic inequalities. The achievement of political equality was, therefore, followed by the demand for socio-economic equality. Alexis de Tocqueville (1805-59), the French author of *Democracy in America* (1835-40), postulated that the discrepancy between political equality and economic inequality would not be indefinitely accepted by the democratic people. He, therefore, held that the first phase of the democratic world revolution, political in nature, would inevitably lead to the second phase, which would be primarily social and economic. He foresaw that the political struggle would be followed, before long, by a struggle between the haves and the have-nots. He noted that the working class had turned from political to social questions, and that they were forming ideas and opinions destined to eliminate economic inequality from society. Thus, Tocqueville anticipated the growth of socialist theory which chiefly concerned itself with the problem of socio-economic equality.

SOCIO-ECONOMIC EQUALITY

The term socio-economic equality embraces both social and economic equality. In fact, these two aspects of equality are so closely linked that they should properly be considered together. It is significant that while legal and political equality may be given *a formal* interpretation as the 'absence of discrimination' with little impact on the socio-economic structure of society, social and economic equality demands a *substantive* interpretation, as the force behind social change. While the idea of legal-political equality arose as the cry of early liberalism, the concept of socio-economic equality was articulated as the goal of socialism. Socio-economic equality signified the further development of the concept of equality. It was, therefore, a more progressive idea which was later adopted by the positive liberal theory.

Liberalism

Liberalism refers to a principle of politics which regards 'liberty' or 'freedom' of individual as the first and foremost goal of public policy. Liberty, in this sense, implies 'liberation' from restraints, particularly from the restraints imposed by an authoritarian state. This principle was evolved in the West in late seventeenth century in order to liquidate feudal privileges of the landowning class and to create favourable conditions for the new entrepreneurial class to enable them to contribute to social progress.

Socialism

Socialism refers to a principle of politics which favours social ownership and control of the means of social production so that all able-bodied persons could be suitably employed in productive work, and all means of social production could be deployed for the fulfilment of social needs.

If the principle of equality is not extended to the economic sphere, the operation of legal-political equality will continue to serve the interests of the richer class without substantial benefit for the masses. As Benn and Peters have significantly observed:

> Under such conditions, a wealthy *elite* would continue to exercise effective political power; judges and legislators would still be drawn from its ranks, and predisposed to favour it. Legal costs would put justice beyond the poor man's reach. Without social equality, 'equality before the law' would remain an empty form (*Social Principles and the Democratic State;* 1975).

Thus, while the demand for legal-political equality was raised to press the claims of the new middle class—the merchant-industrialist class or the bourgeoisie—to political power, the demand for socio-economic equality was put forward to assert the rights of the working class or the proletariat—to enable them to shape their destiny. In other words, the ideal of legal-political equality was advanced in order to replace feudalism by capitalism, while that of socio-economic equality was meant to promote socialism in order to rectify the faults of capitalism. Marxian socialism, which made socio-economic equality its supreme goal, seeks to overthrow capitalist system and establish socialist system in its place with a view to evolving a classless society in the process. In any case, it is evident that while the slogan of legal and political equality was raised as a progressive idea in order to secure liberty, equality and justice for humanity itself, it was reduced to the philosophy of the *status quo*—maintenance of the existing order—as soon as it had won political power for the capitalist class. The slogan of socio-economic equality was then raised in order to bring the mission of 'progress' to its logical conclusion.

Feudalism

Feudalism refers to the system of economic, political and social organization which flourished in the medieval Europe. Economically it was based on large-scale agriculture where social status of different sections of society was determined by land tenure. Land was held by various ranks of landlords in return for homage and military service to be rendered to the king. It was tilled by serfs who were obliged to render labour services and dues to the landlords. All sections of society including clerics, soldiers, administrators and toilers were tied to each other by mutual obligations. With the advent of Industrial Revolution in the mid of the eighteenth century, it became necessary to break this system to ensure freedom of the new entrepreneurial class as well as the new working class.

Capitalism

Capitalism refers to an economic system of the modern age, largely based on industrial production in which the means of social production (land, buildings, mines, forests, machinery and capital), distribution and exchange are owned by private entrepreneurs, and economic activity is primarily devoted to private profit.

The exponents of socio-economic equality argued that the capitalist system had only won formal liberty for the people in legal and political sphere, while a handful of property-owners continued to control the lives of the masses, because the masses had to yield to the whims and designs of the capitalist class for their livelihood. As R.H. Tawney, in his *Equality* (1938), observed:

> There are certain natural resources, certain kinds of property, certain types of economic organization, on the use of which the mass of mankind depend for their well-being. The masters of these resources, therefore, are in a position, in the absence of countervailing measures, to secure exceptionally favourable terms for themselves, and to exercise an unusual degree of control over lives of their fellows.

Socio-economic equality may be distinguished from legal-political equality in respect of its scale of measurement also. Thus, legal equality implies the recognition of the 'equal personality' in each individual, and political equality asserts the 'one man, one vote' principle, but socio-economic equality does not insist on 'equal shares for all'. In other words, whereas legal-political equality postulates literal or near-literal equality, socio-economic equality only demands the reduction of gross inequalities according to the prevalent conception of social justice. In the absence of an absolute standard, such as perfect equality in the socio-economic sphere, socio-economic equality insists on a progressive extension of social benefits to the weaker and underprivileged sections. This leads us to the transition from formal to substantive equality, from negative to positive equality, and from static to dynamic equality. For instance, equality of opportunity in the legal-formal sense may be interpreted to mean that opportunities of education, employment, travel, entertainment, etc. shall be open to everybody without discrimination, but this does not ensure that such opportunities will be actually available to all sections of society. Formal equality may not seek to make any effective dent in the existing socio-economic structure; it may reduce attractive opportunities to a mere piece of decoration which are open to everybody but available only to the chosen few. Socio-economic equality, on the contrary, insists on the progressive equalization of opportunities.

An ideal condition of socio-economic equality was expressed in Louis Blanc's classic formula: 'From each according to his ability, to each according to his need' (1839). This rule was adopted by Marx for application to his projected communist society. This model of society would be characterized by highest technological development, universal labour and a classless structure so as to secure abundant production to meet social needs, ensuring satisfaction of everybody's needs—a condition of perfect happiness. However, for the interim stage of socialist society, this formula was modified as: 'from each according to his ability, to each according to his work'. Lenin (1870-1924) described it as a 'bourgeois right' which was to be retained in the socialist society for practical reasons. This, at least, ensures the 'right to work' and the 'right to maintenance'—the satisfaction of basic needs, if not comforts and luxuries, for each citizen.

> **The only thing sacrosanct is the human being and matters should be judged from the social point of view of human betterment.**
>
> **Jawaharlal Nehru**

Socio-economic equality, therefore, postulates the right to equal satisfaction of basic needs, which implies state provision of education and employment as also of essential services such as cheap transport, housing, fair price shops, hospitals, community centres, public parks, health resorts, etc. State regulation of industrial conditions of work, minimum wages, workman compensation, pensions, etc. are also intended to serve the cause of socio-economic equality.

It is important to note that for the provision of essential social services, the modern state resorts to the policy of progressive taxation which means, the larger the income or wealth, the higher the tax. This policy, usually associated with the 'welfare state', ensures that social services will be financed according to the citizens' capacity to pay while these would be availed of according to citizens' needs. W. Friedman, in his *Law in a Changing Society* (1959), has significantly observed:

> Taxation is one of the most important weapons by which the State can mitigate the two objectionable aspects of unrestricted private property:

first, the inequalities of wealth, and secondly, the power to use property for private profit, and without regard to community purposes...By graded taxation and surtax on high incomes, gross inequalities of wealth are evened out more easily than by the equalization of incomes or the abolition of private property... Taxation is a cheap means by which the state finances its costly social service schemes.

Welfare State

Welfare state refers to a state that safeguards liberty of its citizens and also takes care of satisfying their basic needs, e.g. food, clothing, shelter, health care, elementary education and recreation, etc. — particularly of those who cannot afford these things from their own income or other resources. It makes use of public resources and taxation of the relatively rich to provide for a vast network of social services and social security.

In short, Marxian ideology seeks to secure socio-economic equality through the replacement of the capitalist system by the socialist system, which implies the socialization of the major means of production and making work compulsory for all citizens; on the other hand, liberal theory seeks to promote socio-economic equality by small and piecemeal adjustments within the capitalist system itself.

Distinction Between Formal and Substantive Equality

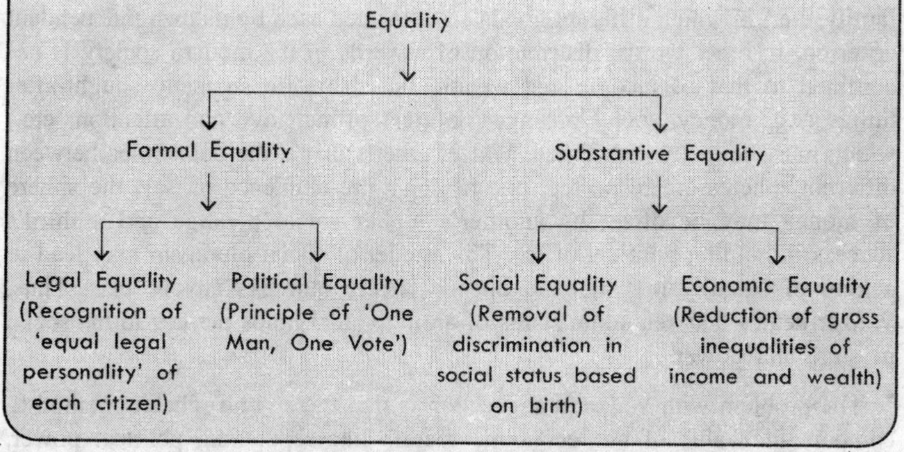

[VI]
SIMPLE AND COMPLEX EQUALITY

Distinction between simple and complex equality presents an alternative classification of distributive equality. In an atmosphere of equality of opportunity, differentials in abilities and efforts are bound to create inequality of outcome. If the state tries to remove this inequality by force, it would not only amount to curbing freedom, but also killing incentive. This will result in general impoverishment of society and the consequent fall in general welfare. On the other hand, if the existing inequalities of income and wealth are allowed to continue and society remains divided by large disparities in standards of living, people will be prevented from understanding and sympathizing with each other's predicament. Such a society will not be able to evolve the feeling of community or fraternity among people which makes society worth living.

Simple equality implies just distribution of the same good (*e.g.* income, wealth, power, etc.) to different persons. It seeks to avoid anyone's exclusive control or 'dominance' over any good which deprives others of their fair share. In practice, this implies that (*a*) the differential rewards received by people should correspond to the real differences in their effort and ability; (*b*) no one's standard of living should fall below a prescribed minimum; and (*c*) the range of inequality should not be so great as to give rise to class divisions. When the principle of equality seeks to contain vast disparities of income and wealth in society, it corresponds to simple equality.

Michael Walzer, in his celebrated work *Spheres of Justice* (1983), has introduced the concept of complex equality which marks a departure from that of simple equality. Complex equality is concerned with just distribution of different goods to different persons. Walzer has argued that the modern society includes a number of spheres of distribution (*e.g.* market, profession, politics, family, etc.) in which different goods are allocated each by its own independent criterion. In other words, distribution of rewards in the modern society is not confined to that of income and wealth, but there are so many sought-after things (*e.g.* money, social prestige, political office, love and affection, etc.) which must be justly distributed. Walzer asserts that if the boundaries between different spheres are respected, one person's pre-eminence in, say, the sphere of money may be offset by another's higher social prestige and a third's success in holding political office. This model of social pluralism may lead to a kind of equality in which no one decisively outranks anyone else. Thus, Walzer denies that economic status of an individual holds the key to his social prestige and power.

The problem with Walzer's suggestion is that there is no reliable method to compare the value of non-economic factors like reputation, political power, education and health, etc. with the value of income and wealth. In the absence of such criteria, it is difficult to attack the disparities created by market society. For example, it would be a poor consolation for a university teacher, scholar, writer, artist or scientist that the low (economic) return of his talents and efforts is compensated by the high esteem in which he is held in society!

In fact, Walzer gives precedence to ethical considerations over economic considerations. Walzer argues that a society of equals lies within our reach. It is implicit in our shared understandings of social goods. These understandings do not produce a vision of 'simple equality' which will lead to immense inequalities through the operation of free market. If the state tries to reinforce initial simple equality, it will end up as a tyrannical state. In our shared understandings we strive for 'complex equality'. According to Walzer,

> Complex equality means that no citizen's standing in one sphere or with regard to one social good can be undercut by his standing in some other sphere, with regard to some other good... No social good *x* should be distributed to men and women who possess some other social good *y* merely because they possess *y* and without regard to the meaning of *x*.

Walzer comes to the conclusion that the distribution of social goods should be determined according to the right reason as applicable in each sphere. Thus, the sphere of politics, or health or education should not be corrupted by the domination of money, for money properly rules in the sphere of commodities; the sphere of office should not (beyond a certain limited point) be contaminated by nepotism, which belongs in the sphere of kinship and love; the sphere of kinship and love should not be dominated by the consideration of profit and loss which are relevant only in the market-place; family organization should not be patterned after male domination which properly belongs to the sphere of military organization.

If Walzer's suggestions are adopted in actual practice, we will certainly have a just society which he intends to create. But he has not indicated the way how to convince the dominant people in different spheres of social life to adopt these rules. *Walzer's scheme of things embodies a strong moral philosophy but it does not provide for equally strong political philosophy.*

Distinction Between Simple and Complex Equality

Equality

↓

Simple Equality	Complex Equality
↓	↓
Distribution of the same good (*e.g.* income, wealth) to different persons	Distribution of goods and other sought-after things, *e.g.* reputation, political office, means of self-esteem, affection, etc.
↓	↓
According to uniform criteria, *e.g.* talent, effort, need, etc.	According to independent criteria based on right reason; *e.g.* different social goods would be chosen for distribution in the spheres of family, market, professional world, politics, sports, art and scholarship, etc.

> **The defect of equality is that we only desire it with our superiors.**
>
> **Henry Becque (1837-99)**

[VII]
LIBERTY AND EQUALITY

When we consider the relation between liberty and equality, it must be realized that different interpretations of these principles lead to different conclusions in this regard. In other words, these principles may be found mutually complementary or contradictory in different contexts.

LIBERTY AND EQUALITY AS COMPLEMENTARY PRINCIPLES

The principle of liberty stipulates 'equal' liberty or freedom for everyone. If freedom of one becomes unfreedom of another, it would be against the spirit of freedom itself. If freedom of the strong destroys freedom of the weak, if freedom of the clever undermines freedom of the simple, and if freedom of the rich turns out to be a constraint on the poor, it would amount to negation of freedom as a universal principle. In this sense, liberty and equality are complementary principles. This view concedes the imposition of reasonable restraints on freedom so that freedom of one does not stand in the way of similar and equal freedom of another. In a primitive society, nobody is allowed to use his physical or manipulative power to harm any other member of the community. With the development of civilization, many new and subtle means of exploitation are evolved. Property is one of such means. While the few cannot enslave society by pooling their physical and mental powers, they can do so by accumulating unlimited property. The property can also be used to hire best talents and labour power. Thus, property is the most potent instrument of depriving others of their freedom. In other words, vast socio-economic inequalities in society are not compatible with the principle of freedom.

So the demand for substantive freedom stipulates the provision of substantive equality. This, in turn, calls for the reduction of vast socio-economic disparities. Those who wish to maintain these disparities—on the ground that the rich have accumulated their riches by 'just' means—try to hide the true relation between liberty, equality and justice. The principle of equality demands a radical change in those social arrangements which enable one section of society to gain undue control over the life of others.

R.H. Tawney (1880-1962), Harold J. Laski (1893-1950) and C.B. Macpherson (1911-87) regard liberty and equality as complementary principles.

IDEA OF EQUALITY AS IMPEDIMENT TO LIBERTY

Some thinkers have envisaged certain situations where the provision of equality obstructs the enjoyment of liberty. French philosopher Alexis de Tocqueville (1805-59), in his celebrated work *Democracy in America* (1835-40), observed that the 'principle of equality', whereby all distinctions of social status are gradually eroded, was the ruling principle of modern history. The principle of equality in this sense encouraged the individual's subservience to public opinion and the extension and centralization of state power. With the extension of democracy in the social sphere, the source of intellectual authority was found in public opinion and this led to the 'tyranny of majority'. Supremacy of public opinion demanded conformity to the generally held attitudes and standards; it further led to believe that a dissenting position must be a wrong one. The net result was the curtailment of individual autonomy and the loss of liberty. In other words, whereas the principle of liberty demands the encouragement of a variety of interests and opinions, the principle of equality tends to promote conformity of opinions and attitudes: hence the antithesis between liberty and equality.

Lord Acton (1834-1902), a British historian, who was deeply influenced by Tocqueville, similarly argued during the nineteenth century that in the modern times, liberty was endangered by the rival doctrine of equality with its tendency to erode independent centres of power and to promote the authority of the state. Thus, Tocqueville and Acton were chiefly concerned with the conflict between liberty and equality in the political sphere, that is in the sphere of use of authority and they sought to resolve this dilemma through decentralization of power, particularly by vesting adequate power in the intermediate voluntary associations. Tocqueville saw free political parties and free press as suitable instruments for safeguarding individual liberty.

In fact, Tocqueville was not against equality as such. He only warned that the demand for equality in the sphere of freedom of opinion should not be pressed to such an extent that it results in the suppression of freedom. John Stuart Mill (1806-73), a British philosopher, was so impressed by this argument that he held that if the opinion of a single individual was different from the rest of society, that society had no right to silence him.

Some writers tend to oppose equality in the economic sphere in the name of safeguarding individual's liberty. Thus, Isaiah Berlin (1909-97), British thinker, in his famous essay 'Two Concepts of Liberty' (1958), argued that the state could only protect negative liberty of individual which consists in not being prevented by other individuals from attaining his goal. On the other hand, positive liberty treats individual his own master. It belongs to his own will and capacity which is beyond the scope of the state. If one cannot fly like an eagle or swim like a whale, one is by no means deprived of political liberty on this count. Similarly, if a man is too poor to afford something on which there is no legal ban—a loaf of bread, a journey round the world, recourse to law-courts—he cannot complain that he has been deprived of political liberty.

Thus, Berlin sought to equate socio-economic inequalities with natural and moral inequalities, and thereby projected a distorted view of equality. He ignored the fact that natural inequalities are unalterable while socio-economic inequalities are the product of social conditions which can be altered to meet the demands of justice. By divorcing liberty from equality, Berlin has done a great damage to his case for liberty itself.

Then F. A. Hayek (1899-1992), an Austrian thinker, in his *Constitution of Liberty* (1960), argued that individual differences in skills and abilities under the conditions of equality before the law result in inequalities of income and wealth. If we try to remove these inequalities by forcing an authoritarian rule, it is bound to destroy individual's freedom. Hayek values freedom as an instrument of social progress. He argues that while extending the scope of freedom, we should not ask how many persons will be benefited by it, but how much progress will be made possible. We should not divide the 'cake of freedom' to ensure 'equal shares for all', but according to each individual's potential to secure social progress. In his view, it is better that some should be free than none, and that many should have full freedom than all should have limited freedom. In other words, let late-running trains get late further if other trains could be run on time.

Hayek's message is clear: Let us strive for achieving high levels of excellence in the chosen few rather than marginal improvement in the majority of mediocres. In his view, the question of social justice should not come in the way of individual prosperity. In his later work *Law, Legislation and Liberty,* Vol. 2 : *The Mirage of Social Justice* (1976), Hayek declared social justice to be a 'mirage', hence an unrealizable principle. Liberty alone is the principle worth pursuing. Hayek wants to solve the problem of individual liberty within the market system, although he conceded that the state should provide for some public services outside the market system. But he has not made it clear as to wherefrom these services will be provided without diverting some resources from the market system. By divorcing liberty from social justice, Hayek has undermined the foundations of liberty itself.

> **A society that puts equality—in the sense of equality of outcome — ahead of freedom, will end up with neither equality nor freedom.**
>
> **Milton Friedman (1980)**

CONCLUSION

Liberty and equality comprise the foundations of a just social order. Conflict between the two arises only from their biased interpretations. In economic sphere, if equality is interpreted as 'identity of treatment', or equal shares for all disregarding merit and need, it not only destroys liberty but makes a mockery of equality itself. As Harold J. Laski (*A Grammar of Politics;* 1938) observed:

> Equality does not mean identity of treatment. There can be no ultimate identity of treatment so long as men are different in want and capacity and need. The purpose of society would be frustrated at the outset if the nature of a mathematician met an identical response with that to the nature of a bricklayer.

It is significant that in the legal-political sphere, a reconciliation of the principles of liberty and equality is not at all difficult. But their relation in the socio-economic sphere is certainly more complicated and capable of conflicting interpretations. Even legal and political equality may be rendered ineffective due to socio-economic inequality. Thus, so long as we do not step into the thorny field of socio-economic life, liberty and equality go together very well. In the historical perspective, the cry for liberty was greatly supported by the idea of equality. As Laski has brilliantly expressed:

> The power, in fact, of the ideal of equality lies in the historical evidence that so far in the record of the State the wills of men have been unequally answered. Their freedom, where it has been gained, has accordingly been built upon the unfreedom of others. Inequality, in a word, means the rule of limited numbers because it secures freedom only to those whose will is secure of respect. They will dominate the State and use its power for their own purposes. They will make the fulfilment of their private desires the criterion of public good (*ibid.*).

In other words, the demand for liberty implied the abolition of special privileges of certain groups, hence equality of all citizens in the legal as well as the political sphere.

But coming to the socio-economic sphere, some champions of liberty would contest the idea of equality. They argue that liberty enables man to acquire unlimited wealth, prestige and power, while equality seeks to limit such opportunity. It discourages initiative and enterprise, stunts potentialities of men and robs society of its valuable assets. Such thinkers deprecate equality as the antithesis of liberty and the road-block to social progress. Still others argue that equality in the economic sphere should be restricted to the provision of a minimum subsistence level for each individual so that the more enterprising, talented and energetic are not deprived of their liberty to prove their excellence and get suitable reward and encouragement. Now, this stand is not very strongly contested by the champions of equality who concede that equality postulates equality of opportunity, not identical treatment; fair shares, not equal shares.

Differential treatment and differential rewards to different persons according to the value of the service rendered by them to society, therefore, do not contravene the principle of equality, nor of liberty. But if this argument is stretched too far, it would become untenable. Those who argue that the state has nothing to do with the existing socio-economic inequalities or that the demand for equality should not be allowed to stand in the way of a purely competitive system, are stretching the principle of liberty too far. They lead to drastic and disastrous conclusions for humanity.

[VIII]
EQUALITY AND JUSTICE

When we consider the relation between equality and justice, different interpretations of these principles would lead to different conclusions. Aristotle had said that justice consists in 'treating equals equally and unequals unequally'. So before deciding the course of justice in a given situation, we should first ascertain as to who are equals and unequals. Aristotle warned that those who are equal in one respect, are inclined to believe that they should be equal in all respects. For example, those who are equal as citizens of a state, may think that they are entitled to equal power, prestige and wealth. When they fail to gain these privileges, they have a feeling of deprivation or the sense of injustice which eventually results in a rebellion. This feeling should not be encouraged in order to maintain peace in society. So the state should not promote the idea of equality.

In the present-day society, those who wish to maintain the prevailing inequalities of power, prestige and wealth, seek to repeat Aristotle's argument in the name of justice. They warn that people should not insist on a radical change in the existing order in order to maintain justice in society. Thus F.A. Hayek (1899-1992), an Austrian philosopher, in his *Law, Legislation and Liberty,* Vol. 2: *The Mirage of Social Justice* (1976), argued that the idea of social justice is baseless. Justice is, in fact, a characteristic of human conduct; a society cannot be just or unjust. If liberty is curtailed in the interest of equality, it would lead to widespread tension and dispute on the question of unjust distribution of life's goods. Pursuit of justice is a matter of procedure; its objective is to promote freedom. It should provide for maximum opportunity to each individual to serve his self-interest according to his own knowledge and wisdom.

> **Justice is a name to which every knee will bow. Equality is a word which many fear and detest.**
>
> **L.T. Hobhouse (*The Elements of Social Justice;* 1922)**

On closer analysis, we find that Hayek invokes the idea of justice in order to vindicate a competitive society model which eulogizes the stronger and the resourceful. He deprecates equality because the idea of equality is intended to give relief to the weaker and the deprived. However, modern social consciousness does not concede the so-called dichotomy between equality and justice. It is now widely maintained that equality will be meaningful only when it is accompanied by a sense of justice. Broadly speaking, justice consists in rightful allocation of benefits and burdens. This condition must always be fulfilled while applying the principle of equality, whether we are dealing with formal equality or substantive equality. Let us take the case of a queue system which exemplifies formal equality. When we form a queue for getting a ticket, it gives us the benefit of having a ticket. In this process, we also bear the burden of waiting for our turn. Queue system is regarded as conducive to justice because it gives equality of opportunity to all candidates for the ticket 'without discrimination' on grounds of social or economic status, race, religion, etc. However, when we allow a separate queue for ladies or senior citizens, who are fewer in numbers, we seek to reduce their burden of waiting time. This is regarded to be just and rightful because we pay special regard to these categories of persons, and also want to help them. In doing so, we enter the arena of substantive equality. In short, we always act with a sense of justice while applying the principle of equality.

If we forget the principle of justice, we might make a mockery of the principle of equality. For example, if a ruler chooses to shoot everyone of his subjects 'without discrimination', and to shoot himself in the end, he might claim to be following the 'rule of equality', but his decision would be termed crazy and inhuman because he would be acting without a sense of justice. Similarly, if a competent lawyer chooses to defend all clients 'without discrimination' between the wicked and the innocent, he would be making a mockery of equality because of his indifference to the dictates of justice.

Again, if somebody hits in my head, it is no consolation for me to be told that I have 'equal' power and liberty to hit him back in his head. I want equality for my 'security'—a positive benefit, and not for the ability of revenge which is at best a method of 'wild justice'. Equality without a genuine sense of justice loses its essence and becomes a source of oppression. Thomas Hobbes (1588-1679), English philosopher, postulated that the state of nature was a state of natural equality (*i.e.* when physical, mental and manipulative powers of all individuals, taken together, were nearly equal), but there was no sense of security for anyone: life of man was 'solitary, poor, nasty, brutish and short'. Then sovereign was established to keep everybody in awe, to enforce law and order throughout his jurisdiction, and to provide protection to people's life and property. We may infer from this argument that natural equality without a sense of justice is a bane, but when it is converted into legal equality informed by a sense of justice, it turns to be a boon. In a nutshell, in the sphere of practical application, the principle of equality is inseparable from the principle of justice.

18

Right to Property

[I]
NATURE AND SCOPE OF PROPERTY

WHAT IS PROPERTY ?

Right to property is derived from the general theory of rights. However, it is a complex issue. In the case of other rights, such as liberty, it is easier to detect where an individual's right is likely to come in the way of another's enjoyment of an equal right, so it is easier to determine its proper limits. This is not so easy in the case of the right to property. Property is either something not made by man but occupied or inherited by somebody by chance, by force, or by tradition, such as landed property; or it is a product of the cooperative effort of a large number of individuals, employing different talents and different amounts of labour, such as buildings, machinery, vehicles and capital assets. But their share in the product of their labour is usually not determined by the value of their contribution. Mostly it depends on external factors, such as the market forces of demand, supply and competition, the conditions of previous investment due to a pre-existing ownership of property, the level of technological development of society and consequent social relations, such as those between master and slave, lord and serf, capitalist and worker, etc. It is an area where there is abundant scope for exploitation.

As a result, the prevailing pattern of ownership of property does not reflect an individual's contribution to the social good, or the service rendered to society. If this is allowed to continue as such, it will not be consistent with the moral basis of granting rights to individuals in society. It must be ascertained how far an individual's right to property amounts to diminishing another individual's title to or share in the property. The fundamental issue is—how can the right to property be made to serve the cause of social justice instead of allowing it to remain a weapon of exploitation and injustice?

Social Justice

Social justice refers to a social policy which seeks to prevent concentration of valuable resources of the community (wealth, prestige and power) in the hands of the chosen few, and to create a social order which will enable the deprived and underprivileged sections to gain a respectable share thereof by virtue of their ability, effort and need.

The right to property is, therefore, called in question particularly when it leads to concentration of wealth in fewer hands, and thus obstructs others from having any significant share in the wealth of society. It is this right that tends to divide society into 'haves' and 'have-nots', and poses a threat to the spirit of fraternity—the sentiment of brotherhood of all men. Vast disparities in possession of wealth, with the resultant disparities in prestige and power, are sometimes sought to be perpetuated by pseudo-religious pretensions—the poverty in this life being interpreted as either an outcome of one's doings in some previous birth, or the price of some other-worldly gain, or at best, a situation divinely ordained. This sort of consolation, which has been a characteristic feature of our belief system throughout our past history, is indeed a very poor consolation. The 'modern consciousness' throughout the enlightened world regards it a device to cover up the existing injustice in society. The true justification for the right to property, and its proper limits, should therefore be sought within the existing institutional framework, without any reference to some supernatural design or the prospect of a divine compensation.

We are always making God our accomplice so that we may legalize our own inequities.

Henri Amiel (1821-81)

SCOPE OF PROPERTY

The term 'property' or 'private property' refers to the possession of material things which are open to personal or selfish use. Material things may also include documents, such as promissory notes, patents, shares, guarantees, etc. which embody an individual's entitlement to property even though such property may not be in his possession for the time being. Birds and animals, like material things, may comprise an individual's property. But property in the form of human beings, that is the right to keep slaves, is not recognized as legitimate property by the modern consciousness although it was so recognized in the past. Modern consciousness regards all human beings, irrespective of their birth and station, always as end-in-themselves, not as means to an end. Thus, no human being, however humble, can be reduced to being the private property of another.

In modern political theory, the right to property has been analysed in different perspectives. Of these, liberal, social-democratic and Marxist perspectives are particularly important.

[II]
LIBERAL PERSPECTIVE

Liberal perspective on property is based on the philosophy of liberalism which has usually regarded the right to private property as an essential ingredient of man's liberty and his right to the pursuit of happiness. Machiavelli (1469-1527), in his *Prince,* has sarcastically pointed to man's extreme love of property in these powerful words: "Men sooner forget the death of their father than the loss of their patrimony." Hobbes (1588-1679) postulated that the state was created for the security of man's life and property. Locke (1632-1704) held that man's right to 'life, liberty and property' was a fundamental natural right, and that the state was created for the protection of this right. Rousseau (1712-78) described the security of property as an essential element of civil liberty provided by the state.

> **Liberalism**
>
> Liberalism refers to a principle of politics which regards 'liberty' or 'freedom' of individual as the first and foremost goal of public policy. Liberty, in this sense, implies 'liberation' from restraints, particularly from the restraints imposed by an authoritarian state. This principle was evolved in the West in late seventeenth century in order to liquidate feudal privileges of the land-owning class and to create favourable conditions for the new entrepreneurial class to enable them to contribute to social progress.

Adam Smith (1723-90), Jeremy Bentham (1748-1832) and other exponents of classical liberalism regarded the institution of private property as an essential instrument of social progress. As Benn and Peters, in their *Social Principles and the Democratic State* (1975), have elucidated:

> Classical economic theory assumed that the sole aim of the individual entrepreneur would be to maximize profit from the use of his property. In doing so, he would use it for the greatest satisfaction of consumer demand. His interest in profit was thus both an explanation for his behaviour and a reason for leaving capital under his control, since it ensured beneficial results for the community at large.

Thus, the right to property comprised the very foundation of market economy and the capitalist system.

Early liberal political theory regarded the possession of property as a proof of an individual's stake in the state as also of his political wisdom, so much so that it insisted on linking the 'right to vote' with property qualification. In short, early liberalism sought to glorify and defend the right to property in the economic as well as the political sphere.

Modern liberal theory, however, which witnessed the cruel operation of the capitalist system and the rise of socialist theory, does not recognize any sacred or absolute right to private property. J.S. Mill (1806-73), who initially made a strong plea for the security of property, later argued that the right to property was not absolute or sacrosanct, and went to the extent of advocating considerable restriction on the rights of inheritance and bequest. He criticized private property in land which was the original inheritance of all mankind, and pleaded for the taxation of rent. Mill argued that the rapid appreciation of the value of land and its rent without any effort on the part of landlords warranted taxation on the income from land with a view to diverting a part of their increased wealth to the use of the community, particularly for the welfare of the working class which was the real producer of wealth from the land.

T.H. Green (1836-82), an ardent champion of human rights, paid due importance to the right to property as an instrument for exercising moral freedom. But he held that when an unrestrained right to property creates conditions under which some men take an unduly large share and others are prevented from acquiring requisite property as a means of their 'self-realization', as in the case of landed property, this right becomes a hindrance to the exercise of freedom in society. Green, therefore, pleaded for reasonable restrictions on the right to property in the interest of the social good. L.T. Hobhouse (1864-1929) went much further when he postulated the theory of the social origin of property. He defined taxation as a measure of securing to society the element in wealth which is the product of social effort, that is which does not owe its origin to the efforts of living individuals, especially of the present owners of property. H.J. Laski (1893-1950) argued that the right to property should be correlated to the function performed by its owner, that is the service rendered to the state, or the contribution made to the common welfare.

In short, modern liberal theory, instead of conceding an absolute right to property, proceeds to investigate the ethical basis of this right and, in the process, indicates the proper limits of the right to property. Morris Ginsberg, in his *On Justice in Society* (1965), has discerned three types of theories of the right to property, though they are not mutually exclusive. These are: natural rights theories; theories of modes of its origin (including the labour theory); and theories of the contribution to the public good.

NATURAL RIGHTS THEORIES

Natural rights theories regard property as a fundamental right independent of particular institutions, though some institutions are more likely to be in harmony with natural law than others. The concept of property as a natural right is of relatively recent origin. As Ginsberg has observed:

> It is worth noting that neither in Stoic nor Patristic doctrine is private property a natural right. 'By nature all things are held in common', is

Stoic doctrine; the Fathers tell us: 'before the Fall' there was 'no mine and thine distinct'. Private property became necessary and is, therefore, justified because man's greed and avarice have to be kept in check.

Natural Law

Natural law refers to a set of rules of good conduct which exist independently of conventional law. These are directly derived from nature which can be discovered through moral intuition and by the application of human faculty of reasoning. Champions of natural law regard it as superior to any other law.

Stoic Philosophy

Stoic philosophy refers to a metaphysical system founded in ancient Greek thought. It was first promulgated by Zeno of Citium around 300 B.C. It stressed the correspondence between man and nature as a whole. Wisdom was held to consist in the knowledge of the whole but to pursue it man had to hold his passions in check. A stoic was taught to endure hardship and adversity with fortitude.

Patristic Doctrine

Patristic doctrine refers to the teachings of Christianity as elaborated by Fathers of the Christian Church, particularly during the medieval times.

Even in the medieval theory of natural law, private property is not a part of that law though it is not contrary thereto. In modern scholastic writings, private property is conceded as a 'secondary natural right', which should be exercised under the conditions imposed by natural law.

Among the exponents of the natural rights theory of property, William Blackstone (1723-80) includes property among absolute rights. But he seems to apply this concept to 'possession', *i.e.* something held in possession for the time being and till it is so held. When property becomes a subject of inheritance and bequest, it no longer remains a natural right, but comes within the purview of civil rights. If a natural right is to be interpreted as a right which exists independently of social enactment, it is difficult to determine whether any form of property, possession or ownership can be treated as a natural right. But Locke conceives of natural rights differently: It is a right which derives its support from inward morality, conscience or the rational faculty of man. The right to 'life, liberty and property' is a natural right because it is not something granted by the state of its own will, but only recognized by the state because it is obliged to do so. Locke argues that the state has no authority to tamper with the right to property because it is duty-bound to protect this right. Although Locke regards property as a natural right, he looks for its origin in human labour, mixed with nature. Hence, his theory is akin to the 'labour theory' of the origin of property.

THEORIES OF MODES OF ITS ORIGIN

The theories of the modes of its origin seek the basis of property in the modes of its origin or acquisition, *e.g.* first occupation, inheritance, labour, etc. Of these, the basis of 'first occupation' is only of historical or academic interest, since this cannot be related to the mode of acquisition of property in the contemporary world. At best, it can be related to inherited property in land, mines, etc. However, the basis of *property as the 'fruit of labour'* is highly important. This basis was invoked by the liberal theory, but not brought to its logical conclusion. In fact, socialist theory has given it a more logical interpretation.

Among the liberal thinkers, Locke is the chief exponent of the theory of property as the fruit of labour. Locke argued that every man by nature has a property in his own person: the labour of his body and the work of his hands are properly his. Whatsoever then he removes out of nature and mixes with his labour becomes his property, 'at least where there is enough and as good left in common for others' *(The Second Treatise of Civil Government,* 1690). The makers of the American Revolution (1776) and French revolution (1789), who defended the institution of property so ardently, looked upon it primarily as the 'fruit of labour'. But the exponents of this theory failed to develop it on a logical basis. As Ginsberg has pointed out:

> Locke recognizes that in his view a person is only entitled to such products of his labour as he can use and that everything beyond this is 'more than his share and belongs to others'... But instead of using his theory as a basis for criticizing existing inequalities, he accepts and justifies them (*On Justice in Society;* 1965).

Locke attributes these inequalities to the consent of men, and argues that nature provides no principles for regulating inequalities.

C.B. Macpherson (*The Political Theory of Possessive Individualism;* 1962) has termed Locke's view regarding the right to property as a typical expression of the idea of 'possessive individualism'. According to this view, man—the individual—is the absolute natural proprietor of his own capacities, owing nothing to society for them. He is, therefore, free to use his capacities in search of satisfactions, provided he does not harm others. Freedom is identified with domination over things as manifested in ownership or possession thereof. Accordingly, society is seen as an aggregate of free and equal individuals related to each other through their possessions, and not as a set of persons held together by reciprocal rights and duties. The relation of exchange, or market relation, is recognized as the fundamental relation of society. Finally, political society is seen as a rational device for the protection of property of individuals where life and liberty are also reduced to their possessions. The position is further crystallized by the introduction of money. As Jeremy Waldron has aptly observed: "In any case, the acquisition of property is limited by Locke's insistence that an owner must not let resources spoil uselessly in his possession. This would be sufficient to generate a rough equality of possessions, were it not for the fact that the invention of money, a conventionally-sanctioned durable means of exchange, made it possible for men to own and get the benefit of much more land than they themselves could use the produce of. This legitimation of inequality, and the emphasis on private acquisition and enclosure in Locke's theory, have led many to see him as an ideologist of early modern capitalism" (*The Blackwell Encyclopaedia of Political Thought,* edited by David Miller; 1987).

Possessive Individualism

The term 'possessive individualism' was coined by C.B. Macpherson (1911-87), Canadian political philosopher, in his noted work *The Political Theory of Possessive Individualism: Hobbes to Locke* (1962) to describe the main assumption underlying modern liberal theory. According to this view, individual is the sole proprietor of his own person or capacities for which he owes nothing to society. He is, therefore, free to use his physical and mental faculties in pursuit of personal satisfactions provided he does not harm others. Freedom is identified with domination over things as manifested in ownership and possession thereof. Society is seen as an aggregate of free and equal individuals related to each other through their possessions, and not as a set of persons held together by reciprocal rights and duties.

It is thus evident that Locke starts with a progressive idea regarding the true basis of property, but ends up with expediency, forgetting logic. Once even minor inequalities are sought to be justified, larger inequalities automatically find their way. The Utilitarian philosophers and economists also started with a progressive idea—the greatest happiness of the greatest number, where each individual was to count as one, and no one as more than one, for arriving at the standard of 'maximum utility'—but they conceded that:

> inequality has to be tolerated as a necessary evil, on the ground that equalization would tend to discourage effort, decrease saving, and, by lessening efficiency, diminish the total available for distribution, and so would not benefit those for whose benefit it is advocated (M. Ginsberg, *On Justice in Society;* 1965).

All these arguments in favour of inequality prepared a strong foundation for the development of the capitalist system with enormous inequalities.

It is important to note that the liberal theorists strongly upheld the liberty of man and deprecated an unjust power of man over man in the political sphere. But they failed to realize that the inequality of property—which they advocated in the economic sphere—in effect meant allowing the capitalists to exercise power over the life and labour of others through their property and thus deprive them of their liberty. Moreover, inequality of property creates conditions of 'leisure' and 'conspicuous consumption' on the one hand, and rigorous labour and sub-human living on the other. All this amounts to oppression, exploitation and injustice, not the freedom so highly valued by the liberal theorists.

Conspicuous Consumption

Conspicuous consumption refers to a pattern of consumption of goods and services designed to display the possession of wealth and a high standard of living. This term was first used by Thorstein Veblen, American sociologist (*The Theory of Leisure Class;* 1899) to suggest that those possessing wealth beyond their needs do not have a sense of security about their social position; hence they tend to spend it lavishly with a view to enhancing their social prestige. In fact, conspicuous consumption is the characteristic of the neo-rich class which emerged due to unprecedented expansion of business and industry in recent times. Its members are not sure whether they are held in high esteem in society like the traditionally rich classes.

Conspicuous consumption by the richer classes sets such standards of social prestige that the ambitious but poorer sections of society are tempted to emulate them by adopting corrupt and immoral practices. In short, conspicuous consumption causes erosion of values, and moral degradation of society.

The basis of property as the fruit of labour was more cogently developed by socialist theory which postulated that the worker has a right to the whole produce of his labour. As Ginsberg has elaborated:

> What is perhaps more distinctive of socialist thought is that a distinction is drawn between property in the means of production and property in the fruits of labour. It is clear that, if the instruments of production are appropriated by a few, the rest are deprived of the freedom to apply their labour. Combining these two points, a conclusion is drawn which is the very opposite of Locke's individualism, namely that property in the means of production must be held in common, that all must be given access to apply their labour, and that the assignment of apportionment of the results should be a matter of collective regulation (*ibid.*).

THEORIES OF CONTRIBUTION TO THE PUBLIC GOOD

According to the third set of theories, the right to property, like other rights, should be tested by its contribution to the public good or well-being. These theories are most significant under the conditions of the present-day world.

With the change in the system of production, especially since the advent of the industrial revolution, and the consequent concentration of capital in fewer and fewer hands, there has been an increasing dissociation of property from labour. There has been a growing realization of the fact that under modern conditions the property has often become a means of control over others' life and labour. Theories of contribution to the public good seek to make the right to property subservient to social justice rather than maintain it as an instrument of personal gratification. This view finds its fuller expression in social-democratic perspective on property.

[III]
SOCIAL-DEMOCRATIC PERSPECTIVE

Social-democratic perspective on property seeks to maintain the right to property on such conditions that serve the purpose of socialism as well as democracy. While socialist principle requires that means of social production should be placed in social ownership and control to make them serve social purpose, democratic principle stipulates the security of individual's property as an essential ingredient of his freedom. Synthesis of these two principles is difficult to achieve. The obvious course of this synthesis would be to allow individual ownership of property under such regulations that it is largely used to serve social purpose. This perspective is best represented in the political thought of L.T. Hobhouse (1864-1929), R.H. Tawney (1880-1962) and Harold J. Laski (1893-1950), all of them being English philosophers.

HOBHOUSE AND TAWNEY ON THE RIGHT TO PROPERTY

L.T. Hobhouse, in his *Liberalism* (1911), focused on the social origin of property. He argued that it is the organized force of society that maintains the rights of owners by protecting them against thieves and depredators. It is the protection afforded by the State and the machinery of law which enables them to enjoy their possessions without disturbance. Those who believe in their absolute right to property forget that without the organized force of society their rights are not worth a week's purchase. As Hobhouse has significantly observed:

> The prosperous businessman who thinks that he has made his fortune entirely by self help does not pause to consider what single step he could have taken on the road to his success but for the ordered tranquility which has made commercial development possible, the security by road, and rail, and sea, the masses of skilled labour, and the sum of intelligence which civilization has placed at his disposal (*Liberalism;* 1911).

Hobhouse maintained that even the demand for the goods which a businessman supplies is created by the general progress of the world. The whole process of production in the modern world was made possible, thanks to the inventions which have been built up by the collective effort of generations of men of science and organizers of industry. If a prosperous person of today dug to the foundations of his fortune, he would realize that it is society which maintains and guarantees his possessions, so also it is society which is an indispensable partner in its original creation.

In his another important work *The Elements of Social Justice (*1922), Hobhouse criticized the use of property as an instrument of power in utter disregard of social needs:

> We find many forms of property which involve power over other persons... The owner of land may be in a position to determine the means by which many people can earn their living... The extent of this power varies partly with the nature of property, partly with the distribution of ownership. If the property is important and limited, ownership may involve a partial or complete monopoly, carrying with it a considerable, perhaps a fundamental, power over the lives of many... If, again, there is no monopoly, but wealth is very unevenly distributed, then the possessors of capital have advantages in contracting with workers which give them a very large measure of control over labour.

This control is more keenly felt in modern industry which has brought into existence new economic structures characterized by concentration of control, unified direction, immense increase in labour force and a vast development of administrators and technicians. This system not only enables the capitalist employer to dictate his terms to the mass of workers but also gives him an opportunity to make huge profits which tend to widen the disparity between the haves and have-nots. The profit motive also impels the capitalist to disregard public needs; he would not undertake such supplies and services which are less profitable but greatly needed by the community. It is, therefore, essential that the right to property should be subject to two main qualifications: (*a*) it is not used as an instrument of power over others; and (*b*) it is exercised with due regard to the needs of the community.

R.H. Tawney, in his *The Acquisitive Society* (1920), deprecated the tyranny of functionless property; he advocated subordination of property to social service. As he observes:

> Functionless property appears natural to those who believe that society should be organized for the acquisition of private wealth... Those, however, who hold that social unity and effective work are possible only if society is organized and wealth distributed on the basis of function, will ask of an institution not, 'What dividends does it pay?' but 'What service does it perform?'

LASKI'S VIEWS ON THE RIGHT TO PROPERTY

The theory of moral limitations on the right to property with due regard to the function performed and service rendered to society is best developed by Harold J. Laski, a great exponent of positive liberalism. He particularly dwelled on the positive dimension of the liberal theory of property. He sought to modify the liberal theory of property under the influence of socialist theory, and finally came up with a scheme by which the right to private property can be maintained as an instrument of the common good.

The Moral Basis of Property

At the outset, Laski deals with the right to property as a part of his theory of rights. Thus, in his *A Grammar of Politics* (1938), Laski observes:

> If property must be possessed in order that a man may be his best self, the existence of such a right is clear...I have the right to property if what I own is, broadly speaking, important for the service I perform. I have the right to own if what I own can be shown to be related to the common welfare as a condition of its maintenance.

In other words, the right to property should be directly related to the function performed; it is not an absolute right. There is no room for functionless property in a just society:

> No Man... has a moral right to property except as a return for function performed. He has no right to live unless he pays for his living. He has no right to live because another has earned what suffices for his maintenance... Those whose property is the result of other men's effort are parasitic upon society. They enjoy what they have not assisted to produce (*ibid.*).

As a liberal thinker, Laski is not averse to the institution of private property as such. He concedes that the possession of property provides for a means of harmony in the shape of security. The man of property has a stake in the country. He gets a sense of security and opportunity to develop creative tastes for art and culture. Poverty means a miserable life which destroys man's creative impulse. The institution of private property cannot be condemned as bad in itself. But what we find in the real world is that any significant property is owned by a small number, and its ownership is not necessarily related to the performance of duties or possession of virtues. Laski draws our attention particularly to the conditions prevailing under capitalism and brings it under severe attack:

> The ownership of property involves the control of capital, and...in a regime of free enterprise the control of capital involves power to direct the lives of those who depend upon the application of capital to production ...A regime of private property makes the State very largely an institution

> dominated by the owners of private property, and...it protects the will and purpose of those owners (*ibid.*).

The capitalists tend to use their private property for maximization of their private profit ignoring urgent social needs. Production is seldom related to social utility; distribution is barely related to social urgency. The class of property-owners indulges in immense, wasteful expenditure while propertyless workers crave for mere subsistence. Social standards are set by the owners of wealth, but they become status symbols; these are slavishly imitated by those who cannot afford them. In short, owners of property corrupt all society:

> They produce goods and services, not for use, but to acquire property from their production. They produce not to satisfy useful demands, but demands which can be made to pay. They will ruin natural resources. They will adulterate commodities. They will float dishonest enterprises. They will corrupt legislatures. They will pervert the sources of knowledge... They compel strikes which result in serious damage to the community (*ibid.*).

Laski now examines the prevalent theories regarding defence of private property, one by one, and shows their faults. The psychological theory seeks to justify property as an incentive to labour. But in actual practice, the owners of property work for private profit, not for the good of the community. Moreover, they amass property which inhibits their descendants from working at all. Thus, property may defeat more incentives than it creates. The ethical theory of property defends it as a return for an individual's effort. But, in actual practice, the amount of reward depends on the capacity to make profit, *i.e.* on manipulation, not on the value of service rendered to society. Property is, then, defended as a nurse of virtues essential to society—love of one's family, generosity, inventiveness and energy. But Laski argues that these virtues have been present in those persons also who have never amassed property at all.

The theory of property as the outcome of supplying effective demand, similarly, does not stand to reason. As Laski powerfully argues:

> There is a demand for slaves in Abyssinia; but most men will, I think, agree that response to the demand ought never to be allowed, There is a demand for obscene literature; but few would respect those who trafficked in it. There is a demand for prostitutes; but the law has a definite answer to those who live by satisfying it (*ibid.*).

The historical argument in defence of property holds that progressive societies are those built upon the regime of private property and that backward societies are, in general, those founded upon a collectivist basis of some kind. There is some truth in it. But it is still fallacious because, viewed in historical perspective, private property has remained a changing conception:

> Property in slaves was valid in Greece and Rome; it is no longer valid

> today. In England, there is great freedom of testamentary disposition; in France, inheritance is regulated with much stringency (*ibid.*).

Historical development throughout indicates progressive limitations imposed on the right to property. Hence, no pervasive right to property can be established on historical grounds. The growth of socialism has been responsible for the decline of *laissez-faire* individualism. It has transformed the character of the modern state as regards its attitude towards private property. As Laski observes:

> The State which had begun the nineteenth century in the terms of *laissez-faire* began, as the twentieth century came into view, to search for a basis upon which it could compromise with socialism... So the taxation of the modern State was built upon the assumption that assessment must be graduated by ability to pay. Its franchise was well nigh universal. It offered free education—if of a low standard—to the people. It began to insure against the hazards of sickness and unemployment. It made things like the provision of houses and pensions in old age a matter of corporate concern (*ibid.*).

Laissez Faire

Laissez faire is a French term which means 'leave alone'. It implied the policy of non-intervention by the state in economic activities of individuals. The phrase was in common usage in mercantile and industrial circles in nineteenth-century England and other parts of the world, to express a belief in the freedom of industry and economic activity from state interference.

Modern consciousness, therefore, does not vindicate the maintenance of functionless property—a class which lives luxuriously by owning the means of production, without a sense of social obligation and without making any contribution to the social good. Laski very strongly argues for the limitation of the right of inheritance on moral grounds. No property can be justified unless it is the result of the performance of socially useful functions and duties. True justification of the right to property may be found in: (*a*) a theory of reward; and (*b*) a theory of industrial organization.

Theory of Reward

Laski proceeds to examine several theories of reward with a view to determining the true basis of the right to property. He rejects the doctrine of equal rewards because there is no justice in an equal reward for unequal effort, as also because needs are also unequal. Another theory which links rewards with the operation of market forces of demand and supply is equally untenable. The market is largely manipulated by experts in advertising and salesmanship who distort social need to create a demand for their own products, and thereby do a disservice to society. This is also true of professions: "The incomes made by skilful special pleaders in the days before the reform of judicial procedure largely represented wealth secured in an effort to defeat the ends of justice" (*ibid.*). The prevailing price system is seldom related to the value of the service performed.

The third theory of reward—*viz.* 'from each according to his ability, to each according to his needs'—is quite attractive. But it is an over-simplification of a complex issue. Who will determine the ability, capacity or power of the individual to do a particular work, and how would it be subjected to a common standard? Also, who will determine the genuine needs of each individual with varying duties, capacities, aptitudes and character? This theory is, therefore, hardly capable of practical application.

Laski comes to the conclusion that any principles of reward must satisfy the two complex conditions: (*a*) that it enables the individual to reach out towards his best self; and (*b*) that it preserves and develops necessary functions of society. This would imply a reconciliation of the interest of the individual with that of society. Apart from a system of rewards on this basis, society will also meet the demands of certain classes—children, old people, disabled and defective persons, who cannot pay their way. This criterion of reward involves provision of a 'common civic minimum', beyond which the reward will increase with the value of the service rendered to society.

Theory of Industrial Organization

The theory of just rewards leads to finding a new basis of industrial organization. Laski outlines an elaborate scheme of industrial organization according to the concept of social justice. Thus, he postulates:

> Industry, in fact, must be made a profession. It needs to be informed by a principle of public service. It must not be merely a body of persons who are turning out goods for profit. It must be a body of persons who perform certain functions at some standard of competent performance (*ibid.*).

Laski, in fact, envisages a thorough transformation of the capitalist system. This involves, in the first place, alteration of the character of the owner of wealth. Laski argues that the owner of the capital should receive a fixed dividend for the service rendered by the loan of his capital. He will no longer profit by the special ability of management, the rise in price or the special privilege of a monopoly. Secondly, it involves alteration in the character of the control exercised in industry. Rules for the industry will be laid by its working force: "Once the functionless owner of capital is removed, an industry becomes an intelligible entity, and rules can be drawn up for its governance upon the basis of the functions performed by each element therein" (*ibid.*).

Besides, more room should be made for the social element in the industrial equation. This implies socialized production of essential commodities, such as electric power, which are necessary for the well-being of the community, but hardly fetch private profit. Then all industries—socialized as well as private—should be regulated by standard hours and standard rates of pay, so that autocratic managerial control is replaced by the democratic method. Finally, recruitment to industrial cadres should be based on proven competence, as required in the case of entry into the bar or medical practice. All these changes are intended to convert functionless property of the capitalist system into an instrument of the social good. This would also eliminate the wide economic disparities which plague our socio-economic-political system. As Laski concludes:

> There is nothing inherently wrong in the notion of private property. There is a sense in which it may be so held as genuinely to express personality and to contribute to its enrichment... It must never be so large in amount that its owner exercises power by reason of its sheer magnitude; it must never be so small that its possessor cannot be himself at his best. The more equal its distribution, the more likely is the contribution of the citizen to be judged in terms of its social value (*ibid.*).

In short, Laski holds that the capitalist system itself can be suitably altered so as to make it serve the cause of social justice. He strongly pleads for determining reward in relation to the service rendered to society; he also advocates curtailing the rights of inheritance so that inheritance is reduced to a provision for immediate security. But still he envisages that some people would be left with the 'capital' to be invested in industry, for which they will get a 'fixed dividend' for the service rendered by the loan of that capital. If Laski's scheme is seriously put to practice, it will eliminate big capitalists. There may, of course, remain a large number of 'shareholders' if private industry is still allowed to continue. In that case, there will remain the cooperative sector side by side with the public sector—a feature of socialist society. Laski apparently seeks to maintain capitalism in a subdued form. He hopes to do away with the exploitative character of capitalism.

[IV]
MARXIST PERSPECTIVE

MARX AND ENGELS ON THE ROLE OF PRIVATE PROPERTY

Marxist theory views 'private property' not as a right of the individual, but as a condition which determines relations of production corresponding to the prevailing stage of historical development. Private property, like the state, has not existed from eternity, not to speak of property as a natural right. The origin of private property was attended by the beginning of exploitation in society. The state was created by the class of property-owners for the protection of its private property. It is, therefore, an instrument of exploitation of the dependent class which does not own property.

> **Exploitation**
>
> Exploitation refers to a form of social oppression in which one party takes undue advantage of the vulnerable position of another party. The stronger party uses the physical and mental capacities—resources, talents and skills, etc.—of its victim for its own profit or gratification of its own desires.

Private property did not exist under early social stage—the stage of 'primitive communism'. The means of production at that stage were very rudimentary and held in common ownership. All production was meant for the common consumption, although it was just sufficient for the survival of the community. It was only with the development of the forces of production that surplus production became possible, and with that came the institution of private property, with the consequent division of society into antagonistic classes—masters and slaves. As Friedrich Engels, in his *The Origin of the Family, Private Property and the State* (1884), has recorded:

> The increase of production in all branches—cattle breeding, agriculture, domestic handicrafts—enabled human labour power to produce more than what was necessary for its maintenance. At the same time…the addition of more labour power became desirable. This was furnished by war; captives were made slaves. Under the given general historical conditions, the first great social division of labour, by increasing the productivity of labour, that is wealth, and enlarging the field of production, necessarily carried slavery in its wake. Out of the first great social division of labour arose the first great division of society into two classes: masters and slaves, exploiters and exploited.

Property as the Basis of Class Division

The origin of private property is, therefore, associated with the division of society into antagonistic classes. Private property may be owned by individuals, but they constitute a specific interest, hence a class. Their interest is antagonistic to the interests of the propertyless class. The form of private property changes with the development of forces of production and consequent changes in the mode of production, but so long as private property exists, its exploitative character does not change. Private property divides society into *haves* and *have-nots,* who assume the positions of dominant and dependent classes respectively. In ancient society, this division takes the form of masters and slaves; in medieval society, it takes the form of lords and serfs; and in modern capitalist society, it takes the form of *bourgeoisie* and *proletariat.* This division is sharpest under the capitalist system. The proletariat by its very definition, is propertyless and dependent on wage-labour. As Marx and Engels, in their *Communist Manifesto* (1848), observed:

> Does wage labour create any property for the labourer? Not a bit. It creates capital, *i.e.* that kind of property which exploits wage labour and which cannot increase except upon condition of begetting new supply of wage labour for fresh exploitation. Property, in its present form, is based on the antagonism of capital and wage labour.

Bourgeoisie and Proletariat

These are the two contending classes in modern capitalist society. Engels' note to the English edition (1888 edition) of *Communist Manifesto* reads: "By bourgeoisie is meant the class of modern capitalists, owners of the means of social production and employers of wage labour. By proletariat, the class of modern wage-labourers who, having no means of production of their own, are reduced to selling their labour power in order to live."

Private property, according to Marxism is, therefore, a divisive factor—a source of conflict, not of harmony; a mode of exploitation, not of cooperation. Private property, in this sense, denotes the means of production, because it is the mode of ownership of the means of production which determines how the 'have-nots' will earn their livelihood, and thereby keeps them in permanent subjugation. Marxism, therefore, advocates the abolition of private property in this sense, not personal property:

> The fruit of a man's own labour, which property is alleged to be the ground-work of all personal freedom, activity and independence... Hard-won, self-acquired, self-earned property... When, therefore, capital is converted into common property, into the property of all members of society, personal property is not thereby transformed into social property. It is only the social character of the property that is changed. It loses its class character (*ibid.*).

Property as the Cause of Alienation

Marxist theory holds the system of private property responsible for the erosion of human values. Marx, in his earlier work *Economic and Philosophic Manuscripts* of 1844, presented a searching analysis of the capitalist system of private property from the humanist angle. This work, usually associated with the thought of Young Marx, is known for its literary style rather than scientific rigour, yet some of its parts are quite relevant for the mainstream of Marxist theory. It is a valuable contribution to the Marxist theory of alienation which represents the humanist aspect of Marxism. Marx argued that under the capitalist system, human labour is reduced to a commodity. The more wealth the worker produces, the poorer he becomes. As Marx observes:

> The worker becomes an ever cheaper commodity the more commodities

> he creates. With the *increasing value* of the world of things proceeds in direct proportion the *devaluation* of the world of men. Labour produces not only commodities; it produces itself and the worker as a *commodity*—and does so in the proportion in which it produces commodities generally (*Economic and Philosophic Manuscripts of* 1844).

Under the capitalist system, the worker has no say in the policy or process of production. The acute division of labour deprives the worker of the creative joy of production. If a worker produced a shirt under the feudal system, he could derive the satisfaction of creating some useful thing; but now he produces only a collar, or only a pocket or some other small portion of the shirt, he is unable to discern his role in the creative process. The whole process is characterized by the loss of purpose. The worker's own product confronts him as something *alien,* as a power independent of the producer. The process of *self-estrangement* or *alienation* under the capitalist system takes place at four levels: (*a*) man is alienated from his own product and from his work process; (*b*) man is alienated from nature as he is forced to work under the artificial atmosphere of a factory; (*c*) man is alienated from his fellow-men because of the severely competitive character of the capitalist economy and the sharp class division of society; and (*d*) finally, man is alienated from himself. He is reduced to an animal existence—for in the fulfilment of his biological needs, his human faculties, including the taste for literature, art, music, etc. evaporate in the process.

In his other important works, particularly *Critique of Hegel's Philosophy of Right* (1843) and *On the Jewish Question* (1844), Marx argues that the constitution of modern representative states is, in reality, the 'constitution of private property'. Modern society is characterized by the real domination of private property. As Lucio Colletti, in his Introduction to *Karl Marx: Early Writings* (1975), has summed up:

> Property ought to be a manifestation, an attribute of man, but becomes the subject; man ought to be the real subject, but becomes the property of private property... The social side of human beings appears as a characteristic or property of things; on the other hand, things appear to be endowed with social or human attributes. This is in embryo the argument which Marx will develop later in *Capital* as 'the fetishism of commodities'.

The phenomenon of *fetishism of commodities* (*commodity fetishism*) was analysed by Marx in his seminal work *Capital,* Vol. I (1867). In short, *fetishism of commodities* implies a feature of capitalist society where social relation between different producers is reduced to relation between the products of their labour. It brings different types of skills and quantities of labour into equivalence with each other in terms of their market values. Thus, the social relationship between a tailor and a carpenter appears as a relationship between a coat and a table in terms of their exchange value in the market rather than in terms of the labour and skills embodied in these products. In other words, the commodity becomes an embodiment of value under the capitalist system of private property, while the human being as worker and real producer of value is reduced to a commodity governed by the market forces of demand, supply and competition. The result is an overall dehumanization of man, his self-estrangement and alienation.

Abolition of Private Property

Under the capitalist system, private property takes the form of bourgeois property which creates its domination over society through the blind laws of market forces. It is devoid of any human sense or human appeal. It is a dehumanizing force: no useful purpose will be served by trying to humanize it. Marxist theory, therefore, does not seek to appeal to the good sense of the property-owners; they themselves are slaves of their private property no less than the workers. So if human values are to be restored, human freedom is to be secured, and a rational system of production and distribution is to be evolved to ensure satisfaction of social needs, the obvious course is the abolition of private property itself.

It is the mass of workers who are the worst victims of oppression, exploitation and injustice under the capitalist system. Their emancipation requires the abolition of the system of private property itself. The owners of private property, though equally enslaved by the system, do not feel the pinch because they are placed in a dominant position. They would never be prepared to part with their private property unless overthrown in a violent revolution. Marx, therefore, appeals to the revolutionary zeal of the working class, to abolish the system of private property and to socialize all major means of production. This will restore human sense and human values. As Marx, in his *Economic and Philosophic Manuscripts of* 1844, declares:

> The transcendence of private property is, therefore, the complete *emancipation* of all human senses and attributes; but it is this emancipation precisely because these senses and attributes have become, subjectively and objectively, *human.* The eye has become a *human* eye, just as its *object* has become a social, *human* object—an object emanating from man for man.

With the abolition of private property comes the end of exploitation also. The abolition of private property does not imply abolition of property as such. It involves changing the pattern of ownership of property, from bourgeois ownership to social ownership, from class ownership to common ownership, although in the transitional phase of the 'dictatorship of the proletariat' it may temporarily be held in class ownership of the proletariat till the classless society comes into existence. Thus, Marx and Engels in their *Communist Manifesto* (1848), have observed:

> The distinguishing feature of Communism is not the abolition of property

> generally, but the abolition of bourgeois property. But the modern bourgeois private property is the final and most complete expression of the system of producing and appropriating products, that is based on class antagonisms, on the exploitation of the many by the few... In this sense, theory of the Communists may be summed up in the single sentence: Abolition of private property.

The capitalist system of private property is based on the distortion of property itself: it denotes a condition under which the product of collective effort is appropriated by a few persons, and used as an instrument of domination over society. As Marx and Engels have elucidated:

> To be a capitalist is to have not only a purely personal, but a social *status* in production. Capital is a collective product, and only by the united action of many members, nay, in the last resort, only by the united action of all members of society, can it be set in motion. Capital is, therefore, not a personal, it is a social power... Communism deprives no man of the power to appropriate the products of society: all that it does is to deprive him of the power to subjugate the labour of others by means of such appropriation (*ibid.*).

In short, Marxist theory views the system of private property as the foundation of capitalism which is characterized by the exploitation of man by man. It, therefore, advocates the abolition of private property in the major means of production to pave the way for a humanistic reorganization of production and distribution, while personal property—a genuine fruit of an individual's labour and the instrument of his freedom—will remain intact. The introduction of socialist system will destroy the exploitative character of property and evolve its developmental character, because it will undertake production and distribution of commodities to fulfil social needs, for social benefit, not for private profit at the expense of the community.

CONCLUSION

Marxist theory of property draws a significant distinction between 'personal property' and 'private property'. It favours full protection of 'personal property' which is the source of security of the individual, and abolition of 'private property' which is an instrument of controlling the lives of others. It is a laudable idea. However, it raises some difficulties in actual practice.

Marxist theory of property is fit for application to a society which is divided into two clear cut classes—*haves* and *have-nots*. But in the present-day society, the size of the middle class has considerably increased and it is steadily expanding. Its problems cannot be analysed in the light of Classical Marxist theory. And when a very large number of shareholders have invested their hard-earned money and savings in big business and industries, then the situation turns out to be more complex. When a middle class person raises his personal property by dint of his talent and effort, and invests his savings in the shares of selected companies for the security of his future, then the dividing line between 'personal property' and 'private property' in the Marxian sense starts blurring. In such a situation, recourse to a violent revolution for the abolition of 'private property' would lose its rationale. However, we must appreciate an important suggestion of Marxist theory, that any form of property should not be allowed to become an instrument of exploitation and control over lives of others.

As long as the right to property provides freedom and a sense of security to the individual, and facilitates the best use of his talent and effort, it must be admired. But when this right gives rise to glaring economic disparities in society and forces the bulk of workers to lead a sub-human life, it must be strictly regulated.

Aristotle, ancient Greek philosopher, taught that a certain amount of private property was necessary for good life and for exercising virtue, but when acquired beyond this limit it becomes a source of vice. Here Aristotle was dealing with the impact of property on personal morality, not with its impact on social organization.

Early socialists, who were deeply concerned with the institution of property as a source of vast socio-economic disparities and social injustice, sought to transform it thoroughly. P.J. Proudhon (1809-65), a French philosopher, went to the extent of saying: 'Property is theft'.

Mahatma Gandhi (1869-1948), Indian social philosopher, sought to assess the role of property in the sphere of social as well as personal morality. His principles of non-possession (renunciation or *aparigraha*) and non-stealing (abstention from theft or *asteya*) deal with personal morality. A person should not acquire any material things beyond his immediate requirement because amassing of wealth is bound to degrade his character. It also amounts to theft because thereby you deprive others of their due share. Gandhi maintained that the earth has enough to satisfy everybody's need, but it does not have enough to satisfy anybody's greed.

Then Gandhian principle of 'bread labour' requires that everybody should do physical labour, apart from his usual duties, and contribute to the production of material things in order to compensate for his consumption. This means that the scarcity of material things in society will not be further aggravated due to their continuous consumption. Gandhi also commended 'bread labour' as an instrument of self-purification. This principle deals with personal as well as social morality.

Finally, Gandhian doctrine of trusteeship largely deals with social morality. It requires the owners of capital and big estate to treat their possessions as the trust of humanity and employ them for social service, not for personal gratification, not to speak of private profit. If these principles are adopted, tyranny of property will automatically disappear and there will be a general uplift of material and moral life of society.

19

Concept of Justice

[I]
IDEA OF JUSTICE

Political thinkers since earliest times have been trying to formulate the concept of justice. However, with the dawn of modern consciousness, especially under the influence of the principles of democracy and socialism, this concept has been thoroughly transformed. As a result, the traditional view of justice has given way to the concept of social justice. In a nutshell, *the problem of justice in the contemporary world is concerned with determining logical criteria for the allocation of goods, services, opportunities, benefits, power and honours as well as obligations in society, particularly in a scarcity situation.* Hence, the quest for justice is concerned with just allocation of benefits as well as burdens.

SPHERE OF APPLICATION

Justice is primarily a problem of moral philosophy. But since it has to be implemented by a political order, it also becomes a problem of political philosophy. Here it is important to note that the quest for justice will not be relevant in a purely authoritarian, purely competitive or purely communist regime. In a purely authoritarian system—whether it belongs to the traditional type or modern type—all allocation is made according to the dictates of an established authority. Hence, there is no use of search for the new criteria of allocation. Then in a purely competitive system, all allocation is decided by the free play of market forces. So there is no scope of applying any new criteria of allocation. Finally, in a hypothetical communist system where the rule of 'allocation according to need' is supposed to be applied, it will be futile to consider any alternative principles of justice. If everybody's needs could be met, the problem of injustice in society would automatically disappear.

Search for justice would, therefore, be relevant only in an open society in a situation of scarcity. In other words, the question of justice would become significant in a situation where there is a widespread demand of social advantages that are in short supply, and where the criteria of allocation of these advantages can be openly discussed and adopted. Moreover, these criteria should be determined in such a manner that they prove to be acceptable to all individuals or categories of the individuals concerned. However, it may be conceded that there can be no final word in this behalf. Hence, suitable channels of appeal and even of protest should be provided within the system so that the prevalent criteria could be revised as and when so warranted by reason.

Authoritarian System

Authoritarian system refers to a system of social or political organization where everything is required to conform to an established order, and it is regulated by the person or group which is recognized as the guardian of that order.

Open Society

Open society refers to a society where there is freedom to criticize the existing order in the light of a new logic and to reform or reformulate the existing institutions by attaining public support for the proposed changes.

Scope of Justice

(Justice = An inquiry into the moral basis of allocation of benefits and burdens in society)

Search for Justice

Not relevant in	Relevant only in an
Purely Authoritarian System (No scope to change the allocation made by the established authority) Purely Competitive System (No scope to change the allocation made by the market forces) Hypothetical communist System (where allocation according to need prevails and there is no scarcity)	Open Society (where there is a free flow of information so that faults of the system can be easily detected; where allocation of benefits and burdens is open to alteration; and where a change in this allocation can be demanded and expected)

PHILOSOPHICAL CONTEXT

Justice is primarily a problem of discovering the 'right' course of action. Here the distinction between 'right' and 'wrong' becomes important. It is sometimes confused with the distinction between 'good' and 'evil', as if 'good' corresponds to 'right' and 'evil' corresponds to 'wrong'. But on deeper analysis we find that these variables represent different sets of value systems. Good is akin to useful, profitable, beneficial, and so on; bad or evil implies harmful, damaging, disadvantageous, etc. In any case, good and bad do not fall in absolute categories. You cannot say that something is either good or bad, and nothing else. In actual practice, something may be good in some respects, and bad in others. In other words, it may be 'partly good' and 'partly bad'. Technically we may say that 'good' and 'bad' constitute a 'continuum'. These could be plotted on two extremes of a scale which permits free access from one extreme to another in any direction. Any course of action or state of affairs may be situated on this scale anywhere between the two ends, according to our assessment or evaluation of its qualities.

But the position of 'right' and 'wrong' is different. These are absolute categories, opposed to each other in the absolute sense. Something can be either right or wrong, and nothing else. It is similar to the distinction between 'true' and 'false'. Something could be either true or false, and nothing else. In short, right and wrong, like true and false, are mutually exclusive categories. Their relationship may be represented by a dichotomy. It is a peculiar dichotomy where negative would prevail over the positive. If something is partly true, it must be false. If something is partly false, then too it must be false. If something is partly right, it must be wrong. If something is partly wrong, then too it must be wrong. In the present context, justice corresponds to right; injustice corresponds to wrong.

Continuum and Dichotomy

Continuum stands for a logical device for representing a range of variables which fall between two opposites. It is based on the assumption that though the two opposites are situated on extreme positions, like the two ends of a straight line, yet they are linked with each other so that they provide for easy access from one extreme to the other. Dichotomy, on the other hand, rules out such a possibility between two mutually conflicting positions. One may either stay on one extreme or the other. These are like the two banks of a big river which are not connected by a bridge or navigation facility.

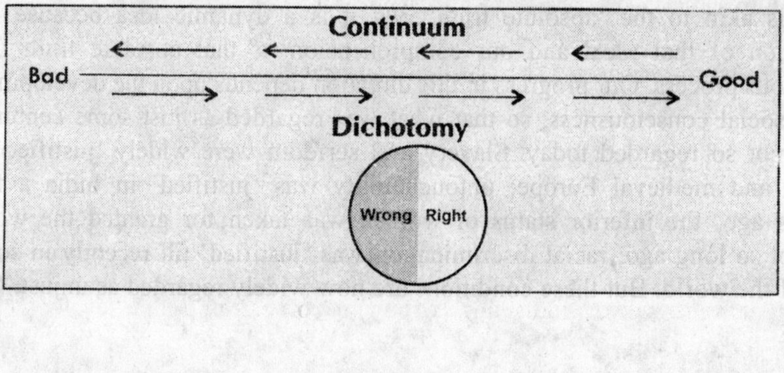

Again, good and bad are marked by quantitative differences. On the other hand, right and wrong are distinguished by qualitative differences. Good and bad are susceptible to measurement and quantification. Utilitarianism deals with good and bad. That is why Jeremy Bentham (1748-1832), the exponent of utilitarianism, founded his 'felicific calculus'. This is concerned with the balancing between the quantities of pleasure and pain. When J.S. Mill (1806-73) focused on the importance of qualitative differences between different types of pleasure, it marked a significant departure from the mainstream utilitarianism. That is also why the mainstream utilitarianism proved to be indifferent to the problem of justice. Bentham advanced a theory of allocation of goods and services without pretending that it was a theory of justice. John Rawls (1921-2002), who accords primacy to the problem of justice, is strongly opposed to utilitarianism. He has pointed to certain situations that satisfy the needs of utilitarianism but they fail to satisfy the needs of justice.

Utilitarianism

Utilitarianism refers to a school of thought founded by Jeremy Bentham (1748-1832), which treats pleasure and pain as the chief motive force behind all human actions. The balance of pleasure over pain derived from a thing or a course of action is termed as 'utility' which is the source of 'happiness'. According to this view, the guiding principle of public policy should be 'the greatest happiness of the greatest number'.

It is important to note that utilitarianism tends to subordinate individual to the collectivity. So when J.S. Mill gives precedence to liberty of the individual over the opinion of the majority, he seems to be distancing himself from the mainstream utilitarianism and coming closer to the idea of justice. Here *Mill accords primacy to the moral worth of a policy instead of subjecting it to cost-benefit analysis.* This tendency to restore the dignity of the individual on moral grounds was brought to its logical conclusion in Rawls's theory of justice.

JUSTICE AS A DYNAMIC IDEA

The term 'justice' implies the quality of being 'just', 'right' or 'reasonable'. It is opposed to what is 'unjust', 'wrong' or 'unreasonable'. It embodies an ideal which is akin to the 'absolute truth', yet it is a dynamic idea because our realization of that ideal and our comprehension of that absolute truth is a continuous process. Our progress in this direction depends upon the development of our social consciousness, so that what was regarded as just some centuries ago is not so regarded today. Slavery and serfdom were widely 'justified' in ancient and medieval Europe; untouchability was 'justified' in India a few decades ago; the inferior status of women was taken for granted the world over not so long ago; racial discrimination was 'justified' till recently in some parts of the world. But these conditions are now widely regarded as unjust. Our changing outlook about these problems and changing public opinion in favour of human liberty and equality are ample proof of the dynamic character of the idea of justice.

It is necessary that the conception of justice should always be based on 'reason'. But man develops his faculty of reasoning according to the social consciousness of his age. The true meaning of justice should, therefore, be determined in the light of prevalent social consciousness, or what D.D. Raphael, in his *Problems of Political Philosophy* (1976), described as 'modern consciousness'. We do not claim that this would represent the perfect idea of justice. Social consciousness is an ever-growing phenomenon, and we should be prepared to accept new and progressive ideas as far as they are supported by reason.

[II]
RELATION BETWEEN LIBERTY, EQUALITY AND JUSTICE

Ernest Barker (*Principles of Social and Political Theory;* 1951) has shown that justice represents a synthesis of the principles of liberty, equality and fraternity. Justice is the thread which runs through all these values and makes them parts of an integrated whole. It reconciles their conflicts and contradictions and gives them the shape of universal principles of governance. Justice is the basic idea behind these values—we hold them in high esteem because they are the manifestations of justice. Justice is the final goal to which all these values should conform.

Why do we demand that human relations in society should be governed by the principle of liberty? Why do we not leave them to the whims of individuals, to the free play of the natural forces of survival of the fittest, to the element of chance, or to irrational traditions and superstitions? Obviously, it is our sense of justice that impels us to postulate that human relations in society should be regulated by 'reason'. Our sense of justice recognizes the dignity of the human being as such. It is the rational nature of man which clothes him with this dignity. It demands that each individual should be treated as an 'end-in-itself, not a means to an end. In this respect, all individuals should be treated as equal to each other. No individual can be treated as superior or inferior to another because of his place of birth, race, religion, language, culture, sex, education or economic status. Irrespective of these differences, all individuals are potentially capable of acquiring excellence and making suitable contributions to the social good. They need equal freedom of personal development in their own right so as to prove their worth to society. That was the idea behind the 'French Declaration of the Rights of Man and of the Citizen' (1789) which reads: "Men are born and remain free and equal in rights. Social distinctions can be based only upon public utility."

Now the principle of liberty will not conform to the principle of justice until the benefit of liberty is equally extended to each individual in society. The idea of absolute liberty is a contradiction in terms. If liberty is defined as the 'absence of restraint', it cannot become a universal principle until it is qualified by the principle of equality. Equality calls for such restraints on liberty that liberty or freedom of one does not become a threat to another's similar and equal liberty. An unrestrained liberty of one or the chosen few will turn out to be the sentence of slavery for the rest of the community. Thus, adherence to the principle of equality becomes necessary in order to resolve the inherent contradiction of absolute liberty. As Barker has elucidated:

> The need of liberty for each is necessarily qualified and conditioned by the need of liberty for all; and the liberty of A will, therefore, be such liberty as he can enjoy concurrently with the enjoyment of similar *and equal* liberty by B and C and D... Because the liberty of each is thus relative to that of others, and has to be adjusted to that of others, it must always be regulated; and indeed it would not exist unless it were regulated (*Principles of Social and Political Theory;* 1951).

On the same principle, any restraint on liberty can only be upheld when it is duly proved that it is imposed in the interests of justice and equality.

The principle of equality is, again, not the final principle of justice. Equality may be defined as the 'absence of discrimination'. In the legal or political sphere, this interpretation of equality will not present much difficulty. This could be interpreted as equality before the law, equal legal personality of each individual, equal voting rights—'one man, one vote' principle, etc. But as we turn to the economic sphere, the mere 'absence of discrimination' may not meet the requirements of justice. When society is divided into different strata due to disparities in possession of wealth, prestige and power—one class enjoying special privileges at the expense of another—the cause of justice will not be served by treating them entirely without discrimination. The principle of justice requires that the deprived and underprivileged sections should be given special protection in all competitive situations. Thus, if an ordinary man in his capacity as worker, consumer or tenant is open to exploitation by the employer, trader or landlord, the law should make reasonable discrimination in favour of the weaker party. It is just like extending the principle of brotherhood or fraternity to the regulation of human relations in society as a matter of right, not charity. The principle of fraternity involves resolving the contradiction of the principle of equality which would otherwise leave the individual at the mercy of the cruel market forces of demand and supply and open competition; this would eliminate the weaker sections, not to speak of securing them equal dignity, opportunity or advantage. But any departure from equality can be vindicated only when it is duly proved that it involves discrimination in favour of the weaker section in the interests of justice and fraternity.

Thus, in the final principle of justice, we seek to regulate human relations in society by the principle of liberty; but liberty is qualified by the principle of equality; and equality is further qualified by the principle of fraternity. The intention is to make sure that each individual gets a fair share in the advantages accruing from organized social life. Each individual gets a common civic minimum beyond which one's work is rewarded according to the value of the contribution made to the public welfare. It must be ascertained that an unduly large share of wealth, prestige and power is not cornered by any privileged section or sections by dint of its money and manipulative power. The principle of justice postulates not merely formal liberty and equality, but the transformation of those social conditions which obstruct the weaker and vulnerable sections from enjoying substantive freedom and equality. This view brings liberty and equality very close to the principle of justice.

[III]
CLASSICAL THEORIES OF JUSTICE

PLATO'S THEORY OF JUSTICE

It would be significant to observe at the outset that the modern concept of justice is different from the traditional concept. Traditional concept of justice focused on the 'just man'. It was primarily concerned with the virtues befitting a man for enhancing his moral worth. It consisted in the performance of his duties attached to his status as determined by the prevalent law, social customs and mode of thought. A typical example of the traditional approach to the problem of justice is provided by Plato's theory of justice which sought to prescribe the duties of different citizens and required them to develop virtues befitting those duties. As Richard Lewis Nettleship, in his *Lectures on the Republic of Plato* (1962), has elucidated:

> Justice, in Plato's sense, is the power of individual concentration on duty. If a soldier is just in this sense, he is, of course, a brave man; if a man in subordinate position is just, he, of course, accepts and maintains authority, or is 'self-controlled'. Justice therefore...is really the condition of the existence of all the virtues; each of them is a particular manifestation of the spirit of justice, which takes different forms according to a man's function in the community. In modern phrase it is equivalent to sense of duty.

Plato prescribes different duties for different classes of citizens whose fulfilment would be instrumental in building up a just social order. Justice results from each element in society doing its appropriate task, doing it well and doing it only. In order to achieve perfect harmony which symbolizes justice, it is imperative that reason must rule within the man as well as within the state.

So, in a just or ideal state, the reins of government shall remain in the hands of a class of philosopher-kings who are supposed to be the living embodiments of wisdom, whereas material production and military defence shall be entrusted to the producer and warrior classes respectively. Thus, in Plato's perfect state:

> the industrial forces would produce but they would not rule; the military forces would protect but they would not rule; the forces of knowledge and science and philosophy would be nourished and protected and they would rule (Will Durant, *The Story of Philosophy;* 1954).

Plato enumerated four cardinal virtues. Of these, the first three were the befitting virtues for each social class whereas justice was the befitting virtue of the social order, as shown in the following chart:

Plato's Theory of Justice

Social Class	*Dominant Trait*	*Befitting Virtue*
Philosophers	Knowledge	Wisdom
Soldiers	Emotion	Courage
Traders	Appetite	Temperance
Virtue befitting the social order		Justice

It is significant that the ideal form of Hindu caste system, as enunciated by the ancient law-givers, strikes a similar note regarding the nature of *dharma* which is equivalent of justice.

ARISTOTLE'S THEORY OF JUSTICE

While Plato's theory of justice represents the radical view in that it sought to change the existing social order of his times, Aristotle's theory of justice embodies the conservative view in favour of maintaining the existing order. In Aristotle's view, justice was concerned with the regulation of human relations. He held that the identical notion of justice in the minds of people was responsible for binding them together, and this was the reason behind the existence of the state.

Aristotle identified three types of justice: (*a*) Distributive Justice; (*b*) Retributive (also called Corrective, Rectificatory or Remedial) Justice; and (*c*) Commutative Justice. The legislator should be concerned with distributive justice whereas the judge should be concerned with retributive and commutative justice. Distributive justice deals with the allocation of honours and wealth. Its basic principle is 'treating equals equally and unequals unequally'. Aristotle preferred to rely on the prevailing custom and customary law for deciding as to who were equals or unequals.

Retributive justice deals with imposition of punishment and payment of damages. It requires full restoration of any loss involuntarily sustained in the course of transactions between individual members of the community. Finally, commutative justice seeks to determine the amount of one sort of goods or services to be rendered in return for another sort in voluntary transaction of buying and selling, or letting and hiring. Its guiding principle should be full equivalence.

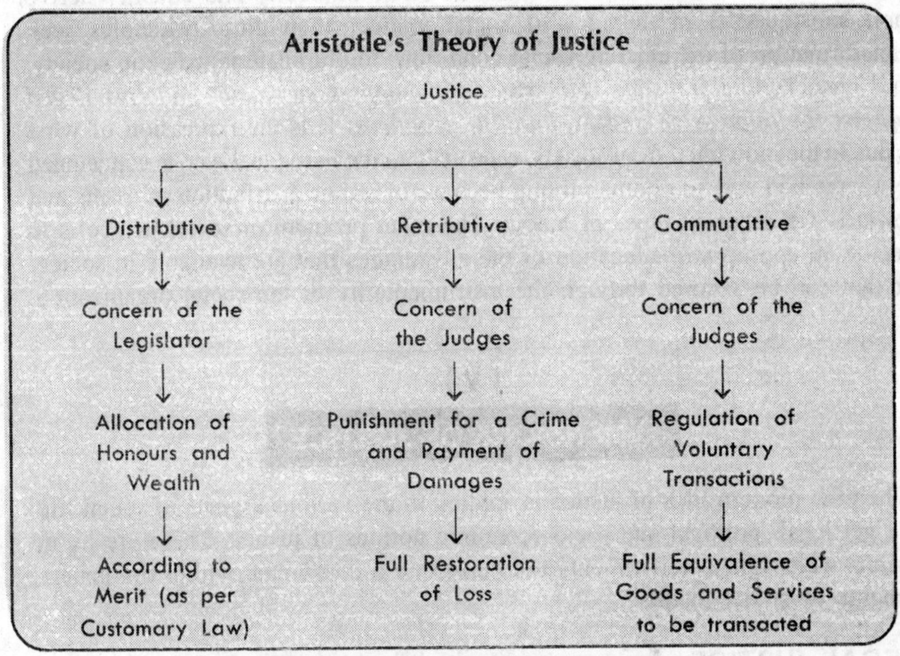

[IV]
MODERN VIEW OF JUSTICE

Whereas the traditional view of justice was largely conservative, the modern view of justice embodies a progressive idea. Traditional view required the individual to conform to the existing social order; modern view of justice seeks to transform society itself for the realization of certain human values. In short, the traditional view of justice has given way to the modern idea of 'social justice'. D.D. Raphael, in his *Problems of Political Philosophy* (1976), has made an important point: "The term 'social justice' tends to issue from the mouths of reformers, and to be regarded with suspicion by those who are satisfied with the existing order."

Human Values

Human values refer to a set of moral principles and beliefs whose upholders pay due regard to human life, human personality, human feelings and human dignity while dealing with others. In this pursuit, considerations of material profit and loss are relegated to the background.

The idea of social justice comprises a force behind social change. It is precisely when people find fault with the existing social order, involving oppressive and exploitative social conditions, that they raise the demand for social justice, seeking suitable changes in social policy so as to secure fair distribution of benefits and burdens. The ideas of liberty and equality derive their substance from the idea of social justice when these principles seek transformation of the existing social conditions to eliminate injustice in society. In a nutshell, *'social justice' is the voice of the oppressed and the underprivileged against the oppressive and exploitative practices.* It is an expression of what is due to the individual from society, especially to the individual who is condemned to a wretched and sub-human living because of unfair distribution of assets and rewards for different types of labour. The main problem of social justice is to decide an appropriate allocation of the advantages that are available in society or that can be secured through the instrumentality of the social organization.

[V]
DIMENSIONS OF JUSTICE

When the modern idea of justice is applied to the various aspects of social life, we get legal, political and socio-economic notions of justice. These are by no means watertight compartments but constitute a *continuum* within the general scheme of social justice.

LEGAL JUSTICE

The term 'legal justice' is broadly applied in two contexts: (*a*) 'justice according to law' (formal justice)—here we do not question the validity of law but focus on the principles of administration of justice according to the prevalent law; and (*b*) 'law according to justice'—here we examine the substance of law itself to ensure that it conforms to the requirements of justice.

Alf Ross, in his *On Law and Justice* (1958), argued that justice consists in an efficient administration of law and that it should not be tested on some imaginary moral values. As Morris Ginsberg, in his *On Justice in Society* (1965), has elucidated:

> Ross accepts what may be called the formal principles of justice as a basis of law. The notion of a legal order implies that decisions shall be made not arbitrarily but in accordance with general rules, and that these general rules (whatever they are) shall be correctly (that is what moralists call impartially) applied; that is by criteria defining the class of cases coming under the rule, and not affected by the subjective reactions of the judge. Justice then is conformity with existing law.

This view represents an outstanding example of the concept of legal justice as 'justice according to law'. It does not question whether a particular law itself is right or wrong, on the plea that there is no scientific way of such verification. A good law is known by its efficiency in attaining its purpose, whatever that purpose may be. In this sense, the problem of justice has nothing to do with the purpose of law; it is solely concerned with the efficacy of law. Justice in totalitarian societies may be distorted not because of bad laws, but because of the power given to judges to disregard fixed rules.

On the other hand, Ernest Barker, in his *Principles of Social and Political Theory* (1951), has dwelled on the concept of legal justice as 'law according to justice'. Barker draws a distinction between 'positive law' and 'natural law' to show that law derives its validity and value from two different sources. Positive law denotes a particular law—the law defined and declared by each community for its own members. On the other hand, natural law is a universal law—a law founded on what is right-in-itself, on what is just everywhere and at all times, for all mankind, on what is valuable whether it is valid or not. Barker demonstrates that this distinction between the two aspects of law can be traced in the political theory of Aristotle, Roman jurisprudence as well as Christian doctrine. After a detailed examination of these theories, Barker comes to this conclusion:

> If we make this distinction, we may say that authority gives validity to law, and justice gives it value. A law has validity, and I am legally obliged to obey it, if it is declared, recognized, and enforced as law by the authority of the legally organized community, acting in its capacity of a State. A law has value, and I am bound to obey it not only legally, and not only by an outward compulsion, but also morally and by an inward force, if it has the inherent quality of justice (*Principles of Social and Political Theory;* 1951).

Barker points out that, ideally, law ought to have both validity and value. Thus, law will be most effective if it conforms to the principle of justice and also has the authority of the state.

Of the two views of legal justice, one represented by Ross and the other by Barker, the latter is definitely more sound. Justice in the legal sphere consists not only in an efficient administration of law, but it postulates that law itself should embody human values according to the prevailing social consciousness. If law does not reflect the changing social values, it will turn out to be a dead weight on the wheels of social progress, only to be discarded in a violent overthrow.

POLITICAL JUSTICE

The term 'political justice' is sometimes applied in a comprehensive sense so as to embrace the restructuring of the entire fabric of socio-economic and political relations. For instance, William Godwin, in his *Essay on Property*

(1793), used the term 'political justice' to denote a moral principle whose object was the 'general good' and which was especially invoked to evolve a genuine system of property. Otto Kirchheimer, in his *Political Justice: The Use of Legal Procedure for Political Ends* (1961), conceived of 'political justice' as 'the search for an ideal in which all members will communicate and interact with the body-politic to assume its highest perfection'.

A more specific usage of the term 'political justice', however, refers to the transformation of political institutions, political process and political rights according to current conceptions of justice. This means, in the first place, the establishment of democratic institutions in political life of the community so that these institutions represent and take care of the interests of the people, not of any privileged class. Thus, representative institutions—the legislature and executive—should be constituted on the principle of universal adult franchise, while the independence of the judiciary should be protected and maintained. This also implies 'rule of law', *i.e.* the principle that government should not be arbitrary, but should be conducted through procedures authorized by legislation passed in the proper form. A constitutional government is also an essential ingredient of political justice in this sense.

Constitutional Government

Constitutional government refers to a type of government in which powers of governance (legislative, executive and judicial powers) are exercised by those who are appointed through the prescribed procedure, in a prescribed manner and under regular legal and political restraints provided by a Constitution. A constitution in this context denotes a set of rules, procedures; practices and conventions which prescribe structures, functions, powers and responsibilities of different organs of government; the procedure of their formation, working and dissolution; relation between the state and its citizens, etc.

In the second place, political justice implies a full guarantee of the liberty of thought and expression, especially the right to criticize the government and its policies. Finally, there should be complete freedom for forming associations and interest groups to enable the citizens to articulate their interests through the normal channels of communication and through political parties as well as to express their approval or disapproval of particular measures, to organize peaceful protests against harmful measures, and to pressurize the working of the government through democratic channels and procedures. In a nutshell, political justice postulates the universal availability of the mechanism for resolving the conflicting claims of different interests in society.

SOCIO-ECONOMIC JUSTICE

The term 'socio-economic justice' comprehends two important elements: 'social justice' and 'economic justice'. Their combination into 'socio-economic justice' is significant because social life of the community cannot be transformed according to the principle of justice unless its economic relations are suitably transformed. The term 'economic justice' may be used in the restricted sense of reordering human relations in the economic sphere, *e.g.* relations between employer and worker, between trader and consumer, between landlord and tenant, between money-lender and borrower, etc. so as to eliminate exploitation of the vulnerable sections of society. On the other hand, the term 'social justice' is used more comprehensively so as to include economic justice and also to restore the dignity of human beings who have lost it due to a lower economic, educational and cultural status. In short, it seeks to eradicate social discrimination at all levels.

When we speak of 'economic growth with social justice', the term social justice suggests that the benefits of economic growth—which are largely economic in nature—should accrue to larger and larger sections, especially to the lower strata of society. The term socio-economic justice, or social justice, in a broad sense, comprehends the reallocation of both material and moral advantages of social life. It denotes a progressive concept and a model of development. The Indian Constitution (1950), particularly its Preamble and the part dealing with the Directive Principles of State policy, is committed to the ideal of justice—social, economic and political. In common parlance, the term 'social justice' is usually applied to comprehend all the three aspects of justice in society—social, economic and political. Of these, the economic aspect is most crucial because economic disparities and injustice are bound to erode the foundations of legal and political justice.

In a nutshell, *the term social justice, in the wider sense, implies a reordering of social life in such a manner that the material and moral benefits of social effort are not cornered by a tiny privileged class,* but *accrue to the masses to ensure the uplift of the lower, weaker and underprivileged sections.* This involves a logical synthesis of liberty, equality and fraternity in their substantive aspects so that: (*a*) liberty of thought and expression, etc. is supplemented by a democratic electoral system free from the decisive influence of money and manipulative power; (*b*) formal equality is not rendered ineffective due to vast economic disparities, especially in the field of seeking justice in the law-courts and availing of educational and career development opportunities; (*c*) special safeguards for minorities and weaker sections are provided in order to raise their dignity and promote the spirit of fraternity; and (*d*) the right to property is subordinated to the common good and the pattern of production of goods and services tends to subserve social needs.

[VI]

PROCEDURAL AND SUBSTANTIVE JUSTICE

Contemporary debate on the nature of justice focuses on the distinction between procedural justice and substantive justice which largely coincides with the essence of social justice. Champions of procedural justice hold that it is necessary to determine a just procedure for the allocation of social advantages, *viz.* goods and services, opportunities and benefits, power and honours; then its outcome will automatically be accepted as just. In other words, the allocation resulting from a just procedure must be treated as just. On the contrary, champions of substantive justice argue that the allocation or distribution of social advantages among various sections of society itself should be just—that is the primary issue; the procedure for making such allocation is a secondary issue, which can be adjusted suitably to meet the requirements of just distribution.

The notion of procedural justice is closely related to the tradition of liberalism. According to this viewpoint, the function of justice is to regulate the mutual relations between individuals and groups. Hence, the quest for justice should aim at evolving reasonable rules which should be applied impartially to all categories. Freedom of contract is the mainstay of procedural justice. It requires the state to ensure that no individual or group would oppress another by force or fraud. Using the analogy of race, the defenders of procedural justice insist on laying down rules of the game; it hardly matters as to who wins or loses in the race. As Norman Barry (*An Introduction to Modern Political Theory;* 1989) has aptly illustrated: "Procedural justice is exemplified in competitions, such as races. A fair race is not one in which the person who wins morally deserves to win but one in which there is no cheating, nobody jumps the gun or has an unfair advantage through the use of drugs." Accordingly, procedural justice treats the rules of market economy as the model rules of human behaviour. It holds that the market mechanism creates necessary conditions for the most efficient use of resources; any artificial social policy designed to disturb this process will lead to the wastage of the rare material and human resources. The exponents of procedural justice include Herbert Spencer (1820-1903), F.A. Hayek (1899-1992), Milton Friedman (1912-2006), and Robert Nozick (1938-2002). Besides, John Rawls (1921-2002) has sought to accommodate the requirements of substantive justice or social justice in his well-drawn scheme of procedural justice.

Liberalism

Liberalism refers to a principle of politics which regards 'liberty' or 'freedom' of individual as the first and foremost goal of public policy. Liberty, in this sense, implies 'liberation' from restraints, particularly from the restraints imposed by an authoritarian state. This principle was evolved in the West in late seventeenth century in order to liquidate feudal privileges of the land-owning class and to create favourable conditions for the new entrepreneurial class to enable them to contribute to social progress.

Procedural justice repudiates all discrimination between human beings on grounds of caste, creed, sex, race, region, language and culture, etc. and accepts equal dignity and moral worth of all human beings. In this respect, it is a progressive idea. But it stretches the principle of open competition too far. Thus, Spencer went to the extent of suggesting that the state should not extend any help to the handicapped and let the weakest go to the wall. Spencer argued that if the state gives any support to the incapable, the imprudent and the weak, it would amount to depriving the capable, the prudent and the strong of their genuine share, and thereby impeding social progress. Spencer's social philosophy implies applying Darwin's principle of 'natural selection' and 'survival of the fittest' to the realm of human relations. It obliterates the distinction between rules of the animal world and those of civil society. Hayek suggested that the state should positively promote competition in society and ensure that the market is not reduced to an instrument of distributive justice. Friedman eulogized competitive capitalism as an essential condition of freedom and wanted government to move out of all welfare and regulatory functions. Nozick contended that the state has no authority to redistribute the property of its citizens who were originally its clients. C.B. Macpherson (1911-87) has rightly pointed out that the free market society destroys the creative freedom of human beings who are constrained to employ their talents, skills and energies to cater to the needs of the market-place instead of pursuing self-appointed goals. Where is the scope of justice under such conditions of constraint?

In contrast, the idea of substantive justice corresponds to the philosophy of socialism. It holds that the test of justice in society consists in ascertaining whether the poor and the underprivileged have adequate opportunity to improve their lot. It demands that the opportunities of self-development should be progressively extended to the underprivileged and disadvantaged sections of society.

Socialism

Socialism refers to a principle of politics which favours social ownership and control of the means of social production so that all able-bodied persons could be suitably employed in productive work, and all means of social production could be deployed for the fulfilment of social needs.

[VII]
RETRIBUTIVE AND DISTRIBUTIVE JUSTICE

Aristotle had defined retributive and distributive justice in consonance with his conservative outlook. In modern times, these aspects of justice must be defined in terms of modern social consciousness. Retributive justice is primarily concerned with determining punishment for a crime. David Miller has identified three conditions to ensure justice in the matter of punishment:

(*a*) that punishment should only be inflicted on those found guilty of wrong-doing, using proper procedure;

(*b*) that punishment be uniformly imposed, *i.e.* the differences in penalty should always correspond to differences in wrong-doing; and

(*c*) that the scale of penalties should be proportionate to the various misdemeanours being punished—neither too severe nor too lax ('Justice' in *The Blackwell Encyclopedia of Political Thought,* edited by David Miller; 1987).

In short, retributive justice requires that punishment should be awarded for a crime duly proved, in proportion to the seriousness of crime; and that it should neither be too severe nor too lax. On the other hand, distributive justice is concerned with the allocation of benefits and burdens according to our notion of justice. David Miller, in his celebrated work *Social Justice* (1976), has defined the problem of social justice as that of determining 'the principles which should be chosen to govern the distribution of wealth, prestige and other benefits among the members of society'. He has identified three criteria which are usually invoked to determine the principles of distributive justice: (*a*) Protection of acknowledged rights; (*b*) Distribution according to desert; and (*c*) Distribution according to need. Each of these criteria has its own merits and demerits. None of these can be commended for the final selection.

Miller has also identified the corresponding social order upheld by each of these criteria. Accordingly, the principle of 'protection of acknowledged rights' gives rise to 'hierarchical order'. Its chief exponent was David Hume (1711-76). The principle of 'distribution according to desert' upholds 'competitive market system'. Its chief exponent was Herbert Spencer (1820-1903). Finally, the principle of 'distribution according to need' corresponds to 'solidarity community'. Its chief exponent was Peter Kropotkin (1842-1921). Miller's classification is shown in the following chart.

Principles of Distributive Justice
(as identified by David Miller)

Criterion of Justice	*Corresponding Social Order*	*Chief Exponent*
Protection of Acknowledged Rights	Hierarchical Order	David Hume (1711-76)
Distribution according to Desert	Competitive Market	Herbert Spencer (1820-1903)
Distribution according to Need	Solidarity Community	Peter Kropotkin (1842-1921)

Now the first criterion, *viz.* the 'protection of acknowledged rights' creates a 'hierarchical order'. In this system people have different ranks or positions depending on how important they are. The very demand for the protection of existing rights and the maintenance of existing ranks implies the denial of any relief to underprivileged sections. For instance, Aristotle's defence of slavery was based on the argument that the slave was incapable of virtue; that he could avail himself of the benefits of virtue only through serving his master. Defenders of Hindu caste system also declared that serving the higher castes amounted to penance for the members of the lowest caste (तपः शूद्रस्य सेवनम्). It is, therefore, impossible to attain the true goal of social justice so long as we adhere to the principle of 'protection of acknowledged rights'.

The second principle, *viz.* 'distribution according to desert' which upholds 'market society' system, is ahead of 'hierarchical order' in the sense that it rules out the privilege based on birth, and determines one's share of social benefits according to one's contribution to the social good. However, it concedes vast disparities of income and wealth as it enables the owners of private property to multiply their wealth by hiring the physical and mental capacities of the working classes at competitive rates. In short, the competitive system tends to widen the gap between rich and poor. Herbert Spencer, the chief exponent of this principle, sought to apply the law of 'survival of the fittest' to social life. He did not hesitate to rule out any assistance to the incapable, the imprudent and the weak.

The third principle, *viz.* 'distribution according to need' is quite laudable, but it has its own difficulties. It will promote social solidarity only if it could be put into practice. But 'distribution according to need' is possible only if there is abundance of goods and services. That is only a hypothetical situation. If this principle is sought to be applied, even partially, in a scarcity situation which is always the case, it will kill incentive and discourage the talented and energetic people from giving their best to society. That would further impoverish society and make the application of this principle more difficult.

Solution to the problem can reasonably be found by a judicious combination of the third and the second principles. In the first place, people should learn to minimize their needs, and make adequate contribution to production for society, as taught by Mahatma Gandhi (1869-1948), Indian social philosopher. The state should then make provision for meeting the minimum needs of people to ensure their survival and basic education. Thereafter reward of for each individual should be determined according to his contribution to the social good.

CONCLUSION

Justice is primarily a problem of moral philosophy. In politics, the concept of justice is used as a guide to public policy. The question of justice arises under two conditions: (*a*) in a scarcity situation—where goods, services, opportunities, etc. are too scarce to satisfy all contestants; and (*b*) in an open society—where allocation of various benefits is not tied to fixed status of various individuals but they are free to demand a fair share on some reasonable ground. In a hierarchical or authoritarian society where all social advantages are allocated to different sections of society according to a predetermined scheme, justice is conceived as the strict adherence to that scheme. In an open society, we may consider two major criteria of allocation: (*a*) allocation according to need; and (*b*) allocation according to desert, merit and ability. In a scarcity situation, it is impossible to meet everybody's needs. If we resort to an equal distribution of social advantages for the purpose of equal satisfaction of everybody's needs irrespective of their contribution, then no incentive will be left to work hard. The result will be less production and a lesser availability of goods and services, etc. for distribution and a general impoverishment of society.

On the other hand, if we introduce a purely competitive system, ignoring needs altogether, some human beings might be constrained to lead sub-human life. This would result in a general moral degradation as well as loss of potential for social progress. Justice, therefore, requires that a provision should be made for meeting some minimum needs of all human beings irrespective of their individual contribution to society. Minimum needs could include means of subsistence, healthcare, some level of education or literacy, and some job opportunities, because a job is not only a means of subsistence but also a means of self-respect. While making allocation according to need, it is imperative that the neediest should get priority. Needs should be determined on individual basis (or family-unit basis). If some groups or classes are declared to be entitled to special concessions, they are bound to develop a vested interest in the system. As a consequence, the claims of the neediest individuals (or family-units) among other categories are bound to be ignored, resulting in injustice.

Once the provision for minimum needs has been made, an additional reward can be given according to desert. Criterion of desert is, again, by no means a simple issue. A purely competitive system is no answer to the question. In a system based on desert, reward will depend on four factors: (*a*) one's talents and skills; (*b*) effort; (*c*) opportunity; and (*d*) social demand. Of these, the first two factors, *viz.* talents and skills combined with effort are hardly controversial, but the last two factors, *viz.* opportunity and social demand might prove to be beyond control of the individual. Talents and effort may go unrewarded or scantily rewarded for want of adequate opportunity. Then variations in social demand might result in overvaluation or undervaluation of talents. As John H. Schaar ('Equality of Opportunity, and Beyond' in *Contemporary Political Theory,* edited by Anthony de Crespigny and Alan Wertheimer; 1971) has pointed out, talents might not be rewarded according to their intrinsic worth due to variations in the prevailing hierarchy of values in different social settings. Thus, soldierly qualities and virtues were highly admired and rewarded in the ancient Sparta, while the poets languished. C.B. Macpherson (1911-87) has lamented on the lack of creative freedom for ordinary human beings in a capitalist system. In view of these constraints, the state should create adequate opportunities for and give suitable encouragement to sublime arts and professions in order to meet the requirements of justice.

Creative Freedom

Creative freedom refers to a concept of freedom which regards man as a *doer* and *creator*. It can be realized only when man gets adequate opportunities for development and application of his uniquely human capacities. Champions of creative freedom believe that the essence of man's freedom lies in fully realizing his creative faculties for the fulfilment of his self-appointed goals. C.B. Macpherson (1911-87), Canadian political philosopher, has argued that in capitalist market society, owners of land and capital wield immense power to exploit the manual and intellectual capacities of ordinary citizens. Under this system, the poor are constrained to sell their capacities according to needs of the market; they have little opportunity to use these capacities for the fulfilment of their self-appointed goals. Thus, capitalist system provides little scope for the poor to enjoy their creative freedom.

20

Diverse Perspectives on Justice

QUEST FOR JUSTICE has been an important concern of political theory since ancient times. In modern times, a significant part of political theory is directly or indirectly related to the problem of justice. This has given rise to diverse perspectives on justice. Of these, the following are particularly important: Liberal perspective; Libertarian perspective; Marxist perspective; Feminist perspective; Subaltern perspective; and Communitarian perspective. An acquaintance with these perspectives will immensely help us in understanding the complexity of the problem.

[I]
LIBERAL PERSPECTIVE

Liberal perspective on justice treats liberty as the central problem of justice. It is important to note that only the idea of substantive liberty will auger well for the realization of justice. This perspective is chiefly represented by Rawls's Theory of Justice.

> **Substantive Liberty**
>
> Substantive liberty refers to a condition in which individual finds himself capable of enjoying his freedom. For this purpose, he should be capable to understand what is good for him and for his society, determine his goals, and then achieve those goals without unreasonable restraints. Where necessary, concrete steps should be taken in the direction of removal of economic and cultural constraints from the life of the deprived sections of society to enable the concerned individuals to enjoy their freedom in the real sense.

RAWLS'S THEORY OF JUSTICE

John Rawls (1921-2002), a contemporary American philosopher, in his celebrated work A *Theory of Justice* (1971), has pointed out that a good society is characterized by a number of virtues. Justice is the first virtue of a good society. In other words, justice is a necessary but not a sufficient condition of a good society. Those who argue that justice should not be allowed to come in the way of social advancement and progress, run the risk of causing the moral degradation of society.

Problem of Distribution

According to Rawls, the problem of justice consists in ensuring a just distribution of 'primary goods' which include rights and liberties, powers and opportunities, income and wealth, means of self-respect, and so on. Rawls has described his theory as the theory of pure procedural justice. It means that once certain principles of justice are unanimously accepted, the distribution resulting from their application will be necessarily just. Rawls has severely criticized those theories of allocation which ignore moral worth of the individual for the attainment of any predetermined goals. He has attacked utilitarianism because in calculating the 'greatest happiness of the greatest number', it does not care if it leads to extreme hardship to any particular individual. For instance, one might imagine a state of affairs in which the maximum amount of happiness would be produced and its distribution to a maximum number of people achieved by the enslavement of a minority. *Rawls has brilliantly argued that you cannot compensate for the sufferings of the dis.ressed by enhancing the joys of the prosperous.*

Utilitarianism

Utilitarianism refers to a school of thought founded by Jeremy Bentham (1748-1832) which prescribes 'greatest happiness of the greatest number' as the goal of legislation and public policy. The balance of pleasure over pain derived from a thing or a course of action represents the amount of happiness. In estimating 'greatest happiness of the greatest number', each individual should be treated as one unit, but in estimating the total amount of happiness derived from a thing or action, this mode of thought does not pay due attention to the disparity in the shares of particular individuals.

Rawls has evolved a unique methodology for arriving at a unanimous procedure of justice. Following the tradition of the 'social contract', Rawls has envisaged an 'original position' by abstracting the individuals from their particular social and economic circumstances. These individuals are symbolically placed behind a 'veil of ignorance' where they are supposed to be deliberating as rational agents. They are totally unaware of their wants, interests, skills and abilities as well as of the conditions which lead to discrimination and conflict in society. But they have an elementary knowledge of economics and psychology, and are also endowed with a 'sense of justice'. Each individual wants to maximize his or her well-being, without being envious. They are self-interested but not egoists. They are not prepared to take a risk or resort to gambling. According to Rawls, in such a state of uncertainty the rational negotiators will choose the least dangerous path. In other words, each individual will hypothetically place himself or herself in 'the least advantaged position' while recommending the criteria of allocation of the primary goods. Hence, each of them will demand greatest benefit for the least advantaged.

Social Contract

The idea of the social contract refers to an agreement among men whereby they relinquish the hypothetical 'state of nature' and enter into civil society. Thomas Hobbes (1588-1679), John Locke (1632-1704), English philosophers and Jean-Jacques Rousseau (1712-78), French philosopher, are regarded the chief exponents of the theory of the social contract. They have given different accounts of the state of nature, the terms of the contract, and the nature of political obligation which comes into existence in consequence of the social contract.

Principles of Distribution

As a result of the hypothetical negotiation under such conditions, *three principles of justice* will be accepted by all, according to Rawls, in the following order: (1) *Principle of equal liberty* (*i.e.* equal right to most extensive liberty compatible with similar liberty of others) which postulates that nobody's liberty will be compromised for any other benefit (liberty in this sense implies equal right to political participation, freedom of expression, religious liberty, equality before the law, etc.); (2) *Principle of fair equality of opportunity,* particularly for acquiring offices and positions; and (3) finally, *Difference principle* which implies that any departure from equal distribution of the primary goods can be justified only when it could be proved to bring greatest benefit to the least advantaged. In other words, a special reward for extraordinary ability and effort to any individual can be treated as just only if it results in the greatest benefit to the least privileged. When these conditions have been fulfilled, the criteria of efficiency can be justly applied in a competitive economy. In other words, the rule of allocation 'to each according to his ability' can be applied only if higher efficiency of the concerned individual results in ameliorating the condition of the least privileged.

Here Rawls introduces the idea of the chain connection which implies that in order to strengthen a chain, we should start with strengthening its weakest link, and then repeat the process by identifying the weakest link on each occasion. As Norman Barry (*An Introduction to Modern Political Theory;* 1989) has elucidated: "Rawls… argues that a 'chain connection' operates between the best and the worst off and that a rise in the expectations of the best off will have the effect of raising everybody else's expectations throughout the system." The justifiability of any special concessions, subsidies or protection depends on empirical facts whether or not such benefits filter down ultimately to help the neediest. As Samuel Gorovitz has significantly observed: "Rawls… is clearly a redistributionist in that he takes the proper function of government to include not merely the maintenance of a social order, but the achievement of distributive justice by placing the highest social value on the needs of the neediest" ('John Rawls: A Theory of Justice' in *Contemporary Political Philosophers,* edited by Anthony de Crespigny and Kenneth Minogue; 1975).

A CRITICAL APPRAISAL

Rawls's theory of justice has been criticized by various schools of thought. *Collectivists* argue that he has discovered the ground for the justification of the existing capitalist system. He has shown that if the rich have the freedom to accumulate wealth, the poor would be automatically benefited. Even if his principle of fair equality of opportunity is strictly enforced, the existing disparities between the rich and the poor will not be substantially reduced. A slight improvement in the condition of the most disadvantaged sections will be treated as an excuse to permit vast socio-economic inequalities.

Some critics argue that the identification of the most disadvantaged sections is very difficult. If income and wealth are treated the sole criteria for identifying such sections, how shall we compensate those who lack ability or who suffer from emotional insecurity?

Marxists contend that Rawls has tried to determine the principles of justice in a hypothetical condition where people deliberate behind a 'veil of ignorance'. Any deliberations without the knowledge of prevailing social and economic conditions are meaningless. Moral systems should always be analysed in the light of class relations and the patterns of ownership of private property.

Libertarians argue that Rawls has sacrificed liberty for the sake of equality. Why should we force the meritorious and industrious to work for the benefit of the most disadvantaged sections? Moreover, enterprising persons must take risks for their advancement in life. Rawls's negotiators are not prepared to take risk. How would they help in social progress?

Communitarians point out that Rawls's political philosophy does not grade any conception of good life as superior or inferior to others. This ethical neutrality evades the opportunity of the pursuit of the common good.

On closer analysis, these diverse critiques seem to be based on biased interpretations of Rawls's theory of justice. In fact, Rawls has tried to combine different value-systems in order to arrive at his theory of justice. Some tenets of these value-systems are thought to be incompatible with each other. Any attempt to combine them must yield a complex model. This applies to the present case also. Indeed, *Rawls's theory of justice represents a convergence of libertarianism, egalitarianism and communitarianism.*

In the first place, Rawls is a *libertarian* because his conception of men negotiating in the 'original position' envisages those who are trying to maximize their self-interest. This conforms to libertarian point of view. Secondly, his first principle of justice accords priority to liberty which cannot be compromised for any other benefit.

Then Rawls is an *egalitarian* because he concedes 'equal' liberty for all. Further, he insists that social-economic inequalities can be allowed only if they satisfy the condition of fair equality of opportunity for all. In other words, he accepts equality as a cardinal principle, and insists that only inequalities shall be required to be justified. Again, he rules that any reward for merit and effort must satisfy the condition that it yields greatest benefit to the least advantaged. Why should the meritorious accommodate the interests of the least advantaged? Here Rawls invokes the principle of the 'chain connection' operating between different individuals. More meritorious enjoy the benefits of their merit in association with the less meritorious lot. A chain is no stronger than its weakest link. Rawls shows that society can be strengthened by strengthening its weakest parts successively. The idea of 'chain connection' brings Rawls very close to the image of a *communitarian.*

It is true that Rawls contemplates to retain the capitalist system on some specified conditions. However, it should not be forgotten that once these conditions are fulfilled, the capitalist system is bound to assume a new humane look. In fact, *Rawls has discovered a method for making procedural justice an instrument of meeting the requirements of substantive justice.* By insisting on the emancipation of the least advantaged on priority basis, he has advanced the principle of moral individualism which requires consideration of individual cases for a favourable treatment, and prevents the better-placed members of the backward classes from taking undue advantage of their class position.

Moral Individualism

Moral individualism refers to a philosophical principle which regards individual as an end-in-itself, endowed with 'dignity'. Accordingly, no human being can be treated as a means to serve an end which lies beyond his conscious existence; no worldly thing can be treated as more valuable than a human being; and no human being can accept an obligation except at his own free will.

[II]
LIBERTARIAN PERSPECTIVE

Libertarian perspective on justice also treats liberty of the individual as its central problem. But it focuses on formal liberty and insists on minimal role of the state in economic activities of individuals. It regards the right to property as an important ingredient of individual liberty. It is largely opposed to the idea of welfare state. This perspective is chiefly represented *by Nozick's theory of justice* as well as *Hayek's view of justice.*

NOZICK'S THEORY OF JUSTICE

Robert Nozick (1938-2002), an American philosopher, in his *Anarchy, State and Utopia* (1974), sought to advance an alternative to Rawls's theory of justice. Whereas Rawls sought to moderate his libertarianism by a modicum of egalitarianism and communitarianism, Nozick adhered to libertarianism in its pure form. If Rawls is known as a 'left liberal' or egalitarian liberal advocating a substantially redistributive welfare state, Nozick may be described as a 'right liberal' or a libertarian committed to a 'nightwatchman' state.

> **Nightwatchman State**
>
> Nightwatchman state refers to the model of a state whose functions are similar to those of a nighwatchman, that is ensuring safety of life and property of its clients, *viz.* its citizens. In other words, it is responsible only for the maintenance of law and order within its territory and defence against external attacks. Its power of taxation is largely determined by the needs of performing this function. Indeed 'nightwatchman state' represents the antithesis of 'welfare state'.

Modes of Acquisition

Nozick ridicules Rawls's approach which seeks to determine the principles of distribution of certain goods as if they have come to us as a gift from heaven. Nozick insists on a realistic approach which should account for the different modes of acquisition of goods and entitlement of different individuals to own those goods. He has identified three sources through which various goods are acquired by individuals:

(*a*) Their selves—their bodies, brain cells, etc. They have absolute right over them. An individual is free to use his limbs and brain to do whatever he likes;

(*b*) The natural world—land, water resources, minerals, etc. Individuals may acquire bits of the natural world through several methods and may become entitled to their use as they like. This is precisely the area where principles of entitlement are required to be determined according to logic; and

(*c*) The things people make by applying themselves to the natural world—agricultural and industrial products, etc. An individual's entitlement to these products may not be questioned. Voluntary transfer of these goods will establish others' entitlement to them.

Principles of Entitlement

People's entitlement to self-ownership of their body and mind—their physical and mental faculties is obvious which needs no further justification. Their entitlement to bits of the natural world and the products of their labour should be based on the principles of justice. Nozick identifies three principles on which this entitlement would conform to justice:

(*a*) *Initial acquisition:* The method whereby an individual comes to appropriate some previously unowned bits of the natural world. Those who come to settle in an uninhabited continent may legitimately acquire its land and natural resources on 'first come, first served' basis, *as long as nobody is made worse off by their doing so.* This means that this mode of acquisition should not result in creating scarcity for others—a condition which may scarcely be satisfied. This is similar to the condition spelled out in John Locke's *Second Treatise of Government* (1690) in the case of similar acquisition, *viz.* 'as long as enough and as good is left for others';

(*b*) *Voluntary transfer:* It applies to all property whether acquired through initial acquisition or by mixing one's labour with the natural world, *i.e.* by means of one's talents, efforts, enterprise, etc. in a market situation. In other words, if I use others' labour and pay them as per market rates, I become owner of the product of their labour. This must be based on voluntary contract, without force or fraud. In all such transactions, an individual shall be treated as 'end-in-itself' and not as a means to others' ends. This is similar to the moral principle enunciated by Immanuel Kant (1724-1804), a German philosopher. Hence, a contract through which an individual sells himself or any other individual to slavery will be void; and

(*c*) *Rectification:* This is precisely the area where the state or the international community will be justified to intervene in order to restore justice. Nozick concedes that the history of the world abounds with involuntary transfers as well as unjust acquisitions of natural resources. As long as economic disparities result from voluntary transfers, Nozick is not bothered. But if some country has gained control over rare natural resources depriving others of their legitimate share, Nozick would step in to register his protest. If Wilt Chamberlain becomes a millionaire because millions of people are willing to pay for watching him play basketball, it is his legitimate right. If the inventor of the cure of a dreaded disease, like cancer, demands exorbitant charges from his patients, there is nothing wrong in this deal for Nozick, because he does not make anybody worse off by treating his patients. But if there is a single source of water which is needed by all human beings, nobody has the right to take it into his control.

A CRITICAL APPRAISAL

Nozick claims to discover the principles of justice for all human beings, but his bias is quite clear. He is an out-and-out champion of a competitive market society which favours the rich and the resourceful, and lets the weak go to the wall. He absolves the rich of all social responsibility, not to speak of social indebtedness. In a very large part of the contemporary world, justice is thought to be the 'voice of the oppressed'. But Nozick wants to maintain the prevailing oppression in the name of justice! Even his principle of 'rectification' is designed to legitimize the huge riches of the manipulators, and hit at the only assets of oil-producing countries because oil is needed all over the world, and its resources are confined to a small region!

Nozick invokes moral principles to demolish a redistributive, welfare state. He approves of taxation only for the provision of the common services, like streets and street lights, police and defence, etc. When a part of taxes imposed on the rich is spent on welfare of the poor, Nozick would term it immoral, as it is akin to 'forced labour'. In Nozick's view, it involves using abilities and efforts of one section as a means to others' ends; it involves involuntary transfer and, therefore, violates the moral principle. The lucky should have freedom to help the unlucky, if they so like! Nozick makes welfare of the poor dependent on charity, not on justice! He is not prepared to concede that the operation of competitive market society may itself create certain conditions of injustice.

In contrast, Rawls's provision for the regulation of social-economic inequalities on the condition of giving greatest benefit to the least advantaged shows his genuine concern for justice.

HAYEK'S VIEW OF JUSTICE

F.A. Hayek (1899-1992), an Austrian philosopher, was a champion of freedom that enables the talents to flourish and thereby promote progress. He placed liberty or freedom above every other political ideal like equality and justice. He particularly attacked the concept of social justice as an unrealizable principle.

In his noted work *Law, Legislation and Liberty: The Mirage of Social Justice* (1976), Hayek argued that the idea of social justice itself is irrelevant. Justice is the characteristic of human conduct, and not of a society. If freedom is curtailed to promote equality, the disputes over the distribution of life's goods are bound to give rise to conflict and controversy. Search for justice is simply a matter of procedure designed to promote freedom. Justice requires that each individual should get maximum opportunity to serve his interest according to his own understanding.

Hayek maintained that society has only limited resources which are not enough to satisfy everybody's needs. If we try to adopt the policy of social justice, the bureaucracy responsible for the implementation of that policy would assume the power of arbitrary distribution of those resources. This will harm the individual freedom. Again, diverse interest groups will start demanding a large share of these resources in order to serve their self-interest. Stronger interest groups will be able to corner the larger share. So the incompetent sections of society will be able to grab an undue share of social wealth. As a result, the competent will suffer. They will be discouraged from giving their best to society. This trend will impoverish society. Such a situation will be inimical to growth of excellence as well as individual freedom.

A CRITICAL APPRAISAL

Hayek is keen to promote excellence in society. He is not worried about the plight of the poor and the unlucky. His way of thinking resembles the railways' policy on late-running trains. When many trains are running late, the railways would try that the trains which are less late should be given way to run on time, and those which are very late could be allowed to be further late. The emphasis is on reducing the number of late-running trains even if some trains become very, very late. Hayek would wish that the distinguished members of society should maintain and enhance their excellence even if the the poor become poorer. Hayek not only rejects social justice, his philosophy also militates against the spirit of humanitarianism.

Humanitarianism

Humanitarianism refers to the spirit of human welfare which impels us to help the needy, the poor and the helpless. It is based on the view that every human being has the right to social assistance in the case of utter necessity. If somebody is in distress, he cannot be left to languish and die. It is the duty of society to come to his rescue and provide him with necessary means of subsistence, medical care and treatment to protect his life.

[III]
MARXIST PERSPECTIVE

CONCERN WITH JUSTICE

Status of the notion of justice in Marxist thought has remained a controversial subject. One view is that Marxism aims at replacing capitalism by socialism for which revolution is indispensable. Inclination towards justice would mean maintaining the existing system with minor changes, and thus making a departure from the basic tenets of Marxism. This view regards the question of justice as irrelevant for the Marxist theory. It holds that the exploitation of workers as described in Marx's *Capital* (1861-79) is the natural characteristic of capitalism. It would be futile to regard it as the problem of injustice and to try to find its solution within the capitalist system. Marx did not seek any reform in the level of incomes and wages within the capitalist system itself, but he wanted to transform the entire mode of production and property relations.

Again, in his *Critique of the Gotha Programme* (1875), Marx rebuked those socialists who became complacent after raising the demand of 'fair distribution' within the existing system. Moreover, in Marxian framework of social analysis, morality is regarded as a part of superstructure, and it is argued that historical changes in the base, *viz.* the mode of production result in corresponding changes in the criteria of right and wrong, just and unjust. Then, how can we determine any enduring principles of justice? Finally, according to Marx, the communist society which will be evolved after the dissolution of capitalism will be free from the conditions involving scarcity and conflict; hence the state and its juridical apparatus will no longer be required in that society.

Base and Superstructure

The terms 'base' and 'superstructure' are used in Marxist theory to describe the relation between economic structure of society and other aspects of social life. In this building-like metaphor, mode of production (*i.e.* the economic structure of society) constitutes the base (or the substructure), while legal and political structure, religion, morals, and other forms of social consciousness constitute the superstructure. It is believed that any change in the base results in corresponding changes in the superstructure.

Should we assume on the basis of the foregoing arguments that Marxism is not concerned at all with the question of justice? On deeper analysis, we may realize that this assumption would not be correct. Marx has repeatedly dubbed workers' exploitation a theft, or even an act of robbery. Again, Marx has conceded moral supremacy of one mode of distribution (*viz.* 'to each according to his need') over another mode of distribution (*viz.* 'to each according to his ability'). This shows his concern with distributive justice. Then, in spite of his adherence to moral relativism, he has shown the way to set up a social system where the ideology or 'false consciousness' emanating from the prevailing mode of production will disappear; hence it would be a morally superior system.

Moreover, Marx firmly believed in freedom and humanism. How can we call him indifferent to justice? Marxism attacks those conditions of dominance and dependence which are the glaring examples of social injustice. It would, therefore, be improper to say that Marxism is not concerned with the problem of justice. He, of course, does not accept a solution which would serve as an excuse to retain capitalism with certain modifications. Marx (1818-83) and Engels (1820-95) have amply shown the extent of injustice which is inherent in the capitalist system itself. This is evident from their concept of surplus value.

CONCEPT OF SURPLUS VALUE

According to Marxist theory, capitalist mode of production involves exploitation of the working class. Marx's theory of surplus value illustrates how this exploitation takes place. According to Marx, labour is the sole creator of value. Of the four elements of production—land, labour, capital and organization—three elements, *viz.* land, capital and organization, are sterile because they are capable of reproducing only what is put in them. They are, therefore, no source of value. Labour is the only variable element which produces value in society. In his *A Contribution to the Critique of Political Economy* (1859), Marx observed:

> The common social substance of all commodities is labour ... A commodity has a value because it is crystallization of social labour. The greatness of its value or its relative value depends upon the greater or lesser amount of that social substance contained in it, that to say, on the relative mass of labour necessary for its production. The relative values of commodities are, therefore, determined by the respective quantities or amounts of labour worked up, realized, fixed in them.

The amount of labour embodied in a commodity should be calculated right from the beginning—the labour employed in producing the raw material, in processing the raw material, in mobilizing the sources of energy used (*e.g.* coal and oil) and in constructing the machinery and building, etc. In saying that the value of a commodity is determined by the quantity of labour employed, we must take into account the quantity of labour required for its production in a given state of society, under certain average conditions of social production, and average skill of the labour employed.

Here it is essential to distinguish between value and price of a commodity. Price is only a monetary expression of value. If the price of a commodity corresponds to its value in monetary terms, it may be described as the *natural price.* But, besides the natural price of a commodity, there is the *market price* which fluctuates heavily depending upon the conditions of demand and supply. The market price is, therefore, sometimes much higher than the natural price of a commodity; sometimes much lower. Under the conditions of a free market economy fostered by the capitalist system, the worker is forced to sell his labour in the open market at the market price. Now, the market price of labour is not determined by its potential value which would be added to the value of the commodity produced by it, but by the value of necessities required for the worker's own maintenance and for the maintenance of his family so that he could bring up his children to replace him on the labour market, in order to sustain the capitalist system itself.

Labour is the only element of production which produces surplus value. In other words, labour is capable of producing much more than what is required to maintain, develop and perpetuate it. Suppose a worker is required to work at an average of thirty hours a week to match the value of the necessities required to maintain him and his family. If he works only to this extent, he does not produce surplus value. But, under the capitalist system, a wage-labourer is forced to sell his labour power to the capitalist where its market price is determined by the law of demand and supply. With the increased availability of the labour force, the market price of labour declines. The capitalist forces the worker to labour to his maximum capacity while he pays him only 'subsistence wages' at the market rate. In this way, the labourer gets back only a part of the value that he produces in the shape of his wages.

Subsistence Wages

Subsistence wages refer to the wages required to meet the requirements of mere survival of the worker and his family.

The value produced by the labour may be divided into two parts: one part comprises that value which is paid to the worker as wages; the other part comprises the value of surplus labour done by him which is not paid to the worker but which swells the pockets of the capitalist and constitutes his profit. Rent and interest are paid out of this surplus value. If the capitalist employs his own capital, land and building, etc., the entire surplus value would go into his pocket; otherwise he will only get the industrial or commercial profit, and some part of the surplus value will be passed on to third parties. In any case, land, capital or organization do not produce any value; the value of these elements is derived from the surplus value produced by labour. With the overthrow of capitalism and socialization of the means of production under the socialist system, the exploitation of surplus value will be eliminated; the value of labour would be paid to the worker or some part of it would be diverted to the provision of common services which will again benefit the worker. Only the worker who produces value will be entitled to maintenance; social parasites would no more be tolerated: 'He who does not work, neither shall eat'.

VISION OF THE SOCIALIST SOCIETY

The remedy of the injustice involved in the capitalist system lies in transition to the socialist system. Socialist system comes into existence after the overthrow of the capitalist system through a proletarian revolution. This system is characterized by social ownership of the major means of production. The production relations of the socialist society are based on co-operation and mutual assistance among the workers liberated from the exploitation. State power is still necessary to be used for the oppression of reactionary forces and also to destroy the values and attitudes fostered by the capitalist system. In due course, as the last vestige of the old system is destroyed, the state as an institution becomes redundant and the stage is set for the 'withering away of the state'. The socialist system is, therefore, envisaged as eventually ushering in the epoch of a classless and stateless society, described as *communist* society.

> **Reactionary Forces**
>
> Reactionary forces refer to the forces that seek to reverse the direction of the ongoing change, or to replace the new system by the old one. In a socialist system, reactionary forces seek to restore the capitalist system.

The socialist system, therefore, stands for that economic and political system which is established by the proletariat after a revolutionary overthrow of the capitalist system. It is coterminous with the 'dictatorship of the proletariat'. This stage does not represent the final goal of revolution; it is only an interim stage of transition from capitalism to communism.

The functions of the state in socialist society are to be determined by the changed relations of production, which may be described under various heads.

Socialization of Production and Distribution

The first socialist state, according to Marxist principles, was established in Soviet Russia after the Bolshevik Revolution (1917) under the stewardship of Lenin (1870-1924). Lenin sought to evolve a programme of action according to Marxist theory for his socialist state, although his own contribution in this sphere cannot be ignored. According to Lenin, the first and foremost function of the socialist state was complete socialization of the means of production and distribution in the sphere of industry as well as agriculture. In his pamphlet on *Economics and Politics in the Era of Dictatorship of the Proletariat* (1919), Lenin recorded:

> In Russia, labour is united communistically insofar as, first, private ownership of the means of production has been abolished, and secondly, the proletarian state-power is organizing large-scale production on state-owned land and in state-owned enterprises on a national scale, is distributing labour-power among the various branches of production and the various enterprises, and is distributing among the working people large quantities of articles of consumption belonging to the state.

The Communist Party of Soviet Russia, immediately after the assumption of power, abolished private ownership of land without compensation to the big landowners, and expropriated the big capitalists, owners of factories, joint stock companies, banks, railways, and so forth, without compensation. Large state farms and cooperative societies of small farmers were also organized.

Raising the Productivity of Labour

Maximization of production for the satisfaction of the masses is an important objective of the Marxist programme. Complete socialization of all major means of production and distribution is meant to ensure production for the masses, not for a particular class. Raising the productivity of labour is another important requisite of this programme. Lenin elaborated this idea in his pamphlet on *The Immediate Tasks of the Soviet Government* (1918) as follows:

> In every socialist revolution, after the proletariat has solved the problem of capturing power, and to the extent that the task of expropriating the expropriators and suppressing their resistance has been carried out in the main, there necessarily comes to the forefront the fundamental task of creating a social system superior to capitalism, namely raising the productivity of labour, and in this connection (and for this purpose) securing better organization of labour.

This objective is secured through large-scale planning. The idea of planning was, in fact, introduced by the socialist system of Soviet Russia which served as a model for many developing countries, including India.

Development of Science and Technology

Maximization of production calls for the fullest development of science and technology and its use in the industrial as well as agricultural spheres. A rational system of production, according to Marxism, implies not only socialization of the major means of production but also the fullest technological advancement to ensure maximum production. Common ownership of the major means of production would create conditions for the fullest development of the forces of production for meeting social needs. Development of science and technology is to be undertaken as an integral part of the programme of socialist reconstruction.

Transformation of Bourgeois Culture

Destroying the vestiges of capitalism involves not only the transformation of the economic system, but also the transformation of bourgeois culture into socialist culture. The cultural function of the socialist state was accorded special significance by Mao Zedong (1893-1976), the chief architect of the socialist revolution in China (1949). Mao has given a new interpretation to the principles of Marxism-Leninism as regards their operational aspect. Marx, Engels and Lenin had, of course, realized that classes could not be abolished in a single stroke, but they had nevertheless assumed that the dictatorship of the proletariat would be a short-lived affair and would be quickly followed by the process of the 'withering away' of the state. Mao, on the other hand, postulated that the class struggle would continue for a very long period after the proletarian revolution. In other words, a socialist revolution on the economic front, followed by the socialization of the major means of production, would not be sufficient by itself; it would have to be continued on the political and ideological fronts for a very long time; may be, for a century or several centuries. In other words, the class struggle between the bourgeoisie and the proletariat continues throughout the stage of socialism, in the political, cultural, ideological and educational fields, though its intensity might fluctuate. This is the gist of Mao's concept of *permanent revolution.*

According to classical Marxist theory, a fundamental change in the *substructure,* namely the mode of production, must bring about a corresponding change in the *superstructure,* namely legal and political framework, morality, culture and ideas. Mao's theory postulates that, sometimes, the superstructure tends to dominate the substructure. In other words, *bougeois* political culture is so deep-rooted in the minds of the people that it may continue to influence their behaviour even after the transformation of the economic foundations of society. The big property-owners may have been dispossessed, yet they may continue to command special attention or consideration or other privileges in society because the prevalent attitudes in society die hard. The people have to be initiated into the socialist political culture with a view to consolidating the forces of socialism. The socialist state must take this function upon itself.

Fighting Against Injustice in the International Sphere

Classical Marxism knew no national boundaries. Marx himself had given the call: 'Workers of the world unite!' But Lenin sought to consolidate 'socialism in one country' before it could be expanded further. After World War II (1939-45), the idea of world communism was abandoned, and various socialist states or communist countries, such as Yugoslavia and Cuba, apart from the USSR and the People's Republic of China, continued to exist as independent nations. The socialist states also adopted the policy of 'peaceful co-existence' which signified a long-term co-existence of the capitalist and socialist states without war between them. Besides, the socialist states recognized their duty to help revolutionary movements of the oppressed classes abroad in their fight against imperialism and neo-colonialism. In fact, neo-Marxists have reinterpreted the future class struggle as the struggle of the new nations against the imperial and neo-colonial powers in the international field.

CONCLUSION

Marxian theory of communism, which seeks to replace capitalist system by socialist system, envisages that eventually a classless society will come into existence. It will be a society no longer divided into antagonistic classes on the basis of ownership of private property. Private property is the source of exploitation and injustice in society. It must be distinguished from personal property which is the source of security for the individual. Marx and Engels in their *Communist Manifesto* (1848) declared:

> The theory of the Communists may be summed up in the single sentence: Abolition of private property.

Marxian communism does not contemplate to abolish personal property which is the fruit of man's own labour, and which is the groundwork of all personal freedom, activity and independence. It includes the property of the petty artisan and of the small peasant. Such property needs to be protected. It is the capitalist system which has destroyed such property. Communist system will safeguard it. But it will not allow private property which is the source of exploitation. As Marx and Engels *(Communist Manifesto)* have further noted:

> Communism deprives no man of the power to appropriate the products of society; all that it does is to deprive him of the power to subjugate the labour of others by means of such appropriation.

Abolition of private property will result in the abolition of classes and class antagonism, and it will pave the way for the free development of all. So Marx and Engels conclude:

> When, in the course of development, class distinctions have disappeared, and production has been concentrated in the hands of a vast association of the whole nation, the public power will lose its political character. Political power, properly so called, is merely the organized power of one class for oppressing another…
>
> In place of the old bourgeois society, with its classes and class antagonisms, we shall have an association, in which the free development of each is the condition for the free development of all.

This picture of the classless society is quite fascinating. But the problem with this view is that it treats the possession of private property as the only source of class distinctions. In actual practice, class distinctions may reappear on the basis of possession of political and bureaucratic power, even after the abolition of private property, giving rise to new forms of dominance and injustice. So the problem of injustice will have to be tackled at many more subtle levels.

[IV] FEMINIST PERSPECTIVE

Feminist perspective on justice seeks restoration of justice for women who remained deprived of equal status and opportunities vis-à-vis men since earliest times. This perspective is based on the philosophy of feminism which is closely concerned with the condition of women in society, the causes of their suffering and deprivation. It aims at the removal of discrimination against women in terms of their rights, opportunities for self-development and share in political power. In short, feminism seeks to secure justice for women in all spheres of life. That is why the main focus of feminism coincides with the feminist perspective on justice. This perspective inquires into various forms of injustice against women prevailing in society and insists on restoring justice in each relevant sphere. Broadly speaking, injustice against women may be found in the following spheres for which suitable measures of redressal must be taken: (*a*) Political Sphere; (*b*) Economic Sphere; and (*c*) Cultural Sphere.

POLITICAL SPHERE

Feminists argue that our society largely discriminates between men and women in the matter of allocation of benefits and burdens. Society has failed to appreciate the full range of contributions made by women for its sustenance, not to speak of giving adequate reward for these contributions. On the other hand, society has also failed to realize the extraordinary constraints under which women work, not to speak of removing these constraints.

Coming to the political sphere, it may be noted at the outset that the advanced nations of Western Europe and North America withheld women's right to vote for a very long time. It was introduced in the United States as late as 1920; in France, it was granted in 1947; and in Switzerland, it was extended to all territories in 1971. Apart from their fight for suffrage, women in Western countries had to launch separate struggles for securing rights connected with citizenship. These included: to pass their citizenship to their children; to retain their citizenship on marriage on the basis of their own nationality (instead of their husbands' nationality); to contend for political office and to hold it; and the right to serve on juries. Now they have won their political rights in all the advanced industrial nations but their actual share in political power is far behind that of men. For instance, nine decades after the women won the right-to-vote in the United States, their share in the House of Representatives is less than 20 percent; in the Senate, it is less than 10 per cent; it is nil at the positions of President and Vice-President. On the occasion of signing of the Charter of Paris in 1990, marking the end of the era of Cold War, women were conspicuous by their absence or near-absence in the group photographs of European heads-of-states or heads-of-governments.

Many reasons are advanced to explain this situation. It is now ruled out that the gross underrepresentation of women at the positions of political power is the outcome of their own choice. One tangible reason of this situation is that the vast majority of successful candidates come from a handful of *elite* professions such as law which require high levels of education, but women get fewer opportunities for higher education. A record of military service or high standing in business also proves a stepping stone to political office. Women lag far behind in this area also. Besides, electoral victory requires large-scale mobilization of funds; party workers are less willing to mobilize such funds for women candidates.

Even where women are elected, they are excluded from responsible positions because of a preconceived notion that they cannot take a tough stand on important issues. It is also believed that women with small children might be constrained to be absent on some important occasions. The position can be changed if the responsibility of bringing up children is equally shared by mother and father, at least in the cases where mother is equally competent. Moreover, experience has shown that women in high positions can also take bold decisions and firm stand at the time of crisis. The political tenure of Indira Gandhi (1917-84), former Prime Minister of India, is the case in point.

Feminists have also identified some typical problems concerning women which prevent them from taking up political career. It is generally observed that women are particularly conscious of their bodily appearance and self-presentation as if beauty is the measure of their success in social life. It is believed that a woman's looks and figure constitute much of her fortune. Again, women are vulnerable to sexual harassment and various kinds of violence including domestic violence, apart from molestation on streets, offices and public places. It is alleged that a woman's vulnerability is directly proportional to her beauty and attractive make-up! Preoccupation with personal care and decoration sometimes prevents a women from thinking of taking up a political career.

Adequate provision of safety, educational and career development opportunities and professional training for women would go a long way in ameliorating the lot of women. This can be secured more effectively if women themselves come forward in the field of active politics. It would not be correct to say that there are no women activists. However, a large number of women activists are devoted to community work at grassroot level. According to Martha Ackelsberg ('Communities, resistance and women's activism' in *Women and the Politics of Empowerment,* edited by Ann Brookman and Sandra Morgen; 1988), women have been "leaders and activists in 'bread riots' and tenant organizations... participated in factory-based strikes that engendered, and depended on, community support...they have led struggles for new and better schools." Again, women have also been leaders in the struggles for environmental justice. In India, women living on mountains particularly played active role in '*chipko* movement' (They hugged the trees to stop their cutting.). They also lodged strong protests against the displacement of tribals due to construction of dams, particularly against Narmada dam. Then women have also led struggles against rape, sexual harassment, domestic violence, etc. all over the world. In short, women activists have largely fought for welfare of women and the society at large, but they have scarcely focused on their own political career.

ECONOMIC SPHERE

Feminists argue that women's contribution to economic life has been largely ignored; hence they have been denied befitting benefits in this sphere. The system of national income accounting ignores the unpaid work done by women for the benefit of family and community. Many feminists argue that most women not only do a lot of domestic work, their services towards child-bearing and child-rearing, etc. constitute 'real work'; they not only consume the worker's time and energy but also involve various skills including some sophisticated skills like cooking, house-keeping, sewing, weaving, embroidery, etc. apart from the operation of domestic appliances. Market value of these services is seldom taken into account. Even working women who make a substantial contribution to family income have to perform most of these services for which they seldom get credit, not to speak of any special reward.

Feminists further argue that women's larger contribution to well-being of men and other members of the family could be justified if it is made voluntarily. But, in fact, it is necessitated by the social conditions where women's occupational choices are constrained by institutional factors, such as employment opportunities and cultural norms which impose larger burden on women. The services rendered by women provide more time and energy for men who are thus enabled to make a significant contribution to society. Thus, women's extra labour benefits not only their men and their families, it also benefits the larger society. Unfortunately, the women doing a huge amount of 'unpaid work' are stigmatized as 'dependent' on men. It is a striking example of 'unjust' distribution of benefits and burdens in society.

CULTURAL SPHERE

Women are also victims of discrimination in cultural sphere. Many common social practices reflect a cultural climate of masculine dominance in which women regularly experience shame, embarrassment and vulnerability. In professional life, men look for excuses to touch the bodies of their women colleagues, and to address them in apparently affectionate but actually mischievous ways. Most of the jokes cracked by men ridicule or sexualize women. In Indian languages, most of the abuses involve insult to women—the mother, the sister and the daughter. Women's attractive looks and voice are widely used in advertising which tend to prejudice their dignity. Women's reputation is regarded to be so delicate that many of the cases of molestation and outraging of modesty of women go unreported due to fear of shame.

In Indian tradition, some saints have deprecated the company of women as the door to hell. In Indian mythology, women have been treated as an object of donation. Many 'great men' sought to save their glory by gifting their wives to strangers. When several contenders stake their claims for marrying the same girl, decision is taken by an authority on the basis of some logic based on 'conventions'; choice of the girl herself is seldom invoked.

Among Hindus, cremation ceremony of the dead body of a person is to be performed by his son, which is believed to ensure the dead person's entry into heaven. It is presumed that if the dead person had only daughters and no son, he would not be entitled to a place in heaven. Our beliefs about other-wordly matters are derived from our experience of wordly matters. In modern times, when girls have proved their talents in all important fields, exaltation of son to the detriment of daughter will have to be abandoned, like so many other superstitions.

In a nutshell, justice for women must be secured in all spheres—political, economic as well as cultural. Without securing substantive justice for women, no society can claim to have established a just social order.

[V]
SUBALTERN PERSPECTIVE

Subaltern perspective on justice is concerned with the plight of those groups in society who are more or less permanently placed in subordinate position because of various constraints inherent in the social structure. In other words, these are exploited, oppressed and marginalized groups. Because of an inherent division of society into the ruling and subaltern groups, a lion's share of all benefits accruing from the total efforts of society is cornered by a tiny class variously described as ruling class, dominant class or the *elite*. And the majority consisting of various subordinate groups who put their abilities and efforts into the creation of these benefits are left with a meagre share thereof. So the subaltern critique of justice raises the question of social justice in most eloquent manner. What is meant by the term 'subaltern'?

The concept of the 'subaltern' was introduced in social theory by Antonio Gramsci (1891-1937), an Italian Marxist, who was imprisoned by Mussolini for his radical views, during the ascendancy of fascism. In his *Prison Notebooks* (1929-35/1971), Gramsci revealed some new dimensions of Marxian thought which included the concept of the 'subaltern'. It is interesting to recall that the Marxian theory of class structure as founded in late nineteenth century was challenged by the *elite* theory in the beginning of the twentieth century. Class theory had envisaged the division of society broadly into two classes on the basis of ownership and non-ownership of means of production. The *elite* theory, as expounded by Vilfredo Pareto (1848-1923), Gaetano Mosca (1858-1941) and Robert Michels (1876-1936), advanced an alternative division of society into *elite* and masses on the basis of distinctive ability or organizational capacity of one group vis-à-vis others. It implied that if ordinary people (the masses) get a lesser share of the cake, they deserve it. This view is designed to vindicate the liberal model of distribution—'to each according to his work', that is the market society model.

The concept of the subaltern, on the other hand, contradicts the *elite* theory and holds that ordinary people contribute substantially to the production of the cake and still get a marginal share thereof because of their exploitation by the ruling class. The ruling class evolves a value-system to suit its own interests, and projects it as the one embodying universal interests. In other words, the subaltern groups (peasants, workers, and other subordinate groups) are made to believe that they are being ruled with their consent. Gramsci described this quality of the ruling class as 'hegemony'. Thus, hegemony signifies the ability of the ruling class to convince the subject classes that their rule represents the common interest.

Hegemony

According to Antonio Gramsci (1891-1937), Italian Marxist, hegemony refers to a web of beliefs and institutional as well as social relations which serve as instruments of domination in society. In the capitalist society, family, school, church and other primary groups (*e.g.* neighbourhood and peer groups) play leading role in creating consent which keeps the system going. Use of force is resorted to only when the instruments of consent fail to work.

In short, while *elite* theory treats the division of society into rulers and the ruled as natural and functional, subaltern theory regards it artificial and exploitative. *Elite* theory eulogizes the role of ruling class in building the whole civilization and downgrades the role of the ruled. But subaltern theory focuses on the significance of the role of the subordinate classes. It even believes that the subaltern groups are capable of organizing themselves and shaping human history. But most of the historians are biased towards the *elite* and they have largely ignored the role of the subaltern groups. Subaltern theory insists on rewriting of history giving due place to the role of the subaltern groups.

Distinction Between *Elite* and Subaltern Perspectives

The Issue	*Elite Perspective*	*Subaltern Perspective*
Division of Society into	*Elites* and Masses	Ruling (Dominant) Class and Subaltern Groups
Reason of the Division	Competence and Organizational ability of the *elite* and lack of these qualities in the masses	Hegemony of the dominant class endowed with ideological as well as economic power and lack of this power in the ordinary people.
Nature of the Division	Natural and Functional	Artificial and Exploitative
Outcome of the Division	*Elites* play the key role; they direct and masses simply follow	Subaltern Groups also play significant role, beside the dominant class, in sustaining the social system
Whether this Division is Alterable	No. Masses cannot be equated with *elites* at any stage	Yes. Distinction between dominant and subaltern groups can be obliterated through revolution
Exponents	V. Pareto, G. Mosca, R. Michels	Antonio Gramsci

In contemporary social analysis, the scope of 'subaltern theory' has been considerably expanded. It is now conceded that any group in society who has been relegated to a subordinate position because of undeserved discrimination, *e.g.* discrimination on grounds of gender, age, vocation, class, caste, race, region, religion, language, culture, etc. should be included in the category of subaltern groups. Their energies, abilities and skills are systematically exploited, but they are deprived of their due reward. Justice can only be restored if their rights are protected, their contribution to society is valued and properly rewarded, and their dignity is restored. It also demands restoration of equitable shares of social benefits for the *elite* and subaltern groups.

[VI]
COMMUNITARIAN PERSPECTIVE

Communitarian perspective on justice is best understood by contrasting it with liberal perspective. As Will Kymlicka, in *Contemporary Political Philosophy—An Introduction* (2002), has observed:

> Liberal visions of politics do not include any independent principle of community, such as shared nationality, language, identity, culture, religion, history, or way of life... Communitarians believe that the value of community is not sufficiently recognized in liberal theories of justice, or in the public culture of liberal societies.

Broadly speaking, liberalism holds that an individual should be left free to pursue his self-interest solely on the condition that his freedom does not come in the way of similar freedom of others. On the contrary, communitarians hold that an individual finds self-fulfilment by accepting the prevalent social roles, practices and situations within the community, and not in isolation from his fellow-beings. Thus, against the liberal concept of 'isolated self' communitarianism introduces the concept of 'situated self'. While liberalism defines the common good as the sum total of individual goods, communitarianism, on the other hand, treats the common good as one entity, which is the source of good for each individual.

Communitarian view also differs from liberal view on the respective status of 'right' and 'good' in determining the principles of justice. Liberal theory of justice, particularly Rawls's theory of justice, accords priority to 'right' over 'good'. Rawls, in his *Theory of Justice* (1971), commended justice as 'the first virtue of social institutions', as truth is the primary consideration in accepting any system of thought. For communitarians, on the other hand, the 'right' implies virtue, and when we accept the 'good', the right has already been taken care of.

Alasdair MacIntyre (1929-), British (Scottish) moral philosopher and an early exponent of communitarianism, in his essay *After Virtue* (1981), observed:

> For what constitutes the good for man is a complete human life lived at its best, and the exercise of the virtues is a necessary and central part of

> such a life, not a mere preparatory exercise to achieve such a life. We thus cannot characterize the good for man adequately without already having made reference to the virtues.

MacIntyre ridiculed the liberal notion of individuals as 'autonomous moral agents' operating in an atmosphere where they are disconnected from social context. In his view, individuals flourish only within the context of socially established cooperative human activity, which is designed to encourage the development of human excellence. He argued that liberals were committed to *moral relativism,* detaching themselves from 'any particular standpoint' in order to practise tolerance. So they could not defend any particular view of justice, nor develop a unified concept of 'the good'. Thus, they have not been able to develop true communities or define moral obligations of the members of society to each other.

Moral Relativism

Moral relativism refers to the view that no moral principle or value system can be treated as universally right and acceptable. Moral Relativism holds that the validity of any moral principle can be established only with reference to a particular social and historical context. This view is opposed to moral absolutism.

Moral Absolutism

Moral absolutism refers to the view that a particular moral principle or value system should be accepted as universally valid for all individuals and societies. So each individual and group must conform to its requirements. Moral Absolutism does not allow freedom to any individual or group to propose or follow any alternative moral principle or value system.

MacIntyre exhorted the people of the West to immerse themselves in the knowledge and traditions of Western culture to enable themselves to reason truly about the contents of justice, the good and virtue. In *Whose Justice? Which Rationality?* (1988), MacIntyre came to realize the pitfalls of moral absolutism, and conceded that liberal tolerance was itself a virtuous practice.

Michael Sandel (1953-), American political philosopher and an exponent of communitarianism, in his *Liberalism and the Limits of Justice* (1982), particularly attacked the form of liberalism exemplified by Rawls's *A Theory of Justice* (1971). He argued that Rawls's 'rational negotiators' who have gathered to determine the principles of justice, represent the disconnected and disembodied people deliberating behind the 'veil of ignorance'. Like many other liberals in the past few hundred years, Rawls tries to understand human beings independent of all activities, desires, ideas, roles, and pursuits that characterize human lives in actual society. Sandel argues: "Is anything left of the person when we subtract all this from his personality?" He laments that the Rawlsian view of the person is woefully impoverished.

Sandel asserts that liberal theories have failed to recognize our 'embeddedness' in a particular time, place and culture. He urges that political theory should help in generating such laws, institutions and practices that are genuinely good for us and instrumental in creating a fully just society. Justice cannot be secured by isolated individuals seeking personal profit (as in markets and political arena), but by those who create a 'deeper commonality' through 'shared self-understanding' and mutual affection. Sandel argues that liberal political philosophy sought to justify a form of individualism which was not founded on concrete social institutions. It was wrong in giving priority to the pursuit of abstract equal justice over a communal, moral good. Liberal perspective implies that 'the self is prior to its ends'. On the contrary, Sandel maintains that the self is not prior to its ends; it is rather constituted by its ends, which are not chosen but discovered by the self by virtue of its being embedded in some shared social context. Sandel contends that Rawls's view of 'unencumbered self' does not correspond with our 'deepest self-understanding'. In his *Democracy's Discontent* (1996), Sandel reiterates his argument and even claims that the decline of democratic politics in the United States in the twentieth-century was due to the wrong ordering of priorities between the self and its ends.

Charles Taylor (1931-), Canadian social philosopher and exponent of communitarianism, in his *Philosophical Papers,* published in 1985, questioned the premise of atomistic individualism which is the hallmark of liberal political theory. He attacked the liberal concept of human beings as autonomous choosers. This concept treats human being only as a manifestation of will, and ignores the complexities of human personality which would develop only when it is situated in a society. Taylor argued that atomistic type of individualism promised freedom for human actors, but ultimately failed to realize that human beings constantly reflect on their life in order to find its meaning. He pointed out that human agency, rights and freedom exist only in their social context whereas modern (*i.e.* liberal) political theory failed to account for the reciprocal relations among individuals and between individuals and society.

In his *Sources of the Self* (1989), Taylor further argued that human agency may be understood only from the premise that persons exist as 'embodied individuals' engaged both in self-interpretation and in constant interaction with others. In this process of moral reflection, they criticize and transform themselves through the interpretation and reinterpretation of their rights and obligations. To impart meaning to their actions, they are constantly guided by moral sources—secular, religious, literary and philosophical.

Michael Walzer (1935-), American political philosopher, may be distinguished from other exponents of communitarianism for his unique contribution in this sphere. While other communitarians have largely produced a communitarian critique of liberal theory of justice, Walzer, in his celebrated work *Spheres of Justice* (1983), has enunciated a communitarian theory of justice, although in some respects it is akin to liberal-pluralist point of view. Walzer argued that the quest for a universal theory of justice was misguided, because it was futile to look for any principle of justice outside the community—particularly its history and culture. The requirements of justice could only be identified in the context of a particular community, its practices and institutions.

According to Walzer, the shared understandings in our society require us to apply the principle of 'complex equality' (as distinguished from 'simple equality') in the distribution of social goods. It implies a system of distribution that does not contemplate equal distribution of the same good (*e.g.* income, wealth or power) according to a uniform criterion (*e.g.* ability, output or need), but rather seeks to ensure that inequalities in one 'sphere' (*e.g.* wealth) do not permeate other spheres (*e.g.* health care and political power). Walzer argued that the modern society includes a number of spheres of distribution in which different social goods are allocated each by its own independent criterion. In other words, the distribution of rewards in the modern society is not confined to that of income and wealth, but there are so many sought-after things in society. Walzer asserts that if the boundaries between different spheres are respected, one person's pre-eminence in, say, the sphere of money may be offset by another's higher social prestige and a third's success in holding political office. This type of social pluralism may lead to a kind of equality in which no one decisively outranks anyone else. Thus, Walzer denies that economic status of an individual holds the key to his social prestige and power.

The problem with Walzer's suggestion is that there is no reliable method to compare the value of non-economic factors like reputation, political power, education and health, etc. with the value of income and wealth. In the absence of such criteria, it is difficult to attack the disparities created by the market society. For example, it would be a poor consolation for a university teacher, writer, artist or scientist that the low (economic) return of his talents and effort is compensated by the high esteem in which he is held in society!

In fact, Walzer gives precedence to ethical considerations over economic considerations. Walzer argues that a society of equals lies within our reach. It is implicit in our shared understandings of social goods. These understandings do not produce a vision of 'simple equality' which will lead to immense inequalities through the operation of free market. If the state tries to reinforce initial simple equality, it will end up as a tyrannical state. In our shared understandings we strive for 'complex equality'. According to Walzer:

> Complex equality means that no citizen's standing in one sphere or with regard to one social good can be undercut by his standing in some other sphere, with regard to some other good... No social good x should be distributed to men and women who possess some other social good y merely because they possess y and without regard to the meaning of x.

Walzer comes to the conclusion that distribution of social goods should be determined according to the right reason as applicable in each sphere. Thus, the spheres of politics, or health or education, should not be corrupted by the domination of money, for money properly rules in the sphere of commodities; the sphere of office should not (beyond a certain limited point) be contaminated by nepotism, which belongs in the sphere of kinship and love; the sphere of kinship and love should not be contaminated by the consideration of profit and loss which are relevant only in the market-place; family organization should not be patterned after male domination which properly belongs to the sphere of military organization.

If Walzer's suggestions are adopted in actual practice, we will certainly have a just society which he intends to create. But he has not indicated the way to convince the dominant people in different spheres of social life to adopt these rules. *Walzer's scheme of things embodies a strong moral philosophy, but it does not provide for equally strong political philosophy.*

21

Concept of the Common Good

[I]
NATURE OF THE COMMON GOOD

WHAT IS THE COMMON GOOD?

Aristotle, ancient Greek philosopher, believed that the state exists 'for the sake of the good life'; it exists to promote moral objectives, justice and the common good. However, in actual practice, different constitutions may exist to pursue different objectives. Making a distinction between 'right' (or normal) and 'perverted' types of constitutions, Aristotle maintained that the 'right' type of constitution pursued the common good, which implied the good of the whole community. D.D. Raphael (*Problems of Political Philosophy;* 1976) has identified the pursuit of the common good as the key feature of the modern state. As he observed: "The State carries out its purpose by laying down laws, backed by force, requiring everyone to refrain from actions (crime and torts) that harm the common good, and to contribute in taxes and other imposts to upkeep of services (such as defence, public utility, and social services) that promote the common good." What is the common good?

At the outset, it may be noted that the notion of the common good is closely related to the idea of justice. Justice is concerned with determining the right criteria for the allocation of benefits and burdens among the members of society. Indeed, only those rules of justice will win respect of all members of society which are beneficial to all, *i.e.* which conform to the prevalent notion of the common good, common interest or public interest. Though these terms are used interchangeably, they are not identical in their meaning and scope. The common good embodies a normative concept. It is concerned with moral standards which are the subject of philosophical discussion. The common interest embodies an empirical concept. It is concerned with the understanding of the persons likely to be affected by a proposed decision. It can be empirically ascertained. Then, the public interest is a matter of judgement by a competent authority who is expected to be sensitive to the needs and aspirations of the people. Those likely to be affected by a decision yet to be taken can make appeals to the competent authority in the name of the public interest. In case there is a dispute about a decision taken in the public interest, it can be resolved through discussion between the decision-makers and those affected by it.

The notions of the common good and the public interest are based on the same logic. *What is described as the common good in moral philosophy becomes the public interest in the realm of politics and administration.* But the common good is more comprehensive than the public interest. In other words, all references to the public interest imply the common good. But all references to the common good cannot be expressed in terms of public interest. For instance, a soldier may die in war so that his country wins the war. It is a sacrifice made for the common good, not 'in public interest'. On the other hand, if government enforces quarantine laws to prevent the spreading of an infectious disease, this step is taken in public interest which also implies the common good. A government official who takes bribe for the welfare of his family may be prosecuted in public interest because he acts against the common good. A good citizen always puts the common good before his own or his family's interest.

Jean-Jaques Rousseau (1712-78), famous French philosopher, in his classic work *The Social Contract* (1762), made a strong case for the pursuit of the common good. He expressed great indignation at the selfishness of men and the brazenness of social and economic interests which appropriate the sacred name of the public good. Then T.H. Green (1836-82), a brilliant English philosopher, in his *Lectures on the Principles of Political Obligation* (1882), declared that the state was an instrument for the promotion of the common good. This tradition of thought on the common good, as founded by Rousseau and Green, led to the development of the communitarian perspective.

The idea of the common good is frequently invoked in order to focus on certain political demands or to vindicate certain acts, decisions or policy measures. References to the common good or public interest abound in political speeches, posters and pamphlets, newspaper editorials, verdicts of the law-courts, arguments of the lawyers, guidelines of the government, and even on international forums. It is a fascinating word which defies any precise definition. It cannot be equated with the good of the state, because a particular form of the state like a tyranny may operate against the common good itself. Nor can it be equated with the good of the majority because the common good may be invoked to stop injustice against minority.

Someone may like to define the common good as the common interest of the civil society. But it is not necessary for the civil society to have a common interest. It may be characterized by conflicting interests. Reconciliation of these conflicting interests may not necessarily represent the common interest, although it is so described in liberal theory. This reconciliation, in many cases, may be the result of bargaining between contending parties; and the process of bargaining is not conducive to arriving at the common good. One possible interpretation of the common good could be given as the good of the community. But it is difficult to identify the good of the community apart from the narrow interests of different individuals and groups comprising it. In any case, this is precisely the area where we should look for a workable definition of the common good.

Distinction Between Justice, Common Good and Public Interest

The Issue	*Justice*	*Common Good*	*Public Interest*
Status	Highest ideal which lends legitimacy to any action, arrangement, policy or decision	An ideal usually invoked to persuade the members of a community to resolve their differences on a matter of common concern	A principle usually invoked to justify a public decision
Scope	Settlement of individual claims and allocation of benefits and burdens among the members of society	Discovering the points on which good of all members of a community would converge	Arriving at public decisions which take care of larger interests of people though some sections may have to share an extra burden
Sphere of Application	Universal, whether at national or international level	Usually confined to the members of a community	Universal, whether at national or international level
Criteria	Subject to constant debate	Subject to constant debate	Usually determined by a competent authority
Who are affected?	Everyone, whether individuals, associations or nations	A community and its members	People of a nation or different nations
Who are concerned with the issue?	Philosophers, jurists, social reformers	Philosophers	Administrators, lawyers, policy-makers of a nation or an international organization

In short, the common good points to a goal which does not give precedence to the interests of a class, party or faction but gives due regard to the interests of all members of society. In other words, *the common good stands for the goal which is regarded by the consciousness of the community as conducive to the welfare of the whole community, transcending the immediate interests of different individuals and groups. If its realization entails some loss or benefit to a particular individual or group, that loss or benefit is not treated as a matter of settling individual claims.* For example, taxation system of a welfare state is designed to accommodate the common good. The measures concerning defence, law and order, public health, expansion of education and environmental cleanliness, etc. are geared to meet the needs of the common good. But disputes may still arise as to whether a particular measure conforms to the common good or not. If people are genuinely interested in the pursuit of the common good, their disputes will never take a violent form.

The nature of the common good is quite complex, but one thing is certain that in the case of a conflict between different groups, the common good shall not coincide with the interests of a particular group. For example, in the case of labour-management dispute, the common good cannot be identified with the interest of the workers or that of the management. Similarly, heavy taxation of the urban population to provide for liberal subsidies to the rural population, or spending the revenue of villages for the advancement of cities cannot be equated with the common good. If we want to test a proposal from the point of view of the common good, we must consider the merit of its beneficiaries rather than the claims of its opponents. When the common good is invoked in the context of claims and counterclaims of the conflicting parties, we wish to remind them of certain objectives beyond their conflicting goals, competition and bargaining which are recognized by the community and which should not be overlooked by them. For example, when we draw attention to the common good in the case of employer-employee dispute in the industrial sector, we wish to remind both parties to the dispute that they should not try to work out an arrangement that would serve the purpose of both parties but which might be repugnant to the interests of the large body of consumers or those of the general public.

Some writers tend to equate the common good with the utilitarian formula of the 'greatest happiness of the greatest number'. This view is misleading. John Rawls (1921-2002), has amply shown how the 'greatest happiness of the greatest number' could be interpreted to mean injustice to the minority. This argument can be extended to the common good also. If the minority is made to suffer in the name of promoting the so-called general happiness, it would be against the spirit of the common good. On the other hand, some champions of individualism argue that insistence on the common good would undermine incentives for the individual to make best use of his talents and efforts. This view is also misleading because if the common good is ignored, no individual would be able to achieve his potential excellence or make full use of his personal assets. As J.K. Galbraith (1908-2006) has pointed out, the rich cannot have full enjoyment of their wealth unless there is adequate provision of public services in society.

METHOD OF PURSUIT

Consistent pursuit of the common good in a society can be ensured only through the process of consensus. Those who focus on social cleavage as part of the basic structure of society cannot be devoted to the common good. For example, in contemporary Indian society, some people focus on rural-urban divide; others focus on caste division. Some sections lay stress on religious differences and induce communalism; others harp on the division based on linguistic or regional interests. Some people focus on the divide across gender; others try to sow the seeds of dissention between white-collar and blue-collar workers. Some politicians, too, capitalize one type of social cleavage or another, and after winning seats in legislative assemblies or the parliament, they try to encash their political support in the bargaining for a share in power.

However, these divisive tendencies should not be confused with those humanitarian movements which aim at the preservation of environment or other laudable objectives. For example, when the so-called developmental activities render some poor tribals or villagers homeless, out of job or sick, the movements aiming at their rehabilitation should not be termed as divisive activities.

Cleavage and Consensus

The existence of cleavage in a society means that society is sharply divided into antagonistic groups on the basis of some more or less fixed attribute. For example, such division may occur along the lines of class, region, religion, language, race, or gender. On the contrary, consensus implies the absence of a rigid division in society on these lines. The existence of consensus in a society may be analysed at two levels: (*a*) As a *process*, it implies that the different groups have resolved their differences and arrived at an arrangement which is best suited to their needs under the existing constraints; and (*b*) As a *condition*, it implies that the different groups in a society have no differences on any issue; that society is informed by a deep-rooted and long-term agreement on all issues. It is a Utopian view of consensus. In modern societies, consensus is achieved only as a process.

Broadly speaking, notion of the common good is concerned with the hopes and aspirations of a larger community beyond the area of self-interests of different individuals and groups. Some people may take to a dangerous path for want of proper knowledge, due to their temperamental weakness, or due to the fascinating effect of fashion or advertisements. Government may frame some rules and regulations or take administrative measures to deal with such situations. For example, advertisements of wine and cigarettes have been banned on radio and television. A cigarette case or its advertisement anywhere must contain a statutory warning: 'Cigarette smoking is injurious to health'. Dangers of drug-abuse and drinking are displayed in the form of warnings at prominent public places. Wide publicity is also given to the measures meant for environmental protection, cleanliness, prevention of diseases, population control, expansion of literacy, etc. All these steps are designed to promote the public interest or the common good.

For a wider understanding of the concept of the common good, it may be analysed in different perspectives. Of these, Liberal, Communitarian, Marxian and Gandhian perspectives are particularly important.

[II]
LIBERAL PERSPECTIVE

Liberal view of the common good regards it as the aggregate of individual goods. According to this view, the common good is not a metaphysical element which exists beyond the experience of ordinary persons. Man is a rational creature. In other words, man is endowed with the faculty .of reasoning which enables him to grasp his own good, and to realize the need of certain rules which are necessary for securing the good of all members of society. These rules are instrumental to the reconciliation of conflicting interests of different individuals and groups. Indeed, the point of their reconciliation represents the common good. Individuals who have a common interest in some issue organize themselves into an interest group. Then the point of reconciliation between different interest groups represents the common interest of society which is coterminous with the common good.

From this point of view, any conflict existing in society is not very deep. Every problem of society is capable of a peaceful solution. Every member of society realizes that we live in a scarcity situation where all wishes or demands cannot be fulfilled. People can fulfil their reasonable demands by making suitable adjustment with others. So they are found to be ready for the necessary adjustment. They can decide about their respective rights and obligations by using their own intellect and by persuading each other to adopt a reasonable course of action. This equilibrium of their respective rights and duties represents the common good. Norman Barry (*An Introduction to Modern Political Theory;* 1989), who uses the term 'public interest' as a synonym for the 'common good', has significantly observed: "Liberal advocates of the doctrine of the public interest...argue that the concept describes the *shared* interests of a community and that its promotion, so far from oppressing individual interests, actually enables individuals to secure advantages which they could not otherwise enjoy."

For liberal thinkers, the rules of the civil society which provide safety of the individual from the oppressive powers of others, constitute the common good. When everybody abides by these rules, then the strong will not oppress the weak; nobody will cheat anybody; everybody will enter into contract with others at his free will; and everybody will sincerely act according to the terms of the contract. State intervention will become necessary only when some anti-social element does not comply with the rules.

The chief exponents of the liberal view of the common good include John Locke (1632-1704), Adam Smith (1723-90), Jeremy Bentham (1748-1832) and

John Stuart Mill (1806-73).

A CRITICAL APPRAISAL

Liberalism regards the rules of the market society as a fit instrument of the common good. It views the free competition, equality of opportunity and allocation according to merit as the rules of proper behaviour.

The problem with these rules is that the reward of an individual's merit and effort would be governed by the market demand, which is beyond individual's control. For instance, in ancient Greek city of Athens, philosophers were highly respected and soldiers held a lower position, but in Sparta, soldiers were held in high esteem and philosophers languished. Similarly, in the present-day consumer society, it is possible that highly talented and sincere poets, artists, scientists and other intellectuals may be constrained to lead a poor standard of living whereas semi-literate property dealers and mediocre businessmen may be rolling in riches. Under the circumstances, the state will have to protect and promote those talents which are indispensable for the preservation of human civilization and culture but whose existence is threatened by the free market competition. Only a welfare state can take care of this situation.

Welfare State

A state that gives protection to the people and those components of human civilization and culture whose existence is threatened by the forces of a competitive market society.

C.B. Macpherson (1911-87), a contemporary political philosopher, has criticized the market society model on the ground that it subjects human talents to the rules of demand and supply. It stunts the natural capabilities of man and destroys his creative freedom.

In a nutshell, liberal interpretation of the common good can only be accepted on the condition that it is linked with the concept of the welfare state.

[III]
COMMUNITARIAN PERSPECTIVE

Communitarianism is an important stream of contemporary political philosophy. It points to the shortcomings of liberalism and attempts to redefine the relation between individual and the community. Liberalism promotes individualism to focus on individual freedom which undermines individual's affinity with the community. When every individual turns to seek his own good, no one is emotionally attached to any one. An individual would manage to have many means of comfort at the expense of his emotional security. In other words, if an individual devotes himself exclusively to the pursuit of self-interest, he cannot secure good life in the fullest sense of the term.

If isolated individuals cannot secure their own good by their efforts, how can we arrive at the common good by aggregating the outcome of their individual efforts? Communitarians hold that only a community is capable of realizing the common good. If all individuals pool their efforts for the attainment of the common good instead of striving to secure their individual good, they would be able to realize the common good more effectively from which they would be able to derive their individual good. This view necessitates individual's first commitment to the community, and not to himself.

For communitarians, individual's own existence and personality are the product of his social situation, roles and conventions which are embedded in society. While liberals leave the individual to pursue his self-appointed goals, communitarians want him to pursue the community-determined goals. While liberals regard the individual to be the sole proprietor of all his faculties, communitarians affirm his indebtedness to society for these faculties. While liberals insist on individual's rights and liberties, communitarians focus on his duties and obligations. Communitarianism insists on our common identity and eulogizes those values and beliefs which are dear to all of us.

Early indications of communitarianism are found in the political thought of Aristotle, ancient Greek philosopher, Jean-Jaqucs Rousseau (1712-78), French philosopher, G.W.F. Hegel (1770-1831), German philosopher, and T.H. Green (1836-82), English moral philosopher. Its contemporary exponents include Alasdair MacIntyre (1929-), Charles Taylor (1931-), Michael Walzer (1935-), and Michael Sandel (1953-).

T.H. Green (*Lectures on the Principles of Political Obligation;* 1882), the forerunner of communitarianism, argued that human beings, as self-conscious creatures, attain the knowledge of the common good in association with the members of their community. Green believed that men knew the common good more intimately than their self-interest or individual good. The common good not only comprehends the good of all members of the community, but their conception of the common good is also identical. The state and politics come into existence for the realization of the common good. The idea of the common good is the foundation of political obligation. Green asserts that the state is authorized to make only those laws which promote the common good; and the individual is obliged to abide by only those laws which conform to the common good. If an individual thinks that he can protect the common good more effectively by opposing a particular order of the state, his political obligation does not stop him from going ahead. It is the consciousness of the common good which induces people to accept their duties. They are prepared to forego their personal choice and self-interest for the sake of realizing the common good. They are convinced that they can attain self-realization only by pursuing the common good.

Alasdair MacIntyre (*After Virtue;* 1981) argued that individuals flourish only within an atmosphere of 'socially established cooperative human activity'. If the state treats individuals as disconnected entities and lets them loose to realize their rights without realizing their duties, the result would be social disintegration and moral disaster. Michael Sandel (*Liberalism and the Limits of Justice;* 1982) asserted that the person can only be understood in the context of his 'embeddedness' in a particular time, place and culture. Only with this understanding a political theory can generate laws, institutions and practices that would be genuinely good for us and contribute to a fully just society. This alone will create a 'deeper commonality' which will be informed by 'shared self-understanding' as well as affection.

Then Michael Walzer (*Spheres of Justice;* 1983) laid down elaborate criteria for the distribution of various social goods according to the proper spheres of their application, where they would contribute to the smooth functioning of the community. Charles Taylor (*Philosophical Papers;* 1985) echoed MacIntyre's attack on the liberal conception of 'atomistic' individuals and confirmed the tenets of communitarianism. Taylor argued that if human beings want their genuine development, they must acknowledge first that they are situated in a society. They can realize their good only through cooperation in pursuit of the common good.

On the whole, communitarian notion of the common good requires the individual to pursue his goals within the structure of society, and to look for his good as part of the good of whole society.

A CRITICAL APPRAISAL

Communitarian concept of the common good insists on cooperation, and not competition between individuals, and thereby promotes social solidarity. It inspires the isolated individuals to establish cordial relations with each other, and shows them the way to obtain emotional security. However, in spite of its strong ethical base, it has no mechanism to ensure that its principles will be adopted as the general rules of behaviour. In a nutshell, *communitarianism embodies a strong moral philosophy, but it is not founded in equally strong political philosophy.*

[IV]
MARXIAN PERSPECTIVE

NECESSARY CONDITIONS FOR THE COMMON GOOD

According to Marxist theory, since the division of human society into two antagonistic classes on the basis of ownership of private property, idea of the common good has become irrelevant. The common good can exist only in a classless society, *i.e.* either under primitive communism (which existed before the rise of civilization), or in a future communist society. Since the state is an instrument of the dominant class for the exploitation of the dependent class, a classless society does not need state power; it is bound to evolve into a stateless society. Under this system, society uses its authority for the protection of common interests of all members of the community which represent the common good.

Primitive communism was a pre-state society where the instruments of labour were of the most primitive kind—the club, the stone axe, the flint knife, the stone-tipped spear, followed later by the bow and arrow. Man's muscular strength was the only motive force employed to operate these elementary tools. These tools were held in common ownership by the members of the primitive community which engaged itself in common labour, such as common hunting, common fishing, and the fruits of this common labour were also shared in common. There was no concept of private property, hence no exploitation of man by man.

The amount of production at this stage was scarcely sufficient for the subsistence of each member of the community; there was no surplus that could be stored in private possession. Hence, society was not divided into *haves* and *have-nots*. In the absence of class distinctions and consequent exploitation, there was no need for a special apparatus of coercion. The common affairs of the community were managed collectively or entrusted to the most respected and experienced members of the community. The concept of state or political power—exploitative class power—was particularly absent at this stage.

On the other hand, *communist society* will come into existence after the socialist stage of historical development. According to classical Marxism, when all means of social production will be placed under social ownership, remnants of capitalism will be liquidated, labour will become universal for every able-bodied person on voluntary basis, and forces of production will have been fully developed, the state will 'wither away'. In this phase of historical development, called 'communist society', economy will be regulated by the principle: 'from each according to his ability, to each according to his need'. In other words, in communist society, the distribution of burdens shall depend on abilities, while the distribution of benefits shall depend on needs. Benefits shall not be treated as the reward of contribution to the common good. It is the picture of an ideal society where men shall shed their selfishness and spontaneously contribute to the common good without the thought of the return. It is hoped that when society undertakes the responsibility to fulfil all their needs, men will use their maximum abilities for contribution to the common good without any specific incentives. The idea of the common good shall be fully realized only in such an ideal society. But before it comes into existence, society will have to undergo various stages of class struggle which must be understood in the present context.

DOCTRINE OF CLASS STRUGGLE

Karl Marx (1818-83) and Friedrich Engels (1820-95) have particularly dwelled on the role of class struggle in the process of historical development. They believed that the struggle between the antagonistic classes—haves and have-nots—had been of fundamental importance in society since the dissolution of the primitive tribal community with its common ownership of the means of production. Thus, the opening sentence of the *Communist Manifesto* (1848) reads: "The history of all hitherto existing society is the history of class struggles." Of these classes one invariably comprises the oppressors and exploiters, and the other includes the oppressed and exploited. So the *Communist Manifesto* proceeds:

> Freeman and slave, patrician and plebeian, lord and serf, guild-master and journeyman, in a word, oppressor and oppressed, stood in constant opposition to one another, carried on an uninterrupted, now hidden, now open fight, a fight that each time ended, either in a revolutionary re-constitution of society at large, or in the common ruin of the contending classes.

With the development of productive forces, men enter into social relations corresponding to the prevailing mode of production. Thus, the ancient society was characterized by the relations between master and slave, the medieval society by those between feudal lord and serf, while the modern society is marked by the corresponding relations between capitalist and worker. Each stage of social development is, therefore, known by the division of society into social classes. Critics point out that Marx has nowhere given a clear-cut definition of class. In the third volume of his *Capital* (1894; edited by Friedrich Engels), he raised many questions about the nature of class without arriving at a definite answer. However, he recognizes that classes are not homogeneous and that varying degrees of social status may give rise to a number of classes. He holds the view that all classes are ultimately divisible by two, one of which controls the means of social production, while the other is forced to thrive on its labour power, and that the antagonism created by this division gives rise to a profound contradiction. Yet it is through this very contradiction that progress is effected.

Accordingly, class struggle is instrumental to social progress. Until the stage of perfect production is reached, class struggle is bound to operate at each stage of social development. The process of class struggle results in the elimination of the contending classes and the emergence of a new class structure corresponding to the new mode of production. As the productive forces change, the class which hitherto controlled them is confronted by a new class, which claims to be able to administer them more efficiently; and just as the merchants and craftsmen were able to challenge the feudal lord of later Middle Ages, so will the wage-earner challenge the capitalist and wrest economic power from him.

Marx and Engels laid special emphasis on the class struggle to transform the capitalist system which had entered a decisive phase. Thus, they declared:

> The modern bourgeois society that has sprouted from the ruins of feudal society has not done away with class antagonisms. It has but established new classes, new conditions of oppression, new forms of struggle in place of the old ones.
>
> Our epoch, the epoch of the bourgeoisie, possesses, however, this distinctive feature: it has simplified the class antagonisms. Society as a whole is more and more splitting up into two great hostile camps, into two great classes directly facing each other: Bourgeoisie and Proletariat (*The Communist Manifesto;* 1848).

They recognized the existence of some other classes on their way to dissolution. The proletariat is distinctively a revolutionary class whom they addressed in particular:

> Of all the classes that stand face to face with the bourgeoisie today, the proletariat alone is a really revolutionary class. The other classes decay and finally disappear in the face of modern industry; the proletariat is its special and essential product.
>
> The lower middle class, the small manufacturer, the shopkeeper, the artisan, the peasant, all these fight against the bourgeoisie, to save from extinction their existence as fractions of the middle class. They are, therefore, not revolutionary, but conservative (*ibid.*).

The proletarian revolution, according to Marx and Engels, would be different from all previous revolutions of history:

> All previous historical movements were movements of minorities, or in the interest of minorities. The proletarian movement is the self-conscious, independent movement of the immense majority, in the interest of the immense majority (*ibid.*).

This revolution would bring about the final emancipation of mankind because there is no class below the proletariat which could be subjected to exploitation when the proletariat comes to power. The proletarian revolution would, therefore, pave the way for the emergence of a classless society.

Whereas G.W.F. Hegel (1770-1831) had envisaged the culmination of social progress through a clash of nations, Marx and Engels anticipated society's march towards perfection through a clash of classes. They believed that mankind's division into classes would cut across their division into nations. Thus, they announced:

> The working men have no country. We cannot take from them what they have not got… National differences and antagonisms between peoples are daily more and more vanishing, owing to the develop[illegible] of the

> bourgeoisie, to freedom of commerce, to the world market, to uniformity in the mode of production and in the conditions of life corresponding thereto (*ibid.*).

In order to exhort the proletariat to prepare themselves for revolution, Marx and Engels inspire them to develop their class consciousness, to identify their class interest and to organize themselves to fulfil their historic mission. Thus, the concluding part of *The Communist Manifesto* reads:

> The proletarians have nothing to lose but their chains.
> They have a world to win.
> Working men of all countries, unite!

A CRITICAL APPRAISAL

According to Marxist theory, as long as society is divided into antagonistic classes, it is not possible for the individual to discover the common good. At best, he can discover his class interest. For example, under capitalism, the interest of capitalist class lies in maintaining the capitalist system whereas the interest of working class lies in overthrowing capitalism and establishing a socialist system so that it eventually turns into communist society. The common good can only be realized in the communist society.

However, in actual practice, the vision of communist society is nowhere realized. Experience of over seven decades of socialism in the former Soviet Union and over four decades in East Europe has shown that it never came close to the image of a classless society. When economic power as the basis of class division is removed, political power brings a new class division into existence. In due course, political power in socialist countries proves to be more oppressive than that in liberal democracies. Liberal democracy, at least, provides for some mechanism of civil liberties which enable the citizens to exercise some control on political power, but under socialist system, the new ruling class not only appropriates economic resources of the state for personal enjoyment, it also suspends civil liberties. Initially the citizens are compensated by the adequate provision of social and economic rights, but when these rights cannot be maintained due to increasing shortages, the system proves to be fragile. That is what precisely happened in the former Soviet Union and its satellites during 1989-91. So Marxian perspective on the common good must be taken with a pinch of salt.

[V]
GANDHIAN PERSPECTIVE

Commitment to the common good is the essence of Gandhian philosophy. Mahatma Gandhi (1869-1948), Indian activist and social philosopher, saw India's independence as an opportunity 'to wipe every tear from every eye'. He wished to transform the destiny of India at a critical juncture through moral regeneration. It was a time when India was groaning under an oppressive foreign rule, abject poverty, vast social and economic inequalities. Further, it was also in the grip of communal tension and hatred. Gandhi preached the gospel of spiritualism, *ahimsa* (non-violence), renunciation (non-possession), dignity of labour and moral courage, etc. for the uplift of man as well as society. His doctrine of trusteeship, his vision of a classless society and his concept of *sarvodaya* (uplift of all) hold the key to his idea of the common good.

DOCTRINE OF TRUSTEESHIP

Gandhian doctrine of trusteeship is addressed to the conscience of the rich and resourceful members of society, particularly landlords and capitalists. It urges them not to consider themselves as the sole proprietors of their possessions, but only 'trustees' of a gift bestowed upon them by God for the service of humanity. This view is in consonance with the basic philosophy of Gandhi. His principle of non-possession *(aparigraha)* implies that worldly possessions make you morally deprave. Hence, one should not take more than his immediate needs. To maintain one's moral strength, material things should be used with a spirit of renunciation.

Gandhian principle of non-stealing *(asteya)* implies that amassing of wealth, or even the possession of more than one's immediate needs amounts to theft because it is meant to fulfil others' needs. In Gandhi's words: "Earth has enough resources to satisfy everybody's need but not their greed." Any attempt to satisfy one's greed means theft. It reminds us of nineteenth-century French philosopher, P.J. Proudhon's famous dictum: "Property is theft."

However, Gandhi does not favour overthrowing the existing economic system. This system has become oppressive because of moral decline. If the organizers of agriculture and industry could be persuaded to act as public servants, they will win wide public esteem instead of the existing hatred. The feeling of class conflict will be replaced by the sentiment of class cooperation. Gandhi wants 'change of heart' of the rich and resourceful persons to enable the society to have full benefit of their talents and efforts without suffering injustice caused by the exploitation of the poor by the rich. As Gandhi wrote in *Amrita Bazar Patrika* (1934):

> What is needed is not the extinction of landlords and capitalists, but a transformation of the existing relationship between them and the masses into something healthier and purer.

Gandhi realized that this was by no means an easy task. As he himself conceded in *The Modern Review* (1935):

> You may say that trusteeship is a legal fiction. But if people meditate over

> it constantly and try to act up to it, then life on earth would be governed far more by love than it is at present. Absolute trusteeship is an abstraction like Euclid's definition of a point, and is equally unattainable. But if we strive for it, we shall be able to go further in realizing a state of equality on earth than by any other method.

Moral regeneration at any stage is really difficult. We need a constant inspiration from Gautam Buddha, Jesus Christ, or Mahatma Gandhi to follow this path. Every step in this direction will give us more enlightenment, peace of mind and genuine happiness.

VISION OF A CLASSLESS SOCIETY

Gandhi's faith in human equality made him a strong votary of a classless society. This means elimination of discrimination on any irrelevant ground. In a country like India, people are discriminated on many grounds, *e.g.* religion, caste, sex, etc. Gandhi taught us to do away with such discrimination. Gandhi preached equality of all religions. As he wrote:

> Temples or mosques or churches... I make no distinction between these different abodes of God. They are what faith has made them. They are an answer to man's craving somehow to reach the Unseen
> (*The Mind of Mahatma Gandhi,* compiled by R.K. Prabhu and U.R. Rao; 1945).

Gandhi strongly defended equality between man and woman. As he wrote:

> My opinion is that, just as fundamentally man and woman are one, their problems must be one in essence. The soul in both is the same. The two live the same life, have the same feelings. Each is complement of the other. The one cannot live without the other's active help. . .But somehow or other man has dominated woman from ages past, and so woman has developed an inferiority complex... But the seers among men have recognized her equal status
> (*Selections from Gandhi* by Nirmal Kumar Bose; 1948).

Caste and division of labour was another ground of discrimination which Gandhi sought to demolish. His gospel of 'bread labour' expected everybody to do physical labour towards production, at least to compensate for the bread that he consumes. Bread is symbolic of various items of one's physical consumption. As Gandhi wrote in *Harijan* (1935):

> If all laboured for their bread and no more, then there would be enough food and enough leisure for all. Then there would be no cry of over-population, no disease and no misery as we see around. Such labour will be the highest form of sacrifice. Men will do many other things either through their bodies or through their minds, but all this will be labour of love for the common good. There will be no rich and no poor, none high

> and none low, no touchable and no untouchable…
>
> If we did so, our wants would be minimized, our food would be simple. We should then eat to live, not live to eat. Let anyone who doubts the accuracy of this proposition try to sweat for his bread, he will derive the greatest relish from the productions of his labour, improve his health, and discover that many things he took were superfluities.

In short, the principle of bread labour is designed to promote three things: (*a*) simple living among all citizens; (*b*) dignity of labour; and (*c*) a sense of equality transcending the prevailing division of labour. Originally caste symbolized the division of labour which strayed on to division of society into high and low ranks. The principle of bread labour would serve to obliterate this ranking. This would even create equality between the rich and the poor. As Gandhi wrote in *From Yervada Mandir* (published: 1945):

> There is a world-wide conflict between capital and labour, and the poor envy the rich. If all worked for their bread, distinctions of rank would be obliterated; the rich would still be there, but they would deem themselves only trustees of their property, and would use it mainly in the public interest.

Above all, Gandhian principle of *ahimsa* (non-violence) is also conducive to the creation of a classless society. When a person avows not to harm anybody, not to cause injury to anybody and not to hurt anybody's feeling, what else is left for the realization of a classless society? Thus, *the vision of a classless society runs throughout Gandhian thought and philosophy.*

CONCEPT OF *SARVODAYA*

The term *'sarvodaya'* may be rendered as 'uplift of all', 'rise of all' or 'awakening of all'. All the meanings of this term closely correspond to each other. In a society where only the few are endowed with knowledge, power, prestige and wealth, and a very large number are languishing, *sarvodaya* wants them to rise above. But since it believes in upliftment of all, it does not envisage a conflict between the high and the low, between the rich and the poor. As a votary of purity of means as well as end, Gandhi was convinced that violent means cannot be used to achieve a non-violent end.

Whereas the principle of *sarvodaya* seeks material upgradation of the deprived and the underprivileged sections, it also envisages moral upgradation of the rich who would offer their riches for the welfare of the poor and service of the community. Thus, they will not only give a proof of self-control and magnanimity, but also raise their own spiritual level.

The idea behind *sarvodaya* was inspired by John Ruskin's *Unto This Last* (1860). Gandhi came across this work in the midst of passive resistance against the racist regime of South Africa. This contained a message of uplift of the last man or the most neglected lot. Gandhi was so impressed by this work that he published its summary in his Gujarati articles under the title of *Sarvodaya.* Ruskin's teachings are very close to Gandhian philosophy. Ruskin rejected the cult of machinery and consumerism as well as the idea of economic man and mercantile economy. Instead, he advocated simple technology, manual labour, communal enterprise and measurement of value in terms of quality of life. Gandhi relied on these teachings to sharpen his own thinking on various issues of social reform.

Comparative Perspective on the Common Good

The Issue	*Liberal Perspective*	*Communitarian Perspective*	*Marxian Perspective*	*Gandhian Perspective*
Object of Commitment	Individuals' Good	Community's Good	Good of one's Class	Community's Good
Constitution of the Common Good	Aggregate of Individuals' Goods	Community as the Source of Everybody's Good	Common Good not feasible in a Class-Divided Society	Community as the Source of Everybody's Good
Attitude towards Conflict	Not very deep; may be resolved through Discussion	No real conflict; Misunderstanding may be removed by focusing on Community's Good	Conflict between Antagonistic Classes cannot be resolved	No real conflict; Adherence to *Ahimsa* and the Common Good will eliminate all conflict
Ultimate Nature of the Good	Material	Material	Material	Spiritual
Grounds of Criticism	Conformity to Market Society model may destory Creative Freedom of the Individual	No machinery to ensure individual Commitment to the Community	Its vision of a Classless Society seems Unrealizable	Relies mainly on Moral Persuation; No Effective Machinery to Realize the Ideal in Practice

Gandhian concept of *sarvodaya* rejects the utilitarian view of 'greatest happiness of the greatest number' in favour of 'greatest good of all'. As Gandhi himself wrote in *Young India* (1926):

> A votary of *Ahimsa* cannot subscribe to the utilitarian formula (of the greatest good of the greatest number). He will strive for the greatest good of all and die in the attempt to realize the idea. He will, therefore, be willing to die, so that others may live... The greatest good of all inevitably includes the good of the greatest number, and therefore, he and

the utilitarian will converge in many points in their career, but there does come a time when they must part company, and even work in opposite directions. The utilitarian to be logical will never sacrifice himself. The absolutist will even sacrifice himself.

Here the term 'absolutist' stands for the person who has absolute faith in *Ahimsa*—one who will never depart from the path of *Ahimsa* in deference to any other ideal. The message of self-sacrifice for the greatest good of all is the essence of *sarvodaya*.

Competition brings out the best in products and the worst in people.

David Sarnoff

22

Concept of Democracy

[I]
MEANING OF DEMOCRACY

The idea of democracy has existed in the tradition of Western political thought since ancient times. The term 'democracy' was first used in the fifth century BC by the Greek historian Herodotus in the sense of 'rule by the people'. This term is derived from a combination of two Greek words: *demos,* meaning 'the people', and *kratien,* meaning 'to rule'. Abraham Lincoln's famous definition of democracy as 'government of the people, by the people, for the people' is very close to its literal meaning. In short, *democracy as a form of government implies that the ultimate authority of governance in this system is vested in the ordinary people so that public policy is made to conform to the will of the people and to serve the interests of the people.*

Several exponents of democracy have treated democracy chiefly as a form of government. John Austin (1790-1859), James Bryce (1838-1922), A.V. Dicey (1835-1922), John Seeley (1834-95) and A.L. Lowell (1856-1943) are some prominent holders of this view. Lowell, for instance, says that democracy is only an experiment in government. Seeley describes it as government in which everyone has a share.

Analysing Lincoln's definition, D.D. Raphael (*Problems of Political Philosophy;* 1976) observes that all government is government of the people; hence 'government of the people' does not convey much. As regards 'government for the people', Raphael argues that a benevolent despotism, as much as democracy, may be government for (*i.e.* in the interests of) the people, though the political experience of Europe, if not perhaps always of Asia, leads one to doubt whether a despotism can for long remain benevolent. So the essential idea of democratic government is 'government *by* the people'.

Benevolent Despotism

Benevolent despotism refers to a type of government where powers of governance are concentrated in the hands of a ruler who is not bound by law, constitution or any other authority, but who tends to rule for the benefit of the people at his own will.

Now the expression 'government *by* the people' also presents some difficulties. Literally this would mean direct democracy, *i.e.* a system where all public decisions are taken by the whole body of citizens. The form of government which existed in fourth century BC Athens—an ancient Greek city-state—is cited as an example of direct democracy. But it was not a democracy in real sense of the term, as it was the government by a tiny section of the people, who were called 'freemen'; majority of the residents of the city-state were slaves or non-citizens; slaves and women had no political rights under that system. So it was by no means the 'government by the people'.

Direct Democracy

Direct democracy refers to a form of government where all public decisions are taken by the general body of citizens at their regular meetings. It is feasible only in very small communities, as in some ancient Greek city-states.

In modern democratic states, we largely have universal political rights. But these states are so large that we cannot imagine to have direct democracy anywhere. So we have evolved the system of indirect or representative democracy. Now we have the 'government by the people through their representatives' who are chosen for a definite period (like two years to six years). Thus, the people get an opportunity to test their representatives who may be re-elected or replaced in view of their promise and performance.

Apparently, 'government by the people' implies that public decisions should be taken with the approval of all the people. In practice, it would be a far cry. In the first place, all people cannot be made to think alike. So people's representatives have to be elected by a majority vote. Then public decisions by these representatives have also to be taken by a majority vote as they would be rarely unanimous. So the strength of people who actually approve of a particular decision is further diluted. However, it may be hoped that in spite of wide differences of opinion on minor issues, all public decisions in a democracy would be taken 'for the people', *i.e.* in the interests of all the people.

The principle of democracy requires that while all public decisions are taken with the approval of the majority, due regard may be given to the view of the minority. The majority must behave in a responsible manner. It should take care of the interests of the minority. It should also try to accommodate the opinion of minority on essential issues. Under normal conditions, where there is a free flow of information and freedom to influence public opinion, those who are in minority today may be in majority tomorrow and *vice versa*. Hence, majority and minority would give due regard to each other and live in a cordial atmosphere. However, *in a multicultural society* where people tend to vote for the candidates belonging to their own caste, region, religion, language or culture, etc., they may be divided into permanent majority and minorities. In such a case, *the principle of democracy requires that different minorities (like racial, religious, linguistic or cultural minorities) enjoy full freedom to preserve their cultural traits and feel fully safe.*

Multicultural Society

Multicultural society refers to a society where people belonging to different cultural groups, that is those who identify themselves with a particular language, region, religion, caste, dress-code, eating habits, etc. live together as equal citizens of the same state.

Democracy as government by the people relies heavily on the wisdom of the people. As Harry Emerson Fosdick (1878-1969) has stated: "Democracy is based upon the conviction that there are extraordinary possibilities in ordinary people." Is it proved by our experience? Sometimes ordinary people falter in their judgement. Sometimes they are swayed by emotions. They are often misled by demagogues. In some quarters, it is suggested that democracy as the rule of mediocres should be replaced by a better system like meritocracy, *i.e.* government by those who have proved their competence. Shall we then get better results?

Demagogue

Demagogue refers to a type of a political leader who tries to win support of the people by appealing to their emotions rather than by giving rational arguments.

It is interesting to note that the idea of meritocracy was introduced by Michael Young (*The Rise of the Meritocracy;* 1958). Meritocracy implied a system of occupational hierarchy where each person will get his appropriate position according to his qualifications, competence and character rather than on the basis of age, gender, race or inherited wealth. It was based on the belief that only a limited pool of talents exists among a nation's children and that such talents should not be allowed to go waste. However, the author of this idea himself was hardly optimistic about its consequences. He felt that such a system would denude the working class of its culture and leadership. Critics of meritocracy argue that society will do better if there is equality of outcome rather than equality of opportunity in an open competition. Accordingly, *democracy would be more conducive to social development than the proposed system of meritocracy.*

All the ills of democracy can be cured by more democracy.

Alfred Emanuel Smith

[II]
CLASSCAL NOTION OF DEMOCRACY

From Ancient to Modern Times

Democracy has a long tradition. But the notions regarding its essence and grounds of its justification have been revised from time to time. Plato and Aristotle saw democracy at work in some of ancient Greek city-states, especially at Athens. Its salient features were: (*a*) equal participation by *all freemen* in the common affairs *of the polis* (city-state) which was regarded as an essential instrument of good life; (*b*) arriving at public decisions in an atmosphere of free discussion; and (*c*) general respect for law and for the established procedures of the community. The Greeks took pride in their customary law and admiringly distinguished it from the 'arbitrary rule' prevalent among the 'barbarians'.

However, the form of democracy prevalent in ancient Greek city-states was by no means regarded as an ideal rule. Plato decried democracy because the people were not properly equipped with education 'to select the best rulers and the wisest courses'. Democracy enabled the men with the gift of eloquence and oratory to get votes of the people and secure public office, but such men were thoroughly selfish and incompetent who ruined the state. Then, Aristotle identified democracy as 'the rule of the many', that is of the more numerous members of the community, particularly the poor ones. In his classification of governments into normal and perverted forms, Aristotle placed democracy among perverted forms since it implied the rule of the mediocres seeking their selfish interests, not the interest of the state. Aristotle observed that no form of government prevalent during his times was stable and this led to frequent upheavals. In his search for a stable form of government, Aristotle, in his *Politics,* tried to analyse the merits and demerits of various forms of government. In the process, he made very interesting observations about the merits and demerits of democracy: "This rule by the poor has some advantages. The people, though individually they may be worse judges than those who have special knowledge, are collectively as good. Moreover, there are some artists whose works are best judged not by themselves alone but by those who do not possess the art; for example, the user or master of a house will be a better judge of it than the builder... and the guest will be a better judge of a feast than the cook."

But the demerits of democracy, in this sense, were no less striking. According to Aristotle, again, democracy *is based on a false assumption of equality.* It arises out of the notion that those who are equal in one respect (such as in respect of the law) are equal in all respects; because men are equally free, they claim to be absolutely equal. The upshot is that ability is sacrificed to numbers, while numbers are manipulated by trickery. Because the people are so easily misled, and so fickle in their views, the ballot should be limited to the intelligent.

With this line of argument, Aristotle came to commend a *mixed constitution,* that is a combination of aristocracy and democracy as the best possible form of government.

Indeed, Aristotle's ideal of the mixed constitution implied the need to restrain unbridled powers of rulers in order to make them people-friendly. Later, ancient philosophers like Polybius (203-121 BC), Cicero (106-43 BC) and Saint Augustine (354-430) sought to carry forward the ideal of the mixed constitution by subordinating the rulers to virtue or to law which was exalted to be above the rule of men.

With the dawn of modern political thought, Machiavelli (1469-1527) (in his *Discourses;* 1531) and Montesquieu (1669-1755) (in his *The Spirit of the Laws;* 1748) took democracy to be a pure form of government that could be safely incorporated into statecraft only as one component of a mixed republican constitution. Then the early exponents of the theory of the social contract, *viz.* Hobbes (1588-1679) and Locke (1632-1704) sought to base political legitimacy on the consent of the people. This theory offered a challenge to traditional dictatorship and the divine right of kings. It recognized the state as an artificial and mechanistic creation of man which was meant to serve his own end. Placing the ultimate source of all governmental authority in individuals who entered into the 'contract' for the creation of the state for the protection of their natural liberty and natural rights, social contract theory laid the foundations for later democratic theory.

Then Jean-Jaques Rousseau (1712-78), another brilliant exponent of social contract theory, introduced the idea of 'popular sovereignty' and became the greatest early theorist of democracy. His theory of popular sovereignty is embedded in his concept of the *general will.* For Rousseau, the state is not only a product of the general will, it continues to function under the guidance of the general will.

General Will

According to Jean-Jaques Rousseau (*The Social Contract;* 1762), the *general will* refers to the point of convergence of the real will of all members of a community. It reflects the true interest of each individual as well as the common good of the whole community. Sovereignty of the *general will* constitutes the foundation of popular sovereignty.

The classical concept of democracy was articulated by some of the modern thinkers, particularly of England, such as A.V. Dicey (1835-1922) and James Bryce (1838-1922).

DICEY'S ACCOUNT OF DEMOCRACY

Dicey, in his famous work *Law and Opinion in England (*1905), treated democracy as a form of government under which majority opinion determines legislation. According to him, it would be unwise in a democracy to enforce laws not approved by the people. He tried to demonstrate elaborately the relation of legislation to the prevailing public opinion. However, he also pointed out that particular laws are the product of a particular historical setting. Since public opinion under democracy is not a uniform phenomenon, it has not produced uniform laws.

BRYCE'S ACCOUNT OF DEMOCRACY

James Bryce is one of the greatest champions of democracy and its most sympathetic critic. In his two monumental works *The American Commonwealth* (1893) and *Modern Democracies* (1921), he chiefly treated democracy as a form of government. He defined democracy as 'the rule of the people expressing their sovereign will through the votes'. Ultimately he reduced it to 'the rule of the majority'.

Justification of Democracy

Bryce finds the justification of democracy in the concept of relativity, that is by comparing its merits and demerits with other forms of government. The test of government, according to Bryce, is the welfare of the people. Thus, the standard of merit of any form of government can be judged by the adequacy with which it performs the chief functions of government: the protection from internal and external enemies, the securing of justice, efficient administration of common affairs, and the bestowal of aid to individual citizens in their several occupations. History shows that these functions can be carried out by democracies as well as by any other form of government. But democracy has an additional merit in that it stimulates men to self-education, because participation by the people in government activities opens wider horizons for the individual and tends to broaden his interests. This participation is the essence of democracy. It is not actual 'rule by the people'. The people in a democracy exercise their authority in two ways: (*a*) they determine the ends towards which their government shall aim; and (*b*) watch over those into whose hands they have placed the actual power of administration.

Bryce does not claim that democracy offers a panacea for all the ills of society. Yet he prefers it to other forms of government because it has brought about considerable improvement in the standard of governance. It has not led to world brotherhood, nor has it dignified and purified politics, but it has provided for better governance in comparison to the past.

Defects of Democracy

Bryce has enumerated six outstanding evils of the existing form of democracy: (*i*) the power of money interests to pervert administration or legislation; (*ii*) the tendency to allow politics to become a trade, entered for gain and not for service; (*iii*) extravagance; (*iv*) the failure to evaluate properly the skilled man, and to abuse the doctrine of equality; (*v*) party politics; and (*vi*) the tendency of politicians to play for votes. However, Bryce points out that the first three of these evils are common to other forms of government also—they are not specific evils of democracy. The last three are, of course, more closely associated with democracy, but they are by no means insurmountable. Democracy has closed some of the old channels of evil; it has opened some new ones; but it has not increased the stream.

Major problems of democracy include self-interest and irresponsibility of power. Democracy has two powerful weapons to fight against these evils: (*a*) law, and (*b*) opinion. The weapon of opinion is a peculiar safeguard; no other form of government provides for it. Steady urbanization in large democracies and the consequent rise of large labour groups has complicated the problem of democracy. The future of democracy depends upon development of human wisdom. While no other government gives to the citizen as does a democracy, at the same time no other government demands so much. Bryce concludes his account of democracy with an optimistic note.

AN APPRAISAL

Bryce has, of course, given an illuminating account of democracy as a form of government. However, he has not deeply analysed social phases of the problem. He has also dismissed without proper weight the growth of self-conscious groups within society. He has underestimated the true significance of industrial democracy. He sees the growth of a large working class and the ideas of proletarian dictatorship as threats to democracy. But he has failed to appreciate their impact which was transforming the concept of democracy itself. However, his contribution as an exponent of classical notion of democracy in the modern times cannot be ignored.

> **Industrial Democracy**
>
> Industrial democracy represents an attempt to introduce the principle of democracy in the sphere of industrial organization, whether an industry is placed under private ownership or public ownership. This expression of democracy largely implies workers' involvement and participation in the decision-making process. It is argued that this arrangement infuses a sense of responsibility among workers, creates greater understanding between the management and workers, prevents industrial conflicts, and raises the productivity of Labour.

GROWTH OF DEMOCRACY

Since the eighteenth century, democracy came to be regarded as a moral standard by which regimes were judged rather than merely as one of the forms of government. During this period, democratic theory and practice focused on the extension of franchise with a view to translating the principle of human equality into practice. However, in actual practice, democracy was first established in the Western world during the nineteenth century. Initially this term stood for 'representative government' where election of representatives was held by a competitive vote. However, only male citizens had the right to vote in elections. In this sense, democracy came to be established in the United States in 1820s and 1830s when a number of States expanded the franchise.

In France, adult male suffrage was abruptly introduced in 1848, but they could not set up a parliamentary government on an enduring basis till 1871. In Britain, parliamentary government had been established on an enduring basis since 1688 but the bulk of male citizens were not granted franchise till 1867. It is worth-noting that in all these systems only male franchise was sought to be introduced. Hence, early democratic systems of modern Western world were at best imperfect expressions of the idea of democracy as they were not based on *universal adult franchise.* Female franchise has been operative in the United States since 1919; in Britain since 1928; in France since 1945; and in Switzerland all women got their right to vote as late as 1971. Thus, even in the Western world, the idea of democracy was materialized only in the twentieth century.

Universal Adult Franchise

Under a democratic system, the provision that each citizen of the state is entitled to vote at the election on attaining the prescribed age (such as 18 years or 21 years)without any discrimination on grounds of gender, race, caste, creed, region, language, culture, etc.

[III]
CONCEPT OF LIBERAL DEMOCRACY

Democracy is an old concept; liberalism is a recent one. Today, liberalism is generally thought to be inseparable from democracy so much so that the term 'democracy' is applied to refer to 'liberal democracy' unless otherwise specified. But as C.B. Macpherson, in his *Democratic Theory—Essays in Retrieval* (1973), has observed: "Until the nineteenth century, liberal theory, like the liberal state, was not at all democratic, much of it was specifically antidemocratic." Classical liberal theory was committed to individual's right to unlimited acquisition of property and to the capitalist market economy which implies inequality not only in the economic sphere but in the political sphere also. Thus, classical liberalism of the eighteenth and nineteenth centuries insisted on property qualification for the right-to-vote. This was contrary to the democratic principle which implies equal entitlement of each individual not only in the matter of choosing a government but also to other advantages accruing from organized social life.

But a combination of the two antithetical principles—liberalism and democracy—became inevitable in a later phase because of historical reasons. Classical liberalism fostered capitalism and free-market economy which were responsible for large-scale industrialization and urbanization. This gave rise to a large working class centred in large industrial cities and forced to live under sub-human conditions created by a cruel, competitive economy. In due course, this class became conscious of its strength and insisted on a voice at the decision-making level. Thus, the liberal state was forced to accommodate democratic principles in order to save its own existence. The outcome of this combination appeared in the form of liberal democracy which represents a combination of free-market economy with universal adult franchise. It is an attempt to resolve the conflicting claims of the capitalists and the masses by giving a voice to the ordinary people at the decision-making level.

Liberal democracy today is distinguished from other forms of political system by certain principles and characteristics, that is its procedure and institutional arrangements. Institutions are necessary for the realization of principles; without principles, the institutions might be reduced to a mere formality. The two must go together.

PRINCIPLES OF LIBERAL DEMOCRACY

Liberal democracy works on certain principles and certain mechanisms. Broadly speaking, principles of liberal democracy include: (*a*) Government by consent; (*b*) Public accountability; (*c*) Majority rule; (*d*) Recognition of minority rights; and (*e*) Constitutional Government.

Government by Consent

Democracy is a government by consent of the people. Rational consent can be obtained by persuasion for which an atmosphere of free discussion is essential. Any regime where the consent of the people is sought to be obtained without freedom of expression of divergent opinions, does not qualify for being called a 'democracy' even if it maintains certain democratic institutions.

In view of the highly technical nature, the large volume and urgency of governmental decisions, it is impractical to consult the people on every detail of every policy. However, discussion of the broad issues is indispensable. Discussion is usually held at two levels: (*a*) among the representatives of the people in the legislative assemblies where members of the opposition have their full say; and (*b*) at the public level where there is direct communication between the leadership and the people. Mass media (newspapers, radio, television, etc.) also serve as effective channels of communication between the leadership and the people. Democratic leadership is expected not to lose touch with popular sentiment on the major outlines of policy as the ruling parties are bound to seek a fresh mandate of the people at regular intervals.

Public Accountability

Liberal democracy, based on the consent of the people, must constantly remain answerable to the people who created it. John Locke (1632-1704) who thought of government as a 'trustee' of the power vested in it by the people for the protection of their natural right to life, liberty and property, nevertheless, felt that it could not be fully trusted. He wanted the people to remain constantly vigilant. *Locke thought of the people as a householder who appoints a nightwatchman for protecting his house, and then, he himself keeps awake to keep a watch on the watchman!* Jeremy Bentham (1748-1832) envisaged liberal democracy as a political apparatus that would ensure the accountability of the governors to the governed. For Bentham, both governors and the governed, as human beings, want to maximize their happiness. Then governors, who are endowed with power, may tend to abuse it in their self-interest. Hence, in order to prevent the abuse of their power, governors should be directly accountable to an electorate who will frequently check whether their objectives have been reasonably met.

John Stuart Mill (1806-73), in his brilliant essay On *Liberty* (1859), declared the aim of his work to elaborate and defend a principle which will establish 'the nature and limits of the power which can be legitimately exercised by society over the individual'. He significantly observed that 'the only purpose for which power can be rightfully exercised over any member of a civilized community, against his will, is to prevent harm to others'. Mill identified the appropriate region of human liberty as including liberty of thought, feeling, discussion and publication, liberty of tastes and pursuits, and liberty of association or combination, provided it causes no harm to others. He asserted that liberty and democracy, taken together, create the possibility of 'human excellence'. In his view, a system of representative democracy makes government accountable to the citizenry and creates wiser citizens capable of pursuing the public interest.

Jean-Jaques Rousseau (1712-78), the exponent of popular sovereignty, postulated public accountability of government in a different way. In his concept of the 'social contract', sovereignty not only originates in the people, it continues to stay with the people in the civil society. People give their consent to vest their sovereignty in the 'general will' which coincides with their own higher self. As a votary of 'direct democracy', Rousseau is convinced that sovereignty cannot be represented. In his words, "The people's deputies are not, and could not be, its representatives; they are merely its agents; and they cannot decide anything finally" (*The Social Contract;* 1762). Rousseau commended an active, involved citizenry in the process of government and law-making. He wanted that all citizens should meet together to decide what is best for the community and enact the appropriate laws.

Rousseau was in favour of a political system in which legislative and executive functions should be clearly demarcated. While he wanted the people themselves to constitute the legislative assembly, the executive function was to be left to the government. In his own words, "The people require a government to coordinate public meetings, serve as a means of communication, draft laws and enforce the legal system" (*ibid.*). Such government shall be constantly accountable to the people for fulfilling the instructions of 'the general will'. Should it fail to fulfil this obligation, it can be revoked and replaced.

Majority Rule

In modern representative democracies, decisions are taken in several bodies—legislatures, committees, cabinets and executive or regulative bodies. Majority rule means that in all these decision-making bodies, from the electorate to the last committee, the issues are to be resolved by voting. Political equality is secured by the principle of 'one man, one vote', which implies that there will be no privileged sections claiming special weightage, nor any underprivileged sections whose voice is ignored. No discrimination is allowed on grounds of religion, race, caste, sex, place of birth, ownership of property, and even educational qualifications. Any restriction of suffrage should be based on a sound reason, that is where the ballot cannot be used in a rational and responsible manner, such as in the case of convicted criminals, the mentally deranged, and those below the legally fixed age.

The principle of majority rule relies on the wisdom of the majority. Minority opinion has the option to enlist the support of larger numbers by persuasion in an atmosphere of free discussion.

Recognition of Minority Rights

The principle of majority rule by no means allows the suppression of minorities. In modern nation-states, there may be several racial, religious, linguistic or cultural minorities who fear discrimination or the tyranny of majority. Minority grievances may take many forms ranging from psychological insults over discrimination in housing, education and employment to physical persecution and genocide. Legal safeguards are, therefore, considered essential for the realization of the democratic principle because their presence helps to raise the level of awareness of both majority and minority and thus promote a favourable climate for democratic politics.

Constitutional Government

Constitutional government means a 'government by laws' rather than by men. Democracy requires an infinitely complex machinery of processes, procedures and institutions to translate the majority will into action. It makes enormous demands on the time, goodwill and integrity of its citizens and public servants. Once the prescribed procedure is set aside, even for a legitimate purpose, it can set a precedent that may be followed for pursuing illegitimate purposes, and the flood-gates of corruption might be thrown wide open. It is, therefore, essential to have a well-established tradition of law and constitution for the stability of a democratic government.

These five principles throw sufficient light on the nature of liberal democracy.

MECHANISM OF LIBERAL DEMOCRACY

Once certain principles of liberal democracy are accepted, the next step is to identify the mechanism that puts these principles into practice. This would enable us to distinguish a liberal-democratic system from other political systems, *viz.* totalitarian and autocratic systems. Champions of liberal democracy recognize certain institutions and procedures as essential characteristics of democracy. The presence or absence of these characteristics will determine whether a system is democratic or not. They firmly believe that a government can be conducted according to will of the people only by adherence to these institutions and procedures. Any other system may have many qualities but it will not qualify as a democracy without these characteristics. The main characteristics of liberal democracy may be enumerated as follows:

More than One Political Party Freely Competing for Political Power

Liberal democracy seeks reconciliation between varying interests and ideologies of different groups. There is no fixed method of securing this reconciliation. When there is a free competition between more than one political parties for power, the people get an opportunity to consider various alternative policies, programmes and personalities to exercise their choice. According to this test, single-party systems do not qualify as democracies. The former Soviet Union and the present People's Republic of China cannot be treated as democracies as they conceded monopoly of power to their respective Communist Parties, in spite of a façade of periodic elections. Liberal democracy requires open competition for power between different political parties on the basis of established and accepted form of procedure.

Political Offices Not Confined to any Privileged Class

In a liberal democracy, a political office or public office can be acquired only through the support of the people, not by birth, tradition or anybody's favour. This feature of democracy distinguishes it from feudalism, monarchy and despotism, etc. In a democracy, all citizens enjoy equal rights and status. Any citizen can have access to political office by following the prescribed procedure and fulfilling certain conditions. Political office can be held only for a limited period which must be relinquished on completion of one's term or other exigency, such as dissolution of the legislature, one's own resignation, etc. Some qualifications, such as age, education, etc. may be prescribed for the candidates of a political office, but nobody can be declared unfit for any office on grounds of caste, creed, sex, language, region, etc. However, in order to secure due representation for all strata of the population, some seats in the decision-making bodies can be reserved for minorities or weaker sections. It is believed that such provision would strengthen democracy rather than weaken it.

Periodic Elections Based on Universal Adult Franchise

Since representative government is the only practicable method of establishing democracy in the present-day world, periodic elections become necessary for this purpose. Each citizen should have the right to vote on attaining the prescribed age (say, 18 years); nobody should be disqualified on grounds of caste, creed, sex, language, region, etc. Voting should be secret so that each citizen can exercise his or her right in this respect without fear or favour. It is true that the principle of universal adult franchise was introduced in modern democracies only gradually, but today it is regarded a necessary condition of democracy.

Periodic elections require that the people's representatives should be chosen for a limited period (say four or five years) so that the party that comes to power is able to implement its policy and programme, but it is obliged to seek renewal of the people's confidence to continue in power. At the same time, the opposition should have an opportunity to bring any shortcomings of the ruling party to the notice of the people, to offer alternative policy and programme with a view to winning the next election.

Protection of Civil Liberties

Protection of civil liberties, such as freedom of thought and expression, freedom of religion, freedom of assembly and association, and personal freedom, *i.e.* freedom from arbitrary arrest, is an essential characteristic of liberal democracy. On the one hand, these freedoms enable the citizens to form interest groups and other organizations to influence government decisions; on the other hand, they ensure independence of the mass media, particularly the press, from government control. Without civil liberties, will of the people cannot be translated into public policy and decision. Civil liberties, therefore, constitute the core of democracy.

Interest Groups

In a liberal democracy, interest groups refer to the groups of people who organize themselves for pursuing their specific, collective interest. They try to serve their interest through obtaining the support of public opinion by publicizing their viewpoint widely, and pleading to government to mould its policy to suit their interest. Examples of interest groups are: trade unions, lawyers associations and chambers of commerce and industry.

Independence of the Judiciary

Freedom of the people cannot be secured if the powers of governance are concentrated in any one organ. Liberal democracy, therefore, insists on the separation of powers between different organs of government. While the executive and the legislature might become interdependent in a parliamentary government, the judiciary must be kept independent of both. While the legislature and the executive in a democracy are dominated by politicians, judges are appointed on merit and they cannot be removed from office in consequence of sudden changes in the political climate of the country. Independence of judiciary enables judges to pronounce their verdict without fear or favour. This strengthens faith of the people in the regime and ensures continuity and stability of the judicial procedure.

CONCLUSION

The above conditions must be fulfilled in a liberal democracy under the normal circumstances. However, some flexibility in these conditions may be conceded under special circumstances, such as emergency. In any case, mere fulfilment of these conditions should not lead us to complacency. In a developing nation like India, an apparent democratic structure may suffer from several inner distortions. For instance, the existence of more than one political party competing for political power may simply involve conflict and competition between certain dominant and vocal interests, such as large manufacturers, big businessmen, rich peasants and landlords, for acquiring a hold on political power rather than for serving the public interest more effectively. Similarly, vested interests may try to foster a feudal political culture among the people so as to reduce them to submissive voters rather than vehicles of social change. Again, there may be no formal restriction on entry to positions of political power, but in actual practice, these positions may remain the sole preserve of a tiny class. Then there may be complete freedom of the press, but the press might be owned exclusively by big business houses who may use it for moulding public opinion so as to serve their vested interests. Also, the freedom of expression might become redundant because of vast illiteracy, mass ignorance, widespread superstitions, abject poverty and general apathy of the people. It is also possible that the judiciary is independent of both the executive and the legislature, but some judges might uphold the values of a bourgeois society and thus dispense a distorted form of justice.

In a nutshell, the mere structure of a liberal democracy is no guarantee of achieving the objectives of democracy. In any case, the prolonged practice of following democratic procedure may create greater political awareness among the people and a general transformation of the attitudes of power-holders.

[IV]
PROBLEMS OF REPRESENTATION

Modern democracy largely works through its representative institutions. In order to understand its working it is essential, at the outset, to distinguish between direct and indirect democracy.

DIRECT AND INDIRECT DEMOCRACY

Direct democracy means the rule by the people of a state, town or other political community by means of direct participation in the management of public affairs. Some examples of direct democracy are found in ancient Greek city-states, some of ancient Indian republics, new English townships, British parish meetings, etc. This system can obviously operate in an area having a small number of citizens who can periodically meet at one place. It is not practicable in the large states of modern times. Today we, therefore, have 'indirect democracy' or 'representative democracy' where government is conducted by the representatives of the people, who are elected at regular intervals. In modern times, the term 'democracy' is used as a synonym of 'representative democracy', unless otherwise indicated.

TYPES OF REPRESENTATION: TERRITORIAL AND FUNCTIONAL

In a representative democracy, elections are usually held on the basis of universal adult franchise. It means that each man or woman, after attaining the prescribed age (such as 18 years or 21 years) is entitled to vote in the general election, without any discrimination on grounds of gender, caste, creed, region, language, culture, etc. All voters of a community are collectively described as the electorate. Now the question arises: on what basis should the electorate choose its representative? This gives rise to two alternative systems of representation: (*a*) Territorial representation, and (*b*) Functional representation.

Under territorial or geographic representation, the whole country is divided into geographical areas of nearly equal population, which are called constituencies. Voters of each constituency are entitled to elect their representative or representatives. With the growth of population or variation in its composition, boundaries of different constituencies may be required to be redrawn from time to time. It is imperative to ensure that any changes in these boundaries do not result in advantage or disadvantage to any political party. This system is simple and convenient. It enables the electorate to know their representative more closely. However, sometimes it may lead to undue prominence of local issues relegating national issues to the background.

Territorial representation system is apparently based on the assumption that each constituency has a uniform interest. But in the contemporary world, population is nowhere divided in this manner. A constituency may include peasants, workers, traders, industrialists, teachers, doctors, lawyers and other occupational groups. In order to take care of the diverse interests of these different types of groups, a case is sometimes made for introducing functional representation. Functional representation implies that the people belonging to different occupations or functions should be allowed to elect their representatives on functional basis. These representatives should vote on issues relating to their specific functions. For instance, those belonging to industry should vote on industrial policy; those belonging to agriculture should vote on agricultural policy; they need not be consulted on matters pertaining to education or foreign policy. Champions of functional representation argue that the representative of a particular territory cannot take care of the interests of all sections of people living in that territory. So the people should send their representatives to decision-making bodies on the basis of their specific economic and professional interests, and not on a territorial basis. Thus, guild socialists of Britain have been strong supporters of occupational representation.

However, in actual practice, functional representation has largely been tried under totalitarian systems, particularly in pursuance of corporatism. As David Robertson has illustrated: "Corporatism... found a political expression, more façade than reality, in the fascist institutions of the 1930s and 1940s... In Spain and Italy legislative assemblies and councils of the state were therefore organized around such trade corporations rather than around geographical constituencies and the 'capricious' functioning of competitive elections. The convenience of corporatist theory from a fascist point of view was evident: it by-passed both class-conflict and democratic elections" (*The Penguin Dictionary of Politics;* 1984).

Democratic systems have largely relied on territorial representation although in the process of decision-making the representatives of specific economic and professional interests are also usually consulted.

THEORIES OF REPRESENTATION

What should be the role of representatives of the people in the process of policy-making? Are they authorized to control the entire process or should they perform a limited function in this behalf? These questions have been answered differently by different theories of representation.

Reactionary Theory of Representation

Its chief exponents are Thomas Hobbes (1588-1679) and Alexander Hamilton (1756-1804). It insists on the need for order and authority which are best maintained by the executive and the parliament. Hobbes particularly eulogized the authority of the monarch. The reactionary theory largely banks on superior knowledge and wisdom of the politicians who are regarded as the best custodians of public interest. People's representatives have a very limited role in this scheme of things—to convey the popular feelings for their consideration and decision. It is, in fact, an elitist theory with no provision of public control.

Hobbes defined representation as acting in the name of another who has authorized the action. So when a representative is authorized to act on behalf of the represented, the latter is bound to accept the consequences of this act. When people authorize a sovereign (by means of the social contract) to act on their behalf, they make him their unlimited representative. This gives rise to absolute sovereignty. The rights once surrendered to the sovereign cannot be withdrawn. It is hoped that the sovereign will always take care of the public interest.

This theory is democratic only so long as it accepts the primacy of public interest in policy-making. But it is undemocratic in practice because it sets aside the democratic procedure.

Conservative Theory of Representation

Its chief exponents are Edmund Burke (1729-97) and James Madison (1751-1836). It is more progressive than the reactionary theory because it grants a measure of public control without encouraging popular participation in the process of government. It is also an elitist theory because it allows people to choose their representatives from an *elite* group. People are free to convey their feelings to their representatives but they must bank on the good sense of these representatives rather than issuing them any instructions. However, if these representatives fail to satisfy them, they can be replaced by other suitable members of the elite group at the next election.

Burke defined the role and duties of a parliamentary representative to put 'great weight' on the wishes of his constituents and listen to their opinions. However, he did not want him to receive instructions from his constituents, but to exercise his own judgement. Burke argued that if a representative surrendered his own judgement to people's opinion, he would betray instead of serving them.

Liberal Theory of Representation

Its chief exponents are John Locke (1632-1704) and Thomas Jefferson (1743-1826). It exemplifies the true spirit of democracy. It upholds equality of all people who are endowed with equal capability to rule. The liberal theory banks on the wisdom of the masses and treats their representatives only as their agents or messengers. In its view, representatives of the people are their true representatives. Instead of using their own judgement, they must translate the judgement of their constituents into concrete policy proposals.

Locke not only wanted that a government should rule with the consent of the people, but also argued that no taxes could be imposed on the owners of property until they themselves agree, either personally or through their representatives. In short, a representative is ultimately accountable to his constituents. He has no special rights or powers, but only special obligations.

Radical Theory of Representation

Its chief exponents are Jean-Jaques Rousseau (1712-78) and the New Left. This theory holds wisdom of the people in highest esteem and goes to the extent of deprecating representative government itself. It holds that wisdom of the people is bound to be diluted through the process of representation. It, therefore, exalts direct democracy as the only truly democratic form of government.

> **New Left**
>
> 'New left' is a general term applied to a variety of political doctrines and social movements which emerged in late 1950s, particularly after the 1956 uprising in Hungary. It originally arose against the Soviet hegemony over the international communist movement and grew stronger in 1960s, particularly in opposition to the American intervention in Vietnam and the military occupation of Czechoslovakia by Soviet Union-backed East European countries. Eventually it came to embrace the intellectuals of varied origins including dissident communists, anarchists, left-wing socialists and cultural critics.

Rousseau argued that so-called representative institutions only substitute the will of a few people for that of the whole community. He concluded that voters are free only at the moment of elections. As soon as they are formally represented, they are once more subjected to an alien will. Rousseau held that participation in self-government is intrinsically valuable, not just instrumentally. People would remain free only when they are politically involved and active throughout; functioning of representative institutions has come to discourage active citizenship.

CONCLUSION

It may be observed that the reactionary theory of representation relegates representation to marginal importance; the conservative theory erodes the spirit of democracy by overemphasizing the gap between *elites* and the masses. The radical theory claims to be most progressive as it pays highest importance to the people, but it tends to rule out representation itself. Hence, the liberal theory of representation may be treated as most logical and in consonance with the spirit of representative democracy.

[V]
ELECTORAL SYSTEMS

In a representative democracy, election is the process by which the members of a community or organization choose one or more persons to exercise authority on their behalf. The provision of election in a democracy is intended to ensure that the government will exercise its powers with the consent of the governed. In other words, election lends legitimacy to the authority of the government. This source of legitimacy is regarded so important in the modern age that some non-democratic or totalitarian systems also try to legitimize their authority through the façade of elections.

The real test of a genuine election is whether the voters have real alternatives before them for exercising their choice or not. On the contrary, in a non-democratic system, such as the former Soviet Union, elections were held but the voter had to vote for or against a single candidate, nominated by the Communist Party. In late 1980s when independent candidates were allowed to contest elections along with party-nominated candidates, the totalitarian system itself began to disintegrate.

Secret ballot is particularly important in democratic elections. When a voter votes in secrecy, he or she can exercise his or her choice without fear or favour. Where there is open voting, such as by voice or by raising hands, a voter will not feel as secure as in the case of secret voting.

An electoral system refers to the method by which: (*a*) a voter is required to indicate his or her choice of a candidate or political party out of those contesting in the election; and (*b*) the votes obtained by a candidate or political party are translated into allocation of seats or offices. When the number of qualified candidate or candidates in a constituency is equal to the number of offices or seats provided in that constituency, that candidate or candidates are declared unanimously elected. But where the number of candidates exceeds the number of seats, voting becomes necessary. The result of voting is determined according to the prevailing electoral system. Actual types of electoral systems are legion. Broadly speaking, three types of electoral systems may be identified as widely prevalent under democratic systems: (*a*) Plurality system; (*b*) Majoritarian system; and (*c*) Proportional representation. Of these, the first two are applied in single-member constituencies while the third is applied in multi-member constituencies.

Plurality System

Under plurality system, technically an election may be won by a simple majority. If there are only two candidates in the field for one seat, there will be no problem in deciding the winner. When there are three or more candidates in a single-member constituency, and the voter is required to vote for one candidate only, the rule of 'first past the post' is sought to be applied to decide the election. It implies that any candidate obtaining the largest number of votes will be declared elected. It is not necessary for him or her to secure a clear majority, that is more than 50% of the total number of valid votes. This practice is widely followed. Thus, the elections held for the British House of Commons, American House of Representatives, Indian House of the People (Lok Sabha) and Legislative Assemblies are based on this system. Its opponents argue that this practice is not fair to the minorities in multicultural societies where their candidates might lose election in most of the constituencies by a small margin.

Again, under the plurality system, the votes scored by different political parties might not correspond to the number of seats won by them in the legislature.

The advocates of this system, however, contend that this system promotes two-party system which results in a balance between the ruling party and the opposition. It makes the majority sensitive towards the minorities, and encourages major political parties to accommodate the interests and viewpoints of the minorities. Simultaneously, it prevents separatist tendencies among the minorities and motivates them to join the national mainstream. Above all, it provides for a relatively stable and effective government.

Majoritarian System

Under majoritarian system, a candidate is usually required to obtain an absolute majority, that is more than 50% of the valid votes cast, to win the election. If there are only two candidates in the field for one seat, there will be no problem in deciding the winner. But when there are three or more contestants in a single-member constituency, and no candidate wins an absolute majority, some method must be evolved to decide the winner. According to the prevalent practice, two methods can be adopted for this purpose:

(*a*) *Alternative Vote:* Under this system, a voter is required to indicate his order of preference for different candidates, that is he or she would mark 1, 2, 3 and so on against the names of different candidates according to his or her order of preference. If no candidate gets absolute majority of first-preference votes, the candidate who gets the least number of first-preferences, is eliminated, and the next preferences of his or her voters are added to the first-preferences of other candidates. This process is repeated till some candidate gets absolute majority who is declared elected. This system is adopted for election to the Australian Lower House as well as for elections of the American and Indian Presidents.

(*b*) *Second Ballot System:* Under this system, a voter is required to vote for one candidate only. If no candidate is able to obtain absolute majority, second ballot is held to decide the winner. Again, several methods may be adopted for this purpose. Thus, for the election of the French President, when such a situation arises, second ballot is held between the two candidates who obtained the largest and the next largest number of votes in the first ballot. Then, for election to the French Assembly, if no candidate is able to secure an absolute majority in the first ballot, then a second ballot is held among those political parties who have obtained 12.5% votes or more of the registered electorate, and then the candidate obtaining the largest number of votes is declared elected. Under this system, constituencies are drawn on a geographical basis on the lines of plurality system; hence this may suffer from the same disadvantages as noticed in the case of the plurality system.

Proportional Representation

This system is particularly adopted in multi-member constituencies in order to secure a fair representation for the minorities as well as the majority. It is a complex system which may be implemented by several methods. Of these, two are most prevalent:

(*a*) *List System:* Under this system, the ballot contains separate lists of candidates of different political parties; the voter is required to mark one list according to his or her choice. In some systems, the voter is allowed to alter the content, the order, or both, of the list itself. Various complicated methods of calculation of seats per list are used. The list system is employed in voting for national elections in Germany, the Italian Chamber of Deputies, the Knesset of Israel, the Swiss National Council, and the legislature of Finland, etc.

(*b*) *Single Transferable Vote:* Under this system, a voter is required to indicate his or her order of preference against the names of different candidates. For each constituency, a quota is set which is usually equal to the total number of valid votes cast, divided by one more than the number of seats available, plus one vote. A candidate who obtains first-preferences equal to the electoral quota or more, is declared elected. His or her 'surplus votes' (that is first-preferences over and above the electoral quota) are redistributed among those candidates whom these voters had given their next preference in proportion to the number of second-preferences obtained by each of such candidates. The candidate obtaining the least number of first-preferences is eliminated and the next preferences of his or her voters are added to the first-preferences of other candidates. This process of redistribution from both sides is repeated till the number of candidates securing the electoral quota equals the number of seats available, who are then declared elected. This system has been used in the national elections of Irish Republic and Malta. Single Transferable Vote system is largely used in multi-member constituencies whereas its elementary version—Alternative Vote system is used in single-member constituencies.

Single Transferable Vote System

$$\text{Electoral Quota} = \frac{\text{No. of Valid Votes Cast}}{\text{No. of Seats to be Filled} + 1} + 1$$

The system of proportional representation has a unique advantage: it enables due representation of all types of groups, such as ethnic groups, women, different interests and ideologies. But it has a disadvantage also. If a nation is deeply divided into different social, economic, racial, religious, linguistic, cultural and regional groups, proportional representation would hardly result in clear majority in the legislature. Coalition government, formed as a result of bargaining between different groups in the legislature, is bound to prove unstable and ineffective. Secondly, provision of proportional representation would encourage formation of political parties on the basis of narrow, sectional interests rather than on the basis of larger national interest representing reconciliation of conflicting group interests. On the whole, this system is not conducive to national integration.

Ethnic Group

Ethnic group refers to a social group whose members identify themselves as a particular group on the basis of similar physical features and similar cultural traits (including language, religion, dress code, etc.), feel unity among themselves, and distinguish themselves from other similar groups.

[VI]
METHODS OF MINORITY REPRESENTATION

The system of proportional representation may solve the problem of minority representation to some extent, but it hardly provides for a final solution in a complex situation. Some other devices have, therefore, been worked out for solving this problem. Of these, two are most important: (*a*) Concurrent majority; and (*b*) Consociational democracy.

CONCURRENT MAJORITY

In the United States, during the first half of the nineteenth century, an acrimonious debate ensued between the North and the South on the question of the abolition of slavery. The South was dependent on the plantation economy for which it pleaded for the continuance of slavery. But the North was advancing on the road to industrialization; it wanted the abolition of slavery to ensure the supply of workers for the newly set up industries. The North enjoyed majority in the American Congress, hence it was most likely to win its case. At this juncture, John C. Calhon (1782-1850), an eloquent spokesman of the South, advanced the principle of concurrent majority with a view to safeguarding the interests of the South which was in minority. In essence, this meant that *any decision should be treated as valid only when due concurrence of all the important sectional interests effected by it has been obtained.* It implied that if the government of a country takes a decision on the basis of numerical majority, the minority affected by that decision should have the power to veto that decision. So Calhon proposed to replace the prevalent federal system of the United States by a constitutional structure wherein each of the important economic, functional or regional interests of the country would have the right to indicate its organ of self-expression, and concurrence of all these organs would become necessary for every important decision.

In America, this proposal was never accepted, but this principle is often invoked on the question of the role of minority in the decision-making process. Again, the right to veto has been provided in the decision-making process of the Security Council of the United Nations as well as in the European Economic Community. This type of provision is indicative of a favourable attitude towards the principle of concurrent majority.

CONSOCIATIONAL DEMOCRACY

This system involves an elaborate arrangement to ensure minority representation. It is regarded particularly suitable for the governance of the societies which are deeply divided by religious, ideological, linguistic, regional, cultural, racial or ethnic differences. It involves four basic principles. Of these, the first two are of primary importance and the last two are secondary:

(1) *Executive Power Sharing:* It entails a grand coalition of the representatives of all significant segments. Alternatively, the presidency and other high offices may be reserved for different segments of society;

(2) *Greater Autonomy of Different Segments:* It implies that decisions on all issues of common concern should be made jointly by the representatives of all important segments; on other issues concerning particular segments, decision-making should be left to the concerned segment. If these segments are geographically distributed, 'federalism' is the most suitable arrangement; otherwise, segmental autonomy should mainly take a non-territorial form;

(3) *Proportionality:* Under this provision allocation of political offices, administrative appointments and public funds is to be made in proportion to the population of each segment; and finally,

(4) *Minority Veto:* It is the ultimate weapon for the minority segments to protect their vital interests. It is possible that the minority participating in a coalition may be outvoted by the majority on an issue involving its vital interest. In such a case, the right to veto may be invoked by the minority for the protection of its position.

Consociational democracy has been tried in many parts of the world. For instance, in Austria, Catholic and Socialist parties formed a coalition from 1945 to 1966; in Netherlands, this principle was adopted from 1917 to 1967; and in Lebanon, consociational democracy remained operative from 1943 to 1957. In fact, consociational democracy provides for a working government in a society sharply divided by multifarious interests. However, in order to promote a true understanding and cooperation among various segments, it is necessary to resolve their differences at the intellectual and emotional levels.

[VII]

CONDITIONS FOR SUCCESSFUL WORKING OF DEMOCRACY

Democracy as a form of government cannot function properly unless it is supported by suitable socio-economic and cultural factors. It is interesting to recall that Alexis de Tocqueville (1805-59), famous French writer, in his notable work *Democracy in America* (1835-40), tried to enumerate the principal causes which tended to maintain the democratic structure in the United States. His list included not only the constitutional structure but also: (*a*) the absence of a large military establishment; (*b*) equality in social and economic conditions; (*c*) a prosperous agricultural economy; and (*d*) the mores, customs and religious beliefs of Americans. For our purpose, this list should be treated only as illustrative and by no means exhaustive or authoritative. Conditions in America have thoroughly changed since de Tocqueville wrote about America. His list may now be modified as follows so as to reflect the contemporary conditions: (*a*) primacy of civil authority over military power; (*b*) larger equality in social and economic conditions; (*c*) a prosperous agricultural and industrial economy; and (*d*) a democratic culture or mode of thought.

In the contemporary world, democracy has been adopted as a form of government in a large number of countries. It is not equally successful everywhere. The successful working of democracy depends upon many conditions. Some of the important conditions may be described as follows:

NATIONAL SENTIMENT

Some thinkers have pointed out that national homogeneity is an essential condition for the success of democracy. For instance, John Stuart Mill (1806-73), in his *Representative Government* (1861), suggested that a mono-national state is essential for the success of democracy. A large number of states have emerged on the globe since J.S. Mill wrote his *Representative Government.* Most of these states include people belonging to different races, religions, languages and cultures. Democracy is working successfully in many of these states. What is therefore needed for the success of democracy is not the uniformity of the people as a nationality but the sense of belonging to a single nation, inspired by the feeling of having a common history, common way of life in the present and a common future as also a common centre of loyalty.

SPIRIT OF TOLERATION

True national sentiment cannot be created without the spirit of toleration. In fact, the spirit of toleration is the keynote of democracy. In a democracy, we do not demand conformity nor assimilation, but different groups are expected to coexist in spite of their differences. We are free to win others by persuation and discussion, not by force or blackmail. The minority is expected to respect the majority; the majority is expected to accommodate minority with full dignity.

Assimilation

Assimilation refers to the process whereby a dominant group imposes its culture so effectively on subordinate groups that they lose their own identity and become virtually indistinguishable from the dominant culture.

Democracy means tolerance, tolerance not merely of those who agree with us, but of those who do not agree with us.

Jawaharlal Nehru

HIGH MORAL CHARACTER

High moral character of the people as well as leaders is another condition for the success of democracy. If people are led by their narrow selfish interests, or leaders are led by mere opportunism, democracy is bound to give way to demagogy, that is the practice of leaders playing with the emotions of the people instead of appealing to reason. On the contrary, a sense of morality and discipline will make the people active in solving social problems more effectively.

WIDESPREAD EDUCATION

An educated electorate is an asset to democracy. Generally the people should be literate if not highly educated so that they are able to learn more and exercise their judgement in the matters of common concern. Free access to the media of mass communication is provided within the democratic structure itself. Only a literate, preferably an educated, electorate can make best use of this facility. For the fulfilment of this condition, the state itself should provide for universal education.

ECONOMIC SECURITY AND EQUALITY

Lack of economic security in the masses is bound to undermine the people's faith in democracy. Similarly, vast economic disparities are bound to destroy the sense of equal dignity of individuals. In fact, democracy without a reasonable level of economic security and equality is a farce.

CONCLUSION

Of all forms of government, democracy alone is meant to serve the cause of the people directly. However, the democratic process calls for a good deal of patience not only at the level of policy-making, but also at the level of policy-implementation. This may not be found to be very effective during the times of crises. It is, therefore, essential that the provision for a temporary suspension of the democratic process during an emergency, and suitable checks against arbitrary use of power should be made within a democratic constitution itself. Moreover, today democracy is regarded not only a form of government, but as a way of life. That is why there is demand for *democratization* at all levels, including factory, office, school and family.

Democratization

Democratization refers to the process whereby those affected by particular institutional decisions are assured to have their say or representation at the decision-making level. This process may be applied in any political, administrative or social institution. For example, democratization implies that members of a political party should have an effective say in drawing out policy and programme of their party; women's organizations should be consulted while making any law affecting women; teachers' and students' organizations should be consulted during the formulation of educational policy; and workers' organizations should have full say in determining the conditions of work as well as in the management of their respective spheres of work.

[VIII]
DEMOCRACY AS A WAY OF LIFE

Conventional exponents of democracy largely treated it as a form of government. Champions of liberal democracy focus on politics as a process of group conflict, party competition and struggle for power, which are sought to be resolved through democratic method. However, some philosophers have tried to shift their focus from this process to the analysis of democracy as a way of life. John Dewey (1859-1952), an American philosopher, is the chief representative of this school of thought.

Dewey's alternative theory of democracy seeks to connect it with the process of how people form judgements, communicate with each other, and come together to solve problems. In his celebrated work *Democracy and Education* (1961), Dewey sought to compare democratic method to the scientific method in which public is conceived as a community of inquirers trying to solve their common problems. Freedom of speech, elections and other democratic institutions maintained by liberal democracy enable people to adopt rational attitudes in politics. A successful democratic politics does not depend on the judgement of each citizen considered separately. When people arrive at the judgement through their constant interaction, their decision is likely to prove sufficiently sound.

> A democracy is more than a form of government; it is primarily a mode of associated living, of conjoint communicated experience.
>
> John Dewey

> The method of democracy is to bring. . . conflicts out into the open where their special claims can be seen and appraised, where they can be discussed and judged.
>
> John Dewey

Dewey defines democracy as a process whereby the majority is formed, particularly through free communication and free association between citizens. When citizens communicate, talk, share their ideas and try them out so as to test their consequences, a democratic public comes into existence in the real sense of the term. In short, the scientific method of inquiry, communication and experimentation before arriving at the conclusion is the hallmark of a democratic public arriving at a judgement about public issues.

Dewey held that the creation of the democratic public was best accomplished in small groups which allowed close communication between their members and coordination in the process of arriving at collective judgement. He argued that membership of voluntary associations and local communities could help individuals to become democratic citizens. But the increasing industrialization, urbanization, geographical mobility and the growth of the state pose a serious challenge to the development of democracy as a way of life. However, its message is clear: We should organize our society into small, coherent communities to give effect to the democratic principle. This corresponds to the current slogan of the environmentalists: *Small is beautiful.*

> Democracy is the art of thinking independently together.
>
> Alexander Meiklejohn

Another implication of treating democracy as a way of life is associated with the demand of *democratization* at all levels, such as in political parties, industrial management as well as university administration. This means that those affected by particular institutional decisions should have their say or representation at the decision-making level. Thus, the members of a political party should have an effective say in drawing out policy and programme of their party; workers should have effective say in deciding production policy and industrial management. Similarly, teachers and students should have a say in deciding the educational policy. In short, democracy as a way of life requires the end of authoritarianism at all levels, including school and family level. This does not mean the end of guidance and supervision by the superiors, but only that the decision should be taken in consultation with and with the consent of those affected by such decision.

Authoritarianism

Authoritarianism refers to a social and political outlook that requires everybody and everything to conform to an established order, *i.e.* to act according to the directions of the person or group who is recognized as the guardian of that order. Authoritarianism rules out the need to obtain explicit or tacit consent of those affected by a decision. It does not permit ordinary people to express their independent opinions, demands or preferences. Neither does it envisage any accountability of power-holders to public opinion, nor any role of public discussion or popular voting in the process of public decision-making.

[IX]
SIGNIFICANCE OF MULTICULTURALISM

The concept of multiculturalism is closely related to the functioning of democracy. When we seek to establish true democracy in a multicultural society, understanding the principle of multiculturalism would prove to be of a great help. Multiculturalism has emerged as an important principle of politics in recent decades throughout the world. Majority of the nations of the world today consist of multicultural societies. In other words, they include people who belong to diverse cultural as well as ethnic groups. Apart from differences in their traditional cultures, some groups have evolved certain non-conventional intellectual and sexual perspectives. Black aesthetics, lesbian and gay pride movements are the case in point. All such groups demand due recognition as normal components of society. The principle of multiculturalism not only extends due recognition to all such diverse groups, it also concedes that none of the cultural perspectives can be treated as inherently superior or inferior to others.

Black Aesthetics

Black aesthetics refers to the set of standards of beauty and art forms as prevalent in the culture of the black races. Historically, white races had managed to gain dominant position in the world; their standards of beauty and art were projected as universal standards. Now black races have not only achieved independence, they have also shown that they are no less intelligent, talented and competent, their aesthetic standards are no longer considered as inferior to those of the white races.

Multiculturalism enables different cultures within a community to flourish and treat each other with mutual respect. Some writers have argued that this is a necessary condition of individual's freedom. Thus, Joseph Raz ('Multiculturalism: A Liberal Perspective', *Dissent,* 1994) observed that individual's autonomy is intimately tied up with access to his culture. It enables him to make good choices befitting a good life if his culture is flourishing and getting respect from others. Hence, the sense of identity is closely linked with individual's self-fulfilment.

The search for identity has become a popular theme of modern literature. The concept of identity in psychological as well as sociological sense seeks to link inner world of the individual with the outer world. It serves as a bridge between individual's self and the community. *It is now widely experienced that the sense of shared community has largely eroded, leaving modern people without a clear sense of identity.* Modern society, particularly the Western society, is characterized by the absence, breakdown, confusion or conflict of norms. In other words, an individual in this society is not sure about the shared expectation of behaviour—the behaviour that would be considered culturally desirable and appropriate. This state of 'normlessness' in society is known as 'anomie'. This results in 'breakdown of the self' which is the primary theme of many plays and novels written today.

In order to máintain peace and solidarity in a multicultural society, it is necessary that all cultural groups, as defined in the wider sense, get due recognition, enjoy due respect and rights as equal citizens, and get due representation in decision-making bodies. Multiculturalism has emerged as a response to this vital demand. In a nutshell, multiculturalism implies an attitude and policy of accommodating diverse cultural groups within the national mainstream of a country. This involves action at two levels: (*a*) different cultural groups of the country, particularly the dominant cultural group, should cultivate an attitude of toleration and accommodation towards other cultural groups in order to give them a sense of security and dignity; and (*b*) the state should secure their members' equal rights as citizens and provide for their due representation in decision-making bodies. This also implies that the existing method of representation of individuals at political level should be replaced by some method of representation of groups, particularly the cultural groups.

Multiculturalism as well as democracy is the order of the day. A multicultural country that fails to cultivate the spirit of multiculturalism may eventually disintegrate. Fragmentation of Yugoslavia first into Slovenia, Croatia, Macedonia and Bosnia-Herzegovina (1991-92) and later into Serbia, Montenegro (2006) and Kosovo (2008) is the case in point.

Democratic community today has immensely grown in size where small cultural groups live along with big cultural groups. It is necessary to infuse a sense of security among small cultural groups in a multicultural society. *In order to secure social justice, it is necessary that the people belonging to different cultures should be given due representation in decision-making organs of government.*

A CRITICAL APPRAISAL

In short, *the concept of multiculturalism brings out the drawbacks of the contemporary liberal democracies.* In the multicultural societies of today, the normal democratic process would set up majority rule which tends to obliterate the identity of diverse cultural and ethnic groups. *To realize the ideal of true democracy, it is necessary to give due recognition and protection to the cultural traits of diverse groups living together.* This problem is not confined to the American or other Western societies. In a multicultural society like India, it is necessary to maintain the identity of various cultural groups for the realization of democracy and social justice. If the majority itself could absorb the cultural heritage of other groups into its own culture, it would set up a healthy tradition. Those who plead for the so-called 'purification' of Indian culture by insulating it from the influence of 'other' cultures, run the risk of heading for moral degeneration of India.

In any case, too much insistence on 'difference' and rejection of the prevalent norms may result in isolation and deprivation of certain minority groups. Those who reject the 'mainstream' culture and devote all energy to learning their own language and culture may ultimately realize that they are unfit to find employment, business opportunities or professional avenues in society. It must be remembered that 'mainstream' culture is not always the 'dominant' culture. It could be the product of interaction between different cultures, combined with the demands of new technology, business environment and professional techniques. It may even contain some 'foreign' influence as well as the vestige of colonial past. The continuance of English language, calendar, dress code and styles of living, etc. in the present-day India is the case in point. One may despise and reject them only at his peril.

Again, some groups in society could be the victims of cultural distortion. They will have to transform their own culture for their emancipation. For example, the inhuman practice of 'untouchability' in India was the product of 'dominant culture'. However, it also vitiated the culture of its victims. That is why B.R. Ambedkar (1891-1956), their undisputed leader, exhorted them to abandon their age-old occupation and practices, migrate from villages to big cities, educate their children, adopt new professions, and finally mix with the mainstream.

> **Man's capacity for justice makes democracy possible, but man's inclination to injustice makes democracy necessary.**
>
> **Reinhold Niebur**

23

Contemporary Theory of Democracy

TRADITIONAL THEORIES OF democracy were chiefly concerned with democracy as a form of government and they looked for ethical justification of democracy. Contemporary theories of democracy largely focus on the nature of democracy in the light of recent sociological findings, and its ethical critiques.

[I] ELITIST THEORY

Elitist theories were originally developed in the field of sociology to explain the behaviour of men in a social setting. Their implications in the field of politics posed a challenge to democratic theory, which was in turn revised by several thinkers. Broadly speaking, the elitist theories hold that every society consists of two categories of men: (*a*) the *elite* or the minority within a social collectivity (such as a society, a state, a religious institution, a political party) which exercises a preponderant influence within that collectivity; and (*b*) the masses or the majority which is governed by the *elite.*

Vilfredo Pareto (*The Mind and Society;* 1915-19) was the first to use the terms *'elite'* and 'masses' to indicate superior and inferior groups in society, although the idea of such division of society was given earlier by Gaetano Mosca (*The Ruling Class;* 1896) and Robert Michels (*Political Parties: A Sociological Study of the Oligarchical Tendencies of Modern Democracy;* 1911). Mosca postulated that the people are necessarily divided into two groups: the rulers and the ruled. The ruling class controls most of the wealth, power and prestige in society and exercises all power, whatever form of government might be adopted. The ruled are not competent to replace it.

Michel propounded his famous 'iron law of oligarchy' which implied that every organization—whatever its original aims—is eventually reduced to an 'oligarchy', that is the rule of the chosen few, based on their manipulative skills. Majority of human beings are apathetic, indolent and slavish and they are permanently incapable of self-government. Then Pareto came to the conclusion that the *'elite'* show highest ability in their field of activity whatever its nature might be, while masses lack the qualities of leadership and fear from responsibility. They feel safe in following the direction of the *elite.*

REVISION OF DEMOCRATIC THEORY

The *elite* theory had empirically demonstrated that democracy as the government of the people is incapable of realization. Champions of democracy found it difficult to repudiate the arguments advanced by the elitist theories. They, therefore, sought to accommodate the *elite* theory in the framework of democratic theory which led to its revision. The elitist democratic theory or 'democratic elitism' was developed by several writers.

Views of Mannheim

Karl Mannheim, who had initially related *elite* theories with Fascism and with anti-intellectualist doctrines, later championed the reconciliation between the *elite* theory and the democratic theory. In his *Ideology and Utopia: An Introduction to the Sociology of Knowledge* (1929), Mannheim argued that society did not cease to be democratic by entrusting the actual shaping of policy to the *elites.* The people cannot directly participate in government, but they can make their aspirations felt at certain intervals, and this is sufficient for democracy. In a democracy the governed can always act to remove their leaders or force them to take decisions in the interests of the many. Mannheim insists on selection by merit and shortening of distance between the *elite* and the masses in order to ensure compatibility between *elite* rule and democratic government.

> **Fascism**
>
> Fascism refers to an anti-democratic theory advanced by Benito Mussolini (1883-1945), the Italian dictator, which exhorted people to set aside all rules, conventions and legal limitations, and religiously follow the dictates of their leader in pursuit of national glorification.

Views of Schumpeter

Joseph A. Schumpeter, in his *Capitalism, Socialism and Democracy* (1942), argued that the forms of government should be distinguished by their institutions, and especially by their methods of appointing and dismissing the supreme makers of law and policy. Accordingly, the 'democratic method is that institutional arrangement for arriving at political decisions in which individuals acquire the power to decide by means of a competitive struggle for the people's votes'. This implies that: (*a*) in a democracy, political decisions are taken by the 'leadership', not by the people themselves; and (*b*) there is a free competition among the leaders for winning people's votes. In other words, democracy is not a government of the people, nor is it a means to give effect to the will of the people; rulers comprise a select group of individuals who may be distinguished from the common people. Role of the common people is reduced to choosing their rulers from the competing *elites*. The redeeming feature of democracy is that, unlike other forms of government, it does not allow political leadership to wield absolute power. It must draw up policies with an eye on gaining a larger support of the electorate than its opponents can obtain. In any case, initiative remains in the hands of the leadership while the people simply respond to it according to their choice. The leaders trade in votes and the better combination of policies will fetch more votes by appealing to wider sections of the political market.

Views of Aron

Raymond Aron, in his *Social Structure and the Ruling Class* (1950), advanced another version of the democratic theory which combines it with the *elite* theory. Liberal democracy, according to Aron, is characterized by a general system of checks and balances and plurality of *elites*. He points out that the Soviet type society is distinguished by a *unified elite* belonging to the Communist Party while the Western type society, that is liberal democracy, is characterized by a *divided elite,* which makes it a *pluralistic* society. With the plurality of *elites,* government becomes a business of compromise. Those in power are well aware of their precarious position. They are not only sensitive to public opinion but are also conscious of the opposition with which they have to change seats in due course. According to this theory, initiative still remains in the hands of the *elite;* the masses are left to play the relatively passive role of choosing the ruling *elite* and to pressurize them in their functioning.

Views of Sartori

Giovanni Sartori, in his *Democratic Theory* (1958), developed his views on democracy which are similar to those of Schumpeter in all essentials. Like Schumpeter, he regards democracy as a procedure in which leaders compete at elections for authority to govern. Sartori argues that the role of the *elite* does not suggest any imperfection of democracy. On the other hand, it is the core of the democratic system. For Sartori, any notion of self-governing people is a delusion. Government is necessarily the business of competent leaders; the people exercise their right to govern only at elections when they select their leaders. The real danger to democracy emanates not from the existence of leadership but from the absence of leadership which would result in the mass being exploited by anti-democratic *counter-elites.* Sartori even envisages the role of leadership in educating public opinion which is otherwise not enlightened enough.

[II]
PLURALIST THEORY

Pluralist theories of democracy fall into two categories: (*a*) the elitist-democratic theories which regard the *plurality of elites* as the foundation of modern liberal democracy, such as those advocated by Karl Mannheim and Raymond Aron; and (*b*) the *group theories* which interpret democracy as a process of bargaining among relatively autonomous groups; the existence and functioning of these groups in a democracy lends a pluralistic character to the polity; this view is regarded to be representing the mainstream pluralist theory of democracy.

In the United States, A.F. Bentley (*The Process of Government;* 1908) and David Truman (*The Governmental Process;* 1951) interpreted democracy as a political game played by a great variety of groups. According to this interpretation, government is the focal point for public pressure and its task is to make policies which reflect the highest common group demand. Thus, democratic society is seen as a pluralist, differentiated society where the management of public affairs is shared by a number of groups having different values, sources and methods of influence.

Robert Dahl, in his *A Preface to Democratic Theory* (1956), developed a model of the democratic process which was described as *polyarchy.* This corresponds to the models developed by Bentley, Truman and B. Latham (*The Group Basis of Politics;* 1952), variously known as *pluralism* or the *group theory.* The term *pluralism* is used here in the sociological sense, that is to describe the *pluralistic* nature of democratic society. Pluralist theory of democracy is closer to pluralist perspective on power than pluralist theory of sovereignty. In this context, the term *pluralism* provides a scientific explanation of the political process. It also refers to a political outlook that recognizes several centers of power in society.

Polyarchy

Polyarchy refers to a model of political process chiefly outlined by Robert Dahl (*A Preface to Democratic Theory;* 1956). It maintains that the policy-making process in a liberal democracy, however centralized it may appear in form, is in reality a highly decentralized process of bargaining among relatively autonomous groups. Accordingly, public policy is an outcome of the interaction among all groups who make claims upon or express interest in a particular issue. The role of government in such a situation is little more than that of an honest broker in the middle.

Pluralism

Pluralism refers to a political outlook that gives due importance to the diverse interests and viewpoints in society. It tends to promote the emergence of several centers of power and authority, rather than accepting the state as the sole controller of people's actions.

The gist of pluralistic democracy may be given as follows: The policy-making process, however centralized it may appear in form, is, in reality, a highly decentralized process of bargaining among relatively autonomous groups, particularly interest groups. In other words, public policy is not a product of the will of the *elite* or the chosen few, as the elitist theories of democracy maintain. On the contrary, it is an outcome of the interaction of all groups who make claims upon or express interest in that particular issue. The extent to which different groups will get their way, is a function of the strength of the groups and the intensity of their participation.

Interest Groups

In a liberal democracy, interest groups refer to groups of people who organize themselves for pursuing their specific, collective interest. They try to serve their interests through obtaining the support of public opinion by publicizing their viewpoint widely, and pleading to government to mould its policy to suit their interest. Examples of interest groups are: trade unions, lawyers associations and chambers of commerce and industry.

In fact, pluralist theory calls for the revision of the democratic theory itself as well as of the elitist theory of democracy. In its view, policy-making is actually done neither by the representatives of a coherent majority, nor by an autonomous and unresponsive *elite,* but is a product of the interaction among various groups. This theory goes to the extent of claiming that since public policy is largely an outcome of the bargaining among groups interested in a given policy issue, the form of government becomes almost insignificant. In other words, whether you adopt the democratic form of government or any other form, the result is not likely to vary significantly. In any case, public policy will reflect the interests of the more organized and vocal groups in society. For instance, the interests of producers are likely to dominate over those of consumers because the former are usually more organized, vocal and influential than the latter.

A CRITICAL APPRAISAL

The elitist and pluralist theories of democracy have added an empirical dimension to democratic theory by incorporating the results of sociological theory and research. In a nutshell: (*a*) the elitist theories concede that policy-making in a democracy is the function of the elite while the people's role is confined to approval and rejection of particular policies made or advocated by the competing elites; and (*b*) the pluralist theories view policy-making in a democracy as a decentralized process characterized by bargaining between competing autonomous groups. *Pluralist theories are more optimistic than elitist theories because they repudiate the authoritarian basis of policy-making in a democracy as implied by the elitist theories.* In any case, both theories arrive at conclusions which are far removed from the essence of democratic theory.

Men, no doubt, differ in their physical and intellectual capacities and other natural gifts. But social inequalities in the present-day society do not always correspond to natural inequalities. In most cases, the phenomenon of domination in society is closely related to economic disparities. The elitist-pluralist theory of democracy tries to justify the phenomenon of domination on grounds of certain outstanding inborn qualities of persons, or on grounds of better organization of certain interests. In effect, it tends to maintain the *status quo*. However, if the economic structure of the society is transformed so that rewards are directly related to the quality and amount of work done, instead of the privileged position and manipulative power of certain persons, the existing system of domination will disappear and the principle of equality based on reason will reign supreme—which is the essence of democracy.

[III]
THEORY OF PARTICIPATORY DEMOCRACY

Concept of democracy implies that ultimate authority of governance should rest with the people themselves. When this idea is sought to be implemented through the mechanism of representative democracy, it is possible that the people may become inactive after choosing their representatives till the next general elections. Moreover, when the size of a democratic community expands geographically and it includes a large population with a variety of composition in terms of race, religion, language and culture, distance between the people and their representatives is likely to widen. For example, in large democracies like India and the United States, a very small section of citizens participates in any discussion; and very few citizens enter into contact with their representatives. Does not this state of affairs point to the erosion of democracy?

Elitist theory of democracy implies that citizen participation is not a necessary condition of democracy. Thus, for Schumpeter, running of government and framing of public policies is the task of professional politicians; the role of ordinary citizens is confined to vote for the politicians, the political parties and the programmes of their choice at the time of periodic elections. In other words, modern democracy is primarily the rule of politicians in which ordinary citizens play a very limited role at regular intervals. Robert Dahl's pluralist theory of democracy also reconciles with a low level of citizen participation. C.B. Macpherson (*Democratic Theory—Essays in Retrieval;* 1973) has observed that Schumpeter-Dahl axis treats democracy as a mechanism designed to maintain an equilibrium. It conceives of democracy as a competition between two or more elite groups for the power to govern the whole society, requiring only a low level of citizen participation. In Macpherson's view, it is a distorted view where democracy is reduced from a humanist aspiration to a market equilibrium system.

Concept of participatory democracy repudiates this model of democracy as it regards people's political participation as the basic principle of democracy. In short, *political participation refers to the active involvement of individuals and groups in the governmental processes effecting their lives.* In other words, when citizens themselves play an active role in the process of formulation and implementation of public policies and decisions, their activity is called political participation. Conventional mode of political participation includes voting, contesting for a public office, campaigning for a political party or contributing to the management of a community project like public safety, cleanliness drive, or the maintenance of a public park, etc. Interestingly, an act of opposition or public protest also involves political participation. For example, signing a petition, attending a peaceful demonstration, joining a protest march or forming a human chain, etc. come within the purview of political participation. Indeed, the various acts of public protest in a non-democratic set-up, like passive resistance, civil disobedience and *satyagraha,* also qualify as political participation. They are the manifestation of a strong awareness of public interest.

Jean-Jaques Rousseau (1712-78), the exponent of popular sovereignty, is regarded the pioneer of participatory democracy. In his classic work *The Social Contract* (1762), Rousseau asserted that sovereignty not only originates in the people, it is also retained by the people in spite of their transition from the state of nature to civil society. Sovereignty cannot be represented, because it cannot be alienated. The people's deputies are not, and could not be their representatives. They are merely agents of the people. *Government is only an instrument to carry out instructions of the general will.* The people must constantly deliberate on public policy and issue necessary instructions to the government. They should also make sure that government does not depart from these instructions; otherwise, it should be revoked and replaced immediately.

General Will

According to Jean-Jaques Rousseau (*The Social Contract;* 1762), the *general will* refers to the point of convergence of the real will of all members of a community. It reflects the true interest of each individual as well as the common good of the whole community. Sovereignty of the *general will* constitutes the foundation of popular sovereignty.

> **Deliberation and debate is the way you stir the soul of our democracy.**
>
> **Jesse Jackson**

> **A basic tenet of a healthy democracy is open dialogue and transparency.**
>
> **Peter Fenn**

> **In a democracy, dissent is an act of faith.**
>
> **J. William Fulbright**

Forms of Political Participation

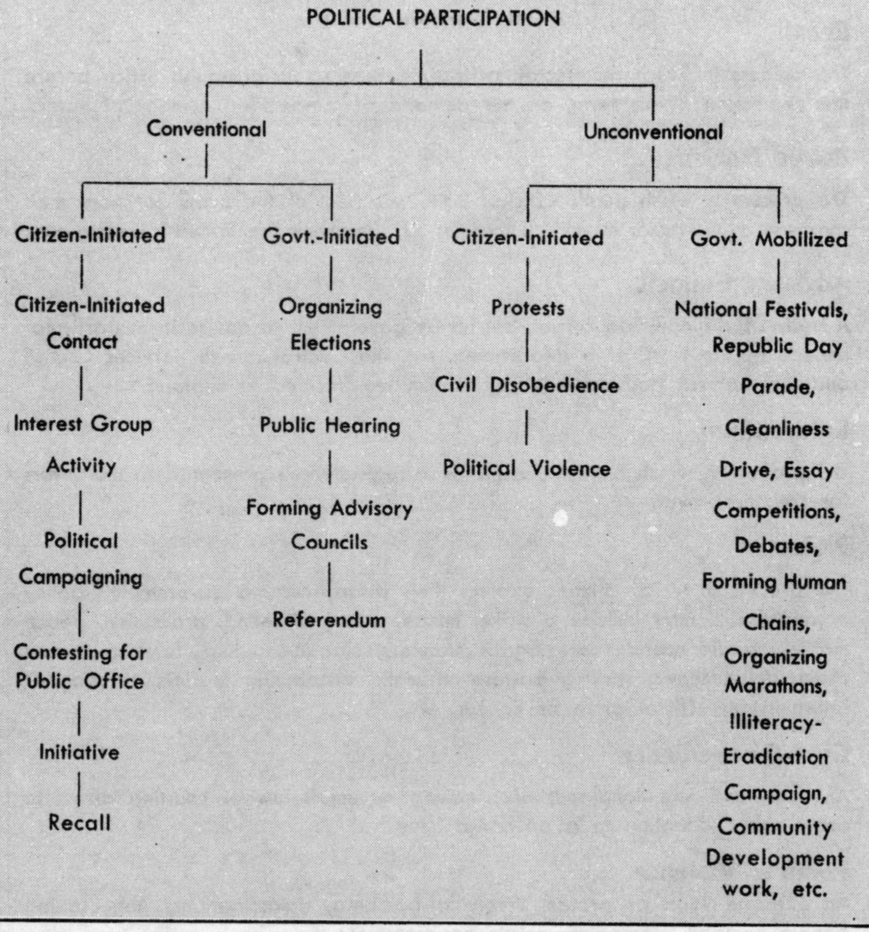

Forms of Political Participation

Political participation involves an active interaction between citizens and government. It is a two-way process. One party initiates and the other responds. Conventional participation includes the recognized methods of democratic functioning. Unconventional participation is less ordinary; and sometimes viewed as less acceptable.

Citizen-initiated Contact

The process in which a citizen contacts public officials by phone, letter, fax, e-mail, etc. or writes a letter to the editor of a leading newspaper regarding a pending piece of legislation or a matter affecting many people. For this purpose citizens may also meet the concerned officials individually or collectively.

Initiative

The process in which citizens may collect a specified number of signatures on a petition whereafter it is entitled to be placed before the legislature for popular vote.

Recall

The process in which an elected official is required to relinquish office before the expiration of his term, on the demand of a specified number of voters.

Public Hearing

The process in which public officials invite members of the public to share their comments on particular matters. Sometimes such comments are invited in writing also.

Advisory Council

A body of distinguished citizens set up by government to advise it on particular aspects of the work of a department, e.g. the Central Health Services Council and the Central Housing Advisory Committee, formed in England.

Referendum

The process in which an act passed by a legislature is presented to the voters for their approval.

Protest

The process in which citizens express their disapproval to government's policy or decision. It may include a strike, hunger strike, picketing, procession, peace march, candle march, carrying of banners, slogan-shouting, forming human chain, street shows, sticking posters on walls, distributing leaflets, refusing or returning an official prize or honour, etc.

Civil Disobedience

An open and intentional act of breaking an unjust law or courting arrest to draw public attention to a particular issue.

Political Violence

An extreme form of protest involving bombing, assassinations, riots, taking people hostage, damaging public property, etc.

> **Democracy is based upon the conviction that there are extraordinary possibilities in ordinary people.**
>
> **Harry Emerson Fosdick**

Present-day champions of participatory democracy argue that representative democracy gives little opportunity to its citizens for any significant participation in the decision-making process. Consequently, under the prevailing system electorates have so little knowledge and understanding of political problems; voters are so indifferent to voting; political representatives are so averse to public accountability; and corruption and abuse of power are so rampant in the whole administration. If people get better opportunities of political participation, they will be inclined to discuss public issues elaborately, keep a strict watch on the activities of politicians, and they shall be able to prevent the corruption and abuse of power. Hence, *citizen participation is not only a necessary condition of good society, but a basic feature of good society.*

In modern large-scale states, the objectives of participatory democracy are sought to be achieved through: (*a*) Decentralization of administration in which many decisions are left to local communities, as in the case of expansion of *panchayati raj* in India; and (*b*) Extensive use of referendum, as in Switzerland. Under this procedure, people's vote is sought on any new law, constitution or constitutional amend·ıent. In Australia, referendum is compulsory on any constitutional amendment. It is a method of combining some features of direct democracy with the mechanism of representative democracy.

In contemporary political theory, *citizen participation* is sought to be *justified* mainly *on three grounds:* (*a*) *Instrumental view* asserts that citizen participation is aimed at promoting or defending the interests of the participant. Before going in for participation, persons calculate the anticipated benefits and costs, and the prospects of attaining their objectives; (*b*) *Developmental or educational view* of participation holds that it enhances the participants' general moral, social and political awareness; and (*c*) finally, *Communitarian view* of participation justifies it on the ground that it contributes to the common good.

In *socialist countries*, the concept of participatory democracy came as *a response to the elitist theory.* Elitist theory had claimed that the division of society into leaders and followers was inevitable. It had, therefore, ruled out the prospects of a 'classless society'. In a way socialist circles accepted this position by recognizing the superiority of the 'vanguard of the proletariat'. Participatory democracy sought to bridge the gap between leaders and followers by encouraging mass participation in the socialist programme and making leaders responsive to the sentiments of the ordinary people. The description of socialist countries as 'people's republic', 'people's democratic republic', etc. was symbolic of this approach. In China, for instance, Mao Zedong (1893-1976) encouraged mass campaigns and followed the policy of 'mass line' which required the leaders and party workers to come close to the masses, explore their sentiments and mould their leadership patterns on those lines.

Vanguard of the Proletariat

The expression used by V.I. Lenin (1870-1924), an exponent of Marxism, to designate the more enlightened, energetic and committed section of the working class which formed the Communist Party. This section was to provide leadership to the working class in its struggle against capitalism, and also to run the government during the socialist phase.

A CRITICAL APPRAISAL

Critics point out that the champions of participatory democracy insist only on increasing citizens' participation within the existing democratic system. They do not suggest any alternative system for its implementation. Indeed, necessary means of participatory democracy already exist within the organization and procedure of liberal democracy. Promotion of participation needs concrete action, not a theory.

Then the advocates of participatory democracy seem to be too optimistic. People's participation in a democracy can reasonably be increased to a small extent. Beyond that it *may* prove harmful. Beneficial results of public decisions, policies and programmes come very late. This process may require imposition of burden on some sections in the public interest. Ordinary people are not endowed with adequate patience and insight that would enable them to make a correct assessment of the situation. If they are encouraged for too much participation, they may take their grievances and disputes to streets, and disrupt normal life.

When ordinary people are reduced to a crowd, it becomes extremely difficult to keep them in discipline or control. When people are moved by excitement, they can hardly be persuaded to stop. As a result, we are faced with frequent gatherings and processions, slogan-shouting, rallies, huge demonstrations, strikes, picketing and *gheraos,* threats to stop water and electric supply and public transport, and incidents of damage to public property. Under the circumstances, it seems that those who have the skill to gather and mobilize crowds will be able to secure fulfilment of their unreasonable demands whereas those who try to present their case peacefully and modestly will go unheard.

[IV]
MARXIST THEORY OF DEMOCRACY

Liberal theory largely identifies democracy by its procedure and institutions. Marxist theory, on the other hand, evaluates any political system with reference to its class character, that is through identification of the antagonistic classes (owners and non-owners of the means of social production) within that system. Marxists criticize the prevalent form of liberal democracy because it harbours the capitalist system in which the majority of people comprising workers is deprived of power.

MARXIST CRITIQUE OF LIBERAL DEMOCRACY

Liberal democracy, by fostering capitalist economic system, exclusively serves the interests of the *bourgeoisie, i.e.* the capitalist class. Marxists, therefore, dubbed liberal democracy the *'bourgeois democracy.'* In spite of its vast paraphernalia of representative institutions, liberal democracy hardly serves the interests of the people on whose behalf power is exercised. According to Marx and Engels, "The executive of the modern state is but a committee for managing the common affairs of the whole bourgeoisie" (*Communist Manifesto;* 1848). Here the term 'modern state' refers to the prevalent model of liberal democracy.

John Plamenatz, in his *Democracy and Illusion—An Examination of Certain Aspects of Modern Democratic Theory* (1978), has enumerated four outstanding reasons advanced by Marxists, anarchists and other like-minded thinkers for calling 'bourgeois democracy' a sham:

(1) Where there are great inequalities of wealth, there, whatever the form of go ernment, power and influence always belong mostly to the wealthy, only because they alone can afford to provide their children with the expensive schooling needed to fit them for positions carrying power and influence;

(2) Where the political system, to work effectively, calls for large organizations, power and influence belong to their leaders rather than to the rank and file;

(3) Where there are great social inequalities, leaders, no matter how modest their social origins, soon acquire the attitudes and ambitions of the privileged and lose touch with their followers; and

(4) Power and influence depend greatly on information, and the wealthy are better placed than the poor both to get information and to control the distribution of it.

These are, no doubt, most familiar points of criticism against liberal democracy involving large economic inequalities. But if we confine our attention to these reasons, it can be argued that if large economic inequalities are removed within the capitalist system, the liberal model can be made to serve as true democracy. But this position would not be acceptable to Marxist exponents of democracy who are convinced that democracy and capitalism cannot go together. In fact, Marxists focus on the defects of the capitalist system itself with regard to its capability of serving as democracy.

Liberal Democracy Exclusively Serves Bourgeois Interests

According to the Marxian standpoint, since the capitalist system of production is designed to serve the economic interests of the bourgeoisie, its political superstructure cannot be made to serve the people. In the economic sphere, society is divided into 'dominant' and 'dependent classes', the 'haves' and 'have-nots', the 'bourgeoisie' and the 'proletariat'; their interests are diametrically opposed to each other. Political power is only a handmaid of economic power. It is, therefore, quite natural that the political institutions of such a system—whatever their outer form—are bound to serve the interests of bourgeoisie. Liberal democracy, which represents the political institutions of capitalist economic system, pays lip-service to 'sovereignty of the people' in order to derive its legitimacy. It operates in a situation where all sections of society—the bourgeoisie as well as the proletariat—accept legitimacy of the bourgeois relations of production and the roles which these impose. In this situation, the state operates as an instrument of preserving the conditions suitable for a market mechanism which continues to serve the interests of the capitalist class.

Liberal Democracy Creates Ideological Misconceptions

Liberal democracy, of course, creates representative institutions and concedes formal equality of political rights. It pretends to create a situation in which government is run by the chosen representatives of the people—the proletariat as well as the bourgeoisie. The workers who have the right to vote *on par* with businessmen and industrialists are led to believe that they have an equal share in governance. Moreover, liberal democracy claims to reconcile the interests of the proletariat with those of the bourgeoisie. This creates an impression that due care of the interests of the workers is being taken. But, according to Marxist theory, these are wrong impressions created by the liberal democracy, because this type of political system simply lends legitimacy to the property relations of the capitalist order which are neither natural nor rational. As John Maguire, in his *Marx's Theory of Politics* (1978), has elucidated: "The modern state, when it 'represents' everybody in this society, is in fact representing the workers only in an illusory manner—representing, as it were, their ideological misconception of themselves." In other words, so long as the capitalist mode of production prevails, society remains divided into two antagonistic classes—capitalists and workers, who represent the dominant and dependent classes respectively. The state as the agent of the dominant class serves the interests of the capitalists at the expense of the workers.

The 'dominant' class has always had an edge over the 'dependent' class in the sphere of ideas. The ideas promoted by the ruling class are the ruling ideas of any age. These ideas may involve injustice, but they are widely accepted as a standard of justice and seldom questioned. Under the spell of bourgeois ideology, the masses are made to believe that they are being ruled with their consent. But they blindly follow the values of bourgeois society against their own interest; their consent is, therefore, a false consent.

Liberal Democracy Tries to Perpetuate the Economic Division of Society

Liberal democracy, in spite of providing universal suffrage, periodic elections, freedom of thought and expression, does not embody an effective mechanism for transforming the economic relations of society in order to serve the common interest. Instead, it tends to perpetuate the economic division of society into 'haves' and 'have-nots' and the values of bourgeois society which support and legitimize this division. It is interesting to recall that liberalism conceded the democratic principle of wider suffrage in a number of Western countries only when it had made sure that its acceptance would not be detrimental to the maintenance of the property relations of the capitalist system. V.I. Lenin, in his *State and Revolution* (1917), significantly observed:

> Democracy for an insignificant minority, democracy for the rich—that is the democracy of capitalist society… Marx grasped this *essence* of capitalist democracy splendidly when…he said that the oppressed are allowed every few years to decide which particular representatives of the oppressing classes shall represent and repress them in parliament.

Thus, liberal democracy, in the Marxist view, is incapable of averting class exploitation; it is a device for keeping the exploiting class or its nominees constantly in power for the purpose of serving its own interests.

[VI]
DICTATORSHIP OF THE PROLETARIAT

According to Marxism, any form of state power implies dictatorship. The character of the state is determined by the character of its ruling class. Thus, 'bourgeois democracy' and 'bourgeois dictatorship' are coterminous; they denote a state characterized by the domination of the bourgeoisie. Similarly, 'dictatorship of the proletariat', 'proletarian democracy' or 'socialist democracy' denotes a state characterized by the domination of the proletariat. It is established by the proletariat after overthrowing the capitalist order by a violent revolution. This is not the final stage of evolution but only an interim arrangement preparing the ground for the abolition of the division of society into dominant and dependent classes, and the consequent 'withering away' of the state itself. It is termed 'dictatorship' because it retains the 'state apparatus' as such, with its implements of force and oppression, not because its organization is fundamentally different from the so-called 'democracy'.

Dictatorship of the proletariat is different from the popular notion of 'dictatorship' which is despised as the selfish, immoral, irresponsible and unconstitutional political rule of one man or a small political clique characterized by the oppression of the masses. On the other hand, dictatorship of the proletariat implies a stage where there is complete 'socialization of the major means of production', *de novo* planning of material production so as to serve social needs, provide for an effective right to work, education, health and housing for the masses, and fuller development of science and technology so as to multiply material production to achieve greater social satisfaction.

DICTATORSHIP OF THE PROLETARIAT IS CONCRETE DEMOCRACY

In popular parlance, 'dictatorship' denotes an antithesis of 'democracy'. In Marxian terminology, so long as the state is in existence, with its vast coercive apparatus, there is no difference whether you call it a democracy or a dictatorship. If democracy means the rule of majority over minority, then the 'proletarian state' is surely more democratic than the 'bourgeois state'. As Henri Lefebvre, in his *Sociology of Marx* (1968), has elucidated: "The dictatorship of the proletariat means concrete democracy, *i.e.* the coercive power of a majority over a minority." The capitalist system of production maintained by the liberal democracy involves domination of the minority—the capitalists—over the majority—the workers in the economic, social as well as political sphere—which is inimical to human freedom. On the contrary, the socialist system of production maintained by the socialist democracy ensures domination of the majority—the workers—over the minority— the former capitalists—and this process continues as long as the state continues to exist. Domination and coercion during this period are necessary to contain the forces of counter-revolution and to destroy the vestiges of the capitalist order. The dictatorship of the proletariat is more akin to democracy not because of its form, but because of the purpose for which the state continues to exist during this period.

Lenin advanced the concept of 'democratic centralism' as a principle of organization of the socialist state as well as the communist party. This was designed to lend a democratic character to the so-called dictatorship of the proletariat.

Democratic Centralism

Democratic centralism refers to the principle of organization of the socialist state as well as the communist party, as enunciated by V.I. Lenin (1870-1924). It implies: (a) that the membership of each body in the political hierarchy (whether of party or state) was to be decided by the vote of the lower body; and (b) that although free discussion on policy matters was to be allowed at the initial stage, any decision reached by the highest body was to be imposed rigidly at all lower levels in the hierarchy.

DICTATORSHIP OF THE PROLETARIAT IS A TRANSITIONAL PHASE

Dictatorship of the proletariat is not intended to last for ever. In fact, Marx associated the term 'dictatorship' principally with the Roman office of *dictatura* where all power was legally concentrated in the hands of a single man during a limited period in a time of crisis. Hence, dictatorship of the proletariat was meant to accomplish a specified function. As Lefebvre, in his *Sociology of Marx* (1968), observes:

> The working class must destroy the machinery of the existing state, but its own state is to last only for a transitional period during which state functions of organization and management are taken over by new social forces...and the state will begin to wither away when a truly rational organization of production becomes possible.

In the past, *i.e.* before the advent of the socialist revolution, changes in the techniques and modes of production had only produced social transformations, but the character of exploitation had not fundamentally changed. Thus, during the period of *domestic* mode of production, slaves were exploited by their masters; during the feudal period, serfs were exploited by their lords; and during the capitalist period, workers are exploited by the capitalists. In all these cases, 'have-nots' are exploited by the 'haves'. But after the socialist revolution, when dictatorship of the proletariat is established, there is a radical change in the character of exploitation in the sense that the former 'haves' are now oppressed by the former 'have-nots'—all property is now socially owned. The abolition of private property—the root cause of all exploitation—is expected to accomplish the elimination of exploitation itself, and to establish a higher social rationality. In the words of Lefebvre: "This implies a qualitative leap, class contradictions disappearing in the new unity, though classes themselves do not vanish literally overnight" (*ibid.*).

Dictatorship of the proletariat is required to exist so long as classes exist. But it will function in such a way that all men will be converted into workers, thereby abolishing the division of society into antagonistic classes:

> As soon as the goal of the proletarian movement, the abolition of classes, shall have been reached, the power of the state, whose function is to keep the great majority of producers beneath the yoke of a small minority of exploiters, will be transformed into simple administrative functions (K. Marx, *Capital,* Vol. 3, edited by F. Engels; 1894).

[VI]
CONCEPT OF PEOPLE'S DEMOCRACY

It is important to note that most of the theories of democracy are concerned with 'liberal democracy', but the concept of 'people's democracy' is associated with Marxist thought. Marx did not reject democracy as such. He attacked 'bourgeois democracy' as a distorted form of democracy, and tried to give an alternative version of true democracy. He was inspired by Rousseau's critique of representative democracy and saw true democracy as an expression of homogeneous interests. But his adherence to class perspective convinced him that a class-divided society cannot have homogeneous interests. Accordingly, the idea of true democracy could only be realized in a classless society, or at best, in a socialist state which represented the uniform interest of the working class.

Marx had anticipated that after the socialist revolution, bourgeois democracy would be replaced by a 'commune system'. Commune refers to a large association whose members work together and own everything in common, including the product of their labour. In the present context, communes were envisaged to be small communities who would manage their own affairs, and would elect their delegates for the larger administrative units, like districts and towns. These larger units would in turn elect their delegates for the still larger administrative areas, culminating in national administration. This system is described as 'pyramidal structure of direct democracy'. Under this arrangement, all delegates would be bound by the instructions of their electorates, and would take their respective place within the pyramidal structure of directly elected committees. In case of violation of instructions of their electors, they could be removed from office. It may be recalled that this scheme was sought to be implemented in the former Soviet Union after the Russian Revolution (1917), and in China after the Chinese Revolution (1949), but it failed in both the countries, primarily due to the lack of attachment to the 'common property', and the absence of incentives for better performance.

Socialist systems on the lines of the Soviet Union were also established in several countries of East Europe after the Second World War (1939-45), under the direct supervision of the Soviet Union. Originally these included Albania, Bulgaria, Czechoslovakia, East Germany, Hungary, Poland and Romania. Some other countries of the world (apart from China) also adopted socialist system on their own. These included Cuba, North Korea, Mongolia, Vietnam, Yemen and Yugoslavia. All of them were ruled by the communist parties of their respective countries, or they formed coalitions with some like-minded minor parties as a temporary measure. Broadly speaking, all socialist systems looked after the homogeneous interests of the working classes. They were described as 'people's democracies' in order to distinguish them from Western-type liberal democracies. With the collapse of socialist systems in Eastern Europe and the Soviet Union (1989-91) and relinquishing of this system by some other countries, people's democracies are now only left in China (People's Republic of China), Vietnam (Socialist Republic of Vietnam), North Korea (People's Democratic Republic of Korea) and Cuba (Republic of Cuba).

It may be pointed out that the term 'democracy' itself stands for government of the people. Hence, the usage of 'people's democracy' seems to be tautological. This term was adopted to indicate a new type of democracy. Conventional use of democracy stands for liberal democracy which is based on a specific procedure of government-formation. Hence, it may be identified as 'procedural democracy'. On the other hand, 'people's democracy' focuses on the substance of democracy, *i.e.* safeguarding the interests of the ordinary people. Hence, it claims to be identified as 'substantive democracy'. In its view, interest of the working classes is coterminous with the interest of the people.

[VII]
DISTINCTION BETWEEN PROCEDURAL AND SUBSTANTIVE DEMOCRACY

Ordinarily the institutions of liberal democracy are recognized as the characteristics of mainstream of democracy. Accordingly, democracy is regarded as a procedure designed to obtain consent of the people for public decisions. It is hoped that when this procedure is adopted, public decisions would be automatically devoted to people's welfare. Champions of liberal democracy regard it the standard by which they would judge any political system. They would never compromise this procedure for any other gain. This model of democracy is, therefore, called 'procedural democracy'.

Defence of procedural democracy implies that 'government *by* the people' would necessarily prove to be 'government *for* the people'. However, some exponents of democracy do not accept this position. They argue that the goal of democracy, *viz.* people's welfare should take precedence over its procedure. In other words, the structure of liberal democracy does not necessarily ensure that it would be conducive to people's welfare. So some critics of liberal democracy advocate necessary adjustment in the procedure and institutions of democracy for the achievement of its goal. Their approach to democracy may be described as 'substantive democracy'.

The debate between the champions of 'procedural democracy' and 'substantive democracy' regarding the true nature of democracy shows that *democracy is essentially a contested concept*. Thus, Marxists argue that the goals achieved by a state are determined by the class character of the state. They contend that when liberal democracy is adopted in the political sphere, it tends to sustain capitalism in the economic sphere which promotes the interests of the capitalist class and exploitation of the working class. So it cannot be regarded as true democracy. Marxists hold that true democracy should promote the interests of the working class which constitutes majority. That is possible only under socialism. Hence, socialism is synonymous with true democracy.

Marxists have evolved an alternative political set up which is described as 'socialist democracy' in order to distinguish it from 'liberal democracy'. While liberal democracy is usually identified as 'political democracy', socialist democracy is described as 'economic democracy' or 'social democracy'.

Champions of socialist democracy regard economic organization of society as the foundation of whole social life. They recognize economic power as the key to political power. Alternative forms of democracy as conceived by these two major schools of thought are shown in the following chart:

Distinction Between Procedural and Substantive Democracy

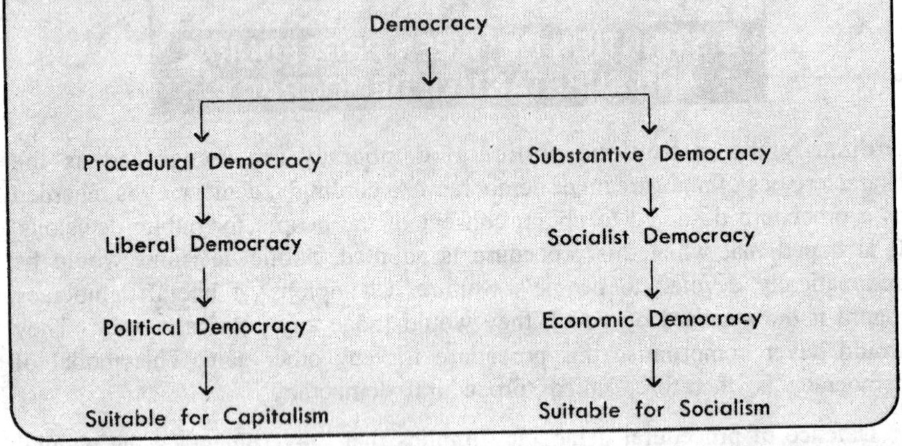

Marxists argue that under capitalism all power is concentrated in the hands of capitalists which is used against the working class. On the contrary, under socialism all power is assumed by the working class and it is applied for the liquidation of capitalism. Capitalism is sustained by liberal democracy which accepts the primacy of civil liberties; socialism sustains socialist democracy which accepts the primacy of social-economic rights. In other words, liberal democracy primarily seeks to protect the individual from arbitrary acts of government; it safeguards his personal freedom, freedom of movement, freedom of thought, expression, faith and worship, freedom of association, right to fair trial, equality before the law, etc. Socialist democracy, on the other hand, makes elaborate arrangements to provide for employment, education, housing, medical care and recreation facilities for the people. Thus, Chinese Government's white paper on 'Building of Political Democracy in China' (2005) focused on the importance of economic development and social stability in establishing a democracy. It asserted that the continued rule of the Communist Party was the most important and fundamental principle for developing socialist political democracy in China.

Liberal democracy allows several political parties to come up and to compete for power, but socialist democracy accepts monopoly of a single political party devoted to the interests of the working class. In a liberal democracy, voters have to elect a suitable candidate from several competing candidates whether sponsored by political parties or fighting the election independently. But in a socialist democracy, voters have to approve the candidate nominated by the ruling political party. In a liberal democracy, elected government is the source of decision-making. But in a socialist democracy, ruling political party is the source of decision-making; organs of government simply ratify the decisions so made. Finally, a liberal democracy requires that bureaucracy and judiciary should remain neutral towards politics, but socialist democracy requires them to be committed to the party in power. Salient features of the two systems are shown in the following chart:

Comparative Study of Liberal and Socialist Democracies

The Issue	*Liberal Democracy*	*Socialist Democracy*
Status of the Major Means of Production	Under Private Ownership	Under Public Ownership
Purose of Production	Primarily Private Profit	Fulfilment of Social Needs
Status of Rights	Primacy of Civil Liberties	Primacy of Social-economic Rights
Status of Political Parties	Several Political Parties Freely Competing for Power	Monopoly of one Political Party representing the Interests of the Working Class
Methods of Election	Election of a Suitable Person from the Competing Condidates	Approval of the Condidate Nominated by the Political Party
Main Source of Decision-Making	The Elected Government	Political Party in Power
Character of Bureaucracy and Judiciary	Politically Neutral	Committed to the Party in Power

Marxists commend socialist democracy as best suited to overcome the defects of liberal democracy. But champions of liberal democracy do not accept this line of argument, and dub the so-called socialist democracy the dictatorship or a totalitarian system, which represents the antithesis of democracy itself.

Indeed, a socialist system cannot be termed as a democracy in real sense of the term, because it fails to safeguard liberty of the individual. *Goals of socialism are certainly laudable, but when the procedure of democracy is set aside on the pretext of achieving those goals, we can no longer claim to remain democratic.* We must try to reform the democratic procedure constantly in order to overcome its shortcomings, but adoption of the socialist system in the prevalent form will defeat the idea of democracy itself.

> In a dictatorship, the people are afraid to tell the truth to their leaders; in a democracy, the leaders are afraid to tell the truth to the people.
>
> Richard J. Needham (1976)

[VIII]
MARXIST THEORY *vs* ELITIST THEORY OF DEMOCRACY

Elitist theory of democracy was developed when Marxist theory was already well-known. In fact, the elitist theory was applied by some writers to vindicate the model of liberal democracy. In any case, the elitist theory shares some of its tenets with Marxist theory while it marks a departure in respect of others.

Both Marxists and elitists agree that so long as society is divided into the 'ruling' and the 'ruled' classes in a subtle manner, real political equality cannot be secured merely through a democratic form of government. However, these theorists differ regarding the nature of the social division and the scope of social change, etc.

NATURE OF DOMINATION

Marxists believe that so long as the institution of the state exists, society remains divided into two economic classes; and that the economically dominant class is *invariably* the ruling class: the political and legal *superstructure* is always raised on the economic *substructure.* In other words, the class holding economic power holds political power *concurrently.* The elitist theory, on the contrary, postulates that society is broadly divided into the *elite* and the masses because of natural differences in the capabilities and aptitudes of different individuals; the *elite* manage to secure and maintain their political power because of their special qualities and cleverness.

Marxists regard the ruling class as a cohesive group which maintains its stronghold on political power until the social order itself is transformed by a socialist revolution. On the other hand, the *elite*-theorists postulate plurality of *elites* so that the competition among several *elites* is responsible for the 'circulation of *elites'*. Marxists envisage an active role of the masses in the revolution; the elitists regard the masses as a passive lot.

NATURE OF THE SOCIAL DIVISION

Marxists believe that the division of society into 'dominant' and 'dependent' classes is a symptom of their mutually antagonistic interests. This inevitably leads to class conflict which is bound to persist as long as this social division continues to exist. Social progress postulates a march towards the goal of establishing a classless society. On the contrary, the elitists hold that the division of society into rulers and subjects is almost instinctive and voluntary; it does not involve any fundamental conflict of interests. The *elites* and the masses compensate each other to evolve an effective social organization. The elitist theory, in this respect, corresponds to Aristotle's defence of slavery who argued that slavery existed in the interests of both—the master and the slave.

NATURE OF JUSTICE AND RATIONALITY

Marxists are convinced that the division of all pre-socialist societies into the 'dominant' and 'dependent' classes does not conform to 'reason'. It necessarily involves oppression and exploitation of the masses, and is therefore a stark embodiment of injustice. Justice can only be restored by eliminating this social division. The elitists, on the contrary, do not see any injustice or irrationality in the division of society into the *elite* and the masses. They treat it as natural, rational and functional; and, therefore, do not plead for revolution to secure social justice.

SCOPE OF SOCIAL CHANGE

According to the Marxists, political domination is based on economic domination. Economic relations in a society depend on the prevalent mode of production. Since the economic structure of society is *alterable,* political domination is also *alterable.* But the *elite*-theorists believe that the domination of the *elite* is inherent in social organization. This phenomenon itself is almost *unalterable.* The scope of social change, according to the elitists, is, therefore, limited to the *circulation of elites*—a process by which an outmoded *elite* is replaced by a new, energetic and promising *elite.*

SCOPE OF DEMOCRACY

The *elite*-theorists argue that democracy can be realized in a liberal society if two conditions are fulfilled: (*a*) there is an *open elite* system, that is the recruitment of *elites* is relatively open so that the especially talented and enterprising persons find adequate opportunity to join the cadre of *elites* and the new *elite* is permitted to replace the dominant *elite* which might have lost its credence; and (*b*) ordinary people are given an opportunity to choose the ruling *elites* at regular intervals, that is there is a provision for periodic elections based on universal suffrage. On the other hand, Marxists believe that true democracy cannot be achieved as long as society remains divided into 'superior' and 'subordinate' classes because of the economic division of society into 'haves' and 'have-nots'. In such a society, periodic elections based on universal suffrage are an eyewash because they cannot bring about an effective change in social relations unless the mode of production is fundamentally transformed. The domination of the bourgeois class is strengthened by the prevalence of bourgeois ideology. The proletariat vote for one or another group of the bourgeoisie, thinking that they are being ruled with their 'consent' and that the system is serving the 'common interest' whereas, in reality, this system exclusively serves the interests of the bourgeoisie. When society is divided into antagonistic classes, all talk of the 'common interest' is a fraud. Marxists are convinced that political equality divorced from real economic equality is devoid of substance. Equality postulates the abolition of social divisions into antagonistic classes. The ideal of true democracy can be realized only in a *classless* society. The elitists do not admit any possibility of a classless society or the termination of the conditions of dominance and dependence.

As regards the possibility of democracy, Marxists distinguish between capitalism, communism and socialism. Under capitalism, the industrial mode of production has been adopted, but society is divided into bourgeoisie and proletariat; production is carried out for private profit, not according to social needs; and exploitation of the proletariat is inherent in the process of production. Under this system the ideal of democracy is incapable of realization. Communism stands for a classless society with a rational system of production; with the highest development of science and technology to ensure maximum production, and where all major means of production are held under common ownership—hence production is undertaken to meet social needs, not to earn private profit; and all members of society become workers—no capitalists, no parasites, no unearned income, no exploitation, no class conflict but a genuine cooperation. Production and distribution of goods and services under this system is governed by the rule— 'from each according to his ability, to each according to his need'—thus fully realizing the ideal of democracy.

Comparative Study of Marxist and Elitist Theories of Democracy

The Issue	*Marxist Theory*	*Elitist Theory*
Nature of Domination	The ruling class holds economic power and political power concurrently	*Elites* dominate in various spheres of life and cleverly manage to use political power also
Nature of Dominant Class	A cohesive group which maintains its stronghold on power until it is overthrown	Plurality of *elites:* constant competition between *elite* groups leading to the 'circulation of *elites*'
Nature of Social Division	Society divided into dominant and dependent classes on the basis of ownership and non-ownership of means of social production; their conflicting interests can never be reconciled	Division of society into *elites* and the masses is almost instinctive and voluntary; not based on fundamental clash of their interests
Nature of Justice and Rationality	Social division is the source of exploitation and oppression of the masses; it involves injustice	Social division is natural, rational and functional; it does not involve injustice
Scope of Social Change	Working class can organize its strength and overthrow capitalism; this will eventually usher in a classless society	Social change confined to the 'circulation of *elites*'; no scope of changing the existing division of society into *elites* and the masses
Scope of Democracy	True democracy possible only in a classless society which is characterized by the rule of the masses	Democracy can be partly realized through an open *elite* system and giving ordinary people an opportunity to choose the ruling *elites* at regular intervals; masses themselves will never rule

Circulation of *Elites*

The expression used by Vilfredo Pareto (1848-1923), an Italian sociologist, to indicate the endless cycle in which one type of *elite* is replaced by another. Pareto distinguished between two types of *elites* on the basis of their psychological orientations: *lions* are marked by conservative 'sentiments' while *foxes* are more innovative and untrustworthy. A constant competition between the two results in one replacing the other alternately. Pareto saw no possibility of the rule of the *elite* being ever replaced by the rule of the masses.

Since direct transition from capitalism to communism is not possible, this is preceded by an interim stage—socialism, which is characterized by the 'dictatorship of the proletariat'. It is a dictatorship because the coercive apparatus of the state is still retained; capitalists are expropriated, the major means of production are socialized; all citizens are required to become workers, full development of science and technology is undertaken. Social division into classes still exists, but the proletariat become the dominant class; oppression is still used to suppress the bourgeois counter-revolution; some rules and institutions of the bourgeois society are still retained—'from each according to his ability, to each according to his work'. However, dictatorship of the proletariat is more democratic than the bourgeois democracy because it is a step forward in the direction of true democracy. Lenin, in his *State and Revolution* (1917), made this point strongly:

> The dictatorship of the proletariat, *i.e.* the organization of the vanguard of the oppressed as the ruling class for the purpose of suppressing the oppressors... *for the first time* becomes democracy for the poor, democracy for the people, and not democracy for the money-bags. The dictatorship of the proletariat imposes a series of restrictions on the freedom of the oppressors, the exploiters, the capitalists. We must suppress them in order to free humanity from wage-slavery, their resistance must be crushed by force; it is clear that there is no freedom and no democracy where there is suppression and where there is violence.

A CRITICAL APPRAISAL

Marxist theory of democracy most emphatically demonstrated the drawbacks of liberal democracy, especially in its inadequacy to win real equality for the masses. Historically speaking, liberal democracy arose in the seventeenth century to win substantive rights for the newly emerging bourgeoisie from the prevailing system of feudalism; Marxism arose in the nineteenth century to demand substantive rights for the newly emerging proletariat from the prevailing system of capitalism. This had a great impact on the liberal theory of democracy itself which had to accommodate the claims of the working classes to maintain its legitimacy.

In any case, the Marxist view of democracy cannot be accepted as the perfect theory of democracy. It has, been critisized on several grounds.

Marxist Theory Rules Out the Existence of Democracy Itself

The principle of democracy is universally identified with the 'sovereignty of the people'. Both capitalists and communists subscribe to this view. The Marxist theory of democracy, however, relies on a narrow construction of the term 'people'. It is concerned with the rights of workers, and denies any rights to capitalists. It does not even recognize the rights of the middle class which is rapidly expanding in the contemporary world.

The cause of democracy will be better served if people of all sections are given equal weightage as regards their share in government. But Marxists insist that the state should be committed to a particular set of interests. That is why under the dictatorship of the proletariat, freedom of thought and expression and freedom of association are severely restricted, and the right to opposition is thoroughly curbed. In effect, there is no question of a free choice as the people have to function within the framework of the prescribed ideology and an all-pervading organization. Now this arrangement may be more conducive to social justice, but it is by no means an example of democracy.

Dictatorship of the Proletariat Holds No Promise of a Classless Society

Marx's vision of future society was based on a benevolent view of human nature. He thought that when the root cause of conflict—the capitalist system of production—was finally terminated, all social conflicts would soon disappear and an era of genuine cooperation would be inaugurated. The twentieth century witnessed proletarian revolutions inspired by Marxist ideology, especially in the USSR (1917) and the People's Republic of China (1949) where Marxian socialism was established. But the actual working of these systems showed a stiff competition for power, sharp political rivalries and cruel suppression of those who sincerely believed themselves to be true Marxists, not to speak of capitalists. The Sino-Soviet dispute in the 1960s emerged as a glaring example of the ideological differences within the communist camp.

The dictatorship of the proletariat was intended to be a temporary phase. But in actual practice, this not only persisted throughout but also fostered a system where differences of status were as sharp as anywhere in the world. Robert M. MacIver, in his *The Web of Government* (1965), drew a vivid picture of the Soviet system to demonstrate this phenomenon:

> The doctrine of the temporary dictatorship is contradicted by the intensive centralization of economic and cultural activities, and the 'stateless' society is relegated to the Greek Kalends. The doctrine of the people's rule is flatly rejected by the rigorous insistence on the party line... There is an

> impressive framework of electoral systems stretching all the way from the local Soviets to the Supreme Soviet of the USSR. There are everywhere People's Courts and People's Commissars. But the voting at elections is practically unanimous, and the one party retains complete control. The doctrine of the abolition of class has been negated by the occupational gradings, but far more thoroughly by the pyramid of power, which rises as steeply as, and perhaps more rigidly than, it did under the Czarist regime.

It may be noted that the advent of the policy of *glasnost* (openness) and end of monopoly of the Communist Party in nominating candidates for the election since the mid of the 1980s in the Soviet Union led to the collapse of the Communist system itself by 1991.

Hegemony of Bourgeois Values Poses a Challenge to the Marxist Road to Social Transformation

Marxist theory had anticipated the collapse of the capitalist system because of its inner contradictions. However, actual experience showed that proletarian revolutions took place only in a part of the world—that, too, where capitalism had not reached its highest stage. On the other hand, the continued success of Western capitalism has been resisting a proletarian revolution. Taking note of this situation, Antonio Gramsci (1891-1937), a brilliant Italian Marxist who was imprisoned by Mussolini, wrote in his *Prison Notebooks* that the dominant economic class does not exercise its coercive force through the state and governmental apparatus alone, but its role in the political realm is matched by the dominant class's hegemony in the social, cultural and moral realm. In other words, the ruling class in capitalist society rules not only by force, but also through the consent of the ruled, because it derives its legitimacy from the cultural and intellectual orientations of the people. This is responsible for the incredible resilience of the bourgeois civilization. Under the circumstances, the Russian model of revolutionary strategy would not be of much avail because it would only destroy one aspect of the power of the ruling class, leaving its general hegemony untouched. Gramsci, therefore, suggested that Marxist revolutionaries should first undermine the hegemony of bourgeois values and beliefs of the people before seeking a political takeover. This view, which had a wide appeal in Marxist circles, in fact, points to a shift in the focus of Marxist ideology and programme.

[IX]
RADICAL THEORY OF DEMOCRACY

Radical theory of democracy contemplates to expand the scope of democracy by recognizing and possibly combining the essential features of procedural and substantive democracy. It is best represented by Macpherson's concept of democracy.

MACPHERSON'S CONCEPT OF DEMOCRACY

C.B. Macpherson (1911-87), contemporary exponent of the radical theory of democracy, has sought to broaden the scope of democracy and to redefine its essential conditions in view of our recent experiences. In his earlier monograph, *The Real World of Democracy* (1966), Macpherson argued that the liberal societies which grant universal suffrage, a choice between political parties and civil liberties have no exclusive claim to the title of democracy.

Democracy is a wider phenomenon. Macpherson identifies three variants of democracy which are equally valid if they fulfil certain conditions. The first variant is, of course, liberal democracy which needs a more humane touch. Secondly, Communist countries might qualify as democracies if they granted full intra-party democracy and opened up their closed bureaucratic systems. Finally, Third World countries, which have no experience of Western individualism, could also conform to the ideals of some historical theories of democracy as far as their governments are legitimized by mass enthusiasm. Thus, in Macpherson's view, different types of systems which undertake to fulfil the aspirations of the masses, enjoy support of the masses and provide an opportunity for the amelioration of the condition of the masses, qualify as democracies irrespective of the structures and procedures adopted by them for serving these purposes.

Third World

The countries of Asia, Africa and Latin America who were the victims of colonial exploitation in the past and are still characterized by a low level of economic and political development as compared to industrially advanced nations of the world. After their independence, they have adopted different types of constitutions, including the Western type or socialist type, in order to cope with the problems of nation-building and economic development. Broadly speaking, their governments are legitimized by mass enthusiasm rather than by individualism.

In his more elaborate work *Democratic Theory—Essays in Retrieval* (1973), Macpherson has attacked the elitist-pluralist theory of democracy as expounded by Joseph Schumpeter (1883-1950) and Robert Dahl (1915-2014) as well as the utilitarian theory expounded by Jeremy Bentham (1748-1832). He has pointed out that the traditional or classical theory of democracy was erected on a moral foundation. It saw democracy as a developmental process, as a matter of emancipation of humanity. The elitist-pluralist theory, or the empirical theory, on the other hand, treats democracy as a mechanism whose essential function is to maintain equilibrium. Under this theory, "democracy is reduced from a humanist aspiration to a market equilibrium system. And although the new orthodox theory claims scientific neutrality, its value judgement is clear enough: whatever works, is right—that is, whatever enables the existing class-stratified society to operate without intolerable friction is best" *(Democratic Theory—*

Essays in Retrieval; 1973). The classical theory had throughout treated democracy as the cry of the oppressed, their claims for recognition as equal human beings—a means by which all men could enjoy and develop their human capacities. The exponents of the elitist-pluralist theory have reduced democracy to a means by which men can register their wants as political consumers in the political market. This theory identifies democracy with a static political system which takes the dominant groups in society for granted, whether they are *elite* groups or strong interest groups. With the acceptance of this principle of domination, the principle of equality is relegated to the background, or even considered redundant.

In contrast, Macpherson has developed a new theory of democracy based on a moralist view and a humanist vision; it will emancipate human beings from the constraints of the prevailing competitive social order of the capitalist world and usher in a new society which will promote 'creative freedom'. According to this view, the essence of man's freedom lies in realizing his creative faculties, that is his truly human capacities for the fulfilment of his self-appointed goals. Macpherson has particularly focused on the prevailing constraints in this sphere. He has argued that the empirical theory interprets democratic politics as a market mechanism and ignores the basic class conflict operating in a market situation. In order to understand the real character of capitalism, Macpherson has pointed to the existence of two elements in Western democratic theory: (*a*) the principle of utility-maximization, and (*b*) the principle of power-maximization. Of these, the first element is quite familiar which treats the human being as a consumer of utilities, *i.e.* inherently as a bundle of appetites demanding satisfaction. This idea played a significant role in the growth of capitalism. This is the essence of the original tenets of utilitarianism. The second element, *viz.* the principle of maximization of powers may be traced to J.S. Mill's modification of orthodox utilitarianism. It is an ethical concept which interprets man as a *doer* and *creator*, rather than merely as a consumer and satisfaction-seeker. In order to explicate this theory, Macpherson draws a distinction between two types of power: (*a*) *developmental power*, and (*b*) *extractive power*. Developmental power refers to man's ability to use his own capacities creatively for the fulfilment of his self-appointed goals. Extractive power, on the other hand, stands for power over others—man's ability to use other men's capacities to extract benefits for himself.

Macpherson on the Genesis of Creative Freedom

The Issue	*Utilitarian View*	*Moralist View*
Conception of Human Nature	As a Consumer	As a Doer and Creator
Goal of Human Life	Maximization of Utilities	Maximization of Powers
Requisite Type of Power	Extractive Power	Developmental Power
Consequence of the Use of Power	Satisfaction of Material Wants	Creative Freedom

Macpherson has brilliantly demonstrated that the capitalist system creates conditions under which non-owners of property enjoy negligible amount of developmental power whereas extractive power remains the sole preserve of the owners of land and capital. The concept *of possessive individualism*—the underlying idea behind liberalism since its inception—asserts that the individual is essentially the proprietor of his own person and capacities, owing nothing to society for these endowments. This idea gives rise to a system in which social relations between individuals are transformed into market relations. In a *simple exchange economy* where means of production are simple and inexpensive, an individual is the owner of the means of production as well as the means of labour. But in a capitalist economy where means of production are complex and very expensive, the means of labour are detached from the means of production. As a result, labour is regarded as a commodity which can be bought and sold in an open market. The means of social production are owned by a small capitalist class which operates them solely with a profit motive, with little regard for humanist values. Members of the working class are forced to sell their labour according to the needs of the market, with little scope for using their energies and skills creatively in an atmosphere of freedom. The power of a horse or machine may be defined as the amount of work it can do whether it is set to work or not. But human being is endowed with an urge for creativity—for making his unique contribution to society according to his talents. These talents are bound to rot in a capitalist economy where demand for work is governed by the calculations of private profit-seekers.

CONCLUSION

Macpherson concedes that the existing liberal democracies have conserved civil and political liberties more effectively than the existing socialist regimes. However, he advocates to combine a system of socialist ownership with the institutions of liberal democracy in order to prevent the use of extractive power and to promote developmental powers of all human beings. He recommends the expansion of welfare-state functions to facilitate allocation of goods and services to the people on grounds of need rather than desert determined by the rules of the capitalist economy. Thus, he seeks to evolve a system in which the advantages of capitalist and socialist societies shall be combined—a difficult proposition indeed! As Norman Barry has observed: "The difficulty with Macpherson's argument is that he evaluates existing liberal democracy by reference to some 'ideal version' of democracy, rather than by comparing it directly to existing alternatives" (*An Introduction to Modern Political Theory;* 1989). Macpherson's ideal is, of course, very difficult to realize in the prevailing scarcity situation. Yet efforts have to be made to meet the conflicting demands on all fronts as far as feasible.

In a nutshell, *democracy as an ideal* can neither be achieved only through political institutions nor only through a transformation of the mode of production.

It *has to be achieved* in all spheres simultaneously: in the legal and political sphere *through constitutional structures;* in the economic sphere *through socialist mode of material production;* and in the cultural sphere *through inculcation of new values of human equality,* and so on.

[X]
CONCEPT OF DELIBERATIVE DEMOCRACY

Concept of deliberative democracy embodies an attempt to reconcile two different models of democratic thought: 'Democracy as a popular rule' and 'Democracy as the bulwark of personal freedom'. Advocates of democracy as a popular rule argue that democratic decision-making should reflect popular will as if people are ruling themselves as free and equal citizens rather than being ruled by the arbitrary will of public officials. On the other hand, advocates of personal freedom argue that democratic decision-making should be the outcome of people's exercise of personal freedom, which implies freedom of thought, speech, press, association and religion, right to hold personal property, freedom to vote and to contest for a public office, freedom from arbitrary arrest and seizure as defined by the concept of rule of law.

Rule of Law

The principle which requires that the law of the land should be properly defined and notified so that the citizens know as to how it will affect them; any action against an individual should be taken only under that law, and not on any other basis. Hence, no one should be arbitrarily arrested, nor punished without a fair trial.

Accordingly, the notion of democracy as a popular rule is primarily concerned with the content of democratic decision-making so that it conforms to the popular will. Institutions and procedures of democracy can be adjusted to meet this requirement. On the other hand, the notion of democracy as the bulwark of personal freedom accords priority to the liberties of individuals. Any decision taken by the institutions which respect these liberties will be treated as legitimate. This view of democracy gives due recognition to the institutions of judicial review, separation of powers, checks and balances, etc., which are designed to protect personal freedom of the citizens.

Judicial Review

In a country with a written constitution, judicial review refers to the power of higher courts to examine the validity of any rule, enactment, administrative order or action in the light of the provisions, underlying principles or spirit of the constitution. If the court declares it to be unconstitutional, it would become null and void.

Now deliberative democracy requires that democratic decision-making should strike a balance between personal freedom and popular rule. It should be used as a means of encouraging public deliberation on issues that are best understood through open, deliberative processes. Deliberative democracy does not subscribe to the model of politics where each individual is fighting to secure his self-interest. It rather promotes a model of politics where each individual is trying to persuade others to find a reasonable solution of public issues. In other words, people in a deliberative democracy try to influence each other through an accepted mode of reasoned argument, that is to win their heart through an appeal to the prevalent value system. At the same time it pays due regard to personal freedom of every individual.

Doesn't this process diminish autonomy of the individual? When others are allowed to persuade me according to their convictions, shall I not be deprived of the opportunity of living according to my choice? Defenders of deliberative democracy tell me that my autonomy doesn't simply consist in living according to my choice. It requires me to have a share in political decisions also, which affect me as well as others. This is made possible only through the mechanism of deliberative democracy.

Deliberative democracy does not rule out division of labour between citizens and professional politicians. While it requires the citizens to participate in deliberation on public issues and thereby supplement the wisdom of politicians, it also demands constant public accountability of politicians. It requires the politicians to report and justify their decisions and actions to the people regularly and thereby help them to deliberate further on important public issues.

Deliberation

Deliberation refers to the process by which people exchange their views with their fellow-citizens as well as their leaders about their common problems and thereby determine their goals as well as their demands.

Among the classical thinkers, Jean-Jaques Rousseau (1712-78), French philosopher, had observed that representative democracy was not conducive to the spirit of democracy. In his view, when legislative function is assigned to representative institutions, these institutions evolve their special interests forgetting the interest of the community. In order to safeguard the interest of the community, each piece of legislation should be ratified by the community itself. The concept of deliberative democracy conforms to this view. Contemporary exponents of deliberative democracy include Michael Walzer (*Spheres of Justice;* 1983), J. Cohen and J. Rogers (*On Democracy: Toward a Transformation of American Society;* 1983), Bernard Manin ('On Legitimacy and Political Deliberation', *Political Theory;* 1987), S.L. Hurley (*Natural Reasons : Personality and Polity;* 1989), and J.S. Fishkin (*Democracy and Deliberation;* 1991).

Genesis of Deliberative Democracy

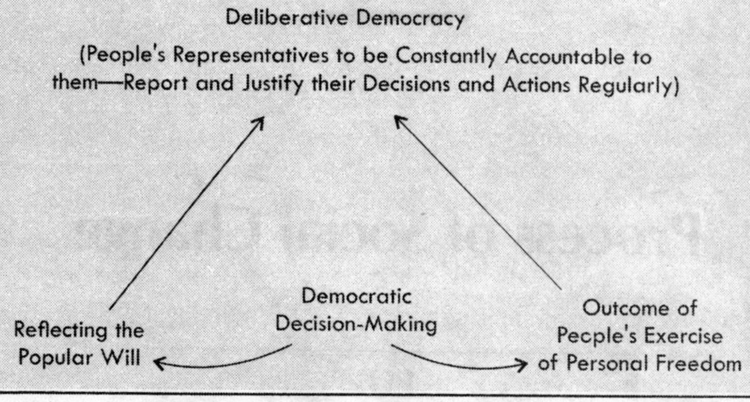

Composition of Deliberative Democracy

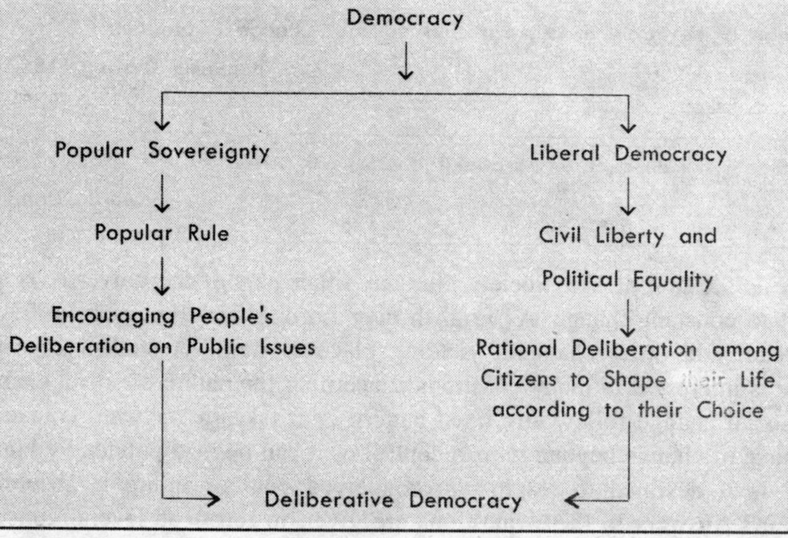

The general theory of liberal democracy expects each individual to form his political attitude by considering the best way to secure his self-interest. On the other hand, the theory of deliberative democracy expects each individual to form his political attitude by considering the best way to secure the 'public good'.

> When citizens bargain and negotiate, they may learn how better to get what they want. But when they deliberate, they can expand their knowledge, including their self-understanding as well as their collective understanding of what will best serve their fellow citizens.
>
> Dennis Thompson (2007)

24

Process of Social Change

[I]
NATURE OF SOCIAL CHANGE

> Change is inevitable in a progressive country. Change is constant.
>
> Benjamin Disraeli (1867)

> All that is human must retrograde if it does not advance.
>
> Edward Gibbon

Change is the law of life. Society, like any other part of the universe, is also subject to constant change. As English poet Lord Alfred Tennyson (1809-92) observed: "Old order changeth yielding place to new." A student of social science is interested in many questions concerning the nature of social change: Does social change follow any fixed pattern or it takes a wayward course? Is the course of change beyond human control or it can be manipulated by human effort? Is it destined to reach a preconceived goal or future is absolutely uncertain? Answers to these questions are given in terms of several concepts like revolution, evolution, development, progress, etc.

Revolution

Revolution refers to a sudden or very fast change in social system which may affect all aspects of social life, e.g. power structure, economy, ways of living, norms and beliefs, and so on. It may be the outcome of mass uprising, mass mobilization, new discovery and inventions, etc. Factors behind revolution may have taken time to reach the point of culmination, but their impact is felt abruptly at a given point of time.

Evolution

Evolution refers to a model of social change where any perceptible change is the outcome of cumulative effect of many short, imperceptible changes. It transforms the old, simple forms of social life into new, complex forms. This model has been borrowed from biological sciences. In other words, it uses the analogy of evolution of plants and animals for explaining the pattern of social change.

Development

Development refers to a process whereby a system or institution is transformed into stronger, more organized, more efficient and more effective form so that it proves to be more satisfying in terms of human wants and aspirations.

Progress

Progress refers to a process whereby a system or institution is transformed into a new order which is regarded better than and morally superior to the old form. Progress is distinguished from other concepts of social change (evolution, development, etc.) as it involves moral judgement and evaluation. While other views of social change try to measure it on empirical scale, the concept of progress applies normative criterion to ascertain its value for humanity.

Auguste Comte (1798-1857), a French philosopher, postulated that with the advancement of science our social organization is transformed from a 'military society' into 'industrial society'. In this sense, military society refers to a form of organization which is characterized by the regimentation of thought and action while industrial society paves the way for freedom of thought. Herbert Spencer (1820-1903), an English philosopher, also described political evolution in terms of transition from 'military society' to 'industrial society'. For Spencer, military society represented the tendency of integration while industrial society was characterized by differentiation. In other words, in military society, relationships among people were governed by the tradition while in industrial society, they became free to enter into voluntary relationships.

Henry Sumner Maine (1822-88), British jurist and legal historian, argued that all progressive societies proceed from 'status' to 'contract'. Status denotes fixed position of the individual within the prevailing social set up whereas contract indicates his freedom to enter into new relations at his free will. In fact, Spencer's distinction between military society and industrial society closely corresponds to Maine's distinction between status and contract.

Then Ferdinand Tönnies (1855-1936), a German sociologist, advanced his famous theory of transition from *gemeinschaft* to *gesellschaft,* that is from 'community' to 'association', for analysing changes in the social organization. A community is based on 'natural will' whereas an association is based on 'rational will'. A community is characterized by cultural homogeneity and enduring relationships whereas an association is marked by cultural heterogeneity and calculative, contractual relationships. Tönnies observed that the loss of sense of community in modern societies was responsible for the social problems created by the breakdown of traditional social structures.

Emile Durkheim (1858-1917), a French sociologist, argued that less advanced societies represent 'mechanical solidarity' (based on similarity between individuals) while modern advanced societies are characterized by 'organic solidarity' (based on complementarities between individuals which necessitate division of labour). Then Max Weber (1864-1920), a German sociologist, described the distinction between traditional and modern societies on a different basis. He observed that traditional society is organized around traditional authority which is based on long-established custom, whereas modern society is ruled by legal-rational authority which rests on the rules framed on rational basis.

Broadly speaking, each of the foregoing theories of social change projects a pattern of change from traditional to modern society. These may, therefore, be compendiously described as conventional theories of *modernization.*

Conventional Theories of Modernization

Exponent of the Theory	*Nationality*	*Pattern of Change*	
		from (Traditional)	*to (Modern)*
Augueste Comte (1798-1857)	French	Military Society	Industrial Society
Herbert Spencer (1820-1903)	English	Military Society	Industrial Society
Sir Henry Maine (1822-88)	English	Status	Contract
Ferdinand Tönnies (1855-1936)	German	*Gemeinschaft* (Community) (Predominated by natural will)	*Gesellschaft* (Association) (predominated by rational will)
Emile Durkheim (1858-1971)	French	Mechanical Solidarity	Organic Solidarity
Max Weber (1864-1920)	German	Traditional Authority	Legal-Rational Authority

In contemporary debates on the nature and process of social change, two theories are considered to be particularly important: (*a*) Marxist theory of revolutionary change; and (*b*) Liberal theory of incremental change.

[II]
MARXIST THEORY OF REVOLUTIONARY CHANGE

Marxist theory of revolutionary change is mainly based on the contributions of Karl Marx (1818-83) and Friedrich Engels (1820-95). In fact, analysis of social change is the central theme of Marxist thought. As Marx himself observed (*Theses on Feuerbach;* 1845): "Philosophers have only *interpreted* the world, the point however is to change it." Changing the world involves changing society as the physical world is governed by its own laws, and it is not amenable to change through human effort. Physical world is subject to 'necessity'; idea of 'freedom' can only be realized in social life.

Necessity and Freedom

As elucidated by Friedrich Engels (*Anti-Dühring;* 1878), necessity refers to the condition under which life of man is governed by immutable laws of nature, e.g. the law of gravitational force, which exist independently of man's will. Man can acquire scientific knowledge of these laws and apply them to his own benefit, but cannot change them at his will. Upto a certain point of historical development, *i.e.* till the emergence of classless and stateless society, human life is governed by 'necessity' whereafter it enters the era of 'freedom'. Freedom denotes a stage when man becomes able to create and recreate his social life at his will. Marx and Engels have described this point of historical development as 'humanity's leap from the kingdom of necessity to the kingdom of freedom'.

Marx and Engels have elucidated the mechanism of social change by their twin principles of dialectical materialism and historical materialism.

DIALECTICAL MATERIALISM

Dialectical materialism indicates the philosophical basis of social change. It may be recalled that G.W.F. Hegel (1770-1831), famous German philosopher, believed that 'idea' or 'consciousness' was the essence of the universe. It was the force behind all historical development. Marx rejected this view and postulated that 'matter' was the essence of the universe, which embodied the force behind all manifestations of social change. For Marx, any stage of social life represented the corresponding material conditions. Thus, Marx advanced his theory of 'materialism' against Hegel's theory of 'idealism'.

Hegel had tried to explain the mechanism of social change through dialectical method. Marx sought to combine Hegel's dialectical method with his philosophy of materialism. The term *dialectical* originally referred to the process whereby ideas are formed and clarified in the course of intellectual debate. A proposition or *thesis* is first advanced, and then challenged by a counter-proposition, or *antithesis.* Since both are apt to be partly true, the normal outcome of the ensuing discussion is a revised proposition, or *synthesis,* that combines the valid elements of each.

In other words, the initial idea or proposition or thesis does not represent absolute truth; the counter-proposition or *antithesis,* which is just the opposite or a negation of thesis, too does not represent absolute truth. When thesis and antithesis clash with each other, they tend to destroy each other's untrue elements (because true elements cannot be destroyed). The resultant proposition, or *synthesis,* which embodies the residual elements both of *thesis* and *antithesis* is relatively free from the untrue elements of the two; it is nearer the truth or perfection as compared to those two. But the *synthesis,* so evolved, may not embody the whole truth. It, therefore, takes the position of a new *thesis* and undergoes the same process of clash with its *antithesis* and the emergence of a new *synthesis.* This process of *negation of negation* continues till it reaches the stage of absolute idea which is free from contradiction.

Mechanism of Hegel's Dialectical Process

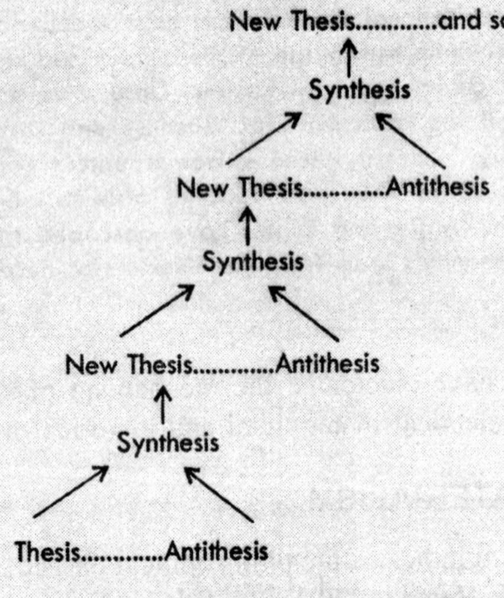

(This process will continue till it reaches the absolute truth.)

Hegel believed that social institutions only reflect the ideas behind them, and that it is the movement of ideas, through the dialectical process, which is responsible for the development of social institutions. Hegel saw nation-state as the highest stage of social evolution, as the embodiment of truth, 'the march of God on earth', the perfect form of social institution. While Marx adopted Hegel's mechanism of social change—the framework of 'thesis', 'antithesis' and 'synthesis'—he refused to recognize the 'idea' or consciousness as the real force behind social evolution. Instead, Marx believed, the social institutions are shaped by the material conditions of life, which are determined by the mode of economic production in society. Thus, Marx sought to replace Hegel's 'dialectical idealism' by his own 'dialectical materialism'. George H. Sabine *(A History of Political Theory;* 1973 edition) has observed that Marx's philosophy is marked by continuity with Hegel's philosophy in important respects:

> In the first place, he (Marx) continued to believe that the dialectic was a powerful logical method uniquely capable of demonstrating a law of social development, and in consequence his philosophy, like Hegel's was a philosophy of history... Though Marx construed his philosophy as a form of materialism, he still used the dialectic to support a theory of social progress in which higher moral values are necessarily realized. In the second place, for Marx as for Hegel the driving force of social change is struggle, and the determining factor in the last resort is power. The struggle is between social classes rather than nations, and the power is economic rather than political, political power being in Marx's theory a consequence of economic position.

> **Just as Darwin discovered the law of development of organic nature, so Marx discovered the law of development of human history.**
>
> **Friedrich Engels (1883)**

Engels (*Anti-Dühring;* 1878) sought to define dialectics as 'the science of the general laws of motion and development of nature, human society and thought'. He identified *three laws of dialectics* which can be illustrated with suitable examples from the material world:

(1) *The transformation of quantity into quality and vice versa:* At certain temperatures (quantity), water is converted into ice or steam (change in quality); water, ice and steam could be identified as the same thing (quality) at different temperatures (quantity);

(2) *The interpenetration of opposites:* Hard and soft are opposite of each other, but in the material world they interpenetrate into each other; iron is hard, but it can be moulded into different shapes which shows that it is also soft; a flower is soft but it can stay in its shape which shows that it is also hard; and

(3) *The negation of negation:* This is the basic principle of progress. *Every stage of social development contains the seeds of its decay;* its decay is followed by a higher stage of development until a perfect society is evolved. In the material world, when we sow a seed, it sprouts. In this process, the seed is destroyed. The seed-bud which appears is negation of the seed. Then it grows into plant. In this process, the seed-bud is destroyed. The plant is negation of the seed-bud. Thereafter ear of corn grows on it and the plant dries and decays. The ear of corn is the negation of the plant. It reproduces seed in larger quantity and better quality. This is the symptom of progress.

Application of the laws of dialectics in social life is demonstrated through the principle of historical materialism.

HISTORICAL MATERIALISM

It is important to note that dialectical materialism represents the philosophical basis of Marxism whereas historical materialism represents its empirical basis. In other words, dialectical materialism is the subject of philosophical speculation, but historical materialism is a subject of social and historical investigation like an empirical science.

At the outset, historical materialism implies that in any given epoch the economic relations of society—the means whereby men and women provide for their sustenance, produce, exchange, and distribute the things they regard necessary for the satisfaction of their needs—exert a preponderating influence in shaping the progress of society and in moulding social, political, intellectual, and ethical relationships. In other words, all types of social relations prevailing at any stage of historical development are determined by the economic conditions.

Marx's argument in this behalf begins with the simple truth that the survival of man depends upon his efficiency in the production of material things. Production is, therefore, the most important of all human activity. Society comes into existence primarily for the purpose of economic production because men in association produce more than men in isolation. A perfect society will secure all the necessities of life to the satisfaction of all its members. But according to the dialectic concept, perfection comes through a very long process. Society, since its inception, has always been subject to internal stresses and strains. Unsatisfied needs are, therefore, the result of the defective modes of production. But as man's knowledge of truth is also imperfect, he has always imagined another world where all his needs would be met. Thus, religion comes into existence as 'the sob of the oppressed creature, the heart of a heartless world, the spirit of conditions utterly unspiritual'. But, in reality, religion is no more than the shadow cast by a defective economic system which will pass away with the removal of those defects. Marx dubbed religion 'the opium of the people', because when no one's needs are fully met in society, religion is the resort of all.

As the process of material production holds the key to man's social life, changes in this process are responsible for all historical development. Marx's description of historical development is based on the concept of historical materialism. As Marx himself observed: "In the social production of their life men enter into definite relations that are indispensable and independent of their will, relations of production which correspond to a definite stage of development of their material productive forces. The sum total of these relations of production constitutes the economic structure, the real basis on which rises a legal and political superstructure" (A *Contribution to the Critique of Political Economy;*

1859). According to this interpretation, mode of production in a given society constitutes its 'base' or substructure; legal and political institutions, religion and morals, etc. constitute its 'superstructure' which are shaped according to the changing character of the base. What is the reason behind changes in the mode of production?

Marx's answer is: "at a certain stage of their development, the material productive forces of society come in conflict with the existing relations of production...within which they have been at work hitherto; from forms of development of the productive forces these relations turn into their fetters... Then begins an epoch of social revolution" (*ibid.*). To understand this process it is necessary to distinguish, at the outset, between 'forces of production' and 'relations of production'. Together they constitute the 'mode of production'. Forces of production comprise two elements: (*a*) means of production (tools, machines, factories, and so on); and (*b*) labour power (the skills, knowledge, experience and other human faculties used in the work). Relations of production are constituted by the pattern of economic ownership of means of production. At every stage of historical development, the owners of means of production constitute the dominant class and those left with labour power only constitute the dependent class.

Man's constant search for improvement of production (with a view to overcoming scarcity, etc.) leads to the development of forces of production. Means of production are improved by scientific discoveries and invention of new techniques and implements while labour power is developed by the acquisition of new knowledge, education and training. The development of the forces of production leads to the *contradiction* between the forces of production and relations of production. The intensification of this contradiction ushers in a stage when the existing relations of production are no longer compatible with the level of development of the forces of production. Its result is the breakdown of the existing mode of production and its superstructure. Thus, for example, with the rise of industrialization in the sphere of forces of production, the pre-existing feudal system in the sphere of relations of production (that is, division of society into lords and serfs) is bound to collapse which is now replaced by a new capitalist mode of production.

This process of historical development can also be explained by the dialectical method. According to the dialectical logic, the established order is a *thesis* which inevitably produces its own *antithesis* in the form of a new mode of production. In other words, as a result of some new invention or discovery, the productive forces come into conflict with the existing relations of production, particularly with the prevailing property system, which instead of furthering their development becomes fetters on the forces of production. As a result of the clash between the existing social relations and the new productive forces, a new revolutionary class emerges which overthrows the existing order in a violent revolution. The old order gives way to the new—slave society is replaced by feudal society; feudal society is replaced by capitalist society; capitalist society is replaced by socialist society. The new order so established represents the *synthesis* of the earlier orders which had been destroyed. According to the dialectical logic, every stage of society which falls short of perfection contains the seeds of its own decay. Marx saw his contemporary capitalist society as an imperfect stage because it was marked by the division of society into antagonistic classes—the haves and have-nots, the *bourgeoisie* and *proletariat,* the dominant and dependent classes—and the consequent exploitation of the dependent class. It was, therefore, doomed due to an interplay of its inherent contradictions.

Marx and Engels identified four main stages of past historical development: (*a*) primitive communism in which forms of production are slight and communally owned; (*b*) ancient slave-owning society in which the means of production are owned by masters and labour for production is done by the slaves; (*c*) medieval feudal society in which the means of production are owned by feudal lords and labour for production is done by the serfs; and (*d*) modern capitalist society in which the means of production are owned by capitalists and labour for production is done by the proletariat—the propertyless workers. At each stage, society is divided into antagonistic classes; the class which owns the means of production and controls the forces of production, dominates the rest, thus perpetuating tension and conflict. At each stage of historical development, the forms or conditions of production determine the structure of society. Thus, 'the hand-mill gives you society with the feudal lord, the steam-mill society with the industrial capitalist'. The structure of society will in its turn breed attitudes, actions, and civilizations. Therefore, 'all the social, political and intellectual relations, all religious and legal systems, all the theoretical outlooks which emerge in the course of history, are derived from the material conditions of life'.

The forces of capitalism had heralded a new era of progress by destroying the feudal system. But Marx saw capitalism itself as a transitory phase. As George H. Sabine (A *History of Political Theory;* 1973 *edition)* has elaborated:

> The abolition of feudalism meant for Marx the rise to power of the middle class and the creation of a political system which made its power effective. In its most developed form, as yet only partially reached, this system would be the democratic republic. The French Revolution, therefore, had been essentially a political revolution. It had transferred social dominance from the nobility and the clergy to the industrial and commercial middle class; it had created the state as a typical organ of middle class repression and exploitation; and its philosophy—the system of natural rights in politics and economics—was the ideal justification and rationalization of the middle class right to exploit the worker.

French Revolution

In European history, French Revolution refers to the culmination of the series of violent political and social upheavals in France (1789-99) caused by the revolt of the middle classes against the prevalent regime. It resulted in the overthrow of King Louis XVI, the end of monarchy as well as the supremacy of nobility and clergy, followed by the establishment of popular sovereignty.

Thus, class-conflict was inevitable during the capitalist stage of historical development, and another revolution was in store. Marx, therefore, anticipated a more profound social revolution by which the rising proletariat would displace the middle class from power as the middle class had displaced the older feudal class. This revolution would pave the way for the termination of the era of exploitation. As Sabine has further elucidated:

> The rising class, too, must have its philosophy, and as the philosophy of the middle class was in substance a claim to the natural rights of property, so a proletarian philosophy must be a socialist claim to the human rights of men without property. But just because the proletariat lay at the bottom of the social structure, with no class below it to be exploited, a proletarian revolution would not merely transfer the power to exploit but would abolish exploitation. It would be the first step to a society without distinctions of social class and a true beginning of history as a record of full human self-realization.

An Outline of Historical Materialism

(Marxian Analysis of the Process of Historical development)

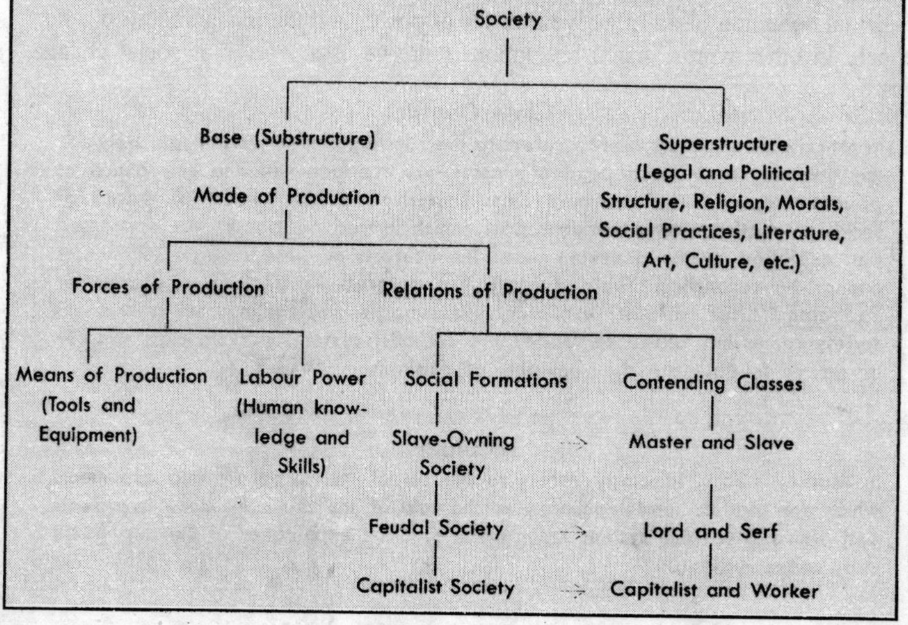

THEORY OF REVOLUTION

Marxist theory of revolution is an integral part of dialectical materialism. According to the dialectic model of analysis, development of *thesis* and *antithesis* takes place slowly and gradually, but as a result of the clash between the two, *synthesis* appears in a sudden stroke. No stage of historical development would end until it has become fetters on the forces of production. The productive forces inherent in any society develop completely before a change takes place, and the change itself would be sudden as when ice turns into water, or water turns into steam. In that sudden revolutionary change, the entire structure of society would be eventually transformed, until the new society in its turn is overthrown and remoulded. Thus, any significant social change—the epoch-making change—is always the product of a revolution. *Revolution is the indispensable midwife of social change.*

Each stage of social development evolves a set of ideas, attitudes and moral values to sustain the existing pattern of social relationships. These ideas lend legitimacy to the system and constitute the dominant ideology. Moreover, the dominant class always has the vested interest in the existing system howsoever outmoded it may be. When the existing system is no longer capable of meeting the demand of the new productive forces, it would still resist any attempts to change it, so that the vested interests of the dominant class are not adversely affected. But the new productive forces must overcome all resistance and have their way. They must smash the existing economic substructure along with the entire superstructure in order to lay foundations of a new socio-economic, legal-political order. The dominant class will not be prepared to part with its power until forced by the new revolutionary class to do so. Revolution is, therefore, an essential concomitant of class conflict or class struggle. It is an essential condition of an effective transfer of power and the inauguration of a new epoch. In other words, social revolution is the necessary lever of social change.

Class Conflict

In Marxist theory, class conflict refers to the constant conflict or struggle between the dominant and the dependent classes which began with the emergence of private property. The dominant class comprised of the owners of means of social production. The dependent class, which thrived on labour, was oppressed and exploited by the dominant class. The interests of these antagonistic classes cannot be reconciled. Their struggle has entered its decisive phase under capitalism. After socialist revolution, this struggle will continue till a classless society comes into existence. Under the socialist system, working class will use its power to liquidate the remnants of capitalism.

Ideology

In Marxist theory, ideology refers to the set of ideas, beliefs and arguments which are used to lend legitimacy to the rule of the dominant class. It projects and promotes a value system under which even the exploitation of the dependent class seems justified.

Each new epoch of social history is, therefore, the product of a revolution. The capitalist system was established by a revolutionary overthrow of the feudal system, as symbolized by the French Revolution (1789). But as the capitalist system had now become fetters on the new forces of production, this must be overthrown by the new revolutionary class—the proletariat—in a revolution. Marx and Engels made it clear in the concluding part of *The Communist Manifesto* (1848): "The Communists disdain to conceal their views and aims. They openly declare that their ends can be attained only by the forcible overthrow of all existing social conditions. Let the ruling classes tremble at a Communistic revolution." Marx and Engels also called for the development of a revolutionary class-consciousness and a strong organization of the proletariat to fulfil their historic mission. Although revolution was inevitable, yet a conscious effort on the part of the proletariat would accelerate the process leading to revolution.

The proletarian revolution would be distinct from all previous revolutions of human history. A revolution in the past was accomplished by a small class, in its own interest, to establish its own supremacy and dominance, for the exploitation of another vulnerable class which came into existence with the introduction of the new mode of production. Thus, the bourgeois revolution was made by a tiny bourgeois class which sought to establish the capitalist system for the exploitation of the proletariat. But the proletarian revolution would be different because it would be a revolution of the majority against the minority, of the masses against the class of exploiters. It is not designed to win power for a particular class for exploitation of any other class, but to put an end to the system of exploitation itself. This would be the final revolution in history to establish socialism in place of capitalism. It would abolish the institution of 'private property' through socialization of the means of production. It would establish a *temporary* dictatorship of the proletariat in order to suppress a possible counter-revolution and to liquidate the remnants of capitalism. It would be a prelude to the emergence of communism. It was hoped that under the loving care of the dictatorship of the proletariat, socialism will blossom into communism.

Dictatorship of the Proletariat

According to Marxism, dictatorship of the proletariat refers to a form of organization of the State that comes into existence when organized working class overthrows capitalism and assumes full control of political power. It is characterized by the socialization of the major means of production, introduction of compulsory labour for every able-bodied person, *de novo* planning of material production so as to serve social needs (*i.e.* to provide an effective right to work, education, health and housing for the masses), and further development of science and technology so as to multiply material production to achieve greater social satisfaction.

Under the dictatorship of the proletariat, classes still exist, with the oppressive mechanism of the state. But this state is different from all previous states. It is not a state of property-holders for the oppression of the propertyless. On the contrary, it is a state of the propertyless for the liquidation of private property along with its ideology and culture. This state would introduce compulsory labour for every able-bodied person, undertake the fullest development of the new productive forces—maximum technological development and gearing the productive process to meeting social needs instead of raising private profit—and pave the way for the evolution of a classless society, and for the 'withering away' of the state itself. Communism will, therefore, blossom from the soil of socialism. No new revolution will be needed to bring about communism. As Lenin in his *State and Revolution* (1917) observed, socialist society is still an imperfect society; it, therefore, retains the bourgeois system of rights: 'from each according to his ability, to each according to his work'. But communism symbolized the perfect system of production with the highest development of the forces of production. It is, therefore, governed by the communistic principle: 'from each according to his ability, to each according to his need'.

> **While the State exists, there can be no freedom. When there is freedom, there will be no State.**
>
> **Lenin (*State and Revolution;* 1917)**

Some later Marxist writers, particularly Mao Zedong (1893-1976), pointed out that the class struggle does not end with the establishment of a communist state, but only takes new forms. Contradictions, which continue to persist even in a communist state—contradictions between progress and conservatism, between the advanced and the backward, between the positive and the negative, even between the productive forces and the conditions of production—must be fought perpetually in order to achieve the goal of communism. Revolution is, therefore, a perpetual and continuing process. This view is usually described as the *doctrine of permanent revolution.*

[III]
LIBERAL THEORY OF INCREMENTAL CHANGE

Liberal theory of incremental change was advanced by Vienna-born philosopher, Karl Popper (1902-94). Liberal thinkers do not believe that human history proceeds according to a predetermined plan which is beyond human control. They regard human being as a rational creature who can apply his intelligence, effort and will power to mould social institutions according to his choice; he can build and rebuild them. As regards the method of social reconstruction, liberal thinkers prefer reform to revolution. Popper has given very strong arguments in this behalf.

REJECTION OF HISTORICISM

In his classic work *The Open Society and Its Enemies* (1945), Popper made his first attack on historicism. Historicism in this sense stands for a belief in overarching laws of historical development, such as those expounded by G.W.F. Hegel (1770-1831), Karl Marx (1818-83) and Oswald Spengler (1880-1936). These laws claim to reveal the inevitability of historical process which is believed to be beyond human control. This also implies that human ingenuity and human faculties are incapable of influencing the course of historical development. Popper argues that historicism is a mask for uncritical attachment to a totalitarian ideology. It uses the belief in the inevitability of history as the justification for acts of tyranny and arbitrary violence. Popper dubs historicism a 'pseudo-science'.

> **Totalitarianism**
>
> **A system of governance in which the State seeks to regulate and control all aspects of life of its citizens—whether public or private. In other words, it seeks to direct all political, economic, social-cultural and intellectual activities of people toward fulfilling certain aims which are determined by the State itself. No citizen has the right or opportunity to criticize the State, or to propose any new aim.**

In Popper's view, all serious science begins with a 'hypothesis' which is subjected to the process of 'falsification' through observation for ascertaining the truth. In other words, for a genuine science, hypothesis should be formulated in such a manner that it should be open to falsification through actual experience. On the other hand, a pseudo-science projects its belief in the form of a statement which is not open to falsification, or it shuns falsification by the constant adoption of qualifications so as to accommodate every conceivable fact. Historicism is a fit example of pseudo-science because it attempts to subsume all of history under a single principle which 'explains' everything. Its belief in historical determinism leaves no scope of any departure from the supposedly inexorable laws of history.

> **Our knowledge can only be finite while our ignorance must necessarily be infinite.**
>
> **Karl Popper**

In *The Open Society and Its Enemies,* Plato, Hegel and Marx are the principal (but by no means the only) targets of Popper's attack. In Plato, he found the philosophical roots or justification of propaganda and totalitarian justice. Plato claimed that he had finally discovered the principles of justice. He wanted to enforce them through the propagation of a 'noble lie', a 'royal fable' or a 'myth' that sought to justify a hierarchical order because nature had made different people by different metals, *viz.* gold, silver and iron. Then Hegel created the myth of nationalism and the worship of the state. He dubbed the state 'the march of God on earth'. Finally, Marx created the myth of class war and violent revolution. In Popper's view, all these 'false prophets' were the advocates of a closed society that suppresses free speech, equal rights and critical deliberation. He argued that science and freedom flourish only in an open society which is prepared to accept new ideas.

Open Society

A society where there is a free flow of information, freedom to criticize the existing order and to reform or reformulate the existing institutions by attaining public support for the proposed changes.

In his another important work *The Poverty of Historicism* (1957), Popper sought to refute all forms of historicism on two grounds: (*a*) In the first place, Popper argued that the growth of knowledge itself exerts its influence on the course of history. Neither the growth of knowledge nor its general effects can be predicted, since to predict knowledge means that we already possess it; and (*b*) Secondly, that social science is of such a nature that it cannot generate laws of total social development, but only laws for fragmented and isolated social units.

Popper argued that the so-called historical laws are, at best, indications of a historical tendency. Marx's law of the increasing concentration of capital simply indicates a tendency. To forecast on the basis of a tendency would be misleading. It would never yield correct result.

FOCUS ON METHODOLOGICAL INDIVIDUALISM

Popper's view of the nature of social science throws a clue for the proper method of dealing with social reconstruction. He attacked methodological holism of Hegel and Marx who sought to propound all-pervading laws of historical development. Methodological holism stands for an approach to the social science which treats social life as a collective entity. According to this view, social behaviour cannot be understood in terms of the behaviour of different individuals. In other words, for the analysis of social life, whole society should be treated as one unit. Historicism purports to pronounce laws concerning society as a whole; hence, it closely corresponds to methodological holism.

Methodological individualism stands for the opposite of methodological holism. In other words, methodclogical individualism asserts that no explanation in social science or history can be valid unless couched wholly in terms of facts about or features of individuals: their properties, goals, beliefs and actions. As a champion of methodological individualism, Popper argued that historicism could not be rationally vindicated because the historical process was singular and unique. It was influenced by the unpredictable growth of knowledge. Thus, the future could not be predicted in accordance with rational scientific method. Popper severely criticized central planning and holistic social engineering as they sought to shape the future of society according to preconceived notions.

CONCEPT OF INCREMENTAL CHANGE

Popper argues that since any attempt at total social change would be futile, it would also be irrelevant to ask as to who is fit to rule. Social sciences should aim to discover the unintended consequences of human action. Hence, the relevant question would be: How can institutions be so devised that they would minimize the risk of bad rulers? Popper warns that rational action must always take account of the imperfections of our knowledge. The safest course would be to make sure that all programmes of change are advanced in small steps so that unexpected ill effects of any action are corrected as soon as they arise, and before they do too much damage. This policy is described as *piecemeal social engineering* or *incremental change*.

The concept of piecemeal social engineering may be distinguished from utopian social engineering in order to appreciate the merits of the former. In common parlance, a scheme is called 'utopian' if it is fascinating but incapable of realizing in practice, or at any rate, the cost of its realization would outweigh its possible benefits. For Popper, any attempt at a revolutionary change involves utopian social engineering.

Utopian social engineering projects a remote, complex ideal like the vision of a classless society. There is very little possibility of complete agreement in society about the desirability of such ideal, and the method to achieve it. It can only be implemented by authoritarian means, which may often involve violence. On the other hand, piecemeal reform calls for the removal of a specific present evil about which there is likely to be a broad agreement in society. So it can be implemented smoothly and peacefully.

Again, a programme of utopian social engineering will take a long time to carry through. The generation that makes great sacrifices and suffers untold miseries in making radical reform may not survive to enjoy its benefits. And the generation which reaps its benefits may not be able to appreciate the sacrifices made by its founders. Piecemeal social engineering obviates the problem of such injustice.

Finally, Popper argues that the nature and growth of scientific knowledge also vindicates the policy of gradualism in the realm of social reform. In his view, progress of science is achieved through step by step approximation to truth, not through the discovery of definitive truth in one go. It advances through successive amendments in its tradition of beliefs and methods. Social reform will also prove most effective if it proceeds gradually, step by step, like the progress of science. Popper does not favour revolution in social structure, but he is not so averse to revolution in the realm of thought, as no blood is spilt in intellectual revolutions.

A CRITICAL APPRAISAL

Popper's concept of incremental change provides new justification of liberal theory, and a new ground for desirability of reform instead of revolution. He has not hesitated to draw moral conclusions from his discussion of scientific method.

However, his preference for gradual reforms remains a debatable issue in the intellectual circles. French socialist, Georges Sorel (1847-1922) had argued that gradual reform never really achieves anything in the long run. Small concession given by the privileged class to the oppressed classes may mitigate their discontent for the time being, but they prove to be ineffective in finding a durable solution to the problem.

However, the champions of reform rightly criticize violence and bloodshed involved in a revolution. In fact, there is no foolproof method of social reconstruction. The advocates of revolution should make sure that the liquidation of one privileged class is not followed by the emergence of a new privileged class in a new garb. And the advocates of reform should make sure that the effect of reform does not evaporate shortly, but it should be used to promote 'equality of opportunity' and reduction of the wide disparities of power, prestige and wealth.

> **Every revolution evaporates and only leaves behind the slime of a new bureaucracy.**
>
> **Franz Kafka (1883-1924)**

25

Concept of Development

[I]
MEANING OF DEVELOPMENT

The concept of development was evolved in the sphere of social sciences for the guidance of new nations who won their independence after the Second World War (1939-45). These nations were described as 'developing nations'. Indeed the idea of development itself was not new. Early indications of this idea are found in the social thought of the nineteenth and early twentieth centuries. It was largely expressed in the theory of social change. The change could be conceived as the transition from simple to complex forms, from less efficient to more efficient forms, or from lower to higher forms. *Development may be identified as a process in which a system or institution is transformed into stronger, more organized, more efficient and more effective form and proves to be more satisfying in terms of human wants and aspirations.* It may be distinguished from progress because development is subject to measurement on empirical scale whereas progress is concerned with moral judgement for which it applies normative criterion.

> **Progress**
>
> **Progress refers to the notion that social change is heading towards a continuous improvement of social conditions of mankind. It is an evaluative concept which seeks to compare the ongoing changes with the vision of an ideal social order. It tries to show that any perceptible social change marks a step in the direction of realizing that ideal.**

Under the concept of development, we first identify some characteristics of an advanced society and then analyse the process of transition of society from its lower forms to higher forms. In other words, development implies a conscious effort for the attainment of a specific goal. The condition of society in terms of its distance from that goal may be described as the level of its development. Thus, J.H. Mittelman (*Out from Underdevelopment: Prospects for the Third World;* 1988) tried to define development as 'the increasing capacity to make rational use of natural and human resources for social ends', whereas underdevelopment refers to 'the blockage which forestalls a rational transformation of the social structure'. Other important definitions of development also tend to convey this idea in more or less elaborate form. Thus, Paul Baran (*The Political Economy of Growth;* 1957) described development as 'a far-reaching transformation of society's economic, social and political structure, of the dominant organization of production, distribution and consumption'. He pointed out that it 'has never been a smooth, harmonious process unfolding placidly over time and space'. Then Walter Rodney (*How Europe Underdeveloped Africa;* 1974) identified development as 'a many-sided process', implying for the individual 'increased skill and capacity, greater freedom, creativity, self-discipline, responsibility, and material well-being'.

In short, people wish to make best use of their natural and human resources in order to achieve their social ends. The process which facilitates their effort in this direction is called 'development'; the factors which hinder them in this effort are called 'underdevelopment'. Since the concept of development was specifically addressed to the 'developing countries' or 'developing nations', it would be essential to understand the status of this set of countries. They are also popularly known as the 'third world'.

[II]
NOTION OF THE THIRD WORLD

The terms 'third world', 'developing countries' or 'developing nations' refer to those countries of Asia, Africa and Latin America which are characterized by: (*a*) A low level of economic and political development as compared to industrially advanced nations of the world; (*b*) A tendency to keep themselves free from the influence of the capitalist world (the first world—comprising the countries of Western Europe, United States, Canada, Australia, New Zealand) as well as the communist world (the second world—comprising the former Soviet Union and the socialist countries of Eastern Europe which were dubbed Soviet satellites). With the dissolution of the second world by 1991, the term 'third world' should have become outdated, yet it still maintains its identity due to long usage; and (*c*) Of these, the countries of Asia and Africa achieved their political independence from colonial domination after the Second World War (1939-45). The countries of Latin America had achieved formal independence from the European colonial domination in the first half of the nineteenth century, but they had remained underdeveloped till the first half of the twentieth century, largely because of their economic dependence on the United States. In fact, the term 'third world' is not very precisely defined as some European countries, which are less developed and whose problems are similar to those of third world countries, are not included in this category because they did not seek to challenge the hegemony of the first or the second world with whom their names were associated.

In the sphere of international politics, third world countries have been following the policy of non-alignment; they refused to join military alliances led by the super powers of the capitalist world (the United States) and the communist world (the former USSR). India is one of the leading countries of the third world. Third world countries do not constitute a separate bloc as against the capitalist and the former communist blocs, yet they sought to maintain close coordination not only to ensure mutual cooperation but to raise a voice against their domination and exploitation by the industrially advanced nations. Although these countries are faced with tremendous problems of socio-economic and political development, yet they constitute such a vast majority of the world's population and world's sovereign states that if they act in unison, they are bound to play a decisive role in the future of world politics.

The usage of the term 'third world' owes its origin to its use in the present sense by the French economist and demographer Alfred Sauvy (1898-1990). Sauvy who coined this term first used it in an article published in 1952. It is interesting to recall that the prevalent social hierarchy of Europe before the French Revolution (1789) was comprised of three estates: the clergy, the nobility and the commoners who were described as the 'first estate', the 'second estate' and the 'third estate' respectively. So the 'third estate' stood for the commoners. The term 'third world' was intended to signify a modern parallel of the 'third estate'. Like the 'third estate', the members of the 'third world' were quite numerous; they were excluded from power; and they were also full of revolutionary potential. Again, the term 'third world' was interpreted as a third social and economic system as distinguished from capitalism prevailing in the first world, and socialism prevailing in the second world.

Since 1950s, this term came to be used widely. Today, the strength of the countries included in the 'third world' exceeds 120, which is more than two-thirds of the countries of the world. Moreover, the population of these countries is around three-quarters of the world's population. These countries may be relatively weak in their resource-base, but the strength of their opinion cannot be set aside by the international community. The countries of the third world do not conform to a uniform system of organization. They are conspicuous by their differences, conflicts and dissimilarities. Yet they are identified by certain common characteristics: (*a*) These countries have a colonial past, and they show resentment against the former colonial powers and against imperialism as such. In the case of Asian and African countries, their independence is relatively recent as they remained under colonial domination of West European countries—chiefly, Great Britain, France, Belgium, Portugal, Holland—till as late as the end of the Second World War (1939-45) and even thereafter; in Latin America, the resentment is directed against the imperialistic policies of the United States; (*b*) Due to the heavy drainage of their resources, and exploitation of their people during colonial domination, these countries find themselves at a very low level of development as reflected in the low per capita income, limited distribution of technology, a predominantly rural society with often as high as 80 to 85 per cent of the population living in rural areas, a small percentage of the population working in manufacturing industries, mass illiteracy (often above 50 per cent), limited educational opportunities with a high degree of educated unemployment, low level of nutrition with consequent diseases and disabilities, limited medical and health facilities, a high birth rate and the consequent population explosion continually threatening the standards of living, a limited social mobility, etc; and (*c*) Politics, bureaucracy and business in these countries are dominated by an educated *elite*, often the Western-educated *elite*, while the masses have little opportunity to influence policy-making; a large number of these countries have been repeatedly subjected to military dictatorship by overthrowing constitutional governments.

> **The third world is not a reality, but an ideology.**
>
> **Hannah Arendt (1972)**

[III]
FROM UNDERDEVELOPMENT TO DEVELOPMENT

The developing countries of today had inherited extremely backward economies at the time of their independence because their natural and human resources were intensely exploited during the period of their colonial domination. Liberal and Marxist writers have given different accounts of the reasons of their underdevelopment; they have suggested different directions for their development.

LIBERAL VIEW

The views of Western writers broadly represent the liberal perspective on the problems of development and underdevelopment. It postulates that all societies undergo a series of stages of political development through which primitive, traditional or premodern societies eventually become modern, industrialized societies. It implies that modern systems are more efficient in solving the problems of state and society in the same way as an industrial system is more efficient than a non-mechanized agricultural system. While a traditional political system is largely concerned with the collection of taxes, maintenance of law and order and defence, the modern system plays an active role in improving the quality of life of its citizens apart from performing the conventional functions of government. Again, in a traditional system, people are not involved in politics;

the government only exercises power over them. In contrast, people are closely involved in politics in a modern system; they communicate their demands and views to government regularly; they often express their approval or disapproval to government policies; and the government in turn relies on legitimacy in order to enlist support and cooperation of the people.

Liberal models of political development lay special emphasis on 'differentiation', which means increasing specialization of roles or a clear-cut division of labour in society; shift from narrow-group identification and loyalty to national identification and loyalty; change from 'ascribed status and role' (determined by tradition) to 'achieved status and role' (determined by performance); and development of appropriate processes and institutions to accommodate these changes.

Western exponents of development and modernization largely project liberal democracy as a model to be followed by the developing nations to secure their development. This is evident from the views of earlier as well as contemporary theorists. Thus, James Bryce *(Modern Democracies;* 1921) and Carl Friedrich *(Constitutional Government and Democracies: Theory and Practice in Europe and America;* 1937) saw political development as a march towards liberal democracy. Then Gabriel Almond and James Coleman (editors, *The Politics of the Developing Areas;* 1960), Gabriel Almond and G.B. Powell *(Comparative Politics: A Developmental Approach;* 1966), and Lucian Pye *(Aspects of Political Development;* 1966) expressed a similar view in a more technical framework. It implied that the new nations would have to develop their political structures as well as economy and social organization in conformity with those of Western-type liberal democracy, failing which they would remain backward. It further meant that third world countries should keep their economies open to free trade and international competition, and rely on market economy for their overall development.

> **Liberal Democracy**
>
> The system of governance based on the principles of liberalism and democracy. Liberalism seeks to mould human relations into market relations by evolving such rules and procedures that would ensure reconciliation of conflicting interests. Democracy implies the formation of government with the consent of the ordinary people. In a liberal democracy—where government is formed by representatives of the people—it is believed that people can exchange their votes for the policies of their choice as in a market-place they can exchange their money for the goods of their choice. They are guided only by their self-interest, and not by any higher moral values.

MARXIST VIEW

On the contrary, Marxist view suggests the path of confrontation with the imperialism, as enunciated in his *Imperialism: The Highest Stage of Capitalism* (1916), had postulated that in the international sphere advanced capitalism had chosen the underdeveloped countries as the target of their exploitation. Lenin had, therefore, exhorted the underdeveloped countries to assume the role of proletariat in the struggle against capitalism. Significance of Lenin's observation lies in exhorting the dependent countries of those days to fight for their independence from the colonial domination.

When it comes to deciding appropriate path of development for the present-day developing countries, Marxist and Neo-Marxist writers have argued that capitalist path will not suit them. The situation prevailing in these countries is basically different from that where the Western countries started their development. Thus, Paul Baran *(The Political Economy of Growth;* 1957) observed that advanced capitalist countries of today had managed accumulation of capital by exploiting their colonial territories. Present-day developing countries have no access to such resources. Capitalists of the developing countries are incapable of developing the forces of production. Hence, capitalist path would hardly promote their progress.

Underdevelopment: Centre-Periphery Model

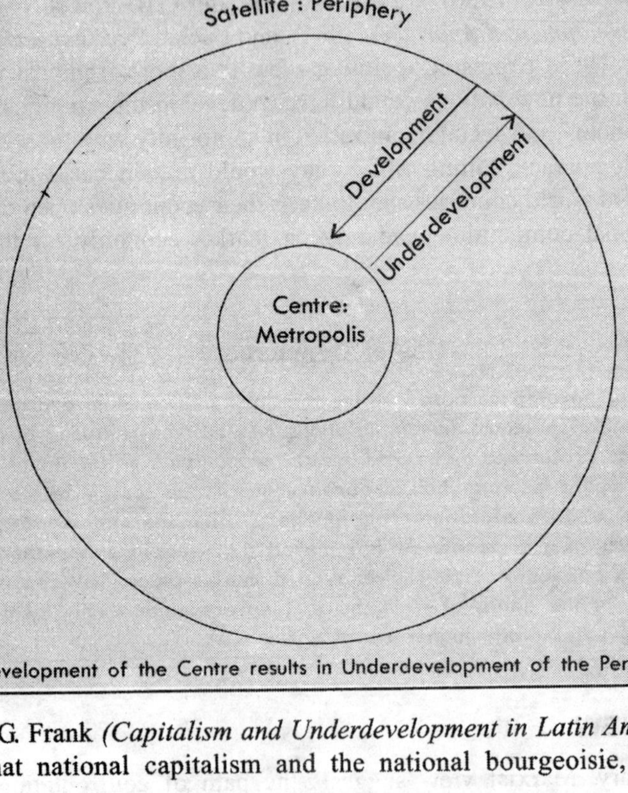

(Development of the Centre results in Underdevelopment of the Periphery)

André G. Frank *(Capitalism and Underdevelopment in Latin America;* 1967) argued that national capitalism and the national bourgeoisie, unlike their counterparts in England and the United States, cannot promote development in Latin America. In the Western countries, capitalism played a different role because it was rooted in imperialism. Frank advanced a centre-periphery model to elucidate the role of imperialism. He likened metropolis to centre and satellite to periphery. They are linked in such a way that the development of the centre leads to corresponding underdevelopment in the periphery. This relationship continued even when satellites had gained political independence. Frank suggested that in order to stop underdevelopment of the new nations, they should be delinked from the capitalist economies. Walter Rodney *(How Europe Underdeveloped Africa;*1974) and B. Cumings ('The Origins of Development of the Northeast Asian Political Economy: Industrial Sectors, Product Cycles, and Political Consequences', *International Organization;* 1984) confirmed Frank's conclusions in the context of Africa and Asia respectively.

Similarly, Samir Amin *(Accumulation on a World Scale: A Critique of the Theory of Underdevelopment;* 1974) argued that the industrialized countries and the less developed countries are integrated in a manner which inhibits capitalism from performing its historical role of developing the productive forces in the underdeveloped countries. Amin also confirmed Frank's conclusions in the context of Africa. Thus, most Marxist and Neo-Marxist scholars have advanced 'dependency theory' in order to explain the phenomenon of underdevelopment. In a nutshell, *exponents of the dependency theory argued that third world countries had remained underdeveloped because their social and economic development was being conditioned by external forces.* Historically, these countries had remained colonies of advanced capitalist nations; their looting and plunder by the metropolitan countries was the initial cause of their underdevelopment. In fact, *industrial growth of the first world was largely secured by the blatant exploitation of the material as well as human resources of the present-day third world countries.* After the liquidation of colonialism, the advanced countries are continuing the process of exploitation of the third world through 'unequal exchange' in the international trade. This explanation marks a departure from the conventional Marxist position which sought to explain the phenomenon of domination and exploitation in terms of forces and relations of production.

Unequal Exchange

The theory of unequal exchange postulates that in the sphere of international trade between developed and developing countries, the developed countries get higher value of the labour inputs of their products (because they use superior technology and produce at a large scale) whereas the developing countries get lower value of the labour inputs of their products (because they use inferior technology and produce at a smaller scale). This theory was advanced by Marxist scholars.

The principal tenet of the neo-Marxist theory of underdevelopment is that underdevelopment of third world countries is not a stage on the road to capitalism;

it is a condition, or symptom of their domination by the capitalist world. Advanced industrial societies of the West have throughout been responsible for economic and political underdevelopment of the third world. Under the present-day conditions, underdeveloped societies are still economically dependent on the export of primary products—various raw materials and agricultural products. Markets for these products are controlled by the capitalist economies; hence they are beyond the control of producing countries. Again, industrially advanced countries invest their capital in the former colonies and use them as suppliers of raw materials and labour at throw-away prices and as potential markets for manufactured goods at the market prices. Thus, former metropolitan countries continue to reap economic profits as earlier without incurring the political costs of colonialism. This strategy of the advanced nations is broadly described as 'neo-colonialism'.

Liberal theory shows third world countries the way to escape from their poverty by linking their economies with the industrially advanced nations. This is an illusion. Neo-Marxists argue that if the underdeveloped nations keep their native economies open to free trade and international competition, this will benefit only the rich countries and widen the gap between the rich and the poor countries. They, therefore, suggest that the suppliers of raw materials in the third world should form their cartels and fix just price of their products in order to prevent their exploitation by the advanced countries of the first world. An example of this type of cartel is provided by the Organization of Petroleum Exporting Countries (OPEC) which was originally set up in 1960.

CONCLUSION

Dependency theory is an answer to the problem of neo-colonial exploitation of third world countries. However, answers must also be found to other social, economic and political problems of these countries. Developing nations will have to adopt a concerted approach for solving their common problems. One response to such a proposal has been south-south cooperation. However, the question of a suitable model of technological development will still have to be solved for which these countries will have to depend on the advanced countries. Moreover, Western technology which is suited to serve the needs of an affluent, highly motivated and small population, cannot be adopted as such for the poor, somewhat apathetic and large population of third world countries. These countries must combine borrowed technologies with indigenous technologies for meeting the requirements of the teeming millions, and also ensure suitable employment opportunities to the vast population. The spirit of cut-throat competition prevailing in the West need not be imported to the third world which still retains some measure of communitarianism inherited from its culture, yet a modicum of competitive spirit must be introduced here as a measure of motivation.

Welfare programmes are indispensable in third world countries, but these should be designed to secure development of human resources and talents lest they generate vested interests of the incompetent and indolent and pra disincentive for the competent and hard-working strata. Moreover, third world countries cannot afford the luxury of consumerism as prevailing in the West. We should not forget that the West is already facing the crisis of human values in spite of its immense material prosperity. The developing countries can exemplify a blend of material and spiritual values to solve the global problems afflicting all humanity.

(Consumerism = growing craze for consumer goods and services).

[IV]
ALTERNATIVE PATHS OF DEVELOPMENT

Development is a complex process. There is no fool-proof method of development. Different schools of thought recommend different paths of development. Of these, four are particularly important: market society model; welfare state model; socialist model; and Gandhian model.

MARKET SOCIETY MODEL

Market society model of development equates development with modernization and projects Western society as a model of modern society. In other words, it implies that the developing societies should try to acquire the characteristics of Western societies in order to accomplish their development. James S. Coleman observes: "A *modern society* is characterized, among other things, by a comparatively high degree of urbanization, widespread literacy, comparatively high per capita income, extensive geographical and social mobility, a relatively high degree of commercialization and industrialization of economy, an extensive and penetrative network of mass communication media, and, in general, by a widespread participation and involvement by members of the society in modern social and economic processes" (*The Politics of the Developing Areas* edited by Gabriel A. Almond and James S. Coleman; 1960). These characteristics of modern society tend to suggest that modernization of the developing societies would result in their 'Westernization'. In political sphere, it calls for evolving the structures of liberal democracy. In economic sphere, it encourages competitive market structure. And in social sphere, it promotes equality of opportunity and respect for merit.

Structure of Liberal Democracy

Distinctive features of the structure of liberal democracy include: (*a*) Representative government based on majority rule with due recognition of minority rights; (*b*) More than one political parties freely competing for political power; (*c*) Periodic elections based on universal adult franchise; (*d*) Political offices not confined to any privileged class; (*e*) Accountability of government to the electorate; (*f*) Protection of civil liberties of citizens (e.g. freedom of thought and expression, movement, association and assembly, etc. including freedom to criticize the government); and (*g*) Independence of judiciary from executive and legislative control.

Exponents of market society model treat economic growth as a necessary condition of development. They argue that each nation will have to pass through various stages of economic growth before reaching the stage of abundance. Thus, W.W. Rostow (*The Stages of Economic Growth: A Non-Communist Manifesto;* 1960) has projected a five-stage model of economic growth, based on economic conditions: (*a*) traditional stage, based on lack of technology and intensive labour in agriculture; (*b*) transitional stage, involving preconditions for take-off based on technological advances; (*c*) take-off stage or self-sustaining economic growth when structural constraints on industrialization have been removed and an entrepreneurial class has emerged; (*d*) the drive to maturity when industrialization has started and the levels of technological development and productivity have risen; and (*e*) finally, high level of mass consumption when society has risen above the level of the fulfilment of basic needs and has turned to widespread use of consumers' durables.

Then A.F.K. Organski (*The Stages of Political Development;* 1965) sought to treat economic growth an integral part of political development and projected four stages of growth: (*a*) primitive unification; (*b*) industrialization; (*c*) national welfare; and (*d*) finally, the politics of abundance.

These theories of development tend to suggest that the developing countries should follow the footsteps of capitalist countries in order to secure their own development. André Gunder Frank (*Sociology of Development and Underdevelopment of Sociology;* 1971) has severely criticized this view. He has pointed out that in the case of Western societies, underdevelopment represented an original stage of traditional society whereas in the case of developing societies, underdevelopment is the consequence of European capitalist expansion. How can they follow the same pattern of development when their starting points are radically different?

Moreover, market society model is not compatible with the spirit of communitarianism which has enlivened the developing societies in the past. They have compensated for their material poverty by a modicum of social solidarity. The members of these societies have held a sentiment of compassion for their neighbours, visitors and those in dire need. On the contrary, market society is motivated by the spirit of competition where self-interest takes precedence over every other consideration. All obligations in a market society are determined by the needs of mutual interest. Even common interest is treated as an aggregate of the self-interests of different individuals. If the developing societies adopt this model, it would weaken the bonds of their social fabric.

In a market society, everything is subservient to 'maximization of profit'. Even higher education, art and culture are geared to fulfil market needs. The activities that promote intellectual development, respect for human values, the spirit of friendship, love and devotion are relegated to the background. Human beings are reduced to self-seeking animals with no permanent bonds of loyalty or commitment to any great ideal. Adoption of market society model by the developing societies may increase their material welfare at the expense of their moral strength.

WELFARE STATE MODEL

Welfare state model represents a modified version of the liberal view which originally stood for market society model. However, originally the idea of the welfare state was introduced by Prince Bismarck (1815-98), German Chancellor during the period from 1871 to 1890. Bismarck wished to strengthen monarchical absolutism in Prussia and to make it most powerful state in Germany. He was opposed both to liberalism and socialism. In fact, he sought to introduce 'state socialism' in an attempt to counter the appeal of socialism. His policy of 'state socialism' included a series of reforms giving workers various forms of social insurance which marked the beginning of the welfare state.

In England, the idea of the welfare state was introduced by Herbert Henry Asquith (1852-1928) during his prime ministership (1908-16). Asquith belonged to the Liberal Party. The National Insurance Act (1911), passed during his regime, protected many workers from the effects of sickness and unemployment. However, fuller expression to the idea of the welfare state was given in the famous Beveridge Report (1942) or the Report on Social Insurance and Allied Services. This Report was prepared by William Henry Beveridge (1879-1963), British civil servant and social reformer. It made wide-ranging suggestions including the proposal for a free national health service, family allowances, government action to maintain full employment, and universal social insurance 'from the cradle to the grave'. This included unemployment, sickness and accident benefits, old-age and widows' pensions, funeral grants and maternity benefits. The acceptance and implementation of most of the recommendations of the Beveridge Report turned England into a model welfare state.

In short, welfare state stands for a state that safeguards the liberty of its citizens, and provides for various types of social services for its citizens, *e.g.* social security (financial assistance in the case of loss of job or any other source of income, death of the bread-winner, prolonged illness or physical disability or any other calamity), free education, public health, poor relief, supply of essential goods and services like foodgrains, milk, fuel and transport to the needy at subsidized rates. For the provision of these services it resorts to the policy of progressive taxation, *i.e.* those who have higher income and wealth are required to pay higher rates of taxes. In effect, it is a method of redistribution of wealth in society which seeks to compensate those who are rendered helpless in an open, competitive market system. It is interesting to recall that before the emergence of the welfare state in England, social services were provided under a system of 'poor relief' where an individual had to compromise his self-respect to avail himself of such relief. But the concept of the welfare state removed this stigma. It was recognized as a system of mutual assistance and self-reliance where all citizens were provided with the means of a respectable living by the nation as a whole. It included the provision of minimum basic needs, housing, employment, adequate standard of living and opportunities for advancement in life.

Eventually, the idea of the welfare state became popular in France, Italy, West Germany, Sweden, Australia and New Zealand, but it was hardly encouraged in the United States which maintained its faith in the merit of an open, competitive system. For the developing countries, the policy of the welfare state became almost indispensable. In the first place, they had to deal with the problem of widespread poverty; secondly, they had a long tradition of social support for the poor and the needy. With the increasing urbanization, the traditional basis of social support for the poor was eroded. So the state had to assume greater responsibility. However, due to extreme shortage of resources, they could set up welfare states only on a subdued scale. To some extent, foreign assistance was also utilized for the purpose. But the functioning of the welfare state in these countries was adversely affected due to bureaucratic inefficiency and corruption.

SOCIALIST MODEL

Socialist model of development may be inspired by either of the two broad streams: (*a*) revolutionary socialism; or (*b*) evolutionary socialism.

Revolutionary socialism is based on the teachings of Karl Marx (1818-83), Friedrich Engels (1920-95) and V.I. Lenin (1870-1924). It believes in class struggle (between capitalists and workers), revolutionary method (for the overthrow of capitalism), full-scale socialization of major means of social production (land, buildings, mines, forests, machinery and capital, etc.), universal labour, focus on the development of technology, and planning for the fulfilment of social needs. This system was established in the former USSR way back in 1917, after the Bolshevik Revolution. Other countries adopted this system either independently or under the tutelage of the then USSR and remained its satellites till the dissolution of the Soviet bloc itself in 1991. Hungary, Poland, East Germany, Czechoslovakia, Bulgaria and Rumania which remained satellites of the former USSR were never included in the third world. None of these remained socialist after the dissolution of the Soviet bloc. Albania alone came out of the Soviet bloc in 1968 and became a part of the third world. It has since relinquished socialist system. Besides, Yugoslavia, Mongolia and Southern Yemen who adopted socialist system independently and remained part of the third world have since relinquished this system. Again, People's Republic of China, Vietnam, North Korea and Cuba, which adopted socialist system independently and remained part of the third world still continue to retain this system although they do not follow it rigidly.

Revolutionary socialist systems are remarkable for protecting the interests of workers, provision of social and economic rights, providing almost universal employment, education and health care, although they hardly care to protect civil liberties and political rights of their citizens.

Evolutionary socialism or democratic socialism seeks to achieve the objectives of socialism through democratic method. It gives precedence to civil liberties and political rights of the citizens and tries to make provision of social and economic rights progressively by expanding the social safety network. Its social policy is based on social justice and welfare of the citizens which are projected as the objects of mass appeal and mass support during democratic elections. In practice, democratic socialist model merges with the welfare state model. That is why the system prevailing in England since 1940s is regarded as an appropriate example of both models. India and a lot of other third world countries try to emulate this model. However, its popularity has declined recently. It is now realized that in a country with huge population, chronic shortage of resources, bureaucratic inefficiency and rampant corruption, it is not possible to cope with the mad rush of demands for subsidies and reservations for the poor and the underprivileged who outnumber those in the general category. So for further social and economic development of the country, emphasis has shifted to liberalization, privatization and globalization. We, in India, are also faced with this situation. However, the policy-makers must be warned that our intellectual tradition, cultural heritage and human value-system are not allowed to suffer because of the all-pervasive commercialization.

Liberalization

Liberalization refers to the policy of removal or relaxation of government control or restriction on economic activity of the people with a view to maximizing its efficiency. It seeks to reduce the state's liability towards welfare of the individuals and promote incentive-based rewards rather than dependence on various subsidies.

Privatization

Privatization refers to the policy of transferring government ownership and control of any sector of economy to private ownership and control in order to improve the standard of its management and to prevent losses to the public exchequer.

Globalization

Policy of globalization holds that economic efficiency can be increased to the maximum if economic activity is allowed to benefit from the resources available at the global scale. It encourages the utilization of capital and machinery available in one part of the world, raw materials in another part, labour in still another part for the process of production and search of markets for the final product all over the world. Its objectives include the minimization of cost of a product, enhancement of its quality, and the maximization of profit from its marketing.

GANDHIAN MODEL

Mahatma Gandhi (1869-1948), Indian thinker and father of the nation, was primarily a moral philosopher. He did not advance any specific theory of development. But the ideas expressed by him on different occasions for the guidance of mankind contain some insights concerning this issue.

Gandhi gave precedence to morality over politics. He saw politics as an instrument of achieving moral goals. His role in the independence movement of India was aimed at securing moral regeneration of India.

Gandhi never wanted India to emulate the ways of the Western civilization. He firmly held that the Western civilization sought to promote consumerism which would lead us to moral decline. Moral regeneration calls for self-control and the spirit of renunciation. Moral strength could not be gained through fulfilment of material needs. As Gandhi wrote in *Young India* (1927):

> I do not believe that multiplication of wants and machinery contrived to supply them is taking the world a single step nearer its goal... I whole-heartedly detest this mad desire to destroy distance and time, to increase animal appetites and go to the ends of the earth in search of their satisfaction. If modern civilization stands for all this, and I have understood it to do so, I call it satanic.

Gandhi was opposed to any notion of development that seeks to multiply material wants and to find the means of their fulfilment. He argued that in the West, people talk of improvement of quality of life in the sense of raising the standard of living. But the key to real improvement of life of man lies in his conscience. It cannot be improved by changing his external conditions. For this, man should be induced to gain knowledge of his duties and devote himself to their fulfilment.

Gandhi taught that man should consume minimum quantity of material things which are necessary to keep him physically fit. Additional consumption would mean grabbing the rightful share of others. As a visionary, he observed:

> Earth has enough resources to satisfy everybody's need but not their greed.

Gandhi warned that a greedy person causes immense harm to nature and society. He who does not control his desires creates scarcity of resources for others. Self-restraint is, therefore, not only beneficial to oneself (as the key to high moral character) but to others as well. Gandhi's principle of 'bread labour' insists that each individual should do, apart from his normal duties, physical labour towards production of goods for his own consumption. This will not only help in meeting the needs of the teeming millions but also raise dignity of labour.

Gandhi argued that in a country like India where a huge work force was available for employment, priority should be given to 'production by the masses' over 'mass production' by machines. It was also necessary to prevent the concentration of wealth. As he wrote in *Harijan* (1935):

> Dead machinery must not be pitted against the millions of living machines represented by the villagers scattered in the seven hundred thousand villages of India. Machinery to be well used has to help and ease human effort. The present use of machinery tends more and more to concentrate wealth in the hands of a few in total disregard of millions of men and women whose bread is snatched by it out of their mouths.

Alternative Paths of Development

The Issue	*Market Society Model*	*Welfare State Model*	*Socialist Model*	*Gandhian Model*
Status of the Individual	Autonomous	Autonomous but Responsible to Social Needs	Fully Responsible to Social Needs	Fully Responsible to Social Needs
Entitlements of the Individual	Opportunity to use full protential in self-interest	Freedom + social security in case of undeserved want	Employment, education, health care and social security	Fulfilment of genuine, basic needs
Status of Rights	Full provision of civil liberties and political rights	Democratic Rights + Social and Economic Rights as far as feasible	Priority to Social and Economic Rights	Duty is prior ro rights
Attitude toward Industrialization	Necessary for Development	Necessary for Development	Necessary for Development	It should be restricted to make use of existing manpower and to fulfil only basic needs
Attitude toward Nature	Indifferent	Indifferent	Indifferent	Very friendly
Goal of Development	Everyone to get suitable reward of merit	Reward of merit in consonance with social responsibility	Respectable living and congenial conditions to serve the society	Build high moral character of individuals, with dignity of labour

Gandhi's principle of non-violence was not confined to dealing with human beings. He wanted to extend it to dealing with nature. In effect, he deprecated the actions that degrade the earth, impoverish nature by over-exploitation of its resources and create inequity among human beings. As he pointed out:

> How can we be non-violent to nature, unless the ethics of non-violence becomes central to the ethos of human culture?

In the present-day society, it may not be feasible to stop industrialization as

Gandhi would have recommended, but Gandhian approach is being increasingly appreciated by the champions of sustainable development. They favour curbs on consumption by the rich to prevent over-exploitation of nature and to save the valuable resources not only for the vast humanity in the present-day world, but also for the future generations.

> **Machinery has its place; it has come to stay. But it must not be allowed to displace necessary human labour.**
>
> **Mahatma Gandhi**

[V]
CONCEPT OF SUSTAINABLE DEVELOPMENT

Development is primarily a positive phenomenon. It stands for improvement of human life in all spheres. But when it comes to economic sphere, some of its side effects may prove to be negative. Economic development demands higher production which involves exploitation of natural resources. In the modern age of gigantic machines operated by huge energy resources to meet ever-growing demand for consumption, the process of exploitation of natural resources has become very fast. Can this process continue indefinitely? Do we have unlimited stock of natural resources? Doesn't their mindless exploitation to match the pattern of our consumption have an ill effect on our environment? If so, what can we do to stop an imminent disaster? These are the questions which have stirred the minds of the champions of sustainable development.

The concept of sustainable development was aptly defined by the now famous *Brundtland Report,* entitled *Our Common Future,* published in 1987. Recognizing that the natural resources are not inexhaustible, it *insisted that the development process should be aimed to meet the needs of the present generation without compromising the ability of future generations to meet their own needs.* In fact, this idea was floated earlier during the Earth Summit held in Stockholm in 1972. This summit expressed a serious concern at the rapid depletion of the exhaustible natural resources. Brundtland Report endorsed these observations and sought to give a new direction to the process of development.

The prominence given to 'needs' of the present as well as the future in the Brundtland Report reflects the concern to eradicate poverty and meet basic needs of the vast humanity. The concept of sustainable development focused attention on finding strategies to promote economic and social development without causing environmental degradation, over-exploitation or pollution. The emphasis on development was particularly welcomed by the developing countries and the groups who were primarily concerned about poverty and social deprivation. The debate on sustainable development has remained a favourite subject of the champions of environmentalism.

[VI] DEVELOPMENT AND ENVIRONMENTALISM

Environmentalism or *ecologism* represents a natural corollary of the doctrine of sustainable development. It seeks to redefine the relationship between human beings and nature, and between human beings themselves. It insists that human beings should no longer operate as the 'masters' of the natural world but as partners with other living organisms. This perspective also calls for a thoroughgoing change in the organization of human world itself.

> **Ecologism**
>
> Ecologism refers to the view that ecology, *i.e.* "the pattern and balance of relationships between plants, animals, people and their environment" *(Collins Cobuild English Language Dictionary)* is a self-sustaining system; that no damage should be done to this system for the satisfaction of human need or greed, as it would be injurious to everyone's life. Ecologism calls for a review of the damage done to the nature in the course of unbridled industrialization, urbanization and multiplication of human wants. It insists that in order to ensure a healthy survival of mankind, the relation between man and nature should no longer be conceived as that of 'master and servant', but as one of friendship and partnership.

At the beginning of human civilization, population was very small. People led a simple life. They were very close to nature. Their needs were very limited. A small amount of production was sufficient to fulfil their needs. Whatever elements (like oxygen, nitrogen, carbon, etc.) they extracted from nature, were replenished through the natural cycles. So the normal consumption by human beings did not cause any damage to nature. The stock of natural resources was so large and their consumption was so little that nobody could anticipate any shortage of these resources in the future.

But with the passage of time, human population multiplied; people's level of consumption rose up, and superior technology was evolved to fulfil their increasing demands. This led to a large-scale exploitation of natural resources so much so that their stock seemed to be depleting. Again, the use of artificial goods in people's day-to-day life increased which took them away from nature. The changing patterns of their consumption began to cause contamination of nature. Under the circumstances, new efforts were needed to restore equilibrium between human beings and nature. In politics, the response to this situation came in the form of environmentalism.

Early hints of environmentalism may be found in E.F. Schumacher's famous essay *Small is Beautiful* (1973) which contained a critique of modern industrial society. He observed: "The modern industrial system, with all its intellectual sophistication, consumes the very basis on which it has been erected." Schumacher warned that the earth and its non-renewable resources should not be confused with the concept of 'capital' which we create and then spend or invest. In fact certain natural resources cannot be created and certainly cannot be increased. By consuming these resources, modern industrial society is running a business which is eating away its own capital. It is digging its own grave.

Advanced industrial societies, with higher rates of production and consumption, are more responsible for environmental degradation and pollution than the developing societies. As Ted Trainer *(Abandon Affluence!;* 1985) observes: Each American uses 617 times as much energy per year as the average for Ethiopians. Unduly higher level of consumption by Americans is also corroborated by other sources of data. They reveal that Americans comprise 6% of world population, but they are responsible for consumption of about 50% of manufactured goods and 33% of energy resources of the world. This leaves very little for the poor countries with vast populations. This trend is not good for the health of Americans themselves, not to speak of its role in the impoverishment of others.

> **Man is complex—he makes deserts bloom and lakes die.**
>
> **Laurence J. Peter (1983)**

Environmentalists argue that the people of advanced nations should reduce the use of private vehicles and increase the use of public transport and bicycles. They should switch over to consumption of green vegetables and pulses from that of fish and mutton. They should promote the use of wind energy and solar energy instead of coal, electricity and nuclear energy. Environmentalists encourage plantation of trees all over the world. In fact, environmentalist movement has motivated many Americans to running, cycling, taking natural food and living in rural areas. Similar trend is visible in other countries of the world also. Environmentalists wish that human beings should maintain friendly relations with nature, and should not damage it. Since they insist on maintaining greenery of nature, their outlook is also described as 'Green movement' or 'Green polities'.

According to environmentalists, the blind race for increasing exploitation of natural resources in the name of development has alienated human beings from nature physically as well as spiritually. In order to restore the harmonious relationship between the two, human beings will have to learn a degree of 'humility' with regard to their environment and to the various types of species on earth. We must realize that the relentless extraction of natural minerals and other resources to feed an increasingly greedy manufacturing system gives rise to environmental degradation and causes immense harm to humanity. It pours various pollutants into the atmosphere which damage the health of all living beings including plants and animals. This process is also responsible for greenhouse effect, global warming and ozone depletion which pose a danger to the very existence of mankind.

Greenhouse Effect

The process involving increase in earth's temperature due to accumulation of carbon dioxide and water vapour in warm air trapped by a mass of cold air. As a result, the heat generated by infra-red rays from the sun is absorbed in the earth's atmosphere and surface temperatures start rising. This would further result in the melting of polar ice.

Global Warming

The process involving extraordinary rise in earth's temperature due to increasing atmospheric pollution. This pollution results from the increasing consumption of petrol and diesel, and soil erosion due to cutting of forests and mountains. It is feared that it will give rise to climate change, the melting of polar ice and consequent rise in sea-level.

Ozone Depletion

Ozone is a concentrated form of oxygen. Its molecule consists of three oxygen atoms whereas a molecule of ordinary oxygen consists of two atoms. The 'ozone layer' exists between 10 and 50 kilometres above the earth's surface. There it absorbs nearly all of the high-energy ultra-violet radiation from the sun, protecting plants and animals from its damaging effects. It is feared that increasing atmospheric pollution has caused depletion of ozone resulting in a hole in the ozone layer over the Antarctica.

We can no longer throw our waste away because there is no "away".

William T. Cahill (1971)

Pollution doesn't respect state boundaries, and it is difficult if not impossible to solve these problems on a state-by-state basis.

S. William Becker (1989)

In order to save mankind from imminent catastrophe, environmentalists wish to dismantle the prevailing large-scale industrial system and to replace it by smaller-scale manufacturing system which would be sustained by a number of self-governing, local communities. In other words, they recommend that the existing system of production at a monstrous scale should be reduced to one at a human scale. Small communities with a moderate level of consumption, and organized at smaller scale represent the model world of environmentalists. That is precisely the idea behind Schumacher's famous dictum: 'Small is beautiful'.

In order to curb the overall levels of consumption, environmentalists also demand reduction in population. It is true that the teeming millions in the third world comprise the major source of its social and economic problems. But it should not be forgotten that their levels of consumption are very low, and proper planning can help in utilizing their immense potential of physical and mental labour. On the other hand, people in the West who are used to comfortable living and extremely high level of consumption also need reasonable population control, apart from the control on their consumption.

Finally, environmentalists insist on moral regeneration of mankind to ensure a just and equitable distribution of resources. If individuals of all countries realize their responsibility to maintain a clean and congenial atmosphere on the globe, they will certainly make it worth living for the present as well as future generations. This idea is aptly expressed in a U.N. slogan: "We have not inherited this planet from our parents; we have borrowed it from our children." Again, the sense of individual responsibility is expressed in another environmentalist slogan: "Think globally, act locally." When mankind is organized into small communities, people are required to act locally. When they are conscious of the effects of their activities on the global environment, they tend to think globally. A still another slogan of British and German environmentalists exhorts people to forget their ideological differences and act together for a better future of mankind. It reads: "Neither left nor right, but forwards."

> **The real owners of the land are not yet born.**
>
> **Indian (Kannada) Saying**

[VII]
CONCEPT OF POLITICAL DEVELOPMENT

General theory of development is largely concerned with the economic activity undertaken by a country for the improvement of quality of life of its citizens, and its social consequences. Since the developing countries are more concerned about their all-round development, it is the focus of their public policy. However, many scholars of politics feel that in order to secure an overall development, a country should also transform its political environment and institutions on the lines of modem nations. The process which seeks to transform political environment and institutions of a developing country in order to make it more efficient to fulfil the changing needs and aspirations of its citizens is described as political development. In other words, *political development denotes the process through which the political system of a developing country acquires the characteristics of a developed country.*

Concept of political development is derived from the liberal tradition of the West. It projects Western liberal democracy as the model of a developed society. Since it is also regarded as the modern society, development is sometimes described as 'modernization', and political development is conceived as 'political modernization'. In short, *modernization stands for the process of transition of a society from traditional values and institutions to modern ways of life.* Generally, traditional values and institutions are regarded as fit for an agrarian economy and society whereas modern ways of life are regarded as fit for industrial and technology-based society. It is believed that only the modern system is capable of fulfilling the needs and aspirations of the modern man.

Different writers have advanced different models of political development. Of these, *two* are particularly important which are *based on similar thinking.* The first model advanced by James S. Coleman and Lucian Pye (*Political Culture and Political Development* edited by Lucian Pye and Sidney Verba; 1965) conceived of political development as political modernization. In its view, a modern political system is more efficient than a traditional political system in the same way as the modern industrial system is more efficient than traditional, non-mechanized agriculture. Traditional political system was primarily concerned with the collection of taxes, law and order and defence but modern political system also plays an active role in improving the quality of life of its citizens apart from performing its traditional functions.

Under traditional political system, people were not involved in politics; government simply exercised power over them. But under modern political system, people are closely associated with politics. They do convey their demands and opinions to government. They do express their support or opposition to government policies and decisions. Government broadly relies on legitimacy of its acts in order to secure the support and cooperation of the people. This model identifies three characteristics of political modernization: (*a*) differentiation; (*b*) equality; and (*c*) capacity. Taken together they comprise 'development syndrome'.

Differentiation refers to the process of progressive separation and specialization of roles, institutional spheres and associations within the political system, *e.g.* the separation of occupational roles from kinship, of legal norms from religion, of administration from politics.

Equality is regarded as the ethos of modernity. It implies the notion of universal adult citizenship, legal equality of all citizens and the psychic equality of opportunity for all to gain excellence according to their respective talents and efforts. The 'subjects' of traditional society become 'citizens' of modern society. Modern political system encourages people's participation in the process of governance. This results in the greater respect for law.

Capacity in this sense denotes the increased capability of political system for the management of public affairs, control of disputes and coping up with the new demands of the people.

The second model of political development was advanced by Gabriel Almond and G.B. Powell (*Comparative Politics: A Developmental Approach;* 1966). Based on the structural-functional analysis of political system, this model identifies three characteristics of political development: (*a*) structural differentiation; (*b*) secularization of culture; and (*c*) expansion of capabilities.

> *Structural differentiation* implies the evolution of distinct structures, organs or institutions for the performance of different functions of political system. It operates at two levels: (*a*) At input level, it envisages the emergence of suitable non-governmental structures for performing the functions of political socialization (family, school, peer groups, etc.), interest-articulation (interest groups), interest-aggregation (political parties) and political communication (media of mass communication); (*b*) At output level, it stipulates 'separation of powers' between different governmental organs for performing the functions of rule-making (legislature), rule-application (executive) and rule-adjudication (judiciary).
>
> *Secularization of culture* denotes the process by which people gradually adopt more rational, empirical and analytical outlook in their political thinking and action. In particular, it requires transition from lower to higher levels of political culture, *i.e.* from parochial to subject, and from subject to participant political culture.
>
> *Expansion of capabilities* refers to an increase in four types of capabilities of political system: (*a*) *regulative capability* (the capability of legitimate coercion to control the behaviour of individuals and groups); (*b*) *extractive capability* (the capability to appropriate the natural and human resources of society and international environment); (*c*) *distributive capability* (the capability to distribute various benefits to individuals and groups); and (*d*) *responsive capability* (the capability to respond to the demands coming from society and international environment). A balanced development requires that regulative and extractive capabilities of political system are suitably matched with its distributive and responsive capabilities.

Political Culture

Political culture refers to those aspects of the culture of a community–including its values, norms and beliefs–which lend legitimacy to its political institutions and ruling classes, and determine status of the individual *vis-à-vis* those institutions and classes. Gabriel Almond and Sidney Verba (*The Civic Culture;* 1965) have identified three types of political culture, although in actual practice these may not be found in pure form: (a) Under *parochial culture,* the individual has a very dim awareness of the existence of a larger political system beyond his village or tribal group; (*b*) Under *subject culture,* the individual is aware of the larger political system but passively accepts its decisions; and (c) Under *participant culture,* the individual becomes an active member of the political system. It creates respect for authority, a sense of individual independence and acceptance of legitimacy of the political system. It is based on the belief that the individual can and should influence the system.

Types of Political Culture

The Issue	*Parochial Culture*	*Subject Culture*	*Participant Culture*
People's Concern for political institutions and processes	Very Little: They hardly differentiate politics as a distinct sphere of life	Only Superficial: People are aware of the political processes and their outcomes but they are hardly interested in playing any role therein	Very Deep: Citizens have a strong sense of their role in politics and their responsibility in this sphere
Political roles of different social organs	Not yet fixed	Dimly fixed	Firmly fixed
Level of Individual's awareness of his political role	Low	Average	High
Individual's Capacity to Influence Political decisions and policies	Negligible	Marginal	Substantial
Prospects of change in political fortunes of people	Not Expected	Thinly Expected	Strongly Expected
Largely found in	Poor, illiterate, under-developed countries	Authoritarian Regimes	Democratic Regimes

Broadly speaking, a traditional society is characterized by parochial culture; a transitional society by subject culture; and a modern society by participant culture. Political culture is a non-institutional element which may sustain certain political institutions, and fail to sustain others. For example, a culture based on 'caste system', 'ancestor worship' or 'divine right of kingship' will fail to sustain democracy. It must be transformed to cultivate belief in human equality for upholding democratic institutions. The process of modernization involves transition from lower to higher forms of political culture which requires to ensure individual's increasing concern with and response to the larger political system. It means that the individual who was initially indifferent to politics, should be gradually drawn into the political process as an increasingly conscious and responsible participant.

If developing societies are able to develop the characteristics of political moderniztion or political development in their political systems, they are likely to prove more efficient in their political functioning. But each of these countries must combine these requisites with its own genius. Because of their large size, complex and multicultural character combined with the heritage of communitarian sentiment, they should not be reduced to competitive market societies in the name of their political development.

Political Modernization and Development: A Comparative Study		
The Issue	*Political Modernization (as conceived by James Coleman and Lucian Pye)*	*Political Development (as conceived by Gabriel Almond and G.B. Powell)*
Structural Changes	*Differentiation* The process of progressive separation and specialization of roles, institutional spheres and associations within the political system	*Structural Differentiation* The emergence of distinct structures for the performance of specific functions both at input and output levels
Attitudinal Changes	*Equality* Transformation of the 'subjects' of the traditional society into 'citizens' of modern society; legal equality and equality of opportunity for all citizens	*Secularization of Culture* Adoption of more rational, empirical and analytical outlook leading to political participation of all as equal citizens
Development of Abilities	*Capacity* Greater efficiency of the political system to manage public affairs, control disputes, and fulfil the needs and aspirations of people	*Expansion of Capabilities* Balancing of regulative and extractive capabilities of the political system with its distributive and responsive capabilities

[VIII]
NATION-BUILDING AND STATE-BUILDING

Concepts of nation-building and state-building are closely related to the concept of political development. These processes are particularly important for the new nations of Asia, Africa and Latin America which are described as 'developing societies'. These are complementary processes which must be taken up together as they would strengthen each other.

Most of the new nations had to face the problem of their political integration so that the people in each country consider themselves part and parcel of a single nation and owe their loyalty to a single centre of power. These states, in fact, represent conglomerations of different racial, tribal, ethnic, religious and regional groups with a weak sense of identity and the common interest. Their integration into a nation-state involves the problem of nation-building and state-building. *Nation-building stands for the process by which people transfer their commitment and loyalty from smaller tribes, villages or petty principalities to the larger central political system.* It involves developing a sense of community among the people within the jurisdiction of a political system and provides for a sense of identification, a common object of their allegiance, an emotional bond and social solidarity. It gives them a national identity cutting across their group loyalties based on religion, race, caste, language, region, culture, occupation, etc. This process integrates the diverse sectors and strata of society and produces the consensus and cooperation so vital to domestic peace and political effectiveness. It involves developing the concept of the legitimacy of the nation as the larger and central political system.

Political Integration

Political integration refers to the process through which individual identifies himself as an integral part of his community while retaining his personal identity in his personality.

However, this process would remain incomplete without undertaking the task of state-building. Respect for authority and for the prevalent method of rule cannot be won until the state itself proves to be capable of fulfilling the needs and aspirations of the people. *State-building implies the process whereby a common centre of power is evolved in order to establish law and order throughout the state and to extend the defensive and welfare services of the state to each and every part of its territory.*

Models of Nation-Building and State-Building

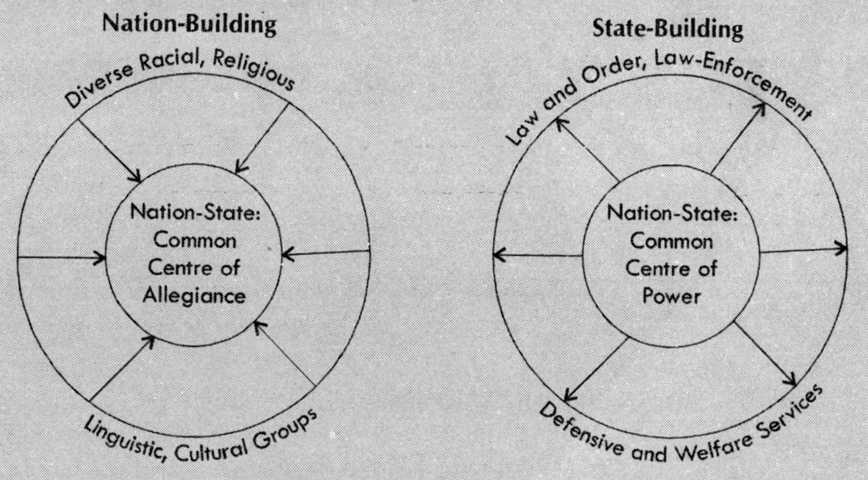

Rajni Kothari, an eminent Indian scholar *(State and Nation-Building: A Third World Perspective;* 1976), has observed that the concept of state-building and nation-building represents the political aspect of a country's development whereas modernization is concerned with its economic, technological and administrative aspects. Western political scientists argue that the developing countries should first attend to the problem of modernization; political development would take care of itself. In other words, the developing countries should focus on raising their Gross National Product (GNP), urbanization, rational bureaucratic establishment, manipulative technology and social mobilization; their political development would automatically follow when these objectives have been achieved. Kothari has rightly pointed out that this view is not corroborated by the European history itself. European countries had achieved national consolidation before embarking on their modernization. So the developing countries should also give precedence to state-building and nation-building before undertaking their modernization.

> The need of the moment is not one religion, but mutual respect and tolerance of the devotees of the different religions. We want to reach not the dead level, but unity in diversity.
>
> Mahatma Gandhi

> In India, the first essential is the maintenance of the unity of the country, not merely a political unity but a unity of the mind and the heart, which precludes the narrow urges that make for disunity.
>
> Jawaharlal Nehru

Further Reading

Books

Anthony Arblaster: *Democracy* (Milton Keynes, Open University Press, 1987).

Om Bakshi: *The Crisis of Political Theory: An Inquiry into Contemporary Thought* (Delhi, Oxford University Press, 1987).

Alan R. Ball: *Modern Politics and Government* (London, Macmillan, 1988).

Leon P. Baradat: *Political Ideologies—Their Origins and Impact* (Englewood Cliffs, Prentice-Hall, 1979).

J. M. Barbalet: *Citizenship—Rights, Struggle and Class Inequality* (Milton Keynes, Open University Press, 1988).

Ernest Barker: *Principles of Social and Political Theory* (London, Oxford University Press, 1951).

Norman P. Barry: *An Introduction to Modem Political Theory* (London, Macmillan, 1989).

Richard Bellamy (*ed.*): *Theories and Concepts of Politics* (New York, Manchester University Press, 1993).

S.I. Benn, R. S. Peters: *Social Principles and the Democratic State* (London, George Allen & Unwin, 1975).

André Bétteille: *Ideology and Social Science* (New Delhi, Penguin Books, 2006).

——: *Inequality Among Men* (Delhi, Oxford University Press, 1977).

Anthony H. Birch: *The Concepts and Theories of Modern Democracy* (London, Routledge, 2001).

T. B. Bottomore: *Classes in Modern Society* (London, George Allen & Unwin, 1965).

——: *Elites and Society* (Middlesex, Penguin, 1964).

Stephen Eric Bronner (*ed.*): *Twentieth Century Political Thought—A Reader* (New York and London, Routledge, 1997).

Alex Callinicos: *Equality* (Cambridge, Polity, 2000).

Martin Carnoy: *The State and Political Theory* (Princeton, Princeton University Press, 1984).

G E. G Catlin: *Systematic Politics* (Toronto, University of Toronto Press, 1965).

James C. Charlesworth (*ed.*): *Contemporary Political Analysis* (New York, The Free Press, 1967).

Thomas Christians, John Christman (*eds.*): *Contemporary Debates in Political Philosophy* (West Sussex, Wiley-Blackwell, 2009).

William E. Connolly: *The Terms of Political Discourse* (Oxford, Martin Robertson, 1983).

Anthony de Crespigny, Alan Wertheimer (*eds.*): *Contemporary Political Theory* (London, Nelson, 1971).

Bernard Crick: *In Defence of Politics* (Harmondsworth, Penguin, 1964).
——: *Socialism* (Milton Keynes, Open University Press, 1987).

Robert A. Dahl: *Democracy and Its Critics* (New Delhi, Orient Longman, 1991).
——: *Modern Political Analysis* (New Delhi, Prentice-Hall, 1991).

Morton R. Davies, V.A. Lewis: *Models of Political Systems* (London, Pall Mall, 1971).

S. C. Dube: *Modernization and Development—The Search for Alternative Paradigms* (New Delhi, Vistaar, 1988).

Vernon Van Dyke: *Political Science—A Philosophical Analysis* (Stanford, Stanford University Press, 1960).

Roger Eatwell, Anthony Wright (eds.): *Contemporary Political Ideologies* (London, Printer Publishers, 1993).

William Ebenstein: *Modern Political Thought—The Great Issues* (New Delhi, Oxford and IBH, 1970).
——: *Today's Isms* (Englewood Cliffs, Prentice-Hall, 1980).

Robert Eccleshal, et al.: *Political Ideologies—An Introduction* (London, Routledge, 1994).

Jon Elster: *An Introduction to Karl Marx* (Cambridge, Cambridge University Press 1986).

Friedrich Engels: *The Origin of the Family, Private Property and the State* (Moscow, Progress Publishers, 1972).

Colin Farrely: *Introduction to Contemporary Political Theory* (London, Sage, 2004)

Keith Faulks: *Political Sociology — A Critical Introduction* (Edinburgh, Edinburgh University Press, 1999).

Carl J. Friedrich: *An Introduction to Political Theory* (New York, Harper and Row, 1967).

W. Friedmann: *Law in a Changing Society* (London, Stevens & Sons, 1959).
—— (*ed.*): *Legal Theory* (London, Stevens & Sons, 1967).

Madhav Gadgil, Ramachandra Guha: *Ecology and Equity* (New Delhi, Penguin India, 1995).

O. P. Gauba: *Dimensions of Social Justice* (New Delhi, National, 1983).
——: *Reading Gandhi* (New Delhi, National, 2009).
——: *Social and Political Philosophy* (New Delhi, National, 2007).

Gerald F. Gaus, Chandran Kukathas (*eds.*): *Handbook of Political Theory* (London, Sage, 2004).

Dante Germino: *Beyond Ideology: The Revival of Political Theory* (New York, Harper and Row, 1967).

Alan Gewirth: *Human Rights—Essays on Justification and Applications* (Chicago, Chicago University Press, 1982).

Morris Ginsberg: *Law and Opinion in England in the 20th Century* (Berkeley, University of California Press, 1959).

——: *On Justice in Society* (Middlesex, Penguin, 1965).

James A. Gould, Vincent V. Thursby (*eds.*): *Contemporary Political Thought: Issues in Scope, Value and Direction* (New York, Holt, Rhinehart and Winston, 1969).

Keith Graham (ed.): *Contemporary Political Philosophy: Radical Studies* (Cambridge, Cambridge University Press, 1982).

Andrew Hacker: *Political Theory—Philosophy, Ideology and Science* (Toronto, Macmillan, 1961).

Jean Hampton: *Political Philosophy—An Introduction* (Oxford, Oxford University Press, 1997).

Derek Heater: *What is Citizenship?* (Cambridge, Polity Press, 1999).

David Held: *Models of Democracy* (Cambridge, Polity Press, 1996).

——: *Political Theory and the Modern State* (London, Polity, 1994).

—— (*ed.*): *Political Theory Today* (Cambridge, Polity Press, 1991).

L. T. Hobhouse: *The Elements of Social Justice* (London, George Allen and Unwin, 1922).

——: *Liberalism* (New York, Oxford University Press, 1911/1964).

John Horton: *Political Obligation* (London, Macmillan, 1992).

Thomas Janoski: *Citizenship and Civil Society* (Cambridge, Cambridge University Press, 1998).

C. E. M. Joad: *Introduction to Modern Political Theory* (Oxford, Oxford University Press, 1974).

Nevil Johnson: *The Limits of Political Science* (Oxford, Clarendon Press, 1989).

Dudley Knowles: *Political Philosophy* (London, Routledge, 2001).

Leszek Kolakowski: *Main Currents of Marxism: Its Origin, Growth and Dissolution* (Vol. 1. The Founders; Vol. 2. The Golden Age; Vol. 3. The Breakdown) (Oxford, Oxford University Press, 1982).

Rajni Kothari: *Rethinking Development — In Search of Humane Alternatives* (Delhi, Ajanta, 1988).

—— (*ed.*): *State and Nation Building:* A *Third World Perspective* (Bombay, Allied Publishers, 1976).

Will Kymlicka: *Contemporary Political Philosophy: An Introduction* (Oxford, Clarendon Press, 2005).

Harold J. Laski: *Liberty in the Modem State* (London, George Allen & Unwin, 1961).

——: *The State in Theory and Practice* (London, George Allen & Unwin, 1961).

Harold Lasswell, Abraham Kaplan: *Power and Society* (New Haven, Yale University Press, 1950).

Henri Lefebvre (*ed.*): *The Sociology of Marx* (London, The Penguin Press, 1968).

Adrian Leftwich (*ed.*): *What is Politics: The Activity and its Study* (Oxford, Basil Blackwell, 1984).

V. I. Lenin: *The State and Revolution* (Moscow, Progress Publishers, 1969).

Michael Lessnoff (*ed.*): *Social Contract Theory* (Oxford, Basil Blackwell, 1990).

John Lewis: *Marxism and the Open Mind* (Connecticut, Greenwood Press Publishers, 1976).

Leslie Lipson: *The Great Issues of Politics: An Introduction to Political Science* (Englewood Cliffs, Prentice-Hall, 1993).

Seymour Martin Lipset (*ed.*): *Politics and the Social Sciences* (New York, Oxford University Press, 1969).

J. R. Lucas: *The Principles of Politics* (Oxford, Clarendon Press, 1967).

Steven Lukes (*ed.*): *Power* (Oxford, Basil Blackwell, 1986).

Robert M. MacIver: *The Modern State* (London, Oxford University Press, 1926).

——: *The Web of Government* (New York, The Free Press, 1965).

C. B. Macpherson: *Democratic Theory—Essays in Retrieval* (Oxford, Clarendon Press, 1973).

——: *The Life and Times of Liberal Democracy* (Oxford, Oxford University Press, 1977).

——: *The Real World of Democracy* (New York, Oxford University Press, 1966/1972).

John M. Maguire: *Marx's Theory of Politics* (Cambridge, Cambridge University Press, 1978).

David Marsh, Gerry Stoker (*eds.*): *Theory and Methods of Political Science* (London, Macmillan, 1995).

Karl Marx: *Economic and Philosophic Manuscripts of 1844* (Moscow, Progress Publishers, 1977).

——, Friedrich Engels: *Manifesto of the Communist Party* (*Communist Manifesto*) (Moscow, Progress Publishers, 1975).

Catriona McKinnon (*ed.*): *Issues in Political Theory* (Oxford, Oxford University Press, 2008).

David MacLellan: *Marxism After Marx: An Introduction* (London, Macmillan, 1979).

Peter H. Merkl : *Political Continuity and Change* (New York, Harper & Row, 1972).

Diana Tietjens Meyers (*ed.*): *Feminist Thought—A Reader* (New York & London, Routledge, 1997).

Ralph Miliband: *Marxism and Politics* (Oxford, Oxford University Press, 1977).

——: *The State in Capitalist Society: The Analysis of Western System of Power* (London, Quartet Books, 1969).

David Miller (*ed.*): *Liberty* (Oxford, Oxford University Press, 1991).

——: *Political Philosophy—A Very Short Introduction* (Oxford, Oxford University Press, 2003).

——: Social Justice (Oxford, Clarendon Press, 1976).

——, Larry Siedentop (*eds.*): *The Nature of Political Theory* (Oxford, Clarendon Press, 1983).

J. D. B. Miller: *The Nature of Politics* (London, Gerald Duckworth, 1962).

Kenneth Minogue: *Politics—A Very Short Introduction* (Oxford, Oxford University Press, 1995).

Manoranjan Mohanty: *Contemporary Indian Political Theory* (New Delhi, Samskriti, 2000).

Lydia Morris: *Dangerous Classes—The Underclass and Social Citizenship* (London and New York, Routledge, 1994).

Thomas Pantham: *Political Theories and Social Reconstruction* (New Delhi, Sage India, 1995).

Bhikhu Parekh: *Gandhi—A Very Short Introduction* (Oxford, Oxford University Press, 1997).

——, *Rethinking Multiculturalism—Cultural Diversity and Political Theory* (Harvard, Harvard University Press, 2002).

Geriant Parry: *Political Elites* (London, George Allen & Unwin, 1969) .

Z. Pelczynski, John Gray (*eds.*): *Conceptions of Liberty in Political Philosophy* (London, The Athlone Press, 1984).

J. Ronald Pennock: *Democratic Political Theory* (Princeton, Princeton University Press, 1979).

John Plamenatz: *Democracy and Illusion* (London, Longman, 1978).

Roscoe Pound: *The Spirit of the Common Law* (New Hampshire, Marshall Jones Company, 1931).

Anthony Quinton (*ed.*): *Political Philosophy* (Oxford, Oxford University Press, 1967).

Ramashray Roy: *Understanding Gandhi* (Delhi, Ajanta, 1996).

D. D. Raphael: *Problems of Political Philosophy* (London, Macmillan, 1976).

John Rawls: *A Theory of Justice* (Oxford, Oxford University Press, 1971).

John Rees: *Equality* (London, Pall Mall, 1971).

David M. Ricci: *The Tragedy of Political Science* (New Haven, Yale University Press, 1984).

W. G. Runciman: *Social Science and Political Theory* (Cambridge, Cambridge University Press, 1969).

Michael Rush: *Politics and Society—An Introduction to Political Sociology* (New York, Harvester Wheatsheaf, 1992).

Michael J. Sandel (*ed.*): *Liberalism and its Critics* (Oxford, Basil Blackwell, 1984).

John Schwartzmantel: *The State in Contemporary Society—An Introduction* (New York, Wheatsheaf, 1994).

Amartya Sen: *Development as Freedom* (New York, Anchor Books, 2000).
——: *Inequality Reexamined* (Oxford, Clarendon Press, 1992).

Manfred B. Steger: *Globalization—A Very Short Introduction* (Oxford, Oxford University Press, 2003).

James P. Sterba (*ed.*): *Social and Political Philosophy—Contemporary Perspectives* (London & New York, Routledge, 2001).

Adam Swift: *Political Philosophy* (Cambridge, Polity Press, 2001).

R. H. Tawney: *Equality* (London, George Allen & Unwin, 1938).
——: *The Acquisitive Society* (New York, Harcourt Brace & Co., 1920).

Andrew Vincent: *Modern Political Ideologies* (West Sussex, Wiley-Blackwell, 2010).

Raymond Wacks: *Philosophy of Law—A Very Short Introduction* (Oxford, Oxford University Press, 2006).

Jeremy Waldon (*ed.*): *Theories of Rights* (Oxford, Oxford University Press, 1984).

Stephen L. Wasby: *Political Science—The Discipline and its Dimensions* (Calcutta, Scientific Book Agency, 1972).

C. W. Watson: *Multiculturalism* (New Delhi, Viva Books, 2002).

C. L. Wayper: *Political Thought* (London, St. Paul's House, 1973).

Sheldon S. Wolin: *Politics and Vision: Continuity and Change in Western Political Thought* (Boston, Little Brown, 1960).

Reference Works

Sonya Andermahr, Terry Lovell, Carole Wolkowitz: *A Glossary of Feminist Theory* (London, Arnold, 1997).

Bill Ashcraft, et al.: *Key Concepts in Post-Colonial Studies* (London, Routledge, 1998).

Frank Bealey: *The Blackwell Dictionary of Political Science* (Oxford, Blackwell, 1999).

Robert Benewick, Philip Green (*eds.*): *The Routledge Dictionary of Political Thinkers* (London, Routledge, 1998).

Vernon Bogdanor (*ed.*): *The Blackwell Encyclopedia of Political Institutions* (Oxford, Blackwell Reference, 1987).

Carles Boix, Susan Stokes (*eds.*): *The Oxford Handbook of Comparative Politics* (Oxford, Oxford University Press, 2009).

Tom Bottomore (*ed.*): *A Dictionary of Marxist Thought* (Oxford, Blackwell Reference, 1991).

Robert E. Goodin, Philip Petit (*eds.*): *A Companion to Contemporary Political Philosophy* (Oxford, Blackwell Reference, 1993).
—— (*eds.*): *Contemporary Political Philosophy—An Anthology* (Oxford, Blackwell, 1997).

Julius Gould, William L. Kolb (*eds.*): *A Dictionary of the Social Science* (Compiled under the auspices of UNESCO), (London, Tavistock Publications, 1964).

Mary Hawkesworth, Maurice Kogan (*eds.*): *Encyclopedia of Government and Politics* (Vols. 1 and 2) (London, Routledge, 1992).

Edward Hyams: *A Dictionary of Modern Revolution* (New York, Taplinger Publishing Co. 1973).

Joel Krieger (*ed.*): *The Oxford Companion to Politics of the World* (New York, Oxford University Press, 1993).

Frank N. Magill (*ed.*): *International Encyclopedia of Government and Politics* (Vols. 1 and 2) (London & Chicago, FD, 1996).

Iain McLean: *The Concise Oxford Dictionary of Politics* (Oxford, Oxford University Press, 2003).

David Miller (*ed.*): *The Blackwell Encyclopaedia of Political Thought* (Oxford, Blackwell Reference, 1987).

William Outhwaite, Tom Bottomore (*eds.*): *The Blackwell Dictionary of Twentieth Century Social Thought* (Oxford, Blackwell Reference, 1993).

J. C. Plano, R. E. Riggs, H.S. Robin: *The Dictionary of Political Analysis* (California, ABC-CLIO, 1982).

Geoffrey K. Roberts: *A Dictionary of Political Analysis* (London, Longman, 1971).

David Robertson: *A Dictionary of Human Rights* (London & New York, Europa Publications, 2004).

——: *The Penguin Dictionary of Politics* (Middlesex, Penguin Books, 1986).

Roger Scruton: *A Dictionary of Political Thought* (London, Macmillan, 1982).

David L. Sills (*ed.*): *International Encyclopaedia of the Social Sciences* (Vols. 1-17) (New York, Macmillan and The Free Press, 1968).

Index

Other Important Books
by
Dr. O.P. Gauba

Students are advised to select relevant titles according to their needs, after glancing through the contents of each title. Please insist on the latest edition/reprint for better results.

All the books are written in a simple language, concise and lucid style, equipped with some reader-friendly features such as flow-charts, comparative charts, explanatory diagrammes, on-the-spot definitions of relevant concepts, historical references and crisp quotations given in boxes.

Social and Political Philosophy

- Nature and Scope of Social and Political Philosophy
- Scientific Temper and Progress (including Nehru's Vision of Science)
- State and Sovereignty (including the context of Kautilya)
- Individual and the State (including the concepts of Human Rights, Accountability and the Curse of Corruption)
- Concept of Democracy (including Macpherson's analysis)
- Concept of Liberty (including Gandhian view of Freedom, Macpherson's and Amartya Sen's analysis)
- Concept of Equality (including Ambedkar's analysis)
- Concept of Justice (including Rawls's theory and Amartya Sen's view)
- Crime and Punishment (including the debate on Capital Punishment)
- Principle of Humanism (including the views of Kant, Vivekanand, Tagore and M.N. Roy)
- Principle of Secularism (including the views of Gandhi and Nehru)
- Principle of Multiculturalism
- Principle of Anarchism
- Principle of Socialism (including the contributions of Narendra Dev, Nehru and Jayaprakash Narayan)
- Principle of Marxism (including Neo-Marxism)
- Gender Perspective (including broad streams of Feminism, status of the Girl-child)
- Ecological Perspective (including Sustainable Development)
- Gandhian Perspective (including Gandhism and Marxism, Gandhism and Rawls's theory of Justice)

Western Political Thought

- Understanding Political Thought
- **Classical Tradition** — Plato; Aristotle
- **Renaissance Tradition** — Nature of the Renaissance; Machiavelli
- **Liberal Tradition** — Broad Streams of Liberalism; Hobbes; Locke; Rousseau; Rawls, Nozick
- **Conservative Tradition** — Basic Tenets; Burke
- **Utilitarian Tradition** — Basic Tenets; Bentham; Mill
- **Enlightenment Tradition** — Nature of the Enlightenment, Immanuel Kant
- **Idealism** — Basic Tenets; Hegel; Green
- **Marxist Tradition** — Basic Tenets; Marx and Engels; Lenin, Rosa Luxemberg, Mao and Gramsci; Neo-Marxism
- **Feminist Tradition** — Basic Tenets; Broad Streams of Feminist Thought
- **Communitarian Tradition** – Basic Tenets; Exponents
- **Environmentalist Tradition** — Basic Tenets; Sustainable Development; Broad Streams of Environmentalism
- **Contemporary Political Philosophers** — Hannah Arendt; Oakeshott